THE NEW TESTAMENT: An Introduction
Second Edition

NORMAN PERRIN
late of the University of Chicago
DENNIS C. DULING
Canisius College

THE NEW TESTAMENT
An Introduction

Proclamation and Parenesis, Myth and History

Second Edition

Under the General Editorship of ROBERT FERM
Middlebury College

HARCOURT BRACE JOVANOVICH, INC.

New York   San Diego   Chicago   San Francisco   Atlanta
London   Sydney   Toronto

Scripture quotations in this publication, unless otherwise noted, are from the Revised Standard Version of the Bible, copyrighted 1946 and 1952, © 1971, 1973 by the Division of Christian Education, National Council of the Churches of Christ in the U.S.A., and are used by permission.

ISBN: 0-15-565726-7

Library of Congress Catalog Card Number: 82-80524

Printed in the United States of America

Cover: Inscription from the Catacomb of Domitilla.

Picture credits appear on page 505.

For Nancy,
in token of my love

PREFACE

The New Testament is both a book and a collection of books. When we read the New Testament we immediately are aware that it is trying to convince us that certain things are true and therefore affect our lives. There is, in other words, a strong element of *proclamation* in the New Testament. Its writers sought to exhort and instruct, to guide and comfort, to advise and encourage, and often to reprimand. Scholars call this *parenesis*.

These considerations account for the first part of the subtitle of this book. The second part of the subtitle derives from the further consideration that the New Testament is a fascinating blend of history and myth. On one level we are being presented with the historical facts of how the Romans crucified a potentially dangerous leader (they crucified a hundred such men) and of the story of a wandering missionary for a new religion or philosophy who ran into trouble with his rivals in the city of Corinth. On another level we are being presented with the same facts as they reveal the nature of God's judgment on the wisdom and power of the world—as they become myths. This theme is developed in the second chapter of this book, and it remains a constant factor in later chapters.

The New Testament tells of events, ideas, and persons surrounding a Jew who lived in ancient Palestine and who spoke the Aramaic language. But Palestine was part of the Roman Empire, and the texts of the New Testament reflect the historical, cultural, and religious circumstances of that larger environment; they were written in Greek, then the international language of the empire. Chapter 1 therefore surveys the world of the New Testament by taking up the history and religions of the Greek and Roman periods, especially those of Judaism. Moreover, the texts of the New Testament can properly be understood historically only if they are placed firmly in the context of the particular circumstances of each phase of the New Testament Christianity from which they came. In order to make this possible, chapter 3 presents a systematic account of the theological history of New Testament Christianity. Chapters 4-12 discuss each part of the New Testament against the background of its place in the spectrum of that history. Chapter 13 concludes with a presentation of Jesus and his teaching.

Special features of this book are:

The treatment of apocalyptic Christianity. The first actual discussion of the literary texts of the New Testament, in chapter 4, deals with a group of texts of which only one, the book of Revelation, is a complete work, and that a comparatively late one. The subject of the chapter, however, is really apocalyptic Christianity, apocalyptic being a movement of the very earliest days, and we therefore discuss it first. Since it continued to be a strong influence in the Christian movement, constantly exhibiting the same features, we have brought together in this discussion a representative sample of the apocalyptic texts to be found in the New Testament.

Emphasis on literary factors. The discussion of the books that make up the New Testament emphasizes literary factors and includes a literary analysis of the longer books. Several years of intensive research on the gospels and the Acts of the Apostles indicate that the authors of these books signaled their intentions by the literary structure they gave to their work and by various literary devices they utilized within that structure.

Social factors in early Christianity. Scholars have attempted to uncover the social contexts of various early Christian communities by analyzing the significance of social environment (whether it was urban or rural, for example), social status, the distribution of power. Where appropriate, such social factors have been commented on in these pages.

The synoptic gospels and the Acts of the Apostles. Considerable space is devoted to the evangelists Matthew and Mark and to the author of the gospel of Luke-Acts of the Apostles. A major development in recent New Testament scholarship has been the recognition that these men were all major theologians in their own right and that the contribution of each to the development of New Testament Christianity was as distinctive as that of the Apostle Paul.

Material ascribed to Jesus in the synoptic gospels. The synoptic gospels (Matthew, Mark, and Luke) contain both the teachings of Jesus and stories about him. All this material, however, reflects the teaching, understanding, and concerns of early Christian communities, and much of it was in fact created by prophets and scribes in those communities. (For support of this view, see Perrin's *Rediscovering the Teaching of Jesus,* chapter 1.) This view of the synoptic gospel material is given serious consideration both in the discussion of the gospels in chapters 8, 9, and 10 and in the discussion of Jesus in chapter 13.

Jesus as the presupposition of the New Testament. It is usual to begin a survey of the New Testament with Jesus—that is, with the historical Jesus—and then go on to examine developments in the later church, understanding those developments as moving forward from the mission and message of the historical Jesus. But in accordance with the views of Rudolf Bultmann, who viewed Jesus as a Jew whose teaching was a "presupposition for the theology of the New Testament,". we have put the chapter on Jesus last. By the time readers have reached this chapter, they will have encountered numerous interpretations of Jesus in the New Testament and will be aware of the difficulties in reexamining his teaching and commenting about his life.

The "exegetical surveys." The seventh general feature of the book is the extensive use of "exegetical surveys." Every major book in the New Testament is surveyed, and when limitations of space have made it impossible to treat a book in this way, it is outlined and the contents briefly discussed. This procedure was chosen deliberately to encourage readers to read the New Testament itself, rather than only a book about it, and to help them understand what they are reading. We regard these exegetical surveys as the heart of the book. They are designed to be read in conjunction with a good English translation of the Bible. The more important of the available translations are discussed in appendix 3.

Changes in This Edition

Those who have used the first edition will want to know why and how it has been revised. I have attempted to preserve what I believed was most distinctive in the first edition, namely, Perrin's overall plan (with the chapter on Jesus coming last), as well as his most characteristic chapters, one on the nature of the New Testament (chapter 2), a second on Mark (original chapter 7, now chapter 8), and a third on the historical Jesus (original chapter 12, now chapter 13). But, in the light of several recent developments in scholarship, I have done much revising and rewriting. The most obvious changes are the replacement of chapter 1 by an extensively expanded and updated treatment of the history and religions of the Greco-Roman world, built up out of appendixes 1 and 2 of the first edition, and the expansion of chapter 5 on Paul into two chapters. The new chapter 5, "Paul: Apostle to the Gentiles," takes up the sources (undisputed letters and Acts), chronology, background, life, "conversion" and call, missionary activity, basis for authority, relation to the Jerusalem church, opponents, and the urban world of the Pauline communities. The new chapter 6, "The Theology of Paul in His Letters," picks up Perrin's exegetical outlines but prefaces them with an expanded discussion of the form(s) of Paul's letters in relation to Greco-Roman letters and of the nature of pre-Pauline traditions. This chapter now concludes with a summary of Paul's theology and a brief discussion of several concrete ethical issues.

For anyone who wishes to follow Perrin's original scheme, which began with "Approaching the New Testament," the first pages of that chapter are at the beginning of this Preface, and the "Techniques and Methods of New Testament Scholarship" are dispersed throughout the book: the chronological listing of books is now in chapter 2; the synoptic problem initiates the section on the history of Christianity in chapter 3; and form criticism is discussed in chapter 13, the chapter on Jesus. These changes were made because it was felt that beginning students need a somewhat more complete introduction to the world of the New Testament and that the methods of criticism can best be studied at the points where those methods have been most productive.

In addition to the changes in chapters 1 and 5, a third major area of revision has been the attempt to enrich the historically oriented material with recent research in social history (see the third feature, above). Such revision is obvious in chapter 5, in the section on the urban world of Paul's communities. But it also is reflected in the historical-religious background in chapter 1; in the rewriting of chapter 3, in which Perrin's "theological history" is modified by an emphasis on the shift from a rural, agrarian, sectarian environment to Hellenized urban centers, with note of the attendant complications presented by the Hellenization of Palestine; and in additions on the "community" to other chapters. For this orientation I am most indebted to Professor Wayne Meeks of Yale University and to his 1979 seminar on the social world of early Christianity, which was made possible by a grant from the National Endowment for the Humanities.

Other changes include the following: a discussion of the types of New Testament books and their chronology in chapter 2; the transferral of Jewish apocalyptic and the Qumran Community to chapter 1 from chapter 4, and the expansion of chapter 4 with discussions of the forms of Q material, the social context of the Q Community, and the structure and special themes of the book of Revelation; the modification of chapter 7 (original 6) with reference to a Pauline "school" and the opponents at Colossae; the addition of the discussions of redaction criticism and the Markan community to chapter 8 (original 7); recent proposals for a Matthean "salvation history" in chapter 9 (original 8; see also the note on "salvation history" in relation to Romans 9–11 in chapter 6); reference to Hellenistic historical writing, Savior figures, and modification of Conzelmann's "salvation history" scheme in chapter 10 (original 9); comments on Johannine traditions, community, school, and a summary of major Johannine theological themes in chapter 11 (original 10); and an expanded discussion of the Jesus tradition and some modifications in accord with Perrin's later analysis in *Jesus and the Language of the Kingdom* (1976). With appendixes 1 and 2 incorporated into chapter 1, the appendixes have been renumbered and two have been added, one on major archeological and textual discoveries and publications, the other on sample religious texts from the Greco-Roman world, including Judaism. I have updated the bibliographies throughout, inserting a Bibliography for Research Papers. Two maps and a time line of Pre-Christian and Christian Eras are new to this edition, and the art now includes a floor plan of the Jerusalem Temple.

Professor Norman Perrin died unexpectedly just before Thanksgiving in 1976. He was a distinguished and internationally known New Testament scholar, an unusually clear-headed thinker and writer, and a spunky personality who had developed and defended his own views on a number of central issues in New Testament interpretation. Perrin had moved through several stages in his scholarly career; he himself would have revised his textbook in accord with his most recent perspective. Since that was not possible, I, his former student and continuing friend, agreed to attempt a revision, not without some initial hesitation.

I would like to acknowledge the following people and institutions for their part in the production of this edition. Bill McLane of Harcourt Brace Jovanovich launched the project and encouraged me to undertake it. Comments were solicited from a number of teachers and scholars, and extremely helpful suggestions were offered by the general editor, Professor Robert Ferm of Middlebury College, who read the manuscript. The difficult task of editing an extensively rewritten manuscript fell to John Holland and Tina Barland, who also made a number of suggestions. Robert Winsor created the design for this second edition, Yvonne Gerin applied her educated taste to the artwork, and Marlene Fein developed the maps and charts. I am deeply grateful to Canisius College for providing a fellowship that allowed me time for writing in the summer of 1981, and for hours of labor from our departmental secretary, Mrs. Lynne Glair, whose efficiency in typing the revised portions and collating them with the first edition was an indispensable ingredient in our progress. To the staffs of the Canisius College library and Christ the King Seminary goes a special word of thanks, and to Father Bonaventure Hayes, librarian at the Seminary, I owe a small debt for help on the Bibliography for Research Papers. Eric B. Dewling prepared the index. I thank my wife, Gretchen, and our children for their reluctant willingness to allow me to sit buried in articles and books. As already noted, I owe much to the National Endowment for the Humanities for a summer at Yale University (1979), where Professor Wayne Meeks taught us about the social world of early Christianity. Finally, I recall, vividly and with fondness, the author of the first edition of this book, and I hope the second edition will continue to be of as much service to students as the first has been.

Dennis C. Duling

A NOTE ABOUT THE RESOURCE BOOKS

The following are the six works continually referred to in the Further Reading section at the end of each chapter and appendix.

Feine, P., J. Behm, and W. G. Kümmel, *Introduction to the New Testament.* New York and Nashville: Abingdon Press, 1975. (Since Kümmel is solely responsible for this edition, it is quoted as Kümmel, *Intro.*) An English translation of a standard German reference work deliberately encyclopedic in scope.

Marxsen, W., *Introduction to the New Testament.* Philadelphia: Fortress Press, 1968. (Quoted as Marxsen, *Intro.*) The English translation of a work by a member of the "Bultmann school," and hence representative of the more radical wing of contemporary New Testament scholarship.

Fuller, R.H., *A Critical Introduction to the New Testament.* London: Duckworth, 1966. (Quoted as Fuller, *Intro.*) Representative of the best Anglo-American scholarship.

Peake's Commentary on the Bible. Revised Edition. London and New York: Thomas Nelson and Sons, Ltd., 1962. (Quoted as *PCB.*) A one-volume commentary on the Bible, largely a product of British scholarship.

The Jerome Biblical Commentary. 2 vols. bound together. Englewood Cliffs, N.J.: Prentice-Hall, 1968. (Quoted as *JBC.*) In effect, a one-volume commentary on the Bible; although there is separate pagination for the volumes on the Old Testament and the New, the two are bound together. It is a product of the growing American Roman Catholic scholarship in the period following Vatican II (1962–1965). All the references are to the part of the volume that deals with the New Testament.

The Interpreter's Dictionary of the Bible. 4 vols. New York and Nashville: Abingdon Press, 1962. (Quoted as *IDB.*) The most comprehensive reference work available in English. The articles vary in quality, but at their best they are very good and always extremely informative. (*IDB Suppl.* is volume 5.)

ABBREVIATIONS AND EXPLANATIONS

Books of the Bible and the Apocrypha are abbreviated to the first three or four letters of their titles; e.g., Gen = Genesis, Matt = Matthew, 1 Cor = 1 Corinthians. We have followed the example of the Oxford Annotated Bible in using *Sir* for The Wisdom of Jesus the Son of Sirach, a book in the Apocrypha sometimes called Ecclesiasticus. The abbreviation *par.* (for *parallel*) is used to refer to passages in the gospels that are parallel to the one cited; e.g., "Mark 13 par." means "Mark 13 and its parallels in Matthew and Luke."

Qumran materials are abbreviated according to the standard established in the official publication *Discoveries in the Judaean Desert,* edited by J. T. Milik and D. Barthélemy (Oxford: Clarendon Press, 1955–   ).

The following is a list of other abbreviations used.

ASV	American Standard Version (of the Bible) = SV
AV	Authorized Version (of the Bible) = KJV
ERV	English Revised Version (of the Bible) = RV
IDB	*Interpreter's Dictionary of the Bible* (4 vols.)
IDB Suppl.	*Interpreter's Dictionary of the Bible* (vol. 5)
JBC	*Jerome Biblical Commentary*
KJV	King James Version (of the Bible) = AV
LXX	Septuagint (the Greek translation of the Jewish Scriptures, transmitted as the Old Testament by Christians)
NAB	New American Bible
NEB	New English Bible
OAB	Oxford Annotated Bible
PCB	*Peake's Commentary on the Bible*
RSV	Revised Standard Version (of the Bible)
RV	Revised Version (of the Bible) = ERV
SV	Standard Version (of the Bible) = ASV
TEV	Today's English Version (of the Bible)

Unless otherwise identified, quotations from the Bible are from the RSV.

"Matthew," "Mark," "Luke," and "John" are used to refer both to the evangelists (gospel writers) and to the gospels themselves. Further definition ("the evangelist Matthew," or "the gospel of Matthew") is given only for the sake of emphasis or where it is necessary to avoid confusion. This usage is purely a matter of convenience and is not intended to imply anything about the actual names of the evangelists.

Publication details of all books and articles quoted or referred to are given in the bibliography at the end of the book, except that individual articles in the resource books (*PCB, JBC,* and *IDB*) are not further listed there.

CONTENTS

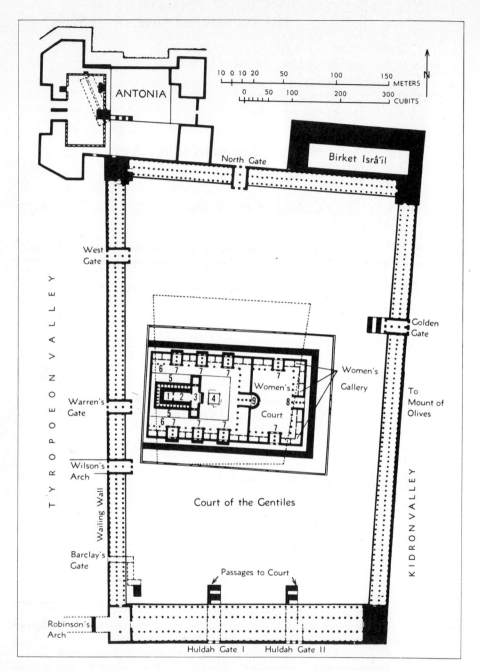

Floor plan of Herod's temple and courts, based on Vincent-Steve: (1) holy of holies; (2) holy place; (3) porch; (4) altar of burnt offering; (5) court of priests; (6) court of Israel (men's court); (7) sanctuary gates; (8) Nicanor gate (?) or Gate Beautiful; (9) Nicanor gate.

TIME LINE
PRE-CHRISTIAN AND CHRISTIAN ERAS

EMPIRES	POLITICAL EVENTS & PERSONS	JEWS & CHRISTIANS	SELECTED LITERATURE

ROMAN MONARCHY
BABYLONIA
PERSIAN EMPIRE
EGYPT
EGYPT
GREEK STATES

600

597—1st Deportation to Babylon
587—2nd Deportation to Babylon

BABYLONIAN EXILE

MYSTERY RELIGIONS

Lamentations
Ezekiel
Deutero—Isaiah
(Trito—Isaiah?)
Haggai/Zechariah

Obadiah

539—CYRUS OVERCOMES BABYLONIA
538—Cyrus' Edict of Toleration
515—Dedication of 2nd Jewish Temple
509—Roman Republic

500

PERSIAN DOMINANCE

440—Greeks defeat Persians at Marathon
480—Greeks defeat Persians at Salamis

Greek Drama

Job?

460–454—Independence of Egypt from Persia
445– ? —Nehemiah governor of Jews

Malachi
Ezra/Nehemiah
Herodotus/Thucydides

428?—Ezra's mission to Jews
401—Independence of Egypt from Persia
(28th, 29th, 30th Dynasties)

Jonah?
Ruth?

400

Joel
Plato's writings
Cynicism (beginnings)

336–323—CONQUESTS OF ALEXANDER THE GREAT

Aristotle's writings

(continued on next page)

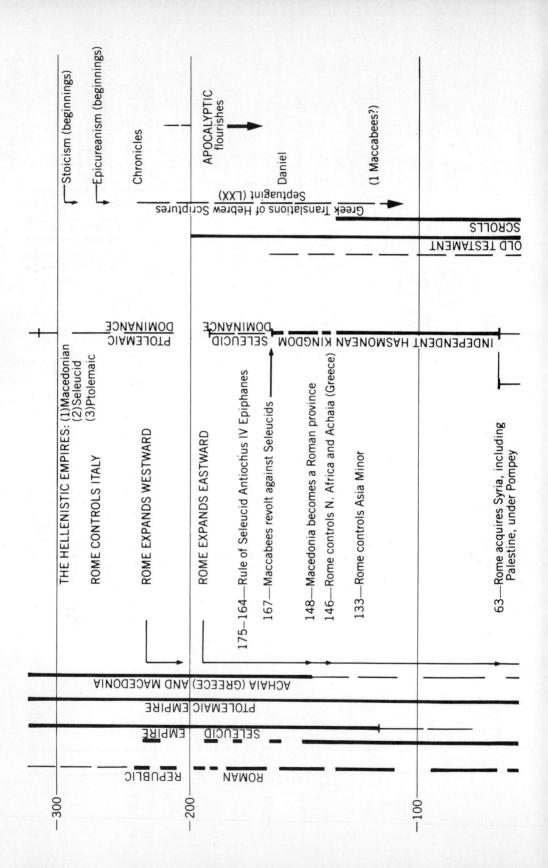

Cicero's Writings

Virgil's writings
Horace's writings

Jesus Teaches
Writings of Philo of Alexandria

Q ?

St. Paul's Writings

Seneca's Essays and Letters
Gospel of Mark
Deutero—Pauline Writings
Luke—Acts
Gospel of Matthew
Josephus' writings
Revelation
Gospel of John
Plutarch's writings
Pliny the Elder and Younger
Epictetus teaches
Tacitus' writings; Pastorals
GREEK TRANSLATIONS OF OT; LATER NT WRITINGS
CORPUS HERMETICUM
Writings of Marcus Aurelius

EARLY CHURCH FATHERS
NEW TESTAMENT APOCRYPHA
DEAD SEA
GNOSTIC WRITINGS
APOCRYPHA AND PSEUDEPIGRAPHA OF THE
RABBINIC TRADITIONS
TARGUMS
Mishnah codified

37–4 Herod the Great
6–4 BIRTH OF JESUS
4 B.C.–A.D. 6 Archelaus
4 B.C.–A.D. 34 Philip
4 B.C.–A.D. 39 Herod Antipas
MINISTRY OF JESUS
Herod Agrippa I 37–44
PAUL
66–70 WARS WITH ROME
ca. 90 COUNCIL OF JAMNIA
132–135 WARS WITH ROME (Bar Cochba Revolt)
ROMAN PROCURATORS IN PALESTINE
ROMAN DOMINANCE

48—Julius Caesar defeats Pompey
44—Julius Caesar assassinated
40–37—Parthians "liberate" Jews in Jerusalem
31—Octavian defeats Antony at ACTIUM
27—ROMAN EMPIRE Octavian

14—Tiberius

37—Gaius Caligula
41—Claudius

54—Nero

66–70—JEWISH-ROMAN WARS
68—Galba, Otho, Vitellius
69—Vespasian
79—Titus
81—Domitian
96—Nerva
98—Trajan

117—Hadrian
132–135—WARS WITH JEWS
138—Antonius Pius

(161–169 Lucius Vevus)

161—Marcus Aurelius
180—Commodus
193—Pertinax
193—Didius Julianus
193—Septimus Severus

PARTHIAN EMPIRE
ROMAN EMPIRE

0
—100

THE NEW TESTAMENT: An Introduction
Second Edition

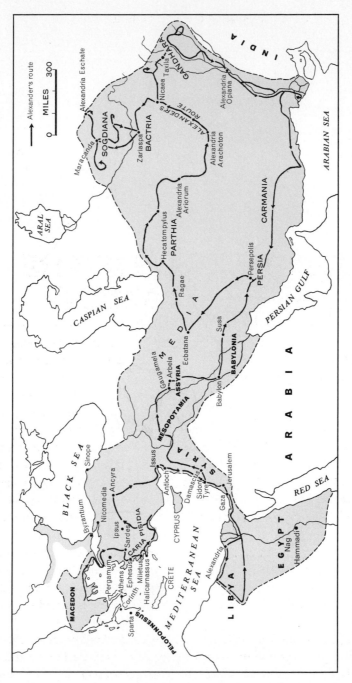

Alexander's Empire.

CHAPTER ONE

THE WORLD OF THE NEW TESTAMENT

The world of the New Testament is a fascinating one. It can be studied from a political science point of view as the arena of struggling empires that waged war until one military dictatorship, the Roman Empire, gained control over the lands that border the Mediterranean Sea. It can be studied from an economic point of view as a vast system of business and finance dominated by international trade, an enforced system of taxation, and large bodies of slave labor. It can be studied from a sociological point of view as a pluralistic assortment of ethnic peoples, high government officials, merchants, small business people, slaves and minorities. This world has its literature, sculpture, philosophy, art, and architecture from the civilizations of ancient Mesopotamia, Egypt, Rome, Greece, and Canaan, the area settled by the ancient Hebrews. Finally, this world gave rise to a diverse and often, from the modern western point of view, exotic religious life. It is impossible in an introduction such as this to study all of these important facets of ancient Mediterranean civilization in detail; but it is important to gain some knowledge of the civilization to bring the New Testament to life as a collection of books of particular times and of particular places.

With this in mind, we shall first characterize the Hellenistic world, that is, the Greco-Roman world and its culture; then we shall backtrack and give a brief sketch of the political history of the Jewish people in order to understand what happened in the period when they were dominated by the Greeks and the Romans; finally, we shall offer a brief description of the Jewish religion in the Greek and Roman periods.

THE HELLENISTIC WORLD:
THE CRADLE OF CHRISTIANITY[1]

The New Testament is a product of the Hellenistic world (Greek *Hellas*, "Greece"), a world that came into being as a consequence of the conquests of Alexander the Great, 356–323 B.C.[2] When Philip II of Macedonia (northern Greece) was assassinated in 336, his brilliant and ambitious son, Alexander, only 20 years old, consolidated his power and then launched a campaign eastward. He gained mastery over the far-flung Persian Empire that extended from western Asia Minor (modern Turkey) to India, and included Egypt. Alexander's first major victory over the Persian king and general, Darius III, took place at Issus in southeastern Asia Minor in 333 B.C. The young commander then moved down the eastern Mediterranean coast, overcame resistence at Tyre and Gaza (332), induced submission of the Jews of Palestine,[3] and was welcomed in Egypt as a conquering hero. There he founded the city of Alexandria, destined to become one of the greatest cities of Hellenistic civilization. Then he moved further eastward, decisively defeated the armies of Darius at Gaugamele, and took possession of the wealth of the eastern cities. When Darius was murdered by the Persian princes, Alexander proclaimed himself "King of Asia" and quickly accustomed himself to the divine honors paid an oriental monarch. When he advanced into India in 326, his weary army refused to follow him. Alexander returned to Mesopotamia, settled in Babylon, and began to consolidate his huge empire. But he was not to enjoy it for long, for in the summer of 323 B.C. he died of a fever. In thirteen years this amazing young man had become master of the whole eastern Mediterranean world.

Alexander was a brilliant military strategist, but there was more to his dream than military conquest. He had been tutored by Aristotle and saw himself as the apostle and emissary of the classical Greek culture. Attached to his general staff were historians, ethnographers, geographers, botanists, zoologists, mineralogists, and hydrographers. His vision was "one world" (Greek

---

[1] For a good summary, cf. A. Toynbee, ed., *The Crucible of Christianity.*

[2] Standard historical treatments are W. Tarn and G.T. Griffith, *Hellenistic Civilization,* chapter 1, and V. Tcherikover, *Hellenistic Civilization and the Jews,* Intro. A brilliant and convincing portrait of the young Alexander has been drawn by Mary Renault in her novel, *Fire from Heaven.*

[3] Throughout this book we shall refer to the area of Canaan, settled by the ancient Hebrews, as Palestine. This is the commonly accepted term in New Testament study. It is derived from the Greek (*Palaistinē*) and Latin (*Palaestina*), words for Hebrew *Pelesheth,* the southern coastal region settled by the "People of the Sea" in the twelfth century B.C., a people from the regions of the Aegean Sea who often made war against the Hebrews who had previously settled in Canaan. The Egyptians called them *prst* and the Hebrews designated them *Pelishti,* hence "the land of the Philistines" (Gen 21:32, 34; Exod 13:17). The Assyrians called the area *Palastu.* The fifth-century B.C. Greek historian Herodotus used the term *Palaistinē* in a broader sense to include the area further inland settled by the Hebrews (cf. esp. Book IV, 36 and Book II, 102–05). The term is used by the first-century A.D. Jewish writers Josephus and Philo of Alexandria. The Roman emperor Hadrian (A.D. 117–138) called the region *Provincia Syria Palaestina* in order to expunge the name *Provincia Judaea* that was based on the Biblical "land of Judah." Cf. Y. Aharoni, *The Land of the Bible. A Historical Geography* (rev. ed. 1979), pp. 78–79.

oicumenē), or one great "world city" (Greek *cosmopolis*). Alexander's conquests "spread Hellenism in a vast colonizing wave throughout the Near East and created, if not politically, at least economically and culturally, a single world stretching from Gibraltar to the Punjab [with] . . . Greek *koinē* ["common" or vernacular] as a lingua franca."[4]

The extent to which Alexander went in his attempt to create a "single world" can be illustrated by two points. First, he wed Persians, including Statira, the daughter of Darius III, and Parysotis, the daughter of Artaxerxes III Ochus; then he induced eighty of his officers to marry local women; in the spring of 324 B.C. during a "feast of fraternization" he gave gifts to 10,000 of his men for marrying Persian women! Second, he built a network of almost thirty Greek cities throughout the empire, a building program that was expanded by later Hellenistic rulers. These became enclaves of Greek culture. Here gymnasia, baths, and theaters were built, and the upper classes spoke *koinē* Greek, wore Greek dress, absorbed Greek learning, adopted Greek customs, and took part in Greek athletics. Palestine, the land of the ancient Hebrews (now known as "Jews" from the word Judah) was no exception to this phenomenon. Furthermore, the process of Hellenization continued through the beginning of the Roman Empire (27 B.C.) and beyond, for the Romans perpetuated Greek culture.

Despite the cultural revolution, the Hellenization of the East was limited. The urban nature of the phenomenon meant that traditional cultures in nonurban regions continued much as before. Indeed, while Hellenization continued in the cities, there occurred a revival of Eastern ways, both spiritually and materially, so that eventually the West began to experience the impact of the East.

The death of Alexander the Great in 323 B.C. led to a bitter political power struggle among his Macedonian generals. In 301 three distinct Hellenistic empires emerged: (1) Macedonia and parts of Greece; (2) the Seleucid Empire ("Syria") from western Asia Minor to Mesopotamia, established by Seleucus; and (3) the Ptolemaic Empire in Egypt and the North African coast, along with some islands in the Mediterranean, established by Ptolemy. There was constant probing of the balance of power between the Ptolemies and the Seleucids in border areas. Following their historical fate as inhabitants of a buffer zone, the Jews were controlled first by the Ptolemies and then, after 198 B.C., by the Seleucids. The Jews soon found that the Hellenizing policies of the Seleucids, especially Antiochus IV, were intolerable. As a result, they revolted in 167 B.C.; they gained their independence gradually, and established an independent monarchy. But there was a new power over the horizon with which the Jewish people would have to contend, and which would ultimately end their independence in 63 B.C.: the power of Rome.

Roman history can be divided into three major periods:[5] (1) the monarchy, traditionally founded in connection with the legend of Romulus and Remus,

---

[4] From the article on Alexander in the *Encyclopaedia Britannica* (1968), vol. 1, p. 576.
[5] R. M. Grant, "Roman Empire," *IDB* vol. 4, pp. 103–09; cf. also E. Lohse, *The New Testament Environment*, Part 2, chapter 1.

about 735 B.C.; (2) the Roman Republic, established in 509 B.C.; and (3) the Roman Empire, which sought to bring peace and order to the faltering Republic in 27 B.C., and which lasted until its western lands began to fall to Germanic invaders from the north in the fourth, fifth, and sixth centuries A.D.

During the later period of the Roman Republic Rome gained control over the Hellenistic empires surrounding the eastern Mediterranean Sea. Although Rome was unable to extend her control as far eastward as the Persians and the Greeks had, the western part of the empire eventually took in Spain, Gaul (modern France), southern Germany, and southern Britain. Each of the Hellenistic empires was subdivided into Roman provinces in the second and first centuries B.C. The formation of Syria as a Roman province brought Palestine under Roman control in 63.

The vast extension of Roman power over the whole Mediterranean region put an immense strain on the Roman Republic. New tax revenues and interest created an expanded economy, a higher standard of living, and a new wealthy class at Rome. But they also brought political corruption, social dislocation, and moral decline. Political bribery was common; abused slaves on the countryside plantations revolted and were often joined by the oppressed poor. Traditional Roman respect for family gave way to childless marriages, divorce, adultery, prostitution, and pederasty. Exploits abroad created instability at home; what seemed necessary was highly centralized, stronger rule, and eventually the Romans looked more and more to the military.

A series of strong leaders emerged in the first century B.C., among them Pompey, Julius Caesar, Antony, and Octavian. By 42 B.C. the armies of Octavian and Antony had decisively defeated those of Caesar's murderers, leaving Italy and the West in the control of Octavian, and the East as far as the Euphrates in the control of Antony. In 31 B.C. Octavian's defeat of Antony's forces at the battle of Actium followed by the subsequent suicides of Antony and Cleopatra in Egypt, meant that Octavian was in a position to assume great power. Upon his return to Rome, he was made *Imperator*, or supreme commander of the army; the Senate conferred upon him the additional titles *Augustus*, the August, and *Princeps*, the first of the Senate. Thus the Roman Empire was born in 27 B.C., and Octavian, called Caesar Augustus, was its first emperor.

Augustus was a wise ruler. He secured the borders of the empire and built roads. The result was a new era of peace and stability (the *pax Romana*). He reorganized the provinces to achieve a more just administration, instituted tax reform, developed a civil service, and engaged in many public works projects, especially in Rome. It was during his reign that Jesus of Nazareth was born.

Not all of Augustus' successors, however, were as capable. Tiberius (A.D. 14–37), though experienced, was unpopular and spent his last eleven years in a life of debauchery on the island of Capri; one of his infamous appointees was the prefect of Judea, Pontius Pilate. Tiberius was followed by his grandnephew and the great-grandson of Augustus, Gaius Caligula (A.D. 37–41) who became absorbed with power, demanded that he be addressed as a god, and proposed that his horse be made a consul (he rewarded this animal with a marble stall and a purple blanket!). He also drained the treasury to pay for his dissolute life and reckless building activities, and he fomented a crisis among the Jews by demanding that statues of himself be set up in the Temple at Jerusalem. The crisis was averted only when he was assassinated by his private Praetorian Guard. Fortunately, his uncle and successor, Claudius (A.D. 41–54), though considered weak in body and mind by his relatives, turned out to be a competent ruler. When Claudius was poisoned by his fourth wife Agrippina, Nero, who was Agrippina's son by a previous marriage, became emperor. Though at first the empire ran smoothly under the direction of the philosopher Seneca, Nero took control and things began to deteriorate. He poisoned Claudius' son, executed his own wife, and arranged for the assassination of his mother. There were other murders. In A.D. 64 a great fire devastated Rome, and Nero found his scapegoat in the Christians. Tradition has it that Peter and Paul were martyred by Nero. Finally, matters got so bad that military commanders seized several provinces and Nero fled from Rome. Upon hearing that the Senate had condemned him to death *in absentia*, the last of the Augustan family rulers committed suicide in A.D. 68.

Widespread unrest in the empire and chaos at home led to a quick succession of emperors: Galba, Otho, and Vitellius. In A.D. 69, Vespasian, a seasoned commander who had been dispatched to Palestine to crush the Jewish rebellion (A.D. 66–70) was popularly acclaimed emperor. Vespasian provided a decade of peace and prosperity for the empire (A.D. 69–79) reminiscent of the Augustan era. Similarly Vespasian's son and successor, Titus, who had concluded the war with the Jews, reigned wisely for two years (A.D. 79–81). But a second son of Vespasian, Domitian (A.D. 81–96), was a tyrant of the first order. He relied on informers, had his enemies murdered, and laid a heavy tax on the people of the empire, especially the Jews. Enamored with his own divinity, he also persecuted the Christians, and it is his reign that provides the backdrop for the most anti-Roman book in the New Testament, the book of Revelation. The following Flavian emperors, as they are called, were some of Rome's best: Nerva (A.D. 96–98), Trajan (A.D. 98–117), Hadrian (A.D. 117–138), Antonius Pius (A.D. 138–161), and the Stoic philosopher-emperor Marcus Aurelius (A.D. 161–180).

This brief sketch of the Roman emperors cannot offer a detailed understanding of the period; it can, however, depict the general flavor and tenor of the times, and especially some of the difficulties faced by Jews and Christians. We shall have more to say about such events in connection with the literature of the New Testament.

HELLENISTIC CULTURE

We have noted that Hellenization was primarily an urban phenomenon. In the cities of the Greco-Roman period, Greek ideas were disseminated, Greek dress was fashionable, and the externals of Greek civilization—stadia, baths, theaters, amphitheaters, hippodromes, fountains, aqueducts, arches, and the like—were highly visible. A new cosmopolitanism emerged in which any city might become a center for the interchange of ideas from all over the world. This was extremely important for the rise of early Christianity. Though it emerged from the Galilean countryside and perpetuated many ideas from its rural and Jewish origins, it moved quickly to the cities of the empire where its beliefs were gradually recast with the mold of Hellenistic thought. In such places its ranks were filled largely, though not exclusively, with believers of low status who nonetheless produced a substantial literature in the Greek language.

What was daily life in the Greco-Roman world like? Generally speaking, safe travel became possible as it had never been possible before, but with it came the spread of disease. Physicians and healers of all sorts were in great demand. There were many advantages of city life, but at the same time the problem of feeding the increasing urban populations was never adequately solved and famine was an ever-recurring possibility. War was prevalent until the Augustan peace in 27 B.C.; thereafter it was confined largely to securing the frontiers—an exception being the wars with the Jews in A.D. 66–70. The practice of enslaving conquered populations was common, and slaves made up a sizable proportion of the population, especially in Rome.[6] It should be realized that though slaves were often abused on some of the plantations, loyal slaves were sometimes given their freedom while those who became secretaries, domestics, tutors, or financial overseers could occasionally accumulate enough money to purchase freedom. The emperor's slaves held especially influential and powerful positions in government. Still, slaves were chattel and their legal rights were limited. There were no great political movements to abolish the institution. It is not surprising, then, that the image of the master and the slave occurs frequently in the New Testament. Below the slave on the social ladder were the free poor who could barely subsist from day to day. The vast wealth of the empire was controlled by a few aristocrats, who often gained honor and status with their public works and philanthropic deeds, but the gap between rich and poor remained great.

Finally, the shift from older, established, local cultures to new, changing, international environments meant for the urban dweller social dislocation. The loss of a sense of belonging to a natural and continuing community must have been a common experience. It is clear that for the vast majority of people the traditional religious systems of ancient Greece and Rome held little meaning. These religions were formalistic and unemotional, and their function had become largely political.[7] The people longed for some form of physical or spiritual healing, some pertinent philosophy of life, some religious peace and harmony within. It is no surprise that with the revitalization of the East much of the populace was attracted to the somewhat more exotic and emotional religious movements of the orient, as well as popular religious philosophies and local religions which shared some of the same features. We will now briefly review some of these intellectual currents and religious movements, as far as possible calling attention to matters that are important for understanding particular parts of the New Testament.

[6] R. MacMullen, *Roman Social Relations*, p. 92; W. Rollins, "Slavery in the NT," *IDB Suppl.*, pp. 830–32; M. I. Finley, *The Ancient Economy*, chapter 3.

[7] F. C. Grant, "Roman Religion," *IDB*, vol. 4, pp. 109–12.

Popular Philosophy

There were a number of philosophies of the Hellenistic Age that we quite popular and that functioned as religions for many who held them. Part the common stock of much Hellenistic thinking about the world was derive from Platonic "dualism." Plato (d. 347 B.C.) presented the view that the transient material world we perceive through the senses is only a shadow of the true reality, that is, the eternal world of abstract ideas known through reason.[8] Plato also believed that the transient, material body was a prison of the divine, immortal soul, and that the good and just man disciplines the body and its emotions, allowing the reasonable side of the soul to achieve virtue, which is knowledge. This philosophical dualism, especially its view that this world is transient, is reflected at points in the New Testament, especially when the earthly realm is described as a shadow of the heavenly realm, for example in the letter to the Hebrews. It also influenced such religious movements which stressed that human origins and destinies lie in a higher world, or that this world is evil, for example, Gnosticism (see below). Early forms of such religious movements provide some of the environment of early Christian writings, especially the gospel of John and the writings of Paul.

Another popular philosophy of the period was Stoicism. Stoicism took its name from the Greek word *stoa*, "a painted portico" where the founder of Stoicism, Zeno (ca. 336–263 B.C.), taught in Athens. The Stoics believed that the world was ordered by a divine Reason, the *Logos* (a Greek term for "word," "reason"). *Logos* was associated with fire, and capable of being identified with God, or Zeus.[9] They also believed that a spark or seed of the *Logos* dwelt within human beings, and that a person could find a place in the world by obeying the spark or seed within. This orientation tended toward world affirmation and the denial of evil; all is according to Reason. The Stoic philosophy sought to teach a person to attain happiness by maintaining inner peace and contentment in a world full of troubles. To be in harmony with Nature meant self-sufficiency, tranquillity, suppression of emotion, and freedom from external constraints and material things. The ethical orientation of Stoicism emphasized the importance of the will and a certain detachment from property, wealth, suffering, and sickness. This led to a cosmopolitan egalitarianism, a focus on the natural and innate rights of all people, including slaves and women, and Stoics often formed brotherhoods stressing these great ethical themes.

The founder of Stoicism, Zeno, was a follower of Crates who, in turn, was a disciple of Diogenes, the first to call himself "dog," from which the philosophical movement called Cynicism derives (Greek *kyōn*, "dog").[10] The Cynics were counter-culture street preachers who attempted to convert people from the quest for fame, fortune, and pleasure to a life of austere virtue as the path to true freedom and happiness. Many Cynics restricted their diets, begged for

---

[8] For the text of the central portion of Plato's allegory of the cave, see Appendix 5.
[9] The religious overtones of Stoicism can be seen in Cleanthes' *Hymn to Zeus*, cf. Appendix
[10] A. Malherbe, "Cynics," *IDB Suppl.*, pp. 201–03.

food, wore short cloaks, carried only a wallet and staff, rejected social institutions such as marriage and the state, and believed that such a practical moral philosophy was "according to nature." This stress on ethics and right living was gradually absorbed into the more moderate and philosophically reflective Stoicism of the lecture hall, but the Cynic way of life was revived as an ideal among first-century Stoics who wished to appeal to the masses. Thus, later Stoics like the ex-slave Epictetus (late first, early second century A.D.) and emperor Marcus Aurelius (ruled A.D. 161–180) highlighted the ethical life.[11] Though there is no evidence to suggest that Epictetus was in direct contact with early Christians—in fact he made unfavorable comments about them—there are nonetheless many parallels between Cynic-Stoic lifestyles and those of early Christians, most visible in austerity and apostolic mission. The Cynic-Stoic style of argumentation and the habit of listing virtues and vices are also characteristic of the apostle Paul (Rom 1:16ff.; cf. also James 2:14ff.).

Another philosopher whose views were influential in the Hellenistic Age was Epicurus (ca. 342–270 B.C.). Epicurus' critics denounced him as lewd, fraudulent, and uneducated. These estimates, as well as the charge of atheism, were denied by Epicurus. He preached that one should not fear the gods, as religion so frequently taught, and that true happiness lies in the individual's attempt to avoid pain and find pleasure in this world.[12]

In the larger Hellenistic world the ideas, beliefs, and sometimes the lifestyle of religious-philosophical leaders were often perpetuated in the "schools."[13] As early as the sixth century, the followers of Pythagoras gathered around him in southern Italy to form a tightly-knit brotherhood or association. Many such schools were formed in Athens, the most famous being Plato's Academy, Aristotle's Lyceum, Epicurus' Garden, and Zeno's open-air Stoa. The school tradition was also highly prevalent among the Jewish Pharisaic teachers, though its ultimate origins probably lay in the prophetic guilds of the Ancient Near East. There were many differences among the various schools, but there were also some similarities which one study has summarized:

> (1) they were groups of disciples which usually emphasized *philia* [love] and *koinōnia* [fellowship]; (2) they gathered around, and traced their origins to a founder whom they regarded as an exemplary wise, or good man; (3) they valued the teaching of their founder and the traditions about him; (4) members of the schools were disciples or students of the founder; (5) teaching, learning, studying, and writing were common activities; (6) most schools observed communal meals, often in memory of their founders; (7) they had rules or practices regarding admission, retention of membership, and advancement within the membership; (8) they often maintained some degree of distance or withdrawal from the rest of society; and (9) they developed organizational means of insuring their perpetuity.[14]

Early Christianity, as we shall see, also developed schools.

[11] Two samples of Epictetus' view of the way to cope with the unpredictability of life are found in Appendix 5.

[2] For Epicurus' view of pleasure, see Appendix 5.

A. Culpepper, *The Johannine School.*

. Culpepper, p. 259.

Religions and Religious Movements

If the Stoic view that everything was ordered according to Reason led to divine providence, there were also those who believed that the plan of the universe was mysteriously difficult to fathom. The early Greeks had come to believe that each person had his or her own "Fortune," "Chance," or "Destiny," deified as the goddess *Tychē* (Latin *Fortuna*). A somewhat more deterministic and less kindly view was called "Fate" (Greek *Heimarmenē*). It was influenced by Babylonian conceptions about the impersonal, fixed order of the stars and planets (who were also deified as gods, goddesses, and demons; in the New Testament, cf. Gal 4:8–10; Col 2:8). Hence the view arose that one's fortune or destiny was determined by the position of the stars at birth; by a knowledge of the stars, or astrology (Greek *astēr*, "star"), one could learn about his or her fate. The study of astrology was extremely widespread in the Hellenistic world, affecting almost every religion or religious philosophy. The most obvious reference to astrology in the New Testament is the star of the Magi (Matt 2:1–12, 16).[15]

Mention of the Magi leads to one of the areas where astrology was highly visible, namely, magic (Greek *magus*, a word borrowed from the Persians referring originally to the priests who practiced it).[16] For those who believed in it, magic was an attempt to gain some control over the mysterious powers that determined one's fate, and especially to provide protection against demonic powers (associated with stars) who brought about war, famine, disease, and family problems. To know the correct formula, and to recite it correctly, was a primitive "scientific" way of dealing with life's evil tragedies. The New Testament mentions a certain Simon from Samaria who practiced magic and attempted to buy Peter's powers (Acts 8:9–24); some details of gospel healing stories can be best understood in connection with magic.[17]

Still another type of religion in the Hellenistic world is the "mystery religion." Mystery religions seem to have originated in different countries but the gods or goddesses of one religion were often identified with those of another because they had similar characteristics. These religions are called "mystery religions" because they stress secret initiations.[18] Our knowledge of these initiations is incomplete. But there were also public celebrations that displayed great pageantry, usually involving the recital or reenactment of a myth to celebrate the death and resurrection of a hero or heroine corresponding to the death and rebirth of vegetation during the cycle of the agricultural year. There was also a sacred meal connected with the ritual. Though by modern standards many of these religions had bizarre qualities, they did promise the initiates immortality, mystical communion with their Deity, and membership in a

---

[15] Cf. Appendix 5 for a brief astrological comment by the Roman author, Vettius Valens.

[16] J. Hull, *Hellenistic Magic and the Synoptic Tradition*, chapters 1–3; A.D. Nock, "Greek Magical Papyri," reprinted in Z. Stewart, *Essays on Religion and the Ancient World*, pp. 176–94.

[17] Cf. Appendix 5 for a magical text which includes the name of Jesus.

[18] Cf. Appendix 5 for an account of the initiation into the Isis mysteries.

close-knit community. Examples of such mystery religions could be found in Greece (the Eleusinian Mysteries at Eleusis, not far from Athens; the religion of Dionysus or Bacchus, god of wine and the vintage harvest); Asia Minor (Cybele, the Great Mother, and her consort Attis, whose priests were castrated in imitation of Attis, driven mad by the jealous Cybele); Syria-Palestine (the Adonis fertility cult); Persia (the religion of Mithras, god of light and patron of the soldier); and Egypt (the religion of Isis and Osiris). Though the mysteries had sacred shrines in these regions, many of them spread to other parts of the empire, including Rome. There is no clearly direct influence of the mysteries on early Christianity, but they shared a common environment and many non-Christians would have perceived Christians as members of an oriental Jewish mystery cult.

A widespread religious movement which surfaced in the Roman Empire was Gnosticism. The term Gnosticism comes from the Greek word *gnōsis*, meaning "knowledge," that is, revealed religious knowledge necessary for salvation. Gnosticism was not a single religion but a diversified and complex religious phenomenon both independent of, and interacting with, Judaism and early Christianity. Discoveries in modern times (the Mandaean literature, the Manichaean papyri, the Nag Hammadi texts[19]) combined with the previously known Hermetic literature have convinced scholars that it was pre-Christian and originated in the East. There is still no consensus, however, on whether its essential ideas were current at the time of the rise of early Christianity. This is of particular interest since the myth of the Gnostic Redeemer, which some scholars believe influenced the way many early Christians understood the meaning of Jesus, can be documented with absolute certainty only in later Gnostic texts.[20] Yet, some form of early Gnosticism was probably in the air and it seems likely that on occasion New Testament writers were influenced by it or attempted to counter it.[21]

Basic to the Gnostic view is the perception that the world is an evil place, and that the only possible means of liberation from it is *gnōsis*—secretly revealed knowledge about God, the world, and the origin, condition, and destiny of humankind. The Gnostic Theodotus once summarized the content of *gnōsis* as:

> Who we were, what we have become;
> Where we were, whither we were thrown;
> Whither we are hastening, from what we are redeemed;
> What birth is, and what rebirth.

> Clement of Alexandria
> *Excerpts from Theodotus* 78.2[22]

Gnostic myths show that the evil world was not created by the good God, but by a second, inferior Deity, and that the true self, the divine self seen as a

---

[19] See Appendix 4 for the discovery of the Nag Hammadi texts.

[20] See Appendix 4 for the argument that the Gnostic Redeemer might have been early, an argument based on the Apocalypse of Adam.

[21] Further discussion may be found in E. Lohse, *Environment*, Part 2, chapter 3; a good introduction is H. Jonas, *The Gnostic Religion*.

[22] E. Lohse, *Environment*, pp. 255–56.

spark of light, is trapped in an alien body with all of its sensual passions.[23] This body-spirit dualism is expressed in another way, that the evil powers attempt to keep the true self in a state of sleep or drunkenness in order to hold the creation of the evil world together. To know the myths—to have *gnōsis*—is to have salvation!

In general, Gnostics believed that *gnōsis* can be taught or that it can be transmitted through a secret ritual, but ultimately it comes from above as a "call," or by a Gnostic Redeemer who descends from the world of light, disguises himself in human form without becoming bodily, teaches *gnōsis*, and returns or reascends. It is precisely the origin of this myth that is debated. Did it exist in New Testament times? Undoubtedly the possibilities for such mythical thinking were current in Mediterranean antiquity whether we label them "Gnostic" or not.[24] However the Gnostic gains his *gnōsis*, he learns that this world and this body are not his true home, that he has been "thrown" into an alien world. Often he totally renounces the body and its passions (asceticism) or, knowing that the world is not his true place and cannot really affect him, he allows himself the utmost freedom (libertinism). Either way, he experiences rebirth and becomes part of the privileged few.

It is clear that the problem of the origin of evil in Gnosticism differs from that found in Genesis, though the Genesis account is sometimes used to interpret that myth. Similarly, the reluctance of Gnostics to think of a Redeemer who can literally take human flesh, suffer, and die conflicts with the view of those early Christians who persisted in believing that Jesus of Nazareth was a god incarnate in the flesh. This latter belief became orthodox. But it must be recalled that this orthodoxy and its literature were only gradually accepted; until they were accepted, Gnostics, Gnostic Jews, and Gnostic Christians continued to exist side by side with other types of Jews and Christians in the period of the early Christian movement.

Gods and Saviors

The Greco-Roman world did not lack gods and goddesses. There are the deities of myth, those who dwell in the heavens or in some mythical mountain to the north, and those who are associated with the rhythms of the seasons.[25] Occasionally these eternal, immortal gods are said to descend, or are sent from heaven to earth, for some important redemptive mission on behalf of humankind, and occasionally they can be identified with historical figures, for example, the identification of the Gnostic Redeemer with Christ in certain Gnostic circles. Essentially they are gods, not human beings.[26]

But there were also human figures known from history and legend who were believed to be so endowed with divinity as to perform superhuman feats,

---

[23] E. Lohse, pp. 262–68; C. K. Barrett, *The New Testament Background*, chapter 5.
[24] C. Talbert, "The Myth of a Descending-Ascending Redeemer in Mediterranean Antiquity," *New Testament Studies* 22 (1975–1976), pp. 418–39.
[25] See above, pp. 11–13.
[26] C. Talbert, "Descending-Ascending Redeemer," pp. 418–20.

to be "supermen." They could be offspring of divine-human unions, but what is most characteristic of them is their wisdom and special powers, including their ability to work miracles.[27] Usually they were considered to be the great benefactors of humankind. In this category were all manner of kings, emperors, military conquerors, politicians, philosophers, physicians and healers, poets, and athletes. The notion of emperor worship, for example, was an adaptation of eastern beliefs about the divinity of the king or pharaoh. But western conquerors fostered such ideas on their marches eastward; in the eastern provinces the Roman emperor was often believed to be divine.[28] At home, the Greeks and Romans cautiously tolerated such views as a means to political unity and stability, but in fact discouraged them. When Roman emperors claimed divine prerogatives, they encountered stiff opposition, though it was customary to pay worthy emperors divine homage after they died. Also, majestic titles were often bestowed on the emperor (or demanded by some!) such as "Lord," "God," "Son of God," and "Savior." Titles of this sort were also given to Jesus.

Especially widespread was the notion of a hero or philosopher who was venerated for his ability to perform miracles or for his great wisdom, or both. Some modern scholars have called such a figure the "divine man."[29] These tremendous abilities were believed to be a manifestation of deity, even if the figure was not an immortal god. Yet, it may be that there was also a special class of "divine men" who, it was believed, were rewarded with the status of immortality at death.[30] One of the most famous was the itinerant Pythagorean philosopher Apollonios of Tyana (Asia Minor) who was said to have been sired by the Egyptian God Proteus, and to have gathered followers, taught, helped the poor, healed the sick, raised the dead, cast out demons, and appeared to his followers after death to discourse on immortality. He lived through most of the first Christian century, and shortly after 217 a "Life" of him was written by Philostratus. There is no evidence that Philostratus drew on the gospels; thus, the lives of famous heroes raise the question whether there are any literary prototypes for the New Testament "gospel."[31]

---

[27] M. Hadas and M. Smith, *Heroes and Gods;* see also D. R. Cartlidge and D. L. Dungan, *Documents for the Study of the Gospels,* esp. Intro.

[28] A Calendar Inscription from Priene in Asia Minor, 9 b.c., treated Augustus as a Savior, stating that ". . . the birthday of the God (Caesar Augustus) has been for the whole world the beginning of the gospel (*euangelion,* "good news") concerning him (therefore, let all reckon a new era beginning from the date of his birth, and let his birthday mark the beginning of the new year)." Cf. D. R. Cartlidge and D. Dungan, *Documents,* pp. 13–14; quoted from F. C. Grant, *Ancient Roman Religion,* p. 174.

[29] H. D. Betz, "Jesus as Divine Man," in F. T. Trotter, ed., *Jesus and the Historian;* P. J. Achtemeier, "Gospel Miracle Traditions and the Divine Man," *Interpretation* 26 (1972), pp. 174–97; for a critique of the category, see D. Tiede, *The Charismatic Figure as Miracle Worker;* C. Holladay, *Theios Anēr (Divine Man) in Hellenistic Judaism: A Critique of This Category in New Testament Christology.*

[30] C. Talbert, "The Concept of Immortals in Mediterranean Antiquity," *Journal of Biblical Literature* 94 (1975), pp. 410–36; see below chapter 10, pp. 295–96.

[31] N. Perrin, "The Literary *Gattung* 'Gospel'—Some Observations," *Expository Times* 82 (1970), pp. 4–7; see further, C. Talbert, *What Is a Gospel?*

There is much more that might be discussed about the general cultural and religious life of the Greco-Roman world;[32] for our purposes, however, it will be more important to narrow the focus to one specific Hellenistic religion, the religion of Judaism out of which Christianity began. In order to set the stage for understanding Judaism, it will first be necessary to retrace our steps and give a brief sketch of the history of the Jews.

HISTORY OF THE JEWS IN THE GREEK AND ROMAN PERIODS

The Hebrews had settled the land of Canaan in the late second millennium B.C.; in about 1000 B.C. there emerged the monarchy of King David and his son King Solomon.[33] About 921 the united monarchy split. First the northern kingdom ("Israel") was crushed by the Assyrians in 721 B.C., and the resulting population created by deportations and importations of peoples became eventually what the New Testament calls the Samaritans, who had a rival holy place, Mt. Gerizim: Then the southern kingdom ("Judah") was destroyed by Neobabylonia which deported its leaders ("the Babylonian Exile") and in 587 destroyed Jerusalem and its holy Temple. Thus began the "dispersion" of Jews from the homeland (Greek *Diaspora*), a phenomenon that continued throughout history.

The Babylonian Exile marked a major turning point in the history of the Jewish people. Many Jews elected to stay in Babylonia and it remained a center of Jewish life and thought for a thousand years. But when Cyrus the Great of Persia overcame Neobabylonia and permitted the Jews to return home by his Edict of Toleration in 538 B.C., groups of exiles returned periodically. First they laid the Temple foundations.They also hoped for the reestablishment of the monarchy under Zerubbabel upon whom they pinned messianic hopes (cf. the prophets Haggai 2:23 and Zechariah 3:8; 6:12). About 515 B.C. a modest Temple was dedicated. Despite Samaritan opposition Nehemiah rebuilt the walls of Jerusalem (437 B.C.). Finally—or perhaps earlier—Ezra, "a scribe skilled in the Law of Moses" (Ezra 7:6) came, bringing with him the sacred Law, or Torah, which included the sacred traditions which embodied the very life of the people. By now, the people no longer spoke its language, Hebrew, but a sister language which had become the standardized international language of administration in the Persian Empire, Aramaic.

Nonetheless, Ezra promulgated the Torah and the people celebrated the festival of Succoth, acts which symbolized Jewish identity. In fact, some marriages with non-Jews were dissolved (Ezra 10:18–44), and the book of Nehemiah stresses the necessity to follow Torah, to avoid trade with non-Jews on the Sabbath, to observe the rule that the land was to lie fallow and that the slaves were to be released every seventh year (the Sabbatical Year), and to pay Temple taxes promptly. All this should not be interpreted to mean that Juda-

---

[32] See F.E. Peters, *The Harvest of Hellenism.*
[33] Standard historical treatments are J. Bright, *A History of Israel,* and M. Noth, *The History of Israel.*

ism had become simply an ingrown, protective, and national-chauvinistic religion legalistically seeking repentance in order to gain God's favor. Archeological evidence indicates that extensive contacts with surrounding nations existed in this period and, in fact, there were temples outside of Jerusalem![34] Indeed, Babylonian ideas of wisdom, astrology, and magic, as well as Persian views of resurrection of the dead and final judgment, made their way into Jewish thinking. Perhaps most important, this was a period of intense literary activity during which time much of what later became Scripture in Judaism was collected, edited, written.[35] Yet, Judaism did evolve emphases on Torah and its interpretation. Gradually prophecy waned and the High Priests gained in political power and religious authority as interpreters of the sacred books. Ultimately, the Torah, centered in the Pentateuch, and its interpretation would rival and even surpass in authority the Temple and the priesthood. Judaism became a "religion of the book," and Torah and its interpretation were central to its life and thought.

Then came Alexander and Hellenization. Archeological evidence indicates that the upperclasses in Palestine were probably already influenced by Greek culture in the third century B.C.[36] Indeed, Greek ways soon entered the city of Jerusalem,[37] while Babylonian astronomical, meteorological, and calendrical speculations seem to have continued to influence the Jews.[38] One gets the impression that Hellenization, had it proceeded at its own pace, might have continued a progressive and uninterrupted alteration of Jewish life and culture, at least in the urban areas. But this did not happen.

When the Seleucid Greeks finally overcame the Ptolemies in 198 B.C., Palestine came under Seleucid domination. Although the Jews welcomed the Seleucids, in 190 B.C. the Romans defeated the Seleucids (but allowed them to remain in office), and forced them to pay an enormous indemnity, which was passed on to their own subjected peoples, including the Jews. Now the fortunes of the Jews took a turn for the worse.

In 175 B.C. Antiochus IV Epiphanes ("[god] manifest") took the Seleucid throne.[39] Antiochus was an eccentric despot who sought to *enforce* Hellenization throughout his empire. When Jason, a priest who was pro-Greek offered a huge sum of money for the High Priesthood and promised to turn Jerusalem into a Greek city, Antiochus accepted and Hellenization proceeded at a rapid pace. But Jason was soon out-bought by Menelaus, a rival for the post. Even-

---

[34] M. Stone, *Scriptures, Sects, and Visions. A Profile of Judaism from Ezra to the Jewish Revolts,* chapter 3 and pp. 78–82; cf. also S. Talmon, "Ezra and Nehemiah," *IDB Suppl.,* pp. 317–28; E. Bickerman, *From Ezra to the Last of the Maccabees.*

[35] See Appendix 1, "The Canon of the Bible."

[36] M. Stone, pp. 27–28, on the basis of the Aramaic papyri from Wadi Dāliyeh.

[37] The Hebrew book of Ben Sirach, or Ecclesiasticus, written about 180 B.C., defends Judaism against Hellenism, but shows strong Hellenistic influences. Ben Sirach was born, bred, and ran a school in Jerusalem.

[38] M. Stone, chapters 4 and 5.

[39] For further history see E. Schürer, *The History of the Jewish People in the Age of Jesus Christ,* revised and edited by G. Vermes and F. Miller, vol. 1. The chief ancient sources for this period are 1 Maccabees and the Jewish historian Flavius Josephus, cf. H. Kee, *The Origins of Christianity. Sources and Documents,* pp. 10–44.

tually civil war broke out among the various rival factions. Antiochus, disgruntled because of his setback in the war with Egypt, interpreted the civil strife in Jerusalem as a revolt against his Hellenizing efforts. He attacked Jerusalem, exterminated all males who resisted, and sold women and children into slavery. The city walls were torn down; the old citadel of the Temple was fortified as a Greek garrison (the Akra). Then Antiochus attempted to obliterate the Jewish religion by forbidding Temple sacrifices, traditional festivals, Sabbath worship, and the rite of circumcision (the sign of the covenant), upon pain of death. Torah scrolls were ordered destroyed, and every town in Judea was commanded to sacrifice to the Greek gods. An altar was erected over the altar of burnt offering in the Jerusalem Temple; sacrifices were offered to the Olympian high god, Zeus. This event was etched on the memory of the Jews as "the abomination of desolation" (1 Macc 1:54, 59; Dan 11:31; 12:11). This was no mere assimilation of Greek ways; it was a threat of the annihilation of traditional Judaism.

The response to these events was the Maccabean Revolt in 167. When Antiochus' emissary came to the little town of Modein and demanded that the people offer sacrifices, Mattathias, of priestly stock, refused. Seeing one of the Jews about to comply, he rushed forward and slew him at the altar and then killed the king's emissary, "acting zealously for the law of God, as Phinehas had done" (cf. Num 25:6–15). Then he and his sons fled to the hills and were joined by many others. At his death, his son Judas Maccabeus took charge and waged a successful guerilla war against the Seleucids, retook Jerusalem, and in 164 restored and rededicated the Temple, giving birth to the Feast of Hanukkah ("Dedication"), or "Lights." Thus began a long war which, despite great odds, ended in victory and the establishment of the Maccabean, or Hasmonean, kingdom, an independent kingdom which lasted until 63 B.C.

In summary, the Greek period, 333 B.C. to 63 B.C., was marked by two trends: the Hellenization of Palestine, and the reaction of the Jews to *forced* Hellenization resulting in the Maccabean Revolt and the independent Hasmonean kingdom. From this history we can see several forces at work: the tendency of some to come to terms with Hellenization; the tendency of others to hold onto the traditional ways; and the willingness of still others to revolt because of "zealousness" for the Law when the traditions are severely attacked. Similar responses will occur in the first century A.D. Moreover, in the period of the independent Hasmonean kingdom, three religious movements appear for the first time: the Sadducees, the Pharisees, and the Essenes. We shall discuss them further when we take up Jewish religion.

In 63 B.C. the Roman general Pompey was invited to settle a dispute between two Maccabeans. He sided with Hyrcanus II and his supporters, one of whom was the ruler of Idumea, Antipater II. From this point forward, however, Palestine was considered to be controlled by Rome and in the reorganization by Augustus, it fell under the administration of the imperial province of Syria. Unlike senatorial provinces Roman troops were stationed in imperial provinces to keep order and were governed by a military governor called a "Legate" who, in this case, resided at Antioch. There were also "districts" that were testy enough to be governed directly by the emperor through his "prefect" (later

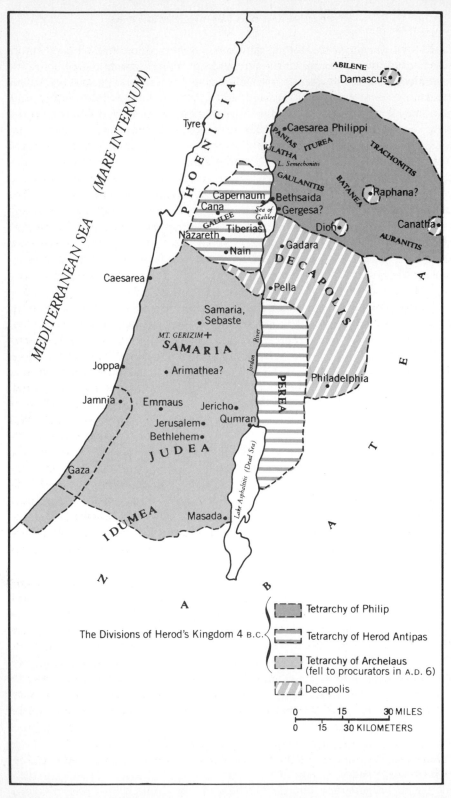

ABILENE

Damascus

Tyre

PHOENICIA

MEDITERRANEAN SEA (MARE INTERNUM)

Caesarea Philippi

PANIAS ITUREA

ULATHA

L. Semechonitis

GAULANITIS

TRACHONITIS

BATANEA

Raphana?

Capernaum
Cana

Sea of
Galilee

Bethsaida
Gergesa?

Dion

Canatha

GALILEE

Tiberias

AURANITIS

Nazareth

Nain

Gadara

DECAPOLIS

Caesarea

Pella

Samaria,
Sebaste

MT. GERIZIM ✝

Jordan River

SAMARIA

Joppa

Arimathea?

Philadelphia

PEREA

Jamnia

Emmaus

Jericho

Jerusalem

Qumran

Bethlehem

JUDEA

Lake Asphaltitis (Dead Sea)

Gaza

IDUMEA

Masada

N

A

B

The Divisions of Herod's Kingdom 4 B.C.

⬛ Tetrarchy of Philip

▦ Tetrarchy of Herod Antipas

▨ Tetrarchy of Archelaus
(fell to procurators in A.D. 6)

▨ Decapolis

0   15   30 MILES

0   15   30 KILOMETERS

Palestine in the time of Jesus.

"procurator"). The chief responsibilities of the governors were civil order, the administration of justice (including the judicial right of life and death), and the collection of taxes which were often farmed out to local tax companies whose income was what they collected in excess, a system open to abuse. The system was policed by the Roman army, in the legions only Roman citizens, in the auxiliary units, local recruits. The Romans were sensitive enough to permit the Jews some special privileges: exemption from military service, from going to court on the Sabbath, from being required to portray the emperor's head on its coins (hence, the need for money changers at the Temple), and from having to offer sacrifices to the emperor as a deity, this being replaced by sacrifices "for Caesar and the Roman nation" twice daily. Furthermore, the Romans were not to represent the image of the emperor on their military standards in areas of heavy Jewish population. Yet, it is also clear that these concessions were not always carried out in practice, and in Palestine there were a number of occasions when more restless elements in the population resisted Roman abuses and followed the tradition of "zealousness for the Law."

In the meantime, the Idumeans Antipater and especially one of his sons, Herod ("the Great"), were crafty enough to shift allegiances to a succession of Romans—Pompey, Julius Caesar, Cassius, Antony, and finally Octavian—and by this means Herod emerged as a powerful puppet king ("ethnarch") under the Romans (ruled 37–4 B.C.). Herod proved to be an extremely capable tyrant. To consolidate his power, he had numerous opponents and relatives executed, including his wife Miramme, thus eliminating the possibility of the return of the Hasmoneans. To win the favor of the emperor he became an ardent Hellenizer. He surrounded himself with Greek scholars and undertook many building projects, including a magnificent and fortified palace. He rebuilt the Temple in Jerusalem with a fortress on its corner (Antonia), and in other non-Jewish areas he built whole cities with the usual manifestations of Greek culture such as theaters, baths, and amphitheaters. Herod also built many military fortifications, most famous of which was the fortress of Masada along the Dead Sea.[40] In his final years, Herod was plagued by domestic problems. He died unloved and unmourned by either family or nation. Before he died, Jesus of Nazareth was born.[41]

Herod's final will, slightly modified by Augustus, divided his kingdom among three sons. Philip (4 B.C.–A.D. 33 or 34) was named "tetrarch" of the largely non-Jewish regions northeast of the Sea of Galilee. Herod Antipas (4 B.C.–A.D. 39) became tetrarch of Galilee and Perea, an area across the Jordan River. Herod Antipas is the king of Galilee in the gospel stories (cf. Luke 13:31–33, "that fox") and is remembered for the execution of John the Baptist (cf. Mark 6:17–29) and, in the gospel of Luke, as well for his contemptuous treatment of Jesus (Luke 23:6–12). He was finally exiled by the Roman emperor, Caligula. The third son, Archelaus, was given Samaria and Judea in the

---

[40] Y. Yadin, *Masada*; "Masada," *IDB Suppl.*, pp. 577–80; cf. Appendix 5.

[41] Sixth-century A.D. calculations of the birth of Jesus were in error by at least 4 years. Modern scholars usually date his birth at 6–4 B.C.

South. He was opposed by his subjects and by his brother, Herod Antipas. Also at this time there was unrest in Galilee caused by a certain Judas the Galilean so that there was soon total revolt in Judea. Archelaus went to Rome to appeal his position, while the Legate of Syria intervened with troops to restore peace. When he returned Archelaus treated his subjects so brutally that he was eventually summoned back to Rome, dismissed, and banished to Gaul in A.D. 6. Except for the short period of the reign of Herod Agrippa I over all of Palestine from A.D. 41 to 44, Samaria and Judea fell under the authority of procurators appointed directly from Rome, as did most of the land after 44. Thus, during the adult life of Jesus, Galilee was ruled by Herod Antipas and Judea-Samaria by the procurator, Pontius Pilate (A.D. 26–36).

Life for the Jews under the procurators was exceedingly difficult. Pontius Pilate, for example, was described by Agrippa I as ". . . by nature unbending and severe with the stubborn," and accused of ". . . the taking of bribes, wanton insolence, rapacity, outrages, countless and continuous murders, endless and most painful cruelty."[42] This portrait is confirmed by the Jewish historian Josephus who chronicled a number of events that provoked the Jews under Pilate and the other procurators, leading to riots, beatings, and executions.[43] Pilate was eventually removed by the Legate of Syria on the complaints of Samaritans, whom he had mistreated. After the interim reign of Herod Agrippa I ended in A.D. 44, the situation under the procurators deteriorated even further. In one case, says Josephus (who likes to inflate figures), 20,000 Jews were killed in a riot which was prompted when a Roman soldier ridiculed some Passover pilgrims with an indecent gesture. There thus emerged within Judaism groups of revolutionaries who looked back to the militaristic Maccabees and their zeal for the Law as great heroes. These "Zealots" were already active in spirit, if not in name, in the period prior to the birth of Jesus. In A.D. 6 or 7, Judas the Galilean and a Pharisee named Zaddok attempted to arouse the people to revolt against the first Roman census. Self-styled prophets and messiahs appeared from time to time and eventually an even more radical group, the Sicarii (Latin *sicarius*, "dagger"), emerged to foment revolution by assassination. Clearly, the policy of the tyrannical and brutal procurators, like that of the Seleucid Hellenizer Antiochus IV over 150 years earlier, met with increasing opposition led by more revolutionary Jews; ultimately, the forces of moderation could not contain them.

The last of the procurators, Gessius Florus (A.D. 64–66), was probably the worst. In the spring of A.D. 66, he robbed the Temple treasury of a great sum of money. The outraged populace mocked him by taking up a collection. Florus took revenge by allowing his troops to plunder part of the city of Jerusalem. Attempts at mediation by the priests failed, and when departing troops did not respond to friendly overtures of the Jewish crowds, the people began slinging insults at Florus. Slaughter ensued. But in a bloody street battle, the people

---

[42] Philo, *Embassy to Gaius*, 38, as quoted in W. Foerster, *From the Exile to Christ*, p. 101; cf. C. K. Barrett, *Background*, pp. 123–24; H. Kee, *Documents*, pp. 50–51.

[43] C. K. Barrett, pp. 123–24.

eventually gained the upper hand, took possession of the Temple mount, and cut off the passage between the Temple and the Roman-held fortress of Antonia. Further attempts at mediation by Agrippa II, leading Pharisees, and the priestly aristocracy could not quell the revolt. The fortress of Masada, taken earlier by the Romans, was retaken by rebels and, at the direction of the son of the High Priest, Eleazar, the sacrifices in behalf of the emperor were stopped. This was, in effect, a declaration of war.

An initial success in routing the army of the Legate of Syria encouraged the rebels and the land was organized for battle. The emperor Nero (A.D. 54–68) dispatched his experienced commander Vespasian, who organized the legions at Antioch and sent his son, Titus, to Alexandria to bring up the fifteenth legion. The newly organized army contained a formidable force of 60,000 troops. Galilee, organized for the Jews by the future historian Josephus, offered only moderate resistance, causing the radicals to believe—with some justification—that the leadership was not fully dedicated. The Zealots under the leadership of John of Gischala sought to replace them with more dedicated patriots, while (if tradition is correct[44]) the Christians fled to Pella across the Jordan. Now Jerusalem found herself in a bloody civil war between the moderate and radical forces. The experienced Vespasian subdued the surrounding areas, deciding to let the Jews exhaust themselves. Then, in A.D. 68, news came of Nero's suicide and Vespasian again delayed. In quick succession, Galba, Otho, and the western commander, Vitellius, became emperor. But the East was not to be denied; Vespasian was also acclaimed emperor and after the assassination of Vitellius, Vespasian left for Rome to assume his role, leaving his son Titus to complete the war.

When in the spring of A.D. 70 Titus began the siege of Jerusalem, the Jewish factions of the city united against a common enemy. Though they fought valiantly, Titus built a wall around the city making it impossible for the Jews to get provisions. Hunger and thirst began to take their toll. Gradually the various walled divisions of the city fell, one by one, and the fortress of Antonia was retaken. Titus attempted to save the Temple, but in the heat of battle it was ravaged by fire. The Jews refused to surrender. Women, children, and the elderly, all were butchered, and the city and most of its walls destroyed. The major battle over, Titus set sail for Rome with 700 handsome prisoners for the victory parade through Rome, commemorated by the arch of Titus, still to be seen in the Roman Forum.

The victory belonged to the Romans. Several fortresses still remained to be subdued, however. The most difficult was the mesa along the Dead Sea fortified by Herod the Great, the fortress of Masada. Commanded by the descendant of Judas the Galilean, Eleazar son of Yair, it was almost impenetrable. The task fell to Flavius Silva who, because of the steepness of the cliffs, built a tremendous wall of earth as a bridge across which the huge battering ram could be rolled into place. When Eleazar saw that the Jewish cause was hopeless, he addressed the garrison; he asked that they kill their families, and

[44] Eusebius, *Ecclesiastical History* 3.5, 3.

then each other. It was done. The Romans finally breached the wall, but there was no battle left to be fought.[45]

With Jerusalem and the Temple destroyed, the heart of Judaism was pierced. What survived was a totally reorganized Judaism under the Pharisees who met at the coastal town of Jamnia, along with those Jewish communities of the Diaspora. To be sure, Palestinian Judaism still flickered—enough that another revolt in Judea broke out in A.D. 132–35, probably in response to the emperor Hadrian's empirewide ban on circumcision (not exclusively a Jewish practice), his attempt to establish a Greco-Roman city (Aelia Capitolina) where the Jewish holy city had stood, and his intention to build a temple to Jupiter Capitolinus on the site of the previous Jerusalem Temple. The leader of the revolt, bar Kosiba, called bar Kochba ("Son of the Star," a messianic title, cf. Num 24:17) by his supporters, but bar Koziba ("Son of the Lie" = "Liar") by his detractors, also failed. Hadrian's plans were carried out; Jews living in Jerusalem were driven out and not permitted to return upon punishment by death. From that time on, Judaism became primarily Diaspora Judaism, a Judaism without a homeland, until the establishment of the state of Israel in 1948.

MAJOR FEATURES OF JUDAISM IN THE GREEK AND ROMAN PERIODS

It is clear from the foregoing sketch that the historical fortunes and misfortunes of the Jews in this period were intertwined with their religious beliefs, many of which were shared by the early Christians. A brief account of these will be an aid to understanding the pages of the New Testament.

God and His People

As Judaism emerged from the Babylonian conquest and exile, it inherited the stress of Israelite religion on monotheism: "Hear, O Israel, the Lord our God, the Lord is one . . ." (Deut 6:4). God's name, Yahweh, had become too holy to pronounce, being substituted with *Adonai* ("lord"). According to Genesis 15 and 17, God had made an agreement, or covenant, with Abraham that the land of Canaan would be given to Abraham and his descendants. This agreement had been sealed by a sign, circumcision of every male child. The covenant meant that the Jews believed themselves to be the special people of God, his elect or chosen people, with a mission to become "a light to the nations." As the writers of the historical traditions of Israel expressed it, God had created the world, had delivered his people from bondage in Egypt, and had given them the land of Canaan. Other covenants, one with Moses, another with David, that is, agreements about the Law and the monarchy, were made. God had revealed himself and his plan for his people; but if the king or the people disobeyed the covenant, they were subject to God's just punishment.

[45] Josephus, *Wars*, VII.8.

Temple and Priesthood[46]

The first Temple was built by Solomon, David's son, in the tenth century B.C., and destroyed by the Neobabylonians in 587 B.C. A modest Temple was rebuilt by the returning exiles in 515 B.C. and further reconstructed on a grand scale in the Roman-Herodian period (see page xx). This reconstruction was begun by Herod the Great in 20 B.C., and it was not completed until about A.D. 60, only to be destroyed a decade later! In the Persian period, the priests gained power in the absence of an actual king and the decline of prophecy; in fact, the High Priest as leader of the cultus and interpreter of religious traditions became the most powerful figure in Judaism.[47] However, the High Priesthood became something of a political position under the Seleucid Greeks; then the Maccabees, who were also of priestly descent (though of an undistinguished line), assumed control of the High Priesthood and eventually assumed royal prerogatives as well, thus succumbing to the politicization of the office. Hence, other priestly parties made their appearance, among them the Essenes and the Sadducees (see below). Under the Herodians and procurators, High Priests were of varying families, and they were appointed to the post; nonetheless, they maintained a measure of political power, for they continued to preside over the central cultus at the Temple and over the religious Sanhedrin, the highest court of Judaism. The destruction of Jerusalem and the Temple in A.D. 70 meant the end of their power.

Apart from the political functions of the priests, their major religious functions consisted of the maintenance of purity by the sacrificial system at the Temple. In Judaism the definition of sin was not only a moral question but also it was concerned with the practice of ritual, notions of sacred and profane, purity and impurity; this distinction is often lost to the modern consciousness. In ancient Israel a whole system of sacrifices had arisen to atone for sin, that is, to set sinful humankind right with the one, holy God. This system was administered by the priests and sacrifices were offered at least twice a day. Even the architectural plans of the successive temples reflect the various degrees of holiness. The outermost area of the Herodian Temple, for example, was accessible to Gentiles; beyond it they could not go "under penalty of death." Moving toward the center in the Sacred Enclosure (for Jews) came the Court of Women, the Court of Israel (men), the Court of Priests and the forecourt where the sacrifices took place, the Holy Place, and finally the Holy of Holies into which the High Priest entered only once a year, on the Day of Atonement. Thus the Temple was the holy center of the holy city in a holy land. Yet, like all oriental temples, it was also the hub of much economic and commercial activity, for it housed the national treasury. Every Jew was expected to pay the annual Temple tax.

[46] D. Gowan, *Bridge Between the Testaments*, chapter 16.
[47] See Appendix 5 for a description of the Jewish High Priest from ben Sirach 50.

Feasts and Fasts[48]

Most Jews followed a lunar calendar which required the insertion of an extra month every two or three years to account for almost 11 days in the solar year. Following the Jewish months, the feasts and one fast are as follows:

1. Nisan 15 (Mar./Apr.) (7 days) — Passover and the Feast of Unleavened Bread (*Pesaḥ* and *Mazzoth*), Exod 12–13.

2. 50 days after Passover, Sivan 6 (May/June) — Weeks (in the New Testament, Pentecost) (*Shavuoth*), Lev 23:15–16.

3. Tishri 1 (Sept./Oct.) — New Year (*Rosh Hashanah*), Lev 23:24.

4. Tishri 10 — Day of Atonement (*Yom Kippur*), Lev 16 and 23:26–32.

5. Tishri 15 (8 days) — Booths (*Succōth*), Exod 23:14–17; Lev 23:34–36.

6. Kislev 25 (Nov./Dec.) (8 days) — Dedication (*Hanukkah*), 1 Macc 4:42–58; 2 Macc 10:1–8.

7. Adar 14 (Feb./Mar.) (2 days) — Lots (*Purim*), Esther.

Three feasts—Passover, Weeks, and Booths—were Pilgrim Festivals, that is, (male) pilgrims were obligated to make a pilgrimage to Jerusalem. "Passover" in popular etymology is a reference to the "passing over" by the angel of death of the houses of the Israelites in Egypt whose lintel and doorposts were marked with the blood of the sacrificial lamb. Originally a nomadic rite of sacrifice to maintain the fertility of the flock, it came to commemorate the exodus from slavery to freedom. This rite was associated with the week-long Feast of Unleavened Bread, originally marking the barley harvest. In the period of the New Testament, goats and lambs were ritually slaughtered at the Temple in the afternoon before the feast began (the Day of Preparation) and the blood was sprinkled on the altar; when the sun was setting, the feast proper began with a common meal at a house or apartment within the city walls of Jerusalem. The pilgrim was obliged to find a room in the city, procure a male yearling sheep or goat for sacrifice, and buy wine, unleavened bread dough, and spices, and to celebrate with a minimum of ten males.

The Feast of Weeks ("Pentecost"), originally a celebration of the fertility of the land at the end of the grain harvest, became associated with the arrival of the Israelites at Mt. Sinai, and hence came to commemorate the giving of the Law at that time to Moses. The third Pilgrim Feast, Booths (*Succōth*), was originally a festival of harvesting grapes when booths were built in the vineyards for grape pickers; it, too, represents events in Israel's history, namely, the wilderness wanderings. *Hanukkah* celebrated the "dedication" of the Temple

[48] H. Schauss, *The Jewish Festivals, History and Observances.*

after its defilement by the Seleucid Greeks, and *Purim* (Lots) celebrated the victory of Persian Jews over Haman who cast lots in his attempt to exterminate them. The book of Esther, which tells the story, was read on this day.

The only prescribed fast in the written Torah (Lev 16)—custom developed others—was *Yom Kippur,* the Day of Atonement. On this fast day, also marked by rest and penance, the High Priest sacrificed a bull for his sins and for the sins of the Aaronic priesthood; then he entered the Holy of Holies and sprinkled its blood on the "mercy seat" of the Ark of the Covenant, the place from which God was merciful toward his people. Combined with this was an originally separate ritual in which two goats were presented by the people, one for God, one "for Azazel." The former was sacrificed to atone for the sins of the people; then the High Priest placed his hands on the latter, shifting to it the sins of the people. A man led it into the desert, after which he purified himself. In this way the sins of the community were driven off into the desert (the "scapegoat").

Synagogue and Prayer

Sacrifice was an enacted prayer, that is, a means of human communication with God, and there were other forms of liturgical prayer, for example, the whole tradition of chants and psalms which in New Testament times had become the special province of a class of Temple priests, the Levites. This form of public prayer was continued even where there was no access to the Jerusalem Temple. When the synagogue (from the Greek for "gathering together") developed sometime in the post-exilic period (the earliest archeological evidence is from the first century A.D.), it served as a "house of prayer," as well as a gathering place for meetings, meditation, and instruction. No sacrifice was offered there. Rather, the synagogue services probably consisted of a recitation of the *Shemā* ("Hear, O Israel, the Lord our God, the Lord is one . . ."), Scripture, sermon, blessing, and, of course, prayer.[49] Prayers could also be offered at any time and any place; yet, they should be oriented toward Jerusalem—specifically the Holy of Holies—and it was customary to offer them three special times a day, namely, morning, midday, and evening. Standing or kneeling with hands raised to heaven were the usual positions.

The Centrality of Torah

In the post-exilic period, Judaism sought God's will more and more in sacred tradition, that is, the written word and its interpretation became the very basis of life. *Torah* meant "instruction," in its widest sense any form of revelation, in a somewhat narrower sense Scripture and its written and (especially) oral interpretation, in a still narrower sense the Pentateuch, and most specifically the legal materials in the Pentateuch. It was therefore "law," but it

[49] See Appendix 5 for some traditional synagogue prayers.

was much more. To study it and to do it were a "delight" (Ps 1:2; cf. Ps 19), and the heroes and heroines of Judaism were frequently those who kept the Torah despite adversity, war, or persecution (Tobit; Judith; Daniel). In the period as a whole, we can observe different attitudes toward the Torah, from the Maccabees and Zealots whose enthusiastic observance of the Law led them to fight and die for it, to the Sadducees who accepted only a literal view of the Pentateuch, or the Essenes who found in it prophecies about their own community of the end-time. In general, something is known about the tendency of the Pharisees and their descendants to expand the written word by the oral tradition in order to apply it to constantly changing conditions. This meant a certain retelling, rewriting, and constant debate, and by the first century we are aware of the appearance of "schools." All this was done "to make a hedge for the Torah" (Sayings of the Fathers 1:1), that is, to keep it from being transgressed. If to preserve the Sabbath commandment (Exod 20:8–10; 35:1–3), one should not work, what is work?

> The main classes of work are forty save one: sowing, ploughing, reaping, binding sheaves, threshing, winnowing, cleansing crops, grinding, sifting, kneading, baking, shearing wool, washing or beating or dyeing it, spinning, weaving, making two loops, weaving two threads, separating two threads, tying [a knot], loosening [a knot], sewing two stitches, tearing in order to sew two stitches, hunting a gazelle, slaughtering or flaying or salting it or curing its skin, scraping it or cutting it up, writing two letters, building, pulling down, putting out a fire, lighting a fire, striking with a hammer and taking out aught from one domain into another. These are the main classes of work: forty save one.[50]

From there it would be necessary to go into more detail. As it developed, the tradition arose among the Pharisees that the Law came from Moses on Mt. Sinai who gave it to Joshua, who gave it to the Elders, who gave it to the prophets, who gave it to the men of the "Great Synagogue." So important was the Torah to the Jews that all phases of life and thought were inspired and guided by it.

Wisdom

The Wisdom literature has an ancient and venerable tradition in the Ancient Near East. Examples from the Old Testament are Proverbs, Job, Ecclesiastes, and some of the psalms; examples from post-exilic Judaism are all late, since practically no literature has survived from the period 400–200 B.C. These examples include such books as the Wisdom of Jesus ben Sirach (Ecclesiasticus), the Wisdom of Solomon, Tobit, Baruch, the Letter of Aristeas, and the Sayings of the Fathers. The Wisdom movement was fostered by "wise men" who were originally part of the royal court, and though its most characteristic form is probably the proverb, it also includes a wide variety of other forms,

---

[50] C. K. Barrett, *Documents*, p. 154, quoting from the Mishnah on the Sabbath.

including the parable. Characteristically, Wisdom deals with the practical knowledge about the world and human relations which will help the individual to prosper and lead a long and fruitful life. Here are examples of the practical, proverbial type:

> A continual dripping on a rainy day
> and a contentious woman are alike.
>
> Prov 27:5

> He [Hillel] used to say:
>   If I am not for myself, who is for me?
>   And when I am for myself, what am I?
>   And if not now, when?
> Shammai said:
>   Make thy Torah a fixed *duty*;
>   Say little and do much;
>   And receive every man with the look of a cheerful face.
>
> Sayings of the Fathers 1:14–15

Such practical wisdom was considered to be from God. But there was also the growth of the Wisdom myth, that is, that Wisdom was the personified expression or extension of God.

> Wisdom found no place where she might dwell;
> Then a dwelling-place was assigned her in the heavens.
> Wisdom went forth to make her dwelling among the children of men,
> And found no dwelling-place.
> Wisdom returned to her place,
> And took her seat among the angels.
>
> Enoch 42:1–2

As in Greco-Roman religions at large, we observe the descent/ascent motif.

Apocalyptic Eschatology[51]

The term eschatology is from the Greek *to eschaton*, "the end," and *ho logos*, "the word," "the teaching," and it means, therefore, "teaching concerning the end of things," specifically teaching concerning the end of the world. A particular form of eschatology is called apocalyptic, from the Greek *apocalypsis*, "an uncovering," "a revelation," and it describes both a movement and a literature that characteristically claimed that God had revealed to a writer the secrets of the imminent end of the world and so had given him a message for his people. As with Wisdom, the literature dates after 200 B.C. and is largely non-Biblical (that is, outside the Old Testament). It reveals a very diversified Judaism prior to A.D. 70, one marked by a number of movements which, if measured by the Judaism that survived the wars, appears in many respects

---

[51] P. Hanson, "Apocalypticism," *IDB Suppl.*, pp. 28–34; see below, chapter 4.

non-normative or unusual. Much of that literature is the literature of apocalyptic eschatology.

There is no absolute agreement about what constitutes apocalyptic eschatology either with respect to its origins or content. It shows influences of Old Testament prophecy and Wisdom literature; but there are also currents of Persian dualism and Babylonian astrology. It is a child of hope and despair: hope in the invincible power of God and the world he created, as well as his plan and purpose for his people, but despair of the present course of human history in that world. The one true God was the creator and the ruler of all within it: that was the primary tenet of Jewish faith. At the same time the actual experience of the people of God in the world was catastrophic: Assyrian and Babylonian conquest; exile in foreign lands; Persian domination; the coming of the Greeks; and finally, the Romans. The burdens of war, occupation, forced Hellenization, and taxation by imperialistic powers produced an intolerable experience of alienation and powerlessness. Human history was a virtual descent into hell. But God was the ruler of all things and, therefore, the tragic events of human history must have been foreordained by him. Thus, there was some divine plan through which the horrors of history would reach a climax and everything would change. The hope was that the world would become much the same as it had been in the beginning of time, a paradise in which God's elect people would be vindicated. This change would be marked by tremendous historical and cosmic catastrophies. In the meantime the people of God had to prepare themselves for the change and watch for the signs of its coming.

The most apocalyptic book in the Old Testament is the book of Daniel, which contains the Son of Man vision in 7:13–14, highly influential in the gospels:

> I saw in the night visions,
> and behold, with the clouds of heaven
> there came one like a son of man,
> and he came to the Ancient of Days
> and was presented before him.
> And to him was given dominion
> and glory and kingdom,
> that all peoples, nations, and languages
> should serve him;
> his dominion is an everlasting dominion,
> which shall not pass away,
> and his kingdom one
> that shall not be destroyed.

There are many other forms of the apocalyptic hope. The Assumption of Moses, a work contemporary with the New Testament, is particularly interesting because of its use of "Kingdom of God," a key concept in the teaching of Jesus.[52] Another form of the hope is associated with the coming of a Son of

[52] See Appendix 5 for the passage in the Assumption of Moses.

David found in the first century B.C. document called the Psalms of Solomon.[53] Despite the variety of the forms of expression, the hope itself is constant for a climactic series of events that will lead to the final, eschatological intervention of God into human history, directly or through intermediary figures. Through these events the world would be forever changed, transformed into a perfect world in which the people of God would be forever blessed for their fidelity, and their enemies and God's forever punished.

This hope is called the "apocalyptic" hope because the characteristic claim of the literature that expresses it is that God has uncovered or revealed to the writer or seer his plan for the further course of history and the coming of the End. This revelation frequently takes the form of dreams or visions, which are then interpreted by a heavenly figure. The dreams or visions generally use symbols to recount the history of the Jewish (or Christian) people and to express the hope for the immediate future. So, for example, Daniel 7 tells in symbols the history of the Near Eastern world from the Babylonian Empire through the Persian Empire to the conquests of Alexander the Great and his ten successors as kings of the Macedonian Seleucid Kingdom of Syria. The final symbol used to represent a king is the "little horn" (Dan 7:8), which represents Antiochus IV Epiphanes, who began persecuting the Jews in 167 B.C. in an attempt to consolidate his empire. The result was the Jewish revolt. The author of Daniel 7 is living at the time of this Maccabean revolt, writing to inspire his people with confidence that the war is the beginning of the End, that it will shortly be ended by the coming of the Son of Man as judge and ruler of the world.

The book of Daniel is pseudonymous, that is, it was written long after the time of most of the events it pretends to prophesy under an assumed name. This is characteristic of Jewish apocalyptic writings, and usually a name of some importance—Abraham, Moses, David, or the like—would be chosen. This feature, of course, lent the writing a certain authority, and there was no modern notion of fraud or copyright. The history would be portrayed in symbolic form leading up to the symbolic vision of the seer. The seer also dreamed and thought in traditional symbolic images, and frequently he alluded to previously written texts that contained them.

These are the most important characteristics of apocalyptic eschatology: a sense of alienation and of despair about history that bred the belief that the world was rushing to a foreordained tragic climax; a hope in God that fostered the conviction that he would act in the climactic moment to change things utterly and forever; and a conviction that it would be possible to recognize the signs of the coming of that climactic moment. Its chief literary characteristics were pseudonymity, symbolism, and quotation from previously existing texts.

Associated with some apocalyptic eschatological texts is the hope for a future redeemer, a Messiah. Originally the term "Messiah" (Hebrew *mashiah*; Greek *Christos*) meant anointed, and in the Old Testament it was applied to any figure that was installed into office by anointing, that is, prophets, priests,

[53] See Appendix 5 for the passage in the Psalms of Solomon.

or kings. Any of these figures was an "anointed one," or messiah. In the eschatological materials, there are several types of expectation. We have just noted a future redeemer and judge, the Son of Man. Other Jews hoped for a descendant of David to come, overthrow the enemies, and reestablish the Davidic kingdom. In the Dead Sea Scrolls (see below), there is evidence for a triple expectation: a prophet like Moses, a royal Messiah of the line of David ("the Messiah of Israel"), and a priestly Messiah ("the Messiah of Aaron"). The following passage combines this with adherence to the Torah:

> And they shall not depart from any maxim of the Law to walk in all the stubbornness of their heart.
> And they shall be governed by the first ordinances in which the members of the Community began their instruction, until the coming of the Prophet and the Anointed (Ones) of Aaron and Israel.

The Manual of Discipline 9:9–11

JEWISH MOVEMENTS AND GROUPS IN PALESTINE

The major radical political movement in Palestine, the Zealot movement, has been discussed; it cut across many party lines and included within its ranks priests, Pharisees, and common folk. Besides the Zealots, there were three major groups, which are first mentioned in the texts of the second century B.C.: Sadducees, Pharisees, and Essenes; references to the first two appear frequently in the New Testament. We shall also note some more esoteric movements and figures.

Sadducees[54]

The Sadducees, whose name seems to be derived from the High Priest Zadok of Solomon's time (tenth century B.C.), were a group largely composed of priests of the Zadokite line. They are first mentioned in connection with the non-Zadokite priest and Maccabee, John Hyrcanus I (134–104 B.C.). Because the Temple was destroyed (in A.D. 70), priestly groups and, apparently, their literatures, disappeared. Knowledge of the Sadducees comes therefore through secondary references to them in ancient Jewish and Christian writings. From all indications, the Sadducees were members of influential Jerusalem families, and therefore of the "upper classes." Historically, they had come into conflict with the Pharisees and thus were opposed to them for political and religious reasons. As priests, they sacrificed at the Jerusalem Temple, dominated the Sanhedrin and, as political leaders, they attempted to maintain cordial relations with their Roman overlords. This conservative political stance was paralleled by a conservatism in religion. They held to a more literal reading of the Torah,

---

[54] A. Sundberg, "Sadducees," *IDB*, vol. 4, pp. 160–63. Important descriptions of Sadducees, Pharisees, and Essenes are found in Josephus, *War* II. 8, 14 and *Antiquities* XX. 9, 1.

which for them was the Pentateuch, and did not accept the oral tradition which was the special prerogative of the Pharisees. They also rejected those views which were most developed in the non-Pentateuchal, post-exilic Scriptures, namely, angels and demons, and the resurrection of the dead (Acts 23:8; Mark 12:18–27). Correspondingly, they were strict in matters they believed were based in the Torah, for example, Sabbath laws. When the war with Rome became imminent, they attempted to mediate, but to no avail.

Pharisees[55]

The name Pharisee is probably derived from the Hebrew *perushim* or the Aramaic *perishaya*, which means "the separated (ones)," though it is debated as to from what or whom they were separated. Like the Sadducees, they first made their appearance in the late second century B.C. under the Maccabees whom they initially supported, but from whom they later separated. After John Hyrcanus took bloody revenge on them for a Pharisee's criticism of his mother, they once again came into their own under Queen Alexandra (76–69 B.C.) and gradually gained in stature. Unlike the Sadducees, most Pharisees were not priests, but lay scholars whose main influence was in their development and preservation of the oral legal tradition mentioned above. Thus, they were rooted in the synagogue and known for pious living (alms, tithing, prayer, and fasting) and interpretation of the Torah, especially in areas such as food purity, crops, Sabbaths and festivals, and family affairs.[56] In these areas, the Pharisees "made a hedge for the Torah." In direct contrast to the Sadducees, they accepted the larger notion of Scripture, as well as newer views such as angels, demons, and the resurrection of the dead. In the New Testament, Jesus is pictured as frequently in debate with the "scribes and the Pharisees," the former having perhaps formed still another, separate group.[57] The Pharisees were divided into various "schools," the most well-known being those of Hillel and Shammai in the first century A.D. Their most renowned teachers became rabbis, though the beginning of the use of this term is also debated. Unlike the Sadducees, then, many of the Pharisaic traditions have been preserved in the so-called rabbinic literature, for it was the Pharisees who survived the war with Rome and reorganized Judaism along Pharisaic lines at the coastal town of Javneh (Jamnia). Here the books of the Jewish Scriptures were decided, the oral traditions collected, and the prayer against the Christians (Nazarenes) and Heretics added to the important set of Jewish prayers, the Eighteen Benedictions.[58] Henceforth, the heart of Judaism was the Torah, the synagogue, and the interpretation of Torah by the rabbis.

[55] E. Rivkin, "Pharisees," *IDB Suppl.*, pp. 657–63.
[56] J. Neusner, *The Rabbinic Traditions About the Pharisees Before 70* (3 vols.).
[57] J. Neusner, "The Formation of Rabbinic Judaism: Yavneh (Jamnia) from A.D. 70 to 100," *Aufstieg und Niedergang der Römischen Welt* II, 19.2, pp. 3–42.
[58] See Appendix 5.

Essenes[59]

The Essenes, who are not mentioned in the rabbinic literature or the New Testament, are described by the ancient writers Philo, Josephus, and Pliny the Elder.[60] They first appear under the Maccabean High Priest Jonathan (161–143/2 B.C.) and subsequently disappear during the wars with Rome, about A.D. 68. Though some Essenes lived in the towns and cities, the discovery of the Dead Sea Scrolls in 1947 and the subsequent excavation of nearby Khirbet Qumran (the ruins of a Jewish "monastery" along the Dead Sea near the Wadi Qumran)[61] have convinced most modern scholars that most of the scrolls were composed and copied by the Essenes, and that Pliny is correct when he says that an Essene community lived there, apparently in the caves in the cliffs. The name "Essene" (Greek *Essēnoi, Essaioi* = probably Aramaic *Hasayyāh*, "Pious Ones," or perhaps *'asayyah*, "healers") reflects possible origins among the *Hasidim*, the "Pious Ones" who temporarily joined the Maccabees in the Revolt of 167 B.C. In any case, the founder of the community was a certain Teacher of Righteousness, a Zadokite priest who opposed one of the Maccabean priests as "the wicked priest" (Jonathan? probably Simon)[62] in the second half of the second century B.C. In fulfillment of this passage which early Christians said prophesied John the Baptist (Isa 40:3: ". . . in the wilderness prepare the way of the Lord . . ."), the Teacher took his followers to the Dead Sea and established a priest-directed, scribal, and apocalyptic community which interpreted the prophecies to refer to themselves. There they worked, copied religious texts, wrote religious literature, worshipped according to their own calendar and customs, baptized, had a common meal, and sought to live pure and undefiled quasi-ascetic lives. Their literature, community organization, and eschatological orientation have become extremely important for understanding the rise of early Christianity, and we shall have reason to make further comparisons in chapter 4.[63]

Magic and Miracle Traditions

We have seen that in the Greco-Roman world at large there was an abundance of magicians and miracle workers, healers and physicians. Palestine was no exception, though some circles were very cautious because of the belief that

---

[59] The literature is overwhelming; classic are F. Cross, *The Ancient Library of Qumran and Modern Biblical Studies*; J. T. Milik, *Ten Years of Discovery in the Judean Desert*; H. Ringgren, *The Faith of Qumran*.

[60] A. Dupont-Sommer, *The Essene Writings From Qumran*, chapter 1.

[61] See Appendix 4.

[62] F. Cross, *Library*, pp. 127–60.

[63] See chapter 4, pp. 96–99.

God, not a powerful human being, was the ultimate source of healing. Nonetheless, Babylonian and Persian beliefs about angels and demons which influenced the apocalyptic literary tradition also influenced popular religious views about the origins of sickness and disease. One widespread view about the origin of evil was based on the interpretation of Genesis 6:1–4, namely, that the "sons of God" (interpreted as angels) lusted after the "daughters of men" (human women) and produced a race of giants (interpreted as demons). In a reinterpretation of a Genesis story in the Dead Sea Scrolls, Abraham is said to have exorcized a demon from Pharaoh by prayer, the laying on of hands, and rebuking the evil spirit (GenApoc 20:16–19). David was said to have done the same thing by playing his harp (LibAntBib 60:1–3) and Noah by medicines and herbs (Jub 10:10–14). Solomon, especially, was remembered for his wisdom—here we note the influence of the Wisdom tradition—and that wisdom included his vast knowledge of magic and medicine. Josephus tells the story of the Jewish exorcist Eleazar who performed the following exorcism:

> He put to the nose of the possessed man a ring which had under its seal one of the roots prescribed by Solomon, and then, as the man smelled it, drew out the demon through his nostrils, and, when the man at once fell down, adjured the demon never to come back into him, speaking Solomon's name and reciting the incantations which he had composed.
>
> Antiquities 8:2, 5

In Josephus and the rabbinic literature, Honi the Circle Drawer was remembered for bringing rain by prayer, and the Galilean *Hasid* ("Pious One") named Hanina ben Dosa is remembered for healing by prayer. When the son of Yohanan ben Zakkai became ill, Yohanan said,

> "Hanina, my son, pray for him that he may live." He put his head between his knees and prayed; and he lived.
>
> Babylonian Talmud, Berakoth 34b

In the stories of the Talmud, the tendency to ascribe the actual healing to God himself is clear, that is, the cure is effected through prayer; nonetheless, it is also clear that particular Holy Men were famous for the ability to heal.[64] Such a man, also, was Jesus of Nazareth.

The People of the Land

We have highlighted some of the major movements and groups, as well as individuals, of Palestinian Judaism: Zealots, Sadducees, Pharisees, Essenes, magicians and miracle workers. There were others. But most of the people were the common people, the ordinary people, whom the rabbis called "the People of the Land." These people are difficult to identify with precision, ex-

[64] G. Vermes, *Jesus the Jew*, chapter 3.

cept that the rabbis considered them with some disdain, presumably because they would or could not keep the Law with precision.

DIASPORA JUDAISM[65]

The focus of our sketch of the history and religion of Judaism has been on Palestine, though it is clear that Hellenism had a profound impact on Palestinian Judaism. But many Jews no longer lived in Palestine; many had stayed in Babylonia, and others were found scattered throughout the cities of the eastern Mediterranean, the largest and most famous being Alexandria where the Jewish community almost formed a state within a state. During the Greek period, Diaspora Jews learned to speak Greek, as did certainly urban Palestinian Jews, and the need arose for Greek translations of the Scriptures.[66] Though there are many problems with recovering the earliest Greek (Old Greek) text and tracing its history in relation to Hebrew and Aramaic texts, both tradition (the Letter of Aristeas) and recovered manuscripts, especially from the Dead Sea Scrolls, indicate that translations were already being made in the second century B.C., that is, prior to the time when the leaders at Jamnia had settled on the precise books of the Bible (Old Testament). The Greek translations (and subsequent translations and revisions) became the holy texts for Diaspora Jews, Greek-speaking Jews in Palestine, and Greek-speaking Christians. Based on the legend of their translation in Alexandria (Aristeas), which stated that 70 (or 72) Greek-speaking priests (from Jerusalem!) translated the Scriptures independently and arrived at precisely the same translations, the Greek version (including a few other books) is still called the Septuagint (LXX). The use of Greek-language Scriptures is an important factor not only in the Hellenization of the Jews, but in the very understanding of the Jewish religion.[67]

Jews had a special status in the Greco-Roman world; as we have seen, they were exempt from emperor worship and were permitted a number of special privileges based on their observance of the Sabbath and the festivals: exemption from military service, going to court on the Sabbath, and certain business arrangements. They were also permitted to settle inter-Jewish legal disputes according to their Law and tradition, and to administer their own funds and send money to Jerusalem, especially the Temple tax. It is a debated question whether Jews also had *civic* rights as citizens of the empire, that is, participation in public life, election of magistrates, and the like. Josephus says they did; other sources during the Roman period indicate they did not, which seems more likely. In their relations with Gentiles, Jewish practices such as the rite of

---

[65] M. Cook, "Judaism, Hellenistic," *IDB Suppl.*, pp. 505–509; V. Tcherikover, *Hellenistic Civilization*, Part II.

[66] E. Tov and R. Kraft, "Septuagint," *IDB Suppl.*, pp. 807–15; K. G. O'Connell, "Greek Versions (Minor)," *IDB Suppl.*, pp. 377–81.

[67] Though debated, many scholars believe that Paul's understanding of the Law (Greek *nomos*) was Greek and based on the LXX, and that this understanding contributed to the rejection of it as a means of salvation.

circumcision and ritual purity laws tended to keep them distinct, and their special privileges under the Romans brought them some ill will. No doubt many Jews of the Diaspora became less inclined to follow the Law as strictly as they did in Palestine, especially since much of it dealt with the Temple. On the other hand, Judaism bore witness to a high sense of morality and attracted proselytes (especially among women, who were not circumcised) and "God-fearers" (especially men who were attracted to Judaism, but not to circumcision).

The New Testament is a product of a religious movement which had its origins in Judaism, but which quickly moved out into the larger Greco-Roman world. It is written in the common Greek of the period (*koinē* Greek), but it also represents at points the religious traditions of the Jews and, of course, the stresses created in the process of separating from Judaism. But eventually Christianity was transplanted into areas where the Jewish Diaspora had preceded it. The New Testament does not represent all of these areas, for example, Egypt—that is, if modern critical theory is correct. It does, however, represent parts of that area, namely, Asia Minor, Greece, and Rome. Our next task will be to take a closer look at the New Testament as a body of literature, and then we shall give a sketch of the history of New Testament Christianity as it moved from its rural Palestinian roots into the cities of the Greco-Roman Empire. From this vantage point we shall proceed to take up in more detail the various religious and theological ideas in the literature of the New Testament.

Further Reading

The following represents a select list, most of which contain further bibliography:

On the history, culture, and religion of the Greco-Roman world, see:

PCB, pp. 712–18, "Pagan Religion at the Coming of Christianity" (R. McL. Wilson).

IDB, vol. 2, pp. 479–87, "Greek Language" (E. C. Colwell); pp. 487–500, "Greek Religion and Philosophy" (F. W. Beare); vol. 4, pp. 103–09, "Roman Empire" (R. M. Grant); pp. 109–12, "Roman Religion" (F. C. Grant).

IDB Suppl., pp. 364–68, "Gnosticism" (E. Pagels); pp. 395–401, "Hellenism" (F. E. Peters); pp. 613–19, "Nag Hammadi" (G. MacRae).

F. Cumont, *Oriental Religions in Roman Paganism.*
E. R. Dodds, *The Greeks and the Irrational.*
A. J. Festugière, *Personal Religion Among the Greeks.*
M. I. Finley, *The Ancient Economy.*
M. Grant, *The World of Rome.*
M. Hadas, *Imperial Rome* (Time-Life).
M. Hades, *Hellenistic Culture.*

J. Hull, *Hellenistic Magic and the Synoptic Tradition.*
E. Lohse, *The New Testament Environment,* Part II.
R. MacMullen, *Roman Social Relations.*
F. E. Peters, *The Harvest of Hellenism.*
W. W. Tarn and G. T. Griffith, *Hellenistic Civilization.*
A. Toynbee, ed. *The Crucible of Christianity.*

On Judaism, history, culture, religion, see:

PCB, pp. 126–33, "History of Israel—II. Post-Exilic" (L. E. Browne); pp. 686–92, "The Jewish State in the Hellenistic World" (W. D. Davies); pp. 693–98, "The Development of Judaism in the Greek and Roman Periods" (M. Black); pp. 705–11, "Contemporary Jewish Religion" (W. D. Davies).

JBC, pp. 535–60, "Apocrypha: Dead Sea Scrolls; Other Jewish Literature" (R. E. Brown); pp. 686–702, "A History of Israel," the latter part of a longer article (R. E. Murphy and J. A. Fitzmyer). This survey of Jewish history in the relevant period is particularly good.

IDB, vol. 1, pp. 790–802, "Dead Sea Scrolls" (O. Betz); vol. 2, pp. 143–49, "Essenes" (W. R. Farmer); pp. 568–70, "Hebrew Religion," the latter part of a longer article (J. Bright); pp. 761–65, "History of Israel," the latter part of a longer article (H. H. Rowley); vol. 3, pp. 774–81, "Pharisees" (M. Black); vol. 4, pp. 160–63, "Sadducees" (A. C. Sundberg); pp. 190–97, "Samaritans" (T. H. Gaster); pp. 476–91, "Synagogue" (I. Sanne).

IDB Suppl., pp. 1–3, "Aaron, Aaronides" (E. Rivkin); pp. 39–44, "Aramaic" (J. Greenfield); pp. 28–34, "Apocalypticism" (P. D. Hanson); pp. 210–19, "Dead Sea Scrolls" (G. Vermes); pp. 277–79, "Essenes" (O. Betz); pp. 312–14, "Exorcism in the NT" (J. M. Hull); pp. 317–28, "Ezra and Nehemiah" (S. Talmon); pp. 475–77, "Jerusalem" (R. Amiran; Y. Israeli); pp. 505–09, "Judaism, Hellenistic" (M. Cook); pp. 577–80, "Masada" (Y. Yadin); pp. 657–63, "Pharisees" (E. Rivkin); pp. 687–90, "Priests" (B. A. Levine); pp. 775–77, "Samaritans" (J. D. Purvis); pp. 807–15, "Septuagint" (P. A. Kraft); pp. 844–45, "Synagogue, the Great" (L. M. Barth); pp. 842–44, "Synagogue, architecture" (E. M. Meyers); pp. 856–61, "Targums" (M. McNamara); pp. 870–72, "Temple of Herod" (M. Ben-Dov); pp. 909–11, "Torah" (J. A. Sanders).

E. Bickerman, *From Ezra to the Last of the Maccabees.*
R. Bultmann, *Primitive Christianity in Its Contemporary Setting,* pp. 59–100.
D. Cowan, *Bridge Between the Testaments.*
F. Cross, *The Ancient Library of Qumran and Modern Biblical Studies.*
W. Foerster, *From the Exile to Christ.*
E. R. Goodenough, *An Introduction to Philo Judaeus.*
P. Hanson, *The Dawn of Apocalyptic.*
M. Hengel, *Judaism and Hellenism.*

K. Koch, *The Rediscovery of Apocalyptic.*
S. Libermann, *Hellenism in Jewish Palestine.*
E. Lohse, *The New Testament Environment.* Part I.
M. McNamara, *Targum and Testament.*
J. Neusner, *The Rabbinic Traditions About the Pharisees Before 70.* 3 vols.
R. H. Pfeiffer, *History of New Testament Times with an Introduction to the Apocrypha.*
H. Ringgren, *The Faith of Qumran.*
D. S. Russell, *Between the Testaments.*
S. Safrai and M. Stern, eds., *The Jewish People in the First Century.* 2 vols.
E. Schürer, G. Vermes, and F. Miller, *The History of the Jewish People in the Age of Jesus Christ,* vol. 1.
M. Simon, *Jewish Sects at the Time of Jesus.*
M. Stone, *Scriptures, Sects and Visions.*
V. Tcherikover, *Hellenistic Civilization and the Jews.*
G. Vermes, *Jesus the Jew.*
Y. Yadin, *Masada.*

Collections of Texts:

General:

C. K. Barrett, *The New Testament Background: Selected Documents.*
D. R. Cartlidge and D. Dungan, *Documents for the Study of the Gospels.*
H. Kee, *The Origins of Christianity. Sources and Documents.*

See also:

S. Baron and J. Blau, *Judaism. Postbiblical and Talmudic Period.*
W. Foerster, *Gnosis: A Selection of Gnostic Texts.* 2 vols.
F. C. Grant, *Hellenistic Religions.*
E. Hennecke and W. Schneemelcher, *The New Testament Apocrypha.* 2 vols.
J. M. Robinson, *The Nag Hammadi Library.*
G. Vermes, *The Dead Sea Scrolls in English.*

There will also be a collection of Pseudepigrapha from about 200 B.C. to A.D. 200 under the general editorship of J. H. Charlesworth to be published in the autumn of 1982. See Appendix 4.

A standard collection of texts that includes the works of Josephus and Philo of Alexandria is the Loeb Classical Library.

Codex Sinaiticus, fourth century (here opened to Luke 20:34-22:20), is the only complete manuscript of the New Testament in uncial (block) script to survive (see Appendix 2 and Appendix 4).

CHAPTER TWO

THE NATURE OF THE NEW TESTAMENT

The center of the New Testament is Jesus Christ. But once that is said, the striking thing about it is its great variety. It contains a variety of books, written in a variety of lengths and styles, and attributed to a variety of authors. Further study will show that its writings come from diverse times and places and encompass an even larger diversity in their forms and contents. A unity in Jesus Christ, but a rich variety in the books written about him—that is characteristic of the New Testament.

In this chapter we shall examine the nature of the New Testament in terms of its books, probable authorship and date, but most importantly its general character as religious literature, a religious literature that contains preaching, exhortation, myth, and history.

THE NEW TESTAMENT BOOKS

When one picks up the New Testament and looks through it, one discovers that it contains a number of books that are named as follows:

The Gospel According to Matthew
The Gospel According to Mark
The Gospel According to Luke
The Gospel According to John
The Acts of the Apostles
The Letter of Paul to the Romans
The First Letter of Paul to the Corinthians
The Second Letter of Paul to the Corinthians
The Letter of Paul to the Galatians

The Letter of Paul to the Ephesians
The Letter of Paul to the Philippians
The Letter of Paul to the Colossians
The First Letter of Paul to the Thessalonians
The Second Letter of Paul to the Thessalonians
The First Letter of Paul to Timothy
The Second Letter of Paul to Timothy
The Letter of Paul to Titus
The Letter of Paul to Philemon
The Letter to the Hebrews
The Letter of James
The First Letter of Peter
The Second Letter of Peter
The First Letter of John
The Second Letter of John
The Third Letter of John
The Letter of Jude
The Revelation to John

A glance at this list shows in the first place that there are twenty-seven books of four basic types: (1) gospels, of which there are four; (2) a book named Acts of the Apostles; (3) letters, of which there are twenty-one; and (4) a final book called Revelation. These four types are in themselves worth some consideration. The first type, gospel, takes its name from the Old English *godspell* ("good discourse"), a translation of the Latin *evangelium* and ultimately the Greek *euangelion* ("good news"). This term *euangelion* was known in the ancient Greek world, among other things for the oral proclamation of good news in emperor worship (see page 14, *n.* 28). The apostle Paul's frequent use of it indicates that it was already well accepted in early Christianity as a term for the oral preaching of good news about the meaning of Jesus Christ for salvation. The gospel of Matthew can use it for Jesus' oral preaching (Matt. 4:23; 9:35; 24:14; 26:13, cf. Mark 14:9). However, designating a written document that narrates the story and teachings of Jesus as gospel seems first to have been done in the gospel according to Mark (1:1). Moreover, though the issue is debated, our view is that the written type, or genre, called gospel is the unique literary creation of Mark. In short, the "gospel" has no precise literary prototype.

The other three types of literature are commonly known in the ancient world. The Acts of the Apostles is an early Christian history book telling about the spread of Christianity from Jerusalem to Rome though, as we shall see, it is not empirical history in the modern sense. Letters in early Christianity are also interesting since there was no precedent in Judaism for the use of letters specifically as scriptural texts. It will be seen that the letters in the New Testament are of different types and, in fact, that some of them are not letters at all! Finally, the New Testament concludes with Revelation, a term that translates *apocalypsis,* the Greek word for "apocalypse." This mode of thinking and its literary embodiment were, as discussed in chapter 1, well known in Judaism.

It should be observed that these four literary forms do not exhaust the extent or subtlety of literary form in the New Testament. Gospels and letters can vary from one another and there are other, smaller forms. Revelation contains letters, the letters of Paul contain hymns and confessions, Acts contains speeches, and the gospels contain discourses, miracle stories, and parables. This group of subtypes could be extended to a much longer list. When one is thinking about whole documents, however, it is possible to say that the New Testament contains these four basic types of literature.

The four literary types are especially characteristic of early Christianity. There have been preserved many other examples of these types which were used and were considered authoritative by most early Christians. There are also some varying types, such as collections of Jesus' sayings and infancy gospels. These are collected in the New Testament Apocrypha and provide very interesting reading.[1]

Christianity added the twenty-seven books to the Bible that was in use by Jews and Christians of the Diaspora, the latter forming the Old Testament, the former the New Testament. The process of deciding on these twenty-seven books took about three centuries—and for some churches in the East, the process continued longer (for further treatment, see Appendix 1, the Canon of the New Testament).

The phenomenon of adopting authoritative books as a normative guide for religious faith and practice is not universal. Some religions lay no stress on sacred texts and their study. But given its origins in Judaism, which had its own scriptural collections, and the eventual separation of Christianity from Judaism, perhaps it was inevitable that Christianity would come to depend on the written word. And once this decision was made, Christian truth would forever be bound in some way to the interpretation of sacred books. Throughout the history of the Christian movement, many crucial issues have had to be decided on how this written deposit was interpreted; in fact, a significant component of the history of western civilization lies precisely in just such interpretations. Our following discussion is a contemporary approach to the interpretation of the New Testament. We will first indicate a historical reconstruction of the development of the twenty-seven books in terms of authorship and date; then we will attempt to give a general picture of the New Testament literature and its meaning.

AUTHORSHIP AND DATE

Another obvious fact that emerges from listing the twenty-seven books of the New Testament is that all but the Acts of the Apostles and the letter to the

---

[1] E. Hennecke and W. Schneemelcher, *New Testament Apocrypha,* 2 vols.; cf. E. J. Goodspeed, *A History of Early Christian Literature,* revised and enlarged by R. M. Grant, chapters 1–5.

Hebrews have some name connected with them. Acts, as we shall see, is the second volume of a two-volume work, the first being the gospel of Luke. Hebrews is unnamed, though the church came to think that it came from Paul, or at least from his inspiration. All the men named as authors are known to us from the New Testament itself. James and Jude were brothers of Jesus (Matt 13:55); Peter, Matthew, and John were among the original group of Jesus' disciples (Mark 3:16–19); Paul is prominent in the Acts of the Apostles; and Luke and Mark are mentioned in 2 Tim 4:11 and elsewhere. All were either apostles or closely associated with apostles, and, indeed, the traditional claim of the church has been that they were either "apostles" or "apostolic men." Were this claim substantiated, it would lead to a particular understanding of the New Testament—that it is largely a historical chronicle of the ministry of Jesus and the life of the early church, for the most part written by men who were either relatives of Jesus or closely associated with him, or by the apostle Paul and men who had been associated with him. This would have very important consequences for our understanding of the New Testament. It is obviously important, therefore, to establish as far as we can the authorship of the books of the New Testament. The question is whether the books of the New Testament themselves show evidence of having been written by the men whose names are attached to them, and New Testament scholars have investigated this question very carefully. The position taken in this book is as follows.

The gospels were not written by eyewitnesses of the ministry of Jesus. They were written in the period between A.D. 70 and 100, forty years or more after the crucifixion, and originally they circulated anonymously. It has to be understood that in the ancient world it was quite common to attach important names to anonymous works, or to write in the name of some teacher or famous person from the past (pseudonymous works, see chapters 7, 12). Many modern scholars believe that authoritative "apostolic" names were attached to the gospels in the second century A.D. We simply do not know who wrote them, though as we shall see, the gospels themselves tell us a great deal about the gospel writers—the evangelists—and their concerns. But they do not tell us their names, and when we speak of "Matthew," "Mark," "Luke," or "John" we do so only for convenience; the actual names of the evangelists are forever lost to us.

Of the thirteen letters traditionally ascribed to Paul, seven were written by him: 1 Thessalonians, Galatians, 1 and 2 Corinthians, Philippians, Philemon, and Romans. Two of these, 2 Corinthians and Philippians, are not single letters but rather collections of several letters and remnants brought together into single letters when Paul's letters were collected and circulated as a group. The other letters are pseudonymous, written by men who used Paul's name, not by Paul himself. These pseudonymous letters fall naturally into two groups. First there is the group comprising 2 Thessalonians, Colossians, and Ephesians. These were written by pupils and followers of the apostle, men who deliberately represented their teacher and who wrote in his name. We call these letters "deutero[secondary]-Pauline." Then there is the group consisting of 1 and 2 Timothy and Titus. These are a generation or more later, written early in the second century A.D. Because they so obviously reflect the concerns of a Christian pastor for the churches committed to his care, they are usually called the "Pastoral Epistles." They belong together with 1 and 2 Peter, James, and Jude, all of which are pseudonymous, and all of which were written between about A.D. 90 and 140. This whole group of letters represents the interests and concerns of the church on the way to becoming an institution in the Greco-Roman world, and we discuss them as "the literature of the emerging institutional church." The reasons for regarding 2 Thessalonians, Colossians, and Ephesians as "deutero-Pauline" and the Pastorals, 1 and 2 Peter, James, and Jude as "the literature of the emerging institutional church" are given in detail in the relevant chapters later.

We may summarize our conclusions with regard to the authorship of the books of the New Testament as follows, giving approximate dates.

A.D. 50–60   Paul writes 1 Thessalonians; 1 Corinthians and [the collection of letters that is now] 2 Corinthians; [the collection of letters that is now] Philippians; Philemon; Galatians; and Romans—probably in that order, though we cannot be sure of the place in the order of the individual elements in 2 Corinthians and Philippians.

All the remaining New Testament literature comes after the fall of Jerusalem to the Romans and the destruction of its Temple, in A.D. 70.

70–90   Pupils and followers of Paul write the deutero-Pauline letters: 2 Thessalonians, Colossians, and Ephesians.

Unknown Christians write what we now know as the gospels of Matthew, Mark, and Luke, the Acts of the Apostles, and the letter to the Hebrews.

80–100   The gospel and letters of John are produced most probably not by one individual but by men who were members of a tightly-knit group. We do not know their names but for convenience we will call them "the Johannine school."

90–100   A church leader named John writes the book of Revelation while in exile on the island of Patmos.

90–140   Leaders in various churches write the pseudonymous literature of the emerging institutional church: the Pastorals, 1 and 2 Peter, James, and Jude.

The reasons for these conclusions and the evidence that supports them are given at the appropriate places in the chapters that follow.

THE NEW TESTAMENT AS A BOOK
AND AS A COLLECTION OF BOOKS

As is clear from the foregoing, the first thing to be said about the New Testament is that it is both a book and a collection of books; it is a text and a collection of texts brought together by the church and declared to be the New Testament. Both descriptions are important. As a book, the New Testament represents a single entity of foundational importance to Christians and Christian churches; as a collection of books it is a variety of documents of different literary forms and sometimes of different religious viewpoints.

There is a real tension between the "text" and the "collection of texts." We can proclaim that the New Testament is a unity, but in actual reading differences in literary form and religious viewpoint may make the reader more comfortable in one part than another. The most famous example is Martin Luther, who found himself at home (to put it mildly) in Paul's letter to the Romans with its view of justification by faith, but who dismissed the letter of James as "a right strawy epistle" because it expressed a very different view. In point of fact these two letters show differences in specific theological doctrine and even in general understanding of what it means to be religious in the world. There are similar differences between the gospel of John and the two-volume gospel of Luke and Acts of the Apostles, or for that matter between Paul's letter to the Romans and his letter to the Thessalonians.

The differences are theological in that the concept of justification by faith is present in Romans and absent in James;[2] salvation history, the view that God is saving his people through a progression of historical events, is present in Luke-Acts[3] and absent in the gospel of John; "faith" reflects quite different concepts in the genuine letters of Paul and in the pseudonymous Pastoral Letters (first and second letters to Timothy, letter to Titus).[4] The religious differences represent different understandings of what it means to be Christian in the world. So, for example, the Thessalonian letters concentrate on the parousia, the (second) coming of Jesus as judge of the world;[5] to be religious is to prepare for that coming by rigorously following the instructions given by and through the Jesus who is to come. In Romans, however, Paul celebrates the benefits of the Cross and exults in the present experience of Christians, and the parousia no longer dominates the field of vision. Although the two viewpoints

---

[2] On this see chapter 12, p. 374.

[3] On this see chapter 10, pp. 301–08.

[4] On this see chapter 12, pp. 384, 389.

[5] *Parousia* is the Greek term for the visit of an important official to a province or district to regulate its affairs. Early Christian writers used it to denote their expectation of the coming of Jesus from heaven to judge the world (e.g., Matt 24:27): "For as the lightning comes from the east and shines as far as the west, so will be the coming [*parousia*] of the Son of man." Modern scholars follow this practice and use parousia as a technical term to denote the early Christian expectation of the imminent coming of Jesus from heaven as Son of Man to judge the world.

can be reconciled in the theology of Paul—but just barely—the fact remains that the Thessalonian and Roman Christians were religious in very different ways.

Another difference among the various books collected in the New Testament, as suggested above, is in their literary forms. In recent years we have become increasingly aware that different literary forms function in different ways. The reader of the realistic (mimetic) narrative of the gospel of Mark is caught up in the story as participant, whereas he is an observer of the sacred drama of the gospel of John. The reader of the letters of Paul, which are real letters, is directly addressed by them, but he has to wrestle with the meaning of the letter to the Hebrews, which is not a letter at all but a theological treatise. Each of these literary forms works differently and so addresses its reader differently, and it is important for the reader to know what kind of text he or she is reading if it is to be understood correctly.

Paralleling the differences in form are the differences in language. Not all language is alike; there are many kinds of language, and each tends to function differently. In the New Testament itself the direct discourse of the Sermon on the Mount is in form and function unlike the exalted revelatory style of the "I am" discourses in John's gospel, as also are the down-to-earth realism of the parables and the exotic imagery of the book of Revelation.

Though the books in the New Testament differ from one another in their understanding of the nature of Christian faith in the world, they are in common wrestling with the problems of that faith and no other. Their authors are at different stages in the development of New Testament Christianity and so face different problems, and they necessarily develop their understanding of the nature and meaning of Christian faith differently. When they face the same problems they sometimes respond to them in different ways. But there is an overall unity in the New Testament: each writer attempts to relate to and to make sense of life in the world by means of his faith in Jesus Christ.

The diversity of the New Testament is matched by the diversity of Christian churches in subsequent Christian history. Over and over again a particular viewpoint in the New Testament is developed historically by a group of churches. Chapter 4 of this book describes "apocalyptic Christianity," a viewpoint represented by many Christian sects even today. The particular perspective of "justification by faith" found in Paul's letters to the Galatians and to the Romans is the central thrust of the churches that owe allegiance directly or indirectly to Martin Luther. Further, both the gospel of Matthew, which, we argue later, is preeminently the "Church's book," and the literature of "the emerging institutional church" are clearly the inspiration of the Catholic church through the centuries. The Luke-Acts understanding and presentation of Jesus as the first Christian, the model and paradigm of Christian faith and practice, is as clearly the foundation of the "liberal" understanding of Christian faith as the literature of the "Johannine school" is the inspiration for centuries of Christian mysticism.

The New Testament represents the whole spectrum of possibilities of what it means to be Christian in the world, and either anticipates or inspires every subsequent development within the Christian churches. The Roman Catholic and the Lutheran, the liberal Protestant and the fundamentalist, the contemplative mystic and the apocalyptic visionary, all find themselves at home in one part or another of this collection from the literature of earliest Christianity.

THE NEW TESTAMENT AS
PROCLAMATION AND PARENESIS

In 1918 Martin Dibelius stated a thesis that has come to dominate the modern understanding of the New Testament: "At the beginning of all early Christian creativity there stands the sermon: missionary and hortatory preaching, narrative and parenesis, prophecy and the interpretation of scripture."[6] In the next year he published a book, *From Tradition to Gospel*, developing his thesis and interpreting the New Testament in its light. There we find, for example, the statement, "In the sermon the elements of the future Christian literature lay side by side as in a mother cell" (page 70). "In the beginning was the sermon" usually summarizes this view, calling attention to the fact that the New Testament texts were the product of preaching, teaching, exhortation, and comforting, and that in turn they preach, teach, exhort, and comfort.

It would be hard to overestimate the element of proclamation in the New Testament. Jesus "proclaimed" the Kingdom of God and in turn the early Christians "proclaimed" Jesus as the one through whom God had acted decisively for the salvation of man. The major form of proclamation in the church is preaching, and the New Testament itself testifies to the centrality of its role. "I must remind you of the gospel that I preached to you," says Paul to the Corinthian Christians (1 Cor. 15:1, NEB); in a crucial passage in Romans he speaks of the word of faith which we "proclaim" (Rom 10:8, NEB).[7] The Acts of the Apostles features frequent and extensive sermons and closes with Paul "proclaiming the Kingdom of God and teaching the facts about the Lord Jesus Christ quite openly and without hindrance" (Acts 28:31, NEB). For all that Acts expresses the theological viewpoint of its author, there can be no doubt that it is correct in the emphasis upon the sermon. Moreover, this emphasis is distinctive to early Christianity. The Jewish synagogue featured homilies, and itinerant Greek philosophers taught publicly, yet no other group in the first century preached in houses and on street corners in quite the same way the Christians did. "In the beginning was the sermon" is not only true of, but special to, early Christianity.

[6] Quoted from the translation of the sentence in N. Perrin, *What Is Redaction Criticism?* p. 15, n. 19.
[7] Paul also uses the verb *euangelizō*, "I announce good news" (1 Cor 15:1), the verb form of *euangelion*, "good news"; cf. above, p. 40, for a discussion of *gospel*. Rom 10:8 uses the verb *kēryssō*, "to act as a herald," i.e., "to proclaim." The noun from this root is *kērygma*, "proclamation," and this is used in the N.T., e.g., Rom 16:25 (RSV translates it "preaching"); 1 Cor 1:21 (RSV, "what we preach"); 2:4 (RSV, "message"). Modern scholars use the word kerygma to denote the proclamation of the N.T. or of the church.

Martin Dibelius also called attention to the role of parenesis in the New Testament, using it as a technical term to describe the activities of the church in exhorting, advising, and edifying her members.[8] It is a rare word, but the Greek from which it comes is found in the New Testament—in Acts 27:9 (NEB) where Paul "gives advice" to the ship's crew and in 27:22 (NEB) where he "urges" them not to lose heart. The rarity of the word makes it a suitable technical term, and it is now used as such by New Testament scholars, but there can be no doubt of the prominence of the activity it designates. Large sections of Paul's letters are fundamentally parenesis or, to use the adjective, parenetical. Even a letter like Romans, which comes near to being a theological treatise, contains four chapters of parenesis, chapters 12–15, and the letter to the Hebrews, which also is a theological treatise, has carefully spaced parenetical sections. In this characteristic the early Christians were not distinctive. Both Jews and Greeks exhorted, advised, composed all kinds of homilies, and constantly attempted to edify one another. But to recognize the twofold emphasis on proclamation and parenesis in the New Testament is to come closer to appreciating its essential nature.

The parenetical material in the New Testament is sometimes specifically Christian exhortation developed from specifically Christian themes such as Jesus as the true High Priest in Hebrews or the humble, crucified Jesus in 1 Corinthians. But at other times the Christian writers simply borrow their material from the moralizing literature of the Hellenistic world, for example, in the "household codes" of the deutero-Pauline letters and the literature of more institutional Christianity.[9]

We have characterized the New Testament literature as fundamentally proclamation and parenesis, and we hope to justify this description in our subsequent discussion of the literature. But this is a very broad and general characterization, and as noted above, there are innumerable subcategories within the literature. Despite this great variety of literature and literary forms, the broad categories of proclamation and parenesis are helpful in approaching the material as a whole.

THE NEW TESTAMENT AS MYTH

One of the hotly debated questions in New Testament scholarship has been how far and in what ways the word *myth* may be used in connection with the texts of the New Testament, more especially with the texts concerning

[8] In modern English all this would be described loosely as "preaching," but in the N.T. there is a real difference between proclaiming the Good News of what God has done through Jesus Christ on the one hand and exhorting, advising, and attempting to edify on the other. It is because of the loose usage of "preaching" in modern English that we are using the two distinct terms "proclamation" and "parenesis" to describe these two different verbal activities in the N.T. In N.T. Greek, "preaching" is a form of proclamation.

[9] See the reference to Stoic-Cynic vice and virtue lists and "household codes," chapter 1, p. 10; chapter 7, pp. 217–18, 223; and chapter 12, p. 378.

Jesus, the gospels. The problem came dramatically into focus in the middle of the nineteenth century in Germany, and it has remained with us ever since. The story is worth outlining so that the reader may better understand the current discussion of myth in the New Testament.

The Enlightenment and the rise of the natural and historical sciences created a grave problem for understanding the New Testament, for the New Testament narratives are full of references to things that are difficult for people living in the post-Enlightenment world to accept literally: angels, demons, miracles, resurrection and ascension, the (second) coming of Jesus on the clouds of heaven, and much more. At the beginning of the nineteenth century in Germany there were two ways of facing this problem. The supernaturalist way was to hold that the narratives were indeed factually true—angels, demons, miracles, and all. The rationalist way was to argue that factual history could and should be reconstructed from the narratives by explaining away the obviously legendary, miraculous, and absurd. Both sides took for granted that factual history was what mattered and that one had either to be able to claim the New Testament narratives as factually historical or to reconstruct factual history from them. Then came D. F. Strauss' two-volume *The Life of Jesus Critically Examined,* published in 1835–36. What Strauss did in effect was to cry "a plague on both your houses" and to introduce the idea of the New Testament narratives as *myth,* an idea that was, to say the least, strenuously resisted.

To understand the impact of Strauss' bombshell and the course of the subsequent discussion among New Testament scholars, it is important to recognize that Strauss' work contrasted myth and factual history, and that he had a particular understanding of myth.[10] For Strauss, myths were not abstract ideas or concepts, but the vivid, dramatic, and pictorial religious images with which primitive peoples expressed themselves. Traditional messianic ideas were clothed in such images, and the events of Jesus' life were portrayed with the same or similar images as a result of religious enthusiasm about him. Many stories about Jesus were legendary, that is, as they passed through the process of oral transmission, they were transformed by myth. In some cases, the additions of the individual authors can be discerned. As an example of mythic coloring, the baptism of Jesus is told in terms of popular, well-known Old Testament images about the way God would speak to the Messiah as a son (Isa 42:1; Ps 2:7), and the expectation that the Spirit would come as a dove in the messianic age (Joel 2:1ff. [2:28ff.]; Isa 11:1ff.). Such an account was not historical, but "mythical," even though an historical event—the actual baptism of Jesus—might have given rise to it. In this particular instance, Strauss believed there was a historical event in the background. Strauss' view that myths were not, strictly speaking, historical narratives meant that the impact of his work was to cast doubt on the historical reliability of the gospel narratives.

The attempt to counter Strauss' concept of the New Testament narratives tried to establish the factual historicity of the gospel of Mark. The so-called

[10] D. Duling, *Jesus Christ Through History,* pp. 177–84.

Markan hypothesis[11] states that Mark is the earliest gospel and hence nearest to the events it relates and so is fundamentally historical in character. A century and more of "life-of-Jesus research" was built upon this hypothesis and only recently has it been abandoned. Today New Testament scholarship in general recognizes that the nineteenth-century emphasis on factual historicity is inappropriate to interpreting a first-century text in the twentieth century. At the same time Strauss' understanding of the nature of myth has become very influential among New Testament scholars who, when they talk about myth, usually mean the narrative embodiment of an idea. In this context the most important scholar is Rudolf Bultmann, whose "demythologizing program" is the most creative and serious contemporary attempt to understand and interpret myth in the New Testament.[12] Bultmann's ultimate indebtedness to Strauss is open and acknowledged, and when he speaks, as he so often does, of *Jenseits* and *Dieseits,* of the "other side" and "this side," then he is heir to Strauss. Bultmann regards myth as a story about the "other side" told in terms of "this side," that is, a story about gods and religious reality told in terms of men and the world. The story of the resurrection of Jesus is myth, a crassly human story about the resuscitation of a corpse and its eventual elevation to a region above the earth via the clouds as a kind of celestial elevator. But the religious reality so described is the spiritual presence of Jesus experienced in the kerygma, the proclamation of the church;[13] it is the power of the proclamation to manifest Jesus and his offer of authentic existence to any generation of people in the world. Bultmann boldly asserts that for him Jesus is risen—into the kerygma of the church. In addition, Bultmann is an existentialist, and as such he claims that myths that speak of the "other side" in terms of "this side" are really talking about the historical reality of being human in the world. So he accepts Martin Heidegger's existentialist analysis of the reality of being human in the world and calls attention to Heidegger's distinction between "authentic" and "inauthentic" human existence. Thus, the resurrection of Jesus is a concrete image which, when preached, opens up the possibility of authentic human existence in the world. By responding to the kerygma, and only by responding to the kerygma, can one achieve the reality of authentic existence. For Bultmann to say that Jesus is risen into the kerygma is the same as to say that the kerygma offers one the genuine possibility of human existence in the world: the myth of the resurrection is now being properly understood and interpreted.

To give another example, the parousia, the idea of the return of Jesus as judge of the world, is as dependent on a view of heaven as spatially "above"

---

[11] On the role of the Markan hypothesis in recent N.T. studies see N. Perrin, *What Is Redaction Criticism?* pp. 3–13.

[12] Bultmann's views on myth and his demythologizing program are to be found in his essays "New Testament and Mythology," "A Reply to the Theses of J. Schniewind," and "Bultmann Replies to His Critics," now in H. W. Bartsch (ed.), *Kerygma and Myth,* and in his book *Jesus Christ and Mythology.* See also Perrin, *The Promise of Bultmann,* pp. 74–85, and the Further Reading at the end of this chapter.

[13] See *n.* 7 for the explanation of this use of "kerygma."

the earth as is the myth of the resurrection-ascension and features the same celestial elevator moving in the opposite direction. But it is also interpretable as dealing with the futurity of human existence in the world; to speak of the parousia of the Son of Man is to speak of the futurity of human existence in the world, that "openness to the future" of which Bultmann and the existentialists speak so eloquently. The success of this particular view of such central New Testament myths as the resurrection and the parousia guarantees its continuing and legitimate role in the interpretation of the New Testament. But this widely held view of myth is not the only possible one, and in fact does not command outstanding support among historians of religion. An urgent challenge confronting contemporary New Testament scholarship is to approach the New Testament with views of myth other than and in addition to the Strauss-Bultmann view.

A second view of myth with which to approach the New Testament is that of Mircea Eliade, the distinguished Rumanian-born historian of religion. "Myth narrates a sacred history; it relates an event that took place in primordial time, the fabled time of the 'beginning.' . . . Myth tells how, through the deeds of supernatural beings, a reality came into existence. . . . Myth . . . relates how something was produced, began to be."[14] Myth can be "known," "experienced," "lived" by means of recitation and ritual. ". . . In one way or another one lives the myth, in the sense that one is seized by the sacred, exalting power of the events recollected or reenacted."[15] These words are immediately applicable to the Jewish Passover and to the Christian sacred meal (Lord's Supper or Eucharist, 1 Cor 11:23–26; Mark 14:17–25; Matt 26:20–29; Luke 22:14–23). Passover celebrates the events of the Exodus, the deliverance from Egypt, in recitation and ritual, and it is believed that there is renewal in an experience that can certainly be described as being seized "by the sacred, exalting power of the events recollected and reenacted." Similarly, in reciting the account of Jesus' institution of the meal that celebrates and interprets his death, the Christian reenacts that meal. In saying "Every time you eat this bread and drink this cup, you proclaim the death of the Lord" (1 Cor 11:26, NEB), Paul is claiming that the Christian experiences the event of the Cross in all its significance.

In a very real sense, therefore, Jews and Christians are constantly involved in something Eliade would recognize as myth; there is for both renewal by a conscious return to a beginning. At the same time there is also another element present in both the Passover and the Christian meal—an orientation toward the future. The Jewish family looks for the coming of Elijah on a Passover night, and Paul finishes the sentence quoted above, "until he comes." In addition, there are the claims that the Exodus events and the Cross of Jesus are historical, occurring in secular as well as sacred time, but the vitality of the celebration comes from their mythic quality rather than from their factuality.

Both the Strauss-Bultmann and the Eliade understanding of myth have to

---

[14] From M. Eliade's article on myth in the 1968 *Encyclopaedia Britannica*, vol. 15, pp. 1132–42, especially p. 1133.
[15] M. Eliade, p. 1135.

be considered seriously by a student of the New Testament. Certainly there are narratives in the New Testament that should be demythologized, i.e., reinterpreted and understood as directly addressing the realities of human existence in the world. Bultmann correctly interprets the resurrection as Jesus being risen into the kerygma of the church, i.e., as affecting the potentialities for human existence in the world under the faith found in response to the kerygma. But Easter is also celebrated as a time of renewal by a return to the power of the First Easter in recitation and ritual. These alternatives are not mutually incompatible; rather, they explore the richness of the possibilities inherent in understanding the resurrection of Jesus as myth.

A further view of myth is that of the French philosopher Paul Ricoeur, as presented in his book *The Symbolism of Evil*.[16] Ricoeur accepts the history-of-religions view of myth. It is a traditional narrative about events that occurred in a primeval time and place; it is foundation for ritual which reenacts it; and it establishes the way people think and act as a means of understanding themselves in the world. However, Ricoeur thinks that more can be said about myth. For modern people, the myth has lost its power to explain reality because its sacred time and place—for example, a garden of Eden—is not connected to time and place as understood by modern scientific history. In other words, if modern scientific facts cannot support all the spontaneous associations of events in the emotional experience of those who believe the myth, something is lost in the attempt to understand it. Paradoxically this act of demythologizing, of interpreting myth in relation to scientific information, opens up the possibility of understanding the *symbolic* function of myth, that is, its power to explore and discover the area of what people believe about the sacred and their relationship to it.

To briefly describe myths (which we are about to do) is almost a contradiction in terms. Myths are narratives that express in symbolically rich language human experiences that resist expression in any objective, descriptive language. Fundamental human emotional experiences such as the feeling that it is "my fault," or that I am unworthy, are subject to many possible meanings and are therefore articulated initially by spontaneous confessions. These are couched in the symbolic language of defilement, of being stained, spotted, or blemished. Similarly, the feeling of guilt is expressed by accusatory language. These confessions objectify and externalize the feelings to a limited extent, but they are still symbolic utterances. An even more basic experience, usually believed to be a universal experience of all humanity, is the experience of not being in touch with oneself, of alienation, which is confessed in symbolic language such as "missing the mark" (the literal meaning of sin) as in archery, or the tortuous road. Symbolic language like this is opaque, that is, it points beyond itself to a situation of human beings that can take other forms of

---

[16] We are deliberately contrasting the views of Bultmann, Eliade, and Ricoeur because it seemed necessary to call attention, at an introductory level, to the different nuances in their views. But at a deeper level they are much closer together than this presentation makes them appear, and Ricoeur constantly acknowledges his indebtedness both to Bultmann and to Eliade.

expression. The experience of being "unclean" can be expressed in many ways. When the symbolic language is taken up into a narrative form and placed in a time and place that cannot be precisely coordinated with historical times and places, it becomes myth. Sin and exile are expressed in the form of a story about the "fall of man" ("man" = 'Ādām in Hebrew) and his expulsion from the garden of Eden. Similarly, the feeling that it is not "my fault," or that I am worth something, can be couched in symbolic language about being clean and pure; innocence is articulated in the language of acquittal; or integration into reality is spoken with the language of being centered, saved from tragedy, or bought back out of slavery (redemption). When this is taken up in narrative form, as we suggested above, the exodus to freedom from slavery in Egypt (celebrated in the Passover) or the sacrifice of an innocent victim for the sin of humankind (celebrated in the Christian sacred meal) becomes an appropriate narrative expression. Finally, we may note that there are also myths of hope about the future which are told in highly symbolic language, and these we call eschatological myths or, if they draw their symbolism from the realm of cosmic catastrophy and the end of the world as we know it, apocalyptic myths. As there are myths of the beginning, so there are also myths of the end.

To return to the New Testament in the light of Ricoeur's symbolism of evil, it is obvious that the New Testament uses the symbols of sin and redemption from sin. It accepts the myth of the rebellion of the primal man, Adam, as a narrative account of the origin of the symbol "sin," and it accepts the symbol "sin" as corresponding to a fundamental aspect of reality experienced in the world. Paul says that "sin came into the world through one man and death through sin, and so death spread to all men because all men sinned" (Rom 5:12). This is the language of the symbolism of evil, and the myth of the fall of Adam is its original narrative context. But in the New Testament there is also a corresponding symbol of "redemption from sin." Paul says: "Then as one man's trespass led to condemnation for all men, so one man's act of righteousness leads to acquittal and life for all men. For as by one man's disobedience many were made sinners, so by one man's obedience many will be made righteous . . . so that, as sin reigned in death, grace also might reign through righteousness to eternal life through Jesus Christ our Lord" (Rom 5:18–21). This is the language of the symbolism of redemption, and its original narrative context is the myth of the redemptive suffering and death of Jesus on the Cross. The myth has its home in the Christian sacred meal, where the suffering and death of Jesus are interpreted as redemptive by means of symbolic language derived ultimately from the passage concerning the suffering servant of God in Isaiah 53. The servant "was wounded for our transgressions, he was bruised for our iniquities; upon him was the chastisement that made us whole, and with his stripes we are healed. . . . the Lord has laid on him the iniquity of us all" (Isa 53:5–6). The early Christians expressed their understanding of the redemptive death of Jesus in Mark 10:45, "For the Son of Man also came . . . to give his life as a ransom for many," and in Mark 14:24, "This is my blood of the covenant, which is poured out for many," which are deliberate allusions to the language of that chapter.[17] But to use the Cross of Jesus as a symbol for redemption requires the narrative myth of the suffering and death of Jesus and that is provided by the brief pregnant references to the death of Jesus at the Christian meal in Mark 14:17–25 and 1 Cor 11:23–26. These references were no doubt expanded into a longer narrative at the celebration of the meal itself, either in the words of the leader of the celebration or in the thought of the participants who would know the crucifixion story. So the use of the symbolism of redemption through the Cross of Jesus requires and presupposes the myth narrated in the account of the suffering and death of Jesus; to use the technical language of New Testament scholarship, it requires and presupposes a "passion narrative." In practice in the New Testament and subsequent Christian history the Cross itself comes to represent the symbolism of redemption, so we may speak quite simply of the symbolism of the Cross and its essential narrative context, the myth of the passion narrative. We are therefore dealing with three things: the experience of a happy, free consciousness expressed by the symbol of redemption (literally, "buying back out of slavery"); a secondary symbol, the Cross, which represents the particular form of redemption Christians believe in; and the narrative myth of the passion of Jesus, in which the Cross has its context and from which Christians first learn of its meaning.

This brief discussion of the element of myth in the New Testament should serve to show that the New Testament is particularly rich in myth, which is one reason for its impact on generations of readers. But the New Testament is not only rich in myth; it is also rich in history. The Jesus who is the central figure in the myth is a man who lived and taught, suffered and died in Palestine in the first century. The New Testament is essentially concerned, therefore, with *both* myth *and* history, and this is a matter we must now discuss.

THE NEW TESTAMENT AS MYTH AND HISTORY

Let us point out again that it is regrettable that the discussion of myth in the New Testament began in an atmosphere of bitter controversy about the reliability of the gospels. In that particular historical context myth was interpreted as false or unreliable narrative, and the battle was joined. "Myth" became a pejorative term concerning the gospels, and the study and interpretation of the gospels labored under a handicap from which it has still not recovered. It must, therefore, be stated once more that myth is a rich, meaningful, and honorable term used in connection with a religious text, including the gospel texts.

One way to make our point is to claim that a myth cannot be true or false; it can only be effective or ineffective. Another way is to state, as Eliade has

---

[17] In the gospel of Mark, as in 1 Corinthians 11, these words are given to Jesus, but they were nonetheless coined in the early church in accordance with a procedure we discuss in detail in connection with the gospel of Mark in chapter 8.

done orally, that no one can self-consciously create a myth. A myth has to arise spontaneously out of the consciousness of the people; it has to correspond to reality as they experience it; and it has to make sense for them of that reality, or a significant part of it. If it does these things, then it is "true," or "effective"; if it does not, it is false and ineffective.

Men and women do in fact and in practice live by means of myth. They understand themselves and their place in the world according to the myths of origins they accept, and their behavior is in many ways determined by the myths to which they subscribe, whether recognized as such or not. In England there is the myth of the "British gentleman"; in America that of the "South." Examples could be multiplied indefinitely: the role of "manifest destiny" in American history, the myth of "Aryan supremacy" in Hitler's Germany, or the nineteenth-century myth of the inevitable progress of humanity that in Europe was shattered by the harsh realities of World War I and its aftermath. Myths operate at the conscious level of verbalization as individuals and groups use them to express their fundamental understanding of themselves and their existence in the world. But they also operate at a more primal level as they are accepted without conscious thought as expressing the way things are, or can be, or should be.[18]

The New Testament is a rich source of myths, and this is not the least of its importance. But it also blends history with these myths and thus introduces an added factor. The Christian myth of origins is built around a historical figure crucified by a Roman official whose name has been found on an inscription. The New Testament interweaves myth and history, which introduces an added element into the discussion. In general, myths do not involve an element of history; they normally take place in a special kind of mythical time, like the seven "days" of God's creation of the world. The history they narrate, like the history of the Flood in Genesis 6–10, is usually not a history that critically-minded historians can investigate. But the myths of the Passover and of the Cross as redemptive are different. Both involve events that took place in historical time, the flight of Jews from Egypt and the crucifixion of Jesus. In some way both myths involve an interrelationship between myth and history.

This interrelationship between myth and history may be considered in three ways: (a) the element of correlation between the claims of the myth and the factual data of the history; (b) the use of myth to interpret and give meaning to history; (c) the history itself as remembered and retold becoming the bearer of the myth. In our discussion we find that these three possibilities are necessarily interwoven, but it is convenient to use them as three approaches to the single problem of the interrelationship of myth and history in the New Testament.

---

[18] A recent discussion of the natural function of myth in the lives of men and women even today is J. Campbell, *Myths to Live By*. As examples of the power of myths, Campbell cites "the economics of the Pyramids, the cathedrals of the Middle Ages, Hindus starving to death with edible cattle strolling all around them, or the history of Israel, from the time of Saul to right now" (p. 22).

A Preliminary Point: The Meanings of "History" in Any Discussion of Myth and History

Before any discussion of myth and history can be meaningful, a further point must be made. There is a range of meanings in the word "history," a range we ought to discuss with some care.

History as the Historical

History means first of all factual history, things "as they actually happened." Here we are concerned with "getting at the facts," reconstructing the data in a way that would satisfy a court of law. A major concern of New Testament scholarship in modern times has been to investigate the factual data of Jesus and the early church, and the results of such an investigation are the presupposition of any contemporary understanding of the New Testament.

History as the Historic

Facts by themselves are not enough for evaluation or understanding. They have to be interpreted; their significance has to be appreciated in the broader context of the totality of human experience. This brings us to a second meaning that can be given to the word *history*, history as the "historic."

As an example outside New Testament studies, there have been many American presidents, and each has made many public speeches: in one sense all are equally "historical." But if we think in terms of their significance for the future, there were few presidents and presidential addresses as "historic" as Abraham Lincoln and his Gettysburg Address. So also the Cross of Jesus is as "historical" as that of any other Jew executed by the Romans, but it is also "historic" in the significance it came to have for future generations in a way the others did not.

We are using "historical" to designate history as what actually happened and "historic" to designate the ongoing significance of a person or event for subsequent generations. German has two nouns for history, and German scholars speak of the former as *Historie* (adjective: *historisch*) and of the latter as *Geschichte* (adjective: *geschichtlich*). Though English does not have two nouns, it has two adjectives, and we have used them. Regardless of the words, the distinction is real and important. Every person or event is historical in that there are facts to be established, and every person or event is historic in that there is an ongoing significance for subsequent generations. But even this distinction does not exhaust the significance of the word *history*: there is also history as "historicity."

History as the Historicity of Human Existence in the World

Every man and woman lives out his or her life in concrete historical circumstances, and the possibilities for that life are in no small measure determined by those circumstances. An Asian peasant has one set of possibilities; a western European, a second; a black American, a third; and so on. Moreover, the possibilities for that life are affected by external historical occurrences: wars, technological advances, natural catastrophes, political decisions. All these and many more can change one's life, sometimes dramatically and drastically. We speak of this as the "historicity" of human existence in the world. But human existence in the world is affected not only by historical circumstances and events, but also by the impact of ideas and the interpretation given to the data present to one's consciousness at all kinds of levels. So, to return to our primary example, we may speak of the historical Jesus as he actually was, or we may speak of the historic Jesus as interpreted in his significance for future generations. But then we must go on to recognize that there is another side to the historic Jesus; that is, there is the historicity of human existence in the world which can be affected by the historic Jesus and by the response of an individual to the impact of that aspect of Jesus.

Each of these possibilities in the meaning of the word *history* is important in discussing myth and history in the New Testament, and we now turn to that relationship.

The Relationship Between Myth and History in the New Testament

The Element of Correlation Between the Claims of the Myth and the Factual Data of the History

The immediately obvious thing about the New Testament myths is that they are built around historical personages and events. The central characters actually lived, and their lives are subject to historical investigation. The ministry of Jesus, the spread of the church in the Hellenistic world, the fall of Jerusalem, and the persecution of Christians that triggered the writing of the book of Revelation are all events that can be the subject of historical investigation. At the same time, each of these persons and events becomes part of one or more of the myths in which the New Testament is so rich.

Let us take as our example the myth of the passion of Jesus as effecting human redemption, the central feature of the Christian sacred meal. Jesus is a historical person, and his death on the Cross is a historical event; both are proper subjects for historical investigation. Our question then becomes, what are the consequences of the results of such historical investigation for the functioning adequacy, i.e., truth of the myth? Or to put it another way, does the historical data about Jesus and his Cross affect the subsequent influence of the myth at the level of the historicity of human existence in the world?

In one way this question is no sooner asked than answered, because the general study of the history of religions, including Christianity, has shown that there is no discernible correlation between the factual element of history and the functioning adequacy of a myth, and we have already acknowledged that this is the case for Christian myth. Christian myths, like all myths, function precisely because they are myth, and the only kind of history by which they may be judged or validated is that of the history of an individual or people in the concrete circumstances of life in the world. In the final analysis, myths may be judged true or false, valid or invalid, effective or ineffective, only by judging their impact at that level; with most myths that is the end of the matter. So in the myth of the passion of Jesus as redemptive the only criterion of truth or validity is its effectiveness on the historicity of the life in the world of the participants in the Christian sacred meal. Whether the narrative recited at the meal, and indeed the passion narrative itself, is historically factual is simply irrelevant. But another factor is at work in this particular myth, as in some others in the New Testament: it is not only claimed that the central figure in the myth was a historical person, but also that *he exemplified the reality that the myth claims to mediate.*

Historical data with regard to Jesus himself is extraordinarily difficult to reach, as we shall see in chapter 13; the evidence seems to indicate, however, that Jesus did not make any claims for himself, but focused attention entirely upon God and the proclamation of the Kingdom of God. The New Testament writers are a different matter: they make extensive claims for him, one being that he exemplified the myth of redemption. In understanding his Cross in terms of Isaiah 53, they necessarily imply that he died with noble dignity and a sure confidence in God, as the righteous servant is in Isaiah 53 described as dying; this claim is made explicitly in 1 Pet 2:21–25 and implicitly in every use of Isaiah 53 in the New Testament. But the manner of Jesus' dying, unlike the significance of his death in the myth, is subject to factual historical investigation. What would happen were it shown that Jesus did not accept his death with the noble dignity claimed in 1 Peter and described in the passion narratives themselves? What if it could be shown that Jesus was carried to the Cross railing against God and his fate? It would surely become difficult to accept the myth, because the claim that Jesus exemplified the myth in his own life, which brings an aspect of the myth into the realm of history as the historical, would be in fact false.

Not all aspects of the narrative of a myth where the myth moves into history as the historical are equally important. For example, the narrative of the Christian sacred meal gives details of Jesus arranging the meal, breaking bread, passing wine to the disciples, saying various words, and so on. All this is in the realm of the historical and has been subject to investigation, with almost entirely negative results. Most New Testament scholars would agree that the narrative is a product of the piety of early Christianity, excepting possibly a core of the words spoken over the bread and the wine, and many scholars, including us, would ascribe even those words to early Christianity. But the effectiveness or validity of the myth is not weakened, since these

"historical details" are either the narrative setting of the myth (the arrangements and so on), or the verbal expression of the symbol (the words over the
bread and wine). In neither case is it claimed that these "historical" elements
embody the myth. They provide the narrative setting or express verbally the
central symbol, but they are not affected by an element of historical factuality
or by the lack of it.

A myth can *distort* history, as myth has certainly distorted the history of
Jesus' last meal with his disciples. Distortion does not matter unless it is
claimed that the history *embodies* the myth. The claim that Jesus embodied the
myth of the Christian sacred meal (the Last Supper) made the manner of his
death significant to the myth, but not the historical details of the meal. A Jesus
carried to his Cross railing against God and his fate would destroy the myth of
the passion as redemptive, but the narrative details of the supper do not matter
except as expressions of the myth.

The element of correlation between the claims of the myth and the factual
data of the history in the New Testament is limited but significant. The significant historical data is what concerns an aspect of the history that is claimed to
embody the myth. That the myth can, and indeed does, distort the history is of
no significance to the functioning adequacy of the myth as myth.

Myth as the Interpretation of History

A striking element in the New Testament is the fact that it narrates a
whole series of events as God's revelation of himself to man and of the working out of man's redemption by God: the coming of Jesus into the world, his
life and teaching, his death and resurrection-ascension, the church's possession
of his spirit, the experience of Christian witness-martyrs paralleling the passion of Jesus, the certainty of his parousia as judge and redeemer, and so on.
The individual variations among the various books are immense, but all can be
interpreted as seeing this complex of events as the central aspect of Christian
faith.

Contemplating such a list of events held to be central to Christian faith
reveals a difference between the first century and the twentieth. For a man of
the first century these events hold together because they are all important at
the level of his existence in the world and at the level of his existence before
God. But in twentieth-century man's distinctions between myth and history,
some of these events are historical—the coming of Jesus into the world, his life
and teaching and death, the various religious enthusiasms in the early
church—whereas others are myth—the resurrection-ascension, the parousia.
Even as sophisticated a man of the New Testament as the author of Luke-Acts
could write about all these things in exactly the same way. On the one hand, he
has "gone over the whole course of these events in detail" and "written a
connected narrative" to give "authentic knowledge" about these matters (Luke
1:3-4, NEB), and then he firmly establishes the birth of Jesus as a factual event
in the context of a census taken for taxation purposes (Luke 2:1-7). On the

other hand, he is personally responsible for introducing into the New Testament narratives of the myth of the ascension as separate from the resurrection, and hence for the ascension narrative of Acts 1:9–11. But today we have to distinguish between the factual history of Roman officials ordering a census for taxation purposes and the myth of Jesus ascending to heaven and disappearing from the disciples' sight on a cloud. That they are held together by the author of Luke-Acts means they are related events so far as the New Testament is concerned. The question is, are they related "events" so far as we are concerned?

The answer surely lies in the myth that interprets the history. The "events" are related at the level of the historicity of human existence in the world. The one interprets the other at the level of its meaning for human life in the world, and hence they can be spoken of in the same breath. The birth of Jesus did change forever the possibilities for a man living in the world; his ascension is a way of saying that there is now a futurity for human existence in the world that was not there before. The myth is a vividly pictorial way of interpreting the history.

Consider also how the New Testament writers use narrative to interpret events. In the crucifixion, for example, Mark has narrative details taken from Psalms 69 and 22, which are concerned with the righteous sufferer and God's vindication of him: Mark 15:23, the offering of the wine mingled with myrrh (= Psa 69:21); 15:24, the dividing of the clothes (= Psa 22:18); and 15:29, the mocking (= Psa 22:7). In his turn Matthew adds another, Matt 27:43, where the words of the taunting are from Psa 22:8. These narrative details are not "true" at the level of factual history but are included because the crucifixion of Jesus is being interpreted as the death of a righteous sufferer whom God vindicated, and hence as the fulfillment of Psalms 22 and 69. In that sense (the only sense that interests the evangelists Mark and Matthew), they are true, and we may therefore say that the narrative interprets the event. Another striking example is Luke's use of Mark's reference to the false witnesses at the trial of Jesus, Mark 14:57–58. Luke is following and using the gospel of Mark at this point, but when he edits the Markan trial scene for his own use he omits this reference (Luke 22:71), only to use it in his account of the trial of Stephen (Acts 6:11). He does this to make the point that the passion of Stephen, the first martyr-witness, is an echo and imitation of the passion of Jesus. That the suffering of early Christians echoes and imitates the passion of Jesus is, of course, a well-known feature of early Christian martyrologies and martyrological thinking. The New Testament expresses it by using features of the passion of Jesus in the account of Stephen's martyrdom; the narrative is interpreting the event. In the New Testament, therefore, the myth interprets the history.

History Itself Functioning as Myth

If the myth interprets the history, or to put it another way, if the narrative interprets the event, we can now claim that the history narrated in the New

Testament is history as the historic (*Geschichte*), and, furthermore, that history as the historic necessarily involves history as the historical and the historical as interpreted by myth. Finally, history as the historic itself comes to function as myth. To speak of history as the historic is to speak of the narration of events that brings out the significance of those events for future generations. The passion narratives in the gospels deliberately narrate the story of the death of Jesus in order to interpret it and to express what the gospel writers, the evangelists, understand to be its significance for them and their readers. The events are, as we have seen, of different orders: some are historical, some are mythical, and some no doubt are simply legendary. But the total configuration is historic; it is history narrated to bring out its significance for the writer and his readers.

Narration of history is almost always concerned with the historic. Factual history belongs in the scholar's study and the law court, and even there it is difficult to attain. The natural tendency is always to narrate in such a way as to express what one holds to be significant in the events, and this is expressly stated in the New Testament. In Mark 1:1 the use of "the gospel of Jesus Christ" indicates that what is to follow is in some sense a sermon, designed to elicit the response of faith; in Luke 1:4 what is to follow is designed to instruct Theophilus in "the truth concerning the things of which you have been informed"; and John 20:31 sums up the purpose of the preceding narratives as having been written so that the reader "may believe that Jesus is the Christ, the Son of God." In our words, the events are narrated to bring out their significance for faith; the history in them is history in the sense of the historic.

But history in the sense of the historic necessarily shades over into myth, since the story of Jesus is told as the focal point of God's revelation of himself to men, the story of the Cross of Jesus is told as the means of man's redemption, the story of the movement of the church from Jerusalem to Rome is told as the story of an essential aspect of the founding of the church, and so on. The time concerned has become a sacred time; the events narrated make possible the reality of Christian existence in the world: the history itself has become myth.

THE NEW TESTAMENT AS TRADITION
AND AS INTERPRETATION OF TRADITION

The texts of the New Testament are to a large extent the result of a long period in which a tradition was established and in which that tradition was instantly interpreted, added to, and further reinterpreted. The parables of Jesus were remembered and handed on as tradition within the Christian communities, but as they were handed on they were reinterpreted both by changes within the texts of the parables themselves and also by the addition of new conclusions or explanations to them.[19] Then, when the evangelists incorporated

---

[19] This process is carefully described by J. Jeremias in his book *The Parables of Jesus*, especially chapter 2, "The Return to Jesus from the Primitive Church."

them into their gospels, they introduced further changes to make them express the meaning they saw in them.[20] Further examples of this process are the apocalyptic discourse in Mark 13 and the hymn Paul quotes in Phil 2:6–11. The discourse in Mark 13 was developed and interpreted in the Christian community before the gospel of Mark was written and then the evangelist himself reinterpreted what he received: giving it a setting, adding a section in which the sufferings of Christians exactly parallel what happened to Jesus in his passion (Mark 13:9), and so on. In Phil 2:6–11, Paul quotes a hymn from the tradition of the church, but he reinterprets as he quotes, for example, when referring specifically to the Cross he adds "even death on a cross," a phrase not found in the original hymn. A fundamental aspect of the New Testament texts is that they are in no small part the end product of a long and constant process of interpretation and reinterpretation. At the same time, their authors were by no means content simply to hand on what they had themselves received, but further reinterpreted the tradition they received. The process does not necessarily end with the production of a given text; Matthew and Luke freely reinterpret a text they themselves received, the gospel of Mark.

Recognizing this fact about the texts of the New Testament not only adds great complexity to New Testament scholarship but is critical to understanding the nature of the New Testament itself. The New Testament is on one hand the product of the vision of reality of individual authors, and it is also the deposit of a long period of Christian experience and Christian tradition. Both these elements are important in understanding the texts themselves, and they enable us not only to focus our attention on the faith and understanding of the authors, but also to reach behind them into earlier stages of primitive Christianity. Furthermore, this constant process of interpretation and reinterpretation of traditional material indicates the dynamic nature of early Christianity. These Christians did not simply depend on their traditions for guidance, but rather interpreted those traditions to give them new meaning in light of their experience as Christians in the world and the expectations they were developing.

Let us examine how the men and women of the New Testament use their own sacred Scriptures—what we would call the Old Testament and the Apocrypha, together with several other texts that didn't make it into either the Jewish or Christian version of the canon, such as the book of Enoch. In the speech of Peter at Pentecost in Acts 2:14–36 there is a lengthy quotation from the prophet Joel (Acts 2:17–21 = Joel 2:28–32). But the fact that the text of the book of Joel has been reinterpreted in the speech is shown by significant additions and changes. In Acts 2:17 "in the last days" and "God declares" have been added to Joel 2:28. In Acts 2:18 "they shall prophesy" has been added to Joel 2:29. In Acts 2:19 there are two small but very significant additions to the text of Joel 2:30—"above" and "beneath." The text of Joel has only one set of portents or signs, the cosmic indications of the coming of "the day of the Lord." But in Acts there are two such sets of signs, those in the sky *above* and those on the earth *beneath*. The significance of this change is apparent when in

---

[20] A very good example of this is to be found in J. D. Kingsbury, *The Parables of Jesus in Matthew 13.*

Acts 2:22 (NEB) Jesus of Nazareth is "a man singled out by God and made known to you through miracles, portents, and signs, which God worked among you through him, as you well know." The signs in the sky above remain outstanding, to be fulfilled at some point in the future, but those on the earth below have been given in the coming of Jesus, the first act of the great divine drama. The text is reinterpreted in the light of immediate experience and imminent expectation. The same is true of the two earlier additions. "In the last days" expresses the Christians' conviction that the text applies to them and that they are the community of the End Time; they are experiencing the first act of the divine drama that will shortly reach its climax in the (second) coming of Jesus to judge the world, the parousia. "And they shall prophesy" emphasizes a matter very important to early Christianity, the possession of the spirit of prophecy, the sure sign that they were indeed the community of the End Time.

Further Reading

For the formation of the canon of the N.T. (i.e., the process by which the collection of books that make up the N.T. came to be the one book of the N.T.), see Appendix 1 at the end of the book.

In this volume the word *text* is used in the literary critical sense of a written (or orally fixed) text, and so we speak of the N.T. as a "text" and a collection of "texts." Another use of the word, more common in N.T. scholarship, is to refer to the original written text of the N.T. as we know it or can reconstruct it from our various sources in manuscripts and versions (early translations). This matter is briefly discussed in Appendix 2 at the end of the book.

For the work on the N.T. as proclamation and parenesis, there is no need to go beyond Martin Dibelius' classic, *From Tradition to Gospel.*

The dilemma of the nineteenth century with regard to the gospels as factual history, the introduction of the idea of the gospels as myth, the subsequent reaction of an ever more sophisticated attempt to derive history from the gospels, and the final counter reaction in Bultmann's return to the kerygma of the church have all been reviewed in H. C. Kee, *Jesus in History,* pp. 1–25. Kee, however, does not go into the question of myth in its present form nor into Bultmann's demythologizing program.

Bultmann's view of myth is presented in two works already mentioned.

H. W. Bartsch, ed., *Kerygma and Myth.*
R. Bultmann, *Jesus Christ and Mythology.*

For a more detailed discussion of Bultmann, his view of myth, and his demythologizing program, see N. Perrin, *The Promise of Bultmann,* especially pp. 74–84, "Demythologizing and the Existential Interpretation of the Documents of Faith." For further information, see also D. Duling, *Jesus Christ Through History,* especially chapters VI–X.

Discussions of Bultmann, his view of myth and his demythologizing program, are of course legion. Among the more readily available are:

P. Althaus, *The So-Called Kerygma and the Historical Jesus*. Althaus is a German scholar more conservative than Bultmann.

D. Cairns, *A Gospel Without Myth? Bultmann's Challenge to the Preacher*.

F. Gogarten, *Demythologizing and History*. Gogarten is a German scholar sympathetic to Bultmann.

I. Henderson, *Myth in the New Testament*.

K. Jaspers and R. Bultmann, *Myth and Christianity: An Inquiry into the Possibility of Religion Without Myth*. A most important debate between Bultmann and a leading existentialist philosopher more radical than he.

G. V. Jones, *Christology and Myth in the New Testament*.

J. Macquarrie, *The Scope of Demythologizing: Bultmann and His Critics*. A perceptive discussion of the issues by a philosophical theologian.

S. Ogden, *Christ Without Myth*. The most important English language discussion of Bultmann's theology and program.

Eliade's view of myth is to be found in his *Encyclopaedia Britannica* article, quoted in the text, and in the following books:

M. Eliade, *The Quest; History and Meaning in Religion;* especially pp. 72–87, "Cosmogonic Myth and 'Sacred History.'"

——, *Cosmos and History: The Myth of the Eternal Return*.

——, *Myth and Reality*.

The present writers know of no other systematic discussion of "the New Testament as Myth and History."

The section on the "New Testament as Tradition and as Interpretation of Tradition" is built on insights gained through the historical critical disciplines of form criticism and redaction criticism. On these see N. Perrin, *What Is Redaction Criticism?* and the literature given there.

The process of constant reinterpretation that lies behind the apocalyptic discourse in Mark 13 is discussed in L. Hartman, *Prophecy Interpreted*.

The reinterpretation of Old Testament texts as they are used in the N.T. texts is particularly discussed in B. Lindars, *New Testament Apologetic*.

The Egnatian Way (Via Egnatia) was the major Roman road across Macedonia, linking the Adriatic and Aegean Seas. Paul traveled this road between Philippi and Thessalonica.

CHAPTER THREE

A HISTORY OF NEW TESTAMENT CHRISTIANITY

To understand the works that constitute the New Testament, it is necessary to know something of the history of the churches in and for which they were produced. Historical information about the Christian movement down to A.D. 140, the approximate date of the writing of 2 Peter, the last work to come into the New Testament canon, is hard to come by. There are a number of reasons for this. As we said in the last chapter, the literature of the New Testament is concerned with proclamation and parenesis, myth and history. But the history lies buried in forms and genres that are not intended to be historical narrative in the modern sense. To get at that narrative we must interpret the forms and genres and evaluate them critically while we attempt to reconstruct history.

A few examples will illustrate the point. Many early Christians lived in expectation that the world was about to end. Therefore they chronicled events, if at all, only in the form of apocalyptic symbolism, as in the books of Daniel and Revelation. It is often difficult for us to pinpoint the person or event in world history to which such an apocalyptic symbol refers. Other Christians told stories which might look like historical narratives at first glance, but which were evidently recounted for didactic reasons, that is, they were intended to instruct and exhort rather than to record facts. The stories they told were history dramatized to give meaning, to involve the reader in the necessity for decision, or to inspire emulation. These stories do not therefore record what the modern reader might like to know about historical events. Still other Christians wrote letters, or letter-like writings, in which references to events were autobiographical, as in the case of Paul. The one New Testament book, the Acts of the Apostles, which purports to present us with a history of the early church, turns out upon examination to be a highly interpreted piece of literature much like other ancient historical writings. Whenever it covers the same ground as some of the autobiographical information given in the letters of

Paul, the two accounts are sometimes difficult to reconcile. The writer of Acts does not intend to give biographical information about the apostle Paul but to challenge us to emulate him.

However difficult it is to reconstruct historical information from the New Testament it is not impossible, once we have learned to read it critically. This is especially the case with the Acts of the Apostles. For example, in Acts 8:1 the author reports a violent persecution of the church in Jerusalem and says that "they were all scattered . . . except the apostles." Now it is unlikely that the Jewish authorities would make a distinction between the apostles and other members of the Jerusalem church, and permit the apostles to stay. What might be a critical interpretation of this odd reference? In Acts 6:1-6 the author reports a dispute between "the Hebrews" (i.e., Jews speaking a Semitic language) and "the Hellenists" (i.e., Greek-speaking Jews) over the distribution of the property held by the community in common. Seven are appointed to take care of the matter, all with Greek names and hence presumably "Hellenists." But these seven are never reported as serving the function for which they were allegedly selected. They appear only as evangelists, and their leader, Stephen, is martyred for a speech criticizing his fellow Jews; this martyrdom is the beginning of a violent persecution of the church. Modern scholars have concluded that there was a real distinction in earliest Jerusalem Christianity between aggressive Hellenistic Jewish Christians, who tended to be critical of Judaism as such, and more conservative Jerusalem Christians, who differed from their fellow Jews only in holding Jesus to have been the Messiah. The aggressive Hellenistic Jewish Christians were persecuted and driven out of Jerusalem; it was not "the apostles" who were permitted to stay, but the conservative Jewish Christians. The Hellenistic Jewish Christians would have been driven out of Jerusalem, not because they claimed that Jesus was the Messiah, but because they developed a criticism of Judaism and of its Law.[1]

If one way to get at the history of the early church is a critical reconstruction of Acts, a second way is source criticism. We shall illustrate the attempt to isolate sources with "the synoptic problem."

The gospels of Matthew, Mark, and Luke are usually called the synoptic gospels (from the Greek *synoptikos,* "seeing the whole together") because they tell much the same story in much the same way. They can be set side by side and read together. But if we do set them side by side it becomes evident that there are likenesses and differences, indicating that there is a literary relationship among them. This relationship is of two kinds. First, in some sections of the gospels it is clear that all three gospels are related to one another; second, there are passages in which it is evident that Matthew and Luke are related to each other but not to the gospel of Mark. We examine each of these phenomena in turn.

---

[1] G. Bornkamm, *Paul,* pp. 13–15; for a comparison of Paul's biographical statements and the book of Acts, see below, pp. 132–33, and for an evaluation of Acts in the light of Hellenistic historiography, pp. 301–03.

The first example of the interrelatedness of all three gospels is the Baptism of Jesus (Matt 3:13–17 = Mark 1:9–11 = Luke 3:21–22):

Matt 3:13–17	Mark 1:9–11	Luke 3:21–22
Then Jesus came from Galilee to the Jordan to John, to be baptized by him. John would have prevented him, saying, "I need to be baptized by you, and do you come to me?" But Jesus answered him, "Let it be so now; for thus it is fitting for us to fulfill all righteousness." Then he consented.	In those days Jesus came from Nazareth of Galilee	Now when all the people were baptized
And when Jesus was baptized, he went up immediately from the water, and behold, the heavens were opened	and was baptized by John in the Jordan. And when he came up out of the water, immediately he saw the heavens opened	and when Jesus also had been baptized and was praying, the heaven was opened,
and he saw the Spirit of God descending like a dove and alighting on him; and lo, a voice from heaven, saying, "This is my beloved Son, with whom I am well pleased."	and the Spirit descending upon him like a dove; and a voice came from heaven, "Thou art my beloved Son; with thee I am well pleased."	and the Holy Spirit descended upon him in bodily form, as a dove, and a voice came from heaven, "Thou art my beloved Son; with thee I am well pleased."

If we look at these passages closely, we find a distinct pattern to their verbal interrelatedness. The pattern is that Matthew and Mark can agree against Luke, and Mark and Luke can agree against Matthew, but *Matthew and Luke do not normally agree against Mark where they share the same material*. A comparison of *words* suggests that Mark is the common factor. In Matthew and Mark Jesus came from Galilee, but this is not mentioned in Luke. The Spirit descends like a dove on Jesus in Mark and Luke; the Spirit descends like a dove *and alights* on Jesus in Matthew. The voice from heaven says, "Thou art my beloved Son; with thee I am well pleased" in Mark and Luke, but "This is my beloved Son, with whom I am well pleased" in Matthew.

This pattern of *verbal* interrelatedness continues throughout the three gospels with only very minor exceptions, and it is matched by a similar pattern in the *order of the events* presented: Matthew and Mark can agree against Luke, and Luke and Mark against Matthew, but Matthew and Luke rarely agree against Mark. Again, Mark appears to be the common factor.

This consistent pattern both in the verbal relationship among the three gospels and the order of the events presented shows that the gospel of Mark was written first and that Matthew and Luke have both used it as a source. This conclusion of the *priority of Mark* is presupposed in our subsequent discussions of the synoptic gospels.

A further phenomenon of the *verbal* relationships among the synoptic gospels is that sections of Matthew and Luke *not* found in Mark are so close verbally that they must be using a common source. The first occurrence of this phenomenon is the Preaching of John the Baptist (Matt 3:7–10=Luke 3:7–9):

Matt 3:7–10	Luke 3:7–9
But when he saw many of the Pharisees and Sadducees coming for baptism, he said to them, "You brood of vipers! Who warned you to flee from the wrath to come? Bear fruit that befits repentance, and do not presume to say to yourselves, 'We have Abraham as our father'; for I tell you, God is able from these stones to raise up children to Abraham. Even now the ax is laid to the root of the trees; every tree therefore that does not bear good fruit is cut down and thrown into the fire."	He said therefore to the multitudes that came out to be baptized by him, "You brood of vipers! Who warned you to flee from the wrath to come? Bear fruits that befit repentance, and do not begin to say to yourselves, 'We have Abraham as our father'; for I tell you, God is able from these stones to raise up children to Abraham. Even now the ax is laid to the root of the trees; every tree therefore that does not bear good fruit is cut down and thrown into the fire."

This material common to Matthew and Luke but not found in Mark is almost always *teaching material*. The first example is teaching of John the Baptist, but the remainder is teaching of Jesus. Other examples of it are the teaching on anxiety (Matt 6:25–33 = Luke 12:22–31), and on judging (Matt 7:1–5 = Luke 6:37–38). The constant appearance of such parallel passages in the gospels of Matthew and Luke has led to the conclusion that they have a source in common in addition to the gospel of Mark, a source consisting mostly of sayings material. The existence of this source is hypothetical since no copy of it has been found, but the verbal relationships between Matthew and Luke show that it did once exist. For the sake of convenience this source is called Q (for the German *Quelle*, "source").

In addition to the sources they have in common, the gospel of Mark and source Q, both Matthew and Luke present a good deal of special material of their own, e.g., sections of the Sermon on the Mount in Matthew 5–7 (Matt

5:17–20, 21–22, 27–29, 33–37; 6:1–6, 16–18, 34; 7:6, 15) and the parables in Luke 15. We may represent the interrelatedness of the synoptic gospels in diagram form as follows.

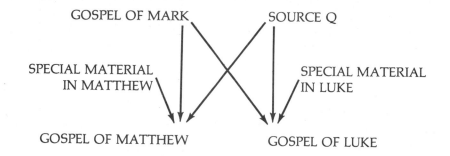

It is clear from this solution (sometimes called the "Two-Source Theory" in reference to the gospel of Mark and the source Q) that we are answering certain historical questions about the priority of sources. Though this solution is not unanimously held,[2] it is still the opinion of the majority. The source Q will be used as the best representative of early Palestinian apocalyptic Christianity, and we discuss it in detail in chapter 4. Similarly, we discuss Mark as the earliest gospel and, in fact, the creator of that genre in Christianity, even though there are some parallels in Greco-Roman literature which in the most general sense are similar. Thus, in our historical reconstructions we shall add to a critical use of the book of Acts source theories, the best of example of which is the Two-Source Theory.

Still another way of attempting to arrive at historical information is what the German scholars after World War I termed *Formgeschichte*, that is, "form criticism," or literally, "form history." Greater appreciation of oral tradition in the ancient world led to the realization that the New Testament writers had made extensive use of traditional material, some written (as we have just seen in the Two-Source Theory), but much of it oral. They also realized that Paul and other writers of the letter in the New Testament constantly quoted hymns, confessions, benedictions, and other elements from the liturgies of the New Testament churches; similarly, they used lists of virtues and vices and lists of the duties of various members of a household—a device commonly used in the Greco-Roman world as a means for ethical instruction. Perhaps even more startling was the belief that the gospel writers were not eyewitnesses to the events they recorded, but that they had picked up more or less fixed oral traditions which had been circulating in the Christian churches before their use by the evangelists in their gospels. "More or less fixed forms" means that the forms, as well as their content, were subject to modification. The object of form criticism was therefore to describe the forms and their variants, then to track them through the various Christian communities where they were given

---

[2] The theory has been challenged in recent times by W.R. Farmer, *The Synoptic Problem* (second edition) and others, but it is still held by most scholars.

shape, modified, and interpreted. Though there is a good deal of subjectivity involved in this process, experienced form critics sought to trace a history of tradition by theorizing about what was early and late. It should be noted that form critics did this with the shorter units, such as parables and miracle stories, not with the whole gospels. By analyzing all of the traditions in the (synoptic) gospels, tracing their histories, and attempting to locate them in communities, form critics could gain an overall impression of the history of earliest Christianity.[3]

Recently there have been some modifications in classical form criticism. Contemporary literary criticism has shown us that more attention should be paid to the function of a particular form within a given community. Anthropological and sociological research into oral traditions and their transmission are modifying the perception of oral tradition in primitive Christianity. Others are exploring the importance of the shift from oral to written material. Though modifications like these are taking place, form criticism in the broad sense still remains a useful tool for attempting to understand the history of early Christian traditions, and their functions in the early churches.[4]

Of special interest in this regard are two other methods, redaction criticism and social historiography. Redaction criticism (*Redaktionsgeschichte*, "the history of redaction") attempts to establish the theology of the New Testament writers by analyzing the way they accepted or rejected, modified or expanded, or otherwise reformulated traditions, as well as how they reordered and regrouped materials to make a certain point, composed new materials, and structured their accounts—all primarily intentional interpretative devices—in order to set forth their own points of view. Although this is a form of literary analysis (as is form criticism), it yields a historical result in so far as it is possible to observe sources and traditions being remolded at a later date. This method has been especially fruitful with Q and the four evangelists, but it has also been used with other literature, for example, the book of Revelation or the Acts of the Apostles. If combined with the Two-Source Theory, it is possible to observe how Matthew and Luke make use of Q and Mark. Furthermore, some scholars have been interested in tracking the trajectories of various larger genres, such as collections of sayings like Q or gospel-like narratives.[5]

One of the main purposes of form criticism was the identification of early Christian communities and their religious life in order to understand how the traditions functioned from community to community. A special contribution in this area is now being made by scholars who are influenced by social historiography.[6] Social historiography describes how various groups of people, or communities, construct and maintain a meaningful world for themselves. People

---

[3] For further illustration of form criticism, see below, pp. 401–05.
[4] C. Carlston, "Form Criticism, NT," *IDB Suppl.*, pp. 345–48; see chapter 13 for further discussion.
[5] J. M. Robinson and H. Koester, *Trajectories Through Early Christianity*.
[6] J. Z. Smith, "Social Description of Early Christianity," *Religious Studies Review* 1 (1975), pp. 19–25; R. Scroggs, "The Sociological Interpretation of the New Testament: The Present State of Research," *New Testament Studies* 26 (1980), pp. 164–79; H. Kee, *Christian Origins in Sociological Perspective*.

like to construct a comfortable world and give expression to their world by sharing beliefs, lifestyles, and values. Moreover, they will attempt to perpetuate their worlds with laws, role models, and in religious communities, rituals. To use the terminology of chapter 2, the rituals are means of reenacting cultural or religious myths, the myths embodying the meaningful world. Very frequently the inhabitants of such a world do not consciously articulate their values but they do express them in an offhand way. Later, the data can be gathered and analyzed to determine a whole set of meaningful social relationships. How, for example, did the early Christians understand power, that is, leadership, group interaction, or conflict? What seemed to be the importance of a rural agrarian background as compared with an urban business or commercial world? Can one gather any data on Christian attitudes toward poverty and wealth, reaction to outsiders, social institutions like marriage, divorce, family life, or slavery? How were Christian myths perpetuated in rituals? The answers to such questions will not always give historical information in the sense of temporal sequence; but occasionally they will contribute in various ways. For example, a description can be made of the transition of primitive Christianity from a rural agrarian background to the cities of the Hellenistic world. This description of a social transition can then be related to whatever generalizations can be made about the theological history of early Christianity as seen in the dating of traditions, sources, and documents.

Finally, a major source for our historical knowledge of the earlier period is the autobiographical material in the apostle Paul. Once we stop the misleading attempt to always harmonize Paul's statements with the highly interpreted picture of Paul in the Acts of the Apostles, the way is opened for the letters to yield valuable historical information about particular events.

THREE IMPORTANT FACTORS IN THE HISTORY OF NEW TESTAMENT CHRISTIANITY

Having suggested an approach to the history of New Testament Christianity, we will now take note of three important facts: (1) the rapid spread of early Christianity; (2) the central importance to Christianity of the fall of Jerusalem and the destruction of the Temple; and (3) the delay of the parousia.

The Rapid Spread of Early Christianity

Christianity spread very rapidly from its rural Palestinian origins into the cities of the Hellenistic world. Jesus of Nazareth was an itinerant, charismatic prophet of Aramaic-speaking, rural Galilee. He was a man who proclaimed to his people that the coming Kingdom of God was already present in his ministry of preaching and healing. He was crucified by the Romans in Jerusalem as a potentially dangerous Zealot-type revolutionary. Within a short time groups of itinerant preachers were scattered about the villages of Syria-Palestine perpetuating his teaching and proclaiming that the End was near. Others were soon teaching and proclaiming among the cities of the Roman Empire where Greek was spoken and understood. All claimed that Jesus himself was in one way or another "the Messiah" and that he was the means of the salvation of the world. How this came about so abruptly we describe in phases of New Testament Christianity below.

The Fall of Jerusalem and the Destruction of the Temple

Another important factor in the history of New Testament Christianity was the fall of Jerusalem to the Romans and the destruction of the Temple in A.D. 70. Jerusalem and its Temple were holy to Christians (many of whom were Jewish) as well as to Jews, and the Pauline letters attest to the special status of the church at Jerusalem and its emissaries. The destruction of Jerusalem and the Temple by the Gentiles sent a shock wave through the Jewish-Christian world and its importance is impossible to exaggerate. Indeed, much of the subsequent literature both of Judaism and Christianity took the form it did precisely in an attempt to come to terms with the catastrophe of A.D. 70. Deprived of the Holy City and the Temple, the Jews turned to the synagogue and the Law, and the result was the Mishnah and eventually the Talmuds. Deprived of the Sacred Place they shared with the Jews through Jesus and the Jerusalem church, the Christians turned to the time of Jesus as a Sacred Time and produced the gospels. Nothing was ever to be the same again for either Jews or Christians.

The Delay of the Parousia

A third important factor in the historical situation of New Testament Christianity is the negative one of what is technically known as the "delay of the parousia." The first Christians were dominated by apocalyptic eschatology, that is, by the expectation of the End, of the coming of Jesus as Son of Man or Lord to judge and to redeem, to destroy and to remake. They expected this to happen imminently, in a matter of months at most, and with this event their world would end and another, different and more perfect, would be created. The evangelist Matthew uses the Greek term *parousia*, a technical term for the visit of a high official, for this expected and anticipated event and it has passed into New Testament scholarship as a technical term. But the months and years passed by, and the parousia simply did not take place. Even though their hopes were raised again with the fall of Jersualem (cf. Mark 13) or when the Christians of Asia Minor were persecuted by the Emperor Domitian about A.D. 95 (cf. the book of Revelation), it became necessary for most New Testament Christians to come to terms with this delay of the parousia, and the attempts to do so have left a deep impression on the New Testament texts. Broadly speaking, there were three alternatives that were taken. In the first place the expectation was simply reiterated even more firmly, as if doubts could be overcome by using a louder voice. This is essentially the procedure of 2 Peter. A second way was to push the parousia into the more distant future, though still maintaining the expectation, and then to make theological sense of the extended interim period. This is essentially the procedure followed by the evangelists Matthew and, especially, Luke. The third way was to claim that the parousia had in effect already taken place, that the Cross and resurrection of Jesus were in fact the "final" (the technical term would be "eschatological") events and that the "new" life was in fact and in practice to be known by Christians now. This is the main thrust of the gospel of John.

THE PHASES OF NEW TESTAMENT CHRISTIANITY

Because of the complex nature of our sources, it is impossible to trace a precise unilinear development of New Testament Christianity; nonetheless, using the methods, key events, and ideas we have noted, it is possible to attempt a dating of New Testament sources and to gain a general impression of some of the important phases of early Christianity.

Palestinian Christianity

The Christian church began as an apocalyptic sectarian movement within ancient Judaism. The term "sect" deserves some discussion, since it is often an emotionally loaded term. As used here,[7] it is a descriptive term referring to a group that begins as a *protest* against the establishment, that is, the dominant economic, political, social, and religious power structures. Whatever the basis—poverty, degradation, denial of freedoms, lack of status, and the like—people experience humiliation and are dehumanized. A sect *rejects the realities assumed by the dominant culture;* it embraces the realities of a counter culture; it is frequently a persecuted minority. Hence, its members reject the signs of status current in the dominant culture and adopt a posture of *equality for all,* regardless of age, sex, wealth, class, or national origin. Within the sectarian community there is the *love and acceptance* usually denied them by the outside world. As a result, there are frequently emotional experiences, for example, spiritual phenomena such as prophesying or speaking in tongues (*glossalalia,* from the Greek *glōssa,* "tongue"). The warm acceptance within the community, and especially from attractive individuals, wins "converts" who make a *free choice* to join.[8] When a person enters the sect, he or she accepts its beliefs and values

---

[7] R. Scroggs, "The Earliest Christian Communities as Sectarian Movement," in J. Neusner, ed., *Christianity, Judaism and Other Greco-Roman Cults;* cf. B. Wilson, *Sects and Society,* Intro.

[8] J. Lofland and R. Stark, "Becoming a World-Saver: A Theory of Conversion to a Deviant Perspective," *American Sociological Review* 30 (1965), pp. 862–74; "Becoming a World-Saver Revisited," *American Behavioral Scientist* 20 (1977), pp. 805–18.

and develops a *total commitment* to the community. Often, at least in groups that come from religions of the Near East (Judaism, Christianity, Islam), the sect is *adventist*, that is, it expects the coming of the Kingdom of God.[9]

The sect has a great deal in common with what in chapter 1 was described as movements taken up with apocalyptic eschatology, for example, the Essenes. Apocalyptic movements, we recall, were born out of despair about the present world and the course of history leading up to it; and yet, there was the hope that the Creator of the world would carry out his plan for creation in the history of his people. Political, economic, social, and religious powerlessness under the Babylonians, Persians, Greeks, and Romans gave rise to alienation, and this in turn evoked a hope for the reversal of the present order and the reestablishment of a paradisical world, or at least a return to the golden age of King David. In Roman times, the dominant powers were Idumean kings and Gentile procurators, usually with the passive support of the upper-class, wealthy, high priestly establishment, while the populace felt burdened by citified Hellenization and excessive taxation. The apocalyptic movements were largely sectarian movements, movements which reacted to the dominant culture of the age. Many of them looked especially for an anointed one, a "Messiah," whether a royal Messiah ("Son of David"), a "prophet like Moses," a "prophet like Elijah" (who was expected to come at the End and prepare the way), or even a priestly Messiah like the Messiah of Aaron. Waiting for such a leader, they were anxious to follow anyone who proclaimed himself to be such in taking up arms against Rome, believing that this would be the sign to begin a war that God would end. In the meantime they prepared themselves for these eschatological events by adhering to the Law of God ever more strictly. Thus, they not only prepared themselves for the coming of the End and assured themselves a favorable verdict at the judgment, but they believed they were helping to hasten the End, for they were convinced that God would act the more speedily in response to the anguish of his people if his people proved themselves especially worthy by obeying his Law.

Early Palestinian Christianity shared most of these convictions; it was an apocalyptic sect within Judaism. The sources indicate that it believed that Jesus of Nazareth was a preacher, exorcist, and healer who was at the least a prophet and charismatic miracle worker. He left home and family and went from town to town (cf. Matt 8:20, 22; Mark 10:29; Luke 14:26; cf. Mark 3:21), addressing the alienated poor and outcast, the "people of the land," with his religious message of hope about the arrival of the Kingdom of God. He accepted all sorts and kinds of people into his company and ate with them. He taught his audience and challenged his opponents with parables reflecting an everyday, rural, agrarian background, the meaning of which was frequently a challenge of the accepted religious and social norms of the day. He gave his special interpretation of the Law. He exorcized demons and healed the sick as a testi-

---

[9] This theme is developed further by J. Gager, *Kingdom and Community*, who bases his analysis on the model of "millenarian" movements.

mony to God's continuing love and care for his people. He was opposed by traditional religious authorities like the scholarly scribal classes and the Pharisees who were deeply concerned about matters of table fellowship and ritual purity. He encountered political opposition from the Herodians and the wealthy and established priestly classes, leading ultimately to his crucifixion by the Romans for sedition against the state.

What we have just described about Jesus could be defended as accurate from a historical-critical perspective; we shall say more about Jesus of Nazareth in chapter 13. But it should be noted that some of Jesus' earliest followers preserved this image of Jesus in part because it was the model for their own lives as Christians. Many of them became wandering charismatic missionaries, leaving home and family, giving up possessions and security, very much analogous with the wandering Cynic street preachers of the Greco-Roman world. Indeed, they were given power to exorcize demons. Furthermore, they developed much more in their thinking about Jesus, for example, they believed that he would soon return as the apocalyptic Son of Man, and that the activity of the Spirit continued among them as the presence of Jesus.

For Palestinian Christianity at large we have concrete literary remains in that we can reconstruct the sayings source Q used by the evangelists Matthew and Luke. On form critical grounds we can isolate elements in these New Testament texts that certainly go back to the early days of Christianity in Palestine. We will begin with the sayings source Q.

As we pointed out above, there is a literary relationship between the three synoptic gospels, and the generally accepted explanation of this relationship is that Mark has been used as a source by Matthew and Luke and that, in addition, Matthew and Luke used a common source consisting mostly of sayings material, a source designated "Q." This source will be discussed in some detail in our next chapter; for the moment it is sufficient to point out that it is dominated by a particular form of eschatology, by the expectation of Jesus returning from heaven as Son of Man. The community that created the source Q proclaimed the imminent coming of Jesus from heaven as Son of Man and prepared for that coming, challenging others to do the same.

A most important point about the Q source is its *form*: it is in the form of sayings of Jesus and stories about him. The Christians of the Q community began their proclamation by repeating Jesus' proclamation of the Kingdom of God. This they could do because Jesus' proclamation of the Kingdom was in fact the proclamation of the eschatological activity of God,[10] and the eschatological activity of God was what they too were proclaiming. So they repeated the proclamation of Jesus in the form of sayings of Jesus. When they came to give a specific form and content to this expectation of the eschatological activity of God, namely that of the coming of Jesus as Son of Man, they were led to this by what they believed to be the spirit of Jesus inspiring prophets in their

[10] This statement about the proclamation of Jesus will be justified in chapter 13.

midst, and so they continued to use the same sayings form.[11] The eschatological teaching that came to them in the name of Jesus through their prophets was cast in the form of sayings of Jesus, and eventually their whole teaching came to take this form. In this way the particular form of Christian tradition in Jerusalem and Palestine took the shape of sayings of Jesus and stories about him, even when the content echoed the concerns of the church and the material was created by the church. Thus the seed was sown that reached fruition in the one distinctive Christian literary form, the gospel.

A prominent feature of Palestinian Christianity, and indeed of New Testament Christianity altogether, was *prophecy*. The Christians were particularly conscious that the spirit of prophecy had returned to them as a community, which they claimed as evidence that they were indeed God's elect and chosen community. The importance they attached to prophecy is evident in the speech attributed to Peter at Pentecost, Acts 2:14–36, which is based on Joel 2:28–32, a passage understood as a prophecy concerning the End Time now being fulfilled among the Christians. It contains two references to prophecy, Acts 2:17 and 2:18, the second having been added to the original text of Joel by the Christian exegete in order to emphasize the role of the gift of prophecy in the End Time and to emphasize further the fact that the Christian community possessed this gift. A further example of the prominence of prophecy in earliest Christianity is that, as Ernst Käsemann has shown,[12] we can trace prophetic sayings that reflect the conditions of primitive Christianity in Palestine in the text of Matthew's gospel: 7:22–23, the warning against false prophets and exorcists; 23:8–10, the warning not to acknowledge any leadership save that of Christ; 5:17–20, with its core in verse 19 and its emphasis on the imminence of eschatological judgment (being called least or great in the Kingdom); 10:41 and 13:16–17, with their reference to "prophets" and "righteous men"; 19:28–29, the sitting on the thrones with the Son of Man; 10:23, the command to urgency in the mission to Israel in light of the imminence of the coming of the Son of Man; and others. Käsemann argues, correctly, that these sayings go back to earliest Palestinian Christianity and show that that movement was dominated by the apocalyptic hope for the coming of the Son of Man in judgment and that prophets were among its charismatic leaders. Käsemann isolates these sayings on form critical grounds as being pre-Matthean and primitive, and his observations bear out what we have claimed on the basis of the sayings source Q. Earliest Palestinian Christianity was a charismatic movement, dominated by the expectation of the coming of Jesus as Son of Man and prominently featuring prophecy among its characteristics.

[11] In anticipation of matters to be discussed in chapters 4 and 13, we may perhaps say that the crux of the matter with regard to both Jesus and early Palestinian Christianity was that they both proclaimed the eschatological activity of God, i.e., God's final, decisive intervention in the history of the world whereby the wicked would be punished, the righteous rewarded, and the world itself transformed, indeed recreated. Jesus used the symbol "Kingdom of God," which expresses the idea of God acting directly; early Christianity used the symbol "Jesus coming as Son of Man," which expresses the idea of God acting through an intermediary figure.

[12] In the essays referred to in the Further Reading section at the end of this chapter, especially "The Beginnings of Christian Theology."

We have seen reflections of Palestinian Christianity in Q, certain passages in Matthew, and the prophetic emphasis in the speech attributed to Peter at Pentecost. Certainly the gospel of Mark in some ways preserves elements of Palestinian Christianity. In our chapter on the gospel of Mark, we shall designate it as an apocalyptic drama and note that the Markan community reflects Christian apocalyptic sectarianism. Jesus is portrayed in Mark as something of a wandering charismatic prophet, preacher and healer, going about the villages preaching and healing. The same themes of discipleship are present: disciples should take only minimal provisions (6:8–9), abandon their families, and be prepared for rejection. Women and Gentiles are welcome. And though Mark may be warning against a false interpretation of apocalypticism (at Jerusalem? cf. Mark 13), he nonetheless is an apocalyptic writer.

Can anything else be determined about the nature of Palestinian Christianity? Certainly some elements in Christian worship originated in Palestine. As far as we know, Jesus did not baptize; early Christians took over the rite of baptism from John the Baptist, who baptized Jesus. This baptism meant forgiveness of sins and was related to the reception of the Spirit (Mark 1:8). The Jewish holy day was the Sabbath, from sundown Friday to sundown Saturday; for Christians, the holy day became Sunday, the day of resurrection, perhaps already known by Paul (1 Cor 15:4; 16:2). The resurrection traditions were Palestinian, some Galilean (Mark 16:1–8; Matt 28:16–20; John 21), some Judean (Luke 24; Acts 1; John 20; cf. 1 Cor 15:3b–5). There are other elements of worship that are based on the Aramaic language: the address of God as "Father" (*Abba;* Gal 4:6; Rom 8:15; Mark 14:36); "praise God" (*Hallelujah;* Rev 19:1, 3, 6); *Amēn* (2 Cor 1:20); and "Our Lord, come!" (*Maranatha!*) which is an eschatological cry in connection with the Lord's Supper (1 Cor 16:20–22; cf. Rev 22:20).

If these terms and views were held by Palestinian Christians in general, do they also represent the Jerusalem Christians in particular? We have no direct literary remains from the Jerusalem church; our impressions come from statements by Paul, a critical appraisal of Acts, and possibly some pre-Pauline traditions embedded in Paul's letters. Otherwise, we must speculate.

Paul's letters show that a generation or so after the death of Jesus there were still conservative Christians in Jerusalem who believed that circumcision was the sign of the covenant people of God, that Christians should therefore be circumcized, and that such views were the proper interpretation of the Torah. Paul himself had come to the opposite view. The Jerusalem leaders, James (Jesus' brother), Peter, and John, had to mediate this dispute, and were moderate in so far as they yielded to Paul on the circumcision issue. So we learn that Jewish Christians ranged from conservative adherants of the Torah to more moderate positions and that although Hellenistic Christians might have held conservative views (as the Hellenistic Jew Paul himself had once held—as a non-Christian!), they were more likely, as a group, to have been less conservative. This division seems to be implied by the solution of the Jerusalem Conference, "we (Paul and company) to the Gentiles, they (Peter and company) to the Jews" (Gal 2:9).[13] Moreover, this division recalls the implied tensions between the Aramaic-speaking "Hebrews" and the Greek-speaking "Hellenists" (Stephen and others) in the Acts of the Apostles. If the Hellenists were driven out of Jerusalem by persecution, this means that the conservative to moderate Jewish Christians remained, and these are the ones whom Paul encountered.

Another part of the Jerusalem Conference compromise, according to Paul, was that ". . . they (James, Peter, and John) would have us remember the poor, which thing I was very eager to do" (Gal 2:10). This is a reference to the literal "poor among the saints of Jerusalem" (Rom 15:26);[14] it implies at least two economic strata in the church of Jerusalem, and probably there were more.

It may be that the Jerusalem church contained spiritualistic and prophetic elements as well. To be sure this is somewhat speculative for the coming of the Spirit on the church in the story of Pentecost in Acts 2 is, in its present form, from a later period. But Acts also knows of a prophet Agabus who was in Jerusalem (Acts 11:28; 21:20) and we may ask whether some of the Jerusalem disciples did not share in the charismatic, prophetic traditions of Palestinians in general.

Another real possibility is that the Jerusalem church possessed stories about the arrest, trial, and death of Jesus not found in Q, for Jerusalem was the scene of these events. Related to this suggestion is that the Jerusalem church gave shape to the interpretation of the Christian sacred meal, the "Lord's Supper," which Paul struggles to establish at Corinth (1 Cor 11). It would be the Jerusalem Christians who would be constantly brought face to face with the physical circumstances of the passion of Jesus. They would need to explain to their fellow Jews how it came about that Jesus, whom they claimed to be the Messiah of God, had suffered an ignominious death at the hands of the Romans. The latter they did by arguing that such events were prophesied beforehand in the sacred Scriptures, especially in the Psalms concerned with a righteous sufferer. The narrative of the crucifixion is practically a mosaic of such references, especially from Psalms 22 and 69.[15] In interpreting the "Lord's Supper" (1 Cor 11:23–26), with its parallels in the synoptic gospels, one can say only that the whole is so obviously Semitic in linguistic cast, so full of allusions to the Passover (celebrated mostly in Jerusalem), and comes to Paul with such authority, that it is hard to see where it could have originated except in the church in Jerusalem.

Finally, we should note that as an urban center Jerusalem was subject to Hellenistic influences, as were numerous cities throughout Palestine.[16] Greek was spoken increasingly in Jerusalem since the period of the Ptolemies in the third century B.C., as bilingual Aramaic and Greek inscriptions show. Indeed,

---

[13] For further discussion of this conference, see below, pp. 142, 144–46, 149–50.

[14] See chapter 5, pp. 145–46.

[15] See chapter 2, p. 59, for explicit allusions to Psalm 22 in Mark 15:23, 24 and Matt 27:43. The offering of "wine mingled with myrrh," Mark 15:23, is from Psa 69:21, as is the similar act in Mark 15:36. The cry of Jesus in Mark 15:34 is from Psa 22:1, and the cry in Luke 23:46 is from Psa 31:5.

[16] M. Hengel, *Judaism and Hellenism*, pp. 103–06.

there were a number of Greek-speaking synagogues in the city. Herod the Great and his successors, though cautious in the Holy City, breathed the air of Greek education and culture. As we have frequently noted, there were also Greek-speaking Hellenistic Christians present in Jerusalem, at least until they were driven out by persecution. Thus, some Christian ideas and practices which would seem to have developed in the wider Greco-Roman world, and to have come from a somewhat later period, could have arisen in Palestine, and specifically in Jerusalem. Nonetheless, the dominant picture of Christianity in Jerusalem is that more or less conservative Jewish Christians were in charge, at least with respect to fundamental issues such as adherence to a stricter interpretation of the Torah and allegiances to the Temple and all that it symbolized in Judaism. Though they may have shared many of the characteristics of Palestinian Christians as a whole—prophecy, spiritual phenomena, the presence of poor in their midst, Messianism (probably of the royal variety)—they had emphases of their own, among which were Torah and Temple conservatism, and traditions such as those surrounding the trial, crucifixion, death, and resurrection appearances of Jesus, and the "Last Supper" tradition of Jesus and his disciples.

Hellenistic Jewish Mission Christianity

Though Christianity began as an apocalyptic sectarian movement within rural, Aramaic-speaking Palestinian Judaism, it rapidly spread into the cities of the larger Greco-Roman world. As a result, major shifts took place in its nature as a religious movement. No longer was it primarily an agrarian and village movement spread by wandering charismatics preaching about the apocalyptic Son of Man; it became more and more a religion transplanted to the Hellenistic cities with their provincial bureaucracies, wealthy patrons, marketplaces and forums, theaters and baths, soldiers and slaves, as well as "ghettos" of ethnic peoples who came seeking fame and fortune. This was a Gentile world where the language of commerce, industry, and government was Greek, the Greek commonly spoken during the Hellenistic era (*koinē*). This was a world full of mystery cults with their heroes and heroines, their sacred meals and shrines, their myths of fertility. Into the hubbub of the Hellenistic cities the Jews of the Diaspora had preceded the Christians, and their synagogues had a natural attraction for the movement that had sprung out of Judaism. In those synagogues, the Bible was not read in Hebrew and spoken in Aramaic, but in Greek translation, the Septuagint. The literature of the New Testament is written in *koinē* and, though its texts contain ideas and practices from the earliest Palestinian churches, it is dominated with the ideas and practices that progressed beyond this initial phase.

From the very beginning of its days in Jerusalem the Christian church numbered among its members active Hellenistic (Greek-speaking) Jews, the "Hellenists" of Acts 6, who were the spearhead of the movement of Christianity into the larger Hellenistic world. They understood the Greek world; they were missionary-minded and theologically venturesome. Even without the persecution that drove them out of Jerusalem they would certainly have become Christian missionaries among their fellow Greek-speaking Jews, among the "God-fearers," and to the Hellenistic world at large. Persecution hastened the process. It is permissible, therefore, to speak of Hellenistic Jewish Mission Christianity, the Greek-speaking Jewish Christianity that carried the Christian message into the Hellenistic world.

The literary monument to this movement is the Acts of the Apostles. The author of Acts is himself a product of the movement, and in his work he has given us a dramatic and dramatized account of it. The speeches he reports are particularly important, for they represent typical samples of Hellenistic Jewish Christian preaching in synagogues, to "God-fearers," and on the street corners of the Greek cities.

Theologically, Hellenistic Jewish Mission Christianity was such that it was almost explosively creative. In it Jewish, Hellenistic, and developing Christian traditions met and interacted with dynamic results that are today the backbone of New Testament theology. An illustration is the developments in Christology. In Palestinian Jewish Christianity Jesus was characteristically "Messiah," i.e., the one anointed (chosen) by God, or "Son of Man," i.e., eschatological judge and redeemer. He was also "Lord" in the Aramaic form *Mar*,[17] and *Mar* is an Aramaic honorific designation used especially of persons with authority to judge. In Hellenistic Jewish Mission Christianity, the Hebrew "Messiah" became the Greek "Christ," but it lost its force so that "Jesus Christ" became practically a proper name rather than meaning "Jesus, the anointed one of God." "Son of Man" was abandoned because in Greek it had no meaning, being replaced by either "Son of God" or "Lord." In Hellenism, Son of God indicated "possessing divine qualities," "exhibiting a divine aura," or the like, and this nuance can be seen in the cycle of miracle stories now found in Mark 5 and 7: the Gerasene Demoniac (5:1–20: the reference to the Decapolis in verse 20 indicates that this is Greek territory); Jairus' Daughter and the Woman with the Hemorrhage (5:21–43); the Syrophoenician Woman (7:24–30); the Man with a Speech Impediment (again in the Decapolis, 7:31–37). In all these, Jesus exhibits an aura of divine power—he heals by fiat, at a distance, or by the touch of his garments, and so on—and there are enough explicit references to Greek places and non-Jewish people, and still enough contacts with Judaism to show that these stories developed in Hellenistic Jewish Christianity. That these stories are designed to exhibit the fact that Jesus is Son of God is seen from the occurrence of the title in the introduction to the whole section (3:11) and in the first story (5:7). "Son of God" was also used in apocalyptic contexts where Palestinian Christianity would have used "Son of Man" (e.g., 1 Thess 1:10, "to wait for his [God's] Son from heaven"). But the major christological development concerned the use of the title "Lord" (Greek *kyrios*). In Hellenism it was

---

[17] *Maranatha*, "Our Lord, come!" noted above (cf. 1 Cor 16:21; Rev 22:20), contains this term.

the most common honorific title, used for gods, emperors, and kings, as well as for men of power and authority everywhere. Hellenistic Jewish Christianity developed this title extensively, so that the confession "Jesus [Christ] is Lord" became the characteristic Christian confession, and the coming of Jesus as judge was now his coming as Lord rather than as Son of Man (e.g., 1 Thess 4:15).

Hellenistic Jewish Christianity was equally creative in other respects. It made extensive and imaginative use of the Septuagint, or Greek Old Testament, as the speeches in Acts show. It adapted and developed the liturgy of the Jewish synagogue for its own use, devising confessions and liturgical formulas of all kinds. It laid great stress on the resurrection, both in liturgy (the formula-like references to "God who raised Jesus from the dead" in Paul's letters are from the Hellenistic Jewish Christian liturgy, as is his christological confessional formula in Rom 1:3–4) and in preaching (the speeches in Acts). When in Rom 10:9 Paul says, "If you confess with your lips that Jesus is Lord and believe in your heart that God raised him from the dead, you will be saved," he is breathing the very spirit of Hellenistic Jewish Mission Christianity.

Gentile Christianity (Apart from Paul)

Christianity began as an apocalyptic sect within rural Palestinian Judaism and moved rapidly into the urban Gentile world through the Hellenistic Jewish Christian mission. But once established in the Gentile world it tended to take on emphases of its own, no longer necessarily dependent on the Palestinian Judaism that spawned it, nor on the Hellenistic Judaism that propelled it into the wider world. It interpreted itself in new ways in response to the challenges of the new environment, and it reached new understandings of itself and its Lord by using the categories available in the Hellenistic Gentile culture. An apocalyptic Jewish sect begun in Palestine and continued as a missionary movement within Hellenistic Judaism now became a cult in the world of Hellenistic religiosity and began to exhibit many of the characteristics of that religiosity. We deal with the details when we discuss Paul and his relations with the church at Corinth in chapter 6; for the moment we will simply draw a general picture of Hellenistic Gentile Christianity as Paul found it.

The Greco-Roman world was a world of contrasts. Greek culture offered a conception of a good, harmonious life in a world in which the reality experienced daily tended to be neither good nor harmonious. Until the Augustan peace in 27 B.C. warfare was constant, and as a result, a family would be living prosperously in a city one year and its members would be dead or sold into slavery the next. The growth of cities and the emphasis on urban living created the need to feed the inhabitants of those cities, a problem never satisfactorily solved, and so famine became an ever-present and all too frequent possibility. Further, the "closure of the Eurasian ecumene,"[18] the establishment of one

---

[18] The phrase is from W. McNeill, *The Rise of the West*.

Eurasian world, led not only to a dramatic cultural interchange, but also to the spread of diseases against which the inhabitants of that part of the world had no natural immunity. All this led to a focus on "fate" and to a longing for salvation from the vicissitudes of life and the ever-present fear of death. There spread through the Hellenistic world a series of "mystery cults," religions promising their initiates security and immortality. The hero, or heroine, of a mystery cult was characteristically a divine figure who had conquered life in the world and achieved immortality and who could promise a share in that conquest and immortality to the believer who would accept initiation into the rites of the cult. The rites were "mysteries" kept rigidly secret from all but the initiates. They generally consisted of some kind of recital or reenactment of the deeds of the hero or heroine, an act of initiation, and the eating of a sacred meal, by which the initiate came to share the divine power and immortality of the deity.

That Christianity could be interpreted as a cult within Hellenism is obvious at first glance. It too had its myth of the hero, the gospel story of Jesus; its initiation rite, baptism; its sacred meal. The Christians did not borrow directly from the mystery cults; it was rather that the Christian faith came to expression most naturally in a way responsive to the particular needs of the environment of which it became a part. Were it not capable of doing so, it could never have been established in that environment. But Christianity did establish itself and in so doing developed different emphases from what had gone before. For one thing, it was difficult to maintain the traditional Jewish-Christian apocalyptic hope with its expectation of the coming of Jesus as Son of Man, and judgment and transformation of the earth. The Greeks thought more naturally in terms of redemption from the world to a higher level of existence than of the transformation of the world itself, and with the spread of Greek culture in the Hellenistic world, this style of thinking became generally accepted. Significantly, the deeper Paul gets into the Hellenistic world, the less we hear about the characteristic apocalyptic hope of Jewish Christianity. Then a real problem was posed by the characteristic Christian emphasis on the resurrection of Jesus and the hope of the future resurrection of the believer. The Greek world thought more naturally in terms of the immortality of the soul than of the resurrection of the body, and that created the problems for the Christian belief dramatized by the author of the Acts of the Apostles (Acts 17, especially verse 32) and amply evident in Paul's first letter to the Corinthians. On the other hand, religious enthusiasm was very much a part of the Hellenistic world in general, and so the Christian emphasis on the possession of the Spirit and its gifts found both ready acceptance and rapid development there. Paul spends no small part of 1 Corinthians attempting to restrain his Corinthian converts in this regard.

But perhaps the most important contribution of Gentile Christianity to the developing Christian movement lay in the sphere of Christology. There are in the New Testament a series of christological hymns that betray a quite remarkably uniform pattern of thought:[19]

Phil 2:6–11

Who, being in the form of God,
  Did not think it robbery to be equal with God.
  But emptied himself,
  Taking the form of a slave.

Becoming in the likeness of men
  And being found in fashion like a man,
  He humbled himself,
  Becoming obedient unto death.

Wherefore God highly exalted him
  and bestowed upon him the name above
  every name,

That in the name of Jesus every knee may bow
  in the heavens and on earth,
  And every tongue confess,
  "Jesus Christ is Lord."

Col 1:15–20

Who is the image of
  the invisible God,
  first born of all
  creation

For in him was
  created everything
  in heaven and on
  earth

Everything was created
  through him and
  unto him.

Who is the beginning,
  the first born of
  the dead.

For in him all the
  fullness was
  pleased to dwell,

And through him to
  reconcile everything
  unto himself.

And he is before everything
And everything is united in him
And he is the head of the body (the church).

---

[19] We are now following in the main Jack T. Sanders, *New Testament Christological Hymns.* © 1971, Cambridge University Press. Used by permission. See also D. Duling, *Jesus Christ Through History*, chapter 2.

1 Pet 3:18–19, 22

Having been put to
  death in the flesh,
Having been made alive
  in the spirit,
Having gone to the spirits
  in prison,
He preached.

Who is at the right
  hand of God,
Having gone into heaven,
Angels and authorities
  and powers having been
  made subject to him.

1 Tim 3:16

Was manifested in
  the flesh,
Was vindicated by
  the spirit,
Was seen by angels,
Was proclaimed among
  the nations,
Was believed on in the
  world,
Was taken up into glory.

Eph 2:14–16

He is our peace,
Who has made both one
And has broken down the dividing wall
    of the fence,
In order to make the two into one new
    man in him
And to reconcile both in one body to God.

Heb 1:3

Who, being the reflection of his glory and
  the stamp of his essence,
Bearing everything by the word of his power,
Having made purification for sins,
Sat down on the right hand of the
  majesty on high.

In these hymns we can see the pattern of a redeemer figure who descends to the earth from a higher sphere, achieves his redemptive purpose on earth, and ascends again to the higher, heavenly sphere.[20] This pattern of thought appears to have influenced both Hellenistic Judaism and Christianity. It is found in the New Testament with quite remarkable consistency wherever there is strong contact with the Hellenistic Gentile world, not only in these hymns, but also in the gospel of John. The understanding of Jesus as a descending-ascending redeemer is one of Gentile Christianity's great contributions to the developing Christian theology.

A special problem for early Christianity was the Hellenistic Gentile tendency to think in terms of "divine men," that is, of men who particularly represented the power of a god, of men who had about them the aura of

---

[20] See chapter 1, pp. 12–13, 27, for further discussion of this idea. Not every hymn has the full pattern.

divinity.[21] We noted above that Hellenistic Jewish Christianity responded to this aspect of its environment by interpreting Jesus in this way, for example in the miracle stories now found in Mark 5 and 7. (Incidentally, Philo of Alexandria, the greatest Hellenistic Jew, responded to the same Hellenistic emphasis by interpreting Moses in a similar way in his *On the Life of Moses*.) In Christianity this emphasis led not only to a particular understanding of Jesus, a "divine man Christology," but also to a particular understanding of the nature of Christian discipleship, namely that Christians now share the glory of their Lord and can confidently expect to overcome in their lives what Jesus overcame in his life and death. In these traditions the death of Jesus would not have been represented as a sacrificial suffering but as a translation to an even more glorious existence. The evangelist Mark is at war with this understanding of Christology, Christian discipleship, and Christ's passion, as we shall see in a later chapter. The Hellenistic Jewish Christian church understood its heroes as "divine men," as we can see from the portrayal of Peter and Philip in the early chapters of Acts and from the note about Paul's garments possessing miraculous powers (Acts 19:12), for example. In Corinth Paul ran into a related problem in that his opponents there, especially those he argues against in 2 Corinthians, understood a Christian apostle as one who exhibited the aura and power of a "divine man," and they claimed it of themselves and wanted Paul to demonstrate it of himself.
Georgi.

The Apostle Paul

The apostle Paul is discussed in some detail in chapters 5 and 6, but he is so important a figure in the development of New Testament Christianity that some brief indication of his place in it must be given here. A man of the Hellenistic Jewish Christian mission, he became its outstanding representative and natural leader. Among his letters, 1 Thessalonians may be regarded as representing the typical emphases, concerns, and problems of the movement. Paul's mission took him ever deeper into the urban Hellenistic Gentile world, and his Corinthian correspondence must be held to represent not only the particular problems he faced in Corinth, but also the characteristic problems Christianity faced everywhere it established itself in a predominantly urban non-Jewish environment: the impact of Hellenistic forms of religious enthusiasm on the Christian understanding of the possession of the Spirit; ethical questions posed by Christians of non-Jewish background; difficulties with the doctrines of the resurrection of Jesus and the future resurrection of the believer; the tendency to think of Jesus and his most immediate representatives, the apostles, as "divine men"; and so on.

A major shift that occurs in Pauline Christianity, and in sharp contrast with Palestinian Christianity, is the *form* of his traditional material. He does not stress sayings of Jesus and stories about him so characteristic of Palestinian Christianity. In 1 Thessalonians, for example, we are theologically very close to

[21] See chapter 1, pp. 13–15. We are especially indebted here to the works of H. D. Betz and D. Georgi.

the Q community; the Thessalonian community, like the Q community, awaits the coming of Jesus from heaven as eschatological judge and redeemer and prepares itself for that coming. But Jesus is now expected as Lord and Son of God, not Son of Man, and the instruction is given in the form of general Christian instruction, not sayings of Jesus. True, there is enough left of the Palestinian emphasis for Paul to say that "we beseech and instruct you in the Lord Jesus," but even when the instruction is from Q material (1 Thess 5:2 = Luke 12:39–40 par.) it no longer has the form of a saying of Jesus. Nor is there anywhere in the Pauline letters the slightest hint that the churches he represents and to which he writes used sayings of Jesus or stories about him as did Palestinian Christianity. When Paul quotes a "word of the Lord" (1 Cor 7:10; 9:14; 11:23; 14:37) he is quoting established Christian tradition, but not in the *form* of a saying of Jesus. Moreover, neither his letters nor the tradition they represent show any interest in a story of Jesus other than the founding of the Lord's Supper (1 Cor 11:23–26) or accounts of the passion (necessarily implied by the frequent references to the Cross) and resurrection (1 Cor 15:3–6).

Between Palestinian and Pauline Christianity, the form of Christian tradition as sayings of Jesus and stories about him has taken a different course. The sayings and stories forms will turn up again incorporated in narratives of the gospels, and variants of them reappear in second-century sources, for example, the Gnostic Gospel of Thomas, a sayings collection. But the focus in Paul has shifted to the message about the death and resurrection of Jesus.

A major historical event in earliest Christianity in which Paul played a leading part was the Jerusalem Conference, of which we have two accounts, one from Paul himself in Gal 2:1–10 and one in Acts 15:1–29. The problem for the historian of New Testament Christianity is that both these accounts are tendentious. Paul is fighting for his view of the faith and for the very existence of his mission in the Gentile world, and no doubt he is interpreting the event he describes. The author of the Acts of the Apostles is writing a generation later, when the issues confronting the Conference were dead and a whole new set of issues had arisen in the churches. Moreover, Acts is in a tradition of historical writing that consciously put speeches on the lips of protagonists in historical events, interpreting their significance for the present reader rather than recording what had been said. The assumption has to be that Acts 15 represents a reinterpretation of the Conference for a later generation and that it is addressed to the issues confronting that generation, rather than being what the modern world would recognize as a historical report.

In the light of these factors and of our general knowledge of this period of Christian history, the most probable hypothesis is that the Jerusalem Conference grew out of the success of the Hellenistic Jewish Christian mission in the Gentile world. It should be emphasized that this success took everyone by surprise. Earliest Christians in general devoted their missionary activity toward their fellow Jews and expected that the Gentiles would be brought into the divine plan by a direct act of God at the End itself. But the Christian mission to the Jews was largely a failure, whereas that to the Gentiles developed into an astonishing movement of vitality and power no one could have anticipated. This created a major problem, namely, how far the new Gentile Christians should also become Jews: should it be demanded of them that they accept circumcision and Jewish dietary laws?

As we have already indicated above,[22] the Jerusalem leaders yielded to Paul on the circumcision issue. In effect, they struck a compromise, requesting that he remember the poor, and that there be a division in the mission: Paul and his followers would go to the Gentiles, Peter and other Jewish Christians would go to the Jews. We shall discuss the subsequent problems raised by this solution in chapter 5.

At this point it should be noted that the result of the Jerusalem Conference was not the "Apostolic Decree" about food taboos found in Acts 15:22–29, for the subsequent history of Paul's work and correspondence shows that he knew of no such decree; moreover, the decree reads like the kind of compromise reached in a later period when the question was not the legitimacy of the Gentile mission, but the relationship between Jews and Gentiles in well-established Christian churches. The Jerusalem agreement left unresolved the question of table fellowship (the practice of eating together) between Jewish Christians who accepted the Jewish dietary laws and Gentile Christians who did not. Paul's account of the situation between himself and Peter in Antioch (Gal 2:11–21) indicates the problems that could and did arise. They were probably not resolved until the Jewish War of A.D. 66–70 effectively removed Palestinian Jerusalem Christianity from the scene, and the compromise now represented by Acts 15:22–29 became possible.

Another problem was that not all members of either side lived up to the spirit of the agreement—by no means a unique phenomenon in human history—and so incidents arose such as the one that called forth Paul's letter to the Galatians. But generally speaking, agreement was a major achievement and made possible the subsequent advances of the Christian movement in the two decades that separated the Jerusalem Council (most probably A.D. 48) from the catastrophe of the Jewish War and destruction of Jerusalem (A.D. 66–70), which changed forever the circumstances of New Testament Christianity.

The Impact of the Fall of Jerusalem

We have attempted to sketch some aspects of the phases through which the Christian movement must have gone before the mission and achievement of the apostle Paul. It should be emphasized that these phases were neither mutually exclusive nor chronologically successive. Any given Christian community could share to a greater or lesser extent the conservatism of the Jerusalem church, the apocalypticism of Palestinian Christianity, the concerns of the Hellenistic Jewish mission, or the emphases of the Gentile Christian churches. Moreover, all these phases coexisted with and influenced each other until everything was changed by the destruction of Jerusalem and the Jerusalem Temple. But it is helpful to recognize the variety of stages through which the Christian movement passed, so to speak, on its way from Jerusalem to Rome, and hence to appreciate something of the variety as well as the unity of the New Testament.

[22] See above, p. 77.

The Jews revolted against Rome in A.D. 66, beginning the war they expected God to end in their favor. But the war went the way of the Roman legions, and Jerusalem fell in A.D. 70. The war deeply affected the Christian communities. Jerusalem and Palestinian Christians were caught in the midst of the conflict. To the Romans they were Jews, but to the Jews they were suspect as Christians; so they fled Jerusalem and Palestine, going to Pella and other places in the Transjordan, to their Christian brethren in the cities and towns of Syria and Asia Minor, and no doubt also to Alexandria in Egypt. They took with them their Jesus traditions—their traditional material in the form of sayings of Jesus or stories about him. This material must have made a tremendous impact on Christianity outside Palestine. It must have been known in part before, but the dynamism of its interaction with the developing theologies of Hellenistic Jewish Christianity and of the Gentile Christian churches was certainly in no small part responsible for the writing of the synoptic gospels, as was also the fall of Jerusalem itself.

We shall return to these points when we discuss the gospels in detail; for the moment we wish to emphasize the importance to early Christianity in general of the Jewish War and the fall of Jerusalem. Practically speaking, it meant that the Christians in the Hellenistic world no longer had to reckon with the influence of the conservatively minded church in Jerusalem. After A.D. 70 there were no influences like those that Paul wrestled with in his letter to the Galatians and no occasion for an altercation like the one he had with Peter in Antioch (Gal 2:11–21). Also, with the effective disappearance of Jerusalem Christianity, and indeed of Palestinian Christianity generally, together with the effects of the sheer passage of time, the three phases of the Christian movement we have been distinguishing thus far simply ceased to exist. After A.D. 70 there was in effect only a Hellenistic Gentile Christianity, which in any one place might have a greater or lesser concern for or with the Judaism from which it was ultimately descended.

The Middle Period of New Testament Christianity

The New Testament texts relate themselves only indirectly or theologically to the events of their historical world, mostly because New Testament Christians awaited the imminent end of that world. But there is enough indirect and theological relationship in the texts for us to be able to say something about what may be described as the middle period of New Testament history, the twenty-five years or so that followed the fall of Jerusalem.

Theologically speaking, the period was characterized in the main by the necessity for coming to terms with the catastrophe of A.D. 70 and the delay of the parousia, by the continuing influence of the apostle Paul, and by the development of Johannine Christianity, associated now with the gospel and letters of John, the "Johannine corpus." Furthermore, in this period the church became more conscious of being a distinct entity with a history in the world and hence with a need to normalize her relations with both Hellenism and Judaism. But before going further we should note that the period began and ended with a resurgence of Christian apocalyptic.

The Resurgence of Christian Apocalyptic

We have said that Christianity began as an apocalyptic sect within Judaism. The earliest Christians awaited the imminent end of the world, which would take the form of the return of Jesus as eschatological judge and redeemer. With the movement into the Gentile world and with the sheer passage of time and the failure of the expected events to occur, other emphases developed. But apocalyptic thinking, thinking of a world about to end and be replaced by a different world, always tended to flare up in response to a crisis, a tendency that has continued throughout Christian history. In the New Testament period one such crisis was the Jewish War. To Christians as well as to Jews it seemed to be the beginning of the End, the beginning of the war that God would terminate by direct intervention in human history. There was a resurgence of apocalyptic expectation among Christians and Jews, and its literary monument in the New Testament is the gospel of Mark. In our later discussion we shall argue that in many respects this gospel is an apocalypse, and it is certainly a product of the resurgence of apocalyptic expectation occasioned by the Jewish War.

The persecution of the church could also have strengthened apocalyptic expectations. It could have led to the belief that the end of history as known was at hand and that God was about to change everything; it was simply a question of hanging on. One such persecution in the New Testament period was under the Roman emperor Domitian (A.D. 81–96), which was most probably the occasion for writing the one completely apocalyptic work in the New Testament, the book of Revelation.

Coming to Terms with the Fall of Jerusalem and the Delay of the Parousia

As we have said, two major factors in the development of New Testament Christianity were the fall of Jerusalem and destruction of its Temple and the delay of the parousia, the coming of Jesus from heaven as eschatological judge and redeemer. Much of the literature now in the New Testament attempts directly to come to terms with these elements in early Christian history. In what we are describing as the "middle period" of New Testament history, there came the gospel of Matthew, the two-volume gospel of Luke and Acts of the Apostles, and the letter to the Hebrews. The gospel of Matthew sees the ministry of Jesus as the new Sacred Time, the fulfillment of the hopes of Judaism, so that Jerusalem is no longer necessary to the Christian. The parousia is still to be expected, but in the meantime there is work to be done in the world. Luke-Acts sees Jerusalem as the place that rejected Jesus and so has been itself rejected. The time of Jesus is the new Sacred Time, and while Christians are still to expect the parousia, they have also to settle down to the long haul of history wherein they must witness. Hebrews sees all that was good in Judaism and the ancient Tabernacle having been superseded by Jesus.

The Continuing Influence of the Apostle Paul

An important aspect of Paul's work was that he trained men to work with and after him in the Gentile Christian churches. Though we have no direct reference to this training in the New Testament itself, it would have been a natural thing to do (Jewish rabbis regularly trained disciples, as tradition has it that Paul himself was trained by Gamaliel, Acts 22:3), and his letters and the narrative of Acts are studded with references to "fellow workers" or "helpers." But the real evidence for the existence of a Pauline "school" are the deutero-Pauline letters, written in the name of Paul and close to his thinking yet sufficiently different from the genuine letters to allow us to conclude they were not written by the apostle himself. These letters—2 Thessalonians, Colossians, Ephesians—all come from what we are calling the "middle period" of New Testament Christianity. Whereas 2 Thessalonians attempts to maintain the earlier hope for the parousia, Colossians and Ephesians represent the church developing her doctrines and settling down to the problems and opportunities of her ongoing life in the Gentile world. They also represent the continuing influence of the apostle a generation after his death in a world where Jerusalem and the Jerusalem church were no longer to be reckoned with but in which what was later to be called Gnosticism was developing as a major problem.

The Development of Johannine Christianity

The gospel and letters of John represent a distinct and distinctive understanding of Christian faith. To move from the synoptic gospels to John's gospel is to move from one world to another, as it is to move from Paul's letters to these letters. Here the Christian faith is developed out of an independent Jesus tradition, one that seems to have only a tangential relation to the synoptic gospels, and it comes to terms with the Hellenistic world as thoroughly and successfully as did the apostle Paul (but in a different way). Unlike Matthew this gospel also has to define Christianity when it becomes separated from Judaism. Indeed, its world-denying tendencies tend to give it a sectarian flavor, despite its distance from Palestinian apocalyptic origins. "Christianity according to St. John" became a major influence on the Christian piety of subsequent centuries. The famous Anglican archbishop William Temple confessed that he felt at home in the Johannine corpus as he did nowhere else in the New Testament, and in this he is representative of countless Christians. This understanding of the faith was hammered out somewhere in Syria during the middle period of the New Testament, most probably by a strong leader with a group of close followers—a Johannine school to which we owe the Johannine corpus, as we owe the Pauline corpus to a Pauline school. Whether the leader's name was John does not matter; what matters is that the "Johannine" understanding of the Christian faith is a major achievement of the New Testament period.

The Final Period: The New Testament Church
on the Way to Becoming an Institution

The New Testament church began as an apocalyptic sect within Judaism, expecting the imminent end of the world. But by the end of the New Testament period it was on the way to becoming an institution *in* the world, one with a credal basis, a distinctive literature, and a fixed organizational structure. The full establishment of these things—a creed, a canon, and an episcopate— did not come until later, but the movement toward them is evident in the final stages of the New Testament history and literature, especially in the Pastoral Epistles (1 and 2 Timothy and Titus). In these letters we have a third-generation Paulinist writing in the name of the illustrious apostle, but the language and thought are those of the church at the beginning of the second century. Sayings are worthy of acceptance if they are "faithful" (1 Tim 1:15; RSV says, "sure"); we are on the way to a creed. The "office of a bishop" is "a noble task" (1 Tim 3:1); we are on the way to the episcopate. The church is "the pillar and the bulwark of the truth" (1 Tim 3:15); we are on the way to the church as an institution. An equally pseudonymous letter written in the name of an illustrious apostle, 2 Peter, speaks of the letters of Paul as a collection and equates them with "the other scriptures" (2 Pet 3:16); and we are on the way to the New Testament canon.

The remainder of the literature in the New Testament belongs to this last period. First Peter, again pseudonymous, is most probably a developed baptismal homily from the end of the first or the beginning of the second century, reflecting the situation of the church under persecution. James' letter, also pseudonymous, is Christian moral exhortation (parenesis) in a style familiar to Hellenism and Hellenistic Judaism, and its view of faith as the acceptance of a doctrinal proposition (Jas 2:18–19) is characteristic of the developing institutionalization of Christianity. The letter of Jude polemicizes against heretics not by setting out a positive theological standpoint in opposition to the heresy, but simply by appealing to the authority of tradition.

All these texts represent, therefore, the church on the way to becoming an institution in the world with a creed, a canon, and an episcopate: needing and using baptismal and moral homilies, viewing faith as the acceptance of doctrinal propositions, and appealing to an authoritative tradition against what is considered heresy. We call this period the period of the emerging institutional church, and its literature is the literature of the emerging institutional church.

Further Reading

This chapter represents an attempt to present systematically the history of earliest Christianity as it appears in the light of form and redaction criticism, supplemented with the social history of Palestinian and Pauline Christianity. There is no exact further reading for the chapter as a whole, but there are good studies available for parts of it.

The idea for distinguishing various phases in pre-Pauline Christianity was put forth by W. Heitmüller, part of whose important article is found in English as "Hellenistic Christianity Before Paul" (German original 1912) in W. Meeks, *The Writings of St. Paul*, pp. 308–19. Heitmüller argued that Paul learned about early Christianity not from the Aramaic-speaking Jerusalem church leaders, but from the Greek-speaking Hellenistic Jewish Christians at Damascus and Antioch. By "Hellenistic Christianity" he meant a mission Christianity carried on by Hellenistic Jews like Stephen, but in the Diaspora. The development was: Jesus—primitive church—Hellenistic Christianity—Paul. A similar conception was developed by W. Bousset in *Kyrios Christos* (1970; original German 1913), and carried on by R. Bultmann, *Theology of New Testament*, and H. Conzelmann, *History of Primitive Christianity*, wherein the term "Hellenistic" was used. In the 1960s F. Hahn, *The Titles of Jesus in Christology*, followed by R. Fuller, *The Foundations of New Testament Christology*, further distinguished "Hellenistic Jewish" from "Hellenistic Gentile" Christianity. Thus one gained a general impression of the development: Jesus—Palestinian Aramaic-speaking Jewish Christianity—Greek-speaking Hellenistic Jewish Christianity—Greek-speaking Hellenistic Gentile Christianity—Paul. Though such developments were not considered strictly successive in the chronological sense, that is, they could be parallel, there was a quite natural tendency to think in terms of a temporal-geographical progression.

More recently, social-historical studies have placed less emphasis on historical-geographical development and more upon the transition from Aramaic-speaking, rural, agrarian, charismatic, and apocalyptic Palestinian Christianity to Greek-speaking, urban, commercial, Hellenistic-cultural Christianity. Especially important for the former is G. Theissen's *Sociology of Early Palestinian Christianity* and, for the latter, Theissen's studies of the church at Corinth and W. Meeks' views of the social world of Pauline Christianity. This perspective has also been affected by the increasingly widespread view now typified by M. Hengel, *Judaism and Hellenism*, that Palestine, especially its cities, continued to be influenced by Hellenization. In short, "Palestinian Jewish" and "Hellenistic Jewish" in the Hahn-Fuller christological studies is being modified toward the viewpoint that much of Palestinian Judaism, already known to be widely diversified in the pre-A.D. 70 period, was indeed Hellenistic. The current revision of Perrin's *Introduction* has attempted to take such developments into account as in harmony with the direction of his scholarship, but without abandoning his original distinctions.

General histories of New Testament Christianity, in addition to H. Conzelmann's *History of Primitive Christianity*, include:

> F. F. Bruce, *New Testament History*, a mine of historical information though many would not accept his view of the historical trustworthiness of the New Testament narratives.
>
> F. V. Filson, *A New Testament History*, also tends in this direction.
>
> M. Hengel, *Acts and the History of Earliest Christianity*, while not actually a history, attempts to shift away from the widespread tendency to treat the book of Acts as a tendentious theological account which is unreliable as a historical source.

H. Lietzmann, *A History of the Early Church*, vol. 1, an earlier, but classic treatment.

Further bibliography on the Acts of the Apostles is cited at the conclusion of chapter 10.

All of our introductions discuss the synoptic problem; for a comprehensive treatment, see W.G. Kümmel, *Introduction*, pp. 38–80. W.R. Farmer, *The Synoptic Problem*, has led the attempt to overturn the usually accepted Two-Source Theory. A good, recent summary is:

IDB Suppl., pp. 845–48, "Synoptic Problem" (F. Neirynck).

Bibliography on Palestinian Judaism and the Greco-Roman world at large can be found at the end of chapter 1. For Palestinian Jewish Christianity, one may also consult the bibliography on Q at the end of chapter 4. In addition, see:

R. Bultmann, *Theology of the New Testament*, vol. 1, pp. 33–62.
R. Fuller, *Foundations of New Testament Christology*, pp. 142–74.
E. Käsemann, *New Testament Questions of Today*, pp. 82–107 ("The Beginnings of Christian Theology") and 108–37 ("On the Subject of Primitive Christian Apocalyptic") discusses apocalyptic in Palestinian Jewish Christianity.

For the sociological perspective, consult:

J. Gager, *Kingdom and Community*.
H. Kee, *Christian Origins in Sociological Perspective*, especially chapter 3.
G. Theissen, *Sociology of Early Palestinian Christianity*.

A systematic discussion of Hellenistic Jewish Mission Christianity in relation to Christology is in R. Fuller, *Foundations of New Testament Christology*, pp. 182–202. A number of authors in the New Testament are, in various ways, treated as representatives of this movement, including Paul, and the authors of the gospels of Matthew and Luke. Bibliographies will be found at the end of chapters 5, 6, 9, and 10, chapter 5 containing materials on the social world of Pauline Christianity.

On Gentile Christianity, see:

R. Bultmann, *Theology of the New Testament*, vol. 1, pp. 63–184, "The Kerygma of the Hellenistic Church Aside from Paul."
R. Fuller, *Foundations of New Testament Christology*, pp. 203–42.
A. D. Nock, *Early Gentile Christianity and Its Gentile Background*.

On the christological hymns, see J. Sanders, *The New Testament Christological Hymns: Their Historical Religious Background*, which has full references to earlier literature.

Other treatments of New Testament Christianity after the fall of Jerusalem are S.G.F. Brandon, *The Fall of Jerusalem and the Christian Church*, and L. Gaston, *No Stone upon Another*. The discussion we have offered of this subject is independent of both of these.

For the church on the way to becoming an institution, see the bibliography at the end of chapter 12.

This manuscript portrays Jesus as the lamb standing on Mt. Zion, surrounded by the 144,000 redeemed (holding lutes). See Rev 14:1–5; 7:1–8.

CHAPTER FOUR

APOCALYPTIC CHRISTIANITY

The Synoptic Gospel Source Q, Apocalyptic Scenarios in the Writings of Paul and His Follower, the Apocalyptic Discourses, and the Book of Revelation

In chapter 1 we noted the development of apocalyptic eschatology and apocalyptic literature in Judaism. In chapter 2 we cited the book of Revelation as the only book in the New Testament specifically called an apocalypse, but indicated that there were other apocalyptic sections in New Testament writings. In our last chapter we claimed that Christianity began as an apocalyptic sect within ancient Judaism and that apocalypticism was a constant element of much of New Testament Christianity, resurging especially when early Christians felt alienated from the dominant social and religious structures, particularly in times of catastrophe or persecution. We must now go on to describe early Christian apocalyptic eschatology in greater detail, for not only is it central to the New Testament, but it has continually provided the impulse among Christians down through the centuries to hope for a new, transformed reality, a "new age," beyond the pains and frustrations of the old, present reality, an "old age," especially when it seemed that this evil world was on the brink of disaster.

In this chapter we shall first recall some of the general characteristics of Jewish Christian apocalypticism and compare the way the Qumran scribes and early Christians each interpreted the Scriptures to show that they were being fulfilled with respect to their own communities. Then we shall take up four parts of the New Testament which are most typical of apocalyptic Christianity: (a) the source Q; (b) apocalyptic scenarios in the writings of Paul and his follower; (c) the apocalyptic discourses: Mark 13 and its parallels; and (d) the book of Revelation. The chapter will conclude with a few general comments about the visions and symbols of apocalyptic literature and note its enduring influence.

SOME CHARACTERISTICS
OF JEWISH-CHRISTIAN APOCALYPTIC

You will recall that the term eschatology comes from the Greek words *to eschaton*, "the end," and *ho logos*, "the word" or "the teaching," and that it therefore means "teaching concerning the end of things." You will also recall that the word apocalyptic is derived from the Greek term *apocalypsis*, "an uncovering," "a revelation." The religious perspective of apocalyptic eschatology is expressed through a broad apocalyptic movement (apocalypticism) that cuts across party lines; the apocalyptic literature produced in the movement is characterized by a seer's vision of the secrets of the impending end of this evil world. Put into writing, apocalyptic literature is a religious message of hope for the apocalypticist's people in times when they experience alienation through hardship or political persecution. The chief characteristics of apocalypticism, which reaches its height under the Greek and Roman domination of the Jews, are these: a sense of alienation and despair about the dominant culture which leads to the conviction that the world is heading toward its destruction, i.e., that this world is in the hands of evil powers and will soon come to an end; a hope that God will intervene at the moment of destruction to save those who are his faithful followers, the elect, and bring about a new paradisical world like that found in the myths of the original paradise; and a belief that it is possible to see the signs of the times in historical events. Apocalyptic literature is typified by the portrayal of history, the present, and the future heavenly world in the form of esoteric symbols of cosmic destruction and renewal often verging on the bizarre; the use of traditional symbolic imagery from a variety of sources which contain myth, wisdom, astrology, and history, and most importantly works of prophecy and apocalyptic; and pseudonymity, that is, ascription of the writing to an authoritative person from the past who (of course) is often able to see the course of history and its end with accuracy.

Jewish and early Christian apocalypticism shared much in common, a statement that can be illustrated by a comparison of the Qumran community (cf. chapter 1 and Appendix 4) and the early Christian communities of Palestine (cf. chapter 3). To begin with the obvious point, both the Qumran community and earliest Christianity were apocalyptic sects within ancient Judaism. The last days of the Qumran community and the first of the Christian coincided, for Qumran perished in the Jewish War of A.D. 66–70. There were many differences between the two communities, the chief being that Qumran was a monastic community that waited for the world to come to it, whereas Christianity went out into the world as a missionary community—but then Qumran numbered no "Hellenists" in its midst. But both communities shared the apocalyptic hope: the men at Qumran expected two Messiahs—a Messiah of Aaron, a priest who would sanctify them, and the Messiah of Israel, a warrior who would lead them in the battle against the Gentiles that would mark the beginning of the End. Indeed one of their texts, 1QM, the War Scroll ("War of the Sons of Light and the Sons of Darkness") is a battle plan for this war, which they would begin and God would end. The Christians expected the Messiah Jesus to come as eschatological judge and redeemer, but they seem to have abandoned the concept of a Holy War, perhaps under the influence of Jesus himself. Members of the Qumran community ate their communal meals in anticipation of the day when they would eat with the Messiahs, as the Christians ate theirs in anticipation of the Kingdom of God (Mark 14:25). Qumran had an initiatory baptism and subsequent ceremonial lustrations, and great pains were taken to ensure an adequate water supply for these rites. Christianity had an initiatory baptism, but no subsequent ceremonial lustrations. The reason for this difference lay in the fact that the Christians were mostly laymen, but Qumran was essentially a community of priests. Both communities reached the point of sharing their goods in common, Qumran rigidly so, Christianity at the beginning according to the tradition of the "voluntary communism" in Acts 2:43–47. Both communities came to be headed by an individual whose office was described by the same term, the Christian Greek *episkopos* ("bishop," literally "overseer"), an equivalent for the Qumran Hebrew *paqid* or *mebaqqer*. Moreover, the "overseers" in both communities had the same responsibilities: the instruction of initiates and the control of the material resources.

But the most important commonality was a similar method of interpreting Scripture. Just as the Qumran scribes interpreted sacred texts to show that they were prophecies about the Qumran community, its history, and its hopes for the future, so also did the early Christian scribes. At Qumran there was developed a special form of interpretation called the *pesher* method. This method was a kind of running commentary on a passage of Scripture interrupted by brief interpretations beginning with the word *pishrō* ("its interpretation [is]" from *pesher*, "interpretation"). Occasionally the method is complicated by employing other, secondary passages of Scripture as part of the interpretation, and these are also interpreted, and sometimes the actual term *pishrō* is missing, but the method is nonetheless clear. A special feature of the method is that words with more than one meaning are interpreted in terms of the odd meaning, or a letter is omitted or altered to give the word a different meaning; in either case, the meaning will contribute to making the prophecy apply to events or persons related to the community or its aspirations. Although whole prophetic books are interpreted in this way, an example from a shorter Old Testament text will help to clarify the method.

The so-called "4Q Florilegium" contains a complex *pesher* based on 2 Samuel 7:10b–14a. It is broken up into three sections: (1) 7:10b–11a and its interpretation which includes an additional passage, Exodus 15:17–18 with its interpretation; (2) 2 Samuel 7:11b and its interpretation; and (3) 2 Samuel 7:11c–14a (in part) and its interpretation which includes an additional passage, Amos 9:11 and its interpretation. This complex *pesher* develops a well-known theme in the scrolls, that the Jerusalem Temple, which has been defiled by the "wicked priest" and his people, has been replaced by the "spiritualized" temple, or the eschatological community of the End, with particular emphasis on

97

its holiness, purity, and eternal qualities. It also interprets the "rest from all thine enemies" promised to David in 2 Samuel 7:11b as referring to the community's "rest" from all the "sons of Beliel" (= sons of the devil). The text of part 3 of the 2 Samuel *pesher*, with the Old Testament text on which it is based, reads:

Old Testament	4Q Florilegium
And Yahweh declares to you that *Yahweh* will make a house for you. *When your days are fulfilled and you lie down with your fathers, then* I will raise up your seed after you *who shall come forth from your inward parts* and I will establish *his kingdom; he shall build a house for my name and I will establish* the throne of his kingdom forever, I will be to him a father, and he will be to me a son.	(And) Yahweh (de)clares to you that he will build a house for you, and I will raise up your seed after you and I will establish the throne of his kingdom forever, I wi(l)l be to him a father, and he will be to me a son.

The interpretation in 4Q Florilegium continues:

This is the Shoot of David who will arise with the Seeker of the Law and who (12) will sit on the throne of Zion at the end of days; as it is written, *I will raise up the tabernacle (succōth) of David which is fallen* (Amos 9:11). This Branch (the same word pronounced *sōccath*) of David which is fallen (is) he who will arise to save Israel (cf. Jer 33:16) (translation mostly by Vermes).

In this somewhat complex *pesher*, phrases from 2 Samuel 7 are omitted which refer to the death of David, the direct descendant of David (i.e., Solomon), and the "house" which refers to the Temple built by Solomon. In this way the text can be correlated with previous interpretations of 2 Samuel 7 in reference to the spiritualized temple. The "seed" can now refer to a more *remote* descendant of David who did not build a temple, but is the royal messiah, or Shoot of David ("Shoot" of David, cf. Jer 23:5; 33:15; Zech 3:8; 6:12). A further interpretation is made by giving a different pronunciation to the term *succōth*, "tabernacle," so that it means "branch." That which is raised up is not the tabernacle of David which is fallen but the Branch of David, who is also the messianic Shoot of David. He will arise at the End to sit on the throne of Mt. Zion with the founder of the Qumran community, the Seeker of the Law.

Though the New Testament Christians did not quote long passages interrupted by commentaries in this fashion, they certainly shared this freedom in interpreting Scripture in terms of themselves and their circumstances. A good example is the quotation from Joel in Acts 2.[1] Joel 2:30 reads, "And I will give portents in the heavens and on the earth, blood and fire and columns of smoke." There is here only one set of portents and signs; the reference to both the heavens and the earth simply means something we would express by an adjective like "cosmic." Now the same is true of the Greek version of the text, the Septuagint, which Acts is using. However, Acts 2:19 adds some words to read, "I will show wonders in the heavens *above* and *signs* on the earth *beneath*." Now we have two sets of portents, and when we get to verse 22 we can see why: the signs on the earth beneath are interpreted as referring to Jesus. "Jesus of Nazareth, a man attested to you by God with mighty works and wonders *and signs* which God did through him in your midst." The argument is then made that David was a prophet whose psalms prophesied about Jesus as the "Lord" and "Messiah" (vss. 22–36), that is, that death would not contain him (Ps 16:8–11) and that he would be resurrected to the right hand of God (Ps 110:1). Aware that the Old Testament psalms might be taken to refer to David himself, the author of Acts objects that David is prophesying about the Messiah who is Jesus. In a speech which he attributes to Peter he says: "Brethren, I may say to you confidently of the patriarch David that he both died, and was buried, and his tomb is with us to this day. (30) Being therefore a prophet, and knowing that God has sworn with an oath to him that he would set one from the fruit of his loins upon his throne, (31) he (David) foresaw and spoke of the resurrection of the Christ . . ." (Acts 2:29). Since we have seen what the Qumran scribes did with the oracle in 2 Samuel 7, it is interesting to observe that verse 30 alludes to the same oracle ("oath"; cf. Ps 132:12). In short, whereas the Qumran scribes interpreted the 2 Samuel 7 text as a prophecy about the Messiah of Israel yet to come, the author of Acts incorporates an interpretation of it as a prophecy already fulfilled in the resurrection of Jesus to become Lord and Christ, that is, the Messiah recently come (cf. also Luke 1:32).

What is behind all of this interpretative labor is the belief that God's plan as foretold in the Scriptures has recently been, is, or will be soon accomplished against physical or spiritual enemies and in behalf of the elect. In Acts, the author has come to think that some of the prophecies foretold in the Scriptures have *already* been fulfilled in connection with the resurrection of Jesus in the past. The author believes that the prophecies no longer refer specifically to his own immediate time as the final days because a long interval of time has passed between the period of Jesus and the period in which he writes; he sees the prophecy as part of a plan being fulfilled over the gradual course of history, including his own time. In contrast, the fervent apocalypticist may portray the past in symbolic form but he believes that the prophecies refer specifically to events in his own, more immediate present and very near future, in a way that past, present, and future virtually flow together and converge on the *Now*. Again, the context for apocalypticism is alienation in the present and a hope for relief in the near future.

[1] This passage is discussed briefly in chapter 2, pp. 61–62.

THE SOURCE Q

You will recall from our discussion of the history of earliest Christianity in chapter 2 that the majority of modern scholars think that Mark was the first gospel, that Matthew and Luke used Mark or something like it, and that since Matthew and Luke were not known to each other, the non-Markan passages in Matthew and Luke which have approximately the same wording come from a lost source. This source is designated Q, perhaps from the German word *Quelle,* "source." (Though we shall have reason to think about a "Q community," it is not to be confused with the Qumran community, despite some common apocalyptic interests.) The material assigned to Q is distributed differently in Matthew and Luke, but it falls in about the same order, Luke usually preserving both content and order slightly better. There are some minor disagreements about the exact extent of Q, especially in passages where the verbal agreement between Matthew and Luke is less precise or where Q seems to overlap with Mark, but scholars can usually account for the former problem in terms of the evangelists' editorial changes and the latter phenomenon by proposing that they shared common oral tradition. Thus, the problems are not insurmountable to those who hold the hypothesis; in fact, the agreement and similarity in language between Matthew and Luke in most Q passages is so clear that scholars are led to the conclusion that the source as it came to Matthew and Luke was written, not oral, and written in the Greek language, not Aramaic.[2] In terms of quantity, Q material makes up about one-third of Matthew and about one-fourth of Luke.

There is no absolutely certain way to date Q, other than to say that it was put in writing before Matthew and Luke used it. Yet, because of its apocalyptic orientation, and the almost unanimous belief that it ultimately emanates from a type of early Jewish apocalyptic Christianity found in Palestine or southern Syria, most judge it to have been written within the first two generations after the death of Jesus. There is also no way to determine any individual who put Q into writing. In short, whatever is said about Q and the type of Christian community it represents must be said on the basis of internal analysis of the material.

Howard Kee in the second edition of his book, *Jesus in History,* page 84, suggests that there are seven basic forms of material in Q:

Narratives	Na
Parables	Pa
Oracles	Or
Beatitudes	Be
Prophetic Pronouncements	PP
Wisdom Words	WW
Exhortations	Ex

---

[2] Cf. the close similarity of lists in H.C. Kee, *Jesus in History,* pp. 85–87; R.A. Edwards, *A Theology of Q,* pp. xi-xiii; and F. Neirynck, "Q", *IDB Suppl.,* p. 715.

Though these forms can be further subdivided, the simplest procedure will be to list Q passages according to these formal categories, and to assume that these passages represent Q. (All the references given are to the gospel of Luke, because it is generally suggested that Luke's order and version of Q comes closer to the original.[3])

PP	3:7–9, 16b–17	John's Eschatological Preaching
Na	4:2b–12	Jesus' Struggle with Satan
Be	6:20–23	Beatitudes: the Poor, the Hungry, the Hated
WW	6:27–36	Promised Reward for Love and Forgiveness
WW	6:37–42	Rewards of Discipleship
Pa	6:43–46	Parables of Moral Productivity
Pa	6:47–49	Discipleship Must Survive Testing: Parable of the House with and without Foundation
Na	7:2–3, 6–10	Healing of the Centurion's Slave
PP	7:18–23	Response to John the Baptist's Question
PP	7:24–35	John's Place in God's Plan
PP	9:57–58 (-62?)	Leave Behind Home and Family
PP	10:2–12	Disciples Commissioned to Extend Jesus' Work
Or	10:13–15	Doom on Unrepentant Cities
PP	10:16	Disciples Share in Jesus' Rejection
PP	10:21–22	God's Gift of Wisdom to His Own
Be	10:23–24	Beatitude: Those to Whom Wisdom Is Granted
Ex	11:2–4	Prayer for the Coming of God's Kingdom
WW	11:9–13	God Answers the Prayers of His Own
PP	11:14–20	Jesus' Defeat of Demons as a Sign of the Kingdom
Or	11:24–26	The Return of the Unclean Spirit
PP	11:29b–32	The Sign of Jonah and the One Greater Than Jonah: Jesus as Prophet and Wise Man
Pa	11:33–36	Parabolic Words of Light and Darkness
Or	11:39–40, 42–43	Woes to the Pharisees
Or	11:46–48, 52	Woes to the Lawyers
PP	11:49–51	Wisdom Predicts the Martyrdom of Prophets and Apostles

[3] H. Kee, *Jesus in History*, pp. 85–87.

PP	12:2–3	What Is Hidden Will Be Revealed
Or	12:4–5	Do Not Fear Martyrdom
Pa	12:6–7	Parable of God's Care
PP	12:8–10	Confirmation of Confession/Denial of Son of Man
PP	12:11–12	God's Support of the Persecuted
Pa	12:22–31	Freedom from Anxiety about Earthly Needs
Pa	12:33–34	Freedom from Possessions
Pa	12:39–40	Parable of Preparedness: The Returning Householder
Pa	12:42–46	Parable of the Faithful Steward
PP	12:51–53	Jesus as the Agent of Crises
Pa	12:54–56	Signs of the Impending End of the Age
Pa	12:57–59	Parable of Preparedness for the Judgment
Pa	13:20–21	Parable of the Leaven
WW	13:24	Difficulty in Entering the Kingdom
Pa	13:25–29	Parable of Exclusion from the Kingdom
PP	13:34–35	The Rejection of the Prophets and the Vindication of God's Agent
Pa	14:16–23	Parable of the Eschatological Banquet
PP	14:26–27	Jesus Shatters Domestic Ties, Summons Disciples to Bear the Cross
Pa	15:4–7	The Joyous Shepherd
WW	16:13	Inevitable Choice between Masters
PP	16:16	The End of the Old Era and the New Age Proclaimed
WW	16:17	Confidence in God's Promise
Ex	17:3–4	Forgiveness within the Community
Ex	17:5–6	Faith within the Community
Or	17:23–37	Sudden Judgment to Fall
Pa	19:12–13, 15–26	Parable of the Returning Nobleman and Rewards for Fidelity
PP	22:28–30	The Promise to the Faithful of Sharing in the Rule of God

It is immediately clear from this list that according to formal classification, Q contains only two *narratives*, or *stories*, about Jesus, namely, Jesus' struggle with Satan, otherwise known as the Temptation story (4:2b–12), and the Healing of the Centurion's Slave (7:2–3, 6–10). Most obvious in this connection is that there is no "passion story," that is, a narrative about Jesus' arrest, trial, suffering, and crucifixion, so important to the four gospels and, if one limits the point to death and resurrection, so central to Paul. Thus, most of the Q material distributes itself into the six remaining forms, that is, into *sayings or discourses spoken by* Jesus, with virtually no chronological or geographical connections; in fact, Q was once known simply as "the sayings source." The narratives usually associated with the form "gospel" are absent; with respect to form, Q is largely a collection of sayings and discourses. Analogies to such a document have been sought in Old Testament collections of prophetic sayings and wisdom sayings, in Jewish collections like the Sayings of the Fathers, and in early Christian sayings collections such as the Teachings of the Twelve Apostles and the Coptic Gnostic Gospel of Thomas, suggesting perhaps there were early Christians interested simply in the words of Jesus as the words of a prophetic wise man, and in his return.[4] The form of Q, then, is important for attempting to understand its significance, and we shall return to this observation.

If we turn to the content of Q, it is clear that it is dominated by apocalyptic eschatology. In fact, only four of the above fifty-two passages (7:2–3, 6–10; 16:13; 11:34–36; 17:3b–4, 6) are not considered by Kee to be explicitly eschatological. The most dominant form of apocalyptic hope that Q exhibits is the expectation of Jesus coming from heaven as Son of Man: Luke 11:30; 12:8–9; 12:40; 17:24; 17:26, 30 (each time with a parallel in Matthew). Richard Edwards has shown[5] that of these six sayings four were created by prophets within the Q community itself (the community that produced the source Q): Luke 11:30; 17:24; 17:26, 30. These four he calls "eschatological correlatives." Käsemann had already shown that Luke 12:8–9 is a product of early Christian prophecy; it is one of what he calls "sentences of holy law" and we would perfer to call "eschatological judgment pronouncements." Under these conditions it is more than likely that the sixth, Luke 12:40 ("You also must be ready for the Son of man is coming at an unexpected hour"), is also early Christian prophetic exhortation. The importance of Jesus as Son of Man to the Q community can be seen in the fact that it refers to Jesus as Son of Man not only in connection with his eschatological judgment, but also in his earthly ministry: Luke 7:34; 9:58; 12:10; and their parallels in Matthew.

The origin of the expectation of Jesus coming from heaven as Son of Man is disputed. It is clear that the ultimate origin is Daniel 7:13–14:

> I saw in the night visions,
> and behold, with the clouds of heaven
> there came one like a son of man
> and he came to the Ancient of Days
> and was presented before him.
>
> And to him was given dominion
> and glory and kingdom,

---

[4] J. M. Robinson, *"Logoi Sophōn* (Sayings of Wise Men): On the *Gattung* (Literary Form) of Q," and H. Koester, "One Jesus and Four Primitive Gospels," in Robinson and Koester, *Trajectories Through Early Christianity*, pp. 71–113 and pp. 158–205 respectively.

[5] R. Edwards, *The Theology of Q*, pp. 41–42 and n. 23.

that all peoples, nations, and languages
>   should serve him;
his dominion is an everlasting dominion,
>   which shall not pass away,
and his kingdom one
>   that shall not be destroyed.

But how we got from that to the sayings in Q is a matter of dispute. There are two possibilities. Either (a) Jesus proclaimed the coming of the Son of Man as eschatological judge without identifying himself with that figure, and then the early church made the identification: Jesus is that Son of Man.[6] Or (b) the early church arrived at the expectation by interpreting the resurrection of Jesus in light of Psalm 110:1 and Dan 7:13–14, and Jesus himself did not speak of the Son of Man as eschatological judge at all. The latter view is correct[7] on the grounds that the expectation did not exist as a firm conception for Jesus to use in his message and that, furthermore, all apocalyptic Son of Man sayings fail the test of the criteria for authenticity of sayings of Jesus (these criteria are discussed in chapter 13), while at the same time exhibiting typical characteristics of early Christian prophecy.

The Q community expected the return of Jesus from heaven as Son of Man with power to execute the eschatological judgment (Luke 12:8–9). He would come suddenly and unexpectedly, but he would most certainly come (Luke 12:40). Faced with the need to give form and content to this expectation, prophets in the community reached back into the past history of the Jews and claimed that it would be like Jonah's coming to the Ninevites (Luke 11:30), like lightning striking (Luke 17:24), or like the judgmental catastrophes associated with Noah and Lot (Luke 17:26, 30). In characteristic fashion, their eschatological hopes in a time of alienation drew on prophetic and apocalyptic ideas and images from the other apocalyptic and prophetic literature.

It is clear from our interpretation of the Son of Man that the Q community was led, at least in part, by spirit-filled, eschatological prophets who spoke for the now departed, but soon to return, Jesus. Prophecy, then, is one of the chief characteristics of the community, a conclusion that is supported by allusions to Old Testament prophetic and apocalyptic literature, explicit references to prophets, and various expressions of eschatological prophecy, such as warnings about impending judgment by John the Baptist and especially Jesus. One example of an explicit reference to prophets is especially instructive, for it shows the attitude of condemnation toward the Jewish "fathers" and "this

---

[6] This view is represented, for example, by H. Tödt, *The Son of Man in the Synoptic Tradition*, and R. Fuller, *The Foundations of New Testament Christology*.

[7] N. Perrin, *Rediscovering the Teaching of Jesus*, pp. 164–99. Perrin's views as to the subsequent development of the Son of Man Christology in the New Testament are to be found in "Towards the Interpretation of the Gospel of Mark" in H.D. Betz, ed., *Christology and a Modern Pilgrimage. A Discussion with Norman Perrin* (a special publication of the Society of Biblical Literature, 1971); *A Modern Pilgrimage in New Testament Christology*.

generation" in an environment of persecution, and it also contains the theme of wisdom, though not in a form most characteristic of Q:

> Woe to you! for you build the tombs of the prophets whom your fathers killed. So you are witnesses and consent to the deeds of your fathers; for they killed them, and you build the tombs. Therefore also the Wisdom of God said, "I will send them prophets and apostles, some of whom they will kill and persecute," that the blood of all prophets, shed from the foundation of the world, may be regarded of this generation, from the blood of Abel to the blood of Zechariah, who perished between the altar and the sanctuary. Yes, I tell you, it shall be required of this generation. (11:47–51)

A similar passage in the form of a typical wisdom saying condemns Jerusalem:

> O Jerusalem, Jerusalem, killing the prophets and stoning those who are sent to you! How often would I have gathered your children together as a hen gathers her brood under her wings, and you would not! Behold, your house is forsaken! And I tell you, you will not see me until you say, "Blessed be he who comes in the name of the Lord." (13:34–35)

Similar prophetic condemnations are especially directed at the Pharisees, for example:

> But woe to you Pharisees! for you tithe mint and rue and every herb, and neglect justice and the love of God; these you ought to have done without neglecting the others. (11:42)

In these passages, we see that part of the problem for the Q community is found in the attitude of some Jews—specifically "this generation," Jerusalem, and Pharisaic leaders—toward prophecy. In contrast, Q appears to be more directed to a larger community of the righteous who will be invited to the joyous messianic banquet in the near future:

> And men will come from east and west, and from north and south, and sit at table in the Kingdom of God. (13:29)

Given this apocalyptic view of the world, what does it take to be a Christian before the End comes? The beatitudes (6:20–23) possibly hint at the social class of some members of that Q community when they affirm that in the future human values will be reversed: the poor, the hungry, those who weep— all will be vindicated in the future kingdom, and those who will yet be hated on account of the Son of Man will be happy. Prophets have been persecuted before, and prophets and (presumably) disciples are being persecuted now; but "in that day" there will be great reward. The stress is on the near future; those who love their enemies will receive a great reward (6:35). In parables, we discover that a tree is known by its fruit (6:43–44), and that it is important to build one's house on a rock (6:46–49). Attachment to riches is also problematic, for one cannot serve God and mammon (16:13). In short, the loving and well-grounded disciple, though perhaps poor and hungry, though persecuted, though hated because of the Son of Man, will receive a reward in the coming Kingdom.

Discipleship, then, is no easy task. Unlike the animals and birds, the Son of Man had no home (9:57); so those who proclaim the kingdom cannot stop to do what for a Jew is an absolute requirement, burying the dead (9:60). Disciples may be sent out like lambs in the midst of wolves, living off those who will take them in, healing the sick (10:2–20) as Jesus healed (7:22) and exorcizing the demons (11:20); the true disciple of the Kingdom should not even go back and say goodbye to his family (9:62); in fact, following Jesus is bound to lead to family divisions (12:51–53). The teaching is clear:

> If any one comes to me and does not hate his own father and mother and wife and children and brothers and sisters, yes, and even his own life, he cannot be my disciple. (14:26–27)

If we attempt to bring together the results of this all too brief description of Q and the community that preserved it, we gain the following impression. Q is almost exclusively a collection of sayings and discourses, almost exclusively attributed to Jesus. It is not a "gospel" in the usual sense, for it lacks the narrative structure, specifically notations of time and place, characteristic of the four gospels, and most importantly, it lacks a passion story. This means that its focus is not on the suffering, death, and resurrection of Jesus, but on his teaching and on his imminent return as apocalyptic Son of Man who will bring salvation to his true followers, the elect, and judgment on this evil generation and its leaders, who most certainly include the Pharisees. Jesus is apparently God's Wisdom, not in a mythical sense (cf. the New Testament christological hymns in chapter 3), but in the sense that he inspires prophets who speak in his behalf, and who, like himself, give wise teachings to sustain the community until he returns. Hence Q has a special interest in prophets and prophetic forms as well as wisdom and wisdom forms. Such teachings, which are often of a practical, parenetic sort, sustain the apocalyptic community, perhaps composed of the poor and disinherited. The disciples of Jesus are persecuted now, but they expect their reward in the future. They may, like the earthly Son of Man, have no real home, for their allegiances are to the Son of Man—to the extent that, if necessary, they break ties with their families. But they are sustained by a morality strongly rooted in love—even love of enemies; moreover, they have a mission to Gentiles, and, like Jesus, are expected to heal.

If one recalls the attempt to give a social-theological description of Palestinian Jewish Christianity in chapter 3, it is clear that Q provides much of the data from which this description emerges. We may well imagine that the prophets of the Q community were wandering charismatic prophets who lacked home, close family ties, wealth, and security. They would have provided an authority structure for the movement, with many sympathetic disciples located in the villages. In this case, one might think not only of a Q community, but other related communities. In them, the model for the alienated Christian who awaits the End is the alienated Son of Man who has no home, and the hope of the alienated Christian is the hope for the Son of Man who will come as judge and savior.

APOCALYPTIC SCENARIOS IN THE WRITINGS OF PAUL AND HIS FOLLOWER
1 Thessalonians 4:13–5:11; 1 Corinthians 15:20–28; 2 Thessalonians 2:1–12

The apostle Paul, whom we shall consider more fully in the following chapters, wrote letters to his mission churches in Asia Minor and Macedonia-Greece, and to Rome in anticipation of an expected visit. The earliest of these letters, 1 Thessalonians, was written from one port city, Corinth in Greece, to another port city, Thessalonica in Macedonia, about A.D. 51 (see below, p. 172). It stresses Paul's joyful thanks that the Thessalonians have remained faithful despite "affliction." Presumably, the Thessalonians were being persecuted by their own countrymen, though the passage where this is most clearly stated (2:14–16) may have been added later. It contains an analogy with persecution of Judean Christians by "the Jews," that is, those who "killed both the Lord Jesus and the prophets, and drove us out, and displease God and oppose all men by hindering us from speaking to the Gentiles that they may be saved— so as always to fill up the measure of their sins. But God's wrath has come upon them at last!" This astonishing "anti-Semitic" comment is certainly not characteristic of Paul's later writings (cf. e.g., Rom 11:25–26). If Paul did say it, he temporarily moved beyond Q in his harsh criticism of "the Jews" in general. In any case, the whole letter is concerned with "affliction." Paul exhorts the Thessalonians in the way of Christian holiness, and he offers encouragement, apparently in response to the Thessalonians' misunderstanding of what may be a traditional confession Paul had taught them, that is, "to wait for his (God's) Son from heaven, whom he raised from the dead, Jesus who delivers us from the wrath to come" (1:10; cf. 2:19; 3:13). The Thessalonians seem to have feared that those who had already died would miss the parousia, and thus not be delivered. Paul responds in 1 Thessalonians 4:13–5:11 with a clarification about resurrection and the parousia.

1 Thessalonians 4:13–5:11 reflects Paul's early belief that the parousia is imminent, that it will undoubtedly occur in Paul's own lifetime (4:17). The language that describes the parousia—the cry of command, archangel's call, and sound of God's trumpet—comes from conventional apocalyptic symbols derived from the Old Testament and Jewish literature (cf. Rev 1:10; 4:11; 8:7–11:19). The passage iterates the Christian apocalyptic hope, and the cloud language could be a veiled allusion to the Son of Man in Daniel 7:13; however Paul uses "Lord" rather than "Son of Man." Moreover, the itinerary—first the rising of the dead, then "we who are alive" joining them, being caught up in a cloud to meet the Lord in the air—goes into physical details not found in Q nor in the apocalyptic discourses of the synoptic gospels. The "thief in the night"

image as a way of expressing the suddenness of the parousia is a widespread Christian image (Matt 24:43; Luke 12:39; 2 Pet 3:10; Rev 3:3; 16:15). 1 Thessalonians 5:8–10 contains a first statement of themes which will be characteristic of Pauline theology in other letters. Thus, in the style and orientation of the apocalypticist, Paul comforts the Thessalonians in their time of persecution.

1 Corinthians 15:20–28, 50–57

Paul established a church at Corinth about A.D. 50. He revisited it and subsequently wrote a number of letters to the Corinthians. One of them, 1 Corinthians, was written from Ephesus about A.D. 55 in response to a number of problems about which Paul had learned by rumor and letter. One of those problems was the denial of the future final resurrection of the dead. In 1 Corinthians 15 Paul responds by commenting on the death and resurrection tradition (15:1–11) and then by arguing that if there is no general resurrection, Christ has not been raised, and if Christ has not been raised, their faith is in vain, and those who have died have perished (15:12–19).

In 1 Corinthians 15:20–28, Paul states that Christ, the first and best ("first fruits") of the dead, has in fact been raised. He speaks of two mythical men, the one in whom all died (Adam who sinned, bringing death into the world, cf. Rom 5:12–21), and the one in whom all will be made alive (Christ). The sequence he develops is: Christ; next, at his coming, "those who belong to Christ," the Christians; then, the enemies ("every rule and every authority and power") will be destroyed, including the last enemy, death; finally—Paul's order and meaning is ambiguous—he delivers the Kingdom to God the Father, and will himself be subjected to God.

Later in 1 Corinthians 15:50–57, Paul mentions that at the last trumpet, the dead will be raised, and ". . . we shall all be changed, in a moment, in the twinkling of an eye. . . ." Death will then be defeated.

2 Thessalonians 2:1–12

The arguments for suggesting that 2 Thessalonians may have been written by a follower of Paul at some later date are taken up in chapter 7. One of the chief reasons is that its apocalyptic scheme in connection with the parousia of Jesus is somewhat different from that in 1 Thessalonians. Here our author argues that the "day of the Lord" will not come until (a) the "rebellion" (political? religious apostasy or defection [under persecution]?), and (b) the "man of lawlessness," or "son of perdition" is revealed. The latter is probably the evil Antichrist figure, a prophet who will inaugurate final rebellion (cf. Rev 13). It is also said that he opposes all gods and takes his seat in the Temple, proclaiming that he is God. Such a vague reference may be a recollection of the Syrian King Antiochus IV Epiphanes who about 167 B.C. desecrated the Jerusalem Temple by setting up an altar to Zeus and sacrificing a pig (cf. chapter 1, p. 17 for "desolating sacrilege," and Dan 12:11; Macc 1:54; Mark 13:14), or to the more recent attempt of Gaius Caligula to have his own statue set up there in A.D. 40. The reference is uncertain. In any case the author of 2 Thessalonians mentions he had told them this "when I was still with you" (verse 5). He goes on to say that though lawlessness is mysteriously at work already, some person or force is holding the man of lawlessness back; when he is revealed, backed by Satan, accompanied by "pretended signs and wonders," and deceiving those who will perish, the Lord Jesus will slay him with the breath of his mouth (Isa 11:4; Job 4:9; Wis 11:20; Rev 19:15) and by means of the manifestation of his parousia (2:8).

It is possible to cite other apocalyptic passages in the Pauline materials, such as 1 Corinthians 7:25–31, which influences his point of view on marriage and divorce, or Philippians 4:4–5, where he stresses rejoicing. But enough has been said about his more obvious sections to indicate that at some points, Paul shares the fundamental ideas of apocalyptic Christianity. What he has done, however, is incorporate them into his view that the whole apocalyptic drama of the End has been set in motion by the sending, death on the Cross, and resurrection of Jesus Christ.

THE APOCALYPTIC DISCOURSES: MARK 13 AND ITS PARALLELS

We come nearer to the actual literary forms of apocalyptic in Mark 13 and in its parallels in Matthew 24 and Luke 21. Apocalyptic discourses, speeches detailing the events to be expected when the End actually comes, are a feature of apocalyptic literature in general. There are examples in the Assumption of Moses 10 (cf. Appendix 5); 1 Enoch 1:3–9; 1 Enoch 46:1–8; 4 Ezra 6:13–28. These discourses follow the pattern of apocalyptic expectation concerning the End, with variations depending on the particular form of the expectation held by the writer. There is usually a description of the "woes," the climactic catastrophes marking the death throes of human history as now known. This is followed by an account of the form of God's eschatological intervention, either directly or through an eschatological redeemer figure. Then there is an account of the final judgment itself and a description of the punishment of the wicked and the eternal blessedness of the people of God that will follow.

Such discourses were written in a certain way. The particular form of the apocalyptic hope held by the writer gave the overall pattern, but the actual content came from two sources: the Scriptures, that is, the writings held by the writer to be sacred, and the experience of the writer and the group he represented. The Scriptures themselves were used in two ways: they were either directly quoted, or they were alluded to indirectly. Sometimes the writer wished to reinterpret an existing text; sometimes he reached his texts by association of ideas, of words, or even of the *sounds* of words (in the ancient world reading usually meant reading aloud, even to oneself, as in Acts 8:30 when Philip *hears* the Ethiopian reading Isaiah 53). So an apocalyptic discourse is usually a mosaic of scriptural quotations and allusions, together perhaps with some references to the experience of the writer and his community, generally couched in scriptural language.

The Christian apocalyptic discourses vary from this general pattern in that they include sections of parenesis in which the writer exhorts his readers directly out of his text. In this respect the discourses follow the Christian practice of combining parenesis with proclamation.

We now offer an analysis of Mark 13 following in the main that offered by Lars Hartman in *Prophecy Interpreted*.[8]

13:1–5a *An introduction to the discourse,* composed by the evangelist Mark to give the discourse its present setting in the gospel as a whole.

13:5b–8 *The first section of the discourse proper.* It quotes Dan 2:28–29, 45 (LXX: "this must take place"), 2 Chron 15:6; Isa 19:2 (the references to nation against nation and Kingdom against Kingdom), and alludes to Dan 7:21; 9:26; 11:4–27; and perhaps 2:40 at various places.

13:9–13 *The first parenetical section.* It couches references to the actual and anticipated sufferings of Christians in language deliberately reminiscent of the sufferings of Jesus during his passion but also allusive of various scriptural passages (Dan 7:25; Psalm 119:46; Dan 6:13–24). Verse 11b alludes to Exod 4:11–17, and verse 12 quotes Mic 7:2, 6.

13:14–20 *The second section of the discourse.* It quotes and reinterprets Dan 11:31 and 12:11 in the reference to the "desolating sacrilege" (in Daniel this is the altar to Zeus set up in the Jerusalem Temple by the Syrians; in 2 Thess 2:1–12 it might have referred to the emperor Caligula in an earlier period). Many modern commentators suggest Mark could have had in mind the events surrounding the defeat of the Jews and the destruction of Jerusalem and the Temple in A.D. 70, thus giving a clue as to the date of Mark. The command to "flee to the mountains" is a quote from Gen 19:16, as is the command for the man in the field not to turn back in verse 16. In verse 19 the description of the tribulation quotes Dan 12:1.

13:21–23 *The second parenetical section.* The reference to the false prophets uses language taken from Deut 13:1–5, but the whole addresses itself to concrete problems faced by the Christian church in a period of intense apocalyptic expectation.

13:24–27 *The third section of the discourse.* Here the quotations are frequent. Verse 24 quotes Joel 2:10 (the sun being darkened) and Isa 13:10 (the moon not giving its light). Verse 25 has the stars falling and the powers of heaven being shaken (from Isa 34:4). The Son of Man reference in verse

[8] L. Hartman, *Prophecy Interpreted*, pp. 145–59.

26 is from Dan 7:13, and verse 27 is a mosaic of Deut 30:3–4 and Zech 2:10 (in the LXX version). There are allusions to Isa 11:10–12; 27:13; and Dan 7:14 at various places.

Verse 27 ends the apocalyptic discourse proper. The remaining verses 28–37 form a loose-knit, final parenetical section that does not contain a single scriptural quotation but does show a good deal of Christian traditional material. It was almost certainly added to the original discourse by Mark himself.

It is not our purpose here to analyze in any detail the parallel discourses in Matthew and Luke; we are not offering a detailed commentary on these passages but only introducing to the reader this particular early Christian literary form. Briefly, Matt 24:4–31 follows Mark with only minor additions and changes, as does 24:32–36 (= the loose-knit parenesis of Mark 13:28–32). But Matthew then adds a whole series of sayings of various kinds that have parallels in Luke in a different context; i.e., they are from Q—Matt 24:37–51. The context for this Q material is not original, since Matthew arranges teaching material in long discourses. Then Matthew further adds a chapter of eschatological parables (Matt 25). Luke 21:8–28 is close to Mark's discourse, yet sufficiently different from it to make it possible that he may be following a version of the discourse different from what Mark has. But it is in any case fundamentally the same discourse.

What the precise form and original date of this discourse might have been is impossible to say. It is the nature of apocalyptic writers to interpret and reinterpret texts, even their own, so that any discourse text we have represents the version of it that came from the hand of the particular evangelist concerned. Mark is such an apocalyptic writer, and he must certainly have reworked the discourse he presents. When we come to discuss the gospel of Mark later, we shall suggest that Mark 13:5b–27 is a product of the evangelist himself, and this point of view helps us to date the final Markan version of the discourse and indeed the gospel of Mark itself (ca. A.D. 70). Yet it should be understood that apocalyptic discourses are such that so complex a discourse could not have been created by one man at one time in one place, but must have grown and developed over a considerable time. Moreover, we can observe Matthew and Luke reworking Mark. Matthew is conservative in his treatment of Mark's discourse, but then Matthew is no longer an apocalyptic writer; he is on the way to becoming a rabbi, as will appear evident when we discuss him in a later chapter. Luke, on the other hand, has a version so different from Mark's and yet so closely related to it that he may be following a different version of the discourse in the tradition of the church, as noted earlier. But it may also be that Luke, who is by no means becoming in any respect a rabbi, is simply exercising the traditional freedom of a writer dealing with an apocalyptic text. As they stand, then, the apocalyptic discourses in the New Testament are testimony to the continuing element of apocalyptic Christianity and should be read as such. But they are also evidence of the particular concerns of the individual writers and they need also be read in this way.

111

THE BOOK OF REVELATION

A Prophetic-Apocalyptic Letter

The book of Revelation is in several respects different from apocalyptic texts of Judaism: it is not pseudonymous, and it takes the overall form of an open letter to seven churches in Asia Minor. So striking are these characteristics that one might ask whether the book which gives its name to the type of literature known as apocalyptic ("revelation" = Greek *apocalypsis*) is really an "apocalypse"! On the other hand, it can scarcely be doubted that the book of Revelation is full of apocalyptic eschatology and illustrates the apocalyptic movement in a context of persecution, in this instance outside of early Palestine. Furthermore, it should be noted that Revelation in its own way is an outstanding example of the complex interaction of history, myth, proclamation, and parenesis—the theme for our book.

You will recall from previous discussions of Jewish apocalyptic that apocalypticists wrote in the name of some famous person from the past—Abraham, Enoch, Daniel, Ezra—and that a number of them attempted to show how the ancient worthy prophesied historical events correctly down to and including the present and near future of the apocalypticist. All of this was to show that the external course of history is determined by God and that the ancient prophets were correct in perceiving the rapidly approaching End down to the period of the apocalypticist. Revelation, however, does not claim to be written by some venerable worthy from the past who prophesies the future. The author explicitly identifies himself as a certain "John" (Rev 1:1, 4, 9; 22:8) and describes himself as having been exiled to Patmos, a small rocky island in the Aegean Sea between Greece and Asia Minor. Thus, John of Patmos is—and claims to be—a contemporary of the events about which he writes. Therefore he does not claim to be writing about the distant past, nor does he claim to have prophesied the events that are now occurring. For Revelation, authority does not come from a famous past worthy who accurately predicted the present, but from Jesus Christ whose martyrdom inaugurated the last days and provides the basis for understanding martyrdom in the present.[9]

Thus John refers to contemporary events. Writing to seven churches in Asia Minor, he reports that the blood of martyrs had already flowed (2:13; 6:9); the "hour of trial" was threatening all Christendom (3:10); the emperor would demand divine worship (13:4, 12–17; 16:2; 19:20), which Christians would have to refuse (14:9–12). This impending persecution inspires John's apocalyptic vision. It also gives clues about the time and place of composition. First, however, a further word needs to be said about persecution of Christians in the Roman empire.

[9] J. Collins, "Pseudonymity, Historical Reviews and the Grace of the Revelation of John," *CBQ,* vol. 39 (1977), pp. 329–43.

The Roman government was tolerant of local religions but at the same time anxious to guarantee overall loyalty to the empire. A polytheistic society presented no problems; local inhabitants were asked to formally acknowledge the gods of Rome, and having done so, they were free to continue their local religious beliefs and practices. As monotheists, the Jews could not acknowledge the gods of Rome; yet their special position was recognized, their religion was accepted by the Roman authorities as a legal religion, and they were freed from the requirement. The Christians, however, were no longer Jews, and were therefore in the position of having to refuse to acknowledge the gods of Rome while lacking the protection of a recognized legal religion. Thus, they were liable to persecution at any time: the local Roman official could demand that they acknowledge the gods of Rome; they would have to refuse and be liable to banishment, torture, or even death. This ever-present possibility hung over the church from the moment it severed its ties with Judaism and is reflected constantly in the New Testament itself.

Another element in the persecution of Christians in New Testament times was the widespread tendency for the Roman emperor to be worshiped as a god (cf. chapter 1, p. 14). This had spread from the East to the West in the Hellenistic world and was more accepted in some places than in others: some emperors demanded it, while others deplored it; similarly, some local Roman authorities pressed for it while others did not. Again, the Jews were in a privileged position the Christians could not share, in that such worship was not required of them.

We gain a very strong impression of the situation of many Christians from the correspondence between Pliny, the governor of Bithynia in northern Asia Minor, and Trajan, the Roman emperor, A.D. 96–117. Pliny writes:

> It is my rule, Sire, to refer to you in matters where I am uncertain. For who can better direct my hesitation or instruct my ignorance? I was never present at any trial of Christians; therefore I do not know what are the customary penalties or investigations, and what limits are observed. I have hesitated a great deal on the question whether there should be any distinction of ages; whether the weak should have the same treatment as the more robust; whether those who recant should be pardoned, or whether a man who has ever been a Christian should gain nothing by ceasing to be such; whether the name itself, even if innocent of crime, should be punished, or only the crimes attaching to that name.
>
> Meanwhile, this is the course that I have adopted in the case of those brought before me as Christians. I ask them if they are Christians. If they admit it I repeat the question a second and a third time, threatening capital punishment; if they persist I sentence them to death. For I do not doubt that, whatever kind of crime it may be to which they have confessed, their pertinacity and inflexible obstinacy should certainly be punished. There were others who displayed a like madness and whom I reserved to be sent to Rome, since they were Roman citizens.
>
> Thereupon the usual result followed, the very fact of my dealing

with the question led to a wider spread of the charge, and a great variety of cases were brought before me. An anonymous pamphlet was issued, containing many names. All who denied that they were or had been Christians I considered should be discharged, because they called upon the gods at my dictation and did reverence, with incense and wine, to your image which I had ordered to be brought forward for this purpose, together with the statues of the deities; and especially because they cursed Christ, a thing which, it is said, genuine Christians cannot be induced to do. Others named by the informer first said that they were Christians and then denied it; declaring that they had been but were so no longer, some having recanted three years or more before and one or two as long ago as twenty years. They all worshiped your image and the statues of the gods and cursed Christ. But they declared that the sum of their guilt or error had amounted only to this, that on an appointed day they had been accustomed to meet before daybreak, and to recite a hymn antiphonally to Christ, as to a god, and to bind themselves by an oath not for the commission of any crime but to abstain from theft, robbery, adultery, and breach of faith, and not to deny a deposit when it was claimed. After the conclusion of this ceremony it was their custom to depart and meet again to take food; but it was ordinary and harmless food, and they had ceased this practice after my edict in which, in accordance with your orders, I had forbidden secret societies. I thought it the more necessary, therefore, to find out what truth there was in this by applying torture to two maidservants, who were called deaconesses. But I found nothing but a depraved and extravagant superstition, and I therefore postponed my examination and had recourse to you for consultation.

The matter seemed to me to justify my consulting you, especially on account of the number of those imperiled; for many persons of all ages and classes and of both sexes are being put in peril by accusation, and this will go on. The contagion of this superstition has spread not only in the cities, but in the villages and rural districts as well; yet it seems capable of being checked and set right. There is no shadow of doubt that the temples, which have been almost deserted, are beginning to be frequented once more, that the sacred rites which have been long neglected are being renewed, and that sacrificial victims are for sale everywhere, whereas, till recently a buyer was rarely to be found. From this it is easy to imagine what a host of men could be set right, were they given a chance of recantation.

Trajan's Response

You have taken the right line, my dear Pliny, in examining the cases of those denounced to you as Christians, for no hard and fast rule can be laid down, of universal application. They are not to be sought out; if they are informed against, and the charge is proved, they are to be punished, with this reservation—that if anyone denies that he is a Christian, and actually proves it, that is by worshiping our gods, he shall be pardoned as a result of his recantation, however suspect he may have been with respect to the past. Pamphlets published anonymously should carry no weight in any charge whatsoever. They constitute a very bad precedent, and are also out of keeping with this age.[10]

The question of possible Jewish persecution of the churches is more complex. Jewish communities tended to be tightly knit, with a certain authority over their own members. Paul says that "five times I have received at the hands of the Jews the forty lashes less one" (2 Cor 11:24), which was a Jewish punishment, just as the reference "three times I have been beaten with rods" (2 Cor 11:25) was a Roman one. Similarly, Mark 13:9 speaks of Christians being "beaten in synagogues" and of standing "before governors and kings for my sake"; these, again, are references respectively to Jewish and to Roman persecution of Christians. Yet, there is no evidence for a concerted, well-planned persecution of Christians by Jews, thus leaving the impression that hostility toward and maltreatment of Christians was sporadic and spontaneous.[11] In short, persecution came primarily from the Romans.

The internal evidence suggests that the book of Revelation was written in a period of impending persecution of Christians living in Asia Minor, and that the persecution was Roman and sparked by demand for emperor worship. If we return to the tendency of apocalyptic to portray events in symbolic form, we discover that though Revelation does not pretend to contain a prophecy of future events by a worthy figure from the distant past, it does refer in 17:10 to a series of seven "kings" of Rome and the writer appears to have lived under the sixth of these. If these were six Roman emperors, beginning with Augustus and omitting the short reigns of Galbo, Otho, and Vitellius, the sixth would be Vespasian, emperor from A.D. 70–79. But Vespasian did not demand worship of himself as a god, and there is no knowledge of a persecution of Christians in Asia Minor during his reign. The conditions implied by the book as a whole simply do not fit. An alternative suggestion would be that the kings refer to those who were deified by the Roman Senate—Julius Caesar, Augustus, Claudius, Vespasian, and Titus—and the sixth is Domition who did demand divine honors.[12] In our discussion of symbolism below, we shall note that the number of the beast, 666, in Revelation 13:18 probably refers to the name Nero who persecuted the Christians in Rome by finding in them a scapegoat for the fire (chapter 1, p. 7). New Testament Christians certainly lived with the memory of the sudden persecution of the Christians in Rome under the emperor Nero, at which time tradition has it that both Peter and Paul perished. However, since this persecution was limited to Rome and the issue was not emperor worship, it is generally agreed that the number 666 refers to a Nero *redivivus*, that is, the

[10] H. Bettenson, *Documents of the Christian Church*, pp. 5–7; the correspondence is dated about A.D. 110.

[11] S. Sandmel, "Jews, NT Attitudes Toward," *IDB Suppl.*, pp. 477–79.

[12] M. Rist, "The Revelation of St. John the Divine," *IB* vol. 12, pp. 354–56, 495.

belief that Nero would come back to life and invade the empire from the East (cf. Rev 13:3, 12, 14; 17:8, 11). Was Domitian the Nero *redivivus*? Certainly this arrogant megalomaniac who was so zealous in claiming his divinity and so ruthless in enforcing divine honors is as likely a candidate as any. Moreover, there is an early Christian tradition that John was banished to the island of Patmos by the emperor Domitian in A.D. 95 and was released some eighteen months later when Nerva became emperor. There is no absolute certainty, but most modern scholarship is inclined to put Revelation in the Domitian persecution.

The author of Revelation identifies himself as a "servant" (Rev 1:1) and a "brother" of the persecuted Christians to whom he writes (Rev 1:9). In many respects John of Patmos clearly stands in the apocalyptic tradition. However, he also implies that he is a prophet by saying that he was exiled "on account of the word of God and the testimony of Jesus" (Rev 1:1; 19:10: "The testimony of Jesus is the spirit of prophecy"), by stating that he was told to prophesy after eating what is certainly a prophetic scroll (Rev 10:11; cf. Ezek 1–3; Shepherd of Hermas 1:3–4, here a heavenly book of prophecy), and by describing his work as "the words of prophecy" (Rev 1:3; 22:7, 10, 18; cf. 22:19). His work also contains many traditional forms of prophecy often colored by apocalyptic; judgment pronouncements (Rev 2–3); symbolic actions like eating the scroll (Rev 10:8–11); 7 blessings (Rev 1:1; 14:3; 16:15; 19:9; 20:6; 22:7, 14); words and promises of God (Rev 1:8; 16:5; 21:5–8); interpretations of visions by intermediaries or the prophet himself (Rev 1:20; 7:13–17; 13:18; 14:4–5; 17:7–18; 19:8b); and many others.[13]

We pointed out earlier that a distinguishing feature of earliest Christianity was the consciousness of the return of prophecy to the community. John of Patmos is such an early Christian prophet, and he describes the ecstatic vision that qualifies him: "I was in the Spirit on the Lord's day . . . " (1:10). The vision itself is an interesting combination of the kind of experience the classical Hebrew prophets claimed as validating their message (for example, Isaiah 6) and the typical visions of apocalyptic writers. John's vision is characteristically apocalyptic; yet at the same time it is shaped by the characteristics of classical Hebrew prophecy. John is an apocalyptic seer, but he is also a prophet, and this "also" is very important to him, just as the possession of the spirit of prophecy was to early Christianity in general.

That John of Patmos can be identified as a prophet is more important to understanding his work than identifying him with some other individual named John in the New Testament. Traditionally it has been claimed that he is the John, son of Zebedee, known to us from the gospel stories, but this is most unlikely. It has also been claimed that he is the "John" of the fourth gospel, but the difference in language and style alone makes this identification quite impossible. However, that he is able to identify himself, and as a prophet (in sharp contrast to the pseudonymity and practice of apocalyptic writers in gen-

---

[13] E. Schluessler Fiorenza, "Composition and Structure of the Book of Revelation," *CBQ* vol. 39 (1977), pp. 351–52, 355.

eral), speaks volumes for the vitality, power, and self-confidence of New Testament Christianity.

There are a number of other interesting components in the book of Revelation. It contains not only apocalyptic and prophetic, but also liturgical, mythical, and parenetic materials and forms. There are antiphonal hymns (4:1–11; 5:9–12, etc.), the *trishagion* ("Holy, Holy, Holy," 4:8c), doxologies (1:6; 4:9; 5:13b–14; 7:12); acclamations of worth (4:11; 5:9b–10, 12); a thanksgiving formula (11:17–18); the *amen* and *hallelujah* responses (22:20; 19:1); a woe oracle (12:12b); the lament or dirge (18:1–24); the curse (22:18–20); and others. The language of myth is also common. The world is viewed as a heaven above, earth in the middle, and hell below, and great portents occur in the heavens and the stars. It is inhabited by angels and demons, and animals that speak and act. There are also a number of traditional myths such as the birth and attempted destruction of the divine child (12:1–6); the sacred marriage (19:6–10, Christ, the Lamb, and his bride); the victory of the good angel (Michael) and his followers over the primeval dragon and his angels (12:7–9); the divine warrior (portrayed throughout Revelation as a martyred lamb who overcomes and rules the universe from his glorious throne); the combat myth (esp. 19:11–22:9); and the divine city (21:9–22:5). Parenetic materials are found not only in the prophetic commands, but in virtue and vice lists (e.g. 9:20–21; 13:4–8; 14:4–5).

Perhaps the most unusual aspect of the book of Revelation is its letters to seven churches in Asia Minor: Ephesus, Smyrna, Pergamum, Thyatira, Sardis, Philadelphia, and Laodicea (see chapters 2 and 3). This is unparalleled in apocalyptic writing and has to be due ultimately to the impact that Paul's letter writing made on the New Testament church. Paul's letters had become so important that the literary form was imitated even by an apocalyptic writer. In Revelation the 7 letters have a common pattern of 5 parts: address and command to write; a prophetic messenger introduced with the formula, "Then says . . .," (sometimes translated with "The words of . . ." [RSV]); a section about the individual church which begins "I know . . ." and concludes with an exhortation; a formula call to hear the message ("He who has an ear, let him hear what the spirit says to the churches"); and a prophetic promise to the martyr as one "who conquers."[14]

The influence of the letter form is even greater than the letters to the 7 churches, for the book of Revelation as a whole has the external form of a letter in that it begins with an opening salutation (1:4–6) and closes with a benediction (22:21). The contrast in literary form between the direct address of the letters and the symbolic drama of the remainder of the book is startling, but no more so than the fact that an apocalyptic writer identifies himself and calls his work a prophecy.

The fact that we have here the outward form of a Pauline letter (chapter 6, pp. 163–68) helps us to grasp the essential thrust of the work. It begins with a salutation in the Pauline style: "To him who loves us and has freed us from our

[14] E. Schluessler Fiorenza, pp. 351–52.

sins by his blood and made us a kingdom, priests to his God and Father, to him be glory and dominion for ever and ever. Amen" (Rev 1:5b–6; compare Gal 1:3–5). But then it continues: "Behold, he is coming with the clouds, and every eye will see him, every one who pierced him; and all tribes of the earth will wail on account of him. Even so. Amen" (1:7). This is a classic statement of the early Christian hope for the return of Jesus as apocalyptic judge and redeemer. Similarly, the closing benediction, "The grace of the Lord Jesus be with all the saints. Amen" (22:21), is in the Pauline style, but it is preceded by a prayer for the coming of the Lord, "Come, Lord Jesus" (22:20). However, this is the early Palestinian Christian Eucharistic prayer *Maranatha*, which Paul himself used at the end of a letter: "Our Lord, come! The grace of the Lord Jesus be with you. My love be with you all in Christ Jesus. Amen" (1 Cor 16:22–24). It is a reminder that for all its surface strangeness, the book of Revelation is not to be separated from the rest of the New Testament. The hope it represents is a fundamental feature of a major part of the New Testament.

Thus far, we have seen that Revelation contains a great deal of apocalyptic eschatology and can be seen as a representative of apocalyptic literature, to which it gives its name, "apocalypse," or "revelation." Yet it is written by one who, in contrast to Jewish apocalyptic, does not assume the role of an ancient worthy in order to predict events moving toward their climactic end, but identifies himself by name as John of Patmos, thinks of himself as a prophet, and as analysis shows, incorporates many prophetic forms. Furthermore he is familiar with and uses liturgical materials and forms as well as mythical themes, and he incorporates letters and the structure of his writing as a whole takes the form of a letter. There are also a whole set of compositional techniques in the work such as the distribution of symbols and images over the whole work, announcements that are developed later, cross references, contrasts, numerical structures, interludes of material, insertions (intercalations) and various combinations of these techniques.

The natural question that arises from these considerations is this: can one really develop an exact analysis and a precise outline of a work as complex as this, a work that includes in its purpose the attempt to stun its readers by the power of its visions so that the readers lose their fear of the present and are caught up in the hope for the future it presents? It may be that a structural analysis is somewhat arbitrary and in a sense a denial of its very quality as a literary text. Nonetheless, frequent attempts have been made, many of them revolving around the book's clear references to the symbolic number 7.[15] One recent outline attempts to take into account the centrality of John's view of Jesus Christ (1:12–20; 19:11–16), his two scroll visions, especially the little scroll application to current political events (10:1–11:14; 12:1–14:30; 15:2–4),

---

[15] J. W. Bowman, "The Revelation to John. Its Dramatic Structure and Message," *Interpretation*, vol. 9 (1955), pp. 436–53; "Revelation, Book of," *IDB* R-Z, pp. 58–71; M. Rist, "Revelation," *IB* vol. 12 (1957), pp. 360–62.

his divisions by 7, his complex compositional technique, and most importantly, his letter form.[16] Expanded, the outline looks like this:

A. 1:1–8 Epistolary Frame
   1. 1:1–3 Prophetic opening and blessing
   2. 1:4–6 Letter salutation
   3. 1:7–8 Vision of the parousia
B. 1:9–3:22 The Community under Judgment
   1. 1:9–20 Inaugural Son of Man vision
   2. 2:1–3:22 Letters to the 7 churches
C. 4:1–9:21 Judgment of the Cosmos: Septets
   1. 4:1–5:14 Introduction: Handing over the Scroll; vision of God on his throne and the Lamb (Liturgy in Heaven)
   2. 6:1–17; 8:1 Vision of 7 seals
   3. 7:1–17 Community of salvation; sealing and glorification of martyrs
   4. 8:2–9:21; 11:15–19 Vision of 7 trumpets
      a. 8:2–5 Liturgy in Heaven
      b. 11:15–19 Hymn in praise of eschatological salvation
D. 10:1–11:14; 12:1–14:20; 15:2–4 The Community and Its Oppressors
   1. 10:1–11 Introduction: Handing over the small scroll
   2. 11:1–14 Perseverance and witness of the community
   3. 12:1–13:18 Enemies of the community (dragon, beast, pseudoprophet)
   4. 14:1–5 Perseverance of the community
   5. 14:6–20 Parousia and judgment
   6. 15:2–4 Hymn in praise of eschatological salvation
C'. 15:1,5–19:10
   1. 15:1,5–16:21 Vision of 7 bowls
   2. 17:1–18:24 Babylon: Antitype to the community
   3. 19:1–10 Hymn in praise of eschatological salvation
B'. 19:11–22:9 Judgment of Hostile Powers; Salvation of Community and World
   1. 19:11–21 Parousia; destruction of the beast and pseudoprophet
   2. 20:1–10 Destruction of the dragon, including the millennium (reign of the Christian community [martyrs] with Christ)
   3. 20:11–15 World judgment; destruction of death and Hades
   4. 21:1–8 The new creation
   5. 21:9–22:5 The new Jerusalem
   6. 22:6–9 Final acts of consummation
A'. 22:10–22:21 Epistolary Frame
   1. 22:10–15 Prophetic closing and blessing
   2. 22:16–21 Conclusions and expectation of parousia

[16] E. Schluessler Fiorenza, *CBQ*, vol. 39 (1977), pp. 362–66; cf. J. Pilch, *What Are They Saying About the Book of Revelation?* pp. 52–58. In her basic outline (ABCDC'B'A') Fiorenza highlights the small scroll prophecy as the center of the letter and thus its strong prophetic character. I (D.D.) have added the subdivisions based on her previous article "The Eschatology and Composition of the Apocalypse," *CBQ* 30 (1968), pp. 537–69.

The Destruction of Satan's Evil Age, the Millennium, God's Eternal Age, and the Divine City

One of the most striking features of Revelation is its final series of visions of the End (Rev 19:11–22:9), reminiscent of the ancient combat myth.[17] The seer has a vision of heaven open and the heavenly Christ, called the Word of God and wearing a robe dipped in blood, astride a white horse. Following him are the heavenly armies clad in white linen, also astride white horses. Opposing this army are the Antichrist (the beast 666, Rev 13:1–10,18) and the kings of the earth with their armies, along with the false prophet (the second beast, Rev 13:11–17), that is, a miracle-working helper, a pseudo-Christ. The Antichrist and the false prophet are captured and thrown into the lake of fire, a place of eternal damnation and punishment, and the rest are slain with a two-edged sword issuing from the mouth of the heavenly Christ. So ends the reign of idolatrous Rome and the Antichrist! Then an angel descends from heaven, binds Satan who is the mythical dragon and locks him in the bottomless pit. The martyrs for Christ are now raised (the first resurrection) and reign with Christ for 1,000 years as priestly judges. However, all is not ended. After the millennium, Satan is released to deceive the nations, called Gog and Magog (Ezek 38–39), and they surround the martyrs and Christ in Jerusalem; but fire comes down from heaven and destroys them, once and for all. Now the devil is thrown into the lake of fire with the Antichrist and the false prophet, and there they are tormented forever. In John's next vision, John perceives God on his great white throne, and from God's presence heaven and earth disappear. The dead (except the martyrs) are raised for judgment (the second resurrection), and Death and Hades, along with those evil ones whose names are not written in the book of life, are also cast into the lake of fire. Next, the seer has a vision of a new creation, a new heaven and a new earth (Isa 65:17; 2; Baruch 32:6; 48:50; 51:3; 1 Enoch 45:4–5), and a new Jerusalem descends to earth, prepared as a bride adorned for her husband. The new age has begun! God and Christ now join the saints in the New Jerusalem in eternal joy and bliss. Finally the seer is transported by one of the 7 angels to a high mountain where he is shown the divine city, the bride of the Lamb, in all of its magnificent glory.

THE VISIONS AND SYMBOLS OF APOCALYPTIC

The visions of the book of Revelation and of apocalyptic in general are strange and arbitrary to the modern reader. But remember that visions play a

---

[17] A. Yarbro Collins, *The Combat Myth in the Book of Revelation;* "The Political Perspective of the Revelation to John," *JBL* 96 (1977), pp. 241–56. Collins argues that the adaptation of holy war traditions meant (a) that Christ and the heavenly armies will defeat the enemies, and (b) that passive suffering and death is necessary for Christians because a martyr's death hastens the End.

real part in the general history of religion. A vivid example from recent North American culture is the "great vision" of Black Elk, a holy man of the Oglala Sioux, as reported by him to John G. Neihardt.[18] Here is a scene taken at random from that vision:

> And as I looked and wept, I saw that there stood on the north side of the starving camp a sacred man who was painted red all over his body, and he held a spear as he walked into the center of the people, and there he lay down and rolled. And when he got up, it was a fat bison standing there, and where the bison stood a sacred herb sprang up right where the tree had been in the center of the nation's hoop. The herb grew and bore four blossoms on a single stem while I was looking—a blue, a white, a scarlet, and a yellow—and the bright rays of these flashed to the heavens. I know now what this meant, that the bison were the gift of a good spirit and were our strength, but we should lose them, and from the same good spirit we must find another strength.[19]

Like John of Patmos, Black Elk is given to understanding the past and to interpreting the future by means of a vision.

The component parts of a vision are conveyed to the seer by his own culture. John of Patmos meditated on the scriptures he inherited from his tradition, and Black Elk on the stories told to him; both were surrounded by the artifacts and sacred elements of their people. The differences between the visions are, therefore, easy to understand; what should be taken seriously is their similarity as visions.

If we return to the book of Revelation, we have seen again and again that apocalyptic draws heavily on the symbolic language of earlier literature, especially prophetic books of the Old Testament, primarily Ezekiel, and apocalyptic literature, notably Daniel. This is part of its quest for a total all-encompassing vision of reality. Several kinds of symbols in Revelation are worth mentioning. Sacred numbers such as 4 (various parts or divisions of the created order), 7 (completeness, totality, fullness), and 12 (Israel) abound. The numbers 4 and 12 are illustrated by Revelation 7:1–8 where the seer has a vision of the 4 angels standing at the 4 corners of the earth holding back the 4 winds (which cause plagues, cf. Dan 7:2–3). A fifth angel ascends from the rising of the sun with God's seal and orders the other 4 to hold back the 4 winds until the servants (=martyrs, cf. 6:11) should be sealed as a form of supernatural protection (cf. Isa 44:5; Ezek 9:1–8). The number of the sealed is 12,000 from each of the 12 tribes of Israel, or 144,000, which refers to the Christian martyrs from all nations (5:9; 7:9), presumably the true Israel. The number 7 is so significant (occurring 54 times) that, as noted above, there have been attempts to outline Revelation by groups of 7.

A final example of numbers symbolism is the famous number of the beast who symbolizes the Roman empire and its imperial line, as well as the Anti-

---

[18] J. Neihardt, *Black Elk Speaks*, pp. 20–47.
[19] J. Neihardt, pp. 38–39.

christ. He forced all the people to place a number on their right hands or foreheads, a number standing for the emperor-beast's name (Rev 13:18). In most texts, the number is 666; in one fifth-century manuscript, the number is 616, which was also known by Irenaeus in the late second century A.D. Who is the mysterious emperor-beast 666 (616)? Many theories have been suggested, but one of the most plausible is that according to the standard way of counting, the numerical value of Hebrew letters of *Nerōn Caesar* (N=50; R=200, etc.) add up to 666. Certainly others knew this explanation since *Nerō Caesar* (minus N=50) equals 616! If this solution be accepted, the evil beast is a new Nero whose identity, as suggested above, is probably Domitian.

Other kinds of symbols in Revelation are colors (cf. Rev 6:1–8, the 4 horses; white = victory, or purity and eschatological happiness; red = war and bloodshed (?); black = economic depression (?); and pale = death); horns (= power, cf. 5:6; 12:3); eyes (= knowledge, cf. 1:14; 2:18; 4:6; 5:6); a sharp sword (= judging and punishing word of God, cf. 1:12; 2:12, 16; 19:15, 21), and so on. The Son of Man symbolism from Daniel 7:13 also occurs in Revelation 1:7, 12–16, as it does in other New Testament apocalyptic writings.

We have already noted that the Q community turned to Dan 7:13, that prophets in that community produced Son of Man sayings to put on the lips of Jesus, and that the apocalyptic discourses also turn to that passage and its central symbol. When one gets to a certain level of experience or expectation, the normal structure of language is simply shattered, and what is experienced or expected can be described only in symbols, often in archetypal symbols that have deep roots in the consciousness of man as man. So it is with the consciousness of evil, sin, and guilt and with the expectation of a cataclysmic, eschatological act whereby evil, sin, and guilt will be no more. The Jewish myth explains the existence of sin as the result of the rebellion of primordial man, Adam, and its natural consequence is the expectation that the act of another representative man would redeem that sin. When Paul says, "as one man's trespass led to condemnation for all men, so one man's act of righteousness leads to acquittal and life for all men" (Rom 5:18), he is reflecting the natural consequence of accepting the myth that sin resulted from the rebellious act of primordial man. In the language of apocalyptic symbolism, the same natural consequence is the idea of the coming of a redeemer figure "like a son of man," a figure human yet more than human, and it is undoubtedly this fundamental propensity of the human mind to think in such terms that accounts for the prominence of Son of Man symbolism in early Christian apocalyptic.

Another example of the human mind's fundamental propensity to embrace myth or symbol when attempting to approach the ultimates of human experience or expectation is Amos Wilder's poetic expression of his experience in the First World War.

> There we marched out on haunted battle-ground,
> There smelled the strife of gods, were brushed against

By higher beings, and were wrapped around
With passions not of earth, all dimly sensed.

There saw we demons fighting in the sky
And battles in aerial mirage,
The feverish very lights proclaimed them by,
Their tramplings woke our panting, fierce barrage.

Their tide of battle, hither, thither, driven
Filled earth and sky with cataclysmic throes,
Our strife was but the mimicry of heaven's
And we the shadows of celestial foes.[20]

We quote Wilder deliberately because he is consciously sensitive to this aspect of apocalyptic, ancient or modern, Christian or secular; but many other examples could be given.

So in thinking of apocalyptic we have to think of the human mind at a level of ultimacy and at that level turning naturally to the use of myth and symbol. In the case of the ancient Jewish and early Christian apocalyptic the ultimacy came from a total despair of the course of human history and an absolute trust in the purpose of God. The result is the visions and symbols we have been discussing.

THE ENDURING INFLUENCE OF
EARLY CHRISTIAN APOCALYPTIC

The most obvious influence of early Christian apocalyptic is the continuing existence of Christian apocalyptic sects and movements. Throughout Christian history, groups of believers have fed their hopes on New Testament apocalyptic literature and calculated the date of the coming of Jesus as Son of Man, as indeed many still do. Similarly, the Beast whose number is 666 (Rev 13:18) has been identified with every tyrant in Western history, including Hitler and Stalin. But this is a literalistic and hence necessarily false understanding of the apocalyptic hope.

More important is the enduring influence of the myths and symbols of early Christian apocalyptic itself wherever the New Testament has been read. In modern times historical scholars have had all kinds of problems with the book of Revelation, but poets and artists have found it an unending source of inspiration precisely because it uses images of immense evocative power. Early Christian apocalyptic does not challenge us to gather together on a hillside to await the coming of Jesus as Son of Man, or to identify the Beast; it challenges

---

[20] Quoted by A. Wilder himself in his article "The Rhetoric of Ancient and Modern Apocalyptic," *Interpretation*, vol. 25 (1971), pp. 436–53. Originally printed in Amos Wilder, *Battle Retrospect and Other Poems*, copyright 1923, Yale University Press. Reprinted by permission.

us to recognize the importance and significance of the myths and symbols it uses so dramatically to express hope in the midst of despair.

Further Reading

For the characteristics of apocalyptic, see:

PCB, pp. 484–88, "Apocalyptic Literature" (H. H. Rowley).
JBC, pp. 536–43, "Apocrypha" (R.E. Brown).
IDB, vol. 1, pp. 157–61, "Apocalypticism" (M. Rist).
IDB Suppl., pp. 28–34, "Apocalypticism" (P.D. Hanson).
P. Hanson, The Dawn of Apocalyptic.
K. Koch, The Rediscovery of Apocalyptic.
W. G. Kümmel, Intro., pp. 452–56.
D. S. Russell, The Method and Message of Jewish Apocalyptic.
C. K. Barrett, The New Testament Background: Selected Documents, pp. 227, 255. A representative selection of texts with introduction and notes.
E. Hennecke and W. Schneemelcher, New Testament Apocrypha, vol. 2, pp. 579–803. A general introduction and then texts in translation with introduction.

Surveys of recent scholarly work on apocalyptic are to be found in Journal for Theology and the Church, vol. 6, Apocalypticism, R. Funk, ed; in W. Schmithals, The Apocalyptic Movement: Introduction. Interpretation, vol. 25, no. 4 (October 1971) is wholly devoted to the subject of apocalyptic; so is The Catholic Biblical Quarterly, vol. 39 (1977).

Systematic investigation of the theology of Q was begun by H. Tödt, The Son of Man in the Synoptic Tradition, pp. 232–74. Further studies are:

H. Kee, Jesus in History, pp. 76–120.
R. A. Edwards, The Sign of Jonah, pp. 41–70.
——, "An Approach to the Theology of Q," Journal of Religion, vol. 51 (1971), pp. 247–69.
——, A Theology of Q.

See also:

IDB Suppl., pp. 715–16, "Q" (F. Neirynck).

A recent book on the apocalyptic discourses has rendered all previous work out of date and indeed almost superfluous: L. Hartman, Prophecy Interpreted: The Formation of Some Jewish Apocalyptic Texts and of the Eschatological Discourse Mark 13 par.

For the book of Revelation, see:

PCB, pp. 1043–61 (N. Turner).
JBC, pp. 467–93 (J. L. D'Aragon).

IDB, vol. 4, pp. 58–71 (J. W. Bowman). Most scholars do not share Bowman's convictions with regard to the structure of the work, but his argument is extremely interesting.

IDB Suppl., pp. 744–46 (E. Schluessler Fiorenza).

W. G. Kümmel, *Intro.* (17th ed.), pp. 457–74.

W. Marxsen, *Intro.*, pp. 274–78.

R. Fuller, *Intro.*, pp. 184–90.

A. Yarbro Collins, *The Combat Myth in the Book of Revelation*.

E. Schluessler Fiorenza, *The Apocalypse*.

——, "Composition and Structure of the Book of Revelation," *CBQ*, vol. 39 (1977), pp. 344–66.

J. Pilch, *What Are They Saying About the Book of Revelation?*

On the visions and symbols of apocalyptic, in addition to the works mentioned in connection with the source Q above, see:

A. Wilder, *Early Christian Rhetoric: The Language of the Gospel*, especially pp. 118–28.

——, "Eschatological Imagery and Earthly Circumstance," *New Testament Studies*, vol. 5 (1958/59), pp. 229–45.

——, "The Rhetoric of Ancient and Modern Apocalyptic," *Interpretation*, vol. 25 (1971), pp. 436–53.

L. Hartman, *Prophecy Interpreted*, pp. 248–52.

W. Beardslee, *Literary Criticism of the New Testament*, pp. 53–63.

The apostle Paul appears to be taking a ride in a swing. Actually, he is escaping from King Aretas by being let down in a basket through a window in a wall of the city of Damascus (2 Cor 11:33; Acts 9:25).

CHAPTER FIVE

PAUL
Apostle to the Gentiles

Paul is a major figure in early Christianity. His letters, plus those the later church believed he wrote, make up over one-fourth of the New Testament, and over one-half of the lengthy Acts of the Apostles (twenty-eight chapters) is given over to the life, journeys, and speeches of this leading New Testament missionary. In terms of sheer bulk of material, Paul literally dominates the New Testament. Moreover, he hammered out an understanding of the Christian faith that is one of the great achievements in Christian theological history. At the same time, some things in his writings, as the author of 2 Peter knew, are "hard to understand" (2 Pet 3:16), and they have always been, like Paul himself, the occasion of great controversy. While he inspired many of the church's greatest thinkers and reformers—Augustine, Luther, Calvin, and Wesley—he has also been accused in more recent times of distorting Jesus' simple message, of laying the groundwork for Christian anti-Semitism, and of perpetuating chauvinistic attitudes about race, politics, sex, and the status of women! A study of Paul and his letters can be as exasperating as it is interesting and challenging, but it can hardly be doubted that one is in the presence of a religious genius.[1]

In this chapter we shall attempt to lay some groundwork for the study of Paul's letters. Our first objective will be to evaluate the sources for his life and thought, especially his undisputed letters in relation to the Acts of the Apostles. Then we shall attempt to establish a relative chronology for his career and give a sketch of his life stressing his background, his "conversion" and call, and his activity as a missionary. Finally, we shall discuss Paul's basis for authority both in relation to the church at Jerusalem and to the mission churches he founded, taking into account his opponents and the general social world of Pauline mission communities.

[1] S. Sandmel, *The Genius of Paul, passim.*

SOURCES FOR THE LIFE AND THOUGHT OF PAUL

The church came to believe that Paul wrote fourteen letters, thirteen of which bear his name (Letter to the Hebrews excepted). It also came to believe that the Acts of the Apostles portrayed the course of his life from his first encounter with Christianity up to his imprisonment in Rome. Both of these assumptions must be evaluated.

Modern scholars do not believe that Paul wrote (or dictated to his secretary) all fourteen letters attributed to him. On the basis of language, style, and content, the letters can be ranked on an ascending scale of probability, from the least likely to have been written by Paul to those which are undisputed. The Letter to the Hebrews is almost universally rejected as Paul's letter, especially because its dominant theme, the heavenly high priesthood of Christ, is not found in the rest of the letters. Indeed, it does not bear Paul's name! We may safely exclude it from the authentic Pauline letters. Only slightly more debatable are the three "Pastoral Letters," 1 Timothy, 2 Timothy, and Titus. In addition to serious problems of language and style, these letters testify to a highly developed church organization not found in the others. They are supposed to have been written by Paul as pastoral advice to his co-workers, Timothy in Ephesus (1 Tim 1:3) and Titus on the island of Crete (Tit 1:5), but especially the latter cannot be coordinated with what is otherwise known about Paul's life unless we accept the unproven theory that he was released from prison in Rome to carry out a further mission. Most contemporary scholars think they date from the early second century. Finally, we note Ephesians, Colossians, and 2 Thessalonians, in that order. In addition to the differences in language, style, and content from the undisputed letters, Ephesians lacks Paul's usual personal touch, and the reference to Ephesus in 1:1 is not present in our earliest manuscripts. Indeed, Ephesians is clearly dependent on Colossians. Many scholars would accept Colossians, despite the distinctive vocabulary and ideas in comparison with the undisputed letters. As for 2 Thessalonians, we are clearly close to Paul and many hold it to be Paul's letter. The difficulty with it is that it seems to imitate 1 Thessalonians and at the same time it has a slightly different eschatology. Thus, those who do not accept these last three as coming from Paul suggest that they may well emanate from a Pauline "school," and they call them "Deutero [Secondary]-Pauline Letters." That is our position, and we shall give more evidence in chapters 7 and 12.

Seven of the fourteen letters—Hebrews, 1 Timothy, 2 Timothy, Titus, Ephesians, Colossians, and 2 Thessalonians—will not be used as sources for the life and thought of Paul himself. Seven undisputed letters remain, namely, 1 Thessalonians, 1 Corinthians, 2 Corinthians, Philippians, Philemon, Galatians, and Romans. Six of these letters are written to congregations in Asia Minor (Galatia), Macedonia (Thessalonica, Philippi), Achaia or Greece (Corinth), and Italy (Rome). Philemon purports to be written to a person, though it is clearly intended to be read to a congregation (Phlm 2, 3 ["you" in verse 3 is plural]). But if we have removed seven letters from Paul, the remaining seven are actually more than seven for at least one of them (2 Corinthians), probably another (Philippians), and possibly a third (Romans), contain letter fragments. The view that some of Paul's letters contain letter fragments is important for establishing a chronology for Paul's life and thought. Before attempting to summarize the relative sequence of letters and letter fragments, let us illustrate the problem briefly.[2]

The most striking features about Paul's letters are radical interruptions in the flow of thought. Though some of these can be explained by his own deviations in the course of his argument, or in a few instances, by later insertions by a student of Paul (or perhaps even a scribe), others show signs of being parts of letters that are accidentally misplaced. In these cases, one can pick up the flow of thought a few verses, or even chapters, later. An illustration of the phenomenon can be seen from the following verses:

> **2 Cor 6:11–13:** Our mouth is open to you, Corinthians; our heart is wide. You are not restricted by us, but you are restricted in your affections. In return—I speak as to children—widen your hearts also.

> **2 Cor 7:2–4:** Open your hearts to us; we have wronged no one, we have corrupted no one, we have taken advantage of no one. I do not say this to condemn you, for I said before that you are in our hearts, to die together and to live together. I have great confidence in you; I have great pride in you; I am filled with comfort. With all our affliction, I am overjoyed.

Here we can observe a continuing discussion. What falls in-between is 2 Corinthians 6:14-7:1, a section that contains language and ideas so characteristic of the Dead Sea Scrolls and so unlike those of Paul (e.g., Belial [Greek: Beliar] for the Prince of demons; the light-darkness dualism; the use of the term "righteousness"; separation from unbelievers) that many believe that it is a non-Pauline fragment inserted into the letter when the letters were brought together as a collection at a later date.

Another example is the following:

> **2 Cor 2:12-13:** When I came to Troas to preach the gospel of Christ, a door was opened for me in the Lord; but my mind could not rest because I did not find my brother Titus there. So I took leave of them and went on to Macedonia.

> **2 Cor 7:5-6:** For even when we came into Macedonia, our bodies had no rest but we were afflicted at every turn—fighting without and fear within. But God, who comforts the downcast, comforted us by the coming of Titus. . . .

This flow of thought indicates that relations between Paul and the Corinthians are being patched up; however, in the intervening section, 2 Cor 2:14-7:4

---

[2] D. Georgi, "Corinthians, Second Letter to the," *IDB Suppl.*, pp. 183–86.

(minus the non-Pauline fragment just considered) Paul's relations with the church are deteriorating. Thus, we can see part of a letter which is 2 Cor 1:1–2:13 and 7:5–17, part of another letter which is within it, 2:14–7:4 (without 6:14–7:1), and we also find mentioned a "tearful letter" (2 Cor 2:3–4; 7:8) which many scholars identify with Paul's self-defense in 2 Cor 10–13. To these three letter fragments, we add chapter 8 which takes up a new theme, the collection of money for the "poor" among the saints at Jerusalem, and chapter 9, which discusses the collection as though it had not been mentioned in chapter 8! If we attempt to reorder these five letter fragments in a sequence with those that are lost, as well as with the movements of Paul and his co-workers, we get the following picture (leaving out the non-Pauline fragment):

1. Paul leaves Corinth and resides in Ephesus (1 Cor 16:8); eventually he writes the "previous letter" (1 Cor 5:9) which is lost.	LETTER I (lost)
2. There comes back an oral report from "Chloe's people" about factions at Corinth (1 Cor 1:11).	
3. There also arrives a letter asking Paul about problems at Corinth (1 Cor 7:1), perhaps brought by Fortunatus, Stephanus, and Achaicus (1 Cor 16:17).	A LETTER FROM CORINTH
4. Paul responds with 1 Corinthians (minus a later addition, 1 Cor 14:33b–36[3]). Timothy's visit is announced (1 Cor 4:17; 16:10; cf. Acts 19:22). Paul also gives instructions about the collection (1 Cor 16:1–4).	LETTER II (1 Cor)
5. Paul sends Titus to hurry up the collection (2 Cor 8:5–6, 10; 9:2; 12:18).	
6. Paul learns (from Timothy or Titus?) that Jewish Christian missionaries come to Corinth, challenge Paul's authority, and say that he lacks charisma (3:1; 11:4–5, 13, 22; 12:11).	
7. Paul writes 2 Cor 2:14–7:4 (minus 6:14–7:1); the church is still loyal, but relations are deteriorating.	LETTER III (2 Cor 2:14–6:13; 7:2–4)
8. Paul now makes a "painful visit" (2 Cor 2:1; 12:14; 12:21; 13:1), which includes an attack against him by a member of the church (2:5; 7:12).	
9. Paul returns to Ephesus and writes the "tearful letter" defending himself against the Jewish Christian missionaries (2 Cor 2:3–4; 7:8). This was probably 2 Cor 10–13 and may have been delivered by Titus (2 Cor 2:12–13; 7:5–7).	LETTER IV (2 Cor 10–13)

---

[3] We shall discuss the addition, or interpolation, of this section in chapter 6, pp. 179–80, 201.

10. Paul was apparently imprisoned in Ephesus at this time (2 Cor 1:8–11), and it was probably from there that he wrote three letters to Philippi (Phil 4:10–20; Phil 1:1–3:1; Phil 3:2–4:9) and another to Philemon at Colossae.

(four letters not written to Corinth)

11. Paul is released from prison, heads north to Troas then to Macedonia to meet Titus who reports that the situation at Corinth has much improved (2:12–13; 7:5–16).

12. Paul writes 2 Cor 1:1–2:13; 7:5–16, a letter of reconciliation that clarifies why Paul has not yet visited them on his way to Macedonia, and what to do about the person who had so offended Paul (2 Cor 1:15–2:4; 2:5–11).

LETTER V
(2 Cor 1:1-2:13; 7:5–16)

13. Paul now writes 2 Cor 8 (about the collection) which he sends with Titus from Macedonia.

LETTER VI
(2 Cor 8)

14. Leaving Macedonia, Paul writes 2 Cor 9 about the collection to all the Christians of Achaia (Greece).

LETTER VII
(2 Cor 9)

15. Paul visits Corinth (cf. Acts 20:2–3).

It is clear from this reconstruction that the isolation of Pauline fragments in 2 Corinthians is a helpful tool in reconstructing Paul's checkered relations with the Corinthian church.

If we now return to the undisputed letters, we can be fairly sure from what Paul says about gathering the collection for the "poor" among the saints in Jerusalem that the sequence 1 Corinthians (cf. 1 Cor 16:1–4), the letters in 2 Corinthians (2 Cor 8, 9), and Romans (cf. 15:25–29) is established.[4] Based on the general conviction that 1 Thessalonians is Paul's earliest letter because of its apocalyptic orientation, that he wrote letters to the Philippians and to Philemon while imprisoned at Ephesus (probably not later at Caesarea or Rome; cf. 2 Cor 1:8–11; Phil 1:12–26), and that Galatians is relatively late because of its similarity to Romans, his last letter (Rom 15:24–29), we may place Paul's letters in the following *tentative* order:

Letter	**Origin**
1. 1 Thessalonians (minus 2:13–16?[5])	Corinth? (2:2; 3:1, 6)
2. "Previous letter" to Corinth (1 Cor 5:9)	Ephesus?
3. 1 Corinthians (minus 14:33b–36[6])	Ephesus (16:8)

[4] W. G. Kümmel, *Intro.*, p. 254.
[5] Some hold that this anti-Semitic statement was added (interpolated) later.
[6] See above, n. 3, and chapter 6, pp. 180, 201.

Letter	Origin
4. 2 Cor 2:14–6:13; 7:2–4 (minus 6:14–7:1)	Ephesus?
5. "Tearful letter" = 2 Cor 10–13	Ephesus?
6. Phil 4:10–20	Ephesus
7. Phil 1:1–3:1 (4:4–7? 4:21–23?)	Ephesus
8. Phil 3:2–4:9	Ephesus (perhaps earliest)
9. Philemon	Ephesus
10. 2 Cor 1:1–2:13; 7:5–16	Macedonia (7:5)
11. 2 Cor 8	Macedonia (8:1)
12. 2 Cor 9 (to Cenchreae near Corinth?)	Macedonia (9:2, 4)
13. Galatians (to north Galatia? cf. 4:13)	Macedonia?
14. Romans 1–15	Corinth? (15:25–26)
15. Romans 16 (to Ephesus? cf. 16:3; 1 Cor 16:19)	Corinth?

We shall indicate what we can hope to reconstruct from Paul's letters in the following section; that will be supplemented with the second major source for his life, the Acts of the Apostles. Acts cannot be used for reconstructing the thought of Paul because Paul's speeches there are free compositions of the author, as was customary in ancient historical writing; it can be used as a secondary source for various aspects of Paul's life if interpreted with critical caution.[7] We can illustrate the difficulty by comparing its version of his first visit to Jerusalem with the corresponding account in Galatians.

Galatians 1:18–24	Acts 9:19b–30; 11:25–26
Then after *three years* at Damascus I went up to Jerusalem (cf. 2 Cor 11:32–33: "At Damascus, the governor under King Aretas guarded the city of Damascus in order to seize me, but I was let down in a basket through a window in the wall, and escaped his hands.")	For *several days* he was *with the disciples at Damascus*. And in the synagogues immediately he proclaimed Jesus. . . . When *many days* had passed the Jews plotted to kill him . . . but his disciples took him by night and let him down over the wall, lowering him in a basket. And when he had come to Jerusalem

---

[7] See above, chapter 3, pp. 65–66, 80, but especially below, chapter 10.

to visit Cephas, and remained with him fifteen days. *But I saw none of the other apostles except James the Lord's brother. (In what I am writing to you, before God I do not lie!)* . . .

. . . And *I was still not known by sight to the churches in Judea;* they only heard it said, "He who once persecuted us is now preaching the faith he once tried to destroy." And they glorified God because of me.

. . . Then *I went into the regions of Syria and Cilicia* . . .

he attempted to join the disciples; and they were all afraid of him, for they did not believe that he was a disciple. But *Barnabas took him and brought him to the apostles,* and declared to them how on the road he had seen the Lord, who spoke to him, and how at Damascus he had preached boldly in the name of Jesus.

So he went in and out among them at Jerusalem, preaching boldly in the name of the Lord. And he spoke and disputed against the Hellenists; but they were seeking to kill him.

And when the brethren knew it, they *brought him down to Caesarea and sent him off to Tarsus (Cilicia)*

11:25–26: So Barnabas went to Tarsus to look for Saul; and when he found him, he *brought him to Antioch (Syria).*

A comparison of the two accounts above shows not only a difference in time references (Galatians: three years; Acts: an indefinite number of days); in Galatians Paul is much more a free agent operating on his own (cf. Gal 2:2: "by revelation"). In Acts, Paul is something of a public hero who disputes with "Hellenists" (Jews who speak Greek and follow Greek ways) and he is thus more in line with the Jewish Christians who bring him to Caesarea and send him to Tarsus; in Galatians Paul is virtually unknown in Jerusalem, for he makes only a short visit with Cephas (i.e., Peter) and meets James. Luke-Acts has the perspective that Paul's relations with the Jerusalem Jewish Christian leaders are relatively smooth and harmonious and that they authoritatively dispatch him on his mission. In Galatians he argues for his independence. It is therefore necessary to make a precise historical analysis to decide whether Paul's anger in Galatians leads him to make errors of memory; he is normally to be trusted since Luke-Acts has its own perspective from a later time and place.

A CHRONOLOGY OF PAUL'S CAREER

Having said something about the sources for Paul's life and about his general background, we shall now attempt to be more precise about the course of his career. Given the nature of our sources, it is important to anchor the chronology of the life of Paul as best possible in world history. In this, two statements, one from the letters, another from Acts are of some help. In 2 Cor 11:32 Paul mentions that he escaped from the governor of Damascus under King Aretas. This refers to King Aretas IV of Nabatea, a monarch who ruled a powerful kingdom of Arabs to the east and south of Palestine and Damascus, the region of Paul's conversion and call (cf. Gal 1:17–18). Since the reign of Aretas IV was 9 B.C. to A.D. 40, Paul was in the region of Damascus after the death of Jesus prior to A.D. 40.

Apart from this reference in the letters, one must turn to Acts and a piece of archeological evidence called the Gallio Inscription found at Delphi in Greece. According to Acts 18:11, Paul had been in Corinth eighteen months when, as a result of Jewish opposition, he was brought before the proconsular governor Gallio. Scholarly evaluation of the Gallio Inscription places the period of Gallio's office most probably from May 1, 51, to May 1, 52. Paul would have arrived in Corinth, then, sometime in 49 or 50. This date seems to be confirmed by the Roman historian Suetonius in his *Life of Claudius* 25, for he speaks of the expulsion of "the Jews" from Rome, an event that can be dated in A.D. 49. Acts 18:2, just prior to Paul's coming before Gallio, states that Aquila and his wife Priscilla had recently come to Corinth because of Claudius' expulsion of the Jews from Rome.

According to Paul's autobiographical statements in Galatians, he had been in Damascus three years (or by Jewish reckoning at least two) and in Syria and Cilicia fourteen years (or by Jewish reckoning at least thirteen), a total of seventeen (or at least fifteen)—if the three is not to be included in the fourteen (Gal 1:18; 2:1)! Then he went to the Jerusalem Conference, to Antioch, and eventually, to Macedonia and Greece. If he arrived at Corinth ca. A.D. 49/50, his conversion and call occurred in the early thirties, some fourteen to seventeen years earlier. There have been attempts to correlate other events in Acts with world history, but none are as important as the Gallio Inscription and Acts 18.

Though tentative, a chronology of Paul's life would look like this:[8]

Paul's date of birth	unknown (probably about the beginning of the century)
Crucifixion of Jesus	ca. 30?
Conversion and call	ca. 32 (perhaps as late as 36)
Jerusalem Conference	48 (49?)
Paul in Corinth	18 months; winter of 49/50 until summer of 51
Paul in Ephesus	about 2½ years (Acts 19:1, 10, 22); probably 52–55

[8] D. Georgi in G. Bornkamm, *Paul*, pp. 12–13; cf. J. Hurd, "Chronology, Pauline," *IDB Suppl.*, pp. 166–68.

Last stay in Macedonia and Greece	probably winter of 55/56
Journey to Jerusalem and arrest	spring of 56
Taken prisoner to Rome	probably 58
Two years' imprisonment in Rome	probably 58–60 (cf. Acts 28–30)
Martyrdom under Nero	probably 60

It must be emphasized that the final dates of the chronology are based on comments in the book of Acts and an early church tradition that Paul was martyred in Rome (1 Clem 5:7; 6:1). In addition, the chronology assumes that Paul was not released to carry on a mission in Spain and did not write the "Pastoral Epistles."

A SKETCH OF PAUL'S LIFE

Having evaluated the sources for Paul's life and attempted something of a chronology, we shall present a general sketch of his life. Again, the letters will be primary sources, but occasional details can be filled in where the data of Acts will permit.

Background

Paul may be called a man of three interacting worlds: he was born, reared, and became active in a strongly-Hellenistic Greek urban environment; he was the son of a proud Jewish family living in the Diaspora; and he became a Christian when, as he said, God revealed his Son to him and called him to preach the good news of Jesus Christ to the Gentiles. It may be said of him that he was a Hellenist, a Jew, and a Christian, and each of the elements in his personal heritage played an important role in shaping the man who must be reckoned the most important figure in the New Testament church.

According to Acts, Paul was born in Tarsus, the capital of Cilicia.[9] Tarsus was a flourishing commercial city and contained many of the religions prevalent throughout the Greco-Roman world. It also had a well-known Stoic philosophical school.[10] In fact, Tarsus rivaled Athens and Rome as an educational center. Paul's letters show that he had a formal Greek education, for he writes (and dictates) Greek well and displays a knowledge of Greek rhetorical devices especially characteristic of Cynic-Stoic preachers of the period. In some of his ethical discussions, Paul cites lists of virtues and vices of the type

[9] A late tradition from Jerome (*De Viris Illustribus* 5; *Comm. in Ep. ad Philemon* 23) says that Paul's family emigrated from Gischala in northern Galilee to Tarsus as prisoners of war. There is no way of proving this. Acts claims that Paul was a Roman citizen from birth (16:37; 21:39; 22:25–29; 25:10–12). If correct, it raises some interesting questions about the status of his father. If he was a prisoner of war, he would have been freed and subsequently granted citizenship. Acts also says that a son of Paul's sister helped him when he was in trouble in Jerusalem (23:16).

[10] See above, chapter 1, p. 9, for the Stoics.

135

known in Cynic-Stoic schools. He also accepts from tradition, perpetuates, and develops views of Jesus Christ that would ring familiar to almost any person living in the broader Greco-Roman world. Anyone who knew the mystery religions would not be surprised to hear of dying and rising with Christ (Rom 6:5). Others would find the tradition that Jesus Christ was in the form of God, took the form of a servant, and was highly exalted by God (Phil 2:6–11) a congenial way of thinking not unlike the notion of descending-ascending redeemers widely known. In the light of this orientation, it is no surprise that Paul himself uses the Greek form of his name—*Paul*, not the Hebrew form, Saul (contrast Acts 9:4, 17; 13:9; 22:7, 13; 26:14, etc.).

There are many other aspects of Paul's thinking that might be derived from his Hellenistic background. But there is one more practical concern that will become important for his mission: his trade. Paul was an artisan, one who worked with his hands (1 Cor 4:12), which the author of Luke-Acts identifies specifically as a "tentmaker" (Acts 18:3), that is, a leather worker who made tents and various other leather products. Paul probably learned his trade from his father as was characteristic in the Greco-Roman world, and this apprenticeship might have been given an impetus by the rabbinical ideal of combining learning with a worldly occupation. Yet, in the world in which Paul worked and traveled, the life of a tradesman was not an easy one. One recent author has concluded, "Stigmatized as slavish, uneducated, and often useless, artisans, to judge from scattered references, were frequently reviled or abused, often victimized, seldom if ever invited to dinner, never accorded status, and even excluded from one Stoic utopia. Paul's own statements accord well this general description."[11] Such a life would have been relieved by the hospitality of those with whom he stayed and the intellectual discussions shared on journeys with traveling companions, in inns, homes, and possibly the workshop, as was the custom among the Cynics. As we shall see, Paul's desire to support himself led to a particular view of his role as missionary, one that was not without conflict at Corinth.

If Paul was indebted to his Hellenistic background, he was no less proud of his Jewish heritage. His most elaborate comment about it occurs in Philippians 3:5–6: "circumcized on the eighth day, of the people of Israel, of the tribe of Benjamin, a Hebrew born of Hebrews; as to the law a Pharisee, as to zeal a persecutor of the church, as to righteousness under the law blameless" (cf. 2 Cor 11:22; Rom 9:3–5; 11:1). This important statement says a great deal about what Paul thought of his Jewishness, that he considered himself a very good Jew. In this connection Acts comments that he was brought up in the city of Jerusalem and educated "at the feet of Gamaliel" (22:3), a famous Jerusalem rabbi of the period. How are these comments to be related to the "Paul of Tarsus" tradition? Clearly we can perceive the tendency of Luke-Acts to orient

[11] R. F. Hock, *The Social Context of Paul's Ministry. Tentmaking and Apostleship*, p. 36; this paragraph is particularly indebted to his study. An alternative perception of Paul's life as a guest in the salons of the urban elite is suggested by E.A. Judge, "St. Paul and Classical Society," *Jahrbuch für Antike und Christentum* 15 (1972), pp. 28, 32.

Paul to Jerusalem Judaism. Is there any evidence in Paul's letters that would reflect a "rabbinic" training, especially with regard to his view of the Torah or, more generally, Scripture and its interpretation? Would Paul have passed his final exams at the rabbinical college? This issue has been hotly debated. Some have said "no," arguing that Paul had no formal education, that his interpretation of Scripture does not adhere to the text enough to be rabbinic, and that the Gamaliel tradition is another example of romantic historicizing and tendentiousness on the part of the author of Luke-Acts.[12] Others, however, have argued that Paul's indebtedness to rabbinic-type Biblical interpretation is quite strong, and that he was in the main rabbinic, despite his view of Torah.[13] The question is complicated by the problem that most sources for specifically rabbinic interpretation are later than the New Testament; moreover, one may well ask difficult questions such as the way a Diaspora Pharisee might interpret the Septuagint to make arguments to largely, but not exclusively, Greek Christians. Certainly, Paul was heavily influenced by his Greek background and education; but there is also evidence for connections with at least an early form of rabbinic Judaism and, indeed, certain aspects of Paul's thought can be illuminated by what are known to be Palestinian Jewish sources.[14] Most important in this regard is the strong apocalyptic orientation in much of Paul's writing. It is safe to say, therefore, that one component in Paul's thought can be rooted in his Jewish background and education.

"Conversion" and Call

It was this combination of background and education in both Hellenism and Judaism that particularly fitted Paul to assume leadership of the Christian movement as it moved out of Palestinian Judaism into the larger Hellenistic world. But there was more to his leadership than this background; there was his "conversion" to Christianity and his call to become an apostle to the Gentiles. How did this take place?

According to Acts, Paul enters the early Christian scene as a bystander at the martyrdom of Stephen (Acts 7:58) and, subsequently, we meet him as a persecutor of the fledgling Christian community in Damascus (Acts 9:1-2). Paul himself does not mention the former incident, but the latter is clearly an unforgettable memory for him. We saw above that in his statement about his Jewish background, Paul included the comment, "as to zeal a persecutor of the church." A further reference of this sort is made to the congregation at Galatia in Asia Minor: "For you have heard of my former life in Judaism, how I persecuted the church of God violently and tried to destroy it; and I advanced in Judaism beyond many of my own age among my people, so extremely zealous was I for the traditions of my fathers" (Gal 1:13-14). As far as can be

---

[12] Recently, S. Sandmel, *The Genius of Paul*, pp. 7, 156.

[13] An important work, with which Sandmel disagrees, is W.D. Davies, *Paul and Rabbinic Judaism*.

[14] E. P. Sanders, *Paul and Palestinian Judaism*, Intro., gives the state of the debate.

determined, widespread systematic Jewish persecution of Christians did not take place; yet, there were some sporadic persecutions and, since Paul was clearly involved, it will be helpful to make a hypothesis about this feature of Paul's past.

Hellenistic Judaism was itself very much a missionary movement. We saw in chapter 3 that Judaism was very attractive to the Hellenistic world, and the synagogues regularly had their circles of "God-fearers," men attracted to Judaism but resisting full proselytization because they were reluctant to accept circumcision and the dietary laws. In Gal 5:11 Paul asks rhetorically, "But if I, brethren, still preach circumcision, why am I still persecuted?" This leads us to conclude that at one time he had in fact "preach[ed] circumcision," that is, he had been an active missionary for Judaism in the Hellenistic world.

If the supposition that Paul was a *Jewish* missionary is correct, it is possible that despite his Hellenistic background, he came into conflict with Hellenistic Jewish *Christian* missionaries on the mission field. It should be remembered that churches outside Jerusalem and the surrounding areas had often been founded by such missionaries and that they had gone a step beyond what even Hellenistic Jews could tolerate: a strong critique of the Temple and Jewish Law (Acts 6:14). Indeed, eventually they developed a view of Jesus Christ that drew on many of the ideas current in the Hellenistic world at large. At any rate, it appears that such Hellenistic Jewish Christian missionaries had been driven from Jerusalem by persecution, while the more conservative Jewish Christians were permitted to remain. Presumably such missionaries would be attractive to the "God-fearers" precisely because they were critical of those very aspects of Judaism that the "God-fearer" found to be stumbling blocks to full proselytization, especially circumcision. Such "God-fearers" were also the object of Jewish missions. Thus, Paul would have come in conflict with the Hellenistic Jewish Christian missionaries and have persecuted them—though one day he would join their ranks.

A discussion of Paul's persecution of the Christians leads to what he frequently links with it, his "conversion" and call (Gal 1:11–17; 1 Cor 15:9; Phil 3:6–7). The subject of Paul's "conversion" has been the occasion of much discussion for it raises fundamental issues such as his attitude toward Judaism, his conception of Torah and covenant, his view of the gospel, and the meaning and significance of his religious experience in later Christendom.[15] We cannot discuss all of Paul's important theological ideas at this point, but a few remarks should be made about this central event. Not surprisingly, any interpretation of it is in part a question of which sources are most important, and what they mean; in part, it is a question of what is meant by the word "conversion."

As mentioned, Paul links his persecution of the Christians, his experience

---

[15] K. Stendahl, "The Apostle Paul and the Introspective Conscience of the West," *Harvard Theological Review* 56 (1963), pp. 199–215, reprinted in W. Meeks, *The Writings of St. Paul*, pp. 422–34 and in K. Stendahl, *Paul Among Jews and Gentiles*, pp. 78–96; E Käsemann, "Justification and Salvation History in the Epistle to the Romans," *Perspectives on Paul*, pp. 60–78; K. Stendahl, pp. 129–33; S. Sandmel, *The Genius of Paul*, chapter 3: "Paul the Convert." Further discussion and literature in H. D. Betz, *Galatians*, pp. 64–66.

of a revelation of Christ, and his call to be a missionary, or in his own words, an "apostle" (Greek *apostolos*: "one who is sent out"). In the letter to the Galatians where Paul immediately sets out to defend the truth of his gospel and thus of his apostleship, he begins, "Paul an apostle—not from men nor through man, but through Jesus Christ and God the Father . . ." (Gal 1:1). All the evidence points to the probability that Paul had never known Jesus of Nazareth, which was apparently a necessary component for being an "apostle" for the author of Luke-Acts (Acts 1:20–26). But Paul argues that his apostleship is not of human origin, an idea he develops in Gal 1:11–17. In typical rhetorical style, he reminds the Galatians, "For I would have you know, brethren, that the gospel which was preached by me is not man's gospel. For I did not receive it from man, nor was I taught it, but it came through a revelation (*apocalypsis*) of Jesus Christ." After telling of his formerly persecuting the Christians, Paul continues, "But when he who had set me apart before I was born, and had called me through his grace, was pleased to reveal his Son to me (literally "in me"), in order that I might preach him among the Gentiles, I did not confer with flesh and blood, nor did I go up to Jerusalem to those who were apostles before me, but I went away into Arabia (i.e., Nabatea), and again I returned to Damascus." The stress in this passage is not so much on changing from one religion (Judaism) to another religion (Christianity) in the usual sense of "conversion" as it is on a special call to be apostle to the Gentiles through direct revelation. There is a striking pattern for this call in the Old Testament prophets Isaiah and Jeremiah, who were set apart while they were still in the womb (Isa 49:1; Jer 1:5); that is, Paul felt "predestined" to his vocation. This does not deny that Paul had an intense religious experience. He says that God revealed his Son "in him" and that the Son, Jesus Christ, revealed the gospel Paul preached.[16] This is, in the first place, a "vision" of the Son. In 1 Cor 9:1, Paul says, "Am I not free? Am I not an apostle? Have I not *seen* Jesus, our Lord?" and in 1 Cor 15:8 after noting resurrection appearances to Cephas, the twelve, five hundred brethren, James, and "all the apostles," he states, "Last of all, as to one untimely born, he *appeared* also to me" and again mentions his apostleship and persecution of the church (15:9). This is, in the second place, an implied verbal revelation as well, and elsewhere Paul mentions his "visions and revelations of the Lord" in which one might hear things (2 Cor 12:1–5).

In all of these texts, Paul's focus is on the revelation and his call to be an apostle to the Gentiles. He relates this to his persecution of the church, and speaks of a change from his "former life." As we shall see, he also has difficulties accepting the Law as sufficient for maintaining a relationship to God (cf. Rom 7), and he does not require circumcision as a prerequisite for becoming a Christian. Yet, his pride in his Jewishness and his analogy with a prophetic call raise the question whether he was ever plagued with a "guilty conscience" for what he had done, and this raises the further question whether the term "conversion" is the appropriate one. Another text, Phil 3:4–9, reinforces this inter-

---

[16] H. D. Betz, *Galatians*, pp. 54, 332–33, notes the tradition preserved in the *Pseudo-Clementine Homilies* (sometime before A.D. 375) that Christ instructed Paul for an hour.

pretation. Paul's Jewish background is, he says, reason for "confidence in the flesh" (verse 4). After giving his most important statement about his Jewishness (verses 5–6), he concludes, "But whatever *gain* I had, I counted as loss for the sake of Christ. Indeed I count everything as loss because of the surpassing worth of knowing Christ Jesus my Lord" (verses 7–8). It is this that leads him on to state the major theme of much of his writing, "the righteousness from God that depends on faith" (verse 9).

The author of the Acts of the Apostles lays great weight on Paul's "Damascus road experience," for he relates the story three times (9:1–19a; 22:1–15; 26:4–20). In fact, his stress on the intensity of the experience has probably contributed to its interpretation as an emotional "conversion" experience. There is, however, a constant element in all three of the accounts in Acts that is in accord with Paul's, and that is the central dialogue between Paul and the risen Jesus: "Saul, Saul, why do you persecute me?" "Who are you Lord?" "I am Jesus, whom you are persecuting." Furthermore, we know that in this kind of traditional material the central dialogue is the oldest part, the nucleus around which the other details cluster as the tradition is transmitted. Whether the detail of the vision of light, which is also a constant in all three stories, was connected to the dialogue, is worth considering; at least it would accord with the notion of a vision. Enshrined in the Acts "conversion" stories are elements that are not inconsistent with what Paul himself says: a revelation of Jesus Christ that included some verbal communication.

However one evaluates Paul's "conversion," it is clear that a revelation of Christ is rooted deeply in his experience, and his letters reflect the vitality and power of one who is driven to accomplish what he believes is God's will for his life. "At long last," says the famous classical scholar Wilamowitz-Moellendorf, "Greek speaks out of a vivid spiritual experience."[17]

In summation, it is possible to say that Paul associated his persecution of the church with two interrelated facts: a revelation of Jesus Christ, God's Son, and a prophetic call to become apostle to the Gentiles. In Paul's statements, there is no emphasis on what has usually been associated with a "conversion," namely, a guilty conscience about his persecuting activities. Rather, his statements indicate that he had thought of himself as a loyal Jew, confident in the "flesh." The accent in these accounts falls rather on his call to become apostle to the Gentiles. The revelation itself had visionary and auditory elements, a fact which seems to be further supported in Acts. Acts, however, elaborates the stories with legend and theological interpretation related to Paul's connections with Jerusalem.

Paul's Early Activity as a Christian Missionary

The conversion of Paul probably took place in A.D. 32 or 33, some two or three years after the crucifixion of Jesus. We do not know the exact date of the

---

[17] Quoted by G. Bornkamm, *Paul*, pp. 9–10.

crucifixion of Jesus, however. It was probably either 30 or 33; so the date of Paul's conversion can be as early as 32 or as late as 36. After his conversion Paul spent three years in Arabia, the Gentile district east of the Jordon River, and Damascus (Gal 1:7–18). We do not know what he was doing there, but considering his character, it is most likely that he was already working as a Christian missionary. If he was, his missionary activity must have been unsuccessful, though it apparently aroused enough hostility that he had to flee Damascus (2 Cor 11:32–33; Acts 9:23–25). He then paid a brief visit to Peter, already in many respects the primary leader of the Christian movement, in Jerusalem (Gal 1:18). Paul always refers to Peter by his Aramaic name (Cephas); they probably always talked to one another in Aramaic. We would give a great deal to know what they talked about, but it was obviously not about the weather, and in view of Paul's vehemence about his gospel not coming from man (Gal 1:12), it is unlikely that the visit was to take part in "a crash course in missionary work with Peter."[18] Paul then went back to his own native district of Cilicia to carry on missionary activity (Gal 1:21–23), and sometime during the next fourteen years Barnabas, a leader of the church in Antioch, brought him to Antioch to help in the Hellenistic Jewish Christian missionary activity in Syria.

At Antioch on the Orontes, the third city in the Roman Empire after Rome and Alexandria, the cultural crosscurrents of the Hellenistic world came sharply into contact. Antioch was the capital of the Roman province of Syria located on the best land route between Asia Minor and Syria and Palestine, and hence between East and West. Here Greek civilization and philosophy interacted with oriental culture and religion more directly and on more equal terms than almost anywhere else, and the establishment of a Christian community here was therefore an event of the greatest possible importance for the growth and development of the New Testament church. The New Testament itself says that "in Antioch the disciples were for the first time called Christians" (Acts 11:26).

Paul's coming to Antioch marked the beginning of the most important phase of his life and work. Now he had the active support of a strategically located and missionary-minded Christian church, a church that was developing and attracting a whole group of active and potential missionaries. With its support Paul began the missionary work that is the concern of the Acts of the Apostles. Acts 13:3–14:26 reports a first missionary journey that took him and his companions to Cyprus and the southern part of Asia Minor. No trace of this journey is preserved in Paul's letters, and we do not know whether it took place before or after the Jerusalem Conference. Acts has it before and sees the Conference as a direct consequence of the success of this journey. But Acts also has it immediately following a visit to Jerusalem by Barnabas and Paul, "the famine visit" of Acts 11:27–30; 12:25. That visit is not mentioned in Galatians, even though Paul is telling under oath the story of his relationship with Jerusalem down to the Conference. It is probable, therefore, that the Confer-

---

[18] G. Bornkamm, *Paul,* p. 28.

ence was made necessary not by the success of the first missionary journey, but by the success of the work in Antioch itself, and that the missionary journey of Acts 13 and 14 was a result of the decision to authorize Paul and Barnabas to go into the Gentile world.

The Mission in Asia Minor, Macedonia, and Greece

Paul now began the most active phase of his missionary work, deliberately going out into the Gentile world from his base, the Hellenistic Jewish mission church in Antioch. It is unlikely that this missionary work took the form of the three neatly defined missionary journeys of Acts 13:3–14:26; 15:40–18:22; 18:23–21:17; but the general picture given in Acts is probably correct. Paul would have begun this phase of his work in Cyprus and Asia Minor (Galatia), readily accessible from his base in Antioch. He must have then moved west following the overland route from Antioch to the west, and made the momentous decision to go further west into Macedonia and Greece rather than to turn south to the west coastal region of Asia Minor, whose churches are the concern of the book of Revelation, or northeast to the area of Bithynia and the Black Sea. Acts 16:6–10 presents this decision as a result of a direct revelation to Paul.

From this point, Paul's letters and Acts agree for a time on the essentials of Paul's itinerary; Philippi (1 Thess 2:2; Acts 16:11–40)—Thessalonica (the letter to the Thessalonians itself; Acts 17:1–9)—Athens (1 Thess 3:1; Acts 17:16–34)—Corinth (1 Thess 1:1; 3:6; Acts 18:1–17). Three of these mission congregations (Philippi, Thessalonica, Corinth) have letters written to them. Indeed, it appears that Paul shifted his center of activity from Antioch to Ephesus, his next stop.

In 1 Thessalonians we learn that Paul and his companions had "suffered and been shamefully treated at Philippi" (1 Thess 2:2), a comment that seems to receive some support from Acts 16:19–24 where they are whipped by command of city officials and thrown into prison, an account that is otherwise expanded with miracle stories. Paul later wrote the Philippians thanking them for their financial support when he was in Thessalonica, for this support was unusual (Phil 4:15–16; cf. 2 Cor 11:8–9). Paul displayed a deep affection for the Philippians. After leaving them, he probably followed the main highway (the Via Ignatia) to Thessalonica, a seaport and the capital city of Macedonia (modern Salonika). In 1 Thessalonians, Paul encouraged the Thessalonians, among whom he had worked so hard (2:9), for their steadfast faith in the face of persecution by their fellow countrymen (2:14),[19] i.e., they had become Christian from a Gentile background (1:9; contrast Acts 17:1–9). In the letter, which touches on apocalyptic eschatology, he mentions that Timothy had been dispatched from Athens (3:1, 6), to which he now comes, possibly via Beroea (Acts 17:10–15). We have no letter to the Athenians; the author of the Acts of

---

[19] See above, n. 5, on 1 Thess 2:13–16 as a possible later addition.

the Apostles presents us with one of its most magnificent Hellenistic Jewish mission sermons in the mouth of Paul (Acts 17).

Paul then went to Corinth, a thriving cosmopolitan seaport and capital of Greece. As we noted in connection with the Gallio Inscription, Paul arrived there in A.D. 49 or 50 and stayed about eighteen months. There he established (at the house of Stephanas? 1 Cor 1:16; 16:15) a lively community of mainly Gentile Christians that was nurtured by Apollos (1 Cor 1:12; 3:5–6), whom Acts claims had been an Alexandrian Jew and an eloquent man well versed in the Scriptures (18:24–28). Probably Paul wrote 1 Thessalonians at this time. Paul's subsequent correspondence with the Corinthians indicates many problems related to their Greek background, as well as his conflict with other apostles who challenged his authority. We shall say much more about these subjects below.

From Corinth Paul went to Ephesus. The Acts itinerary takes him from Ephesus to Palestine and up to Antioch from where he retraced his steps through Asia Minor back to Ephesus (Acts 18:18–23; 19:1), thus launching a third missionary journey (down to 21:17). Though this account is full of legendary material, it is undoubtedly accurate in placing Paul at Ephesus for a long period of time, perhaps two and a half years (19:8, 10). 1 Corinthians was written there (1 Cor 16:8), as well as parts of 2 Corinthians, and if Paul was imprisoned there, as many believe (2 Cor 1:8–11), perhaps also the "prison letters" Philippians and Philemon were written there. He appears to have made a quick trip to Corinth from Ephesus (2 Cor 2:1; 12:14; 12:21; 13:1); eventually he left on a journey through Macedonia where he continued his correspondence with the Corinthians (2 Cor 1:8–10, 15–16; 2:12–13; 7:5; 9:2). He may also have written Galations about this time. Finally, he made his third and final trip to Corinth (2 Cor 13:1). His previous correspondence with the Corinthians indicates that he was interested in the collection for the "poor" among the Christians at Jerusalem (1 Cor 16:1–4; 2 Cor 8; 9). At Corinth Paul shows the same interest when he writes his most mature letter, Romans. Despite the dangers involved (Rom 15:31), he clearly indicates his intent to fulfill his promise about the collection (Gal 2:10). It was not only an act of charity; it symbolized the unity of the church (2 Cor 8; 9; Rom 15:25–32). Perhaps his anxiety about the "unbelievers in Judea" (Rom 15:31) was correct; the author of Luke-Acts tells the story that Jews from Asia in Jerusalem claimed that Paul spoke against the Law and the Temple, that he was arrested, and that there was even a plot on his life. According to Acts, Paul appealed his case to Caesar, which was the right of every Roman citizen (Acts 21:1–18:16).

The journey to Rome was begun probably in either A.D. 56 or 58. Paul was taken as a prisoner. According to the conclusion of Acts, Paul spent two years in Rome under house arrest, nonetheless preaching "quite openly and unhindered." As we shall see in our discussion of Luke-Acts, this statement is theologically motivated, but it probably is true that Paul was an active missionary even while a prisoner. Our knowledge of Paul ends at this point, since Acts ends here and no undisputed letters are preserved from this or any later period; possibly Philippians and Philemon were written during the Roman captivity, though we have preferred the imprisonment in Ephesus. Ecclesiastical tradition has it that Paul was released from his captivity, visited Spain, and returned to Rome a second time as a prisoner. But the tradition may well be only a historicization of the plans Paul details in Rom 15:24–29, and it seems most probable that Paul's first imprisonment in Rome ended with his death.

THE AUTHORITY OF PAUL AS APOSTLE

It is clear from Paul's letters and Acts that there are delicate problems that he encountered in his claim to be an apostle to the Gentiles. He had never known Jesus; he had been a persecutor of the church; in many ways he was dependent on various traditions of the Hellenistic Jewish churches, and even the Jerusalem church; yet, there was Paul's claim that his call originated in divine revelation; that though it was agreed to by the leaders of the Jerusalem church, it was independent of any human agency; and that the Gentile churches Paul founded had a special relationship with him based on his authority as an apostle. It should come as no surprise, then, that there were those who constantly challenged his authority as an apostle. Such issues have generated a great deal of discussion, partly because they are related to a number of classical questions about early Christianity, such as whether its "spirit" and vitality can be contained within the institutional church: for example where do Paul and "his" churches fit within a spectrum of possibilities from a "sect" wrestling with its relation to the world and its origins in Judaism to a more independent, rational-legal institution *of* the world?[20] In considering such important questions, we shall have to limit ourselves to three issues: Paul's relationship to the Jerusalem church, his authority in the Gentile churches, and the opposition that developed against him on the mission field.

Paul and the Church at Jerusalem

Paul's relationship to the church at Jerusalem developed in the main from the results of the Jerusalem Conference (Gal 2:1–10; cf. Acts 15). As noted in chapter 3, this was a major event in early Christianity, and Paul appears to have launched his mission westward into Asia Minor and Macedonia-Greece after the Conference about A.D. 48. His precise relationship to the Jerusalem church has been highly debated because it is affected by the relative weight put on Galatians and Acts and, of course, on the interpretation of Paul's statements. Paul himself says that he went to the Conference with Barnabas, that he took Titus with him, and that he went up "by revelation" (Gal 2:2). However one interprets this term "revelation," one would infer from Paul's version that he was the dominant figure at the Conference. In Acts, however, Barnabas and Paul are *sent* as delegates from the church at Antioch, and the Conference is

---

[20] J. Schütz, *Paul and the Anatomy of Apostolic Authority;* B. Holmberg, *Paul and Power.*

clearly dominated by James and especially Peter. Though Galatians is written some years after the Conference and Paul is writing in the heat of controversy, it will be the primary source. Yet, Acts is undoubtedly on target in saying that the Conference was occasioned by Judean Christians who came to Antioch demanding that Christians be circumcised, for Paul states that Titus, a Greek, was not compelled to be circumcised (Gal 2:3). The issue, of course, is Law and covenant, and the influx of Gentiles into the Christian movement. Must one become a Jew to become a Christian (Gal 2:3, 7; Acts 15:1, 5–6)? There appear to have been three parties to the debate: a group of conservative Jewish Christians who, quite naturally, considered that the Torah was still in effect and that circumcision was necessary (in Gal 2:4 Paul calls them "false brethren" to whom he did not yield); the Jerusalem leaders, James, Peter, and John; and Paul, Barnabas, and Titus. What lay in the balance was the mission to the Gentiles, the heart of Paul's mission and, presumably, the Antioch church. If we take Paul seriously, the first group lost the debates and a compromise was reached between the second and third groups: Peter was entrusted with the "apostleship" to the circumcised, and Paul was entrusted with preaching to the uncircumcised Gentiles (Gal 2:7). Yet, Paul's language makes it unclear whether he was granted the status of *apostle* at that time, and there is the lingering doubt that Paul was as independent as he suggests. If Paul was not a full apostle at the time, but something more like a delegate from Antioch with Barnabas, the situation was ripe for a challenge to his apostleship from the conservative party. Galatians itself shows that this happened, for Paul writes that later he had to defend his freedom at Antioch when "certain men from James," whom Paul calls "the circumcision party," caused Peter to withdraw and not eat with the Gentiles (Gal 2:11–14). What did it mean that the "pillars" James, Peter, and John gave Paul and Barnabas "the right hand of fellowship" (Gal 2:9) in apparent victory over the conservatives? How was this compromise solution viewed? Why was Peter so inconsistent? Did James change his position? And did Paul himself abide by the decision, "we to the Gentiles, they to the circumcised" (Gal 2:9)? In 1 Cor 9:20, he states: "To the Jews I became as a Jew, in order to win Jews; to those under the law I became as one under the law—though not being myself under the law—that I might win those under the law." Again, it should be said that we are at the heart of the relationship of early Christianity with Judaism, and at the heart of the message of Paul. If the Jerusalem Conference compromise did not hold, and if Paul's status as apostle at that time was not absolutely clear, the Jewish Christian conservatives had a legitimate case against him.[21]

The second major decision of the Conference also relates to the authority of Paul, namely, "only they (Peter, James, and John) would have us remember the poor, which thing I was very eager to do" (Gal 2:10). This refers to the collection (1 Cor 16; 2 Cor 8; 9; Rom 15) for which Paul was willing to risk his life in going back to Jerusalem (Rom 15:25–32). How should this collection be

[21] H. D. Betz, *Galatians*, pp. 81–83, discusses the essential issues.

interpreted? Some have suggested that this was like a tax, in analogy with the collection of the Temple tax on all Jews.[22] If so, it implies that Paul was a representative of the Jerusalem "mother church," and submissive to it. However, there are a number of features about the collection—its limitation to Paul's "Gentile" churches, its one-time (not annual) occasion, and its destination for literally "the poor"—which make the Jewish Temple tax an inappropriate analogy. Yet, the collection was more than *only* an act of charity; it was also an act of gratitude, an indication of the independence of the Gentile churches, and—despite Paul's defense of his apostleship in Galatians—a sign of the unity of the church. In short, Paul did not submit to the Jerusalem church, but neither did he wish to offend it.[23] One can only ask: how would the conservatives who believed in the importance of the Law have responded? Or anyone who believed that circumcision was the mark of God's people?

Paul's Authority in the Gentile Churches

It is clear that in the communities he "fathered," Paul is something of an authority figure, even though he has occasion to warn against it (e.g., 1 Cor 1:10–17; 3:5–14). He exhorts those in his communities to imitate him (1 Thess 1:6; Phil 3:17; 1 Cor 4:16; 11:1). His letters, as we shall see, are full of parenesis: exhorting, comforting, rebuking, making all sorts of "value judgments" about what Christians should be and do. He has many co-workers, some of whom are clearly subordinate to him. In one instance, he seems to rank persons with certain spiritual gifts (1 Cor 12:28: "God has appointed in the church first apostles, second prophets, third teachers, then workers of miracles, then healers, helpers, administrators, speakers in various kinds of tongues"), and he places his one self-designation, "apostle," at the top (cf. Eph 4:11) and those who are causing problems, "speakers in various kinds of tongues," at the bottom. In another instance, he mentions "bishops" and "deacons" (Phil 1:1). Was Paul rebelling against the authority of the Jerusalem church while at the same time establishing his own power structure? At first glance it might seem so; but the issues are more complicated.

The exhortation to imitate Paul should be seen in the context of Paul's view that the gospel is a gospel of lowliness exemplified by the Cross of Christ, and that the apostle's difficult life "imitates Christ": "Be imitators of me, *as I am of Christ*" (1 Cor 11:1; cf. Phil 3:17–18). Paul puts this in terms of a paradox: God's power lies in weakness (1 Cor 1:10–4:21) and, as we shall see, he will cite this form of power against certain kinds of opponents. This power also expresses itself in love, and behind his parenesis is the one who loves his

---

[22] E.g., the German scholars, K. Holl and E. Stauffer, and K. Nickle, *The Collection. A Study in Paul's Strategy.*

[23] See the recent discussion in B. Holmberg, *Paul and Power*, pp. 35–43 who, however, thinks of the collection as "compulsory"; contrast H. D. Betz, *Galatians*, p. 103.

churches and wants to see them grow. "Knowledge (*gnōsis*) puffs up, but love (*agapē*) builds up." Thus, Paul believes that as an apostle "of Christ" and "in Christ" he could *command* Philemon to release his slave Onesimus, but he appeals to him "for love's sake" (Phlm 8), giving him the free will to make his own decision (Phlm 14). It is true that he views some of his co-workers as subordinate; but the relationship was an intimate, personal one, characterized by such terms as "faithful," "trusted," "beloved." His ranking of spiritual gifts needs to be seen in context. The stress of 1 Cor 12 as a whole is on the *unity* of the church which was being torn apart by fractions, and though Paul recognizes that there are different functions in the congregation, all of them are necessary. Finally, we may catch a glimpse of certain persons with authority at Philippi who are referred to as "bishop" and "deacon," but these terms were scarcely very distinct until a later time, and were sometimes equivalent to "presbyters" or "elders." Indeed, Paul thinks of his apostleship as being a "deacon" (2 Cor 11:23, *diakonoi* = "servants" [RSV]).

Paul did hold authority in his churches, but not in the sense of an official of the church today. It is rather the authority of "charisma," that is, his communities responded to him not as any ordinary person but as one who was in a special way in touch with a loving, self-sacrificing God. He used this recognition to challenge the *status quo* in the name of what he believed to be the gospel of Jesus Christ and Christian freedom. Others, of course, could challenge him or claim greater "charisma" and oppose him.[24]

Paul's Opponents on the Mission Field

It is difficult to identify Paul's opponents from the occasional remarks he makes since it is necessary to reconstruct what they were saying about him from what *he* says about them. What he says about them is usually based on hearsay from co-workers who traveled back and forth between him and the churches, or from letters. In addition, there is the problem of interpreting Paul's rhetorical comments and the ever-present tendency of Acts to smooth over Paul's conflicts with the Jerusalem church. These problems have led to several theories. Some interpreters have attempted to view Paul's opponents as the same everywhere, often suggesting that they followed him from place to place;[25] others argue that the opponents differ from place to place, and even that there are different types of opponents at the same place at different periods;[26] one interpreter argues that Paul is not sufficiently informed to know who they are, and so we cannot know either![27] Nevertheless, the attempt to identify them is important because it sheds light on the diversity of early Christianity and, most important in this context, Paul's own point of view.

[24] This section is especially indebted to J. H. Schütz, *Apostolic Authority.*

[25] W. Schmithals, *Paul and the Gnostics,* argues that Paul's opponents everywhere were Jewish Christian "Gnostics."

[26] G. Bornkamm, *Paul,* is typical.

[27] W. Marxsen, *Intro.,* pp. 45–47.

The Letter to Philemon and the Church at Thessalonica

Philemon is a personal letter to an individual (at Colossae? Cf. Colossians 4:9) and though it was read publicly, it does not reflect opposition to Paul by opponents in a church.

Some scholars have attempted to identify a group of opponents in Thessalonica on the basis of 1 Thess 2:1–12 where Paul is defending the manner in which the gospel had been presented to the Thessalonians. Paul writes that he and his companions had presented themselves *without* error, uncleanness, guile, without seeking to please men, to use words of flattery, to cover their greed, without attempting to gain glory from men. Were there opponents who, in Paul's view, did precisely that? If so, they sound like Gentile charletans who have traits similar to their Jewish Christian missionary counterparts at Corinth. However, Paul's style is typical of missionary and philosophical rhetorical defense.[28] It is possible that there was no actual group of opponents disturbing the church at Thessalonica.

Philippi

In Phil 3:2–3, Paul writes, "Look out for the dogs, look out for the evil-workers, look out for the incision (*katatomē*). For we are the true circumcision (*peritomē*) who worship God in spirit, and glory in Christ Jesus, and put no confidence in the flesh." There is here a pun on the term circumcision, and with it Paul is warning the Philippians against those who stress it, *Christians* of Jewish background. It is, however, unlikely that these are the conservative Jerusalem Christians, for they seem to think of the Law and therefore circumcision as a means of attaining spiritual perfection. The note about spiritual perfectionism, in fact, makes them closest to the opponents encountered in Corinth (1 Cor 15:12–19). As in 1 Corinthians, Paul counters with the humility of the crucified Christ, and in this case with strong words: "For many, of whom I have often told you and now tell you even with tears, live as enemies of the cross of Christ. Their end is destruction, their god is the belly, and they glory in their shame, with minds set on earthly things. But our commonwealth is in heaven, and from it we await a Savior, the Lord Jesus Christ, who *will* change our lowly body to be like his glorious body, by the power which enables him even to subject all things to himself" (Phil 3:18–21). These Jewish Christians may have held views of perfection which were eventually developed in second-century Gnosticism.[29]

---

[28] Again, 2:13–16 may be a later addition; see above, *n.* 5.

[29] H. Koester, "Philippians," *IDB Suppl.*, p. 666, refers to them as "Gnosticizing" Jewish Christians "who preached law and circumcision as a means for reaching perfection."

After Paul had established a congregation at Galatia and moved on, there appeared a group among the Galatians that unsettled the church. They preached a "different gospel" than Paul's, suggesting that they were Christian, but they had a Jewish background since the heart of their message was a stress on the Law and they pressured the Galatians to accept circumcision. Thus, they attacked Paul's version of the gospel and accused him of dispensing with circumcision to "please men"(1:10). Paul does not clearly identify them; he nonetheless attacks them sharply, saying that they "want to make a good showing in the flesh" (their boasting? cf. 6:4; more probably circumcision itself), even though apparently they do not keep the Law, and they stress circumcision to avoid being persecuted "for the cross of Christ" (6:11–16). In good rhetorical style, Paul "knifes" those who have "bewitched" (3:1) the Galatians with one of his sharpest word plays: "I wish those who unsettle you would castrate themselves" (5:12)!

Who were these Jewish Christian "Judaizers"? In the past some scholars have suggested that they were the Jerusalem conservatives (possibly Christians of a Pharisaic origin, cf. Acts 15:1, 5) who followed Paul wherever he went. There is a certain cogency to this view since Paul defends his apostleship in Galatians by recounting the stories of the opposition of the "false brethren" who wanted circumcision for Titus at the Jerusalem Conference (2:3–4) and by the Antioch incident when Peter separated himself from the Gentiles in the fact of "certain men from James," that is, "the circumcision party" (2:11–12).[30]

A major problem with the identification of the Judaizers with the Jerusalem conservatives is that Paul fears that the Galatians will again become slaves to the "elemental spirits," which are probably demonic powers (angels or stars, or both) believed to control "this evil age" (Gal 4:3, 9). Paul links such beliefs with the comment that the Galatians will return to observing days, and months, and seasons, and years, that is, calendrical observations characteristic of astrology. Such "syncretistic" views were widespread in the Hellenistic world. Were these the views of the "Judaizers"? If they were, would the Jerusalem conservatives have held such Hellenistic views? Perhaps, though they are not typical of the Pharisees we know about. One also wonders, because of Paul's defense of his independence, if the Judaizers have not charged that he is too dependent on the Jerusalem Christians (chapters 1-2). These problems have led to other alternatives. Some have suggested that there were two sets of opponents, the Jerusalem conservatives and the more syncretistic group;[31] however, Paul does not explicitly identify two groups. Others have proposed a group of recently circumcised *Gentile Christians* within the church, or a group of

---

[30] For a recent modification of this view, cf. G. Howard, *Paul: Crisis in Galatia.*

[31] E.g., the German scholar W. Lütgert, and D. Ropes, *The Singular Problem of the Epistle to the Galatians.*

Jewish Gnostic Christians.[32] A popular view modifies this to suggest that they are Jewish Christian missionaries rooted in a form of syncretistic Judaism found in Asia Minor (cf. the Corinthian opponents, 2 Cor 10–13). If so they did not follow the precise position of the Jerusalem conservatives, though from Paul's point of view, they were at one with them in the essential issue, their stress on circumcision and the Law. This theory is widely held today.[33] If we accept it, and we are inclined to do so, it is necessary to explain Paul's references to the Jerusalem Conference and the Antioch incident as Paul's way of viewing what the Jerusalem conservatives and the opponents *held in common* and what, to Paul, was the major threat to his gospel: the demand for circumcision and adherence to the Law.

Corinth

At Corinth we observe various phases in the development of the congregation beginning with 1 Corinthians and continuing through the various letter fragments of 2 Corinthians. In 1 Corinthians, from reports that have come back (to Ephesus) via "Chloe's people," Paul has learned that there is quarreling at Corinth, that various factions are proud of their special relationships with their "spiritual fathers," i.e., those who baptized them or those in whose name they were baptized (1:10–17; 3:1–9). These are Paul, Apollos, Peter, and perhaps Christ. As a result, these groups boast of special human wisdom (1:26–30; 3:18–23; 4:6–7) and brag about their special knowledge (*gnōsis,* cf. 8:1–3) and their unique spiritual gifts (2:12). Some of the Corinthians considered themselves more spiritually advanced than others, especially in their ability to "speak in tongues" (*glossalalia*), an ecstatic spiritual phenomenon. It appears that claims were being made for a kind of religious perfection, for some of the Corinthians believed that they were living the life of resurrection *already* (15) and that the community was a redeemed heavenly body (11-12). Others interpreted their freedom to mean they were "strong," not "weak" (8-10). Such views led to various ethical problems. One man boasted of living with his father's (second) wife which was legally incestuous; others were going to houses of prostitution (5-6). Still others were refraining from intercourse (7:1). The "strong" disturbed the "weak" by eating meat sacrificed to pagan gods

---

[32] Esp. J. Munck, *Paul and the Salvation of Mankind* (cf. 6:13, "those who are [now] being circumcised") and W. Schmithals, *Paul and the Gnostics,* respectively. Many critics do view the evidence as pointing to a proto-Gnosticism in Galatia; there is a good deal of discussion of "knowledge" in the Corinthian correspondence, and later Gnostics certainly used Paul, cf. E. Pagels, *The Gnostic Paul,* esp. pp. 101–14 (Galatians), just as they used the gospel of John; cf. chapter 11 below on "The Johannine School."

[33] H. D. Betz, "Galatians," *IDB Suppl.,* p. 352, cites Bornkamm, Wegenast, Koester, and Georgi. Betz himself asks if they might not be Jewish Christians who composed the Qumran-like views found in 2 Cor 6:14–7:1; cf. above, pp. 129–30. In his commentary, Betz resists identifying them precisely.

(8,10). The place of women in worship had become a problem (11:2–16). The rich abused the Lord's Supper by eating all the food and getting drunk before the poor arrived (11:17–34). In general, the church was in a state of crisis.

It is clear from all this that the Corinthians had interpreted Paul's view of freedom from the Law and special Christian wisdom in terms of Hellenistic religious "enthusiasm." The Hellenistic world tended strongly to think of religion as a manifestation of the power of the deity, of the ability to work miracles, of the experience of various kinds of ecstatic phenomena, of superior knowledge. Paul himself was a man of the Hellenistic world and had undoubtedly encouraged the Corinthians' spiritual enthusiasm, but the developments in Corinth were getting out of hand and were destroying the unity of the church both religiously and socially. In this context, opposition to Paul has arisen *within* the congregation: "Some are arrogant, as though I were not coming to you. But I will come to you soon, if the Lord wills, and I will find out not the talk of these arrogant people, but their power. For the kingdom of God does not consist in talk, but in power. What do you wish? Shall I come to you with a rod, or with love in a spirit of gentleness?" (4:18–21).

In 2 Corinthians we can observe a growing opposition to Paul sparked by "outsiders," and subsequently an easing of the opposition. After the visits of Timothy and Titus (the latter to help facilitate the collection, 2 Cor 8:6; 12:18), there came to Corinth the ones Paul labels sarcastically "superlative apostles" (2 Cor 3:1; 11:4–5, 11) and describes as "false apostles, deceitful workmen, disguising themselves as apostles of Christ" (11:13). They are clearly of Jewish background (11:22), they are complimentary of each other (10:12, 18), and they bear "letters of recommendation" (3:1–3). Paul says they preach "another Jesus" and have "a different spirit" (11:4). We can say a little more about them by their attack on Paul and Paul's defense. They say of Paul, "His letters are weighty and strong, but his bodily presence is weak, and his speech is of no account" (10:10; cf. 11:6). Much of Paul's defense centers around "boasting," that is, he can also boast, but he boasts about his trials as an apostle, making comparisons between his supposed "weakness" and his conviction that God demonstrates his power through weakness exemplified in the Cross (13:4). Clearly, then, his opponents were boasting about their superiority. Paul goes on to say that he, too, has had "visions and revelations of the Lord" (12:1); that the signs of a true apostle were performed "in all patience" when he was among them, that is, signs, wonders, and mighty works. Miracles, then, were being performed by the "superlative apostles." The Corinthians have even come to question what Paul might be doing with the collection as a result of these "enthusiasts" from the outside. Can we illumine them any further?[34]

Another feature of the Hellenistic world was the phenomenon of the professional propagandist of a new religion or philosophy. We say "religion or

---

[34] D. Georgi, "Corinthians, First Letter to the," and "Corinthians, Second Letter to the," *IDB Suppl.*, pp. 108–86, is a major source for this section. See also H. Conzelmann, *1 Corinthians* (Hermeneia), pp. 14–16.

philosophy" because in Hellenism the two had coalesced. Both were ways of successfully coming to terms with the reality of life in the world, and representatives of both sought converts or new adherents on the street corners of Hellenistic cities. These religious or philosophical propagandists, these missionaries, were very much of a type and exhibited the same general characteristics. They proclaimed the power of their divinity or hero or philosopher through stories of his miraculous achievements, including the overcoming of death. They themselves demonstrated the power of their faith or philosophy through miraculous healings, acts of prophecy or clairvoyance, and accounts of their own wonderful experiences. Moreover, they expected to live from the results of their labors. Those in the Stoic-Cynic tradition often lived by begging, which was both a livelihood and a means of attracting attention to themselves and their message. In the Hellenistic world, the Christian faith must necessarily have acquired missionaries of this type, and indeed, to many Paul must have seemed such a one. For Paul, the similarity was superficial.

Ultimately, Paul seems to have made some headway with the Corinthians, for 2 Corinthians shows some reconciliation (2 Cor 1:1–2:13; 7:5–16) and Paul finally made his awaited visit in behalf of the collection (2 Cor 8, 9).

Rome and Ephesus

The problem of identifying opponents at Rome centers around the meaning of the admonitions to the Romans in 14:1–15:13 and the question whether these admonitions have any relation to opponents mentioned in Romans 16:17–20. In 14:1–15:13 Paul admonishes "the weak" and "the strong" not to despise or pass judgment on each other, but to live in unity, harmony, and love. Do these seemingly concrete parenetic statements (contrast Rom 12–13), which focus on disputes over food and observances of special days, refer to actual groups at Rome about which Paul has learned indirectly, or, because he has not yet been there and the groups are not identified, do Paul's comments simply sum up his past experiences with factions? Clearly, he had had to counter opponents on food matters and special observances before (cf. Gal 2:12; 4:10), and differences between "the weak" and "the strong" on such matters were similar at Corinth (1 Cor 8, 10). This problem—actual groups or general parenesis—has been much debated recently, in part because it is bound up with the form and purpose of Romans, Paul's most mature letter.[35] If the general form of Paul's letter to the Romans as a whole is a "letter-essay,"[36] it is possible that Paul is doing both: he may be speaking about what he has learned about Rome, and doing so in the light of his painful experiences with

---

[35] K. P. Donfried, ed. *The Romans Debate*; E. Käsemann, *Commentary on Romans*, pp. 364–428.

[36] M. L. Stirnewalt, "The Form and Function of the Greek Letter-Essay," in *ibid.*, pp. 175–206; K. P. Donfried, "False Presuppositions in the Study of Romans," in *The Romans Debate*, pp. 145–46. Cf. the possibility above that the opponents in 1 Thessalonians are simply rhetorical.

his other churches. If the compromise solution is accepted, then it is difficult to identify any specific groups. Those who have attempted to identify them suggest a conflict between more "conservative" (perhaps Jewish, or at least more ascetically-oriented) Christians and (less ascetic) Greek Christians influenced by Hellenistic enthusiasm and spiritual freedom. If the conflict is one of "Jew and Greek" in relation to Christianity, it can be integrated into the whole of Romans more easily.

A compromise solution to Romans 14:1–15:3, however, is complicated by a more explicit reference to *outside* opponents in Romans 16:17–20. In this passage Paul recommends that "the brethren" avoid those who oppose "the doctrine which you have been taught," thereby creating dissensions and difficulties. "For such persons do not serve the Lord Christ, but their own belly, and by fair and flattering words they deceive the hearts of the simple-minded" (16:18). Then Paul commends their obedience and concludes with a typical letter-closing benediction (verse 20).

Before any comparison of this passage to 14:1–15:13 can be made, we must take note of complications. The opponents passage interrupts the context in chapter 16, being preceded by a little "letter of recommendation" for Phoebe, "a deacon of the church at Cenchreae (the eastern harbor area of Corinth) and greetings to twenty-six persons who are named and others in families and house-churches who are not (Rom 16:1–3; 16:4–16); and *despite* the letter-closing benediction of the opponents passage (verse 20), it is followed by greetings from Paul and seven friends and co-workers, as well as an un-Pauline "doxology" which scholars believe has been added later—in part because in some manuscripts it occurs after chapter 14, and in the earliest Romans manuscript (P[46]), it occurs after chapter 15! Was the opponents section originally part of chapter 16? If it was, did the highly unusual chapter 16 belong to the letter to the Romans? How does Paul know so many people at Rome, and how does this comport with the fact that he had not been there, and that he writes a general "letter-essay" to this church? Or do chapter 16 *and* its attack on opponents belong to the "letter-essay" and give it a more concrete situation which would, in turn, illumine the admonitions in 14:1–15:13? Most modern critics have argued that because chapter 16 contains greetings to Aquila and Priscilla who had been expelled from Rome at the time of the Edict of Claudius (A.D. 49) and had subsequently moved to Corinth and then to Ephesus (1 Cor 16:19; Acts 18:2), and because it also contains a greeting to Epaenetus, "the first fruits" (= convert) of *Asia* (16:5), the "letter of recommendation" accompanied by greetings was sent to an Asian church with which Paul was well acquainted, namely, the church in Ephesus. This is given some added weight by the fact that Rom 15:33 also has a final benediction. Some argue that Rom 16 could have been attached to a copy of the Romans letter and dispatched with Phoebe to Ephesus as Paul's statement to the churches of Asia, especially since he was headed for Jerusalem and had written to Rome, other key centers. If this is correct, and if 16:17–20 was part of chapter 16, we have evidence of opponents in Ephesus. But the question has recently been reopened and it has been argued that Paul could have had acquaintances in the Roman church since Nero had rescinded the Edict of Claudius in A.D. 54 and many of those who had been expelled were able to return to Rome. In fact, it has been suggested that one might then correlate the opponents passage with 14:1–15:13 and so explain the tensions between "the weak" and "the strong" by the recently returned Jewish Christians—especially in connection with food (verse 18: "such persons serve their own belly"). In this connection, we may recall that the opponents at Philippi are accused with: "their god is the belly" (Phil 3:19). But can the *internal* problems of 14:1–15:13 be easily equated with the *outside* opponents in 16:17–20? In the former case, Paul recommends unity, harmony, and love; in the latter, he counsels separation from the agitators. And what of the final benediction in Rom 15:33?[37] Whether in Ephesus or Rome, and we lean toward the former, it is clear that the opponents are viewed by Paul in language reminiscent of opponents in other areas, especially Philippi and Corinth.

Any discussion of the authority of Paul the apostle and his opposition on the mission field should take account of at least the following points: (1) the diverse nature of the sources of Galatians and Acts in connection with Paul's relation to Jerusalem; (2) Paul's emphasis on his "conversion" and call; (3) the possibility that not all Jewish Christians interpreted the Jerusalem Conference as Paul did; (4) the role of the collection as *at least* a symbol of unity in the church; (5) Paul's opposition to any group that sought to require circumcision and the Law as a prerequisite to becoming a Christian, for this was a hindrance to Christian freedom; (6) the probability that in most of the Hellenistic churches conflicts arose because Paul's opposition to such a prerequisite was interpreted to mean that the Christian was superior in his wisdom and new-found freedom, a superiority that was fostered by Hellenistic religious "enthusiasm"; and (7) the fostering of this enthusiasm by other Hellenistic Jewish Christian missionaries who came to Paul's churches and contributed to discord by attacking his authority on "charismatic" grounds. When this opposition occurred, Paul's response was to claim that his own authority was rooted in a different sort of "charisma," namely, the power of a loving God who acts through weakness. And the foundation for this claim was the Cross of Christ. In this way, Paul sought to put limitations on the misinterpretation of the freedom he himself had preached against slavery to circumcision and the Law. In this manner, he hoped to maintain Christian unity.

As 2 Peter put it, some things in Paul's letters are "hard to understand"; the second-century ascetics and Gnostics took up his writings as their own, using them as a basis for their denial of self and world in all of their ambiguity; but the Great Church accepted them, too, in part because it accepted the interpretation of Paul found in Luke-Acts, the Pauline school represented by the deutero-Paulines, and the Pastoral Letters. Later, these became (along with Hebrews) a major part of the New Testament canon.

[37] G. Klein, "Romans, Letter to the," *IDB Suppl.*, pp. 752–54.

Is this simply a story of Jews and Gentiles, and of church conflict? In large measure, yes. But it is also the story of a religious genius, a man of charisma, who felt called to an exciting and dangerous journey. In response to the charismatic enthusiasts, Paul boasts of his weakness:

> But whatever any one dares to boast of—I am speaking as a fool—I also dare to boast of that. Are they Hebrews? So am I. Are they Israelites? So am I. Are they descendants of Abraham? So am I. Are they servants of Christ? I am a better one—I am talking like a madman—with far greater labors, far more imprisonments, with countless beatings, and often near death. Five times I have received at the hands of the Jews the forty lashes less one. Three times I have been beaten with rods; once I was stoned. Three times I have been shipwrecked; a night and a day I have been adrift at sea; on frequent journeys, in danger from rivers, danger from robbers, danger from my own people, danger from Gentiles, danger in the city, danger in the wilderness, danger at sea, danger from false brethren; in toil and hardship, through many a sleepless night, in hunger and thirst, often without food, in cold and exposure. And, apart from other things, there is the daily pressure upon me of my anxiety for all the churches. Who is weak, and I am not weak? Who is made to fall, and I am not indignant? . . . And to keep me from being too elated by the abundance of revelations, a thorn was given me in the flesh, a messenger of Satan, to harass me to keep me from being too elated. Three times I besought the Lord about this, that it should leave me; but he said to me, "My grace is sufficient for you, for my power is made perfect in weakness." I will all the more gladly boast of my weaknesses, that the power of Christ may rest upon me. For the sake of Christ, then, I am content with weaknesses, insults, hardships, persecutions, and calamities; for when I am weak, then I am strong (2 Cor 11:21b–29; 12:7–10).

The Pauline Communities

It is clear from the above that within Paul's communities there was friction about his authority, and that other missionaries made claims of authority in opposition to Paul.

Several other features of Paul's churches should be mentioned.[38] If Jesus' parable teaching and the collection of Jesus' sayings called "Q" reflect a village or agrarian setting in (Syria-)Palestine, Paul's letters reflect the urban culture of Hellenized cities in the eastern provinces of the Roman Empire. The commercial and political language of the centers all over the Roman Empire (including those of Palestine) was Greek. Paul, who was a Jew reared and, at least par-

---

[38] W. Meeks, "The Social World of Pauline Christianity," *Aufstieg und Niedergang der römischen Welt* (to be published).

tially, educated in Tarsus, traveled the Roman roads appealing to Greek-speaking Gentiles, some of whom were undoubtedly on the fringes of Diaspora synagogues ("God-fearers"). Thus, Pauline mission Christianity was an urban phenomenon.

Within the Greco-Roman cities, the Christians met in "house-churches" (cf. 1 Cor 16:19; Phlm 2; Rom 16) where they worshipped, discussed, had communal meals, and in general carried on their common life, including the reading of letters from apostles.[39] Such houses had to be large enough for a number of Christians—other "households" and individuals—in which to meet. The "household" itself was not just a family, but included relatives, household slaves, hired hands, and occasionally professional or trade partners and tenants. Whole households were sometimes baptized into Christianity at once (1 Cor 1:16). This undoubtedly created some conflict since a typical household was hierarchically organized from the head of the household (*pater familias*) down; yet, as Christians, they were supposed to be of equal status. The house-churches were of course local; but Paul reminded them that they were linked to a larger group in their own geographical areas (2 Cor 1:1) and, indeed, to the "church of God" itself (1 Cor 1:2), an idea that the later Pauline school developed. For Paul himself, this is implied in the collection.

What kinds of people became Christians? This question has been extensively studied, especially in relation to Corinth.[40] In the past it was argued that as a whole Christianity was a lower-class social movement. It is certainly true that its egalitarian emphasis, both in the Jesus tradition and in Paul's theology, attracted adherents from the lower classes, that is, people who because of their status (artisans, freedmen, slaves, the poor in general) were alienated from social and political power. But it is equally clear that it attracted members of the upper classes who often provided leadership. The "house-church" is a phenomenon which implies a house large enough for a number of Christians to assemble in; at Corinth there were without doubt *some* of "noble birth," and perhaps also some "wise" and "powerful" in the worldly sense (1 Cor 1:26). A study of particular individuals in Paul's churches, some of whom have political positions or offer special services, or can afford to travel bears this out. We know, for example, of the Lord's Supper controversy at Corinth where it appears the wealthy were wont to think of the supper as a Hellenistic banquet, or as a dinner party at one of the clubs. They ate their own meals and got drunk while others remained hungry (11:21). In this situation, "those who have nothing" were humiliated (1 Cor 11:17–34). Paul's solution is that they should wait for one another, or if the wealthy are hungry, they should eat at home (11:33–34).

Although conflicts arose in the Pauline communities the members strove to maintain a united front before others so that Christianity might be positively perceived by "outsiders" or "nonbelievers." This attitude had some precedent

[39] A. J. Malherbe, *Social Aspects of Early Christianity*, chapter 3.
[40] See the writings of the German scholar, G. Theissen.

among Diaspora Jews, but the language of Paul also suggests something of a "sectarian" movement. The Christians are "chosen," "beloved," and "holy ones" who reflect family relationships, that is, "father" to "children" along with the relationship "brother" or "sister." Pauline Christianity had rituals of entrance (baptism, Rom 6) and perpetuation (the Lord's Supper, 1 Cor 10:16–17; 11:23–25). Paul thinks of ethical behavior in terms of "imitation"—his "children" should imitate him as he imitates Christ (1 Cor 11:1), and there is also exclusion of the radical nonconformist (1 Cor 5:2, 11). Nevertheless, the communities are not totally exclusivistic. For Paul, the new era meant abolishment of the distinctions between Jew and Gentile, slave and free, male and female (Gal 3:28). Christians are not asked to break off all relations with outsiders (1 Cor 5:9–13); they are permitted to be entertained at the homes of non-Christians and even to eat "meat offered to (pagan) idols"—*if* the practice does not offend the conscience of a Christian brother (1 Cor 8; 10:23–30). Were these communities "sectarian?" Yes—and no. W. Meeks writes:

> In the letters we see Paul and his followers wrestling with a fundamental ambiguity in their conception of the social character of the church. On the one hand, it is formed as an eschatological sect, with a strong sense of group boundaries, reinforced by images of a dualistic tendency and by foundation stories of a crucified Messiah raised from the dead as the root symbol of the way God's action in the world is to be perceived and followed. On the other hand, it is an open sect, concerned not to offend "those outside" but to attract them to its message and if possible to its membership. It has other forms of self-description and basic symbols which point toward universality and comprehensiveness: it is the people of the one God, including both Jew and Gentile. Indeed, Christ is the "last Adam," the "new *anthropos* ['man']," the image of God and therefore the restoration of humanity to its created unity.[41]

Further Reading

The literature on Paul is extensive. In this chapter, we shall give a general bibliography plus some works that have special relevance to the subjects discussed; further bibliography will be given in the following chapter, and the student is advised to consult both.

There are several "classic" single volumes on Paul:

A. Deissmann, *Saint Paul: A Study in Social and Religious History.*
M. Dibelius, and W.G. Kümmel, *Paul.*
A. D. Nock, *Saint Paul.*

[41] W. Meeks, " 'Since Then You Would Need to Go Out of the World': Group Boundaries in Pauline Christianity," in T.J. Ryan, ed., *Critical History and Biblical Faith. New Testament Perspectives,* p. 22.

W. D. Davies, *Paul and Rabbinic Judaism.*
H. J. Schoeps, *Paul: The Theology of the Apostle in the Light of Jewish Religious History.*
S. Sandmel, *The Genius of Paul.*

Still standard as a general work today is G. Bornkamm's *Paul* in two parts: *I. Life and Work; II. Gospel and Theology.* Part I is most significant for this chapter. Bornkamm uses the insights of Dieter Georgi, some of whose works are listed below. Another account is in *JBC,* J. A. Fitzmyer's "A Life of Paul" (pp. 215-22). Fitzmyer gives excellent bibliographies down into the 1960s.

On the evaluation of Acts as history, see J. Knox, "Acts and the Pauline Letter Corpus," E. Haenchen, "The Book of Acts as Source Material for the History of Early Christianity," and P. Vielhauer, "On the 'Paulinism' of Acts," collected in L. Keck and J. L. Martyn, *Studies in Luke-Acts* (pp. 279-89; 258-78; 33-50, respectively). Somewhat technical but valuable for various approaches is A. J. Mattill, "The Value of Acts as a Source for the Study of Paul," in C. Talbert, ed., *Perspectives on Luke-Acts,* pp. 76-98. On special problems see the following commentaries:

H. D. Betz, *Galatians.* (Hermeneia)
H. Conzelmann, *1 Corinthians.* (Hermeneia)
E. Haenchen, *The Acts of the Apostles.*
E. Käsemann, *Commentary on Romans.*
E. Lohse, *Colossians and Philemon.*

Other useful treatments are:

PCB, pp. 870-81, "The Apostolic Age and the Life of Paul" (W. D. Davies).
IDB, vol. 3, pp. 681-704, "Paul the Apostle" (A. C. Purdy).
IDB Suppl., pp. 166-67, "Chronology, Pauline" (J. C. Hurd); pp. 648-51, "Paul the Apostle" (J. C. Hurd); and the relevant *IDB Suppl.* articles listed below by book, especially pp. 183-86, "Corinthians, Second Letter to the" (D. Georgi).

The "Introductions" have discussions of the chronology of Paul's life and work:

W. G. Kümmel, *Intro.,* pp. 252-55.
W. Marxsen, *Intro.,* pp. 17-23.
R. Fuller, *Intro.,* pp. 6-15.

Especially significant for Paul's background today is E. P. Sanders, *Paul and Palestinian Judaism;* most important for the attempt to understand Paul's "conversion" as a call is K. Stendahl, "The Apostle Paul and the Introspective Conscience of the West," reprinted in W. Meeks, *The Writings of St. Paul,* pp. 422-34, and in K. Stendahl, *Paul Among Jews and Gentiles,* pp. 78-96; this provoked a response from E. Käsemann, "Justification and Salvation History in the Epistle to the Romans," *Perspectives on Paul*, pp. 60–78, to which Stendahl replied, pp. 129–33.

Much excitement in recent years has centered on the discussion of Paul's "divine man" opponents in 2 Corinthians, precipitated by D. Georgi, *Die Gegner des Paulus im 2. Korintherbrief: Studien zur religiösen Propaganda in der Spätantike*, a truly magisterial work. One can gain an impression of Georgi's views in *IDB Suppl.*, pp. 183–86, "Corinthians, Second Letter to the." Other discussions of Paul's opponents can be found in the commentaries cited above and in G. Bornkamm, *Paul*, pp. 18–22, 32–35, 82–84 (at Philippi); pp. 174–76 (restatement in Romans), and *PCB*, pp. 877–78. Especially important for Romans 16 is K. P. Donfried, ed., *The Romans Debate*, where Donfried's article "A Short Note on Romans 16" occurs (pp. 50–60) defending its place in Romans.

We have also drawn on several works attempting to describe the "social world" of Paul:

R. F. Hock, *The Social Context of Paul's Ministry. Tentmaking and Apostleship.*
B. Holmberg, *Paul and Power.*
A. J. Malherbe, *Social Aspects of Early Christianity.*
W. Meeks, " 'Since Then You Would Need to Go Out of the World': Group Boundaries in Pauline Christianity," in T. J. Ryan, ed., *Critical History and Biblical Faith. New Testament Perspectives*, pp. 4–29.
W. Meeks, "The Social World of Pauline Christianity," *Aufstieg und Niedergang der römischen Welt* (to be published).
J. H. Schütz, *Paul and the Anatomy of Apostolic Authority.*
J. H. Schütz, "Steps Toward a Sociology of Primitive Christianity: A Critique of the Work of Gerd Theissen," an unpublished paper distributed to the "Social World of Early Christianity" Group of the American Academy of Religion/Society of Biblical Literature Annual Meeting, December 27–31, 1977, San Francisco Hilton Hotel. The writings of Theissen in this area have made a tremendous impact on many scholars.
G. Theissen, *The Social Setting of Pauline Christianity.* Trans. John H. Schütz.

For a brief analysis of 1 Thessalonians, see:

PCB, pp. 996–1000 (W. Neill).
JBC, pp. 227–33 (J. T. Forestall).
IDB, vol. 4, pp. 621–25 (F. W. Beare).
IDB Suppl., pp. 900–01 (J. Hurd).
W. G. Kümmel, *Intro.*, pp. 255–62.
W. Marxsen, *Intro.*, pp. 30–36.
R. Fuller, *Intro.*, pp. 19–23.
W. Meeks, *Writings*, pp. 3–10.

The first five works listed above all accept 2 Thessalonians as Pauline, whereas the others see it as pseudonymous. This division is representative of responsible New Testament scholarly opinion on the matter.

For Galatians, see:

PCB, pp. 973–79 (J. N. Sanders).
JBC, pp. 236–46 (J. A. Fitzmyer).
IDB, vol. 2, pp. 338–43 (J. Knox).
IDB Suppl., pp. 352–53 (H. D. Betz).
W. G. Kümmel, *Intro.*, pp. 294–304.
W. Marxsen, *Intro.*, pp. 45–58.
R. Fuller, *Intro.*, pp 23–31.
W. Meeks, *Writings*, pp. 10–22.

For the Corinthian correspondence, see:

PCB, pp. 954–72 (C. S. C. Williams).
JBC, pp. 254–75 (1 Corinthians: R. Kugelman), pp. 276–90 (2 Corinthians: J. O'Rourke).
IDB, vol. 1, pp. 685–98 (S. M. Gilmour).
IDB Suppl., pp. 180–86 (D. Georgi).
W. G. Kümmel, *Intro.*, pp. 269–93.
W. Marxsen, *Intro.*, pp. 71–91.
R. Fuller, *Intro.*, pp. 40–51.
W. Meeks, *Writings*, pp. 22–66.

For Philippians, see:

PCB, pp. 985–89 (G. R. Beasley-Murray).
JBC, pp. 247–53 (J. A. Fitzmyer).
IDB, vol. 3, pp. 787–91 (B. S. Duncan).
IDB Suppl., pp. 665–66 (H. Koester).
W. G. Kümmel, *Intro.*, pp. 320–35.
W. Marxsen, *Intro.*, pp. 59–68.
R. Fuller, *Intro.*, pp. 31–38.
W. Meeks, *Writings*, pp. 94–101.

For the letter to the Romans, see:

PCB, pp. 940–53 (T. W. Manson).
JBC, pp. 291–331 (J. A. Fitzmyer).
IDB, vol. 4, pp. 112–22 (F. W. Beare).
IDB Suppl., pp. 752–54 (G. Klein).
W. G. Kümmel, *Intro.*, pp. 305–20.
W. Marxsen, *Intro.*, pp. 92–109.
R. Fuller, *Intro.*, pp. 51–57.
W. Meeks, *Writings*, pp. 66–94.

For the letter to Philemon, see:

PCB, pp. 994–95 (C. F. D. Moule).
JBC, pp. 332–33 (J. A. Fitzmyer).
IDB, vol. 3, pp. 782–84 (M. E. Lyman).
IDB Suppl., pp. 663–64 (W. G. Rollins).
W. G. Kümmel, *Intro.*, pp. 348–50.
W. Marxsen, *Intro.*, pp. 69–70.
R. Fuller, *Intro.*, pp. 38–40.
W. Meeks, *Writings*, pp. 101–04.

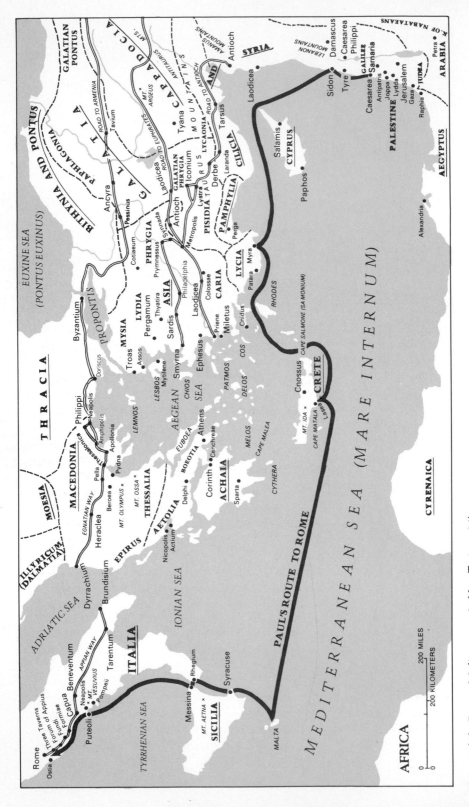

Rome and the Eastern Mediterranean in New Testament times.

CHAPTER SIX

THE THEOLOGY OF PAUL IN HIS LETTERS

Paul of Tarsus, educated in the Greek tradition, a Diaspora Jew with Pharisaic training, of the tribe of Benjamin, former persecutor of the Christian church, had a "religious experience": he received a revelation of Jesus Christ which he associated with his call to become apostle to the Gentiles. He became a Christian missionary who was especially equipped by his background and training to communicate his gospel to the non-Jewish inhabitants of the Roman Empire. With zeal he planted house-churches in the major urban centers of Asia Minor and Macedonia-Greece. Although he would stay for a short period, we mainly catch glimpses of him on the move, as he established a small community where none had existed, or on his travels. He usually supported himself as a tentmaker. Often he encountered opposition from political authorities and religious opponents. How did he nurture his communities once he had moved on to another location? How did he stay in touch with them? One way was by letters. In this chapter we shall examine Paul's letters and attempt to gain some understanding of them. After looking at how Paul's letters compare with other letters of his period, and noting a few of the traditions he followed in them, we shall read his correspondence with the aid of interpretative outlines. The chapter will conclude with a brief summary of some of his main theological ideas and his approach to ethical problems.

PAUL AS A WRITER OF LETTERS

When Paul was prevented from visiting a community for a period of time, he continued a dialogue with it by means of oral reports from travelers, co-workers, or delegations, and such intermediaries delivered his letters. Thus his communication continued, the reports supplementing the letters and vice versa. Paul's letters were normally dictated to a secretary (*amanuensis*; cf. Rom 16:22: "I, Tertius, the writer of this letter, greet you in the Lord"); yet, Paul would sometimes give his stamp of authority to a letter by composing the last lines (1 Cor 16:21; Gal 6:11; cf. 2 Thess 3:17; Col 4:18). The letters were usually written to the whole community or communities in a specific geographical area and read publicly to those gathered in the house-church. In 1 Thess 5:27, he stresses that his letter be read publicly, and as we shall see, this tradition is carried on in his name by his school (2 Thess 3:14–15).

How do Paul's letters compare with other letters of the period? This is an important question because an understanding of the medium in which he writes will be an important aid in understanding his message. We are fortunate to have access not only to more "literary" types of letters from classical litera-ture, including the "letter-essay," but to a large number of "nonliterary" papy-rus letters discovered by archeologists.[1] These include personal letters to friends and relatives, business letters, and various kinds of governmental, mili-tary, diplomatic, and legal correspondence. The writers of these personal let-ters, for example, clearly attempted to maintain friendly, cordial relationships (*philophronesis*) between themselves and their recipients just as Paul did in his letters (esp. 2 Cor 1:1–2:13; 7:5–16; Phil 1:3–3:1a; 4:1–20). Furthermore it is clear that Greco-Roman letter writers follow a rather set pattern, or form, and that Paul modifies it. To illustrate this point, we offer as an example a typical personal letter from the papyri and compare it to Paul's most personal letter, the letter to Philemon.

Apion's Letter to His Father Epimachus[2]

Apion to Epimachus his father and lord, many greetings. Before all things I pray that you are in health, and that you prosper and fare well continu-ally together with my sister and her daughter and my brother. I thank the lord Serapis that when I was in peril on the sea he saved me immediately. When I came to Miseni, I received as viaticum [journey money] from the Caesar three pieces of gold. And it is well with me but I urge you, my lord father, to write me a little letter: first, about your welfare; second, about my brother and sister; third, so that I may do obeisance to your hand, because you have taught me well and I have hopes therefore of advancing quickly, if the gods are willing. Greet Capito much and my brother and sister and Serenilla and my friends. By Euctemon I am send-ing you a little picture of myself. Furthermore, my name is [now] Antonis Maximus. Be well, I pray. Centuris Athenonica [my military unit]. The following send their greetings: Serenus the son of Agathus Daemon, and

---

[1] W. Doty, *Letters in Primitive Christianity*; C. Roetzel, *The Letters of Paul*, chapters 2 and 3; N.A. Dahl, "Letter," *IDB Suppl.*, pp. 538–41. For a definition of the letter-essay, see below, p. 188.

[2] H. Kee, *The Origin of Christianity. Sources and Documents*, pp. 264–65.

... the son of ... and Turbo the son of Gallonius and ... the son of ...
[Farewell].

[On the back]
To Philadelphis for Epimaxus from Apion his son

Give this to the first cohort	of the Apamenians to /?/
	Julianus An ...
the Liblarios, from Apion	so that he may convey it to
	Epimachus his father.

The Letter to Philemon

Paul was in prison (probably in Ephesus) and there he met a runaway
slave, Onesimus (Greek: "useful"), whom he converted to Christianity. According to Roman law, runaway slaves had to be returned to their masters and
were liable to severe punishment, even death; anyone who helped a slave was
liable to his master for damages. In this instance however, Onesimus' master,
Philemon, was a Christian, and so Paul (in his letter) carefully blended punctilious observance of the slave law with shrewdly conceived appeals to Philemon.
Philemon is addressed as a "beloved fellow worker" and commended for his
love and faith. Paul assures him that as an apostle, he could command him to
do his duty, but prefers to appeal to his free will. In passing Paul puns that
Onesimus had been "useless" to Philemon, but now he was "useful" to both of
them (verse 11). Paul then offers to pay any damages incurred. He again makes
a pun in writing that he "wants some benefit" (*onaimēn*) from Onesimus (verse
20), and writes he is confident of Philemon's obedience. He asks him to prepare for his coming and he concludes with greetings and a benediction.

We may now compare the letter to Epimachus and the letter to Philemon
to illustrate the extent to which Paul uses conventional letter-writing forms.

		Papyrus Letter	**Philemon**
A.	**Introduction**		
I.	Salutation		
	1. Sender	Apion	Paul; Timothy
	2. Recipient	Epimachus	Philemon; Apphia; Archippus; his household
	3. Greeting	"Many greetings"	Grace to you and peace from God our Father and the Lord Jesus Christ
II.	Thanksgiving/prayer	Prays for their well-being and thanks God for a safe journey	I thank God always when I remember you in my prayers

	Papyrus Letter	Philemon
B. Central Section		
III. Body	Statement about wages; hopes for advancement	Paul asks Philemon to "accept" the slave Onesimus
IV. Parenesis or other commands	Urges father to write to him about the family	Receive him as you would me . . . Charge that to my account . . . Refresh my heart in Christ . . . Prepare a guest room for me . . .
C. Conclusion		
V. Greetings to . . .	Capito; my brother; my sister; Serenilla; my friends	Absent, but present in other letters; implicit in "you" (=recipients)
Greetings from . . .	Serenus; –?–; Turbo; –?–	Epaphras; Mark; Aristarchus; Demas; Luke; my fellow workers
VI. Closing or benediction	Absent due to text mutilation; usually, "Farewell"	The grace of the Lord Jesus Christ be with your spirit

These parallels speak for themselves; Paul follows the customary letter form, making three interesting changes. Whereas the customary Greek letter usually has a simple "farewell" as a closing, Paul's letter has a religious benediction. Indeed, other letters of Paul have several common "closing" elements: the "peace wish"; the kiss; an apostolic command; or a doxology. The second and third changes become also customary in Paul, namely, the change of the simple "greetings" (*chairein*) to the similar Greek term "grace" (*charis*), which is one of Paul's key theological terms: it refers essentially to God's free gift of salvation in Jesus Christ. The other change is that Paul adds the typical Jewish greeting, "Peace" (*Shalōm*), but Christianizes it with "peace from . . . our Lord Jesus Christ." This greeting formula is highly characteristic of Paul's letters. All of Paul's letters have this overall structure, although of course, he modifies it to fit special circumstances. In the letter to the Galatians, where Paul is angry about the opponents, his salutation launches into a definition of his apostleship (Gal 1:1: "Paul, an apostle—not from men nor through man, but through Jesus Christ and God the Father, who raised him from the dead"). Then he goes immediately to the controversy, omitting the usual "thanksgiving," normally a highly complimentary section to the recipients. Romans has a somewhat analogous adaptation; since Paul has not been to Rome, the salutation contains a long summary of his gospel and defines his apostolic mission (1:1–7). Although his salutations usually speak to the specific situation of the recipients, he sometimes alters them with materials from the liturgical tradition. The central section contains the body and the parenesis. The body of the letter covers the major themes of the letter, as we shall see in our exegetical surveys. He usually begins with some formula of request ("I beseech you . . .") or disclosure ("I would not have you ignorant . . .") and closes with some statement about his itinerary. He omits this only in Galatians to whom he is unable to return, and so he refers to his previous visit (4:12–15).

Undoubtedly because of the limited scope of the letters our examples above are not very parenetic. Paul usually has a longer ethical exhortation section or homily ("sermonette") at this point. This does not mean that he omits parenetic exhortations in the body of the letter for shorter clusters of moral maxims about Christian virtues or virtue and vice lists common in the Hellenistic schools may crop up almost anywhere, but the lengthier parenetic sections normally occur after the body of the letter and before the conclusion. We shall have occasion to deal with several important ethical matters in Paul's letters below.

We have already noted various possibilities for the conclusion of Paul's letters. The "peace wish," like the term "peace" in the greeting, reflects the Hebrew *Shalōm*, that is, well-wishing for one's health, though Paul sometimes uses it as an occasion for recalling a major theme in the letter (1 Thess 4:9). Then come greetings and often another reference to "grace." As Paul opens with "grace" and "peace," so he closes with "peace" and "grace." As in Hellenistic letters, a prayer request may be added (1 Thess 5:25; Rom 15:30). "The kiss" which follows has sometimes been thought to be a liturgical sign, that is, that after the reading of the letter the Christians would celebrate the liturgy. It is more likely a sign of affection within the Christian family. Then finally comes the benediction with its word of grace— occasionally related to a threat (1 Cor 16:23; cf. 1 Thess 5:27; Gal 6:17), or perhaps an apocalyptic cry, probably from the eucharistic liturgy (1 Cor 16:22: "Our Lord, come!" cf. Rev 22:20).

Our model of comparison has been Paul's most personal letter. Even that, however, has its public side since it was intended to be read to those gathered in the house-church (Phlm 2), probably at Colossae (cf. Col 4:9). Moreover, this is not the only type of letter in the Pauline corpus since we find a letter of recommendation for Phoebe (Rom 16:1–2; cf. 2 Cor 3:1–3 a reference to the opponents' letters of recommendation); letters stressing thanksgiving (Phil 1:3–3:1a; 4:10–20); a response to a previous letter (1 Cor 7–15); an apologetic letter, also containing advice (Galatians); a parenetic letter of exhortation (1 Thessalonians); and a "letter-essay" (Romans 1–15). Although these are in part contained *within* Paul's letters, they are all well-known types in the Greco-Roman world.

As we have said it was essential for Paul to stay in touch with his communities in order to continue his conversations with the believers and to challenge the views of the opponents. These letters employed the conventional forms of the day, modified in the direction of Christian faith and practice. As such, Paul's letters were an expression of his role as apostle to the Gentiles.

OUTLINE OF LETTER STRUCTURE

		1 Thessalonians	1 Corinthians	2 Corinthians	Galatians	Philippians	Romans
INTRODUCTION	**I. SALUTATION**						
	A. Sender	1:1a	1:1	1:1a	1:1–2a	1:1	1:1–6
	B. Recipient	1:1b	1:2	1:1b	1:2b	1:1	1:7a
	C. Greeting	1:1c	1:3	1:2	1:3–5	1:2	1:7b
	II. THANKSGIVING	1:2–10 2:13 3:9–10	1:4–9	1:3–7	None!	1:3–11	1:8–17
CENTRAL SECTION	**III. Body**	2:1–3:8 (possibly 3:11–13)	1:10–4:21	1:8–9:15 (letter fragments) 10:1–13:10 (letter fragment)	1:6–4:31	1:12–2:11 3:2–4:1 4:10–20	1:18–11:36
	IV. ETHICAL EXHORTATION AND INSTRUCTIONS	4:1–5:22	5:1–16:12 16:13–18 (closing parenesis)	13:11a (summary)	5:1–6:10 6:11–15 (letter summary)	2:12–3:1 4:2–6	12:1–15:13 15:14–32 (travel plans and closing parenesis)
CONCLUSION	**V. CLOSING**						
	A. Peace Wish	5:23–24	—	13:11b	6:16	4:7–9	15:33
	B. Greetings	—	16:19–20a	13:13	—	4:21–22	16:3–15(?)
	C. Kiss	5:26	16:20b	13:12	—	—	16:16(?)
	Apostolic Command	5:27	16:22	—	6:17	—	—
	D. Benediction	5:28	16:23–24	13:14	6:18	4:23	16:20(?)

Reprinted from *The Letters of Paul: Conversations in Context* by Calvin J. Roetzel, p. 28 (slightly modified). Copyright John Knox Press 1975. Used by permission.

TRADITIONS IN PAUL'S LETTERS[3]

In reading Paul's letters, it will be helpful to identify the way in which he makes his points by drawing on traditions. Though Paul claimed that he was not *taught* his gospel (Gal 1:11–12), he did remain at Damascus (among Christians?) three years, visited Peter and James at Jerusalem for a little over two weeks, associated with Christians in the areas of Syria and Cilicia, and he notes that his gospel was recognized at the Jerusalem Conference. At these locations, he undoubtedly became acquainted with christological confessions and hymns, liturgical formulae, and "words of the Lord." Moreover, he was deeply immersed in the Scriptures and argues from them in ways he learned from his Pharisaic background. He was also educated in the Greek traditions, as his use of rhetorical devices, literary conventions, and parenetic traditions show. Certainly, Paul did not live in a vacuum; others had gone before him.

Scholars trained in various types of literary criticism have learned to recognize and isolate a number of these influences as they appear in Paul's discussions. They often interrupt Paul's line of argument, are sometimes introduced by well-known terms for transmitting traditions, and have a certain poetic or hymnic style; they contain basic christological ideas (not always Paul's), and have a number of atypical terms and phrases. Here are a few typical examples.

- A death-resurrection-appearance tradition is recognizable by technical terms for transmitting oral traditions ("delivered . . . received"), by a formal pattern, and a number of atypical terms and phrases:
  (For I *delivered* to you as of first importance what I also *received*,)
  that Christ died for our sins in accordance with the scriptures
  that he was buried
  that he was raised on the third day in accordance with the scriptures,
  and that he appeared to Cephas, then to the twelve.   (1 Cor 15:3–5)
- A christological confession:
  . . . if you confess with your lips that Jesus is Lord and believe in your heart that God raised him from the dead, you will be saved.   (Rom 10:9)
- A christological creed that does not accord precisely with Paul's views of Jesus as the preexistent Son of God:
  (. . . the gospel concerning his Son)
  who was descended from David according to the flesh and designated Son of God in power according to the Spirit of holiness by his resurrection from the dead . . .   (Rom 1:3–4)
- A christological hymn in Phil 2:6–11 (see above, chapter 3, p. 83).
- A Lord's Supper tradition with the technical terms for transmitting tradition:
  For I *received* from the Lord what I also *delivered* to you, that the Lord Jesus on the night when he was betrayed took bread, and when he had

[3] A. M. Hunter, *Paul and His Predecessors*; C. Roetzel, *The Letters of Paul*, chapter 3.

given thanks, he broke it, and said, "This is my body which is for you. Do this in remembrance of me." In the same way also the cup, after supper, saying, "This cup is the new covenant in my blood. Do this, as often as you drink it, in remembrance of me."   (1 Cor 11:23–25)

- A baptismal liturgy:
(For as many of you as were baptized into Christ have put on Christ.)
There is neither Jew nor Greek,
There is neither slave nor free,
There is neither male nor female;
For you are all one in Christ Jesus.   (Gal 3:27–28; cf. 1 Cor 12:13; Col 3:11)

- A prayer doxology:
Thanks be to God through Jesus Christ our Lord.   (Rom 7:25)

- A "word of the Lord" (that is, a tradition believed to be from Jesus):
To the married I give the charge, not I but the Lord, that the wife should not separate from her husband . . . and that the husband should not divorce his wife.   (1 Cor 7:10–11)

- A parenetic tradition listing or cataloguing vices and virtues:
Now the works of the flesh are plain: immorality, impurity, licentiousness, idolatry, sorcery, enmity, strife, jealousy, anger, selfishness, dissension, party spirit, envy, drunkenness, carousing, and the like . . . But the fruit of the Spirit is love, joy, peace, patience, kindness, goodness, faithfulness, gentleness, self-control . . .   (Gal 5:19–22)

- A proverb:
Bad company ruins good morals.   (1 Cor 15:33)

We conclude by noting that Paul was immersed in the Scriptures (mainly what became the "Old Testament") and frequently used them as a source to buttress his position. Most of his allusions and quotations come from the Greek Septuagint, but many of his arguments rely on methods which, however strange to modern ears, were known among the Jewish scholars of his day. We cite two examples:

- A known Jewish "midrashic" (interpretative) legend given Christian meaning:
(In speaking of the Israelites' wilderness wanderings after the Exodus from Egypt, Paul refers to the Rock.)
I want you to know, brethren, that our fathers were all under a cloud, and all passed through the sea, and all were baptized into Moses in the cloud and in the sea, and all ate the same supernatural food (e.g., manna, cf. Exod 16:4–35), and all drank the same supernatural drink (Exod 17:6; Num 20:2–13). For they drank from the supernatural Rock which followed them, *and the Rock was Christ.* Nevertheless with most of them God was not pleased; for they were overthrown in the wilderness. Now these things are warnings to us, not to desire evil as they did. . .   (1 Cor 10:1–6; cf. Tosefta, *Sukkah* 3:11, etc.)

• A word association between "will" (a Greek term translating "covenant" in the Septuagint) and "covenant," and an interpretation of the *collective noun* "descendants," i.e., "seed," or "offspring":

To give a human example, brethren: no one annuls even *a man's will*, or adds to it, once it has been ratified. Now the promises were made to Abraham and to his offspring. *It does not say, "And to offsprings," referring, to many; but, referring to one, "And to your offspring"* (Gen 12:7, etc.), *which is Christ.* This is what I mean: the law (of Moses) which came four hundred and thirty years afterward, does not annul a covenant (with Abraham) previously ratified by God (like a will), so as to make the promise void. For if the (willed) inheritance is by law, it is no longer by promise; but God gave it to Abraham by a promise.

Why then the law? It was added because of transgressions, *till the offspring should come to whom the promise had been made. . .* (Gal 3:15–19a)

In our outlines below, we shall occasionally identify such traditional elements in order to understand how Paul makes his points as a mature apostle, standing not in isolation, but in the stream of Hellenistic Jewish Mission Christianity.

Having used Philemon as a model, and noted some sources in Paul's letters, we shall now begin to give brief exegetical outlines of his letters to churches. These outlines are no more than guides to aid you in reading the letters themselves. With the structure or outline given below you will find a great deal of help in the comments given on individual points in the *Oxford Annotated Bible*, or in Wayne A. Meeks' *The Writings of St. Paul*, both of which print the text of the Revised Standard Version with introduction and comments.

First Thessalonians

According to the itinerary established above, Paul entered Macedonia and established his first European house-church in Philippi, to which he later wrote several letters from prison (probably from Ephesus). He then traveled the major Roman highway, the Ignatian Way, westward across Macedonia to Thessalonica, the capital of Macedonia, where he established another congregation. While there Paul and his companions had worked hard to support themselves, but they had been treated shabbily (1 Thess 2:2). Acts suggests that their major opposition came from Jews who resented Paul's preaching in the synagogue and who were jealous of the conversion of "God-fearers" to Christianity. As a result, the Jews incited the rabble to riot and Jason, whose house was the center of activity, along with some of the brethren, were brought before the city authorities and charged with treason against Caesar because of their messianic beliefs. The brethren then sent Paul and his companions away by night (Acts 17:1–9). We cannot be sure of all this since Paul himself—if the highly anti-Jewish passage is from Paul[4]—says that both the converts and the opposition

---

[4] See chapter 5, *n.* 5.

came directly from Gentiles (1 Thess 2:14). In any case the small band of missionaries, after some time there (Acts 17:2 says only three weeks), moved on to Athens. Paul and his companions wanted to return to Thessalonica but, as he says, "Satan hindered us" (1 Thess 2:18); so he sent Timothy from Athens (1 Thess 3:1) and went on to Corinth. He arrived there about A.D. 49 (the Gallio Inscription) and he stayed about eighteen months (Acts 18:12–17). 1 Thessalonians was probably written from Corinth, ca. 51.

The primary teaching of 1 Thessalonians, as we have seen, is in the area of eschatology. Paul presents the Christian faith as essentially a matter of believing that Jesus is God's Son, that God has raised him from the dead, and that the risen Jesus will shortly return to the earth as judge and redeemer. He presents the Christian life as essentially a matter of preparing oneself for the coming of Jesus as judge and redeemer, and he gives form and content to the expectation of the coming of Jesus, the parousia. They synoptic gospel source Q has the same understanding of the Christian faith and the Christian life, and it also has the same concern to give form and content to the expectation of the parousia. But though 1 Thessalonians is in many respects close to Q and to the characteristic theology of earliest Christianity, it is also distinctively Pauline. In 5:9–10 we find a first statement of themes that were to become characteristic of the Pauline theology: the concept of Jesus offering to human beings salvation from the wrath of God, and that of Jesus dying "for us so that . . . we might live with him." With respect to the letter's form, there is an unusually long thanksgiving for the Thessalonian's steadfastness in the face of persecution (1:2–3:13).

1:1 *Characteristic Christianized salutation.*

1:2–3:13 *Thanksgiving.* Paul normally uses this to set the tone of the whole letter and to express his understanding of the situation he is addressing. 1:2–10 is a more customary thanksgiving. 1:10 is a formula-like representation of the essence of Hellenistic Jewish Mission Christianity. 2:1–16 recalls and interprets Paul's work in Thessalonica; 2:1–8 may imply Hellenistic Gentile "Divine Man" opponents, but could also be rhetoric. 2:13–16 is possibly a later addition, a second thanksgiving, and not from Paul. 2:17–3:13 resumes expressing Paul's affection and concern for the Thessalonian Christians.
   2:1–16 *Recollection and interpretation* of Paul's work in Thessalonica.
   2:17–3:13 *An expression of Paul's affection and concern* for the Thessalonian Christians.

4:1–12 *Parenesis.* An exhortation to holiness and love.

4:13–5:11 *Instruction with regard to the coming of the parousia.* This section is the real concern of the letter. It reiterates the common early Christian apocalyptic hope, but it uses "Lord" rather than "Son of Man" for Jesus as apocalyptic judge and redeemer, and it goes into physical details not found in the words of the Christian prophets of Q or in the apocalyptic discourses of the synoptic gospels. As noted, 5:9–10 is important as a first statement of the themes that came to be characteristic of the Pauline theology.

5:12–22 *Final Parenesis.* A hint at some form of organization in 5:12 is followed by a stress on work and a *cautious* encouragement about charismatic gifts (cf. 1 Cor 12, 14).

5:23–28 *Conclusion.* Peace wish, request for prayer, the kiss, command for letter to be read, and benediction.

Philippians

Philippi, named for Philip II of Macedon (father of Alexander the Great), was located on the Ignatian Way, eight miles north of the seaport of Neapolis, and was the site of Paul's first European congregation. It was established in the period before Paul went on to Thessalonica, Athens, and Corinth, hence about A.D. 49. Acts emphasizes the importance of Paul's entering Europe by recording that Paul went to Macedonia in response to a vision (16:9–10),[5] and the author of Luke-Acts stresses the Philippi mission by recording these stories: the conversion of Lydia and the baptism of her household; Paul's exorcism of a demon from the slave girl who supported her masters by practicing divination. As a result of the second story Paul and Silas were dragged before the city magistrates and charged by the Jews with being anti-Roman, for which they were imprisoned. They do not take the opportunity to escape during an earthquake. They convert their jailer and baptize him and his family. Paul is finally released and demands an apology because of his Roman citizenship (Acts 16:12–40). Although the exorcism and earthquake episodes have clear legendary features, some of the account is credible. In any case, we know from the letter about four converts (Phil 2:25–30, Epaphroditus; 4:2–3, Euodia, Syntyche, and Clement), and other fellow-workers "whose names are in the book of life" (4:3). The community was basically Gentile (3:3) and there was some local organization (1:1: "bishops"; "deacons"). There is no assurance that Paul visited Philippi again, although it is highly likely he did (Phil 2:24; cf. 2 Cor 13:1; Acts 20:1–6).

As we suggested above, Philippians probably contains three letter fragments. Chapter 3:1a ("Finally, my brethren, rejoice in the Lord") appears to be a final statement or at least near the end of a letter. But 3:2 launches off into a defense against opponents! Also 4:10–20, which occurs rather late in the letter, is a thanksgiving for a gift.

4:10–20 *Part of a letter of thanks to the Philippians* for the revival of their concern for Paul and the gifts sent to him at the hands of Epaphroditus. Paul notes

---

[5] The "we-passages" begin here, see below, p. 294.

that he accepted money from the Philippians while he was at Thessalonica, thus breaking his usual pattern (4:15). Paul appears to be at the beginning of an imprisonment, for he expects acquittal at an upcoming trial (1:25,26; 2:24).

1:1–3:1 *A further letter of thanks* for the concern the Philippians have expressed for Paul, who is now enduring a considerable period of imprisonment. Epaphroditus has been very ill, but is now recovered and will be rejoining the Philippians shortly. This letter characteristically combines thanksgiving and parenesis and includes some of the most moving passages in the Pauline correspondence as well as the great hymn to Christ in 2:5b–11. As noted in chapter 3 the hymn portrays the descending-ascending-redeemer figure, that is the redeemer has a pre-earthly existence ("in the form of God"; "to be equal with God"), who descends to take on an earthly existence ("empties himself"; "in the likeness of men"; "in fashion like a man"; "taking the form of a slave [or servant]"), dies, and is exalted to a post-earthly existence where he is glorified and worshipped as a god. If the basics of the hymn were "pre-Christian," Paul himself probably added "the death on the cross" (verse 8b), one of his favorite emphases.

3:2–4:9 *The remnant of a sharply polemical letter warning the Philippians of the dangers of an enthusiastic "circumcision" party.* The opponents have traits reminiscent of those of both Galatia (circumcision) and Corinth (enthusiasm). As in Galatians and 2 Corinthians, Paul combats them with an autobiographical statement (3:4–11). The characteristic apocalyptic hope is still present (3:20–21). This letter clearly does not belong with the others and must have been written either before or after them. The attitude of thanksgiving for dangers passed and harmony achieved, which the others breathe, leads to conjecture that this one was written earlier.

The conclusion as a whole mentions "Caesar's household" (4:22) and 1:13 mentions the "praetorian guard." The former refers to imperial administration throughout the empire and the latter can refer to the bodyguard of a governor, as well as of Caesar himself.

The second of these letters was certainly written in prison, and the first probably was also. The only imprisonment reported in Acts is that in Palestine and Rome, but we have already concluded that Acts is not a trustworthy source for historical detail concerning Paul or the early church. The letters themselves assume constant intercourse between the imprisoned Paul and the church in Philippi, a factor difficult to imagine if the distance was that between Philippi and Rome. And the letters breathe the same kind of atmosphere as that of Galatians and the Corinthian correspondence. For these reasons modern scholarship tends to assume that Paul was imprisoned in Ephesus during his long stay there and that this correspondence originated there. Paul himself speaks of facing death in Asia (2 Cor 1:8–10; cf. his figurative comment in 1 Cor 15:30–32), and the letters date, therefore, from about A.D. 54–55.

The Corinthian Correspondence[6]

The city of Corinth is strategically situated "between two seas" (Gulf of Corinth; Saronic Gulf) that join the Peloponnesus to the Greek mainland. Destroyed by Rome in 146 b.c., it was rebuilt by Julius Caesar in 44 b.c. It rapidly grew and Caesar Augustus made it the capital of Greece in 27 b.c.

Corinth was a natural seaport—its eastern harbor area was called Cenchreae and its western harbor area Lecheion—and it became a center for shipbuilding, commerce, industry, and government. It was also a sports center, one of the four major locations for the Isthmian games held every two years. The bustling seaport was highly cosmopolitan, populated with Roman officials, merchants, businessmen, soldiers, and sailors. It naturally gained a notorious reputation as a "city of sin" in ancient literature, so that the verb korinthiazein, "to live like a Corinthian," meant "to lead a dissolute life," and korē korinthē, "a Corinthian girl," became synonymous with a prostitute. So Strabo quotes the proverb, "Not everyman's concern is a trip to Corinth."[7] Yet, it had a religious life typical of a Hellenistic city. Its patron deity was Aphrodite Pandemos, a goddess of love, whose temple stood behind the city on a great rock.[8] Sanctuaries of Demeter (of the Eleusinian mysteries not far away)[9] and of Poseidon (in connection with the games) have been recently excavated.[10] Columns of the Temple of Apollo, the sun god, still stand. There were also sanctuaries to the Egyptian goddess Isis and god Serapis, and the Asian Mother of the gods. Moreover, there has been discovered on the Lechaion Road leading into Corinth a marble slab which contains an inscription in Greek letters, "(Syna)gogue of the Hebr(ews)." Though it is in a style later than Paul's period, such buildings were continually built on traditional sites.

The apostle Paul reached Corinth from Athens about a.d. 49 or 50 and he stayed there about eighteen months (the Gallio Inscription; Acts 18:1–11). There he established a Christian community. As we have seen in our discussions above, the apostle returned to Corinth twice (2 Cor 13:1) and wrote at least seven letters to the Corinthians who show their tendencies to quarrel with each other, to lapse into their pre-Christian ways (especially Hellenistic enthusiasm), and to become influenced by Hellenistic Jewish missionaries who challenged Paul's authority as an apostle. Since we have discussed these problems in some detail, we shall proceed to our exegetical outline of 1 Corinthians, written from Ephesus (cf. 1 Cor 16:8) about a.d. 53 or 54.

---

[6] H. Conzelmann, 1 Corinthians, pp. 11–12.

[7] Quoted in E. Haenchen, The Acts of the Apostles, p. 533, n. 3.

[8] Strabo's claim, Geog., VIII 378, that the sanctuary was so rich that it had over 1000 "temple prostitutes" refers to its golden age, not the time of Paul, and at any rate is probably based on a confusion with Asian temples; cf. H. Conzelmann, 1 Corinthians, p. 12.

[9] See chapter 1, pp. 11–12.

[10] C. L. Thompson, "Corinth," IDB Suppl., p. 180.

The body of the letter falls naturally into two parts, the first dealing with matters reported to Paul in Ephesus by messengers from a Chloe (1:10–6:20), and the second with questions raised in a letter to him from the Corinthian community (7:1–15:58). The whole is given a unity because the root of both sets of problems lies in the Corinthian religious enthusiasm.

1:1–3 *Christianized salutation from Paul and (an unknown) Sosthenes* (cf. Acts 18:17).

1:4–9 *Thanksgiving,* characteristically setting the tone of the letter, noting an apocalyptic hope, their spiritual gifts, and their call to Christian fellowship.

1:10–6:20 *The matters reported to Paul in Ephesus.* This section of the letter has four main parts.

1:10–4:21 *The factions in Corinth.* The basic problem in the Corinthian church was factionalism brought about by "enthusiasm." The Corinthian Christians developed a view of baptism in which the baptized persons identified themselves with the person who baptized them. Evidently they regarded baptism as a kind of magical rite by which they came to share the power they attributed to the person who baptized them. Moreover, once baptized they felt themselves to be "spiritual" in a way other people were not, to possess "wisdom" in a way other people did not. The quarrels between them were, therefore, quarrels among a spiritual and wise elite, all of whom recognized their distinctiveness from the rest of the world. Paul's argument against this view is fundamentally that the wisdom of the world is folly to God and that what the world would count folly ("Christ crucified, a stumbling block to Jews and folly to Gentiles," 1:23) is in fact the power and wisdom of God. He applies this directly to the Corinthians, most of whom were from the lower classes (1:26–31; cf. 6:11), that is, not wise, powerful, or of noble birth in the eyes of the world (1:26–31). Paul nonetheless allows for a special kind of *Christian* wisdom for those who understand the crucifixion; in fact, if the Corinthians had understood *this* Christian maturity, they would not be split into factions. The theme of the "weakness" of God, i.e., the Cross, as the basis for unity, will be a constant theme in the letter as Paul attempts to "build up" the church, and oppose enthusiastic misunderstandings.

5:1–13 *Incest and sexual sins in general.* Corinth was notorious for its sexual immorality, and apparently the Christian congregation was too tolerant in this matter. The reference in 5:3–5 is to the kind of act of solemn judgment at the Christian Eucharist isolated and discussed by

E. Käsemann.[11] 5:9 mentions the "previous letter." The Corinthians can associate with pagan *outsiders,* "since then you would need to go out of the world." Paul is concerned with immorality *within* the community.

6:1–11 *Litigation before pagan courts.* Christians will participate in Christ's final judgment of the world, including its magistrates. They must, therefore, fittingly settle their disputes out of court, *within* the community. Verses 9–11 contain a "vice list."

6:12–20 *The claim of the enthusiasts that "all things are lawful."* As truly "spiritual" men, the Corinthian enthusiasts were indifferent to things of the body, and one form of this indifference was an extreme libertarianism, including the freedom to visit Corinth's notorious brothels. Against this Paul argues strenuously for a moral spirituality.

7:1–15:58 *The questions raised by the Corinthians in their letter to Paul.* The Corinthian Christians had written to Paul asking for guidance on a number of practical matters. He responded as a pastor to his people, and the result is a fascinating account of an early Christian attempt to face the practical problems of living in the world—and perhaps also an illustration of the adage, "The more things change, the more they remain the same." Five particular problems are discussed: marriage and celibacy; Christian freedom and the problems of idolatry; the regulation of Christian worship; the true nature of spiritual gifts; and the future resurrection of the dead. Paul frequently introduces a new subject with the words, "now concerning" (7:1, 25; 8:1; 12:1; cf. 16:1, 12).

7:1–40 *Marriage and celibacy.* Paul wrestles here with all the problems of marital and sexual relationships, problems complicated in Corinth because one form of the Corinthian spirituality was an asceticism in which newly-converted Christians denied their wives and husbands their conjugal rights. Thus, on the one hand visiting prostitutes (6:12–20); here, sexual asceticism. From the standpoint of an overall understanding of Paul, it is important to note that the perspective from which the advice is given is that of the imminent end of the world (verses 26–31), that is, the Corinthians should keep the *status quo* because "the appointed time has grown very short" (verse 29). Paul clearly prefers that the Corinthians remain single as he is (7:1, 7, 8); but this, he acknowledges, could easily lead to more sexual immorality (at the brothels? fornication?). "It is better to marry than to be aflame with passion" (7:9). Given marriage, he clearly recommends that the partners fulfill their mutual sexual obligations (3–5). He draws on a "word of the Lord" forbidding the woman to separate from her husband and the man to divorce his wife (cf. Mark 10:1–12; Matt 5:32; 19:9; Luke 16:18). Yet, in the case of mixed marriages that

---

[11] E. Käsemann, "Sentences of Holy Law in the New Testament," in his collected essays, *New Testament Questions of Today,* pp. 66–81.

follows, he gives his own advice which indicates that neither the believing husband nor wife should *divorce* the unbelieving partner, again revealing an equality in this matter, the believing partner "consecrating" the unbelieving partner, and making "holy" their children. Paul suggests, however, that the unbelieving partner may "separate"—presumably meaning divorce—a modification of the "saying of the Lord" in new Christian circumstances. Nothing is said of the Torah command to produce children (Gen 1:28); presumably the apocalyptic situation prevails. Paul finally turns to the question of "the virgins." In verses 25–35, he refers to the betrothed; the same meaning is probable for verses 36–38, though the case is less clear (traditionally it was rendered "daughter," e.g., the refusal of fathers to offer their daughters' hands in marriage).

8:1–11:1 *Christian freedom and Christian love: the question of eating meat sacrificed to other gods.* Living as a Christian in a "pagan" society presented many problems for the newly baptized Christian's relationship to the world around him. For example, if you went out to dinner at a "pagan" friend's house, you might be served meat from the marketplace which had been previously sacrificed to "pagan" gods and subsequently sold, a common practice in Hellenistic cities. In general, this could imply a kind of worship at the god's table, and an acknowledgment of the god. This meat would have been strictly forbidden in Judaism and, as the Apostolic Decree in Acts shows, within some circles in Christianity as well (cf. Acts 15:28). Or possibly you might be invited to dinner at one of the many pagan sanctuary dining rooms where you might be offered a succulent menu of roast pork, just sacrificed. Clearly, no Jew could eat this either! Could the Christian? This was a crucial question at Corinth, and Paul had to deal with it as one of the questions posed to him.[12] Moreover, the passage is complicated. Chapter 9, a defense of Paul's apostleship, seems to break the trend of thought, giving rise to letter-fragment theories. We shall consider it as a unity.[13] Still further problems exist. In 8:1–13, 10:23–11:1, Paul seems to agree with the Corinthian enthusiasts when he says (a) "we know that all of us possess knowledge" (8:1); (b) that idols do not really exist (8:1, 4–6); (c) that fundamentally it is permissible to each such food in the name of Christian freedom (8:8; 10:26–27, 29b–30); but (d) he is concerned that "the weak" might be troubled in conscience if they see a Christian brother or sister "at table in an idol's temple" (8:10) or if someone (non-Christian?) informs a Christian at a non-Christian's house (or temple) that the meat has been (purchased in the marketplace and) offered in sacrifice

---

[12] C. L. Thompson, "Corinth," *IDB Suppl.*, p. 180, gives some recent archeological evidence bearing on such questions.

[13] For comments on this see H. von Soden, "Sacrament and Ethics in Paul" in W. Meeks, *Writings*, pp. 257–68; H. Conzelmann, *1 Corinthians*, pp. 137–38.

(10:28). In these cases, the Christian will be concerned for the "weak" Christian's conscience. It would seem that Paul is wrestling with a dilemma: he concedes a superior Christian knowledge but backs off in view of the conscience of "the weak."

It would appear that the course of Paul's argument here is important. His orientation is stated at the beginning: " 'Knowledge' puffs up, but love builds up," suggesting that "we know that all of us possess knowledge" is a slogan of the enthusiasts. Love is superior to knowledge, and Christian freedom operates out of love for one's brother or sister. Paul may not have been totally clear in his beliefs about the existence of idols, but he is consistent in his opposition to a freedom that leads to superior knowledge without love. That is the danger of "enthusiasm." In the process, Paul defends his apostleship (9:1–27), first on the grounds that he has had a vision of the Lord, and second, that his missionary activity has been successful. He also repudiates the argument that he was not really an apostle because he earned his own living rather than living off the results of his missionary labors, as did the propagandists of religion and philosophy generally in the Hellenistic world.

11:2–34 *The regulation of Christian worship.* The apostle now turns to a series of problems connected with Christian worship. The first (11:2–16) is the necessity for a woman to cover her head in worship, and it is immediately noticeable how ill at ease Paul becomes in questions concerning women. Paul's argument falters and in the end he falls back on a "church rule" (verse 16). We shall discuss this passage in more detail below. The second passage deals with the observance of the "Lord's Supper" (11:17–34). At Corinth the Christian sacred meal took place in connection with a communal meal which was becoming something of a Hellenistic banquet; the rich were eating and getting drunk and were thus humiliating those who had nothing. Paul recalls the tradition of the Lord's Supper (verses 23–25) to indicate the solemnity of the sacrament in connection with Jesus' death. Satiation and sacrament are thereby separated.

12:1–14:40 *The true nature of spiritual gifts.* A major feature of Corinthian religious enthusiasm was the proliferation of religious phenomena connected with religious ecstasy: utterances of wisdom and knowledge, faith, gifts of healing, working miracles, prophecy, "distinguishing between spirits," speaking in tongues, and interpretation of tongues (12:8–10). This in itself would not be extraordinary since other religions in the Hellenistic world exhibited the same phenomena. Indeed, it is Paul who states that these are spiritual gifts. What is interesting is Paul's perspective. As with the previous section, the middle chapter (13) is somewhat of an interruption in so far as it is a self-contained "poetic" section similar to Hellenistic and Jewish wisdom poetry of the period, and it is only loosely connected with chapters 12 and 14 (12:31; 14:1). A second passage on denying women the right to speak at house-church meetings (14:33b-36) interrupts the context; it does not represent Paul's views elsewhere (esp. 11:2–16), and is similar to comments from the later Pastoral Letters (1 Tim 2:11–15). We shall consider it below.

In chapter 12 Paul's remarks show that in general he accepts (had encouraged) various spiritual phenomena, but he denies that a Christian can say "Jesus be cursed!" (an ecstatic cry of the enthusiasts marking a contrast with "Jesus as Lord" statement or perhaps a spontaneous comment by Paul to contrast with the latter), and he draws on the general Hellenistic idea (esp. in Stoicism) of the body and its members to stress the unity of the church. In chapter 14 it is clear that some of the Corinthians consider the highest gift to be "speaking in tongues" (*glossalalia*). Paul has prepared for this by giving his own rank of charismatic gifts (12:27–30) with *glossalalia* and its interpretation last (12:27–30). In chapter 14, he states that incommunicable ecstatic experiences like *glossalalia* are permissible, but sets limitations: only two or three, each in turn, to be followed by an interpretation (14:27–28). Otherwise, they do not contribute to the "upbuilding" or "edification" of the church as a whole, as does the communicable act of prophecy, which he prefers. Paul stresses, then, *his* higher gifts (12:31: apostles, prophets, and teachers come first, cf. 12:28), and indicates in a "love hymn" of three stanzas the "more excellent way" (chapter 13).[14] Not only speaking in tongues, but prophecy and many other gifts and virtues—knowledge of God, working miracles, giving one's possessions to the poor, and martyrdom—are nothing without love (13:1–3). In beautifully active language containing 15 verbs, Paul next describes the nature of love (*agapē*) and its power (13:4–7), and concludes with the eschatological theme that while the other gifts will pass away, love is indestructible (13:8–13). 14:33b-36 is usually held to be an interpolation.

15:1–58   *The future resurrection of the dead.* A major problem for Paul in Corinth was that the Christian enthusiasts there believed that at their baptism they already began to share the resurrection life. Paul has to argue carefully for a future resurrection of the dead. A second problem was that for a Greek it was natural to think of the immortality of the soul but not of the resurrection of the body. Paul has also to argue for a future resurrection of the body. A most interesting passage in this section is verses 3–5, where Paul quotes an early liturgical formula, or confession, concerning the death and resurrection of Jesus and where he apparently understands his own vision of Jesus as a resurrection appearance.

16:1–18   *Some further matters.* Paul concludes his letter by discussing the arrangements he was making concerning the collection for the Christians in Jerusalem and his own future itinerary. 16:13–18 is parenetic.

14 G. Bornkamm, "The More Excellent Way," in *Early Christian Experience,* pp. 180–93.

16:19–24 *His closing* includes greetings from Asia by his own hand, the kiss, a curse, the *Maranatha* ("Our Lord, come!"), which is an Aramaic prayer going back to the earliest days of Palestinian Christianity, and a final benediction.

Second Corinthians

This letter is not a unity but rather a collection of fragments and larger remnants of a whole correspondence between Paul and the church at Corinth when a group of "superlative apostles" had an impact on the Corinthian Christian enthusiasts. The various parts were probably put together when the apostle's letters were circulated as a group toward the end of the first century. They were originally written over a period of time shortly after the writing of 1 Corinthians, around A.D. 55. Parts were written in Ephesus (2:14–6:13 and 7:2–4, minus 6:14–7:1; 10–13), the rest probably in Macedonia (1:1–2:13 and 7:5–16, cf. 7:5; 8, cf. 8:1; 9, cf. 9:2). The remnants of six letters are in this collection, and to read the first three in their proper order is to become caught up in a very dramatic struggle.[15]

2:14–6:13; 7:2–4 *Paul's first letter of defense against his new opponents.* This is part of a letter that Paul wrote to defend himself and his authority against opponents who came to Corinth bearing letters of recommendation from Christian communities in which they had previously worked, and who rapidly assumed positions of authority in the Corinthian Christian community. Paul calls them "peddlers of God's word" (2:17) and offers in his own behalf a moving account of the humility of the true ambassador for Christ.

10:1–13:14 *The "tearful letter."* Apparently Paul's first letter of defense against his new opponents failed in its desired effect, and he paid a flying visit to Corinth where, however, he found the church in open rebellion against him; one opponent was even able to humiliate him publicly (2:5; 7:12). He returned to Ephesus and wrote a further letter to Corinth "out of much affliction and anguish of heart and with many tears" (2:4). This is traditionally known as the "tearful letter," and 2 Corinthians 10–13 is a remnant of it.

In these chapters a picture of Paul's opponents takes shape as he parodies and attacks them, and they represent an aberrant form of Christianity in the Hellenistic world. They boast of their achievements in the name of Christ, and they boast of their Jewish heritage; they are "superlative apostles." They are given visions and revelations as a special sign of their status, and they offer "signs and wonders and mighty works" as

---

[15] Our analysis is indebted to that in G. Bornkamm, *Paul*, pp. 244–46. Bornkamm himself gives an excellent picture of Paul's relations with the church at Corinth, pp. 68–77. See also D. Georgi, "Corinthians, Second," *IDB Suppl.*, p. 184, and our discussion above, pp. 129–31.

proof that Christ speaks through them. Against all this Paul offers the "foolishness" of his own boasting. He appeals to the original effectiveness of the gospel he preached in Corinth, to the fact that he supported himself in Corinth so as not to be a burden on his converts, and alludes to his own Jewish heritage and his sufferings as a servant of Christ. Above all, he appeals to the Corinthian Christian's own sense of what they owe him and his gospel and to the example of Christ himself who was "crucified *in weakness*" (13:4, a deliberately ironic contrast to the power in Christ his opponents claim) but who lives by the power of God.

1:1–2:13; 7:5–16   *The letter of reconciliation.* Paul sent the "tearful letter" to Corinth by the hand of Titus, whom he must have charged with the task of attempting to restore the situation there. The letter and Titus' visit were successful—the Corinthian Christians were probably appalled by the realization of what they had done to the apostle to whom they owed so much—and Paul wrote a letter rejoicing in the resumption of good relations between him and the Corinthian Christian community. This and the following two letters were probably written in Macedonia.

8:1–24   *A letter of recommendation for Titus.* This is part of a letter of recommendation for Titus as organizer of the collection for the saints in Jerusalem.

9:1–15   *A letter concerning the collection for the saints in Jerusalem.* This is part of a letter concerning the collection for the saints.

6:14–7:1   *A non-Pauline fragment.* Neither in terms of ideas nor vocabulary does this have any claim to come from the apostle Paul. It appears, rather, to reflect the influence of ideas characteristic of the Qumran community. We have no idea how it came to be included in a collection of Paul's letters to the Christians in Corinth.[16]

Galatians

Paul addresses this letter to "the churches of Galatia" (Gal 1:2). There are two possibilities for this location: (*a*) the central plateau region of Asia Minor around modern-day Ankara, Turkey; or (*b*) the southern coastal region of east central Asia Minor, also in modern-day Turkey. Those who defend the former possibility ("the North Galatian theory") take Galatia in its ethnic sense to refer to the Indo-Aryan Celts or Gauls (*Galloi*>*Galatai*) who settled there early in the third century B.C. Those who defend the latter possibility ("the South Galatian theory") take Galatia in its Roman provincial sense, for Rome added the southern regions to Galatia in 25 B.C. There are good arguments for each

---

[16] H. D. Betz, "2 Cor 6:14–7:1: An Anti-Pauline Fragment?" *Journal of Biblical Literature* 92 (1973), pp. 88–108, suggests that the fragment holds a position opposed to that represented by Paul in Galatians.

location.[17] The South Galatian theory has in its favor the fact that in Acts (13–14) Paul is said to have visited the cities in this region (Perga, Pisidian Antioch, Iconium, Lystra, Derbe) on his "first missionary journey" (cf. also 16:1–5). If so, the letter was probably written rather early in Paul's career. The South Galatian theory has against it a number of speculative arguments based on a problematic chronology in Acts which conflicts at points with Galatians. In favor of the North Galatian theory is the probability that Paul will not return (Gal 4:20), which suggests that Paul wrote this letter late in his career; this tends to be confirmed by his references in 2 Corinthians about opponents, and in Galatians and Romans about major theological ideas. If the churches of Galatia were in the north he may have written from Ephesus, Corinth, or as suggested above, from Macedonia where the latest portions of 2 Corinthians were written, but before Paul reached Corinth where Romans was written. We suggest that he wrote from Macedonia about A.D. 55 or 56.

We have already sketched out the occasion for this letter, the disturbances created by opponents coming into Galatia. They may be called "Judaizers," but probably not in the sense that they are conservative Pharisaic Christians from Jerusalem. Like the Jerusalem conservatives, they demanded circumcision and the Law; but they also had highly syncretistic views, and seem to have believed Paul was not really so independent of Jerusalem (Gal 1–2). Whoever they were, they so irritated the apostle that he launched into one of his most heated apologies to defend himself. In fact, the genre of the letter itself might be called an "apologetic letter."[18] Not only does Paul defend himself but he curses his opponents at the beginning (1:8–9) and defends his supporters at the end (6:16), making it something of a "magical letter," while at the same time employing all kinds of rhetorical arguments to this end. Most unusual about the letter's structure, as we have seen, is its omission of any thanksgiving section (p. 166).

The letter to the Galatians is Paul's defense of his gospel, and hence his apostleship. The heart of that gospel is the message of "freedom," freedom from all that boxes up a person, from that which represses one religiously, racially, nationally, socially, and sexually. It is a spiritual phenomenon, a position of faith in Jesus Christ "who gave himself for our sins to deliver us from the present evil age according to the will of our God and Father" (1:4). Paradoxically, Paul attempts to defend this freedom with a kind of rhetorical logic which draws on human experience, scriptural proof, liturgical tradition, past friendship, indeed the Torah itself. But ultimately freedom speaks for itself.[19]

1:1–5 *Salutation.* In the greeting itself Paul begins his argument against his opponents in Galatia. He defends the divine nature of his apostleship and gives a terse summary of the gospel that he intends to defend.

---

[17] W. G. Kümmel, *Intro.*, pp. 295–304.
[18] H. D. Betz, *Galatians*, pp. 14–25, analyzes this genre in great detail.
[19] H. D. Betz, *Galatians*, pp. 28–33. Betz's outline of the letter is somewhat different and based on rhetoric.

1:6–9 *Amazement and anathema.* At this point in his letters Paul normally offers a thanksgiving for the faith of those he is addressing, but here he plunges immediately into polemic, expressing amazement at the state of affairs in the churches of Galatia and cursing the preachers of a false gospel.

1:10–2:21 *A personal and historical defense of Paul's gospel.* In the first major section of the letter Paul defines and defends his understanding of the gospel against that of his opponents. The section has three parts.

> **1:10–24** *The divine origin of Paul's gospel.* This is an invaluable autobiographical account of Paul's conversion, call, and early activity as a Christian missionary (see above, pp. 137–44). Paul roots his gospel in a revelation of God's son and in traditional prophetic fashion, a call to become apostle to the Gentiles. He tells of his brief visit to Peter and James in Jerusalem after three years.

> **2:1–10** *The approval of Paul's gospel by the leaders of the Jerusalem Christian community.* After fourteen years Paul attends the Jerusalem Conference with Barnabas, taking Titus, who is not compelled to be circumcised. The conservative party loses to Paul and Barnabas when James, Peter, and John agree that Paul and Barnabas will direct their mission to the Gentiles, while they go to the circumcised. The collection for the poor in Jerusalem is agreed upon. Paul is concerned with defining his mission to the uncircumcised Gentiles who, because of the decision reached in Jerusalem, are free from the need to accept circumcision as they become Christians. His opponents apparently were arguing the opposite, namely that Gentiles who become Christians had also to become Jews by accepting circumcision.

> **2:11–21** *The altercation with Peter in Antioch.* We indicated in our review of the history of New Testament Christianity that a major problem following the success of the Christian mission to the Gentiles was organizing table fellowship between Christians who accepted Jewish dietary laws and Christians who did not. Apparently Peter wavered on this issue, but Paul did not. In reflecting on this incident and its significance, Paul reaches one of his great statements on the nature of Christian faith. The heart of Paul's gospel as he was eventually to hammer it out was "justification by faith," which essentially involves the ability of a person to stand before the judgment seat of God and be approved. Paul came to believe that obedience to the Law ("works") could not earn this approval; approval is possible only through faith in Christ.

3:1–4:31 *A defense of Paul's gospel on ground of the Jewish Scriptures.* Paul's opponents in Galatia were Judaizers, who strongly emphasized the Jewish Law. Paul now turns to an argument based on that Law and on the Scriptures as a whole, no doubt not only to meet his opponents on their own grounds, but also to satisfy himself of the authenticity of his own position. This second major section of the letter is involved and complex, but it may be divided into seven parts.

3:1–5 *The gift of the spirit.* Paul here appeals to the very features of Hellenistic religious enthusiasm manifested by Christians in the Hellenistic world that were to be a major problem for him in Corinth. Here they are a validation of the gospel he preached in Galatia.

3:6–9 *Abraham as the prototype of justification by faith.* In Jewish tradition Abraham was the father of many nations because he believed God's promises and kept God's Law; he kept the covenant. Genesis says that Abraham "believed God and it was reckoned to him as righteousness" (Gen 15:6). Paul quotes this text, but he does not relate it to the Law. Rather, he argues that Abraham's act of belief was *before* the giving of the Law to Moses on Mount Sinai (Exod 20); so justification by faith takes precedence over justification by works of the Law, even if the latter were held to be possible at all.

3:10–14 *The curse on reliance on works of the Law.* Proceeding by a typically Jewish method of argument from Scripture, Paul now strings together a series of quotes to show that anyone who relies on the Law and does not do all that the Law commands is under a curse. Thus, as Hab 2:4 says, "the righteous shall live by faith" (cf. Rom 1:17).

3:15–18 *The promise to Abraham has priority over the giving of the Law.* Still following a typically Jewish method of arguing from Scripture, Paul turns to Gen 12:7, "To your decendants I will give this land." In the Hebrew Old Testament the word translated as "descendants" is a collective noun, and for this reason it is singular and not plural. From this grammatical point Paul argues that Gen 12:7 refers to a single descendant, one person, not a whole people, and that this descendant is Christ.[20] He then argues that Law—referring to the giving of the Torah on Mt. Sinai—came 430 years after the covenant with Abraham. Since no one annuls a ratified will (=covenant), Abraham's covenant based on promise is still in effect.

3:19–29 *The role of the Law from Moses until Christ.* The point at issue between Paul and his opponents was the Jewish Law. For Paul did not deny its promises; but he considered it had already fulfilled its function between the time of Moses and of Christ as a "custodian" (*paidagōgos*), that is, a slave who watched over and protected schoolboys until they reached puberty. With the coming of Christ it had been superseded. Paul recalls a baptismal formula with its social implications to reinforce his point: "There is neither Jew nor Greek, there is neither slave nor free, there is neither male nor female; for you are all one in Christ Jesus" (3:28).

4:1–20 *The freedom of Christians as Sons of God.* This is a magnificent celebration of the new relationship with God that Christ made possible

[20] See above, p. 171. Cf. also Gen 13:15; 17:8; 24:7 for this promise.

for the believers. In his use of "Abba! Father!" (verse 6) Paul is aware of the significance of the mode of address that Jesus taught his disciples to use in prayer, and the whole passage is an impassioned plea to the reader not to abandon that which Christ has made possible. A return to the Law, to the "weak and beggarly elemental spirits" (verse 9: probably a reference to stars and planets personified and understood as forces controlling one's life) and to the observance of a calendar of festivals (verse 10) would be such an abandonment. This passage is our clearest indication that Paul's opponents in Galatia were Judaizers, advocating observance of the Jewish Law and festivals together with a typically Hellenistic admixture of astrology.

4:21–31 *The allegory of Sarah and Hagar.* Abraham had two sons, one by Sarah's slave woman, Hagar, when Sarah was barren; another by Sarah according to the promise of God, despite Sarah's old age and barrenness. Thus, the promise was fulfilled in Isaac, the very one whom according to God's command Abraham was willing to sacrifice, and thus risk cutting off God's promise. Paul says Hagar represents the covenant of law, "the present Jerusalem," and slavery; Sarah represents the covenant of promise, "the Jerusalem above," and freedom. Christians are children of promise, of the free woman.

5:1–6:10 *Parenesis.* Paul now exhorts his readers to preserve and to use correctly the freedom they have in Christ. He attacks his opponents as turning the Galatians back to a "yoke of slavery" (5:1–12). In 5:19–24 he uses typical vice and virtue lists, contrasting the spirit with the flesh.

6:11–18 *Closing.* Paul takes the pen from his secretary and writes with large letters. Even here he cannot avoid a parting shot against his opponents. With a remark about the rigors of his apostleship, he ends with his benediction.

PAUL'S LETTER TO THE ROMANS

The letter to the church at Rome is unquestionably the most important of Paul's letters, and is to many the most important text in the New Testament itself. Historically, it has been highly influential in some of the major religious and cultural revolutions in western civilization. To read Romans is to read not only an occasional letter, but to wrestle with one of the most profound pieces of religious and theological literature ever written.

The church at Rome was not founded by Paul; in fact, its precise origins are a mystery. All roads led to Rome, and there were those professing all kinds of religion on them, including Judaism and Christianity. The tradition that Peter was martyred in Rome may be accurate,[21] but there is no evidence that he was the first to bring Christianity there. It is known from reports and inscrip-

---

[21] R. Brown, "Peter," *IDB Suppl.*, p. 657.

tions that in the early first century Rome contained a large number of Jewish synagogues, mainly Greek-speaking, and that from time to time anti-Semitism ran high.[22] From the Roman historian Suetonius (*Life of Claudius* 25.4) we learn that in A.D. 49 Claudius expelled the Jews from Rome because of a disturbance which Suetonius believed was instigated by a certain "Christus." The probable cause, however, was a dispute over Christus, that is, a dispute between Jews and Jewish Christians. Perhaps, then, the church in Rome arose among Diaspora Jews there. At any rate, Acts 18:2 claims that the Jewish *Christian* Aquila and his wife Priscilla were among the expelled Jews. By the time Paul wrote his letter to the Romans there was a sizable Christian congregation there, but the general orientation of the letter suggests that it was largely, but not exclusively, Gentile (e.g., 1:5–6, 13–15; 11:13; 15:15–33). Since the letter was written about two or three years after the Decree of Claudius was rescinded by Nero in A.D. 54, we may suppose that some Jews and Jewish Christians had returned to Rome. If chapter 16 was part of the letter,[23] Aquila and Prisca (Priscilla) were among them (16:3). Therefore, by the mid-fifties Paul wrote to an established church at Rome; it consisted of a majority of Gentiles and a minority of Jewish Christians, the latter having perhaps recently returned from exile.

Why did Paul write his letter to the Romans? Some scholars have used this historical knowledge to suggest there was tension between "the weak" and "the strong" (Rom 14:1–15:13) directly related to the return of the Jewish Christians after A.D. 54, that is, "the strong" represented the Gentile Christian majority, and "the weak" represented the Jewish Christian minority. The major dispute between the two parties was over eating practices (14:20–21). There is a certain plausibility in this because of Paul's concern with Jews and Gentiles in the letter as a whole. Other scholars derive the purpose of Paul's letter from several statements he makes in passing. In the thanksgiving Paul says he wishes to impart to the Roman Christians some spiritual gift to strengthen them, but quickly adds—cautiously, no doubt—"that we may be mutually encouraged by each other's faith, both yours and mine" (1:12). His general rule has always been not to preach the gospel in anyone else's mission territory (15:20; cf. 1 Cor 3:10; 2 Cor 10:13–17), but he can also say, ". . . I am eager to preach the gospel to you also who are in Rome" (1:15). Yet, Paul certainly does not think of Rome as his mission territory; rather, he wishes to see the Romans "in passing" as he goes on to Spain, and to receive their encouragement (15:24). If he gets their approval Rome will then be something of a power center from which he can move on, as had been initially Antioch and later Ephesus. Some, indeed, have seen this desire for acceptance as the major purpose of the document since Paul was aware that the controversies he had been embroiled in might have led to a false impression of him and his gospel. However, other scholars believe that the letter is not intended to be read only

---

[22] W. Wiefel, "The Jewish Community in Ancient Rome and the Origins of Roman Christianity," in K. P. Donfried, ed., *The Romans Debate*, pp. 100–08.

[23] Some include chapter 16, see K. P. Donfried, "A Short Note on Romans 16," in K. P. Donfried, ed., *The Romans Debate*, pp. 50–60, and the discussion above, pp. 152–54.

by the Christians at Rome. One view is that it is in part a draft of what Paul actually wants to say in defense of himself in Jerusalem. More common is the theory that it is a circular letter to several churches. Another widely accepted suggestion is that Romans is Paul's "last will and testament" which grew out of Paul's anxiety in the face of the dangers that faced him at Jerusalem and which contains a summary of his views as he had developed them from his conflicts with Judaizers and enthusiasts.[24] His polemical passages may thus be part of the Cynic-Stoic diatribe *style*, not directed to specific opponents. This view tends to be reinforced by parallels in Romans with his expressed views in Galatians, Philippians, and Corinthians.[25]

- Justification by faith alone and not by works of the Law (Gal 3 and 4; Phil 3; Rom 1–4; 9:30–10:4).
- Abraham as the type of justification by faith (Gal 3; Rom 4).
- Adam as the mythical embodiment of the fall of man and Christ as the head of the new humanity (1 Cor 15:22–28; Rom 5:12–21).
- Natural man subject to Law, sin, and death (1 Cor 15:56–57; Rom 7:7–25).
- The sending of the Son of God in the flesh for our redemption and the testimony of the Spirit that we are the children of God (Gal 4:4–7; Rom 8).
- The unity of the church described as one body with many members (1 Cor 12; Rom 12:4–8).
- The conflict of "weak" and "strong" over food matters (1 Cor 8,10; Rom 14:1–15:13).

The suggestion that Romans is Paul's last will and testament gains some support from recent comparison with other ancient letters, suggesting that it is a "letter-essay." As such it is an actual letter sent to specific persons about specific subjects, but *at the same time* it is ". . . supplementary in some way to another writing usually by the same author or substitute for a work projected by him, and the idea of instruction is presented in the author's purpose to clarify, abridge, aid in memorizing, defend his thesis, recount history."[26] In other words, Romans could have been written both to a specific situation of which Paul had some knowledge and at the same time have summed up his major ideas on the basis of his other letters. Stirnewalt, who has studied the "letter-essay" makes this conclusion about Romans:

This great document, which summarizes and develops the most important themes and thoughts of the Pauline message and theology and which elevates his theology above the moment of definite situations and con-

[24] G. Bornkamm, "The Letter to the Romans as Paul's Last Will and Testament," *The Romans Debate*, pp. 17–31; *Paul*, chapter 10.

[25] G. Bornkamm, *Paul*, pp. 93–94.

[26] M. L. Stirnewalt, "The Form and Function of the Greek Letter-Essay," in *The Romans Debate*, pp. 176–77.

flicts into the sphere of the eternally and universally valid, this letter to the Romans is the last will and testament of the Apostle Paul.[27]

Exegetical Survey of Paul's Letter to the Romans

1:1–7 *Salutation.* Paul extends this conventional salutation to include a definition of the gospel (verses 3 and 4), which is traditional rather than distinctively Pauline.

1:8–15 *Thanksgiving.* This sets the tone and indicates the purpose of the whole letter, as it so often does. Paul hopes for mutual exchange of faith and the opportunity to preach the gospel.

1:16–17 *Summary statement of Paul's understanding of the gospel.* The righteousness of God is an active concept, with God as the acting subject. It refers to the power of God to act in accordance with his own true nature as creator and redeemer, to establish human beings as righteous before him. This state of acceptance in God's sight is God's own gift; it cannot be achieved by works of the Law, it is accessible only to one act, the act of faith. This is the climactic statement of Paul's characteristic doctrine of justification by faith, and one should compare the earlier statement of it in Gal 3:10–11 and Phil 3:9.

First Major Section: The World's Need for Justification by Faith, 1:18–3:20

1:18–32 The judgment of God is revealed against the sin of man. Gentiles have sinned and are without excuse; God's power and deity have been revealed to them in his creation. Their sin is clear from their sensuality (1:24–27). Paul associates their actions with vices in a typical vice list (1:28–32).

2:1–11 The Jews are every bit as much under the judgment of God as are the Gentiles. But if they "do good," they will also have glory and peace. In both instances, Paul states, "The Jew first and also the Greek" (2:9,10), on which see 1:16 and chapters 9–11.

2:12–29 God judges the Jews by the standards of the Law of Moses, and the Gentiles by the "law" of their conscience. But the Jew may not rely on outward observances; true circumcision is a circumcision of the heart.

3:1–8 The Jews nonetheless have an advantage in that God has directly revealed his will and purpose to them in their Scriptures.

3:9–20 But all men, Jews and Gentiles alike, have fallen under the power of sin. Ultimately, then, the Jews are not any better off.

[27] M. L. Stirnewalt, p. 206.

Second Major Section: The Nature of God's Saving Act in Christ, and of Man's Appropriation of That Act, 3:21–4:25

3:21–26 *Restatement of the doctrine of justification by faith.* Having established that the whole world, Jewish and Gentile, needs justification by faith because it is estranged from God by its sin, Paul now restates the doctrine to include the actual form that the redemptive activity of God has in fact taken: the Cross of Christ. Paul's emphasis on the redemptive power of the Cross of Christ is a major feature of his theology. The crucifixion of Jesus was a stumbling block to the Christian claim that Jesus was the Messiah, the Son of God. How could it be that the Messiah, the Son of God, had been allowed by God to suffer a felon's death on a cross, subject to the power of the Jewish and Roman authorities? The word of his mouth should have had the power to blast them from the face of the earth. Paul must have had this difficulty a thousand times in his years of attempting to convince his fellow Hellenistic Jews that Jesus was the Christ, and he must have spoken out of real personal experience when he said, "We preach Christ crucified, a stumbling block to Jews and folly to Gentiles" (1 Cor 1:23). A crucified redeemer figure was "folly" in the Gentile world, because the characteristic redeemer figures in that world were either heroes of the mystery cults or "divine men." Hellenistic Jewish Mission and Gentile Christianity met this problem by transforming Jesus into a "divine man" and his death into an apotheosis. In the more purely Jewish world the Christians developed a "passion apologetic," an apologetic for the passion and Cross of Jesus attempting to show that it was in accord with the will and purpose of God as revealed in the Scriptures. But as time went by, the Christians came more and more to accept the fact of the Cross as a fact and among themselves to develop an understanding of its meaning rather than an apologetic for its necessity; they moved from a passion apologetic to a soteriology of the Cross.

Paul played a major role in the development of a soteriology of the Cross, that is, in an understanding of how the Cross of Christ changes forever the relationship between God and human beings. The Jews, and early Christianity in general, expected the relationship to be changed by the eschatological act of God, and among Christians the form of this expectation was the return of Jesus from heaven as apocalyptic judge and redeemer when the relationship between God and man would be forever changed. But in Paul's thinking, this change has already taken place in the Cross of Christ. The whole world, Jewish and Gentile, is estranged from God by its sin, but the estrangement is not to be eradicated by an act of God in the future. It has already been eradicated by an act of God in the past: the Cross of Christ.

Paul never tires of this theme. The world is estranged from God by reason of its sin, but God has done something about it. This "something" is the Cross of Christ, and Paul is constantly concerned to find ways of explaining how the Cross of Christ eradicates the estrangement of human beings from God created by their sins. In Rom 3:25 he turns to religious sacrifice and uses the word normally used for the sacrifice that propitiates an angry deity, *hilastērion*, translated in the English Revised Version of the Bible, "whom God set forth to be a propitiation." But God is the acting subject, and how can God be said to propitiate himself? Hence in the Revised Standard Version the translation is "whom God put forward as an expiation," in the New English Bible, "the means of expiating sin," and in Today's English Version, "the means by which men's sins are forgiven." But *hilastērion* is the name the Greek-speaking Jews gave to the "mercy seat" in the Holy of Holies, described in Lev 16:2, 11–17. Paul, also a Greek-speaking Jew, may be saying that the Cross of Christ is the place where the sin of man meets the forgiveness of God. The fact is that we are at a point where language fails us. The fundamental convictions involved are that (*a*) people are estranged from God and doomed for all eternity because of sin; and (*b*) God himself has changed this situation through the Cross of Christ. The fundamental need of human beings is met by God in the Cross of Christ. This is the deepest conviction of Paul, and, indeed, of New Testament Christianity in general, and the language of direct discourse simply fails us.

The act of God that will eradicate human estrangement is "to be received by faith" (RSV) and is "effective through faith" (NEB). Paul reaches this view through reflection and as a result of his controversy with the Judaizers in Galatia and elsewhere. Whatever it is that God has done in the Cross of Christ, it is effective for any given person only insofar as that person responds to it by the act of faith. "Faith" as Paul understands it is another concept that defies the power of the language of direct discourse. The word means "belief," "trust," "obedience," and what Paul is trying to find words to express is something like the following: just as Jesus gave himself totally to God and humanity by accepting the necessity for the Cross, so must human beings give themselves totally to God-as-revealed-in-Jesus in order to appropriate for themselves the power of that Cross.

A final point is the meaning of the verb to *justify* and the noun *justification*. The concept is ultimately derived from the law court, and the reference is to an act of judgment. God has given humanity a standard by which to live—to the Jews his Law, to the Gentiles the conscience in their hearts—and ultimately one must stand before God and be judged by that standard. If one has achieved it he will be declared "righteous," and the divine act of declaring one righteous is the act of justification: God justifies the person who is righteous in his sight. Paul's whole argument is that no one can achieve the necessary righteousness, and so God has established a new possibility: a person will be justified by God—i.e., declared "righteous" by him—if that person has faith in Jesus, and this is a possibility for Jew and Gentile alike. The Jew has failed to live up to the Law and the

Gentile to the conscience in his heart, but God nonetheless declares them righteous in his sight because of the righteousness of Jesus (who more than fulfilled all norms), which they appropriate to themselves by the act of faith.

3:27–31 *It is faith and not works that matters.* Paul's constant controversy with the Judaizers led him to the oversimplified antithesis: *either* gladly accept by the act of faith what God has done in Christ *or* justify yourself before God by the quality of your own life. It is easy enough to say that it should have been in some respects a question of "both . . . and," but in the heat of controversy contrasting emphases become sharpened to radical antitheses. Paul's argument is that justification must be by faith and not by Law, because only the Jews had the Law, whereas the purpose of God must be the justification of all. Everyone is capable of the act of faith.

4:1–25 *Abraham himself was justified by faith and thus is the father of all who believe in the God who raised Jesus from the dead.* Paul's position here turns on the fact that it is in Genesis 15 that it is said of Abraham, "he believed the Lord, and he reckoned it to him as righteousness" (Gen 15:6). Not until Genesis 17 is the requirement of circumcision laid on him as on his descendants (Gen 17:11). Faith is anterior and hence superior to circumcision as a means of being justified before God. This is a typically rabbinic method of argument. For his earlier formulation, see Gal 3.

Third Major Section: The New Life in Christ, 5:1–8:39

5:1–5 *The consequence of justification by faith: peace with God and joy in life.*

5:6–11 *The grounds for the possibility of justification by faith: the Cross of Christ.* In one of his most lyrical passages, Paul expresses his fundamental convictions by using two images: the image of justification, taken as we have seen from the language of the law court, and the image of reconciliation, taken from the language of personal relationships. Both are ways of talking about the plight of man before God—the need for justification, the need for reconciliation—and both are ways of talking about the Cross of Christ—the means by which God has changed the plight of man before him. One is "justified by his blood" or "reconciled by his death." Two further notes are sounded: (*a*) the whole work of justification or of reconciliation is a work of God and hence an outpouring of his love of humanity; and (*b*) the person who is justified or reconciled by the death of Jesus is further "saved" by Jesus' life. This latter point is Paul's version of the claim of the Corinthian enthusiasts that they knew already the power of the risen Lord, that their life in Christ was already the resurrection life. Paul does not deny this; he is willing to claim that Christians in this life share in the power of Jesus' resurrection and that their lives are already transformed by the power of that resurrection. But there is always for Paul what modern scholars tend to call an "eschatological reservation." However much a person now knows of the power and quality of the resurrection life, there is still the resurrection to come. However much one is now justified or reconciled, one still needs to be "saved from the wrath to come," i.e., from the still outstanding, final, eschatological judgment of God. There is in Paul an inevitable element of tension between his ability as a man of the Gentile world to interpret the Christian faith in terms of Greek religious enthusiasm and his necessity as a Jew to think in terms of a Last Judgment. We can understand Paul correctly only if we recognize that for all his enthusiasm for the effectiveness of the Cross of Christ, for all his glorying in the present experience of Christ's risen life, he nonetheless never loses touch with the typical early Christian apocalyptic hope for a second coming of Christ as judge and redeemer. So in this passage, although we are already "reconciled," we still need to be "saved." Logically it is inconsistent, but it has fed the piety of centuries because it has been found to correspond to the reality of Christian religious experience.

5:12–21 *The myths of Adam and Christ.* In our discussion of the early Christian apocalyptic hope, we said that a reason for its enduring power was the correspondence between the myth explaining the existence of evil in the world as the result of the wrongdoing of a primal ancestor and the myth explaining the removal of evil from the world as an activity of another human or humanlike figure. Paul now develops this correspondence of myths more exactly by claiming that just as the wrongdoing of the one man Adam led to the existence of sin and evil in the world, so also the possibility of the removal of sin and evil from the world is the result of the righteousness of the one man Jesus Christ. For Paul's previous statement, see 1 Cor 15:22–28.

6:1–14 *Dying and rising with Christ.* In the Gentile world where Paul preached it was natural to think of sharing the power and destiny of a cult hero, a Serapis or a Mithras. In responding to the imagined protest of an opponent with whom he is in dialogue—a characteristic Hellenistic literary device—Paul interprets the Christian initiatory rite of baptism as a sharing in the death of Christ. He then states the Christian *shall* be united with Christ in a resurrection like his, maintaining the "eschatological reservation." Paul then interjects a parenetic passage of exhortation in the characteristic New Testament manner (verses 12–14).

6:15–7:6 *The two analogies: slavery and marriage.* To drive home his point, Paul turns to two analogies: slavery and marriage. A slave is totally responsible to one master, but only to one. Similarly, a wife is totally responsible to her husband, but only as long as he lives. So Christians were once slaves to sin and married to the Law, but now they are slaves of righteousness, and the Law is dead for them.

7:7–25 *The meaning and function of the Mosaic Law.* As a Jew Paul inherited the understanding of the Law of God as given through Moses as the supreme gift of God's grace, given to man that he might know and do the will of God in the world and so inherit the blessings of all eternity. But as a Christian he had come to see that under the Law Jesus himself stood condemned, since according to the Law, "cursed be every one who hangs on a tree" (Deut 21:23, quoted in Gal 3:13), i.e., in his crucifixion Jesus was, according to the Law, accursed of God. Paul must have maintained this argument in his days of opposition to Jesus and to faith in Jesus. But he revises the meaning in Galatians to show that Christ took the curse of the Law upon himself in behalf of the Christian, for according to God's direct revelation to Paul, Jesus was not accursed of God; he was God's own Son, and Paul must have begun to question the validity of the Law. In his days as a Christian preacher Paul was forced into controversy with his Judaizing opponents in Galatia and Philippi, and no doubt elsewhere, where the question at issue was the validity of the Law, but where the real issue was the freedom of the Christian mission to be *Christian* (as Paul had come to understand the meaning of that term), and not simply Jewish. So Paul was again forced to question the validity of the Mosaic Law, and indeed to deny it. Now in this passage from Romans, he brings his reflections together, and out of his own experience of the crucified Christ and of the Judaizing controversy fashions his classic statement on the ultimate significance of the Law given by God to the Jewish people as the supreme gift of God's grace: the Law in and of itself is not sin; it is "holy and just and good" (7:12); sin brings about death. But one knows what sin is through the Law. Only when one is forbidden to do something by the Law does one become aware that what he does is forbidden. "Apart from the Law sin lies dead . . . but when the commandment came, sin revived and I died" (7:8, 9). So, though the Law was intended to help, it did not; it became a tool of sin. The Law is spiritual, but humans are carnal, "sold under sin. I do not understand my own actions. For I do not do what I want, but I do the very thing that I hate. . . . Now if I do what I do not want, it is no longer I that do it, but sin which dwells within me" (7:14–15, 20).

It is often supposed that this passage is autobiographical and that Paul was reflecting on his own soul-searching as he attempted to fulfill the Law as a Pharisee. But it seems more likely that the use of the first-person singular is a literary device. We have no evidence that Paul thought this way about the Law before his vision of the risen Christ, who should have been accursed of God but was in fact vindicated by him, or before his conflicts with the Judaizers. But the literary device makes it a most powerful passage, because the experience depicted does correspond to the reality of the experience of countless men and women who have conscientiously attempted to fulfill an established code of conduct. "The good that I would I do not: but the evil which I would not, that I do" (Rom 7:19, KJV) is a cry from the heart of conscientious humanity.

8:1–39   *The new life in Christ and its details.* Paul has paused to give his apology for the Law (7:7–25). Now in what is probably the greatest sustained passage from his letters, perhaps the greatest sustained passage from Christian literature altogether, Paul depicts the details of the possibilities of the new life in Christ. These are life in the Spirit, life as free sons of God, life as eschatological hope and love. Christ has accomplished what for Paul the Law was not able to do: Christians are no longer condemned, slaves to sin in the flesh and to die; Christians are free spiritual beings who live with the promise that nothing—none of the world's powers—can separate them from the love of God.

Fourth Major Section: The Place of Israel in God's Plan for the Salvation of All Mankind ("Salvation History"), 9:1–11:36

Nothing could have plagued Paul personally more than the problem of his Jewish heritage. He had grown up proudly in the consciousness of being a member of the people of God, the people whom God had chosen to be his people and to whom he had revealed his will and purpose directly in his Law. Yet the people of God had rejected God's own Son. Paul must have spent a lifetime arguing to Jews that Jesus was God's own Son because his life, death, and resurrection had been foretold in the Scriptures and trying to explain to Gentiles how it was that the people of God had not recognized the Son of God. Now he was proudly preaching a gospel that claimed a Gentile could be justified on the basis of responsiveness to the dictates of his conscience. What then remained of the superiority of the Jewish people as the people of God? The most natural answer would have been, Nothing! especially when facing the problems created by the conservative Jewish-Christian party at Jerusalem, or Judaizers who demanded circumcision and adherence to the Law. Or since most of the Jews had rejected Jesus, the answer could even have been, Less than nothing! But Paul wrestles with the problem on his own terms and comes up with an answer scholars normally discuss under the rubric of the German word *Heilsgeschichte.*

Heilsgeschichte means literally "salvation history"; the term is used to designate the concept in which God is active in history as he reveals himself and saves his people. It is not simply "secular" history (*Weltgeschichte*), but God working out his plan *through* secular history, at crucial points intersecting with secular history.[28]

Paul has come to a crucial point in his argument—and here we do not find parallels in his earlier letters, though he clearly comes close in his discussion of Abraham as the Christian's true "father" (Rom 4; cf. Gal 3), and in his comments about "to the Jew first and also to the Greek" (Rom 1:16; 2:8–9). The problem is this: if God now justifies each *individual* sinner—Jew or Gentile—on

---

[28] *Heilsgeschichte* is a common way of looking at history in the Bible; we shall discuss the concept further in connection with Matthew's, and especially Luke's, theological perspectives.

the basis of *faith* in Christ, what about his promises to "his people" Israel as a totality? Paul has thus to relate justification by grace through faith to God's plan in history, to *Heilsgeschichte,* and specifically to the rejection of God's Son and messiah by most of Israel. Paul argues that everything that has happened must be in accordance with the will and purpose of God, and that purpose is the salvation of all humanity, Israel and the Gentiles. Except for a remnant, however, Israel had failed to recognize that righteousness was ultimately attained only by faith. Israel remained obdurate in its insistence on a righteousness attainable by obedience to an external Law, "and seeking to establish their own, they did not submit to God's righteousness" (10:3). But God has not rejected the people of Israel, and the Gentiles should not feel superior to them. If God can break off some of the branches (the Jews who do not believe) of a cultivated olive tree and graft on branches of a wild olive shoot (the Christians), he could just as easily break off the wild branches and graft in old branches—if they believe—especially since they are natural branches. The rejection of God's Son by "the rest" of Israel has the consequence that the Gentile now has an opportunity to hear the gospel (11:11–12). The word of God to Israel has not failed—after all the promise to Abraham means that his true descendants are those who believe. To be sure, this is not "Israel" as a whole, as a nation, but it is an "Israel." What then of Israel as a whole? Paul argues that there is an eschatological mystery here: while the full number of Gentiles come in, part of Israel will remain outside; nonetheless, in the end all Israel will be saved.

All this is argued in detail and with copious reference to Scripture, and yet the modern reader cannot help but feel that there is something very strained about the whole argument. The world of Romans 1–8 is one world; the world of Romans 9–11 quite another. Romans 9–11 is a testimony to the agony of the spirit of a conscientious Jew who has come to believe that God's own people have rejected God's own Son as well as God's own gospel. A major fact of life in the New Testament is that the Christian mission to the Jews was a miserable failure, while that to the Gentiles was a sensational success, and Romans 9–11 is one Christian Jew's attempt to accept and to understand this reality. It should be read today with sympathy and understanding for the agony of the human spirit that gave rise to it.

Fifth Major Section: Parenesis, 12:1–15:33

As there is always in the New Testament texts, in Paul's letter to the Romans there is both proclamation and parenesis, and Romans 12–15 is the parenetical section of the letter. In Rom 12, we hear echoes of 1 Corinthians 12, that is, though there are many members with differing spiritual gifts, there is one body (12:3–8). This is followed by a series of general exhortations about behavior, both with respect to life within the community and in relation to those outside (12:9–21). Chapter 13 contains Paul's recommendation to be subject to the governing authorities (see below) and the gospel tradition about love. Rom 14:1–15:3 discusses the relation of "the weak" to "the strong," concluding with an itinerary where he expresses the hope of going on to Spain and relays his anxiety about taking the collection to Jerusalem.

The closing contains an appeal to prayer on Paul's behalf and a benediction (15:33).

Romans 16

We have already discussed this passage in some detail. It contains a letter of recommendation (16:1–2), greetings to 26 people by name and others, and "the kiss" (16:16). Then comes a startling comment about opponents (17–20) which includes another benediction (verse 20), greetings from Paul and his companions (21–23), and finally an un-Pauline doxology (25–27).

PAUL'S THEOLOGY AND ETHICS: A SUMMARY

From our brief exegetical outlines of Paul's letters, it will now be helpful to put together a summary of some of his basic ideas.

Paul never met the historical Jesus. Yet, as a result of a religious experience in which he believed he had encountered the crucified and risen Christ, the persecutor of Christians abandoned his former life and carried out his "call" to preach the "good news" to the Gentiles. As recovered from his surviving letters, the heart of this good news is not the perpetuation of the teaching of Jesus or having a "Christ-like" moral life in the sense of following in the steps of Jesus of Nazareth; rather, the center is "the Christ-event," that is, Jesus' death on the Cross and his resurrection from the dead. For Paul, the Cross-resurrection opens up the whole meaning of the divine plan and purpose of the one true God of Israel, and therefore the whole meaning and purpose of human existence. When properly understood, the Christ-event fulfills God's ancient promises, namely, that salvation is not only for those who are, and become part of, God's chosen covenant people as a national entity "Israel," with its religious heritage grounded in the Torah; it is rather for the whole human race and predicated on belief in the Christ-event itself. Salvation is good news about God, his purposes, his relation to humankind, the nature and destiny of humanity, human freedom and ethical responsibility, faith, hope, and love—in short, all of reality. The "Christ-event" is a creative act, a foundational "myth," which gives meaning and purpose to human existence in the world.

For Paul, this event is a *powerful* event, signaling that the final period of history has begun, that the end is imminent. It is therefore an eschatological event.[29] Paradoxically, however, God's power is manifested in weakness, for the

---

[29] This view has been persuasively put forward by E. Käsemann and his followers. For a recent discussion, see E. P. Sanders, "Perspectives on 'God's Righteousness' in Recent German Discussion," in *Paul and Palestinian Judaism*, pp. 523–42.

mysterious Cross-resurrection is not understood by the wisdom of the world. It is power and yet weakness: it is power present both in manifestations of the Spirit of God through spiritual gifts, and of the love of God who gives of himself and commands that believers do the same. For the Christian, then, spiritual enthusiasm and weakness are to be held in balance: enthusiasm without the Cross leads to self-seeking pride and "knowledge"; yet, the new life in Christ is manifested by spiritual security and gifts of the spirit.

At the same time, the "Christ-event" is a gift of God's grace. For Paul, the total self ("body") contains within a struggle between the "spirit," the higher self, and the "flesh," the self subject to attack by sin, a power Paul frequently personifies. It is sin in the flesh that leads the self to rebel against God, and this rebellion manifests itself in all forms of wickedness and vice. The self cannot overcome this evil power by itself; it therefore cannot overcome evil by good works—including those prescribed by the Torah. In fact, God in his anger would be justified in rendering the verdict of "guilty" on evil humanity. But he has not done so for those who believe in his act of power. In other words, "the righteousness of God" is the powerful movement of God toward human beings in which by his free gift of grace—the Christ-event—sinners are made just, or "justified," that is, acquitted on the basis of a trusting belief. The good news is the "power of God for salvation for everyone who has faith" (Rom 1:16). By this faith the believer enters a new community and becomes part of a new humanity. The ritual of baptism means that the believer shares in Christ's death and the promise of participating in Christ's resurrection. This new life in the Spirit is sustained in worship, especially in the common meal, the Lord's Supper, which commemorates Christ's death. It is also manifested by charismatic gifts and can be characterized as "life" and "peace." By God's action "in Christ," then, the whole world and everyone in it is offered reconciliation with the Creator.

Much more could be added to this brief statement but it is obvious that Paul's view of the good news about Jesus Christ led him into conflict with his own Jewish religious traditions at the crucial point: the understanding of the Torah and its function among God's elect, covenant people, Israel. It is highly debated whether Paul, as a Hellenistic Jew of the Diaspora, fully appreciated his full religious tradition about the Torah when he spoke of "works of the Law";[30] whether he did or not, it is clear that if the sign of God's covenant people is circumcision as stated in the Law, Paul's view that Gentiles could become part of the new community without circumcision, and his perspective that Christ is the "end of the Law," led toward a different idea of the community. Once the gospel was preached to the Gentiles on this basis, the conflict with those who upheld the more traditional view of the Torah was inevitable. Although the mature Paul could cite the baptismal formula, "neither Jew nor Greek . . . in Christ Jesus" (Gal 3:28), and hope for the ultimate inclusion of the mother, Israel, who had given birth to her children, the Christians (Rom 11), the way was prepared for the emergence of a separate and distinct institution, the church.

[30] J. A. Sanders, "Torah," *IDB Suppl.*, pp. 909–11; contrast M. Cook, "Judaism, Hellenistic," *IDB Suppl.*, pp. 505–09.

No matter how one evaluates his overall theology, Paul will certainly be seen as a profound religious thinker. But what about his practical, ethical advice? We cannot enter into a full discussion of his ethical teachings at this point[31] but we can, however, indicate his general orientation to ethical issues and cite a few concrete examples.

Much of Paul's ethical advice is drawn from conventional morality in his time. Christians, like Jews, should settle their disputes outside the pagan courts (1 Cor 6); lists of vices and virtues reflect popular Hellenistic morality. There are also sources for authority such as the Old Testament (e.g., 1 Cor 10), Christian tradition (1 Cor 11:23–25 on the Lord's Supper; 1 Cor 15:3b–5 on the resurrection), and more concrete "words of the Lord" on issues like divorce (1 Cor 7:10–11) and the apostolic right to financial support (1 Cor 9:14). Conventional morality and the appeal to tradition, along with Paul's eschatological orientation toward the end of the world and his tendency to put parenetic sections at the end of his letters, have led some interpreters to suggest that Paul's ethical teachings are a time-bound, subsidiary, and ultimately irrelevant part of his thinking.[32] But whatever one may think of Paul's ethical views on specific subjects, it would be inaccurate to say that they are totally unrelated to his theology as a whole. The form of the letter is sufficiently flexible to permit moral exhortation to occur at almost any place and, in fact, 1 Thessalonians might be called a "parenetic letter," while 1 Corinthians is dominated by responses to practical, ethical concerns of the Corinthian church. For Paul himself, then, the parenesis is finally inseparable from his gospel proclamation; ethics grows out of the Christ-event; the moral imperative is rooted in the theological indicative. Thus, while he often draws on authority and conventional morality, some of which has a clearly time-bound quality, Paul's theology contains impulses for ethical reflection that go beyond what is typical of his contemporaries.

If Paul's ethical statements are in the service of his gospel, then they must be coordinated with his view of God's eschatological act of power and grace in the Christ-event. Though the final period of history has begun, the consummation still lies in the future. Meanwhile, Christians have received a taste of the future in the activity of the Spirit (Rom 8:23), both in the individual and in the community. This is expressed in *Christian freedom within the bounds of love.* When freedom is threatened, especially by adherence to the Law, Paul rushes to defend the gospel; at the same time, he checks the abuse of freedom by appeals both to love as the highest spiritual gift for interaction within the community, and to the eschatological reservation. At times, Paul himself is willing to be accommodating (1 Cor 9:19–23), though he is cautious about this principle.[33] More important, we see him struggling with the issue of freedom and

---

[31] For a good, readable introduction, see P. Richardson, *Paul's Ethic of Freedom;* also W. Schrage, "Ethics in the NT," *IDB Suppl.,* pp. 284–86. For elaboration of concrete issues that follow, a good introduction is V. P. Furnish, *The Moral Teaching of Paul.*

[32] A recent defense of the view that Paul's ethical parenesis consistently falls short of his fundamental orientation toward love (*agapē*) is found in J. Sanders, *Ethics in the New Testament,* chapter 3.

[33] P. Richardson, *Paul's Ethic of Freedom,* chapter 4.

love in his willingness to admit that there is a special wisdom for "the strong," but that maturity should never be the occasion for causing "the weak" to stumble (1 Cor 8, 10; Rom 14–15). Finally, though the goal might not actually have been met, it finds one of its best expressions in the baptismal formula of Gal 3:28:

> There is neither Jew nor Greek,
> there is neither slave nor free,
> there is neither male nor female;
> for you are all one in Christ Jesus.

We are now in a position to cite some of Paul's concrete cases.

1. Sex, marriage, and divorce.   At Corinth, Paul had to counter two extremes: the enthusiasts who championed a libertine ethic with the slogan, "All things are lawful" (1 Cor 6:12; 10:23), and the ascetics who fought the evil of physical desire with the slogan, "It is well for a man not to touch a woman" (1 Cor 7:1). Paul responded to specific questions about sex, marriage, and divorce in 1 Cor 7 by taking a middle ground, and by defending the view that the Corinthians remain as they are because the End is near, a practical solution geared to Christian service without anxiety. He clearly preferred celibacy, but as a "gift" (verse 7), not as proof of superior moral status. Yet, he recognized the power of strong sexual desire and did not put marriage down. Drawing on his Pharisaic heritage, he declared that sex belongs in marriage with one partner; otherwise, sexual immorality (*porneia*) results. He said nothing of the other major rabbinic argument, that marriage is necessary for the propagation of the race (cf. Gen 1:28). Paul argued that sex is a mutual responsibility of husband and wife as equal partners, conceding the possibility of temporary abstinence for prayer, again by mutual agreement (verse 6).

What, then, of divorce? In Roman law, either partner could divorce the other, and divorce was common. Jewish law reflected patriarchal traditions. The Law of Moses permitted divorce only by the husband if the wife ". . . finds no favor in his eyes because he has found some indecency in her . . ." (Deut 24:1). The conservative school of Shammai interpreted this to mean that adultery was the only basis for divorce; the liberal school of Hillel said it meant for "any cause." Paul drew upon a "word of the Lord" forbidding divorce altogether, probably as a protection for the woman (Mark 10:2–12; Luke 16:18; contrast Matthew's "except for unchastity" [Matt 5:32; 19:9], probably a reflection of the Shammai position). Yet, Paul did not hold the Jesus word sacrosanct, for in an aside (if it was not interpolated by a scribe), he admitted "separations" would occur, that there should not be second marriages, and that if reconciliation is impossible, the wife (and the husband?) should maintain a single status. If an already married partner *becomes* Christian (nothing is said of a Christian marrying a non-Christian!), Paul recommended that the couple stay together, for marriage is holy, and so the children of holy marriages are holy. Perhaps the non-Christian partner of a marriage will become Christian; yet, if the unbelieving partner wants to separate, the Christian partner is not bound to the marriage. In all of this we observe the apostle accommodating his own preference for celibacy, yet maintaining a position between the poles of libertine and ascetic ethics, and doing so in the light of his eschatology.

2. Attitudes toward women.   In assessing Paul's view of women, it should be recalled that the religious and cultural background out of which he came was patriarchal, that is, a woman was dominated by her father before marriage and by her husband after marriage; her main functions were childbearing (preferably a son) and child rearing, being a wife and sexual partner, cook and housekeeper.[34] A second point to recall is that in looking at Paul's views one must exclude works of the Pauline school (esp. Colossians and Ephesians) and the Pastorals (1, 2 Timothy, Titus); this is an important point since these later letters perpetuate the patriarchal tradition of subordination (Col 3:18; Eph 5:24; 1 Tim 2:9–15). 1 Timothy, in fact, argues that women are not to teach or have authority over men (women are to remain silent) because Eve, not Adam, was deceived; indeed, she ". . . will be saved through bearing children, if she continues in faith and love and holiness, with modesty" (2:15). Another passage that shares this general perspective is 1 Cor 14:33b–36; this passage, as we have seen, interrupts the context in such a way that modern critics believe it is an interpolation by a later scribe, perhaps a member of Paul's school or one from the circles that produced the Pastorals.

This last passage is the strongest indication of subordination in Paul's own letters but it does not come from Paul. Five important passages remain. We have seen that in Gal 3:28, Paul states "neither male nor female . . . in Christ Jesus," clearly indicating that in the new community old distinctions shall be done away with. We have also seen that in 1 Cor 7, Paul balances evenly the roles of men and women in marriage (7:2, 3, 4, 10–11, 12–13, 33–34 [twice]). None of this sounds like the patriarchal tradition. Furthermore, there are clear references to women who have achieved prominence as leaders in the churches. Euodia and Syntyche "labored side by side" with Paul at Philippi (Phil 4:2–3). In Rom 16:1 Paul commends "our sister Phoebe, a deacon of the church at Cenchreae (the eastern port at Corinth)." The masculine term "deacon" implies at least a functional position in the church (Phil 1:1), and elsewhere Paul uses it of his own role as "servant" or "minister."[35] She is also called a "helper" (*prostatis*), which in Hellenistic literature and inscriptions is clearly a term of authority ranging in meaning from "benefactor" to "presiding officer" of a religious cult. Does this one use of the term in the New Testament have the same meaning? Perhaps. In any case, there follows the long list of greetings to persons among whom are Prisca (Priscilla) and Aquila who are given preeminance, Prisca now being mentioned first (cf. 1 Cor 16:19 where Aquila is mentioned first, though greetings are given from the church in "their house" in Ephesus). The order of names clearly indicates her importance inso-

---

[34] R. Harris, "Woman in the Ancient Near East," *IDB Suppl.*, pp. 960–63; P. Trible, "Woman in the OT," *IDB Suppl.*, pp. 963–66; R. Scroggs, "Woman in the NT," *IDB Suppl.*, pp. 966–68.
[35] See below, pp. 211–12.

far as it departs from the usual practice of the day (cf. Acts 18:26). Although there is a good deal of speculation as to how to interpret these passages, it is clear that in Paul's communities, women are not viewed in traditional patriarchal fashion, that in fact they can be seen on a par with men and may have held positions of importance, if not authority.

We come, then, to what appears to be Paul's most "chauvinistic" passage, 1 Cor 11:2–16, a passage that is exceedingly difficult to interpret. Here Paul insists that women should wear a head covering when they pray and prophesy in church, and he gives several arguments to support this view. First, he appears to establish a hierarchy of subordination: God is the "head" (kephalē) of Christ, Christ is the "head" of man/husband, and man/husband is the "head" of woman/wife. Paul uses a play on words: "Any man who prays or prophesies with his head covered dishonors his head (=Christ), but any woman who prays or prophesies with her head unveiled dishonors her head (=man/husband)." In part he has the creation of woman in mind, for in verses 7–9 he states that a man may worship with a bare head because he is "the image and glory of God" (Gen 1:26), but the woman should be veiled because she is the glory (image, of course, is absent) of man according to the order of creation (Gen 2:18–23). Does "head" refer to a subordinationist hierarchy, or is it simply a metaphor for the order of creation?[36] If the latter view holds, Paul does not appear as "chauvinistic" as he might in this passage. These problems of interpretation are compounded by another: the woman should wear a veil "because of the angels" (verse 10). What does this mean? Because of demonic angels who lust for human women (cf. Gen 6:2, the basis for the Jewish tradition of the fall of the angels)? Angels who also participate in worship? No one knows. But the following comment is clear: "in the Lord" men and women have equal status for if originally woman came from man, man is now born from woman, "and all things are from God" (verses 11–12). This comment sounds a good deal more like Paul's balancing of the sexes in 1 Cor 7. In chapter 11, his final comments on the issue of veils indicate his frustration: for a woman to pray without her head covered is improper, against nature, and against Paul's rule in the churches! What lies behind this contrived argument appears to be this: equal status at Corinth has led to a denial of sexual differentiation, that is, freedom has led to potential abuse. In the process we learn that Paul attempts to reassert his Gal 3:28 point of view (verses 11–12), "neither male nor female," and that women do speak in church insofar as they pray and prophesy. Paul's ethical premise of freedom within the bounds of love prevails, despite the difficulties it creates for him at Corinth.

3. Slavery. Slavery was an accepted institution in Greco-Roman society and, due to manumission and subsequent marrying, some estimate that by the end of the first century five-sixths of the population of Rome was servile or had a servile background.[37] It is therefore not surprising that slavery is an accepted

---

[36] R. Scroggs, "Paul and the Eschatological Woman," *Journal of the American Academy of Religion* 40 (1972), pp. 283–303; V. P. Furnish, *Moral Teaching*, p. 99.

[37] W. Rollins, "Slavery in the NT," *IDB Suppl.*, pp. 830-32; S. Bartchy, *First-Century Slavery and 1 Corinthians 7:21.*

institution in the New Testament in general, and that the "master"/"slave" terminology is frequently found, both literally and metaphorically. Paul, for example, states, "Were you a slave when called? Never mind. But if you can gain your freedom, avail yourself of the opportunity (this clause could be translated as "by all means, [as a freedman] live according to [God's calling]"). For he who was called in the Lord as a slave is a freedman of the Lord. Likewise he who was free when called is a slave of Christ. You were bought with a price; do not become slaves of men" (1 Cor 7:21–23). As we saw in the case of Philemon and Onesimus, Paul did not attempt to overturn the institution of slavery; he did, however, appeal to Philemon to accept, and perhaps to release or even to return his slave. Ultimately this appeal was directed to Philemon's Christian freedom, and there is no doubt about the solution for which Paul hoped.

4. Homosexuality.   Paul does not appear preoccupied with homosexuality, but what he does say is in line with most moral philosophy of the period, that is, he condemns homosexual practices. In 1 Cor 6:9, male homosexuality[38] is included in a vice list and in Rom 1:26–27 both male and female homosexual practices are viewed as the consequential activity of those (Gentiles) who refused to acknowledge the one true God. Since we know of no instance of homosexuality in Paul's churches, we gain no impression of how he would have related a specific case to his ethic of freedom within the bounds of love. But it is clear from the context as a whole that his major point is that *all* have sinned and are in need of the gift of God's grace (Rom 1:16–3:31).[39]

5. The state.   Rom 13:1–7 is Paul's chief comment about the state, and it has been the source of much church-state reflection down through the centuries. Frequently, the view here that God has instituted the governing authorities, and every person should be subject to them, has been interpreted in a quietistic sense. This seems reinforced by Paul's appeal to conscience (verse 5). Nonetheless, the total context points to a specific issue—paying one's taxes—and it should be recalled that a minute Christian movement that had as yet had no major conflict with mighty Rome would naturally pick up the Hellenistic Jewish position in relation to the Empire.[40]

THE IMPACT OF THE APOSTLE PAUL

It is impossible to overestimate the importance of the apostle Paul to the New Testament and to subsequent Christendom. His vision of the nature of Christian faith came at the crucial moment when circumstances were trans-

[38] V. P. Furnish, *Moral Teaching*, p. 70, translates: "men who assume the female role in sex" and "men who have sex with them."

[39] Much misunderstanding of Biblical literature as a whole surrounds this subject; for further study, one should consult V. P. Furnish, *Moral Teaching*, chapter 3, and M. Pope, "Homosexuality," *IDB Suppl.*, pp. 415–17, and their bibliographies.

[40] V. P. Furnish, *Moral Teaching*, chapter 5; G. Krodel, "Rome, Early Christian Attitudes toward," *IDB Suppl.*, pp. 756–58.

forming Christianity from an apocalyptic sect within Judaism into a missionary cult within Hellenism and beyond that into a world religion. In this process Paul came to play a major part, not only because he was a leader in the missionary movement, but even more because his view of the nature of Christian faith blended together the three aspects of its heritage—Judaism, Hellenism, and a distinctive Christian experience—into a new whole. Paul's vision of the nature of Christian faith became normative. The author of 2 Peter had to wrestle with it (2 Pet 3:15–16), and as we stated at the beginning of chapter 5, he had a tremendous influence on later thinkers such as Augustine, Luther, Calvin, and Wesley. Moreover, he trained followers who not only served the church during his lifetime, but who also lived to provide leadership in the next generation. The very existence of 2 Thessalonians, Colossians, Ephesians, and the Pastorals is eloquent testimony to Paul's continuing influence. Finally, Paul's letter writing provided the impetus toward the formation of the New Testament itself. The first step in establishing the New Testament as a distinctive body of literature was taken when his letters to individual churches were recognized as being important to all churches and were copied and circulated. For Paul himself, "Scripture" was what we would call the Old Testament, but it is in no small part due to him that there is now a New Testament.

Further Reading

General studies, works pertaining to the life of Paul and his churches, introductions, and commentaries are cited in the bibliography at the end of chapter 5.

For Paul as a writer of letters, see:

JBC, pp. 223–26, "New Testament Epistles" (J. A. Fitzmyer).
IDB, vol. 4, pp. 113–15, "Letter" (O. J. F. Seitz).
⨯ IDB Suppl., pp. 538–41, "Letter" (N. A. Dahl).
W. G. Kümmel, Intro., pp. 247–52.
W. Marxsen, Intro., pp. 17–29.
R. Fuller, Intro., pp. 16–19.
R. Funk, Language, Hermeneutic, and Word of God, "Language as It Occurs in the New Testament: Letter," pp. 224–74.
W. Doty, Letters in Primitive Christianity.
C. Roetzel, The Letters of Paul.
K. H. Schelke, "The Letters of Paul," in K. Rahner, Sacramentum Mundi, vol. 4, pp. 198–203.
M. L. Stirnewalt, "The Form and Function of the Greek Letter-Essay," in C. P. Donfried, The Romans Debate, pp. 175–206.

For traditions in Paul's letters, see:

D. Duling, Jesus Christ Through History, pp. 43–52.
A. M. Hunter, Paul and His Predecessors.
C. Roetzel, The Letters of Paul, chapter 3.

General studies of the theology of Paul:

F. Amiot, *The Key Concepts of St. Paul.*
C. K. Barrett, *From First Adam to Last: A Study in Pauline Theology.*
M. Barth, *Justification. Pauline Texts Interpreted in the Light of the Old and New Testaments.*
G. Bornkamm, *Paul,* Part 2.
R. Bultmann, *Theology of the New Testament,* vol. 1
L. Cerfaux, *Christ in the Theology of St. Paul.*
———, *The Church in the Theology of St. Paul.*
H. Conzelmann, *An Outline of the Theology of the New Testament,* pp. 155-282.
C. H. Dodd, *The Meaning of Paul for Today.*
J. Fitzmyer, *Pauline Theology: A Brief Sketch* (= *JCB*, pp. 800–27).
W. G. Kümmel, *The Theology of the New Testament,* pp. 250–350.
R. Rubenstein, *My Brother Paul.*
E. P. Sanders, *Paul and Palestinian Judaism.*
S. Sandmel, *The Genius of Paul.*
D. H. Whitely, *The Theology of St. Paul.*

Collected Studies:

G. Bornkamm, *Early Christian Experience.*
N. A. Dahl, *Studies in Paul.*
E. Käsemann, *Essays on New Testament Themes.*
———, *New Testament Questions of Today.*
———, *Perspectives on Paul.*
W. Meeks, *The Writings of St. Paul,* Part 2.
K. Stendahl, *Paul Among Jews and Gentiles.*

Studies of questions pertaining to Paul's ethics:

IDB Suppl., "Ethics in the NT" (W. Schrage), pp. 284–86; "Woman in the Ancient Near East" (R. Harris), pp. 960–63; "Woman in the OT" (P. Trible), pp. 963–66; "Woman in the NT" (R. Scroggs), pp. 966-68; "Homosexuality" (M. Pope), pp. 415–17; "Rome, Early Christian Attitudes toward" (G. Krodel), pp. 756–58; "Slavery in the NT" (W. G. Rollins), pp. 830–32.
V. P. Furnish, *Theology and Ethics in Paul.*
———, *The Moral Teaching of Paul.*
J. L. Houlden, *Ethics and the New Testament.*
P. Richardson, *Paul's Ethic of Freedom.*
J. Sanders, *Ethics in the New Testament,* chapter 3.
R. Schnackenburg, *The Moral Teaching of the New Testament.*

Title page of the book Thomas the Contender, *one of the Gnostic texts discovered at Nag Hammadi, Egypt (see Appendix 4).*

CHAPTER SEVEN

DEUTERO-PAULINE CHRISTIANITY
and The Letter to the Hebrews

Pseudonymity is a common phenomenon in ancient literature, a phenomenon shared also by the New Testament. There is no more remarkable example than the six letters supposedly written by Paul, which were not: 2 Thessalonians, Colossians, Ephesians, and the Pastorals (1 and 2 Timothy and Titus). We say categorically "were not," but modern New Testament scholarship is divided on the authenticity or pseudonymity of several of these letters. The Pastorals are accepted by almost all scholars as pseudonymous, Ephesians by most, and Colossians and 2 Thessalonians by some. We are satisfied that all six are pseudonymous, and we proceed on the basis of this opinion, giving arguments for the opinion as each letter is discussed.

That letters are written in the name of the apostle Paul, and indeed that quite elaborate steps are taken to claim his name—2 Thessalonians exactly imitates the greetings of 1 Thessalonians—speaks volumes for the influence of the apostle. The writers were most probably pupils of the apostle who consciously imitated their teacher, wrote in his name, and totally identified themselves with him. This was permissible in the ancient world; indeed, in that world it was an accepted literary practice. This means that we are in the presence of a Pauline "school," analogous to the many schools that existed in the Greco-Roman world, from the rabbis to the Stoics.[1]

The letters fall into two groups because of their concerns and most probable dates. 2 Thessalonians, Colossians, and Ephesians probably date from the seventies or eighties of the first Christian century and reflect the concerns of the generation immediately following the death of the apostle. The Pastorals are at least a generation later and reflect the concerns of the church at the beginning of the second century. For that reason we will discuss here only 2

---

[1] See chapter 11, pp. 364–67, for a discussion of the Johannine school.

Thessalonians, Colossians, and Ephesians, leaving the Pastorals until we discuss emergent institutional Christianity in chapter 12.

SECOND THESSALONIANS

2 Thessalonians is so like 1 Thessalonians and yet so different that it must be an imitation of 1 Thessalonians written to meet a later situation. Verbal similarities begin with the first verse and continue throughout; yet, there are many un-Pauline phrases. The same is true of stylistic peculiarities. Both characteristics point to a heavy reliance on 1 Thessalonians. Indeed, the structure of the two letters is similar enough that 2 Thessalonians imitates what may be an interpolated, second thanksgiving in 1 Thess 2:13–16.[2] Despite these appearances of imitation, there are very real theological differences between the two letters, the most important being that of eschatological perspective. In 1 Thessalonians the parousia, the coming of Jesus from heaven as apocalyptic judge and redeemer, is imminent. When Paul speaks of "we who are alive, who are left until the coming of the Lord" (1 Thess 4:15), he clearly expects the event in his own lifetime. But 2 Thess 2:1–12 sets out an elaborate program of what must first happen before that event can occur. Not only has the apocalyptic imagery changed, but the whole tenor of the expectation is different. The End is no longer imminent. Yet, Paul's subsequent correspondence, especially 1 Corinthians, maintains the eschatological perspective of imminence found in 1 Thessalonians. Another notably non-Pauline feature of the letter is the idea that the judgment of God will be a reward for the persecuted Christians and a persecution of the persecutors (1:5–10). This way of thinking is not only non-Pauline, it belongs to a generation later than Paul's, more poetically expressed in Rev 16:5–7 and 19:2. Furthermore, the generation following Paul tended to ascribe to Jesus attributes and functions that Paul's generation reserved to God, a tendency that was a natural consequence of a developing Christology. So in 2 Thessalonians we read of "our Lord Jesus Christ himself, and God our Father, who loved us and gave us . . ." (2:16), or we find the prayer, "May the Lord direct your hearts to the love of God and to the steadfastness of Christ" (3:5). This is a subtle christological step from "Now may our God and Father himself, and our Lord Jesus, direct our way to you; and may the Lord make you increase and abound in love to one another . . . so that he may establish your hearts unblamable in holiness before our God and Father . . ." (1 Thess 3:11–13). The two are close enough together to be related, but in 2 Thessalonians the Christology represents a later thinking and piety.

The best understanding of 2 Thessalonians, therefore, is to see it as a deliberate imitation of 1 Thessalonians by a member of a Pauline school. In two verses, we read of an oral report and another letter purporting to be from Paul (2:2, 15; cf. 3:14, 17) indicating that the parousia has *already* come. Since such a letter cannot be 1 Thessalonians, it must represent opponents who believe in a kind of apocalyptic enthusiasm. Perhaps they have interpreted the

---

[2] G. Krodel, "2 Thessalonians," in G. Krodel, ed., *Ephesians, Colossians, 2 Thessalonians, The Pastoral Epistles* (Proclamation Commentaries), pp. 77–79; cf. chapter 5, n. 5.

persecutions that the Thessalonians are suffering as the "day of the Lord" (2:2). Some of the Thessalonians have stopped working and are living in idleness. Do the letter and the oral report come from an alternative, rival Pauline school? In any case, a Paulinist writes 2 Thessalonians using 1 Thessalonians as a model, exhorting the community to keep the Pauline traditions, warning against opponents who teach a kind of apocalyptic enthusiasm, admonishing certain members of the church not to be idle and telling them to work and earn their own living. In so doing, the author stressed a delay of the parousia in a sense that went beyond anything Paul himself envisaged. He reveals a situation of persecution and the response to it reaching the stage we know from the book of Revelation, itself a text from the end of the first Christian century; and his Christology is somewhat advanced from, though clearly related to, that in 1 Thessalonians. The letter is apocalyptic, and like other apocalyptic, is intended to be a source of encouragement and hope for those who are in crisis and suffering persecution; but the persecution context is one that is a generation after Paul. Nonetheless, our author is clearly in the Pauline tradition and immensely dedicated to the apostle. The analysis of the letter itself is a comparatively simple matter.

1:1–2 *Salutation,* an imitation of 1 Thess 1:1.

1:3–12 *Thanksgiving,* together with the awareness of persecution and the expectation that God will reward the persecuted and punish the persecutors.

2:1–12 *The problem of the delay of the parousia* is dealt with by developing a scenario of things that must come first: "the rebellion," the revelation of "the man of lawlessness, . . . the son of perdition, who opposes and exalts himself against every so-called god or object of worship, so that he takes his seat in the temple of God, proclaiming himself to be God." Satan will be involved, and pretended signs and wonders. Such references sound like a recollection of events associated with the destruction of Jerusalem and the Temple in A.D. 70, on which see the discussion of Mark 13 above (chapter 4) and in chapter 8.

2:13–3:5 *Thanksgiving and parenesis.* The church must hold fast to the Pauline traditions ("the things which we command," 3:4.) The pattern of thanksgiving, admonition, and benediction occurs twice (2:13–16; 3:1–5).

3:6–16 *Closing appeals, rebukes, and prayer.*

3:17–18 *Autographic conclusion.* In itself an argument for pseudonymity, this note is based on the genuine note in Gal 6:11. See also 1 Cor 16:21.

COLOSSIANS

The authenticity or pseudonymity of the letter to the Colossians is a difficult historical question. Most New Testament scholars who review the evidence and arguments do in fact decide in favor of authenticity. Of the six reference works we are constantly recommending as further reading, only one, Marxsen's *Introduction to the New Testament,* decides for pseudonymity.

The data on which authenticity or pseudonymity has to be decided is not in dispute in the letter to the Colossians; the dispute is in the interpretation of the data. The data themselves and the questions they raise may be summarized as follows:

Factors Indicating Pseudonymity

Language and Style

The vocabulary of Colossians is not homogeneous with the indubitably certain Pauline letters. There are twenty-five words not found elsewhere in Paul and thirty-four not found elsewhere in the New Testament; so the vocabulary is, to say the least, distinctive. In style, synonyms are heaped together (e.g., 1:9; 1:22) and "the style is cumbersome, wordy, overloaded almost to opaqueness with dependent clauses, participial and infinitive constructions, or substantives with *en* (in). For example, 1:9–20 is one sentence (cf. 2:9–15)!"[3] All this contrasts markedly with the normal Pauline style. On the other hand, a number of expressions and stylistic peculiarities in Colossians are found elsewhere in the New Testament only in the genuine Pauline letters.

These linguistic factors could be due to pseudonymity, in part different from and in part deliberate imitation of Pauline vocabulary and style. Or they could be due to an intentional use of the opponents' vocabulary and to the very extensive use in this letter of traditional material—hymns, confessions, lists of virtues, household codes, and the like. The letter does employ a great deal of traditional material, and it can be argued that this accounts for the non-Pauline language and style. If this is the case, the non-Pauline language and style are not indications of pseudonymity. But then it could be retorted that such an extensive use of traditional material is itself non-Pauline. In Phil 2:6–11 Paul does quote a hymn, and in Rom 1:3–4 a liturgical formula, and so on, but never to the extent of such material in Colossians. So the argument from language and style seesaws back and forth.

The Absence of Pauline Concepts

Several of the concepts particularly characteristic of Paul—righteousness, justification, law, salvation, revelation, fellow Christians as "brethren" (apart from the Greeting)—are noticeably absent from Colossians. Of course, some of them are missing from any one genuine Pauline letter; nevertheless, the mortality rate in Colossians is particularly high.

The Presence of Concepts Not Found in the Earlier Letters

Colossians has a whole series of concepts that are either new in the Pauline corpus or a significant development over anything in the earlier letters. The most important of these are the following.

[3] W. G. Kümmel, *Intro.*, p. 341.

Christology.   The Christology of Col 1:15–23 is an advance on anything to be found earlier. In 2 Cor 4:4 (NEB), Christ is the "image" of God, and in Rom 8:29, God predestines Christians "to be conformed to the image of his Son, in order that he might be the first born among many brethren."[4] But in Col 1:15 "He is the image of the invisible God, the first born of all creation." No longer does Christ reflect a likeness to which others can be conformed, but he is now seen as a true representation of God, making visible what heretofore was invisible. He is no longer the first born among the believers who in part share that new birth at their baptism and will share it completely at their resurrection, but rather the first born of all creation. Moreover, he is now the goal of all creation, "all things were created through him and for him" (Col 1:16). In 1 Cor 8:6, God is the goal of creation, "from whom are all things and for whom we exist." "*We* exist," rather than "all things exist," because Paul himself never reaches the pan-cosmic thinking of Colossians, even though in Rom 8:19–23 he is on the way to it. If we argue that these developments in Colossians occur because the author is quoting a christological hymn, as indeed he is, it still remains a fact that he is identifying himself with what he quotes, and the differences between Colossians and Romans or the Corinthian correspondence still remain.

The church as the body of Christ.   In Col 1:18 Christ is the head of the body, the church, where the "body" is a cosmic reality (1:18, 24; 2:19; 3:15), but in Rom 7:4; 12:5; 1 Cor 12:12–31, it is a metaphorical way of expressing mutual interdependence of Christians in the church.

Steps toward the church as an institution.   Perhaps the most important developments in Colossians are not so much those *from* as those *toward:* developments toward the kind of thinking characteristic of the church becoming an institution rather than of the freer, more charismatic days reflected in the indubitably genuine Pauline letters. A first instance of this is the references to Epaphras as "a faithful minister of Christ on our behalf," to the gospel "of which I, Paul, became a minister," and to Paul's ministry as "a divine office" in 1:7, 23, 25. These references are a significant step beyond the use of the same Greek word, *diakonos,* in any earlier letter. In Phil 1:1 ("deacons") and Rom 16:1 ("deaconess") a specific office is not clearly indicated. In Rom 13:4, 5, the word is used of the worldly "governing authorities," in Rom 15:8, of Christ as a "servant" to the circumcision, and in 1 Cor 3:5, 2 Cor 6:4, 11:23, it is used of Paul and others as "servants" of God or of Christ. In these last instances the Revised Standard Version uniformly uses the English word *servant* rather than *minister.* Only in 2 Cor 3:6, which the Revised Standard Version translates, "God who has qualified us to be ministers of a new covenant," do we come even near to the usage in Colossians. But even here there is a significant difference, and a glance at the word in 1 Tim 4:6, "If you put these instructions before the brethren, you will be a good *minister* of Christ Jesus," shows us

---

[4] In the quotations the word translated "image" is always the same word in Greek (*eikon*). But the English translations vary and to make our point we have given the translations that use "image." So 2 Cor 4:4 is NEB (RSV "likeness"), Rom 8:19 is RSV (NEB "likeness"), and Col 1:15 is RSV (NEB also "image").

where the difference lies: the use in Colossians is a move *from* the earlier Pauline letters *toward* the use in the Pastorals.

A further step from the earlier letters toward the Pastorals is the understanding of "Christ Jesus" as the subject of the authoritative tradition the believer "receives" and in which he "lives" (Col 2:6). Here is the understanding of Christian faith as accepting authoritative tradition being the basis for Christian living, which is characteristic of the literature of the emergent institutional church but is foreign to Paul himself. Paul accepts this role of tradition only in connection with the details of Christian living (1 Cor 7:10) or the liturgical practice of the churches (1 Cor 11:23–26), *never* as providing the essence of Christian faith.

One last point is the role of baptism. In Col 2:11 baptism is the Christian equivalent of Jewish circumcision: it is the formal signification of membership in the community. In the earlier letters circumcision is a Jewish rite now abandoned by Christians (Rom 2:25–29; 3:1; 3:30; 4:9–12), and baptism is the dynamic means of entrance into a new and different life (Rom 6:3–11). Moreover, for all that Col 2:11–14 uses the language of Rom 6:3–5, baptism has become more formal and less eschatological. In Colossians we are on the way toward 1 Peter, itself part of the literature of the emergent institutional church, of the church becoming an institution, where "Baptism . . . now saves you, not as a removal of dirt from the body but as an appeal to God for a clear conscience, through the resurrection of Jesus Christ" (1 Pet 3:21).

A further development from the earlier letters applies both to Colossians and to Ephesians: it is the verb in both letters that expresses the activity of Christ in reconciliation. "In Christ God was reconciling the world to himself" (2 Cor 5:19) is the starting point for the developments in Col 1:19–20 ("to reconcile to himself all things") and in Eph 2:16 ("reconcile us both [Jew and Gentile] to God in one body through the cross"). But 2 Cor 5:19 uses *katallassein*, as the earlier letters uniformly do, whereas Colossians and Ephesians as uniformly use *apokatallassein*. Both verbs mean "to reconcile," but there is a small yet significant difference between them.

Each scholar evaluates the data differently, but for us the cumulative weight of the evidence indicates pseudonymity, and the new concepts developed in Colossians provide the decisive impulse for that conclusion.

The Opponents at Colossae

Colossae was located in the Lycus River Valley in Phrygia, in the interior of western Asia Minor east of Ephesus. It was not far from Laodicea and Hieropolis where there were also churches (Col 4:13–17). As far as we know, Paul himself had never been there although it was in his general area of missionizing. From the letter we may state that the church at Colossae was a Gentile church (1:21, 27; 2:13).

The letter to the Colossians (especially chapter 2) indicates that there are certain opponents there who hold a "philosophy." This philosophy is not in accord with the one who on the Cross became Lord over all the "principalities and powers" (1:16; 2:15). It is in accord with the "elements of the universe" (cf. Gal 4:3) who demand "worship of angels," Jewish cultic practices (food, drink, festivals, new moons, and sabbaths), ascetic rigor of devotion, self-abasement and severity of the body, and regulations such as "Do not handle, Do not taste, Do not touch." We also hear of "wisdom" and "knowledge" (2:3). To whom do these beliefs refer? Who are these opponents? These are much discussed questions. To complicate matters, there is a difficult phrase in verse 18 translated "taking his (the opponent's) stand on visions" (RSV) that can be read "which he has seen, upon entering." The term "entering" here has frequently been held to refer to entering the secret sanctuary of a mystery cult.[5] If this is accurate, perhaps the initiate had an ecstatic vision of the cosmos as he was being initiated, having already been instructed in proper beliefs, especially angel worship. Still another recent theory is that "worship of angels" means that there is here a vision of entering into heaven in a mystical fashion and participating with the angels who are themselves worshipping.[6] In view of such difficulties, it is not surprising to find a vast number of theories as to the identity of the fascinating Colossian opponents. Some have suggested that the cultic regulations point to sectarian Judaism such as can be found at Qumran. Others, probably more plausibly, have noted parallels in Hellenistic Judaism, especially "Wisdom" speculation, or Pythagorean philosophy. A very widespread view based on language ("wisdom," "knowledge," "fulness"), the boasting and arrogance of adherents, and the connection with the redeemer myth in Col 1:15–20 is that the "philosophy" looks like an early form of Gnosticism, that is, pre-Gnosticism.[7] In this regard we may recall that the Gnostic despaired of this world since it is under control of evil and hostile powers which have imprisoned one's true spiritual self in a material body. The Gnostic sought release in the form of a true "knowledge" (*gnōsis*) enabling him to know of his origins from the God of Light, his status as an alien in this world, and his destiny in returning to the world from which he came. Later Gnosticism developed a Gnostic redeemer myth which stated that the redeemer brought the knowledge necessary for salvation; this, however, cannot be definitely proved for New Testament times. In any case, it will be illuminating to point to a third-century Gnostic text, the "Gospel of Truth":[8]

The Gospel of Truth is joy for those who have received from the Father of Truth the grace of knowing Him through the power of the Word, which has come forth from the Pleroma (the Word), which is in the

[5] See chapter 1, pp. 12–13.

[6] F. O. Francis, "Humility and Angelic Worship in Col 2:18," *Studia Theologica* 16 (1962), pp. 109–34.

[7] This is especially dominant in German scholarship, cf. E. Lohse, *Colossians and Philemon,* pp. 129–30, ". . . can be termed Gnostic or, if a more cautious designation is desired, pre-Gnostic. . . . The cult . . . probably took the form of a mystery."

[8] The "Gospel of Truth" as we have it is a third-century text, one of the Gnostic texts discovered at Nag Hammadi in Egypt in 1946. On this gospel see E. Hennecke and W. Schneemelcher, *New Testament Apocrypha,* vol. 1, pp. 233–41 and 523–31. Our quotations are from the translation given in Hennecke-Schneemelcher, pp. 523, 525, and 530. For the discoveries at Nag Hammadi, see Appendix 4, pp. 467–68.

thought and mind of the Father (and) which is he whom they call "the Saviour," for that is the name of the work which he is to accomplish for the salvation of those who were ignorant of the Father; for this name "the Gospel" is the revelation of hope, since it is a discovery for those who seek Him.

Therefore if anyone possesses knowledge, he receives that which is his own and draws it back to himself. For he who is ignorant is deficient, and it is a great thing which he lacks, since he lacks what will make him perfect. Since the perfection of the All is in the Father, it is necessary that the All ascend to Him, and that each one receive that which is his own, (the things) which He has written down beforehand, having prepared them to be given to those who came forth from Him.

If anyone possesses knowledge, he is a being from on high. If he is called, he hears, replies, and turns towards Him who calls him in order to ascend to Him, and he knows in what way he is called. Since he knows, he performs the will of Him who called him. He desires to please Him (and) receives rest.

He will speak about the place from which each one has come, and (each) will hasten to return once more to the region from which he derived his true condition, and to be delivered from that place, the place wherein he has been, since he tastes of that place and receives nourishment and growth (therein).

The pre-Gnosticism at Colossae was a form that had borrowed widely from Judaism, building into its particular way of salvation Jewish elements such as dietary laws and observances of religious festivals and the Sabbath (Col 2:16–17). It also accepted the idea of "elemental spirits of the universe," i.e., supernatural intermediaries between God and the world, who had to be placated because they controlled life in the world and the destiny of man. Therefore one had to know what days were favorable or unfavorable, what was under the control of malevolent supernatural beings and hence taboo, and what was under the control of beneficent beings and hence permitted to the man of "knowledge" (Col 2:20–23).

The author of Colossians meets the problem by claiming, in effect, that Christianity is superior to any form of Gnosticism. Christ is superior to the supernatural beings, as the salvation he offers is superior to that offered by Gnostic "knowledge." The author rebukes those falling into the heresy for disqualifying themselves from enjoying the true riches available in Christ. In doing this, the author interprets both Christ and the Christian faith very much in Gnostic terms, and the letter is an interesting blend of Pauline and Gnostic ideas.

Exegetical Survey of the Letter to the Colossians

1:1–14 *Salutation, thanksgiving, and intercession.*
    1:1–2 *Salutation,* somewhat shorter than is usual.

1:3-14 *Thanksgiving and intercession.* As we have noted often in Paul himself, and now in the Pauline school, the Thanksgiving indicates something of the concerns of the letter. In verse 7 Epaphras is strongly and emphatically supported in his position in the Colossian church. Nowhere in the genuine letters does Paul show such esteem for a fellow worker as is here exhibited for Epaphras. The Intercession fades over into the Hymn to Christ (1:15-20). For all the periods and paragraphs in the English translations, in the Greek, 1:9-20 is one long sentence.

1:15-23 *Christology and parenesis.*

1:15-20 *The christological hymn.* We have already given an analysis of the structure of this hymn, so we have no need to repeat that here. There is, however, a strong case for the hypothesis that originally it was not a hymn to Christ at all but to another redeemer figure from the Hellenistic world. The language is characteristic of an ancient Wisdom myth which was further developed in later Gnosticism, and one theory is that we have here an early form of the Gnostic myth of the redeemer.[9] This does not mean that the language and concepts are any less Christian; it simply means that early Christianity was as eclectic as any other religious movement in the Hellenistic world and was adopting material offered to it by its cultural environment.

It is possible that we can go even further into the functional context (*Sitz im Leben*) of this hymn, because verses 12-14 contain reminiscences of the baptism of Jesus ("beloved Son," Mark 1:11) and of texts relating to baptism elsewhere in the New Testament.[10] We come close to the dynamics of New Testament Christianity in its "middle period" by envisaging a church adapting a known hymn to a redeemer to express faith in Christ as *The* Redeemer and using it in baptismal rites. Then the author of Colossians, wishing to focus attention on Christ as *The* Redeemer, takes it up and uses it in his letter.

1:21-23 *Parenesis.* In what we recognize as a fashion typical of the New Testament as a whole, the christological hymn is followed by an exhortation to the readers based on it. This concludes on the note of Paul as a "minister of the gospel," which leads into the next section.

1:24-2:5 *The apostolic office.* We have noted that Colossians has a more advanced concept of the office of "minister" (1:7, 23, 25) than we find in the undisputed Pauline Letters, and that this indicates a higher level of formal church organization. In this section the Paulinist is more formal than his teacher, but he has learned from him a preparedness to suffer in and for the ministry of the church (cf. 2 Cor 1:5-6; 4:10). Moreover, the Christian

[9] E. Käsemann, *Essays on New Testament Themes*, p. 154. See also the subsequent discussion in J. Sanders, *New Testament Christological Hymns*, pp. 79-80.

[10] "Deliverance" ("he has delivered us from . . .") is especially associated with the deliverance of the Jews from Egypt, which in Christianity became a type of baptism (1 Cor 10:2). "Forgiveness of sins" is certainly associated with baptism (Mark 1:4; Luke 3:3; Acts 2:38), and "redemption" is very much a liturgical word (Rom 3:24; 1 Cor 1:30). For detailed arguments see E. Käsemann, *Essays*, pp. 160-62.

message takes on more Hellenistic emphases. The word of God is the hidden "mystery" now made manifest; the Christian knows "the riches of the glory of this mystery"; he is warned "in wisdom"; he becomes "mature." Though "mystery" turns up at Qumran, this is language characteristic of Hellenistic religion in general. At the same time, definitely Jewish or specifically Christian emphases are also to be found: "the word of God," "the energy which he [Christ] mightily inspires within me," "faith in Christ." This passage is a good example of how different religious traditions came together in what we may call Hellenistic Christianity after Paul.

2:6–23 *Warning against the false teaching.* It will be noted that we regard this section as beginning at 2:6 (NEB, TEV) rather than 2:8 (RSV).

> **2:6–7** *The nature of Christian faith.* In Col 2:6, the Paulinist takes up a Jewish technical term, the verb *to walk, to go,* the Hebrew verb from which the Jewish scribes took their term for legally binding decisions, *halachah.* So he is using technical terms when he says, "As therefore ye received Christ Jesus the Lord, so walk in him" (ERV), and "Christ Jesus" has become the subject of tradition handed on formally in the church and received as authoritative by the church member. We are moving from anything found in the undisputed Pauline Letters (1 Cor 11:23; 15:3: "receiving," "delivering") to the concept of Christian faith found in the Pastorals as essentially the acceptance of authoritative tradition about Jesus Christ, and of responding by accepting directions as to how the Christian should "walk."

> **2:8–15** *Warning against the false teaching as doctrine.* Since the central element in true Christian faith is "Christ Jesus" as the subject of authoritative tradition, it is essential for the Paulinist to claim that Christ Jesus as understood in orthodox Christian tradition is superior to the spiritual powers and beings who figure so prominently in various Hellenistic religions. This he does by contrasting the "human tradition" concerning "elemental spirits of the universe" with the Christian concept of Christ as the supreme spiritual being. In Christ "the fullness (*plērōma*) of the deity dwells"; he "is the head of all rule and authority," who, moreover, has proven spectacularly successful in making available to those who believe in him a salvation infinitely superior to anything offered by the "principalities and powers" over whom, indeed, Christ triumphed in his Cross.

> A most interesting aspect of this section is the dynamic blend of developments of Pauline ideas (which the author clearly knows well) with ideas taken from Hellenistic religions. The term *plērōma,* a key word in the Christology of this passage, is a technical term in later Gnosticism. Furthermore, Col 2:11–14 must be read against the background of Rom 6:4–11. The differences in the two passages are sufficiently great for us to regard the Colossians passage as written by a Paulinist rather than by Paul himself, but the pupil has understood his teacher and is legitimately developing his insights to meet the

needs of a later generation and a different situation. Similarly, Col 2:15 develops for still another situation a metaphor Paul uses in 2 Cor 2:14.

2:16–23 *Warning against the false teaching as practice.* The Paulinist now argues against the religious and ethical practices encouraged by the false teaching at Colossae. He argues against the Jewish dietary laws and festival and Sabbath-day observances that the false teaching encourages: "All such things are only a shadow of things in the future; the reality is Christ" (2:17, TEV). This statement is not only telling, it is also a further example of the eclectic blending of Hellenistic and Jewish-Christian ideas in deutero-Pauline Christianity. The distinction between shadow and substance (with the worldly being the shadow and the eternal the substance) is Hellenistic, and indeed Platonic, to the core; but the reality to come in the future is a note from Jewish-Christian eschatology. The Paulinist further argues against "visions" and the "worship of angels" by claiming that they are not proper to the church that is the body of Christ and wholly dependent on its head. Here the church's need for an integrated structure and a disciplined organization come to the fore and necessarily push out the charismatic freedom of an earlier day typified by Paul and his revelatory visions. Finally, in this section the author again takes his point of departure from the Pauline concept of dying with Christ in baptism and holds that this sets the Christian free from an asceticism that would be a form of service to those very elemental spirits to which he died in baptism. This argument applies to a later and different set of circumstances a view that Paul expressed in Gal 2:19–21 and in Romans 6, namely that in baptism the believer died to the Jewish Law and its demands.

3:1–4:6 *Parenesis.* There now follows a long parenetical section. Col 3:1–4 accepts the claim characteristic of Hellenistic Christian religious enthusiasm as a whole (and apparently a part of the false teaching at Colossae), namely that already *in the present* the Christian enjoys the power of the resurrection life. The Paulinist tends to accept this, where Paul himself had rejected it (1 Cor 15; Rom 6:5), but he maintains that there is still something that will only be known in the future: "Your real life is Christ, and when he appears, then you too will appear with him and share his glory!" (3:4, TEV). A similar note of traditional Pauline eschatology is sounded in 3:6, "the wrath of God [i.e., the final judgment] is coming."

Col 3:18–4:1 is the first example in the Pauline corpus of a literary form typical in Hellenistic moral instruction, a household code.[11] Such codes were originally developed by Stoic philosophers and were widely used in the Hellenistic world. They are a feature of the deutero-Pauline literature and the emergent institutional church in the New Testament,

---

[11] The Germans have a technical term for such lists: *Haustafeln*. Other examples in the New Testament are: Eph 5:2–6:9; 1 Tim 2:8–15; 6:1–2; Tit 2:1–10; 1 Pet 2:13–3:7. There are none in the undisputed Pauline letters.

but not of the genuine Pauline letters. Except for the references to "the Lord" and the "Master in heaven," this code in Col 3:18–4:1 has no specifically Christian elements. What we have here is most probably the Christianization of a previously existing list of "moral principles governing family life in popular Greek philosophy and Jewish *halacha*."[12]

4:7–18   *Final greetings and benediction.* Note the references to Onesimus (Philemon), Mark (4:10), and "Luke the beloved physician" (4:14).

EPHESIANS

In the case of Colossians, only one of the six reference works recommended as further reading decides for pseudonymity. In the case of Ephesians, however, four of the six decide for pseudonymity, and the other two (*PCB* and *JBC*) recognize the difficulties in maintaining Pauline authorship. Indeed, the difficulties are insurmountable. They are summarized in the following section.

Factors Indicating Pseudonymity

Language and Style

There are forty words in Ephesians that are not found elsewhere in the Pauline corpus. Many of them appear in later New Testament writings and in the Christian literature immediately following the New Testament period. Further, synonyms are heaped together in an absolutely non-Pauline manner, e.g., 1:19 has four separate words for "power." Then there is a passion for long involved sentences, going far beyond anything even in Colossians, e.g., 1:15–23; 3:1–7; 4:11–16. The King James Version and English Revised Version represent this feature of the letter far more accurately than the Revised Standard Version, New English Bible, or Today's English Version which have broken up the sentences as an (admittedly necessary) aid to translating them.

Relationship to Colossians

A glance at the margin of the Revised Standard Version or of a Greek critical text shows that Ephesians constantly quotes and develops Colossians. About one-third of the words in Colossians are found in Ephesians; of 155 verses in Ephesians, 73 have verbal parallels in Colossians; only short connected passages from Ephesians have no parallel in Colossians (e.g., Eph 2:6–9; 4:5–13; 5:29–33). Three examples will illustrate the point.

---

[12] M. Dibelius, quoted by W. Marxsen, *Intro.*, p. 183.

Colossians	**Ephesians**
3:12–13 Put on then,	*4:1–2* I therefore, a prisoner
as God's chosen ones,	for the Lord, beg you to lead
holy and beloved,	a life worthy of the calling
compassion, kindness,	to which you have been called,
lowliness, meekness,	2) with all *lowliness* and *meekness,*
and *patience,* 13)	with *patience,*
forbearing one another	*forbearing one another*
and, if one has a complaint	in love. . . .
against another, forgiving	
each other; . . .	
3:16–17 Let the word of	*5:19–20*
Christ dwell in you richly,	
as you teach and admonish	. . . addressing
one another in all wisdom,	*one another in*
and as you sing	
psalms and hymns and spiritual	*psalms and hymns and spiritual*
songs with thankfulness	*songs,* singing and making melody
in *your hearts to* God.	*to* the Lord with all *your heart,*
17) And whatever you do,	20) always and
in word or in deed,	
do *everything*	for *everything* giving thanks
in the name	*in the name*
of the *Lord Jesus,* giving	*of* our *Lord Jesus* Christ
thanks *to God the Father*	*to God the Father.*
through him.	
4:7–8	*6:21–22* Now that you also may know
Tychicus	how I am and what I am doing, *Tychicus*
will tell you all about	
my affairs; he is	
a *beloved brother and*	the *beloved brother and*
faithful minister and fellow	*faithful minister*
servant *in the Lord.*	*in the Lord*
	will tell you everything.
8) *I have sent him to you*	22) *I have sent him to you*
for this very purpose, that	*for this very purpose, that*
you may know how we are and	*you may know how we are and*
that he may encourage	*that he may encourage*
your hearts, . . .	*your hearts.*

This dependence on a previous letter is unparalleled in the Pauline corpus, and as an argument of pseudonymity it is reinforced by observation of the fact that Ephesians depends verbally to a great extent on other Pauline letters, except for 2 Thessalonians. The same man could have written the two letters, Colossians and Ephesians, in much the same language within a short time; this is the usual way of arguing for the Pauline authorship of Ephesians, but he would scarcely have reached back into his memory for constant reminiscences of earlier letters written to meet quite different needs.

Theology

Ephesians repeats the Pauline doctrine of justification by faith (2:5, 8–9), but in many respects the theology of Ephesians is simply non-Pauline, even if Colossians is counted among the genuine Pauline letters (which we, of course, do not). Eph 2:19–22, where Christians are "members of the household of God, built upon the foundation of the apostles and prophets, Christ Jesus himself being the cornerstone . . ." is inconceivable as a statement by the apostle, even if Col 2:7 is reckoned as Pauline, and much more so if it is not. The reference to the "holy apostles" as recipients of special insights into "the mystery of Christ" in Eph 3:4–5 is impossible as a Pauline statement because Paul never distinguishes apostles in this way and never regards them as "holy" in a way other Christians are not. Ephesians uses the word *church* (*ekklēsia*) uniformly and exclusively for the universal church (Eph 1:22; 3:10, 21; 5:24,25,27). In the genuine Pauline letters and in Colossians (4:16) it is also used for the local congregation. Indeed, the ecclesiology of Ephesians is a striking development toward the understanding of the church as the "Great Church" characteristic of later centuries but not characteristic of Paul. In Eph 3:4–6 the "mystery of Christ" is the unity of Jews and Gentiles in the body of Christ. Not only is this a reflection on an achieved result for which Paul himself was still fighting, but the ecclesiology swallows the Christology. While on the subject of Christology, note that in Ephesians Christ is the subject of the verb *to reconcile* (Eph 2:16), whereas in Col 1:20 God is the subject. In Eph 4:11 Christ appoints the apostles and prophets; in 1 Cor 12:28 God does this. Much more could be said, but we have here enough to indicate why on the theological grounds even scholars who accept Colossians as Pauline regard Ephesians as pseudonymous; for those of us who accept Colossians as pseudonymous, the issue is even clearer.

Literary Character of Ephesians

One last point to be made is that Ephesians is not really a letter at all. If we observe a distinction made in our discussion of "Paul as a writer of letters," that the letters are written because of some particular conflict, set of problems, or at least an occasion in Paul's life (Romans), then Ephesians is not a letter—at least in the usual Pauline sense.[13] All of these features are missing, even though Paul had clearly made Ephesus a kind of "mission headquarters" and had spent considerable time there.[14]

[13] N. A. Dahl, "Ephesians, Letter to the," *IDB Suppl.*, p. 268, in contrast to much prevailing opinion, says: "It belongs to *a type* of Greek letter—genuine and spurious—which substitutes for a public speech rather than for private conversation." (Italics added)

[14] See the frequently made suggestion that Romans 16 was directed toward Ephesus, pp. 152–54 above.

The Occasion for the Writing of Ephesians

If Ephesians was not a letter in the more usual Pauline sense, it must now be determined, if possible, why it was written.

The Lack of an Address

Though the opening salutation parallels the Pauline letters, the best manuscripts and all modern critical Greek texts and responsible translations omit any reference to Ephesus. "At Ephesus" was added by a scribe in a later transmission of the text. Since titles of the letters such as "To the Romans" or "To the Ephesians" come from the period when Paul's letters were collected, these titles ("superscriptions") cannot be used to argue for the destinations of the letters. The address read simply, "To the saints who are also faithful in Christ Jesus" or, since in Paul's letters "who are" is normally followed by a place name, the Paulinist could have written, "To the saints who are——and faithful in Christ Jesus" ("and" = "also" in Greek), and the reader would have had to fill in the place name.[15] In short, we have a "letter" with no address. Because of the general nature of the writing, this suggests that it was an "open letter" addressed to the church at large.

Relationship of Ephesians to Other Letters Attributed to Paul

Ephesians knows and makes extensive use of Colossians; in addition, however, Ephesians shows familiarity with all the other letters attributed to Paul except 2 Thessalonians. Particularly interesting parallels are:

> Rom 8:28 = Eph 1:11; Rom 8:29 = Eph 1:4–5
> 1 Cor 4:12 = Eph 4:28; 1 Cor 6:9–10 = Eph 5:5;
>   1 Cor 11:3 = Eph 5:23; 1 Cor 12:28 = Eph 4:11;
>   1 Cor 15:9–10 = Eph 3:8.
> 2 Cor 1:22 = Eph 1:13; 4:30.
> Gal 2:20 = Eph 5:2, 25; Gal 4:4 = Eph 1:10.

In the *Interpreter's Dictionary of the Bible*, volume 2, pages 110–11, from which we have taken these references, G. Johnston gives many, many more. These parallels allow us to suppose that Ephesians was originally written to accompany the collection of Pauline letters while it was circulated as a distinct body of literature, which must have happened sometime in the last quarter of the first century. This possibility has been argued in America by E. J. Goodspeed and in

---

[15] W. Meeks, *The Writings of St. Paul*, p. 123, n. 1. The difficulty with this suggestion is that there is no parallel practice of leaving place names blank. Some scholars believe that because Marcion had the superscription "To the Laodiceans" in the second century, and because Col 4:16 states that Colossians should also be read "in the church of the Laodiceans," it was originally intended for Laodicea. Except for the fact that as far as we know Paul had not been to Laodicea, this hypothesis faces equally difficult problems.

England by C. L. Mitton. It tends to be dismissed in Germany,[16] but the fact remains that it represents a reasonable explanation of the contents of the "letter" itself.

Exegetical Survey of Ephesians

1:1–23 *Salutation, thanksgiving, and intercession.*

> **1:1–2** *Open salutation.* This of course, is typically Pauline, but it lacks a specific addressee.

> **1:3–14** *Thanksgiving.* It has been said that the most monstrous conglomeration of sentences in the Greek language is found here,[17] and, indeed, any successful translation of it is a tribute to the translator's ingenuity. But the Thanksgiving does make clear the general concern of the "letter," the unity of all men in Christ.

> **1:15–23** *Intercession.* All men everywhere should grasp the magnitude of the hope that awaits them in the church of which Christ is the head. The mythical idea of the world as the body of the cosmic "man" has been transferred to body of the church.

2:1–3:21 *The glory of the one holy church.*

> **2:1–10** *By grace are we saved through faith.* The basis for the glory of the church is that all men, including the writer and his readers, are brought into it as they are saved by grace through faith.

> **2:11–22** *We, Jew and Gentile, are reconciled in Christ.* The readers were once Gentiles, "separated from Christ, alienated from the common wealth of Israel, and strangers to the covenants of promise, having no hope and without God in the world"—the rhetoric of this section which develops the idea that Christians are citizens in a great city-state, the church, is magnificent. They have been reconciled and brought into the one body of the church by the work of Christ.

> In this section we find one of the great christological hymns:

> > [For] he is our peace,
> > Who has made both one
> > And has broken down the dividing wall
> > of the fence [the enmity],
> > In order to make the two into one new
> > man in him [making peace]
> > And to reconcile both in one body to God
> > [through the Cross]

> The strophic arrangement has been lost in the text itself because the author quotes and interprets as he writes. A first interpretation is the

---

[16] W. G. Kümmel, *Intro.*, pp. 354–56. Some suggest that it was "a tract dressed up like a letter" (R. Fuller, *Intro.*, p. 66) or an adaptation of a baptismal liturgy or homily (cf. 1 Peter) "intended to be read to new converts in a group of churches in the southwestern part of the province of Asia (modern Turkey)" (W. Meeks, *Writings*, p. 122).

[17] E. Käsemann, *Die Religion in Geschichte und Gegenwart*, 3rd ed., vol. 2, col. 519.

addition of the words we have put in brackets. This method of interpretation by addition is typically Pauline. As we pointed out earlier,
Paul himself interprets the "became obedient unto death" of the
hymn in Philippians 2 by adding "even death on a cross." It is possible that the hymn in Ephesians 2 originally had a first stanza celebrating the redeemer's participation in creation as does the hymn in
Colossians. Be that as it may, the stanza that is in fact quoted deals
with reconciliation, a major theme in deutero-Pauline Christianity.
Not only has Christ broken down the dividing wall between Jews and
Christians (the wall that separates Jews and Gentiles in the Temple
precincts at Jerusalem? or the proto-Gnostic barrier between heaven
and earth?), thus creating one man out of two; in a series of images
the church is viewed as a holy temple of the Spirit.

3:1–21 *Intercession and doxology.* The fundamental structure of this passage is an intercession begun in 3:1, broken off in 3:2, resumed in
3:14–19, and concluded by a doxology in 3:20–21. The intercession is
a prayer for the Gentile members of the church, that they may know
all the riches membership in the church offers the believer. Eph
3:2–13 is a parenthetical interruption concerning Paul's mission to the
Gentiles, and it testifies to the importance of Paul's work among the
Gentiles to a subsequent generation, as the Acts of the Apostles also
does.

4:1–6:20 *Parenesis.* Now the characteristic element of exhortation.

4:1–16 *The unity of the faith and of the church.* As in 1 Cor 12 and Rom 12,
there is mention of gifts of the Spirit in the church; however, the
church is again viewed as the body of which Christ is the head (cf.
1:22–23).

4:17–32 *The necessity to put off the old and to put on the new.*

5:1–20 *Instruction to shun immorality and impurity.* This section develops
negatively from a list of vices (verses 3–7) and then positively from a
list of virtues (verses 8–20). Such lists of vices and virtues are, like the
household codes, characteristic of Hellenistic moral philosophy.

5:21–6:9 *The household code.* This is a further and more developed Christianization of a household code such as that found in Col 3:18–4:6.
5:31–33 develops the image of the church as the bride of Christ.

6:10–20 *The armor of God and the warfare of the Christian.*

6:21–24 *Closing reference to Tychicus, and benediction.*

DEUTERO-PAULINE CHRISTIANITY AS A MOVEMENT

A major aspect of the importance of deutero-Pauline Christianity is that it
shows the influence of the apostle living on in the church. The Paulinists were
those who were taught by their master, who possessed and meditated on his
letters, who developed further some of his ideas, who carefully and conscientiously attempted to meet in his spirit the challenges and needs of the

churches, and who wrote formally in his name. It must have been these men who were responsible for the collection of his letters and their circulation as a corpus. The literature they left behind represents the influence of Paul and his ideas a generation or so after his death, and it gives us valuable insights into the nature of the Hellenistic Christianity of that generation.

The problems of the Paulinists in that generation, what we have called the "middle period" of New Testament Christianity, are interesting, and so are the ways they were met. From 2 Thessalonians we learn that a major difficulty was the delay of the parousia. By now Jesus should have come on the clouds of heaven to judge the world, but he had not done so. The Paulinist who wrote 2 Thessalonians meets this problem just as his teacher had, and hence virtually repeats 1 Thessalonians, which he clearly knows well and obviously regards as a tract for his own time and as an answer to the problem he and his church are facing. Yet there are subtle differences between the two letters. Paul himself had expected the parousia in a very short time, whereas the Paulinist knows that it has now been a very considerable time and parousia is still delayed. So in presenting the scenario for the parousia, the Paulinist attempts to make sense of this delay.

The second problem faced by Hellenistic Christianity after Paul comes to the fore in Colossians—the increasing threat of ideas that became characteristic of second-century Gnosticism. At this stage the church freely adapted such ideas and terms and met the danger by an "anything you can do we can do better" claim. Later the threat grew more deadly, and the church had to develop an authoritative body of literature from which Gnostic texts were excluded, a canon; an authoritative statement of faith that the Gnostic could not accept, a creed; and a succession of officers who were the source of authority in the church, an episcopate. These structures probably would have developed even without the threat of Gnosticism, but the life and death struggle with that movement as it became a specific Christian heresy encouraged and speeded up the process.

A further insight into the situation of Hellenistic Christianity a generation after Paul can be gained from 2 Thessalonians: the church had to come to terms with the increasing possibility of persecution.

A last such insight gained from 2 Thessalonians is that through this middle period of New Testament Christianity the Christology was developing. The author of 2 Thessalonians attributes to Jesus what the previous generation had attributed only to God. The author of Colossians moves christological thinking a long step forward by taking insights about the nature and function of a redeemer and applying them to his understanding of Christ, developing particularly the idea of Christ as active in creation, as embodying in himself the fullness (*plērōma*) of the godhead, and as reconciling everything unto himself as the head of the body, the church. The Paulinist of Ephesians, whose special concern is the single universal church in which Jew and Gentile are one, develops further the concepts of Christ as reconciler and head of the body, the church.

Christ as reconciler is a major theme of Colossians and Ephesians. It is also a major theme in Paul's letters, e.g., Rom 5:10; 2 Cor 5:18–19. Indeed 2 Cor

5:19 "in Christ God was reconciling the world to himself, not counting their trespasses against them," is obviously the point of departure for what happens in Colossians and Ephesians: Col 1:19–20, "For in him all the fulness of God was pleased to dwell, and through him to reconcile to himself all things whether on earth or in heaven"; and Eph 2:16, "[that he] might reconcile us both to God in one body through the cross." Colossians and Ephesians even use a different form of the verbal root, *apokatallassein*, a verb found only in Christian writers; Paul uses *katallassein*, a verb used in secular Greek to denote human reconciliation, and indeed so used by Paul in 1 Cor 7:11. The difference is small but significant. Paul always uses the verb metaphorically, one metaphor among others (e.g., justification, redemption, propitiation, or expiation) used to portray the saving work of God in Christ. In Colossians and Ephesians the reconciliation is a metaphysical reality and no longer a metaphor.

A similar development takes place in connection with Christ as the head of the body, the church. Paul himself nevers speaks of Christ as the head of the body, the church, and when he speaks of the church as the body of Christ (as he does in Rom 12:5; 1 Cor 12:12–26), the expression is a metaphor for the mutual interdependence of Christians in the church. But in Col 1:18, Eph 1:23, and 5:23, the church as the body of Christ is a cosmic reality, and Christ as its head is what gives it life, power, and direction. These are developments beyond Paul, nevertheless taking their point of departure from him.

Another feature of deutero-Pauline Christianity, and indeed of Hellenistic Christianity after Paul altogether, is the increasing use, with only comparatively light Christianization, of Hellenistic religious and philosophical literary material. Paul himself uses Hellenistic literary forms and metaphors, as he uses Jewish rabbinical methods of arguing from Scripture, but the hymn in Philippians 2 is a Christian literary product and not a Christianization of a hymn to a Gnostic redeemer. Nor is there in the genuine Pauline letters a "household code," as featured so prominently in the parenetical sections of both Colossians and Ephesians. Christianity, as typified by Colossians and Ephesians, was settling down in the Hellenistic world and making increasing use of material presented to it by the cultural environment to which it was increasingly integrated.

The theme of reconciliation in deutero-Pauline Christianity leads naturally to the major theme of Ephesians: the unity of Jew and Gentile in the one body of Christ. In Ephesians "church" invariably means the one universal church, in sharp contrast to Paul's normal use of the word, and the fact that Ephesians is concerned with the one universal church is an important factor in the development of New Testament Christianity. Up until this time the Christian movement had been an apocalyptic sect within Judaism and a cult within Hellenism. Paul took the concept a stage further when in his Corinthian correspondence he addressed "the church of God which is at Corinth . . . together with all those who in every place call on the name of our Lord Jesus Christ" (1 Cor 1:2; compare 2 Cor 1:1). Here the local Christian congregation, still uniformly Paul's concern, was one manifestation of the broader movement of "those who call on the name of the Lord Jesus." But when Ephesians speaks of "the church, which is his body, the fulness (*plērōma*) of him who fills all in all"

(1:22–23), or of "God who created all things, that through the church the manifold wisdom of God might now be made known to the principalities and powers in the heavenly places" (3:9–10), or uses the benediction "to him be glory in the church and in Christ Jesus to all generations" (3:21), then the reference is to the one universal church. Christianity is no longer a sect or a cult within a broader movement but self-consciously the means whereby God works out his purpose in the world, the one all-encompassing unit that represents God to men and by means of which men come to God. It is when we come to Ephesians in the New Testament that we must begin to speak of the Christian Church, with a capital C, and no longer of Christian churches. The theme of Ephesians is the Church Universal, the One Body of Christ, and we have now reached the self-understanding that was to characterize and sustain the Christian Church through the long centuries of the Middle Ages.

Our discussion of Ephesians called attention to the magnificent rhetoric of Eph 2:11–22, magnificent not so much because the author has polished his phrases as because he is here at the heart of his concern: the unity of Jew and Gentile in the Church of God. Jerusalem is now fallen to the Romans, the Temple is no more, there is no longer a Jerusalem church from which emissaries can come arguing that the Christian must also be a Jew. The circumstances that led to Paul's great battles in Galatia, Philippi, and elsewhere are now no more, and the author of Ephesians can celebrate in sonorous phrases the unity of Jew and Gentile in the One Church of God. But even here we catch a glimpse of a major concern of New Testament Christianity in its middle period: the necessity to come to terms with the destruction of the Jerusalem Temple.

> So then you are no longer strangers and sojourners, but you are fellow citizens with the saints and members of the household of God, built upon the foundation of the apostles and prophets, Christ Jesus himself being the cornerstone, in whom the whole structure is joined together and grows into a holy temple in the Lord; in whom you also are built into it for a dwelling place of God in the Spirit.
>
> Eph 2:19–22

This celebrates the unity of Jew and Gentile within the church of God, this church now viewed as the New Temple. In this way the author deals with the catastrophe of the destruction of Jerusalem and its Temple by the Romans.

Eph 2:19–22 also shows the church girding its loins for its own future. The church is "built upon the foundation of the apostles and prophets," Christ Jesus is "the cornerstone." The days of the free, charismatic enthusiasm that provided the dynamism for the beginning of the churches are over; we have a first glimpse of the firm and careful structure that enabled the church to survive and, indeed, to mold the centuries that were to come in the West.

THE LETTER TO THE HEBREWS

Three other letters called the Pastorals (1, 2 Timothy, Titus) purport to have been written by Paul and are sometimes included under the heading "deutero-Pauline" Christianity. They are, however, sufficiently different from the three deutero-Paulines just discussed to raise the question whether they actually come from a "Pauline school" attempting to perpetuate Pauline ideas in the same way. We have therefore decided to postpone discussion of them and consider them with the literature of institutional Christianity in chapter 12. Rather, although there is even less reason for considering the "letter" to the Hebrews with the Pauline school, we take it up here as a matter of convenience.

General Discussion

In addition to the "seven" undisputed letters of Paul, the three deutero-Pauline letters, and the three Pastorals, the fourteenth "letter" which church tradition came to associate with Paul's name is the "letter" to the Hebrews. Yet, the letter to the Hebrews is extraordinarily difficult to fit into any survey of the New Testament. Like Melchizedek of whom it speaks, it is "without father or mother or genealogy" (Heb 7:3), and we would be tempted to add also "without offspring." In the New Testament it has neither antecedents nor descendants and is not part of any movement; it is simply a text of such excellence that it forced its way into the canon of the New Testament. As for who wrote it, the famous church father Origen (about 185–254) had the last word, deciding that the name of the author was known only to God. Nor do we know more about the persons to whom the text was addressed. The address "To the Hebrews" was given to it in the early church because the subject matter is concerned with the Jewish cultus; there is nothing said in the book about the original addressees.

Hebrews is known in the New Testament as a letter, but its only characteristic of a letter is that it closes with a greeting (13:22–25). Hebrews is to be understood fundamentally as a sermon. Recent study has suggested that it might be "homiletic midrash" (a special Jewish sermonic interpretation) on the Old Testament Psalm 110, for the psalm contains one of the two instances where the High Priest Melchizedek is mentioned in the Old Testament (cf. Gen 14:17–20).[18] This is an especially interesting suggestion because an eschatological midrash on Psalm 110 has been discovered among the Dead Sea Scrolls, and there Melchizedek, "the priest of the Most High," is represented as a heavenly angelic being.[19] In Hebrews, the sermon is a mixture of proclamation and parenesis, and it represents the kind of discourse the Christian church was developing to meet the needs of its members. It is not a missionary sermon designed to convert non-Christians; it is directed to believers who are in need of exhortation, guidance, and comfort.

Hebrews must have been written before A.D. 96 because in that year Clement, bishop of Rome, wrote a letter in the name of the church in Rome to

[18] G. W. Buchanan, *To The Hebrews* (Anchor Bible); R. Fuller, "The Letter to the Hebrews," in G. Krodel, ed., *Hebrews-James 1 and 2 Peter-Jude-Revelation*, pp. 6–15.
[19] A. S. van der Woude, "Melchizedek," *IDB Suppl.*, pp. 585–86.

the church in Corinth, a letter known as 1 Clement, and in it he quotes Hebrews (1 Clem 17:1; 36:2–5). Some scholars suggest that Hebrews was written before A.D. 70 because its theme of the sacrificial cultus implies that the Temple of Jerusalem was still intact. This seems unlikely in the light of other internal evidence in the text. Heb 2:3 speaks of the message of salvation as being "declared at first by the Lord, and . . . attested to us by those who heard him," which is very close to the language of Luke 1:2 and suggests that the writer belongs at least to the generation of the author of Luke-Acts, about A.D. 85–90. The references to the sacrificial cultus are not to the Jerusalem Temple, but to its predecessor, the tent sanctuary, or tabernacle, of the time of Moses (cf. Exod 25:9; 33:7). In fact, the author's argument might have been derived wholly from Scripture, not a knowledge of the actual Jerusalem Temple of his own day. Moreover, his discussion of the tent sanctuary is in terms of a heavenly reality and of an earthly copy of that reality, of heavenly substance and earthly shadow. For example, Heb 9:1–5 describes the "earthly sanctuary . . . a tent," but in 9:11, "the greater and more perfect tent (not made with hands, that is, not of this creation)" appears with Christ. Heb 9:23–24 speaks of "the heavenly things" and the "copies of the heavenly things," of "a sanctuary made with hands, a copy of the true one." This kind of thinking is characteristic of Hebrews altogether, and it shows that the author is not concerned with the physical fact, but with the spiritual reality of which the Old Testament tabernacle was always only a shadow and copy.

The writer of Hebrews speaks very frequently of the Jewish sacrificial system; yet he thinks about it in terms of substance and shadow, of reality and copy of reality, thoroughly Greek ideas stemming ultimately from Plato and highly characteristic of a first-century Hellenistic Jew, Philo of Alexandria. So the author of Hebrews has to be regarded as a product of Hellenistic Judaism; he is a Jew of the Diaspora converted to the Christian faith, and his Greek way of thinking about his Jewish heritage has prepared him to interpret that faith as the revelation of the reality of which Judaism was always a copy.

To whom was Hebrews originally addressed? The writer is a Hellenistic Jewish Christian, and his arguments presuppose that he is writing to others who think as he does, i.e., to a Hellenistic Jewish Christian community. Since Clement of Rome knows and quotes the text within what could only have been a few years of its writing, that community may well have been in Rome. This view is supported by the greetings from "those who come from Italy" in Heb 13:24.

The Structure of Hebrews

A feature of Hebrews is the careful alternation of proclamation and parenesis that gives it its distinctively sermonic form. It has no introduction, but plunges immediately into proclamation. Its structure is as follows:

Proclamation: Jesus as Son of God and Savior of Men, 1:1–3:6
Parenesis: 3:7–4:13

Proclamation: Jesus as High Priest, first statement of the theme, 4:14–5:10

Parenesis: Christian maturity, 5:11–6:20

Proclamation: Jesus as High Priest, development of the theme, 7:1–10:18

Parenesis: 10:19–39

Proclamation: Jesus as the pioneer and perfector of faith, 11:1–39

Parenesis: 12:1–13:17

Closing benediction and greetings: 13:18–25

Exegetical Survey

1:1–3:6 *First aspect of the proclamation: Jesus as Son of God and savior of men.* The preacher dwells on Jesus as Son of God and as savior of men, and, further, as the merciful and faithful High Priest who has expiated the sins of the people. But men are flesh and blood, and so Jesus had to share their nature. Sharing the nature of men and sufferings he has not only redeemed men but can help them since he understands their temptations.

Here we have a major feature of Hebrews. On the one hand, Jesus is the "heavenly" High Prest, making the true sacrifice for the sins of the people; on the other hand, he is of the same flesh and blood as those he sanctifies. In a later generation this was to develop into the Christology of the great creeds, where Jesus is declared to be both truly God and truly man. What we have here is a development from the Jewish way of thinking concerning the High Priest. He represented the people before God, and this he could do because he was one with them. But he also represented God before the people, and in doing this came to be thought of as partaking in some way in the aura of divinity, especially when he came out of the Holy of Holies, which he and he alone might enter and even then only one day in the year. Against this background it is easy to see how the writer of Hebrews who regards Jesus as fulfilling both functions perfectly as compared to the imperfect fulfillment in the person of the Jewish High Priest, came to use the language he does.

Note also in Heb 2:9 the characteristic Hellenistic myth of the descending-ascending redeemer, as in the New Testament christological hymns.

3:7–4:13 **First section of parenesis.** This section is built around Psa 95:7b–11. Verses 7b–10 are concerned with the journey of the Israelites through the wilderness, interpreting it as God testing his people. The people failed this testing, hence their failure to reach the perfect "rest" of God (verse 11). The Christians must not similarly fail, and if they can but endure, they will inherit the promised "rest" in which they will share the glory of God's own Sabbath rest. The priesthood of Melchizedek in Ps 110:4 is cited in 5:6, 10.

4:14–5:10 *Second aspect of the proclamation: Jesus as High Priest* (first statement of the theme).

5:11–6:20 *Second section of parenesis: Christian maturity.*

7:1–10:18 *Third aspect of the proclamation: Jesus as High Priest* (development of the theme). The theme of Jesus as High Priest is now developed in various ways, each designed to exhibit the superiority of the high priesthood of Jesus over what it superseded.

7:1–28 *Jesus is High Priest after the order of Melchizedek.* The shadowy figure of the priest-king Melchizedek blesses Abraham the father of the Jewish people in Genesis 14, and this is interpreted as indicating that his order is superior to that of any Jewish priesthood.

8:1–6 *Jesus has made the one perfect sacrifice.*

8:7–13 *He is the mediator of the new covenant that replaces the old, obsolete one.*

9:1–14 *The priesthood of Jesus is the perfection of which the Jewish Levitical priesthood had only been the promise.*

9:15–22 *The new covenant is superior to the old, since the death that ratified it is a death redeeming men from their transgressions under the old.*

9:23–10:18 *Shadow and substance in regard to the sanctuary and the sacrifice.*

10:19–39 *Third section of parenesis.*

11:1–39 *Fourth aspect of the proclamation: Jesus as the pioneer and perfector of faith.* The writer's definition of faith indicates his Hellenistic Jewish heritage. Faith as "the assurance of things hoped for" reflects the Jewish model of promise and fulfillment, and faith as "the conviction of things not seen" reflects the Greek model of appearance and reality.

The idea of listing the heroes of the faith is Jewish. In Sir 44:1 we read, "Let us now praise famous men, and our fathers in their generations," and there follows a list from Enoch to Simon the High Priest (Sir 44:16–50:21). The heroes listed in Hebrews 11 were all faithful men of God, but they did not receive the promise. God had reserved the promise for Christians.

12:1–13:17 *Fourth section of parenesis.*

13:18–25 *Benediction and greetings.*

Further Reading

For 2 Thessalonians, see:

PCB, p. 1,000 (W. Neill). Treats the letter as Pauline.

JBC, pp. 227–29, 233–35 (J. T. Forestell). Pauline.

IDB, vol. 4, pp. 625–29 (F. W. Beare). A good discussion. The letter is treated as Pauline, but with reservations.

IDB Suppl., pp. 900–01 (J. C. Hurd). Pauline and prior to 1 Thessalonians.

W. G. Kümmel, *Intro.*, pp. 262–69. Pauline.

W. Marxsen, *Intro.*, pp. 37–44. Deutero-Pauline.

R. Fuller, *Intro.*, pp. 57–59. Deutero-Pauline.

For Colossians, see:

PCB, pp. 990–95 (C. F. D. Moule). "Substantially Pauline."
JBC, pp. 334–40 (J. A. Grassi). Pauline.
IDB, vol. 1, pp. 658–62 (G. Johnston). Pauline.
X *IDB Suppl.*, pp. 169–70 (F. O. Francis). "Disputed."
W. G. Kümmel, *Intro.*, pp. 335–50. Pauline.
W. Marxsen, *Introl*, pp. 177–86. Deutero-Pauline.
R. Fuller, *Intro.*, pp. 59–65. Pauline.

For Ephesians, see:

PCB, pp. 980–84. Undecided on question of authorship.
JBC, pp. 341–49 (J. A. Grassi). Undecided.
IDB, vol. 2, pp. 108–14 (G. Johnston). Deutero-Pauline. Has a good discussion of relationship between Ephesians and the Pauline corpus as a whole.
X *IDB Suppl.*, pp. 268–69 (N. A. Dahl). Hangs together with Colossians; Paul probably authored neither.
W. G. Kümmel, *Intro.*, pp. 350–66. Deutero-Pauline.
W. Marxsen, *Intro.*, pp. 187–98. Deutero-Pauline.
R. Fuller, *Intro.*, pp. 65–68. Deutero-Pauline.

All the above discuss the Colossian heresy. In addition, see:

E. Lohse, *Colossians and Philemon*, pp. 2–3, 127–31.
F. O. Francis and W. Meeks, *Conflict at Colossae.*
J. Burgess, "The Letter to the Colossians," in G. Krodel, ed., *Ephesians, Colossians, 2 Thessalonians, The Pastoral Epistles* (Proclamation Commentaries), pp. 41–47.

For the letter to the Hebrews, see:

PCB, pp. 1008–19 (F. F. Bruce).
JBC, pp. 381–402 (M. M. Bourke).
IDB, vol. 2, pp. 571–75 (E. Dinkler).
X *IDB Suppl.*, pp 394–95 (F. F. Bruce).
W. G. Kümmel, *Intro.*, pp. 388–403.
W. Marxsen, *Intro.*, pp. 217–22.
R. Fuller, *Intro.*, pp. 144–50.

Also:

R. Fuller, "The Letter to the Hebrews," in G. Krodel, ed., *Hebrews-James 1 and 2 Peter-Jude-Revelation*, pp. 1–27.

The Wailing Wall, believed to be a remnant of the outside western wall of the Jerusalem Temple, rebuilt by Herod the Great and destroyed by the Romans in A.D. 70. Today Jews still mourn the loss of the Temple here.

CHAPTER EIGHT

THE GOSPEL OF MARK:
The Apocalyptic Drama

In chapter 2 we observed that in the most general sense there are four kinds of books in the New Testament: gospels, chronicles or "acts," letters, and apocalypses. With Mark we reach the one unique literary form produced by early Christianity: the gospel. Other movements produced letters, chronicles, and apocalypses, but only Christians wrote gospels, and the first Christian to do so was the evangelist Mark. We must therefore consider his achievement very carefully.

THE TRADITIONAL MATERIAL USED BY MARK

You will recall that in our treatment of the theological history of New Testament Christianity (chapter 3), the gospels of Matthew, Mark, and Luke are called the "synoptic" gospels because they can be put side by side and read together; they tell much the same story in much the same way. The question of their literary relationship, called the synoptic problem, is answered by the majority of New Testament scholars with some version of the two-source theory, i.e., Mark and Q are sources for Matthew and Luke, and Mark is therefore the earliest gospel. You will also recall that Form Criticism attempts to isolate the smaller forms within the New Testament, to determine their various functions in a series of early Christian communities (*Sitz im Leben*) and to trace the history of the transmission of these traditional forms. This perspective also leads to the view that the New Testament can, among other things, be described as tradition and the interpretation of tradition (chapter 2). Nowhere is this more evident than in the synoptic gospels. They make extensive use of traditional material that had been circulating in the churches. So we speak of the synoptic tradition, meaning by that the traditional material used by three synoptic evangelists. This traditional material took the literary form of sayings of Jesus and stories about him, but much of the teaching came from prophets and leaders of the church, and many of the stories reflect the situation and concerns of the church. A remarkable feature of earliest Christianity is precisely that the church cast its teaching in the form of sayings of Jesus and reflected its situation and concerns in stories about him.

A number of sayings thought to come from Jesus and a number of the stories about him undoubtedly circulated in isolated form. A good example is the tradition of the founding of the "Lord's Supper" which is not only in the gospels but in 1 Cor 11:23–26. Probably the traditional account of the meal included some teaching about discipleship. The Lukan account has such teaching (Luke 22:24–27), while similar Markan teaching (Mark 10:42–45), which contains themes similar to those found in the "Lord's Supper" (cf. Mark 10:45 and 14:24),[1] was probably passed on in a eucharistic setting. It is reasonable to suppose that Mark inherited from the tradition an account of the "Lord's Supper," which interprets the death of Jesus in its significance for the believer and which teaches about discipleship in light of the death of Jesus.

Eventually some sayings and stories were gathered into collections. Many scholars in the past thought that the most extensive unit was a connected passion narrative, an account of the arrest, trial, and crucifixion of Jesus. Not only does the passion story have numerous references to time and place, giving it some semblance of realism, but it is full of references to the fulfillment of scripture, and it was thought that the story was told to explain why the Messiah was crucified. Though stories of Jesus' passion may have been told, recent studies of that story in Mark's gospel have concluded that Mark himself composed it out of a number of isolated traditions.[2] If so, the notion of a pre-Markan passion story as a connected account in literary form seems unlikely.

Other suggestions for collections of sayings and stories have been proposed. One is that Mark inherited a cycle of miracle stories portraying Jesus as exhibiting the traits of a Hellenistic "divine man," the stories now in Mark 5 and 7. Further, a cycle of controversy stories in Mark 2 concerning forgiveness of sins, eating with tax collectors and sinners, fasting, and keeping the Sabbath lack evidence of specifically Markan literary traits in the way they are linked together, and Mark may well have inherited them as a unit.

It is also probable that Mark inherited the collection of parables now in Mark 4 as a collection. A careful analysis of the chapter shows that the parables were put together before Mark used them and that he has fitted them into his narrative and added the secrecy motif of verses 10–12.[3] Our earlier discussion of apocalyptic Christianity indicated that the apocalyptic discourse now in Mark 13 was a product of that element of earliest Christianity. Yet, it

---

[1] Mark 10:45 and 14:24 both interpret the death of Jesus in terms of the suffering servant passage of Isaiah 53, and both were apparently originally in a Semitic language, either Hebrew or Aramaic.

[2] W. Kelber, ed., *The Passion in Mark.*

[3] See especially J. Jeremias, *Parables of Jesus*, pp. 13–15. Cf. also *n.* 12 below.

was indicated that Mark has totally reworked the discourse. This is especially clear not only from Markan vocabulary and style in 13:5b–27, but also from specific historical allusions (13:5b–6, 14, 21–22; cf. 13:2).

One last possible pre-Markan unit of tradition is a cycle of stories giving an account of (a) a feeding, (b) a crossing of the lake, (c) a controversy with Pharisees, and (d) teaching concerning bread. Mark has two such cycles of stories:

6:30–44 Feeding of the five thousand	8:1–10 Feeding of the four thousand
6:45–56 Crossing of the lake	8:10 Crossing of the lake
7:1–13 Dispute with Pharisees	8:11–13 Dispute with Pharisees
7:14–23 Discourse about food and defilement	8:14–21 Incident of "no bread" and discourse about the leaven of the Pharisees

What is more remarkable is that the gospel of John, normally so different from the synoptic gospels, has the same cycle of tradition:

John 6:1–14	Feeding of the five thousand
6:15	Attempt to make Jesus a king
6:16–21	Crossing of the sea
6:22–51	Coming of the people and discourse on bread

Possibly Mark inherited two versions of the same cycle of tradition and certainly 6:7–8:21 does not move as smoothly as the other sections, which may indicate that he is using two versions of the same tradition.

Several scholars add other items to the list of pre-Markan units of tradition we have given, and others argue against some of them. But it is generally agreed that some such list is the extent of the connected units of tradition Mark had been able to collect. Apart from these, there are only small or isolated units of tradition, and therefore the organization of the traditional material into an integrated structure is something Mark himself has done. The structure of the gospel of Mark is the work of the evangelist, and it is very important for an understanding of what he was trying to do and say. Before taking up this structure, we must consider an important method for studying the gospels as a whole.

REDACTION CRITICISM

As important as form criticism is and always will be, it suffers from one handicap. In its concern for the forms and tradition underlying the written texts of the New Testament it tended to do less than justice to the originality and creativity of the writers of those texts, particularly the synoptic evangelists Matthew, Mark, and Luke. This imbalance was corrected immediately after

World War II with the rise of the discipline of *Redaktionsgeschichte*, literally "redaction history" but more often translated "redaction criticism." Redaction criticism assumes the work of form criticism on the individual forms and the history of the tradition of the church. It goes on from there to inquire into the use made of this material by the final author of the text, into his redaction of this material (the German word *Redaktor* means primarily "editor") and what it tells us about his theological viewpoint. As developed in Germany the discipline takes its point of departure from an ability to distinguish between tradition and redaction of tradition and to determine the theological view implied by that redaction. But once it was recognized that the final author was in fact an *author* and not merely a transmitter of tradition, it became natural and inevitable to inquire into his total literary activity as revealing his purpose and theology, not only into his redaction of previously existing tradition. In this connection redaction criticism shades over into general literary criticism, especially in the redaction critical work carried on in America, where the influence of general literary criticism is strong on New Testament scholars.

We may illustrate the work of redaction criticism by turning again to the accounts of the baptism of Jesus, which we used in chapter 3 as the basis for a discussion of the interrelatedness of the synoptic gospels. This time, however, we are concerned only with the relationship between Luke 3:21–22 and its source, Mark 1:9–11.

Mark 1:9–11	Luke 3:21–22
In those days Jesus came from Nazareth of Galilee and was baptized by John in the Jordan. And when he came up out of the water, immediately he saw the heavens opened and the Spirit descending upon him like a dove; and a voice came from heaven, "Thou art my beloved Son; with thee I am well pleased."	Now when all the people were baptized and when Jesus also had been baptized and was praying, the heaven was opened, and the Holy Spirit descended upon him in bodily form, as a dove, and a voice came from heaven, "Thou art my beloved Son; with thee I am well pleased."

A consideration of Luke–Acts as a whole combined with Luke's version here shows that all the emphasis is on the descent of the Spirit on Jesus. His baptism has become but one of the three circumstances (a general baptism ["all the people"], his baptism, the fact that he was praying) that set the stage for the descent of the Spirit, whereas in Mark the baptism and the descent of the Spirit are equally significant. Incidentally, the introduction of the theme of Jesus at prayer is characteristic of Luke's gospel. He does it in at least six places where it is not to be found in his sources (3:21; 5:16; 6:12; 9:18, 28, 29). The emphasis in Luke's gospel is on the fact that the ministry of Jesus began not with his baptism but with the descent of the Spirit on him. This becomes important when we recall that in Acts, his second volume, the ministry of the church begins in exactly the same way. In Acts 2 the ministry of the church begins with the descent of the Spirit at Pentecost, which in Acts 1:5 is interpreted in advance as a baptism. The author clearly intends to set these two things—the ministry of Jesus and the ministry of the church—in close and formal parallelism with one another, and this becomes an important clue to his theology, as we shall see when we come to discuss Luke-Acts in detail. The parallelism helps to explain why the descent of the Spirit at the beginning of Jesus' career receives the emphasis it does in Luke's gospel.

If one follows the two-source theory, it is possible to make observations about how Matthew and Luke modify Mark to fit their own points of view. With Mark the matter is more difficult, and one has to theorize about Mark's use of his traditional material as hypothetically isolated by a method such as form criticism. As the previous section indicates, some conclusions about Mark's tradition can be put forward, but there are also areas of disagreement. Hence, redaction critics of Mark have usually relied somewhat more on stylistic, compositional, and structural considerations. In the example just cited, there undoubtedly existed a tradition about Jesus' baptism by John which contained well-known Jewish apocalyptic ideas such as the heavens opening up and a divine voice as signs of the time of salvation. But it is more evident that the naming of Jesus as a "beloved son" is central to Mark, for the view that Jesus is "Son of God" is a major focus of his gospel. A similar account identifying Jesus occurs in Mark 9:7 and a Gentile acclaims him Son of God near the end in Mark 15:39. There are other important passages (e.g., 14:61 ff., cf. 3:11; 5:7). Indeed, Mark opens his story: "The beginning of the gospel of Jesus Christ, the Son of God" (Mark 1:1). The redaction critic will be led to the conclusion that when at the beginning of his public ministry, Jesus is baptized, Mark uses "son" language known from the royal psalms about the enthronement of God's divine king (e.g., Ps 2:7: "Thou art my son . . .") and this will have to be related to Mark's overall portrayal of Jesus.

Redaction criticism is one of the newest developments in the historical criticism of the New Testament, and it has already made possible immense advances in our understanding of the theologies of the synoptic evangelists. Our chapters on the gospels of Matthew and Mark and on Luke-Acts are built on the insights of redaction criticism, as defined in America to include aspects of literary criticism.

MARK AND THE APOCALYPTIC DRAMA

We have seen that many of the church's traditions were passed on in the form of sayings of Jesus and stories about him, even though such sayings and stories often illustrate ideas of a later date than the time of Jesus. Mark follows this convention. He too addresses his teaching to the church of his own day in the form of a story of Jesus teaching his disciples. He presents the problem and challenge of discipleship by telling a story about Peter. At one and the same time he is talking about Jesus and Peter and also about the risen Lord and the Christian disciple of the time at which he writes. The Jesus who addresses the disciples in Galilee is addressing the members of the church for which Mark writes.

237

The gospel narratives blend stories about Jesus' past ministry in Galilee and Judea and the present ministry of the risen Jesus in and through his church. There also are previews of the future ministry of Jesus as Son of Man, especially in the gospel of Mark, for when in Mark 2:10 the Son of Man has authority on earth to forgive sins and in 2:28 to abrogate the Sabbath law, he is exercising the authority it was anticipated that he would exercise when he came on the clouds of heaven.

In the gospel of Mark, past, present, and future all flow together. The past of the ministry of Jesus in Galilee and Judea, the present of the ministry of Jesus in and through his church, the future of the ministry Jesus will exercise when he comes as Son of Man all come together in the narrative of Mark's gospel. In this way the evangelist brings to a climax the tradition he inherits and its literary conventions.

One reason why Mark can write as he does is that in some respects he thinks in apocalyptic terms. He holds strongly the early Christian apocalyptic hope for the imminent coming of Jesus as Son of Man; moreover, he thinks of himself and his church as caught up in the events that mark the end of history. Mark sees a cosmic drama unfolding, a drama in three acts. Each act involves men who "preach" and who are "delivered up." In Mark 1:7 John is described as "preaching" and in 1:14 he is "delivered up."[4] Then Jesus comes "preaching the gospel of God" (1:14), and he is to be "delivered up" (9:31 RSV, "delivered into the hands of men"; 10:33 RSV, "delivered to the chief priests"). After Jesus is "delivered up" the Christians "preach" (e.g., 1:1, "The beginning of the gospel of Jesus Christ," which implies that Mark is concerned to preach the gospel of Jesus Christ as Jesus preached the gospel of God; and, further, 13:10, where "the gospel must first be preached to all nations"). In their turn the Christians are to be "delivered up" (13:9–13). We may represent Mark's fundamental conception as follows:

(a) John the Baptist "preaches" and is "delivered up."
(b) Jesus "preaches" and is "delivered up."
(c) The Christians "preach" and are to be "delivered up."

When the third act is complete the drama will reach its climax in the coming of Jesus as Son of Man (13:26).

It is because Mark thinks in this way that he can write as he does. For him past, present, and future have flowed and are flowing together in the sequence of events that began when John the Baptist preached, continued with Jesus preaching, continued further with the followers of Jesus preaching, and will end with Jesus coming as Son of Man.

This kind of thinking is characteristic of apocalyptic writers; such writers think naturally of a drama that began in the past, continues in the present they

---

[4] The Revised Standard Version has "arrested," but the verb is the same one (Greek: *paradidonai*) used of the fate of Jesus in the passion predictions (9:31; 10:33), and in the Gethsemane story (14:21, 41), and of the fate of Christians under persecution in 13:9–13. It means "to deliver up, to betray."

and their readers are experiencing, and will reach a climax in the imminent future with the coming of the End. Thinking in these terms, Mark can allow past, present, and future to merge in his narrative since the time represented is the apocalyptic time of history hurrying to its climax and end.

THE STRUCTURE OF THE GOSPEL OF MARK

When he wrote his gospel, Mark did not have the resources of such externals as divisions and headings to outline the structure of his work. He had to rely on internal indices of the movement of his narrative, and he did so in two ways: by giving geographical references and by offering summary reports. The geographical outline of the gospel is fairly clear: from 1:14 to 6:13 we are in Galilee; from 6:14 to 8:26 beyond Galilee; from 8:27 to 10:52 moving from Caesarea Philippi to Jerusalem; and from 11:1 to 16:8 we are in Jerusalem. From time to time Mark offers his readers reports of what is going on in the narrative. Such summaries are recognized at 1:14–15, 21–22, 39; 2:13; 3:7–12; 5:21; 6:6b, 12–13, 30–33, 53–56; 10:1. They would be expected at transitions in the narrative, and if we observe the coincidence of a geographical shift and a summary, we have the following natural divisions: 1:14–15; 3:7–12; 6:6b.

Note that there are two stories about people being given their sight, the blind man at Bethsaida (8:22–26), and blind Bartimaeus (10:46–52). They occur where the geography shifts, and they also symbolically enclose the section of the gospel where Jesus tries to make his disciples see the necessity for his suffering and its significance for an understanding of discipleship—signally failing to do so (8:27–10:45).

A last aid to a structural analysis of the gospel is that both the apocalyptic discourse and the passion narrative have introductions (13:1–5a and 14:1–2, 10–12), which on linguistic grounds give every indication of having been composed by the evangelist himself.

All this gives the following structure of the gospel of Mark:

1:1–13	**Introduction**
1:14–15	*Transitional Markan summary*
1:16–3:6	**First major section**: the authority of Jesus exhibited in word and deed
3:7–12	*Transitional Markan summary*
3:13–6:6a	**Second major section**: Jesus as Son of God and as rejected by his own people
6:6b	*Transitional Markan summary*
6:7–8:21	**Third major section**: Jesus as Son of God and as misunderstood by his own disciples
8:22–26	*Transitional giving-of-sight story*
8:27–10:45	**Fourth major section**: Christology and Christian discipleship in light of the passion
10:46–52	*Transitional giving-of-sight story*

11:1–12:44	**Fifth major section:** the days in Jerusalem prior to the passion
13:1–5a	*Introduction to the apocalyptic discourse*
13:5b–37	**Apocalyptic discourse**
14:1–12	*Introduction to the passion narrative* with intercalation, verses 3–9
14:13–16:8	**Passion narrative**

We would argue strongly that the structure we have found is provided by the evangelist himself. We have observed such factors as can be shown to be characteristic of the evangelist and his gospel; this has been deliberate, because recognizing how Mark has structured his gospel is important to understanding the gospel itself and the evangelist and his purpose.

THE GOSPEL OF MARK AND THE PASSION OF JESUS

It is often said, accurately, that the gospel of Mark is "a passion narrative with an extended introduction,"[5] and W. Marxsen claimed that Mark composed his gospel "backwards" from the passion narrative.[6] Certainly the passion of Jesus looms large in Mark, and our structural analysis bears this out. Every major section of the gospel ends on a note looking toward the passion, and the central section, 8:27–10:45, is concerned with interpreting it:

3:6	the plot "to destroy" Jesus
6:6	the unbelief of the people of "his own country"[7]
8:21	the misunderstanding of the disciples[8]
10:45	the Cross as a "ransom for many"
12:44	the widow's sacrifice, which anticipates Jesus'

All through the gospel, the passion and the parousia of Jesus stand in a certain tension with each other. For example, our structural analysis shows that the apocalyptic discourse of Mark 13, in which the parousia is the central concern, is parallel to the passion narrative of 14:1–16:8. They both have introductions, neither one is subordinated to the other, and there is an element of carefully organized parallelism in that the events predicted for the Christians in 13:9 are exactly what happens to Jesus in the passion narrative. Furthermore, there is a careful relationship between the uniform "after three days" of the prediction of the resurrection in 8:31 (and 9:31; 10:34) and the "after six days"

---

[5] Originally said by M. Kähler, *The So-Called Historical Jesus and the Historic Biblical Christ,* p. 80, n. 11.

[6] W. Marxsen, *Mark the Evangelist,* p. 31.

[7] This is a favorite way of thinking about the ministry of Jesus in light of his passion in the New Testament (compare John 1:11 "He came to his own home; and his own people received him not").

[8] The disciples misunderstand the necessity for the passion, and this note of misunderstanding prepares the way for the interpretation of the necessity for and significance of the passion that dominates 8:27–10:45, and that is also misunderstood.

of the transfiguration in 9:2. Since the transfiguration anticipates the parousia, the sequence would seem to be: after three days, the resurrection; after six days, the parousia. Moreover, 9:9 indicates that the event represented by the transfiguration comes after the resurrection and will be of concern to the disciples then: "he charged them to tell no one what they had seen, until the Son of Man should have risen from the dead." Finally, there are the references to Galilee in 14:28, "*after* I am raised up, I will go before you into Galilee," and in 16:7, "he is going before you into Galilee; there you will see him." We hold these to be references to the anticipated parousia. They are, therefore, a final indication of a consistent movement in the gospel through the passion, including of course the resurrection, to the parousia. Mark is addressing people in a situation like that of the women at the tomb, aware of the resurrection and awaiting the parousia in "trembling and astonishment" (16:8).

THE EVANGELIST AND HIS READERS

From time to time in his gospel, the evangelist indicates the state and status of his readers. Mark 9:9 shows that the "disciples" Mark is addressing are now between the resurrection and the parousia. Mark 14:28 and 16:7 also imply this: the readers know the resurrection and anticipate the parousia. They are like the women at the tomb; indeed, the state of the women represents the state of Mark's readers. But more important than any of these references is the apocalyptic discourse in 13:3–37, which is certainly addressed directly to Mark's readers and must be held to mirror their situation. They are being led astray by false Christs (verses 5–7); they are undergoing tribulation and persecution (verses 8–13); and they are seeing "the desolating sacrilege set up where it ought not to be" (verse 14), which has led to more tribulation and to an increase in the activity of false Christs and false prophets (verses 19–23). But the End is near, the Son of Man will soon be seen "coming in clouds with great power and glory" (verse 26); one must now "Take heed, watch" (verses 33–37).

The readers are, therefore, living in a state of heightened apocalyptic expectation, and this is as it should be, for the parousia is indeed imminent. But at the same time, they are being led astray by false Christs and false prophets. We do not know who these people were, but Kelber's careful exegesis of 13:5b–6, 21–22[9] indicates that they were men claiming to be the Risen Jesus himself, i.e., they were "parousia pretenders." The time envisaged is that of the Jewish War of A.D. 66–70. The war led to an upsurge of apocalyptic expectation among both Jews and Christians and to tribulation for Christians, who to the Romans were Jews and to the Jews were Christians. Many had to flee, and they were all subject to the blandishments of the "parousia pretenders."

The reference to the "desolating sacrilege" in Mark 13:14 is ultimately a

---

[9] W. Kelber, *The Kingdom in Mark*, pp. 113–16. For comments on the Markan community, see below, pp. 256–57.

reference to the altar of Olympian Zeus set up in the Jewish Temple by the Syrian king Antiochus IV Epiphanes over two centuries before (cf. chapter 1, p. 17), but the immediate reference is most probably to the desecration and destruction of the Temple by the Romans in A.D. 70 (cf. vs. 2). This shattering event would have brought the apocalyptic expectation to a fever pitch—such an event *must* be the beginning of the End—and Mark writes to support this view, to encourage his readers to wait and hope, and to instruct them that as Jesus himself had to go through his passion to his glory, so too they must be prepared for discipleship that involves suffering.

The readers of Mark are, therefore, the men and women of the church caught up in a resurgence of apocalyptic expectation occasioned by the circumstances of the Jewish War, especially by the destruction of the Jerusalem Temple, but led astray by a false teaching. The gospel is written to exhort and to instruct readers who await an imminent parousia in the period immediately following the fall of Jerusalem and the destruction of the Temple.

MARK, THE GENTILE MISSION, AND GALILEE

If Mark is concerned with readers who stand between the passion and the parousia, who are reeling under the shock of the destruction of the Jerusalem Temple, and who are to anticipate the parousia in Galilee (14:28; 16:7), is he then concerned with *Palestinian* readers? This would be a natural conclusion to draw and some scholars do so in fact, most notably Marxsen.[10] But there are two reasons why this specific geographical limitation will not bear the weight of the evidence: Mark's concern for the Gentile mission (the Hellenistic Jewish Christian mission to the Gentiles) and his symbolic use of "Galilee." We consider each in turn; they are important in determining the readers to whom Mark addressed his gospel, and also to other points in understanding the gospel. It is in fact impossible to separate Galilee from the Gentile mission in Mark's gospel, but we will come at the matter from the two different starting points.[11]

Mark's Concern for the Gentile Mission

Mark has a strong concern for Gentiles and the Hellenistic Jewish Christian mission to them. This is evident in his explicit references to the conversion of Gentiles: the Jews reject Jesus "the son" and the gospel goes to "others" (12:9–11); "the gospel must first be preached to all nations" (13:10); the elect are "from the ends of the earth" (13:27); "the gospel is preached in the whole

[10] W. Marxsen, *Intro.*, p. 143, and *Mark the Evangelist*, pp. 92–95, 151–89, 204–06.

[11] In what follows we are indebted to R. H. Lightfoot, *Gospel Message of St. Mark*, "appendix"; G. Boobyer, "Galilee and Galileans in St. Mark's Gospel," *Bulletin of the John Rylands Library*, vol. 35 (1952–53), pp. 334–48; C. F. Evans, "I will go before you into Galilee," *Journal of Theological Studies*, vol. 5 (1954) pp. 3–18.

world" (14:9). Then there are remarkably many references to Gentiles in the miracle stories in chapters 5 and 7: The Gerasenes are Gentiles, the Decapolis is composed of Greek cities, the woman is a Greek (7:26), and the healing of the deaf mute takes place in the Decapolis. True, Mark is using a cycle of stories developed in the Gentile mission, but that he uses them shows his interest in that mission. Finally, the whole gospel comes to a christological climax when the centurion confesses Jesus as Son of God in 15:39. The centurion is a Gentile, and the title Son of God, itself so prominent in the gospel of Mark, is primarily a Gentile rather than Jewish title. There were, as we have seen, Gentiles in Palestine; but the concern for the Gentile mission also points to the possibility of areas beyond Palestine.

Mark's Symbolic Use of "Galilee"

In 14:28 and 16:7 Galilee is the location for the parousia, and as with so much else in connection with the parousia, it is likely to be symbolic rather than literal. The gospel itself seems to treat Galilee symbolically. Jesus is located there explicitly until his rejection in "his own country" (Galilee) in 6:6a. Then his disciples are sent on a mission, presumably to Galilee, but Jesus himself never works there again. So when in 14:28 and 16:7 he is said to "lead" the disciples to Galilee (the verb translated "go before" in the RSV actually means "to lead"), the natural thought is that he is leading them to the place of their missionary activity. But both in chapter 6 and in 14:28 and 16:7 it is extremely unlikely that this missionary activity is considered in strict geographical terms. The fact that Mark is allowing past, present, and future to flow together in his narrative makes it most probable that the references are to the disciples' activity and the place where the Lord has sent them or has led them to, including the Gentile world at large. Further, there is evidence that in Jewish thinking "Galilee," itself a district of marked ethnic mixing, could be and was a symbol for the work of God in the whole world: Matt 4:15 speaks of "Galilee of the Gentiles"; there is an addition to Isa 8:23–9:6 in the Septuagint that seems to claim that God will pour forth the light of his salvation on "Galilee of the Gentiles"; and in Ezek 47:1–12 the river of life flows from Jerusalem toward Galilee. It is a reasonable claim that in Mark 14:28 and 16:7 "Galilee" has come to symbolize the Christian mission to the whole world, not simply Galilee in the literal geographical sense. In short, the references to the destruction of the Jerusalem Temple and the implication of the parousia in "Galilee" may give clues about the time during which Mark was written, but yield no certainty as to the precise location of its recipients.

EXEGETICAL SURVEY OF THE GOSPEL OF MARK

1:1–13 *Introduction.* Mark defines his work as "the gospel of Jesus Christ, the Son of God" (1:1, 11), that is, the "good news" of the divine human drama in which Jesus Christ is the chief protagonist. This drama began with John the Baptist's preaching, continues with Jesus coming into Galilee preaching the Gospel of God, and will continue further with the preaching of the gospel of Jesus Christ, the Son of God, by the church, including the evangelist Mark, and will shortly reach its climax when Jesus comes into "Galilee" again as Son of Man.

A necessary preliminary to the story, a kind of overture to the whole, is the mission of John the Baptist and the baptism of Jesus. Mark provides a brief account of these, carefully leading up to the moment of revelation when the status of Jesus as Son of God is revealed by the voice of God from heaven.

1:14–15 *Transitional summary.* The drama begins.

1:16–3:6 First major section: *the authority of Jesus exhibited in word and deed.* This section is dominated by the sheer authority of Jesus. He calls Simon and Andrew, and they leave their father immediately to follow him (1:16–20); he exhibits his authority in Capernaum in teaching and healing (1:21–34); he cleanses a leper (1:40–45); he heals a paralytic at Capernaum (2:1–12); he calls another disciple who immediately leaves everything to follow him (2:13–14). Mark 2:15–27 is a series of controversy stories exhibiting the authority of Jesus in various ways: to deny convention by eating with the outcast "tax collectors and sinners"; to disregard fasting regulations; to abrogate the Sabbath law, in both working and healing on the Sabbath. The rubric for this section as provided by the evangelist himself is found in 1:27. "What is this? A new teaching! With authority he commands even the unclean spirits, and they obey him."

This section on the authority of Jesus includes two Son of Man sayings both emphasizing the earthly authority of Jesus as Son of Man to forgive sins (2:10) and to abrogate the Sabbath law (2:28). It will be remembered that in 1:11 the divine voice at his baptism identified Jesus as Son of God. Now he is being identified in his full authority as Son of Man.

In this section there are a number of miracle stories:

1:21–28	the man with an unclean spirit
1:29–31	Simon's mother-in-law
1:32–34	a summary report of many healings
1:40–45	the leper
2:1–12	the paralytic at Capernaum
3:1–5	the man with the withered hand

These stories have a definitive function: to exhibit the authority of Jesus in deeds, just as his teaching and his calling of disciples exhibit it in words. The miracle stories also introduce a theme that will be developed throughout the gospel until it reaches a climax in 14:62, the theme of the "messianic secret."

This theme is introduced in a summary report, "he would not permit the demons to speak, because they knew him" (1:32–34). It was certainly written by Mark himself; so evidently the theme of the demons "knowing Jesus," i.e., knowing the secret of his identity as Son of God (see 3:11–12) and being commanded to keep silent about it is Mark's concern. What he intends to achieve by it will become evident as we trace the theme through the gospel to its climax.

The section ends on a note anticipating the passion, the plot to destroy Jesus (3:6).

3:7–12 *Transitional summary.* This is the longest of the summary reports composed by the evangelist himself, and it marks the transition from the first to the second major section of the gospel. It also introduces a theme that is important in the next section of the gospel, the miracles of Jesus as exhibiting his power as Son of God. In the first section the miracles are one of several things that exhibit Jesus' authority; here in the transitional summary they are particularly significant in their own right, and their importance is that they exhibit the authority of Jesus as Son of God. This summary also develops the idea of the messianic secret. Whereas in 1:32 the demons simply "knew him," in 3:11 they make their knowledge explicit: "You are the Son of God."

3:13–6:6a **Second major section:** *Jesus as Son of God, and as rejected by his own people.* Two themes dominate this section. The first is the power of Jesus as Son of God exhibited through miracles, as in the following references.

4:35–41   "even wind and sea obey him"

5:1–20   the Gerasene demoniac: "What have you to do with me, Jesus, Son of the Most High God?"

5:21–24a, Jairus' daughter: "they were overcome with amazement."
35–43

5:24b–34 the woman with the hemorrhage: "And Jesus, perceiving in himself that power had gone forth from him . . . "

The miracle stories are longer and more elaborate than in the first section of the gospel, and the emphasis on the supernatural in Jesus' power is more marked. He is shown as a Hellenistic "divine man," with power over wind and sea and with power to raise the dead, as one who is openly confessed as Son of God, the touch of whose garments has the power to heal. There are major questions of the origin of these stories and of the use to which Mark is putting them. But these are best discussed after we have reviewed the very similar stories in the next section of the gospel.

The second theme dominating this section is Jesus' being misunderstood and rejected. He is misunderstood by his friends (3:21); he is in tension with his family (3:31–35); and finally, he is rejected by the people of his own country (6:1–6a). This final rejection is the note of anticipation of the passion on which the section ends.

Mark inserts his parable chapter (4:1–34) in this section. It is inherited from the tradition of the church more or less as a unit,[12] and Mark inserts it here because it is a convenient place and because it enables him to begin a theme that becomes prominent in the next section (6:7–8:21) and dominant in the fourth (8:27–10:45): the theme of the disciples and discipleship.

The disciples appear originally in the first major section of the gospel, where their immediate response to Jesus' call was an aspect of the presentation of Jesus' authority. In this second section they figure more prominently, and characteristic Markan ideas and themes appear in connection with them. The section begins with an account of their formal appointment as a group (3:13–19), and in the parable chapter Mark makes a special point about them. They are privy to "the secret of the Kingdom of God" and so are in an especially privileged position compared to "those outside." In a summary report (4:33–34), again composed by Mark himself as are all of the summary reports, their privileged position is further emphasized: "privately to his own disciples he explained everything." Mark makes a great deal of the privileged position of the disciples and of their total failure to understand Jesus. The later theme is developed more and more strongly in later sections of the gospel until it reaches a climax in the flight of the disciples (14:50) and the denial by Peter (14:66–72).

Note the careful balancing of the occurrences of christological titles. The introduction established Jesus as Son of God (1:1 and 1:11), accompanied by the special revelatory circumstances of the heavens opening and the divine voice speaking. The first major section had two occurrences of Son of Man (2:10 and 2:28), and these are now balanced by two occurrences of Son of God (3:11 and 5:7). This careful placement of titles is a major means whereby Mark presents his christological teaching.

6:6b *Transitional summary.* This is the shortest of the transitional summaries in Mark's gospel, but the shift in emphasis between the second and third sections of the gospel is not great.

6:7–8:21 **Third major section:** *Jesus as Son of God, and as misunderstood by his own disciples.* This section does not move as smoothly as do the others, probably because Mark is reproducing two different versions of the same cycle of tradition and finding it difficult to fit them into the overall movement of his narrative. But the two overall themes of the section are clear; indeed, if we accept the thesis that Mark is using a duplicated cycle of tradition, the second, the misunderstanding of the disciples, becomes even clearer.

The first theme of this section is a continuation of the presentation of Jesus as Son of God by reason of his miracles:

[12] Mark has inserted 4:11–12 into the parable chapter. This is evident from the fact that the question in 4:10 now has *two* answers, 4:11 and 4:13, and that both answers are introduced by "and he said to them," a phrase that is a hallmark of Markan literary composition.

6:30–44   The feeding of the five thousand.
6:45–52   Jesus walks on the water, presumably enraptured—"He meant to pass them by" (verse 48).
6:54–56   A summary report emphasizing that Jesus' garments have the power to heal (compare 5:28).
7:24–30   The Syrophoenician woman's daughter, healed at a distance.
7:31–37   The deaf man with a speech impediment. This is much more in the spirit of the stories in the first section (compare 7:37 with 1:27). But Mark can and does link the stories together in the various sections by returning to former emphases (compare 1:27 with 4:41 and 7:37).
8:1–9   The feeding of the four thousand.

Although these stories continue the theme of Jesus as Son of God (e.g., in the deliberate link between 6:56 and 5:28), the title "Son of God" does not occur. Mark is very careful in his use of christological titles. Having balanced the two "Son of Man" references in 2:10 and 28 with the "Son of God" references in 3:11 and 5:7, he does not use another title until the "Christ" of 8:29.

Mark clearly is reinterpreting the miracle stories he presents in these two sections of his gospel. In the form in which he inherited them from the tradition of the church they presented Jesus as a Hellenistic "divine man," and Mark preserves the traits by which they do this. But he then introduces the note of secrecy (3:11; 5:43; 7:36, but not in the story of the Gerasene demoniac, see 5:19). This element of secrecy would strike his readers as startling, because the purpose of such stories is normally precisely to proclaim the power and authority of the "divine man," a tendency that Mark preserves unaltered in the story of the Gerasene demoniac. Mark goes a step further by the careful balancing of the christological titles, whereby Son of God is interpreted in terms of Son of Man, and still further in his narrative structure, which subordinates everything to the passion.

The second theme of this third major section of the gospel is that of the disciples and their misunderstanding of Jesus. The section begins with an account of the mission of the twelve (6:7–13) and of their return (6:30), into which is intercalated the account of the death of John the Baptist (6:14–29). Such intercalation is a favorite compositional technique of the evangelist Mark. Mark does not report this mission of the disciples as a success. He cannot do so, of course, because he is developing the theme of the misunderstanding and failure of the disciples: in 6:51–52 (note "their hearts were hardened," verse 52); in 7:18 (". . . are you also without understanding?"), and in 8:14–21, the climax to this section (with its final note, "Do you not yet understand?").

8:22–26 *Transitional giving-of-sight story.* Mark moves from the third section to the fourth, as he does from the fourth to the fifth, with a story of Jesus giving sight to a blind man (8:22–26; 10:46–52). These stories enclose the fourth section of the gospel (8:27–10:45), in which Jesus attempts to lead his disciples to "sight" (i.e., understanding) and fails to do so. They are certainly used in ironic symbolism, and their function here is therefore quite different from the previous functions of miracle stories in the gospel.

8:27–10:45 Fourth major section: *Christology and Christian discipleship in light of the passion.* This is the most homogenous and carefully constructed of all the sections in the gospel. It begins geographically at Caesarea Philippi to the north of Galilee and has the external form of a journey from there to Jerusalem. The stages of the journey are clearly marked by further geographical references: 9:30 Galilee (9:33 Capernaum); 10:1 Judea and beyond Jordan (10:1 is also a summary report, the last such in the gospel); 10:32 the road to Jerusalem. The section is built very carefully around three passion prediction units, which have a fixed pattern: prediction of the passion and resurrection by Jesus, misunderstanding by the disciples, teaching by Jesus concerning discipleship. Each of these follows a geographical reference. The section indicates that true discipleship means "following" Jesus "on the way" to the passion.[13]

Geographical reference:	8:27	9:30	10:32
Prediction:	8:31	9:31	10:33–34
Misunderstanding:	8:32–33	9:32, 33–34	10:35–41
Teaching:	8:34–9:1	9:35–37	10:42–45

The section has the following structure:

8:22–26	Bethsaida transitional giving-of-sight story	
8:27	**Caesarea Philippi**	
	8:27–30	Fundamental narrative of Peter's confession
	8:31–9:1	**First prediction unit**
		Prediction, 8:31
		Misunderstanding, 8:32–33
		Teaching about discipleship, 8:34–9:1
9:2	"After six days . . ."	
	9:2–8	Transfiguration
	9:9–13	Elijah as forerunner
	9:14–29	Appended incident and teaching on discipleship
		Disciples and boy with the dumb spirit, 9:14–27
		Teaching to disciples, 9:28–29

---

[13] D. Duling, "Interpreting the Markan Hodology," *Nexus* 17 (1974), pp. 2–11; E. Schweizer, "The Portrayal of the Life of Faith in the Gospel of Mark," *Interpretation* 32 (1978), pp. 387–99, reprinted in Mays, *Interpreting the Gospels*, pp. 168–82.

9:30	**Galilee (9:33 Capernaum)**	
	9:30–37	**Second prediction unit**
		Prediction, 9:31
		Misunderstanding, 9:32
		Teaching about discipleship, 9:33–37
	9:38–50	Appended incident and teaching on discipleship
		Nondisciple practicing exorcism, 9:38–40
		Teaching to disciples, 9:41–50
10:1	**Judea and beyond Jordan.** Intercalated units of incident and teaching to disciples	
	10:2–12	Divorce
		The Pharisees and divorce, 10:2–9
		Teaching to disciples, 10:10–12
	10:13–16	Receiving the Kingdom of God
		The presentation of the children, 10:13
		Teaching to disciples, 10:14–16
	10:17–31	Entering the Kingdom of God
		The man with the question, 10:17–22
		Teaching to disciples, 10:23–31
10:32	**The road to Jerusalem**	
	10:33–45	**Third prediction unit**
		Prediction, 10:33–34
		Misunderstanding, 10:35–41
		Teaching about discipleship, 10:42–45
10:46–52	Jericho transitional giving-of-sight story	

Taken together, the three prediction units are extraordinarily interesting. The first summarizes the divine necessity for the passion and is entirely in the present tense. The second provides a hinge in that the first part anticipates Jesus being delivered into the hands of men, but still uses the present tense (RSV is quite wrong in translating 9:31 "The Son of Man will be delivered . . . "; ERV is more accurate, ". . . is delivered . . . ") and then puts the second half of the prediction into the future tense, "they will kill. . . . " The third puts the whole prediction into the future and introduces specific references to Jerusalem and the details of the passion itself. This care in composition, and Mark has composed the predictions himself very carefully, provides an element of movement to the plot of the gospel. In this central section we look back over what has happened to make the passion necessary—the plots, rejections, misunderstanding, all foreseen by God—we pause for these solemn moments of revelatory teaching, and then we move forward to Jerusalem and the passion itself.

The predictions and the prediction units not only provide the framework for this section of the gospel, they are also the main thrust of the teaching on Christology and Christian discipleship. The first prediction follows Peter's confession of Jesus as the Christ (8:29), and so follows the pattern of interpretation of Christology by coordinating titles as in the first and second sections of the gospel. Peter's confession is correct only if "Christ" is understood as the Son of Man who "must suffer," and Peter's reaction indicates that his confession was in fact a false one. The second and third prediction units continue the development of a true Christology by using "Son of Man," and they also implicitly continue the corrective reinterpretation of Peter's confession of Jesus as the Christ. These units provide the key elements to the teaching on discipleship in light of the necessity for Christ's passion: as the master went, so must the disciple be prepared to go. The first unit stresses the need to take up the Cross in following Jesus (8:34–37); the second, the necessity for servanthood (9:35); and the third defines servanthood in terms of the Cross (10:45). There is, further, more general teaching on discipleship between 10:1 and the third prediction unit, probably introduced here in a general context of teaching to disciples.

The first and second prediction units each have appended to them an incident and teaching to the disciples, and the incidents are curiously related. In the first (9:14–27) the disciples are failures as exorcists, while in the second (9:38–40) a nondisciple is successful as an exorcist using the name of Jesus. In this way Mark pursues dramatically his theme of the misunderstanding and failure of the disciples. The third prediction unit has no such appendix; the ransom saying in 10:45 is the climax of the whole section, in some respects its summary, and so brings it to an end.

The one unit in the section we have not so far discussed is the transfiguration-Elijah unit (9:2–13); it is carefully linked to the first prediction unit by the "after six days" of 9:2, which so significantly contrasts with the "after three days" of the resurrection in 8:31 (and 9:31; 10:34). In Mark's gospel and purpose, the transfiguration is an anticipation of the parousia, especially in 9:9, the command to secrecy "until the Son of Man should be risen from the dead." This indicates that the event symbolized by the transfiguration will be of special importance after the resurrection, and hence this event is the parousia. The same point is made by the contrast between the "after three days" used of the resurrection (8:31; 9:31; 10:34) and the "after six days" used of the transfiguration (9:2). Here is an element of Mark's consistent thrust through the passion, including the resurrection, to the parousia.

The transfiguration is, then, an anticipation of the parousia, and its link to the first prediction of the passion and resurrection prepares the reader to appreciate his own position. Like the disciples, he now stands between the past passion and resurrection and the imminent parousia. The transfiguration unit also furthers Mark's christological purpose by a characteristic juxtaposition of titles. Having presented a confession of Jesus as the Christ, Mark now reminds the reader that Jesus is also the Son of God (9:7), again in a special revelatory manner and with the implication that both need correction and interpretation by a use of Son of Man, a point he makes explicit at his christological climax in 14:61–62.

The discussion of Elijah is added at this point (9:11–13) because of the reference to Elijah in 9:4. It is a convenient moment for Mark to present the early Christian understanding of John the Baptist as Elijah, the forerunner of the Messiah, an understanding of the role of the Baptist that he shares.

The motif of the messianic secret is continued through this section (8:30–9:9).

10:46–52 *Transitional giving-of-sight story.* Bartimaeus "sees" and follows "on the way."

11:1–12:44 Fifth major section: *The days in Jerusalem prior to the passion.* The entry (11:1–10) presents all kinds of problems at the level of the historical life of Jesus, but Mark's purpose in presenting the narrative is clear. It fulfills Zech 9:9:

> Lo, your king comes to you;
> triumphant and victorious is he,
> humble and riding on an ass,
> on a colt the foal of an ass.

Already in Jewish exegesis of scripture the irony of the king coming in such a humble fashion is apparent. The Babylonian Talmud preserves a traditional exegesis that claims that if Israel is worthy the Messiah will come in might "upon the clouds of heaven" (i.e., in fulfillment of Dan 7:13); if it is not worthy he will come "lowly, and riding on an ass" (i.e., in fulfillment of Zech 9:9).[14] Mark implies that Israel was unworthy, and so the Messiah entered Jerusalem in this way.

Mark 11:11–25 is an interesting example of the author's compositional technique, because he interprets the cleansing of the Temple (11:15–19) by intercalating it into the account of the cursing of the fig tree (11:12–14, 20–25). Mark thus comes to terms with the catastrophe of the destruction of the Temple by understanding it as the judgment of God on a place become unworthy and by seeing the tradition of Jesus' cleansing the Temple as anticipating that judgment.

The remainder of the section offers a series of units relevant to the situation of Jesus in Jerusalem immediately before the passion: a parable interpreting the fate of Jesus (12:1–12); a series of three controversy stories, the first two featuring adamantly hostile authorities and the third an individual who can be swayed and become sympathetic (12:13–17, 18–27, 28–34). The constrast is no doubt deliberate. Then there follow two inci-

---

[14] Sanhedrin 98a: The tradition is in the name of Rabbi Joshua ben Levi, about A.D. 250, but it exhibits the kind of understanding possible in Jewish and Jewish-Christian exegesis.

dents featuring scribes, a denial that Messiahship should be understood in terms of a Son of David, i.e., a warrior leader in the tradition of David (12:35–37), and a denunciation of scribes (12:38–40). The section closes on the widow's sacrifice, which anticipates the sacrifice of Jesus.

13:1–37 The apocalyptic discourse. Our structural analysis of the gospel shows that after 12:44 there are no more summaries, no more transitional units or stories, only the twin climax of the apocalyptic discourse with an introduction (13:1–5a) and the passion narrative with an introduction (14:1–2, 10–11). Moreover, the prophecy of the destruction of the Temple (13:2) indicates that Mark is writing after the destruction of the Temple in A.D. 70. Mark wrote the introduction, and it is standard to date an apocalyptic work by the latest historical incident it refers to as prophecy.

In dealing with apocalyptic Christianity in chapter 4, we discussed the composition of the discourse Mark uses in his chapter 13, and earlier in this chapter we took up the situation of Mark's readers as reflected in that discourse. It remains only to be added here that the parenesis with which the discourse ends (13:28–37) is most probably a Markan addition. Certainly this parenesis reflects a particular emphasis in Mark's message to his readers. Similarly, the careful parallel of the apocalyptic discourse and the passion narrative reflects Mark's desire to have his readers see their situation as they watch for the parousia as necessarily and profoundly affected by the passion of Jesus.

14:1–16:8 The passion narrative. We discuss this section of the gospel unit by unit.

14:1–11 *The introduction.* Here Mark takes a traditional account of an anointing of Jesus in Bethany and intercalates it into the introduction to the passion narrative. The intercalation has the ironic effect of juxtaposing the plots of the authorities and the connivance of Judas Iscariot with an anointing of Jesus as the Messiah ("anointed one").

14:12–25 *Jesus' last meal with his disciples.* The parallel in 1 Cor 11:23–26 indicates that Mark is using a traditional account of the Last Supper, but the emphasis on the betrayal is a characteristically Markan emphasis, as is the language in Mark 14:21 ("is betrayed" is *paradidotai* from *paradidonai*, the verb used in the passion predictions, 9:31 and 10:33). This language was traditionally used by early Christians of the passion of Jesus,[15] but Mark develops it, especially in the predictions.

14:26–31 *Prediction of the flight of the disciples and the betrayal by Peter.* Again, Mark is moving his readers carefully to the climax of themes very important to him. Note also 14:28, the movement toward the anticipated parousia in "Galilee."

14:32–52 *The betrayal and the arrest.* This narrative represents Markan redaction of a traditional narrative and reflects the Markan emphasis

---

[15] N. Perrin, "The Use of [para]didonai in Connection with the Passion of Jesus in the New Testament," *Der Ruf Jesu und die Antwort des Gemeinde*, pp. 204–12.

on the disciples' failures: they do not watch as they were commanded to do (14:37, 38), and they flee from the scene of Jesus' arrest (14:50). In 14:41 it further reflects the traditional language used of the passion of Jesus, "the Son of Man *paradidotai* . . . ."

14:53–72 *The betrayal by Peter and an intercalated account of the night trial before the Sanhedrin.* First there is the intercalated account of the night trial before the Sanhedrin (14:55–65). It is evident that Mark himself composed this narrative,[16] and it brings his christological concerns to a climax. The High Priest challenges Jesus as "Christ, the Son of the Blessed," i.e., Son of God (14:61), thus bringing together the two titles that have been separately juxtaposed with Son of Man earlier in the gospel. Jesus accepts the titles (14:62), thus formally abandoning the messianic secret by using "I am," which is a formula of self-identification for deities, divine men, and redeemers in the Hellenistic world, and indeed in the ancient Near East at a much earlier period (Exod 3:14–15). Jesus himself uses such a formula earlier in Mark (6:50), as had the "parousia pretenders" of Mark 13:6. Then Jesus goes on to interpret both Christ and Son of God in terms of Son of Man, the last and climactic such reinterpretation in the gospel. The messianic secret is now revealed: Jesus is both Christ and Son of God, but as such has to be understood in light of the emphases associated with Son of Man.

The betrayal by Peter is also a climax, a climax to the presentation of Peter as representative disciple typifying in himself the promise and failure of discipleship as such: the confession (8:29); the misunderstanding (8:32); the leader at the transfiguration (9:5); the responsible person at Gethsemane (14:37). Here he betrays Jesus, as had been predicted after the Last Supper (14:30–31) and then collapses (14:72) in a scene that Aristotle would have recognized as "cathartic."

15:1–47 *The trial before Pilate and the crucifixion.* This section is probably in the main pre-Markan tradition, and we have already noted how heavily it quotes or alludes to the Old Testament, especially in the crucifixion scene itself where 15:23 = Psa 69:21; 15:24 = Psa 22:18; 15:29 = Psa 22:7; 15:34 = Psa 22:1; 15:36 = Psa 69:21.

An incident of particular importance, in view of earlier elements in the gospel, is the Rending of the Curtain: "And the curtain of the temple was torn in two, from top to bottom" (15:38). The curtain separated the innermost part of the Jerusalem Temple, the Holy of Holies, which only the High Priest might enter and where God was particularly to be experienced, from the remainder of the Temple. Its tearing probably symbolizes in the church's tradition an interpretation of the death of Jesus as removing the last barrier between God

---

[16] J. Donahue, *Are You the Christ? The Trial Narrative in the Gospel of Mark.* SBL Dissertation Series 10, 1973.

and man. But in Mark's gospel it picks up the interpretation of the cleansing of the Temple by means of the fig tree incident (11:13–25) and emphasizes that the Temple not only no longer exists, it is no longer needed. In other words, it is part of Mark's attempt to come to terms with the catastrophe of the destruction of the Temple.

The next verse (15:39) is also very important to Mark, for the centurion's confession of Jesus as Son of God is the climax of Mark's christological concern. It is the first and only confession of Jesus by a human being in the gospel that is not immediately corrected or reinterpreted, and the reason is that after 14:62 the reinterpretation of a confession of Jesus as Christ or Son of God by a use of Son of Man is complete, the messianic secret is finally revealed, and such a correct confession is now possible. That a Roman centurion makes the confession symbolizes Mark's concern for the Gentiles, also to be seen in his reference to Galilee (14:28 and 16:7).

16:1–8   *The resurrection.* We are again dealing with specially Markan material, and we saw earlier in 16:7 the movement to the parousia in "Galilee" and the situation of the women as representative of the situation of Mark's readers. Furthermore, 16:7, "tell his disciples *and Peter,*" must be read in the light of 14:72 as implying a restoration of Peter and expressing Mark's hope for a similar happy issue out of the problems afflicting the readers Peter represents in his narratives.

A problem in connection with 16:8 is whether it truly is the ending of the gospel. It seems abrupt, and we can see that the early church regarded it as insufficient, because in the course of transmitting the text of the gospel of Mark two endings were added: a shorter addition to verse 8 and a longer addition that the King James Version has as verses 9–20. All modern translations properly relegate these endings to the margin. Moreover, 16:8 ends with a conjunction, *gar* (*kai ephobounto gar*), and this is a barbarism unlikely to be found at the end of any Greek book. It is difficult, however, to imagine that the text of the gospel could have been accidentally mutilated at a sufficiently early period for all our existing textual traditions to reflect it and not have had the mutilation repaired by the author himself or someone close to him who knew the original ending. This is an extraordinarily difficult issue, and commentators are equally divided. The ending as it stands in 16:8 is appropriate to the gospel as a whole with its consistent thrust through the passion to the parousia and its view of the readers as standing between those events. For this reason we incline to accept the gospel as ending at 16:8.

FURTHER OBSERVATIONS

Having completed our exegetical survey of Mark's gospel, we can make further observations on some of the points touched on in our earlier discussion and exegesis.

The Major Role of Christology in the Gospel of Mark ⟩

The gospel begins with Jesus Christ, the Son of God (1:1), and that Jesus is the Son of God is a main feature of the revelatory scene of the Baptism. Then the two occurrences of Son of Man in the first section (2:10, 28) are balanced by two of Son of God in the second (3:11; 5:7); the titles "Christ" and "Son of Man" juxtaposed in the story of the confession of Peter at Caesarea Philippi (8:27–34) are immediately followed by the use of Son of God at the transfiguration (9:7). Further, Christ, Son of God, and Son of Man are juxtaposed at the trial before the Sanhedrin (14:55–65), and Son of God is the title in the climactic confession by the centurion (15:39). Mark uses Son of Man to correct and interpret a false understanding of Christ and Son of God prevalent in the church for which he writes. The Christology expressed by the use of Son of Man has a threefold emphasis: on authority on earth (2:10, 28), apocalyptic authority at the final judgment (8:38; 13:26), and necessary suffering (8:31; 9:31; 10:33–34, the passion predictions). The threefold christological emphasis expressed by the use of Son of Man in Mark is Mark's answer to the false Christology he is combating and his great contribution to the development of New Testament Christology.

The Purpose of the Gospel ⟩

We are now able to make a statement about the purpose of the gospel in which we will gather points made throughout this chapter. Fundamentally, Mark is an apocalypse in its purpose. For all that he writes realistic narrative, the intent of the evangelist is precisely that of the apocalyptic seers in the discourses in Mark 13 and its parallels or that of John of Patmos in the book of Revelation. He addresses his readers, whom he sees standing between the passion and the parousia of Jesus, to prepare them for the imminent parousia. Like an apocalyptic seer, he views himself and his readers as caught up in a divine human drama, for him the divine human drama that began when John the Baptist "preached" and was "delivered up" and that entered its second act when Jesus came into Galilee preaching the gospel of God. This drama ended its second act when Jesus himself was "delivered up" and rose from the dead, and reached its third act when the church began to preach the gospel of Jesus Christ the Son of God. It is hurrying to the climax of the church being "delivered up" and of Jesus' "coming on the clouds of heaven" to "Galilee."

As preparation for the parousia, Mark seeks to instruct his readers in a correct understanding of Christology and a true understanding of Christian discipleship. This he does not by writing letters to churches and by telling of visions, as did John of Patmos, nor only by putting prophetic words on the lips of Jesus, as in the discourses, nor only by a mixture of remembering, interpreting, and creating Jesus tradition, as in the case of the source Q. Rather, Mark takes the bold and imaginative step of telling the story of the ministry of Jesus

255

so that the concerns of the risen Jesus for his church in the present come to the fore. For him the ministry of Jesus in the past in Galilee and Judea, the ministry of Jesus in the present in the churches for which Mark writes, and the ministry of Jesus that will begin in the future with his parousia in "Galilee," are all the same ministry and can all be treated together in a narrative in which past, present, and future flow together into the one apocalyptic time. He utilized the literary techniques of apocalyptic writers, of the scribes who produced the source Q, and of the editors and transmitters of the synoptic tradition, but he nonetheless created a new literary genre, the gospel: a narrative blend of proclamation and parenesis, of myth and history, a literary type distinctive to early Christianity.

The Markan Community

Apocalypticism emerged among Jews and early Christians who experienced alienation from dominant social and religious structures, especially in times of catastrophe and persecution. The gospel of Mark was an apocalyptic drama written in the wake of the wars with Rome. Its purposes—to warn readers to beware of false prophecy, to encourage them to hold on to their hope in the imminent parousia, and to teach them that discipleship involves suffering in the face of persecution—place it within the general horizon of apocalypticism. More specifically, Mark came out of and wrote for a Christian apocalyptic sectarianism.[17] In his story Jesus appears as something of an apocalyptic charismatic prophet, preacher, and healer. Similarly, the disciples are called to become preachers and healers (1:39; 3:14–15; 6:13). Like the Cynic-Stoic wandering philosophers, they abandon everything (10:28) and take on their mission only the bare essentials (6:8–9: "a staff; no bread, no bag, no money . . . sandals . . .," one tunic). Throughout the gospel the field of activity is not in the cities, but in the villages. Furthermore, the disciples must be prepared to be rejected by (6:4), and to abandon, their families and join together with true mother, brothers, and sisters (3:20–21, 31–35). This new family includes women (1:31; 10:30; 15:41) and children (9:33–37; 10:13, 16), and Gentiles are welcome (5:1–20; 7:24–30; cf. 15:39). Riches can be an obstacle (10:17–27). Jesus' proclamation of the Kingdom brought into being an apocalyptically oriented community for which John and Jesus are models: as they "preach" and are "delivered up," so the followers "preach" and are "delivered up." But discipleship in the eschatological community, for all its trials and

---

[17] H. Kee, *Community of the New Age: Studies in Mark's Gospel*, chapter IV. Cf. p. 105: "In his portrait of Jesus, Mark speaks to and from a community which is influenced both by the Jewish-Hasidic-Essene-apocalyptic tradition, with its belief in cosmic conflict about to be resolved by divine intervention and the vindication of the faithful elect, and the Cynic-Stoic style of gaining adherents by itinerant preaching, healing, and exorcisms from village to village, existing on the hospitality that the local tradition offered." For Kee, the traditional association of the gospel with Rome is, from this perspective, unlikely; he suggests possibly a rural region in southern Syria. See, however, the following section.

sufferings—at least for those who understand and are faithful—has its reward: eternal life in the age to come (10:31).

AUTHORSHIP AND PLACE OF COMPOSITION OF THE GOSPEL

The gospel was originally circulated anonymously; when in the second century it became important to give the gospels authoritative names from the early days of the church, it was ascribed to John Mark, a companion of Paul (Phlm 24; Col 4:10; 2 Tim 4:11; Acts 12:12, 25; 15:37, 39). In the second century Mark was also believed to have been with Peter at Rome (1 Pet 5:13; Papias in Eus *E.H.* III, 39.15: "Lost" letter of Clement of Alexandria). How valid this ascription was we have no means of knowing. All we know about the author is what we can deduce from the gospel itself. Our earlier discussion shows that he has strong links with Palestine and the Palestinian form of Christian tradition, he shares and indeed strongly expresses the characteristic early Christian apocalyptic hope, he is deeply concerned for the Gentile mission of the church, and he wrote shortly after A.D. 70. If "John Mark" can be held to meet these qualifications, well and good; if not, equally well and good. His name is irrelevant; we have called him "Mark" simply for convenience.

The church's tradition claimed that the gospel of Mark was written in Rome, and again we have no way of judging the validity of this claim. The gospel must have circulated quite rapidly since both Matthew and Luke knew and used it within a generation, which seems to indicate a location at an important church center. Moreover, the gospel was accepted into the Christian canon even when it was regarded as little more than an abbreviation of the gospel of Matthew, again indicating the support of an important church center. All that we learn from the gospel itself is that it has a special concern for the Gentile mission and should be located within that mission. Rome is, therefore, a possibility, but then so is almost any other ecclesiastical center. To understand the gospel, however, neither the name of the author nor the place where it was written is absolutely indispensable; so we will not concern ourselves with these matters any further.

THE INTERPRETATION OF THE GOSPEL OF MARK

From the very beginning, the gospel of Mark presented problems to its interpreters because of tensions within the gospel itself: a tension between the purpose of the evangelist and the actual needs of the church within a generation of the writing; and a further tension between the evangelist's purpose and the literary form he chose to express that purpose.

The evangelist followed an apocalyptic purpose, writing within the circumstances of the resurgence of apocalyptic during and immediately after the Jewish War of 66–70. Nevertheless, for all the resurgence of apocalyptic at that

257

time (and at subsequent times of persecution or catastrophe), apocalyptic itself was on the verge of an inevitable decline in the Christian churches. The parousia simply did not take place as was frequently anticipated and expected, and the churches and the Christians were faced with the necessity not only of coming to terms with the delay of the parousia, but also with finding a way of living and working out their faith in a world that continued to exist despite all their hopes, expectations, and prayers to the contrary. In this context the gospel of Mark received its first and perhaps its most dramatic reinterpretation when Matthew and Luke both took it and independently did essentially the same thing with it: they transformed the apocalypse into a foundation myth. They transformed the time of Jesus (which Mark had seen as the same as his own time and that of the parousia, a kind of apocalyptic time) into a kind of Sacred Time. They separated it from all other time by providing it with a beginning, the birth stories, and an ending, the resurrection-ascension (Luke) and the resurrection-commissioning of the church (Matthew). They also made it a Sacred Time by various literary devices that emphasized the element of the sacred and the miraculous in that time. Then they provided the reader with a structured means of relating to that Sacred Time and of living through its power and significance. Now the gospel story became the myth from which Christians lived, as the Jews lived from the myth of the Exodus and as primitive peoples lived from the myth of their totemic ancestors, and so on. It was now the gospel *story*, no longer the gospel as the proclamation of the immediacy and imminence of God's activity, as it has been for Paul and Mark. The apocalypse had become a foundation myth, and apocalyptic time had become Sacred Time, meeting the needs of a generation later than Mark's, and indeed of a hundred generations to come.

The other element of tension was that between the purpose of the evangelist Mark and the literary form through which he expressed that purpose, between his apocalyptic purpose and his realistic narratives. There is no doubt that the narratives of Mark are realistic. They are so realistic that as perceptive a modern literary critic as Erich Auerbach ascribes their realism to the personal reminiscence of an eyewitness and participant.[18] Our discussion has shown that the personal reminiscence is only an echo or shadow, if indeed there is any personal reminiscence at all, but there can be no doubt of the realism of the narratives. With the dwindling of apocalyptic concern in the churches, the apocalyptic purpose of Mark came to be lost, and what remained was the realistic nature of the narratives. In the second and third centuries there was an increasing conflict with Gnosticism, to which we referred in our last chapter, and the Gnostic Christian movement did indeed produce many "gospels" expressing its teaching in the "words" of Jesus, especially in "secret" words of Jesus to his disciples, or in post-resurrection revelatory discourses. The more orthodox church combated the Gnostic Christian movement by emphasizing the apostolic authority of *its* gospels, and under these circumstances a tradition developed that the gospel of Mark was built up largely of the reminiscences of

[18] E. Auerbach, *Mimesis*, p. 36.

Peter.[19] So Papias, bishop of Hierapolis around the middle of the second century, is supposed to have claimed, "The Elder said this also: Mark, having become the interpreter of Peter, wrote down accurately all that he remembered of the things said and done by the Lord. . . ."[20] This tradition is of dubious historical worth, but it is a tribute to the realism of the narratives in Mark's gospel.

This realism provides us with the first clue to the interpretation of Mark's gospel: the narratives are meant to be understood. The evangelist himself takes pains to help his readers by explaining the value of coins (12:42) and by giving the Roman equivalent for the name of a place (15:16).[21] So we must welcome and utilize the patient work of historical scholarship that helps us understand the references and allusions in the narratives. We need to appreciate the significance of the charge of blasphemy in 2:7—the forgiveness of sins was not only reserved to God, it was reserved to God at the End Time—or the force of the plot in 3:6—Pharisees and Herodians were mortal enemies; and much more. We need to know enough about the references and allusions in these narratives for them to become realistic to us and not strange or foreign.

A second clue lies in the fact that narrative functions in a certain way: it draws the reader into the story as a participant. The reader is *there* as the one who took up his cross challenges the disciples to be prepared to take up theirs (8:34), or as he who gave his life interprets the giving as a "ransom for many" (10:45). Similarly, the reader is caught up in the dark hours of the passion and hears Peter's protestations of loyalty (14:26–31), and so shares the catharsis of his breakdown in the courtyard (14:72). The natural function of narrative is to help the reader hear the voices, take part in the action, get involved in the plot. The effectiveness of the evangelist Mark as a preacher is that he has cast his message in a narrative rather than in the direct discourse of a letter or a homily. We appreciate once again the significance of the realism of Mark's narratives, for it enables the reader to be caught up into the narrative as a participant.

Now we can take the important step of recognizing the affinities and differences between Mark and John of Patmos, the author of the book of Revelation. Both are experiencing a period of turmoil and an accompanying resurgence of apocalyptic; one because of the Jewish War and the other because of a time of persecution of the church. Both address their readers directly out of their narrative: Mark by a parabolic discourse, sections of teaching on discipleship, an apocalyptic discourse, and so on; John of Patmos by letters to the churches and interpretations of his visions. Both have essentially the same purpose: to prepare their readers for the imminent parousia. But there is an

---

[19] This tradition is discussed in R. Fuller, *Intro.*, pp. 104–06; W. Marxsen, *Intro.*, pp. 142–43. Details of the tradition in original texts with translations are to be found in V. Taylor, *The Gospel According to St. Mark*, pp. 1–8.

[20] Eusebius, *Ecclesiastical History III.* 39.15. V. Taylor, *The Gospel According to St. Mark*, pp. 1–2.

[21] In the latter instance causing endless difficulties for modern commentators because the soldiers lead Jesus into the *aulē* (courtyard), which is an open space, and Mark explains it as a *praitōrion*, which is a building. Nonetheless, the intent to explain is clear, if not the explanation itself.

extremely important difference between them. Mark's narratives are deliberately realistic; John's deliberately symbolic. The one captures the imagination of his readers by drawing them into his narrative as participants, the other by the sheer power of his symbols to challenge, evoke, and sustain.

We can now recognize that like all apocalyptic, the gospel of Mark needs to be demythologized. The Jesus who comes on the clouds of heaven as Son of Man is probably for Mark already a symbol; certainly he is a symbol for us. He is a symbol of the realities and the possibilities for meaning of human existence in the world. We must allow Mark to catch us up into his narratives as participants and to challenge us with the teaching and example of the Jesus these narratives are concerned to portray, as well as by the example of another kind set by the disciples and opponents, recognizing that in all this we are dealing with symbols of the realities and possibilities of life in the world.

Further Reading

Since the whole chapter is concerned with one book, the further reading is not broken down in accordance with the structure of the chapter, as has been the case previously. Works particularly important at a given place in the chapter are to be found in the footnotes. The references here are more general.

PCB and *IDB* represent the ongoing attempt in Britain to maintain an essentially historicizing approach to Mark, except for Perrin's article in *IDB Supplement.*

> *PCB*, pp. 799–819 (R. McL. Wilson).
> *JBC*, pp. 21–61 (E. J. Mally).
> *IDB*, vol. 3, pp. 267–77 (C. E. B. Cranfield).
> *IDB Suppl.*, pp. 571–73 (N. Perrin).

R. H. Lightfoot pioneered what today would be called a redaction critical investigation of the gospel. No one of the books we are about to list is concerned solely with the gospel of Mark, not even the third, but all are important to the study of the gospel.

> R. H. Lightfoot, *History and Interpretation in the Gospels.* The Bampton Lectures, 1934.
> ——, *Locality and Doctrine in the Gospels.*
> ——, *The Gospel Message of St. Mark.* Consists of lectures originally given in 1949.

Lightfoot's work and insights were carried further and developed by his pupils, and there is now an excellent commentary on the gospel, deliberately written at a nontechnical level, that embodies them: D. E. Nineham, *The Gospel According to St. Mark.*

Recent German language work on the gospel flows from W. Marxsen, *Mark the Evangelist.* Subsequent developments have been reviewed in H.D. Knigge, "The Meaning of Mark," *Interpretation,* vol. 22 (1968), pp. 53–76, and in H. Kee, "Mark's Gospel in Recent Research," *Interpretation*, vol. 32 (1978), pp. 353–68 (the whole issue is dedicated to the interpretation of Mark; it is reprinted in J. L. Mays, ed., *Interpreting the Gospels*, pp. 115–82).

An important recent book taking the evangelist Mark seriously as an author is T. Weeden, *Mark—Traditions in Conflict*. For an introductory review of many problems, see P. J. Achtemeier, *Mark* (Proclamation Commentaries).

The insights and ideas represented in this chapter are, however, very largely those of the present writer and his students.

N. Perrin, "The Son of Man in the Synoptic Tradition," *Biblical Research*, vol. 13 (1968), pp. 1–23.

——, "The Composition of Mark IX. 1," *Novum Testamentum*, vol. 11 (1969), pp. 67–70.

——, "The Literary Gattung 'Gospel'—Some Observations," *Expository Times*, vol. 82 (1970), pp. 4–7.

——, "The Christology of Mark: A Study in Methodology," *Journal of Religion*, vol. 51 (1971), pp. 173–87.

——, *What is Redaction Criticism?* pp. 40–63.

——, "Towards the Interpretation of the Gospel of Mark," *Christology and a Modern Pilgrimage: A Discussion with Norman Perrin*, pp. 1–78.

V. Robbins, "The Christology of Mark." Ph.D. dissertation, University of Chicago Divinity School, 1969.

W. Kelber, *The Kingdom in Mark*.

——, ed., *The Passion in Mark*. Contributions by Donahue, Robbins, Kelber, Perrin, Dewey (as well as Weeden and Crossan) attempt to show Mark's contribution to the composition of the passion story. (Cf. *n.* 2 above.)

——, *Mark's Story of Jesus*.

J. Donahue, *Are You the Christ? The Trial Narrative in the Gospel of Mark*. SBL Dissertation Series 10, 1973.

D. Duling, "Interpreting the Markan Hodology," *Nexus* 17 (1974), pp. 2–11.

A scribe at work in a way that has not changed through the centuries.

CHAPTER NINE

THE GOSPEL OF MATTHEW:
Christianity as Obedience to the New Revelation

The gospel of Matthew is the first book in the New Testament because it was found to be the most useful of all the texts for the church's use through the centuries. It is very much a "church book," written specifically to meet the needs of the church as a developing organization, and it succeeded magnificently. It provided a basis on which the church could build its life, a clear set of instructions for procedure in its affairs, and an understanding of its past, present, and future that made sense of its ongoing life in the world.

THE EVANGELIST AS A MAN OF THE HELLENISTIC JEWISH CHRISTIAN MISSION

The earliest church tradition about the gospel of Matthew comes from the same author who connected Mark with the apostle Peter at Rome (see above, p. 257), Papias, a bishop of Hieropolis in Asia Minor (ca. A.D. 130–140). As recorded by the fourth-century historian Eusebius in his *Ecclesiastical History* 3.39,16, the tradition states: "Then Matthew put together [variant: wrote] the sayings in the Hebrew (probably Aramaic, cf. Acts 21:40; 22:2; 26:14; John 20:16) dialect and each one translated (interpreted?) them as he was able." This tradition and others based on it (e.g., Irenaeus, *Against Heresies* 3.1,1) are referring to the tax collector whom the gospel of Matthew alone calls "Matthew" (9:9; cf. Mark 2:14; Luke 5:27) and specifically identifies as Jesus' disciple (10:3). However, there are a number of problems with the Papias tradition. The gospel of Matthew as we know it is not a collection of sayings; it was not written in Hebrew or Aramaic, but Greek; and it makes very extensive use of the gospel of Mark, building on it as a foundation. All this makes it impossible that the Papias tradition about Matthew is correct. Undoubtedly the ascription of this gospel to Matthew, disciple of Jesus and eyewitness to his life, is the church's later attempt to give special authority to what it considered the most important of its gospels. These factors suggest that, like the other gospels, it first circulated anonymously. Since the gospel presupposes the destruction of Jerusalem in A.D. 70 by its comment that the angry king destroyed the murderers of the king's son and burned their city (Matt 22:7; cf. 24:15–18 par. Mark 13:14–16), and since it appears to be cited by Ignatius of Antioch by the early second century (*To the Smyrnans* I,1 [Matt 3:15]; *To Polycarp* II,2 [Matt 10:16b]), it was probably written about a generation after Mark, about A.D. 90.

"Matthew" has a deep concern for the mission of the church to the world at large. The climax of his gospel is the scene of the Great Commission, where the risen Jesus commands his disciples to "make disciples of *all nations*" (28:19). Yet, there are points within the gospel where "Matthew's" Jesus states his own mission is to "the lost sheep of the house of Israel" (10:5; 15:24), and there are indications that Matthew is concerned with the mission of the church to the Jews. Moreover, in developing his own understanding of Christian faith, he is in constant dialogue with what is going on in Judaism at the same time, and so his gospel reflects much that is Jewish, for example, a concern with the Torah and Jesus as the fulfillment of Scripture. Was Matthew himself a Hellenistic Jew or a Gentile interested in Jewish matters? Was the church as he writes still within the orbit of Judaism, in the process of breaking its ties with Judaism, or now separated from it as a distinctly Christian entity?

To address these questions, it is necessary to examine some of the historical factors facing the church in the late first century. You will recall from previous chapters that the destruction of Jerusalem and its Temple was a shattering problem to both Jews and Christians. For Jews, it meant that the Temple and its worship were no longer available as a way of knowing God in the world and Jerusalem was no longer the center of pilgrimage for the great religious festivals, especially the Passover. Furthermore, the Jewish War had effected a shift in the balance of power and influence among the various sects and parties active in Judaism before the war. The most important of these were the Pharisees, the Sadducees, the Essenes, and the Zealots.[1] The Pharisees were the popular religious leaders devoted to studying and interpreting the Law and obeying it, and to practicing forms of piety such as synagogue attendance, prayer, almsgiving, and punctilious payment of tithes. Since it was difficult to understand how a law written centuries earlier applied to all the circumstances of a changed and changing culture, the Pharisees developed an oral tradition of interpretation of the Law that answered any questions. Fundamentally, the Pharisee understood the Law as revealing the will and purpose of God for men in the world, by obedience to which they achieved the blessing of God (the choice of the masculine is deliberate; a Pharisee regularly thanked God that he had not been born a woman!). The Sadducees, on the other hand, were Jerusalem aristocrats primarily concerned with the Temple, which they controlled,

---

[1] See chapter 1, pp. 30–32 for discussions of the sects and parties in Judaism, and chapter 4, pp. 96–99 for a comparison of Essene and early Christian apocalypticism.

and with the organization of the Jewish state under the authority of the High Priest. They were practical politicians, fully capable of accepting ultimate Roman authority and of accommodating themselves to that authority. The Essenes were a sectarian movement, the major group of which had relocated to the shores of the Dead Sea at Qumran where they lived as a monastic-type order. A priestly community, they opposed the Sadducean priesthood and Temple at Jerusalem and interpreted the Scriptures eschatologically to refer to their own history and messianic hopes for the future. The Zealots were the violent revolutionaries. In their zeal for God and his people they took to the sword against their enemies and God's, even when those enemies were among their own people. They were prepared to kill and to die for their beliefs, and they provided the backbone of the final resistance to Rome, holding out in their fortress at Masada after Jerusalem itself had fallen.

Of these four main parties within Judaism, only the Pharisees could survive the Jewish War. The Zealots perished in the fighting and in attempts to start it up again when it was all over. Likewise, the Essenes opposed the Romans and were destroyed by them. The Sadducees were forced into the dilemma of either active opposition to Rome or betrayal of their own people, and with the destruction of the Jewish state and the Jerusalem Temple, the center of their power and influence, indeed their very reason for being, was gone. The Pharisees, however, had the resources for rebuilding after the holocaust. The Temple was no more, but synagogues could be founded and built. That other pillar of Judaism, the Law, remained, and this was their particular preserve. The forms of piety independent of Jerusalem and the Temple remained, and these had always been the emphases of the Pharisees. Moreover, while the other parties were discredited by the war, the Pharisees were able to maintain their standing among the people.

Left in control of a shattered Judaism, the Pharisees rose to the challenge. They set up a new center at Jamnia, in the remote northwest of the ancient territory of Judah, and there they began to settle the canon and text of Scripture (determining the extent of what Christians now call the Old Testament), to codify the interpretation of the Law, and in general to systematize matters of belief and practice. The Judaism that survived the centuries into the modern world ultimately stems from the work of the Pharisees at Jamnia. It is usually called rabbinic Judaism, because its center is the authoritative interpretation of the Law by the rabbis. In essence, it is Pharisaism redefined in view of the changes necessitated by the destruction of Jerusalem and the Temple.

Matthew writes his gospel in constant dialogue with the developments going on at Jamnia. This dialogue seems not to have been with Jamnia directly, but rather with the synagogue and Jewish community as it responded to what was happening there. So the diatribe against "the scribes and Pharisees" in Matthew 23 does not reflect a conflict between Jesus and the scribes and Pharisees of his day, but one fifty years later between Matthew and their descendants spreading their influence from Jamnia. The church he writes for is closely related to a synagogue "across the street" in any Gentile city with a strong Jewish element in its population. A likely location for such a city is Syria.

Antioch in Syria was the location from which the Gentile mission was launched, but it also contained a sizable Jewish population, as did other Syrian cities. Syria was not far from Palestine and Matthew's gospel contains definite links with Palestinian Christianity, especially Matthew's fondness for using the term Son of Man in the apocalyptic sense (10:23; 13:37–41; 16:28 [for Kingdom of God, Mark 9:1]; 19:28), and other Palestinian Christian traditions can be isolated on form critical grounds (5:17–20; 7:22–23; 10:23; 10:41; 19:28–29; 23:8–10). Thus, a city in Syria meets the conditions of the gospel, and this suggestion is reinforced by the probability that Ignatius of Antioch referred to the gospel, as mentioned above in connection with its date.

The dialogue with a Judaism influenced by Jamnia, the close contact with Palestinian traditions, Greek as the gospel's original language, and the possibility that Syria is the place of origin, point to the probability that "Matthew" is a Hellenistic or Greek-speaking Jewish Christian.[2] Thus, he reveals himself to be a man who stands in the tradition of the Hellenistic Jewish Christian mission. The author of Luke-Acts is also a man of the Hellenistic Jewish Christian mission, but where he represents the movement into the Hellenistic world, the evangelist Matthew represents the continuing links with and concern for the Jewish element in the movement. It is this phenomenon which most characterizes him, and it is this phenomenon which should receive careful consideration in further attempts to understand Matthew's message and purpose.

THE EVANGELIST AND THE PROBLEMS OF THE CHRISTIANITY OF HIS DAY

The Jews of Jamnia had to struggle with the problem of the destruction of Jerusalem and the Temple. Matthew wrestles with the same problem and he does so in dialogue with Jamnia Judaism. This gives a special tone to his work and a particular slant to his solution to the problem. A second area of Matthew's concern is that, like all writers of the middle period of New Testament Christianity,[3] he must address the problem of the delay of the parousia. Third, as in the deutero-Pauline letter to the Ephesians, he faces the difficulties of a Christian movement that is becoming a self-conscious entity in relation to Judaism.

The Fall of Jerusalem and the Destruction of the Temple

Matthew and the Pharisees at Jamnia struggled with the shattering effects of the fall of Jerusalem and the destruction of the Temple. The Pharisees turned to the Scriptures, the record of God's past revelation to his people, and

---

[2] Several scholars today suggest that "Matthew" might well have been a Gentile; for a discussion, cf. J. P. Meier, *The Vision of Matthew*, pp. 17–25.
[3] See above, chapter 4, pp. 88–90.

organized them into a fixed canon of texts they could interpret and build on. Then they began codifying their interpretation of these texts, and the application of their teachings to the changing situations of life in the world. They were concerned particularly with the Law, the Torah, the first five books of what in Christian hands became the Old Testament, for this was to them God's fundamental revelation of his will to his people. This interpretation and application was first transmitted orally, but under the leadership of Rabbi Judah ha-Nasi it was codified in writing as the *Mishnah* ("teaching"), a process completed about A.D. 200. Once collected in writing, the Mishnah became in turn the basis for further discussion, interpretation, and application. The next development of the Mishnah became known as the *Gemara* ("completion"), and it was added to the Mishnah to make up the *Talmud* ("teaching"). The Palestinian version of the Talmud (known as the *Jerusalem Talmud*) existed, but was never completed. The Babylonian Talmud was finished about A.D. 550, and it became and remains the textbook of Judaism, the basis for Jewish life. It is an immense work, covering in encyclopedic fashion every aspect of life that could be imagined or discussed in the five centuries during which it was produced. It is divided into thirty-six tractates, or books, and it contains something like two million five hundred thousand words.

It is interesting to compare the evangelist Matthew with the rabbinic Judaism that produced the Mishnah and other parts of the Talmud. At the risk of oversimplification, we may say that for both the basis of everything else was the fundamental revelation of the Torah. The rabbis saw the Torah further developed by the teaching of the Mishnah and brought to completion by the Talmud. Matthew, on the other hand, sees the Torah "fulfilled" and redefined in the teaching of Jesus (Matt 5:17–20) and completed in the teaching function of the church (Matt 28:16–20, especially verse 20). For both the rabbis and Matthew, revelation is primarily verbal and always requires authoritative interpretation. By emphasizing this aspect of their religious heritage and developing it further, both managed to come to terms with the fall of Jerusalem.

The New Revelation in Jesus

A major emphasis of the gospel of Matthew is, then, that Jesus is the fulfillment of Scripture. The teaching of Jesus fulfills the Torah, and the events of his life fulfill what the prophets speak of. The most striking example of this latter claim is Matthew's careful use of "formula quotations." These are quotations from the Jewish Scriptures always preceded by a formula, such as "all this took place to fulfill what the Lord had spoken by the prophet," or something similar, and always followed by the narration of an incident from the life of Jesus in which the Scripture is fulfilled. These are as follows:

Matthew	Jewish Scripture	Incident from the Life of Jesus
1:22–23	Isa 7:14	The virgin birth
2:5–6	Mic 5:1(2); 2 Sam 5:2	The birth in Bethlehem

Matthew	Jewish Scripture	Incident from the Life of Jesus
2:15	Hos 11:1	The flight to Egypt
2:17–18	Jer 31:15	The massacre of the innocents
2:23	Unknown; Isa 11:1?	Jesus dwells in Nazareth
4:14–16	Isa 9:1–2	Jesus moves to Capernaum
8:17	Isa 53:4	The healing ministry of Jesus
12:17–21	Isa 42:1–4	The healing ministry of Jesus
13:35	Psa 78:2	Jesus' teaching in parables
21:4–5	Isa 62:11; Zech 9:9	Jesus' entry into Jerusalem
27:9–10	Zech 11:12–13; Jer 18:1–13; 32:6–15	The fate of Judas

Of course, it was a commonplace of Christian apologetic that Jesus fulfilled the Jewish Scriptures, but Matthew carries the fulfillment of the Jewish revelation in Jesus to new heights with these careful formula quotations, none of which have parallels in his sources, Mark and Q. They are clearly important to him, and also to us in attempting to understand his gospel. For Matthew it is not a returning to the Torah, but moving forward to the fulfillment of the Torah and the Prophets in Jesus.

Another way Matthew makes this same point is by organizing the teaching of Jesus into five major discourses and by calling attention to them by ending each discourse with a formula, "when Jesus finished these sayings," or the like, as follows:

Matthew	Subject of Discourse	Formula Ending
5:1–7:27	The sermon on the mount	7:28
10:5–42	The missionary discourse	11:1
13:1–52	Teaching in parables	13:53
18:1–35	Christian community regulations	19:1
24:3–25:46	Apocalyptic discourse	26:1

The careful arrangement of these discourses and their formula endings inevitably recalls the five books of the Torah and necessarily implies that here is the *new* Torah, the new revelation that supersedes the old.[4]

The New Revelation as Verbal and as Requiring Interpretation

The insight that Matthew presents the teaching of Jesus as the new Torah leads us to the recognition that for Matthew, as for the Pharisees at Jamnia,

---

[4] B.W. Bacon, *Studies in Matthew* (1930), whose views, or variants on them, are widely held; for critical discussion and an alternative, see J.D. Kingsbury, *Matthew: Structure, Christology, Kingdom,* pp. 1–25. Cf. *n.* 11 below.

revelation is primarily *verbal,* and as such requires authoritative interpretation with changing times and circumstances. Matthew's attitude becomes clear in 5:17–20, again a passage without parallel in his sources. Here Jesus is said to come to fulfill "the law and the prophets," i.e., the Jewish Scriptures.[5] Here greatness in the Kingdom of Heaven depends on keeping the commandments of "the law and the prophets" as fulfilled by Jesus and on teaching men to do so. A similar note is sounded at the beginning of the diatribe against the scribes and Pharisees,[6] "The scribes and the Pharisees sit on Moses' seat; so practice and observe whatever they tell you" (Matt 23:2–3). The passage continues, however, "But not what they do; for they preach, but do not practice." In other words, Matthew honors above all the activity of scribes and Pharisees at Jamnia in interpreting the authoritative revelation; his quarrel with them is about the details of their interpretation and practice. For Matthew the heart of the matter lies in the verbal revelation of "the law" and its authoritative interpretation by "scribes and Pharisees." The Christian revelation is "the law" as definitively interpreted by Jesus: there remains, therefore, the authoritative further interpretation of this revelation by the Christian equivalent of "scribes and Pharisees."

For Matthew that equivalent is "the disciple." An interesting aspect of his presentation of the ministry of Jesus is that he carefully avoids any mention of the disciples of Jesus *teaching.* He regularly summarizes Jesus' activity as "proclaiming the Kingdom," "healing," and "teaching" (4:23; 9:35; cf. 11:1), but when the disciples are commissioned by Jesus (10:1–7), they are to heal and to proclaim the Kingdom, *not* to teach. In the gospel of Matthew only Jesus teaches, and that teaching is the new Torah, the fulfilled revelation. But after the revelation is complete, and the situation has become such that the revelation now needs authoritative interpretation, *then* the disciples begin to teach. At the *end* of the gospel the resurrected Jesus says to the disciples: "Go therefore and make disciples of all nations, baptizing them . . . *teaching them to observe all that I have commanded you;* and lo, I am with you always, to the close of the age" (Matt 28:19–20, the Great Commission). The commandment in italics sums up the major emphasis of the gospel of Matthew: the teaching of Jesus is the new revelation, and it requires the authoritative interpretation of disciples.

Matthew speaks of "disciples" because he is bound by the literary conventions imposed by the form of a gospel. This convention limits him to terms that are realistic in the situation of Jesus and his ministry. But he also readily

---

[5] The Jewish Scriptures are traditionally divided into three parts: "the Law" (Genesis to Deuteronomy); "the Prophets" (Joshua, Judges, Samuel, Kings, Isaiah, Jeremiah, Ezekiel, and the twelve minor prophets); and "the Writings" (Psalms, Proverbs, Ecclesiastes, Song of Solomon, Lamentations, Ruth, Daniel, Chronicles). The last group was achieving canonical status during the New Testament period. Matthew is conservative in this regard, recognizing only "the Law and the prophets"; Luke, on the other hand, has "the law of Moses and the prophets and the psalms" (Luke 24:44), where the third group is recognized and designated by the name of its first book.

[6] A scribe was an interpreter of the Law, generally addressed as "rabbi," whereas a Pharisee was a member of the party or sect of the Pharisees. Many scribes were in fact Pharisees, but the two terms were not synonymous even though the New Testament writers tend to treat them as such (see above, p. 31).

uses the term because the Greek word for disciple, *mathētēs*, means "learner." In contrast to Mark who portrays the disciples as those who misunderstand Jesus, Matthew views them as sometimes having "little faith" but as nonetheless growing in understanding and ultimately to be entrusted with the new revelation. So when Matthew is thinking of disciples, he is thinking of a Christian equivalent to the Jewish "scribes and Pharisees." He does not object to the *function* of a "scribe and Pharisee." On the contrary, he applauds it: "Therefore every scribe who has been trained for the kingdom of heaven is like a householder who brings out of his treasure what is new and what is old" (Matt 13:52). A scribe is an official interpreter of the revelation; in Matthew's view, the need is for scribes "trained for the kingdom of heaven" for official interpreters of the revelation as fulfilled in Jesus Christ.

The Delay of the Parousia

The fall of Jerusalem and the destruction of the Temple lead Matthew to respond that the promises of Torah are fulfilled in Jesus as a new revelation to be further interpreted. What then of belief in the parousia which was perpetuated among many Christians prior to A.D. 70?

Matthew maintains the traditional Christian hope of the parousia. He has a fondness for using Son of Man for Jesus in apocalyptic contexts, and, indeed, he is the first evangelist to use the Greek word *parousia* in its technical Christian sense as referring to the return of Jesus as Son of Man: "What will be the sign of your coming (parousia) and of the close of the age?" (Matt 24:3; see also 24:27, 37, 39). That Matthew anticipates the parousia and the end of the age is very clear. But it is more distant for him than for the evangelist Mark. Whereas in Mark all history is hastening to its imminent climax and end, in Matthew there is still a period of time and history left before the end; this is the period of the church. In it the church works and witnesses (24:14; 28:16–20), and at its end the church will be judged (13:36–43). As far as Matthew is concerned, the delay of the parousia allows time for the work and witness of the church, and the parousia itself becomes especially a judgment of the church. Thus he finds a solution to the delay of the parousia in the challenge to understand the role of the church as a self-conscious entity in the world.

THE CHURCH AND THE CHURCH'S BOOK

Matthew is much concerned with the Christian church as an entity distinct from the Judaism it came from. This can be seen, for example, in that he is the only evangelist to use the Greek work for church, *ekklēsia:* "And I tell you, you are Peter, and on this rock I will build my church" (16:18) and "If he refuses to listen to them, tell it to the church" (18:17). Both these instances are important to understanding the gospel of Matthew.

The first of them, 16:18, occurs in Matthew's version of the incident at Caesarea Philippi. In Mark 8:27–9:1 we have a firmly structured incident:

8:27–29   Peter's confession
8:30   Command to secrecy
8:31   First passion prediction
8:32–33   Peter's misunderstanding and Jesus' rebuke
8:34–9:1   Teaching on discipleship

Mark is Matthew's source; yet the incident has been very significantly edited and redacted by Matthew:

16:13–16   Peter's confession
16:17   *Blessing of Peter*
16:18–19   *Commissioning of Peter as the founder of the Christian church*
16:20   Command to secrecy
16:21   First passion prediction
16:22–23   Peter's misunderstanding and Jesus' rebuke
16:24–28   Teaching on discipleship

What has happened is that Matthew has combined two quite different traditions: a confession by Peter, which he takes from Mark, and a blessing and commissioning of Peter by Jesus, which he inserts between the confession and the command to secrecy. Where this second tradition came from we do not know, but it has been plausibly suggested that it is the remnant of an account of a resurrection appearance to Peter,[7] otherwise lost to us. The effect of the conflation of the two traditions is to focus the reader's attention on Peter's role in the church and on the authority of the church on earth, emphases foreign to the original Markan narrative and yet characteristic of Matthew. Matthew has another version of the saying that appears in 16:19 in his discourse on Christian community regulations in 18:18. The second occurrence of the word *ekklēsia* in Matthew, 18:17 (twice), is in the discourse on Christian community regulations, 18:1–35. This discourse has a core in Mark 9:42–50, but Matthew expands and develops it until it is an embryonic "church order" regulating the life of the Christian community, the church. All communities require such regulations and Matthew is responding to this need.

Whereas Mark had called his work a "gospel" (1:1), Matthew opens his account with "The *book* of the genesis of Jesus Christ, the Son of David, the Son of Abraham" (1:1). Indeed, with a few exceptions (cf. 4:23; 9:35) Matthew rarely uses "gospel" except when following Mark; he is not preaching the gospel, but organizing an interpretation of the revelation given in Jesus Christ. The new revelation is related to the old revelation. Jesus is descended from Abraham, the father of the Jewish people, but also the one to whom a promise was given to the nations. He is descended also from the first great king of

---

[7] For example, R. Fuller, "The 'Thou Art Peter' Pericope and the Easter Appearances," *McCormick Quarterly,* vol. 20 (1966/67) pp. 309–15; R. Brown, K.P. Donfried, J. Reumann, *Peter in the New Testament,* pp. 83–101.

Israel, King David and his royal line, giving him the proper credentials to be a royal Messiah; Matthew further develops the Son of David theology in the miracle stories (9:27; 12:23; 15:22; 20:30; 21:9, 15; 22:42, 45), indicating that even a Gentile who addresses Jesus as Son of David is healed (15:22). He is also—some claim most importantly—Son of God, as Israel was Son of God.[8] Matthew's five major discourses, plus Jesus' temptation of forty days and forty nights and the first discourse delivered from a mountain, have sometimes suggested to scholars that Matthew thinks of him as a new Moses giving a new Torah. He is "Lord" and is frequently addressed as such. He is, finally, Son of Man as Matthew indicates in apocalyptic contexts. Matthew's goal is to build a church on the foundation stone of Peter that will guard and interpret the revelation, going out into all the world to make "disciples from among all nations" (28:19–20). But the final guarantee of the church is not the primacy of Peter nor the efficiency of the regulations nor even the trustworthiness of the interpretation; it is the presence of the risen Christ among its members. The gospel ends with the promise of the risen Lord to the disciples: "and lo, I am with you always, to the close of the age" (28:20). Moreover, in the discourse on community regulations this same note is sounded: "For where two or three are gathered in my name, there am I in the midst of them" (18:20).

Matthew is providing the basis for the church's life—the new revelation in Jesus Christ. The revelation is essentially verbal, "teaching," and as such it requires authoritative interpretation. To this task the church is commissioned to go into all the world as bearer and interpreter of this revelation. In this task the church will be strengthened by the risen Lord in its midst, until that final movement when it, like all the world, will be confronted by the judgment of the Son of Man and his angels. It can readily be seen how in the gospel of Matthew the church came to find "its book."

THE IDEA OF SALVATION HISTORY

In Biblical literature, an author will frequently think in temporal terms, that is, of past, present, and future. An apocalyptic writer writes in this fashion, with his sights fixed on the present and near future; so does the ancient Biblical "historian," with his focus on the past and present. But the history the ancient Biblical historian sees is not merely the factual recounting of events; his concept of history is a history of the world in which God may be known, a history that is both a history of people and their affairs and a history of God's affairs with people. As the history of God's affairs with people, of God's activity on behalf of people, it is *salvation* history, the history of the salvation of humanity at the hand of God. There is then a world history, a history of people and their affairs in the world, and a salvation history, a history of God and his activity directed toward the salvation of people. These two run side by side, and at

---

[8] On Son of David, see below, *n.* 12. J. Kingsbury, *Matthew*, pp. 40–83, structures Matthew's gospel in relation to Son of God.

certain points they intersect, but salvation history is not exhausted in world history. The salvation history of God's activity on behalf of people began before the creation of man and before the beginning of world history, and it will continue after the parousia has brought world history to an end.

The New Testament writer who has most often been thought to have a concept of salvation history is the author of Luke-Acts.[9] But there are also indications that Matthew had, at least implicitly, a concept of salvation history. We noted above Matthew's view of Jesus' limited mission to the Jews, especially to the "lost sheep of the house of Israel" (10:5; 15:24) in the course of Jesus' life; yet the Great Commission of the resurrected Christ at the end of the gospel stresses a mission to "all nations" (28:19). Matthew is in dialogue with Jews in Jamnia, or more specifically the synagogue "across the street" influenced by Jamnia. He is wrestling with the problem of the destruction of the face of Jerusalem and the destruction of the Temple, and he affirms the Law and its teachers (5:17–20; 23:2–3); yet, Jesus is the new revelation who fulfills the Law and the Prophets and is described with various christological titles, and his disciples continue the interpretation of Scripture and are commanded to have a righteousness which exceeds that of the "scribes and Pharisees" who are sharply condemned (5:20–48; 23). As a Christian, Matthew is a man of the Hellenistic Jewish Christian mission (probably in Syria) and the church is a self-conscious entity distinct from Judaism, requiring its own regulations. To all of this should be added Matthew's references to teachings and events of Jesus' life as the time of fulfillment, specific temporal references (e.g., "then," some ninety times; "in those days," 3:1, cf. 24:3, 19, 22 [twice], 29; "from that time on Jesus began . . . ," 4:17, 16:21; ". . . to the close of the age," 28:20; cf. 24:3), and the segmentation of Jesus' life into distinct periods. Clearly Matthew's view of the new revelation in Jesus Christ suggests a distinction between a "period of Israel" and a "period of Jesus" beginning with John the Baptist (cf. the temporal references and Kingdom proclamation in 3:1 and 4:17). The difficult question is whether these two phases should be extended to three; i.e., whether "period of Jesus" and "period of the church" can be distinguished and if so, when the latter begins. It is clear that Matthew follows in the steps of Mark insofar as he lets the story of Jesus, the disciples, and their opponents speak to problems in his own day. This tends to blur the distinction between the period of Jesus and the period of the church and to suggest only a two-phase salvation history. But he has gone beyond Mark in thinking of the church as a self-conscious entity with its mission to the world, and he certainly places central significance on the Great Commission in that regard (28:16–20). This would point to a three-phase salvation history. Thus, while Matthew has not yet developed a salvation history to the extent of Luke-Acts, what has been said above tends to favor a move toward a three-phase periodization, the period of Israel, the period of Jesus, and the period of the Church ". . . until the close of the age." We shall have more to say about this phenomenon.[10]

[9] See below, chapter 10, pp. 301–09; cf. Paul's view, chapter 6, pp. 195–98.
[10] See below, pp. 288–89.

THE STRUCTURE OF THE GOSPEL OF MATTHEW

The gospel of Matthew is built on the foundation of the gospel of Mark, but Matthew has edited and redacted it so that all is changed. As Matthew presents his "book," it falls naturally into five parts:[11]

1. **Introduction, 1:1–4:17.**   This part explains who and what Jesus is: the new revelation of God.

2. **The ministry of Jesus to Israel, 4:18–13:58.**   As the new revelation of God Jesus fulfills the old revelation and hence, fittingly comes first to the people of God whose leaders nevertheless oppose him.

3. **The ministry of Jesus to his disciples, 14:1–20:34.**   In the face of opposition, Jesus continues to minister to Israel but turns his attention more and more to his disciples and prepares them for their work in the world.

4. **Jesus in Jerusalem, 21:1–25:46.**   The drama now approaches its climax as Jesus confronts the Jewish leaders and teaches his disciples concerning the final judgment.

5. **The passion, resurrection, and Great Commission, 26:1–28:20.**   The drama reaches its climax in the passion and resurrection of Jesus and in his commissioning of his disciples. This mission, which is sporadically anticipated, is to all the nations.

EXEGETICAL SURVEY OF THE GOSPEL OF MATTHEW

Introduction, 1:1–4:17

1:1–17   *Genealogy.* "The book of the origin of Jesus Christ, the son of David, the son of Abraham," is the superscription of the whole gospel. Among the Jewish rabbis, Son of David became a favorite title for the expected Messiah. It emphasized the Messiah's descent from David and his coming as fulfilling God's promise to David in 2 Samuel 7. Matthew, in dialogue with developing rabbinical Judaism, uses the title frequently of Jesus (1:1; 9:27; 12:23; 15:22; 20:30; 21:9, 15; 22:42, 45), strengthening the claim that Jesus is the Jewish Messiah, but doing so in relation to Jesus' miracle working.[12]

---

[11] Dissatisfaction with B.W. Bacon's attempt to structure Matthew around the five great discourses (see above, p. 268) is widespread; though Kingsbury's alternative structure finds some support (1:1–4:16; 4:17–16:20; 16:21–28:20), there is as yet no general agreement; cf. D. Harrington, "Matthean Studies Since Joachim Rhode," *Heythrop Journal* 16/4 (1975), pp. 375–88.

[12] D. Duling, "The Therapeutic Son of David: An Element in Matthew's Christological Apologetic," *New Testament Studies* 24 (1978), pp. 392–410.

The genealogy traces the descent of Jesus back through the royal line of King David to Abraham, the father of the Jewish people, to whom was given the promise of becoming the father of many nations (Gen 17:4). It is divided into three divisions of fourteen names (the numerical value of David's name in Hebrew is fourteen [$D=4$; $W=6$; $D=4$]). Matthew stresses Jesus' significance as the fulfillment of the Jewish heritage and possibly anticipates the Great Commission of Jesus to the disciples to go to all nations (28:19).

1:18–2:23 *The birth and infancy of Jesus.* Each sequence in the story is said to fulfill Old Testament Scripture, e.g., Virgin Birth (LXX Isa 7:14); Bethlehem birth (Mic 5:2; 2 Sam 5:2); flight into and return from Egypt (Hos 11:1); weeping over slaying of infants (Jer 31:15); the residence in Nazareth ("He shall be called a Nazōrean," a prophecy not explicitly found in the Jewish Scriptures). Matthew's flight-to-Egypt story allows him to stress the exodus theme through a formula quotation: as Israel (= God's son) had come out of Egypt, so now Jesus as God's son (Hos 11:1; "Out of Egypt I have called my son"). The "son" idea will be important in the upcoming baptism and temptation stories. The section is an excellent example of prophecy fulfillment through the use of formula quotations.

3:1–4:17 *The prelude to the ministry.*

3:1–6 *John the Baptist in the wilderness* (= Mark 1:1–6).[13] Matthew brings John the Baptist into close contact with Jesus, giving him exactly the same message as Jesus (3:2 = 4:17) and making his ministry also a fulfillment of prophecy. As Jesus' immediate precursor, he shares in the act of fulfillment. He is described in terms reminiscent of the description of Elijah in 2 Kings 1:8.

3:7–10 *John's warning to Pharisees and Sadducees* (= Luke 3:7–9). Matthew depicts the leaders of Israel as a homogenous group, a united front opposed to Jesus; in this passage they are opposed to John whom Matthew closely links with Jesus. John's language here is echoed by Jesus in 7:16–20 and 12:33.

3:11–12 *John predicts the coming of Jesus* (= Mark 1:7–8). These verses reflect the Christians' belief that their baptism is superior to John's. The idea of the separation of the good from the evil at the last judgment is dominant in Jesus' eschatological teaching in Matthew 24–25. Matthew is further paralleling John the Baptist and Jesus. This part of John's message has no parallel in Mark.

3:13–17 *The baptism of Jesus* (= Mark 1:9–11). Although Matthew carefully parallels John the Baptist and Jesus in several ways, he also carefully subordinates John to Jesus by adding verses 14–15, which have no parallel in his source, the gospel of Mark. "Righteousness," a favorite term of Matthew's (cf. 5:17–20), is introduced; the theme of

---

[13] We give the parallels from Mark or Luke (indicating Q material) where appropriate, but not where the parallels are weak or scattered through the source.

Jesus' sonship is expressed through a combination of words from Psalm 2:7 and Isaiah 42:1.

4:1–11 *The temptation of Jesus* (= Mark 1:12–13). Mark 1:12–13 simply mentions the temptation of Jesus in the wilderness, while both Matthew and Luke (Luke 4:1–13) share a tradition in which Jesus meets the temptations by quoting Deuteronomy (Matt 4:4 = Luke 4:4: Deut 8:3; Matt 4:7 = Luke 4:12: Deut 6:16; Matt 4:10 = Luke 4:8: Deut 6:13). The passages in Deuteronomy reflect the Jewish interpretation of their people's journey through the wilderness as a testing by God to determine their fitness to inherit the Promised Land (Deut 8:2–3). Again, Jesus, like Israel before him, is identified as Son of God (4:3, 6).

4:12–17 *Jesus goes to Galilee and begins to preach* (= Mark 1:14–15). Mark 1:14–15 makes this the beginning of the apocalyptic drama, but Matthew makes it the conclusion to his introduction. Verse 14 introduces Matthew's formula quotation (Isa 9:1–2) which identifies Galilee as "Galilee of the Gentiles," apparently anticipating the church's mission to all nations (28:16–20). In verse 17 Jesus takes up the message that John had proclaimed. The preliminaries are complete; the new revelation can now begin.

The New Revelation: The Ministry of Jesus to Israel, 4:18–13:58

4:18–22 *The call of the four fishermen* (= Mark 1:16–20). The ministry begins with the challenge to "follow" Jesus, as it will end on the note of "Go and make disciples . . . ." Note that Matthew does not call these men "disciples" until 5:1 when they begin to listen to the teaching, the verbal revelation.

4:23–25 *Summary of the characteristic activity of the ministry* (= Mark 1:39). Verse 23 is a framing summary stressing teaching, preaching the good news of the kingdom, and healing every disease and infirmity; after a section on teaching (5–7) and healing (8–9), Matthew repeats essentially the same summary (9:35).

5:1–7:29 *The First Book of the New Revelation: the Sermon on the Mount.* This takes place on a mountain, whereas the comparable discourse in Luke is on a plain. Matthew is stressing the parallel to Moses receiving the Torah on a mountain, the previous revelation now being superseded (Exod 19:3–6). The first book of the new revelation concerns the personal aspects of Christian piety and behavior.

5:3–12 *The Beatitudes* (= Luke 6:20–23). "Blessed" in the sense used here refers to the fortunate, happy condition of a person blessed by God. The reference is to the blessed conditions that will obtain after Jesus has returned as Son of Man. These are eschatological blessings, and Matthew is using them to set the whole teaching in the context of eschatological expectation.

5:13–16 *Salt and light: the disciples' special status* (= Luke 14:34–35; 11:33).

5:17–20 *The essential nature of Christian faith: obedience to the new revelation.* This is a key passage in Matthew's gospel; it expresses the evangelist's understanding of the essence of Christian faith: obedience to the new revelation as it is interpreted by the Christian equivalent of "scribes and Pharisees." In Judaism, obedience to the revelation in the Torah was expressed by the concept of "righteousness." Righteousness was the quality of obedience one must have achieved to be able to stand before God, and "the righteous" are those who have achieved it. For Matthew the quality of the Christian's obedience to the new revelation must exceed that of the "scribes and Pharisees" to the old. By this means they will "enter the Kingdom of Heaven," i.e., enter into that state of blessedness Jesus will establish for the "righteous" when he comes as Son of Man.

5:21–48 *The antitheses* (partial parallels only in Mark and Luke). In a series of antitheses Matthew expresses aspects of the new revelation in contrast to the old. In each instance the new is an intensifying or radicalizing of the old.

6:1–18 *Instruction on almsgiving, prayer, and fasting* (Matt 6:9–13 = Luke 11:2–4). Almsgiving, prayer, and fasting are forms of Jewish piety independent of the Temple. Even while the Temple stood the Pharisees emphasized them, and after its destruction they developed them still further. Matthew is here in dialogue with the developments going on at Jamnia, and his acrimonious tone indicates its intensity. Matthew is close enough to the Pharisees to quarrel violently with them and denounce them vigorously. Note his constant use of the epithet "hypocrites," which occurs as a refrain throughout the denunciation of the "scribes and Pharisees" in Matthew 23.

6:19–34 *Various images describing the truly righteous man.*

7:1–12 *Various maxims illustrating the new righteousness.*

7:13–27 *Warnings designed to stress the necessity for obedience to the new revelation.* These warnings constitute the ending to the Sermon. They end it on a note of eschatology as the Beatitudes had begun it on a similar note.

7:28 Contains the formula ending to the first book of the new revelation.

8:1–9:34 *The miracles of Jesus.* Matthew characteristically arranges his material in blocks. He follows his first revelatory discourse with a block of ten miracle stories interwoven with teaching on discipleship. In 4:23 and 9:35 the summaries of the characteristic activity of Jesus' ministry stress healing, and nine of the ten miracles are healing miracles. The collection of ten miracles perhaps recalls the ten plagues of Moses in Egypt (Ex 7:8–11:10). In general, Matthew tranforms the miracles by introducing or expanding dialogues.

8:1–17 *The first three healings: the leper, the centurion's servant, and Peter's mother-in-law.* In Matthew 8:17 a formula quotation (Isa 53:4) stresses the healing focus of Jesus' ministry. The faith of the centurion, a Gentile, is emphasized.

8:18–22 *First discipleship section: sayings on discipleship.*

8:23–9:8 *The second three miracles: the stilling of the storm, the healing of the demoniac, and the cure of the paralytic.* The stilling of the storm deserves special comment because here we see Matthew's own understanding most clearly.[14] Matthew's source is the account of the same miracle in Mark 4:35–41, and it is instructive to observe his redaction of that source. In Mark the story has the natural form of a miracle: Jesus and his disiciples embark in a boat, accompanied by other boats; a great storm arises; the disciples appeal to Jesus, and he calms the storm. The following dialogue ends on a note of wonder. In Matthew there is no mention of any other boats. The dialogue takes place *before* the storm is calmed, and Jesus is addressed as "Lord" (Mark: "teacher"); he in turn addresses the disciples as "men of little faith," a frequent reproach by Jesus in this gospel (6:30; 8:26; 14:31; 16:8), and only in this gospel. Matthew has redacted the traditional miracle story to make it an allegory of the church. The one boat is the little ship of the church, beset by the storms of persecution, and the disciples are the members of the church who fail because of their "little faith" and need the presence of their Lord to help them, which presence they have.

9:9–17 *Second section on discipleship: the call of Matthew, eating with "tax collectors and sinners," fasting.* Eating with "tax collectors and sinners" is important in the Hellenistic Jewish Christian mission because in Palestine they were ostracized and treated as *Gentiles*. Since table fellowship between Jews and Gentiles in the Christian church was a major problem in the mission, Jesus' attitude to "tax collectors and sinners" was for Matthew an important aspect of teaching on discipleship. Fasting was also important because it was a form of piety stressed by the Pharisees at Jamnia.

9:18–34 *The last four healings: the ruler's daughter and the woman with a hemorrhage, the two blind men, the dumb man.*

9:35–38 *Summary of the characteristic activity of the ministry.* Matthew has inherited from Mark 6:6b–11 an account of a teaching journey by Jesus, followed by the commissioning of "the twelve" for a missionary journey. The teaching journey further summarizes the activities characteristic of Jesus' ministry—preaching, teaching, and healing (9:35; cf. 4:23).

10:1–11:1 *The Second Book of the New Revelation: The Missionary Discourse.* The commissioning of "the twelve" becomes the occasion for the second rev-

---

[14] We are now following G. Bornkamm, "The Stilling of the Storm in Matthew," in G. Bornkamm, G. Barth, H. J. Held, *Tradition and Interpretation in Matthew*, pp. 52–57.

elatory discourse. The discourse itself contains originally disparate elements (10:5–42). Matt 10:5–6 reflects the Christian mission to the Jews rather than the Hellenistic Jewish Christian mission. In 10:7 Matthew gives to the disciples the exact proclamation of Jesus (4:17) and John the Baptist (3:2). John the Baptist, Jesus, and now the Christian church are the succession of the new revelation. Notice, however, that the disciples are *not* commissioned to teach, as they are when the revelation is complete. Matt 10:9–16 seems to be a development from some traditional "handbook" for the missionaries of the Hellenistic Jewish Christian mission, since Luke 10:4–12 has a similar set of instructions. 11:1 contains the formula ending to the second book of the new revelation.

11:2–12:50 *Opposition by leaders; the people's lack of understanding.* Matthew ends his account of the mission of Jesus to Israel by focusing attention on Jesus himself, developing a Christology, and interweaving with it an account of the opposition by leaders and the people's lack of understanding. It is a skillful blend of Jesus as the Jewish Messiah and the difficulties he faced among the Jews themselves.

11:2–6 *John the Baptist's question* (= Luke 7:18–23). Jesus is the Christ (Messiah) as his ministry testifies.

11:7–15 *Jesus' testimony to John* (= Luke 7:24–30). John is the Elijah expected by the Jews to come as the forerunner to the Messiah.

11:16–19 *Parable of the Children in the Market Place* (= Luke 7:31–35). Neither John the Baptist nor Jesus have been recognized or accepted by "this generation" (cf. 12:38–39).

11:20–24 *Woes on the Galilean cities* (= Luke 10:13–15). The cities that have rejected Jesus will be judged accordingly.

11:25–30 *The "thunderbolt from the Johannine sky"* (= Luke 10:21–22). These verses are astonishing because their style is associated with the gospel of John rather than Matthew. Yet they represent a major Matthean christological statement: Jesus is the revealer of knowledge of God, a knowledge that he reveals to his intimates. "Yoke" is a metaphor much used by the Jewish rabbis of obedience to the Law, the "yoke of the Torah." Matt 11:25–30 therefore contrasts the burden of the old revelation to the ease and joy of the new.

12:1–14 *Jesus in controversy with Pharisees* (= Mark 2:23–28; 3:1–6). Matthew here gives two stories of Jesus in controversy with Pharisees, taken from a collection of five such stories in Mark 2:1–3:6. He had given the other three earlier (9:1–8, 11–13, 16–17), interpreting them as dealing mainly with discipleship.

12:15–21 *Jesus as servant of God.* A further christological statement is made by a formula quotation.

12:22–24 *A healing and two reactions* (= Mark 3:19b–22). A healing evokes two reactions: the crowd raises the question whether Jesus might not be the Son of David; the Pharisees denounce him as an emissary of Beelzebub.

12:25-37 *Jesus denounces the Pharisees* (= Mark 3:23-30). The opposition between Jesus and the Pharisees sharpens. Matthew expands and intensifies the tone of his Markan source.

12:38-42 *The sign of Jonah* (= Luke 11:29-32). Jesus rejects a Pharisaic request for a "sign" that would vindicate his authority and denounces "this evil and adulterous generation." The sign will be the sign of Jonah; that is, Jesus' resurrection will be his vindication over "this generation" that rejected him.

12:43-45 *Further denunciation of "this generation"* (= Luke 11:24-26).

12:46-50 *The true family of Jesus* (= Luke 8:19-21). Matthew stresses, in contrast to the crowds' misunderstanding, that the true family of Jesus consists of those like the disciples who accepted him and his revelation.

13:1-52 *The Third Book of the New Revelation: the Parables of the Kingdom.* Like Mark, Matthew has a collection of parables, but he increases their number and makes special use of them. He has just called attention to the true family of Jesus as those who accept his revelation. Now Jesus addresses the parables of the Sower, the Weeds, the Mustard Seed, and the Leaven to "the crowds" (13:1-33). Matthew concludes this half of his parable chapter with a formula quotation (13:34-35). Jesus then turns to the "disciples," the true family, and gives them the explanation of the Weeds and the parables of the Pearl and the Net.

13:1-35 *The Sower, Weeds, Mustard Seed, and Leaven.* The Sower (13:1-9) with its explanation (18-23 = Mark 4:1-9; 13-20) interprets the ministry of Jesus as rejection and acceptance. The intercalated verses (10-17 = Mark 4:10-12) contrast those who accept Jesus with those who reject him and add a formula quotation. The parable of the Weeds (13:24-30) continues the theme of acceptance and rejection, this time in the context of the coming "harvest," i.e., final judgment of God. The parables of the Mustard Seed and the Leaven (13:31-33 = Mark 4:30-32 = Luke 13:18-21) in Matthew's context and use are means of interpreting the rejection of Jesus and of holding out the hope of ultimate acceptance, if not by all the Jews then certainly by the rest of the world at large. 13:34-35 contains the formula quotation (Ps 78:12).

13:36-50 *Interpretation of the Weeds; the Treasure in the Field, the Pearl, and the Net.* Matthew 13:36 shifts from the crowds to the disciples. In this new context the parable of the Weeds is interpreted as an allegory of the earthly ministry of Jesus as Son of Man and of his coming apocalyptic judgment. Notice the Matthean promise of blessing to the "righteous" in verse 43, and compare it with 5:20. In Matthew, the parables of the Treasure in the Field and the Pearl refer to the blessing that awaits the "righteous," those who accept Jesus' revelation and obey it. The parable of the Net is a restatement of Matthew's characteristic view of the judgment that will separate the evil from the righteous.

13:51–52 *The Christian scribe.* As a climax to his parable chapter, Matthew adds this description of the ideal of acceptance and obedience, the scribe "trained for the kingdom of heaven."

13:53–58 *The climactic rejection.* 13:53 contains the formula to the end of the third book of the new revelation. Matthew ends his third revelatory discourse with the theme that Jesus is not honored "in his own country and in his own house," and because of lack of belief, he is not able to work many miracles.

The New Revelation: Jesus Instructs His Disciples, 14:1–20:34

The ministry to Israel now having reached the climax in the inability of Jesus to find faith among "his own," Matthew turns to the second stage of the new revelation, which occurs in the relationship between Jesus and his disciples.

14:1–16:12 *Preliminary instruction.* In this section Matthew is closely following his source, the gospel of Mark.

14:1–12 *The death of John the Baptist* (= Mark 6:14–29). Matthew abbreviates the story as it occurs in Mark, and he subordinates other elements in the story to his theme of John's death being the occasion for the withdrawal of Jesus with his disciples.

14:13–21 *The withdrawal of Jesus and the feeding of the Five Thousand* (= Mark 6:30–44). Matthew is still abbreviating Mark's narrative in the interest of his withdrawal theme. Jesus, having compassion on the crowds, heals them and feeds them. In Matt 14:19 the disciples play more of an intermediary role than they do in Mark 6:41; they are becoming the church that mediates the sacraments.

14:22–33 *The walking on the water* (= Mark 6:45–52). Again Matthew is abbreviating Mark, in this instance to make room for the redactional insertion of the incident of Peter also walking on the water (Matt 14:28–31). Peter becomes a paradigm of the "disciple" who has "little faith" and so needs the help of his "Lord"; compare 8:23–27, another sea miracle. Matthew ends the account with a formal confession of Jesus as the Son of God (verse 33). In Matthew's thinking the story has become a paradigm of the relationship between Jesus and his followers in the Christian church, and so a formal confession is in place here.

14:34–36 *Healings at Genneseret* (= Mark 6:53–56).

15:1–20 *Dispute with "scribes and Pharisees" about the tradition of the elders* (= Mark 7:1–23). In the dispute with the scribes and Pharisees Matthew is following Mark, but he uses it as a starting point for instruction of the disciples.

15:21–39 *A group of three miracles* (= Mark 7:24–8:10). Matthew is still following Mark closely, shortening somewhat as he goes. Jesus claims he was sent only to the lost sheep of the house of Israel (cf. 10:6), but he nevertheless heals a Gentile woman because of her faith (cf. 8:10, the centurion). The crowds glorify the God of Israel in response to Jesus' healing, i.e., Matthew has created a summary (15:29–31) from Mark's healing of the deaf mute (7:31–37). Jesus has compassion on the crowds and feeds the Four Thousand, the disciples again acting as intermediaries (cf. 14:13–21). The one real change is that a healing of a deaf mute in Mark 7:31–37 is generalized into a healing of many sick persons in Matt 15:29–31.

16:1–4 *The sign of Jonah* (= Mark 8:11–13). This is another version of the pericope found earlier in the gospel (12:38–40). Matthew has added verses 2–3, taken from Q (= Luke 12:54–56), and the reference to Jonah. He also has the request coming from "Pharisees and Saddu-cees" (Mark: "Pharisees"), indicating further opposition from the Jewish leaders (cf. 3:7).

16:5–12 *Warning against the teaching of Pharisees and Sadducees* (= Mark 8:14–21). Again from Mark, with "Pharisees and Sadducees" substi-tuted for Mark's "Pharisees and Herod."

16:13–20:34 *The predictions of the passion and resurrection and instruction on life in the Christian community.* This section is Matthew's equivalent of Mark 8:27–10:52 (he omits 8:22–26). In general, he follows Mark but adds con-siderable material, and the additions transform Mark's teaching on disci-pleship into instruction on life in the Christian community.

16:13–28 *Caesarea Philippi* (= Mark 8:27–9:1). We pointed out earlier that Matthew adds the blessing and commissioning of Peter to the narrative in Mark 8:27–9:1. Further changes are the addition of "and then he will repay every man for what he has done" (verse 27) and the modification of Mark's "before they see the Kingdom of God come with power" to "before they see the Son of Man coming in his Kingdom." These changes transform the Markan understanding of discipleship as preparedness to accept suffering as one followed Jesus to his Cross and awaited the parousia, into the Matthean form of discipleship as living the life of obedience to the new revelation in the church until the coming of Jesus as Son of Man.

17:1–8 *The transfiguration* (= Mark 9:2–8). This reproduces Mark with the significant addition of verses 6–7, where Jesus reassures the disci-ples who are afraid. We saw in 8:23–27 and 14:22–33 that this is a very important theme to Matthew, representing his understanding of the reality of life in the church. Matthew keeps Mark's theme of Jesus' divine sonship.

17:9–13 *The coming of Elijah* (= Mark 9:9–13). Matthew adds his verse 13 to Mark's narrative, stressing the identification of John the Baptist and Elijah.

17:14–20[15]   *The healing of the epileptic boy* (=Mark 9:14–29). Matthew shortens Mark's narrative to make room for verse 20, which introduces another of his favorite themes, the disciple in the church as a man of little faith (see also 6:30; 8:26; 14:31; 16:8).

17:22–23   *The second prediction* (= Mark 9:30–32). Matthew abbreviates the prediction and then breaks up the carefully-structured Markan prediction unit by introducing his fourth revelatory discourse.

17:24–27   *The temple tax.* An early Christian legend, reproduced here by Matthew because it features the prominence of Peter, the foundation stone of the church, in verse 24.

18:1–35   *The Fourth Book of the New Revelation: Christian Community Regulations.* In this discourse Matthew follows Mark where he can, but he adds material from Q and special material of his own to make the whole a revelatory discourse.

18:1–5   *Greatness in the Kingdom* (= Mark 9:33–36; 10:15; 9:37). Matthew uses the latter part of Mark's second prediction unit to introduce the discourse.

18:6–9   *On temptations* (= Mark 9:42–48).

18:10–14   *The parable of the Lost Sheep.* Matthew interprets the "little ones" of Mark 9:42 as members of the Christian community and then uses the parable of the Lost Sheep to reassure them that God will take care of them. The parable has a quite different application in Luke 15:3–7.

18:15–22   *Two community regulations.* In verse 15–20 Matthew greatly expands a saying from Q (= Luke 17:3) by adding references to the need for witnesses to the church, to the authority of the church (18:18 = 16:19), and to the promise of the presence of the risen Lord in the church. All told, 18:15–20 is a major Matthean statement about the church. In verses 21–22 Matthew reproduces a regulation concerning the necessity for reconciliation within the community from Q (= Luke 17:4).

18:23–35   *The parable of the Unmerciful Servant.* Matthew brings his discourse to a close by using the parable of the Unmerciful Servant to reinforce the regulation concerning the necessity for reconciliation within the Christian community. Note the characteristic emphasis on the eschatological judgment in verse 35.

19:1–20:34   *The journey to Jerusalem.* Matthew concludes his revelatory discourse with a characteristic formula and resumes his close following of Mark as he portrays the journey of Jesus from Galilee to Jerusalem. As in Mark, the journey features teaching on discipleship, and the differences reflect the different understandings of discipleship by Matthew and Mark.

---

[15] Verse 21 is omitted in the earliest Greek texts and relegated to the margin in the best modern translations.

19:1–12 *Marriage and divorce* (= Mark 10:1–12). Matthew now gives his characteristic formula for ending a discourse and then goes on to reproduce a pericope from Mark as a community regulation on marriage and divorce. Note the addition of "except for unchastity" in verse 9, which brings the teaching into line with that of the strictest Jewish rabbi of the period, Rabbi Shammai, and the addition of verses 10–12, introducing the note of "celibacy" into the life of the church.

19:13–15 *The blessing of the children* (= Mark 10:13–16).

19:16–30 *The rich young man* (= Mark 10:17–31). The Markan incident is made into a community regulation by the addition of verse 28, which introduces the eschatological promise for those who will accept the challenge to leave all for the sake of discipleship.

20:1–16 *The parable of the Laborers in the Vineyard.* Matthew inserts this parable into the Markan narrative to illustrate the theme of the reversal of values in the coming Kingdom of the Son of Man (verse 16). But the parable fits that purpose uneasily, and it is an example of a parable of Jesus steadfastly resisting an attempt to serve a later and different context.

20:17–28 *The third prediction unit: prediction-misunderstanding-teaching* (= Mark 10:32–45). This essentially reproduces Mark's third prediction unit. In our discussion of the gospel of Mark we saw how carefully structured were the three prediction units (Mark 8:27–9:1; 9:32–37; 10:32–45) with their constant theme of prediction-misunderstanding-teaching on discipleship. Matthew broke up the first two by various insertions, but he left the third practically intact. Even in Mark the third unit has what are to all intents and purposes Christian community regulations (Mark 10:42–44); so as it stands the narrative serves Matthew's particular purpose.

20:29–34 *The healing at Jericho* (= Mark 10:46–52). In Mark this is a transitional giving-of-sight pericope, but Matthew simply reproduces it with a characteristic doubling of the healing as blind Bartimaeus becomes two blind men. Matthew is fond of healings in pairs (8:28–34; 9:27–31). Note the address "Son of David."

Jesus in Jerusalem, 21:1–25:46

This section narrates Jesus' activity in Jerusalem before the beginning of the passion itself. For the most part Matthew follows Mark 11:1–13:37, but with some very significant changes and additions.

21:1–23:39 *The final clash between Jesus and the Jewish leaders.*

21:1–11 *The entry* (= Mark 11:1–10). Matthew follows Mark in the main, but he adds the formula quotation in verses 4–5 and changes one animal to two to make the narration agree exactly with his own understanding of the quotation.

21:12–17 *Jesus in the Temple* (= Mark 11:11a, 15–19, 11b). Mark intercalates the cleansing of the Temple into the fig tree incident to interpret the cleansing by means of the fig tree. Matthew has no such purpose; so he restores what must have been the original unity of the cleansing. Note that verses 14–16 have no parallel in Mark, they represent Matthew's characteristic emphasis on the healing ministry of Jesus. The children respond to Jesus' healing with the same cry as that found in the entry scene, "Hosanna to the Son of David!" This arouses official indignation.

21:18–22 *The fig tree incident* (= Mark 11:12–14, 20–25). What in Mark had been a testimony to the judgment of God on the Temple and a way of coming to terms with the fact of its destruction becomes in Matthew an example of the power of faith.

21:23–27 *The question of Jesus' authority* (= Mark 11:27–33). This follows Mark in narrating a clash between Jesus and the Jewish authorities.

21:28–32 *The parable of the Two Sons.* The true son of God is he who accepts Jesus as his revelation.

21:33–46 *The parable of the Wicked Tenants* (= Mark 12:1–12). In the main this follows Mark, but the addition of verse 43 stresses that the Christians and not the Jews are now the heirs of God.

22:1–14 *The parable of the Marriage Feast* (= Luke 14:16–24). Matthew interprets the parable as testimony that after the Jews rejected Jesus and killed him, the heritage passed to the Christians. But even the Christian must have the wedding garment of true obedience. Note the allegorical reference to the destruction of Jerusalem in A.D. 70 (22:7).

22:15–46 *Three questions in dispute between Jesus and his opponents* (= Mark 12:13–37). Matthew now follows Mark in narrating three questions that cause disputes between Jesus and the Jews: Tribute to Caesar, the Resurrection, and the Great Commandment. Since his source already had a strong element of conflict between Jesus and his Jewish opponents, Matthew engages in no extensive redaction, except that he carefully omits the sympathetic answer of the scribe and Jesus' praise of him in Mark 12:32–34. He then places the concluding remark at the end of the question about David's Son (22:46) and thereby formally brings to an end all debate between Jesus and his opponents. The rejection is complete and the conflict over; there remains now only the working out of the consequences.

23:1–36 *The woes against the Pharisees.* Mark 12:38–40 has a warning against the scribes; in Matthew it becomes a carefully organized diatribe against his opponents, the scribes and Pharisees at Jamnia, and their influence. It is not their *function* he is against, very much to the contrary, but their practice.

23:37–39 *The lament over Jerusalem* (= Luke 13:34–35). This is a Christian lament over Jerusalem that interprets its destruction as the judgment of God for its rejection of his emissaries and which anticipates a restoration at the parousia. A saying developed in the church to help Christians come to terms with the destruction of Jerusalem, it is used by both Matthew and Luke.

24:1–25:46 *The Fifth Book of the New Revelation: the Apocalyptic Discourse.* The apocalyptic discourse proper, Matt 24:1–36, in the main follows Mark 13:1–32. But Matthew omits Mark's ending of the discourse and goes on to add apocalyptic teaching that he takes from Q (Matt 24:37–51 = Luke 17:26–27, 34–35; 12:39–40, 42–46) and then a series of parables (the Ten Maidens, Talents, Last Judgment). As Matthew interprets them, the first two are concerned with the coming of the Son of Man and his judgment (25:13, 29–30), and the third directly describes that judgment.

The third parable, the Last Judgment, is the last element of the teaching of Jesus in the gospel, and it sums up many prominent themes: the need for "righteousness" to enter the Kingdom; righteousness consisting of an obedience expressed in deeds; the fact that the Son of Man will repay everyone according to his deeds; the need for mercy, especially to those who are weak. It is thus a fitting climax to Matthew's presentation of the teaching of Jesus.

The Passion, Resurrection, and Great Commission, 26:1–28:20

26:1–27:66 *The passion and death of Jesus.* 26:1 contains the formula ending to the fifth book of the new revelation. In his account of the passion and death of Jesus Matthew follows Mark closely, with only minor redactional changes. We follow our division of the Markan narrative.

26:1–16 *The introduction* (= Mark 14:1–11). An important change here is the introduction of a fourth passion prediction in verse 2, which links the narrative more closely to the previous teaching of Jesus.

26:17–29 *Jesus' last meal with his disciples* (= Mark 14:12–25). Mark does not identify the betrayer until the Gethsemane scene (14:43); Matthew indicates who it is here (26:25).

26:30–35 *Prediction of the flight of the disciples and the betrayal by Peter* (= Mark 14:26–31).

26:36–56 *The betrayal and the arrest* (= Mark 14:32–52). Matthew makes minor editorial changes that heighten the theme of the fulfillment of Scripture: adding verses 52–54 and rewriting verse 56 (= Mark 14:49b) to read, "But all this has taken place, that the scriptures of the prophets might be fulfilled."

26:57–75 *Betrayal by Peter and intercalated account of the night trial before the Sanhedrin* (=Mark 14:53–72). The only significant change is that Matthew edits the dialogue between Jesus and the High Priest to make it a formal statement of the person of Jesus before the spiritual head of Judaism: "I adjure you by the living God, tell us . . . You have said so . . ." (verses 63–64).

27:1–2 *Jesus is delivered to Pilate* (= Mark 15:1).

27:3–10 *The fate of Judas.* Only Matthew has this narrative of the fate of Judas as fulfilling a formula quotation (Zech 11:12–13; cf. Matt 26:15).

27:11–66 *The trial before Pilate and the crucifixion* (= Mark 15:2–47). Matthew introduces several editorial changes in this narrative. In verse 19 he emphasizes the innocence of Jesus, and hence by implication, the guilt of the Jews, and in verses 24–25 he makes the guilt of the Jews explicit. In verse 43 he uses Ps 22:8 to add to a narrative already saturated with allusions to that Psalm. Then in verses 52–53 he inserts a whole series of supernatural events, including a temporary resurrection of "the saints" to stress the fact that God is at work in these events and that new life will emerge from the death of Jesus. Finally, in verses 62–66 he adds the incident of the Guard at the Tomb. This is a late composition, very probably by Matthew himself, designed to forestall a possible claim that the resurrection was a lie because the disciples had stolen the body of Jesus.

28:1–20 *The resurrection of Jesus and the Great Commission.* At this point Matthew begins to go beyond Mark, necessarily so since Mark has no account of the resurrection as such, only of the women at the tomb.

28:1–10 *The empty tomb* (= Mark 16:1–8). The main changes here are that additional verses 2–4 further emphasize the supernatural nature of these events, and in verses 9–10 Matthew goes beyond the Markan ending to provide an appearance of Jesus and an explicit command of the risen Lord himself for the disciples to go into Galilee.

28:11–15 *The report of the guard.* This is a narrative loaded with anti-Jewish polemic.

28:16–20 *The Great Commission.* This climax to the gospel of Matthew relates the intended reader to what the gospel has narrated. Jesus has given the new revelation to his disciples, and it is now their responsibility to go into the world and make new disciples. Thus the reader becomes a "disciple," heir to the new revelation and to the task of interpreting and obeying it, as well as making further disciples. In this way the reader appropriates the revelation to himself and locates his place in the scheme of things. There will be an extended interval between the passion and the parousia, and during this interval he is to accept, interpret, and obey the revelation, and at the same time persuade others to do the same. But he will not be alone in this task; always the risen Lord will be with him, to the close of the age.

The narrative is not so much a resurrection appearance as an account of the risen and exalted Lord commissioning the church and its members. Certainly it represents the message of the evangelist

Matthew to his readers, as it reveals the convictions that inspired his writing of the gospel: Jesus as the medium of the new revelation that fulfills and decisively reinterprets the old; the disciple as recipient of the revelation he is to obey so that the quality of his obedience exceeds that of the scribes and Pharisees. These are the themes that have dominated the gospel. But now new elements are added. In language recalling the Son of Man vision in Daniel 7:14, Jesus explicitly claims the authority that had before been his only implicitly (verse 18). Now, for the first time, the disciples are commissioned to "teach," to interpret the revelation. Now also the church is given the baptismal confession that will separate it from the world and dedicate it to its Lord (verse 19). Finally, the gospel ends on a note sounded earlier (8:25–26; 14:27; 18:20): the distinguishing mark of the church and the source of its power and authority is the presence of the risen Lord in its midst.

THE INTERPRETATION OF THE GOSPEL OF MARK BY THE EVANGELIST MATTHEW

The material in the gospel of Matthew comes from three sources: the gospel of Mark, the sayings source Q (indicated in our exegesis by = Luke), and a separate source or sources of material peculiar to Matthew. Matthew may have composed some of this last material himself. But whatever the source, it is organized on the basis of the structure of the gospel of Mark. Matthew diverges from that structure by making additions and insertions, or by rearranging related material, such as teaching or miracles, into large blocks. But by and large he organizes his gospel on the basis of the structure of the gospel of Mark, and from 14:1 to 28:10 he follows Mark's order exactly.

The fundamental changes in the gospel of Matthew compared to Mark are the birth stories at the beginning and the resurrection appearance and commissioning scene at the end. Mark himself gives only enough of an introduction to locate the story and identify the characters before he plunges into the first act of his three-act apocalyptic drama. But Matthew does not think in terms of a three-act apocalyptic drama, but rather of the time of Jesus as a special, sacred time. By adding a genealogy and a series of stories on the birth and infancy of Jesus, by emphasizing Jesus as the new revelation fulfilling the promise of the old and superseding it, he is able to set the time of Jesus off from all previous time as the time of fulfillment.

The time of Jesus is then a special kind of time—of fulfillment, of revelation—and Matthew makes this point over and over in various ways. He uses the formula quotations to claim the time of Jesus as the time of fulfillment. He organizes the teaching of Jesus into five discourses, each ending with a formula, and the first taking place on a mountain, to claim that the teaching of Jesus is the new verbal revelation, the new Torah. Though he abbreviates miracle stories, he consistently heightens the sense of the miraculous, having two or many healed where in his source only one was healed, to stress the awesome nature of Jesus and his ministry.

But Matthew not only separates the time of Jesus from all previous time, he also separates it from all following time. He has, as we have seen, a concept of salvation history. Whereas Mark had deliberately involved his readers in the story and left them at the empty tomb awaiting the parousia in fear and trembling, Matthew just as deliberately separates his readers from the story by the Great Commission, in which Jesus appears as the risen and exalted Lord. The Great Commission envisages a time before the parousia, which will be of a different order from the time of Jesus. The revelation has now been given, and the need is for interpretation of that revelation and obedience to it. Now the disciples are to go out into all the world and make disciples; now, for the first time, the disciples are to *teach*, to interpret the revelation. Moreover, they are to organize into a church with a distinctive rite and formula of initiation: baptism in the name of the Trinity. Finally, the disciples will constantly be helped and their teaching authenticated by the presence of the risen Lord in their midst.

In our previous chapter we claimed that despite its realistic narrative the gospel of Mark was essentially an apocalpyse. We can now claim that at the hands of Matthew the apocalypse became a foundation myth. In the gospel of Matthew the time of Jesus is separated from all preceding and succeeding time and becomes what can only be called Sacred Time, the time of fulfillment and revelation. Moreover, the Christian church is constituted on the basis of this Sacred Time—the Sacred Time of Jesus is the time of Christian origins—and lives out of the relationship to that time. The life of the church, and the life of Christians in the world, is made possible by the interpretation of the revelation, and by the concept of the presence of the risen Lord in the church and of the fellowship of the community of believers with him. This may well be called foundation myth: a myth of origins to which the involved group relates by carefully organized means. Matthew's concept of salvation history and his foundation myth go hand in hand.

THE INTERPRETATION OF THE GOSPEL OF MATTHEW

The evangelist Matthew has a distinctive theology and view of the church. Both are built on essentially Jewish models. The concepts of the fulfillment of a previous promise, of a verbal revelation authoritatively interpreted, of a carefully organized and structured community of believers—for all these Matthew is indebted to his Jewish heritage. One could, of course, find parallels in the varied religious communities in the Hellenistic world, but the fact is that Matthew inherited them from Judaism, and he developed them in debate with the changes in Judaism going on at Jamnia. But Matthew's views are not simply Christianized Judaism. He is indebted to his distinctively Christian heritage at many points, especially for the concept of the risen Christ present in the church. Even though Jewish rabbis were to come to speak of the presence (*shekinah*) of God wherever two or three gathered to study the Torah, the Matthean view of the risen Lord present in the church, helping, sustaining, and guiding the "disciples" has its roots in the Hellenistic Christian concept of the presence of the Lord in the cultic worship of the community. Matthew is always a man in the tradition of the Hellenistic Jewish Christian mission.

By the intent of its author, the gospel of Matthew cries out for the interpretation it has in fact received through the centuries: as a text enshrining a revelation subject to authoritative interpretation within the Christian community. Its author expected this "book of the origin of Jesus Christ" to become the subject of authoritative interpretation within the church. More than that, this is what happened to the whole of the New Testament of which it became the first book. The centuries have treated it as the enshrinement of revelation and authoritatively interpreted it within the church, which would have delighted the evangelist himself. Even today, when a Christian claims, "the Bible says . . . ," expression is being given to the stance and attitude of the evangelist Matthew.

Further Reading

W. G. Kümmel, *Intro.*, pp. 72–86.

W. Marxsen, *Intro.*, pp. 146–54.

R. Fuller, *Intro.*, pp. 113–18.

PCB, pp. 769–98 (K. Stendahl).

JBC, pp. 62–114 (J. L. McKenzie).

IDB, vol. 3, pp. 302–13 (F. C. Grant).

IDB Suppl., pp. 580–83 (R. G. Hamerton-Kelly).

Recent work on the gospel is influenced by Günther Bornkamm and his pupils, who pioneered the redaction critical approach to the gospel.

G. Bornkamm, G. Barth, and H. J. Held, *Tradition and Interpretation in Matthew.*

G. Bornkamm, "The Risen Lord and the Earthly Jesus: Mt 28:16–20," *The Future of Our Religious Past* (ed. James M. Robinson), pp. 203–29.

Other useful studies include:

R. Brown, *The Birth of the Messiah.*

L. Cope, *Matthew, A Scribe Trained for the Kingdom of Heaven.*

W. D. Davies, *The Sermon on the Mount.*

———, *The Setting of the Sermon on the Mount.*

J. Fenton, *The Gospel of St. Matthew.*

M. Goulder, *Midrash and Lection in Matthew.*

H. Green, *The Gospel According to Matthew.*

R. Gundry, *The Use of the Old Testament in St. Matthew's Gospel.*

D. Hare, *The Theme of Jewish Persecution of Christians in the Gospel According to St. Matthew.*

M. Johnson, *The Purpose of the Biblical Genealogies.*

J. D. Kingsbury, *Matthew.* (Proclamation Commentaries)

——, *Matthew: Structure, Christology, Kingdom.*

——, *The Parables of Jesus in Matthew 13.*

J. Meier, *Law and History in Matthew's Gospel.*

——, *The Vision of Matthew.*

E. Schweizer, *The Good News According to Matthew.*

D. Senior, *The Passion Narrative According to Matthew.*

K. Stendahl, *The School of St. Matthew.*

J. Suggs, *Wisdom, Christology and Law in Matthew's Gospel.*

W. Thompson, *Matthew's Advice to a Divided Community.*

S. Van Tilborg, *The Jewish Leaders in Matthew.*

Among the many articles on Matthew, we may note:

D. Duling, "The Therapeutic Son of David: An Element in Matthew's Christological Apologetic," *New Testament Studies* 24 (1978), pp. 392–410.

G. Strecker, "The Concept of History in Matthew," *Journal of the American Academy of Religion*, vol. 35 (1967), pp. 219–30.

J. D. Kingsbury, "The Jesus of History and Christ of Faith in Relation to Matthew's View of Time—Reactions to a New Approach," *Concordia Theological Monthly*, vol. 37 (1966), pp. 500–10.

For important theories and sketches on Matthew, see:

D. Harrington, "Matthew Studies Since Joachim Rhode," *Heythrop Journal* 16/4 (1975), pp. 375–88.

Interpretation 19 (Jan., 1975), pp. 3–74.

J. L. Mays, *Interpreting the Gospels.* This book reprints the *Interpretation* articles.

Detail from The Liberation of St. Peter *by Raphael (1483–1520), Vatican Stanze, Rome. Peter's cell is illuminated by the light of an angel who miraculously helps him to escape (Acts 12:1–10).*

CHAPTER TEN

THE GOSPEL OF LUKE AND THE ACTS OF THE APOSTLES:
The Idea of Salvation History

It was a great disservice to readers of the gospel of Luke and the Acts of the Apostles to separate them since they were originally written to be read together as a single work in two volumes (Luke 1:3: ". . . to write an orderly account for you, most excellent Theophilus . . ."; Acts 1:1: "In the first book, O Theophilus, I have dealt with all that Jesus began to do and teach . . ."). But when the New Testament texts were collected, the four gospels were put in a group separate from the remainder, and the gospel of Luke was separated from the Acts of the Apostles. This separation led to the title "gospel" being given to the first volume and "Acts of the Apostles" to the second. The title "gospel" came from the title of the gospel of Mark, which the author himself called a "gospel" (Mark 1:1); the title "Acts of the Apostles" came about simply from the contents of the second volume. As far as we know, the author did not entitle his two-volume work, though he does refer to it as "a narrative of the things which have been accomplished among us" (Luke 1:1). Here we treat the two-volume work as the unity it is intended to be and refer to it as Luke-Acts.

THE AUTHOR AS A MAN
OF THE HELLENISTIC JEWISH CHRISTIAN MISSION

Second-century Christians identified the author of the third gospel, and therefore the Acts of the Apostles, as Luke, the follower of Paul (Irenaeus, *Against Heresies*, 3.1.1–2) and physician (the Muratorian Canon). This identification refers to the Luke who was a fellow worker of Paul while he was in prison (Philemon 24), who was also described as "the beloved physician" (Colossians 4:14) and loyal companion of Paul (2 Timothy 4:11), and who was probably a Gentile (Colossians 4:11). The second-century view that the author

293

of Luke-Acts was Luke the physician and companion of Paul has led to several obvious questions. Is it possible to discern in Luke-Acts a specialized medical language? In the late nineteenth century the answer to this question was a decisive yes. But since the studies of Henry Cadbury this has been denied. Cadbury has shown that Luke's supposed medical terms were commonly used by other writers of the times.[1] It is therefore impossible to prove by analysis of language that Luke-Acts was written by an ancient physician. Is it possible to show that our author was a companion of Paul? Since the apostle Paul is portrayed as the heroic missionary in the latter part of Acts, we ask ourselves if the Acts' portrayal of Paul's life accords with what Paul says about his life, if Paul's thought in the letters is well represented in Paul's speeches in Acts (cf. Acts 13:16–41; 17:22–31), and if a companion of Paul's wrote certain sections of Acts in the first person plural as though their author were present with Paul (the "we-passages": 16:10–17; 20:5–15; 21:1–18; 27:1–28:16). The first question about the life of Paul has already been answered when it was determined that Acts conflicts with Paul on many points and can be used only as a secondary source.[2] Likewise, studies have shown that Paul's speeches in Acts differ significantly from what is known about his theological beliefs as expressed in the letters.[3] Finally, recent work on the "we-passages" indicates that they may not be direct comments by a companion of Paul, or from some diary source of that companion, but are typical of the first-person style of ancient sea voyage narratives in general.[4] Internal analysis, therefore, does not support the view that the author of Luke-Acts (who, by the way, does not see Paul as Paul sees himself as "apostle," cf. Acts 1:21–22; but cf. 14:4, 14) was Luke the physician, his loyal companion. To find out who the anonymous "Luke" is, we must once again look more closely at the two-volume work itself.

Luke-Acts was written in the generation immediately following the fall of Jerusalem, in what we are calling the middle period of New Testament Christianity. The author knows and uses the gospel of Mark, which we have dated shortly after A.D. 70. Furthermore, his view of the church and its faith shows movement toward the institutionalism and theology characteristic of a later period. So a date of A.D. 85, plus or minus five years or so, is appropriate.

By this time the characteristic phases of the Christian movement before the fall of Jerusalem no longer existed in the same way. What we find is a growing Gentile Christianity more or less concerned with the Judaism it ultimately descended from. In the deutero-Pauline letters, Christianity was becoming a real part of the Hellenistic world and moving toward a more structured, institutionalized entity. In the gospel of Matthew, Christianity was also moving toward a self-conscious entity over against Judaism, but still in

---

[1] H. Cadbury, *The Style and Literary Method of Luke.*

[2] See above, pp. 132–33; A.J. Mattill, "The Value of Acts as a Source for the Study of Paul," in C. Talbert, *Perspectives on Luke-Acts,* pp. 76–98.

[3] P. Vielhauer, "On the 'Paulinism' of Acts," in L. Keck and J.L. Martin, *Studies in Luke-Acts,* pp. 33–50, and in W. Meeks, *The Writings of St. Paul,* pp. 166–75.

[4] V. Robbins, "By Land and by Sea: The We-Passages and Ancient Sea Voyages," in C. Talbert, *Perspectives on Luke-Acts,* pp. 215–42.

dialogue and in dispute with Judaism. Both the deutero-Pauline letters and the gospel of Matthew make creative use of the traditions of an earlier period. In his turn, the author of Luke-Acts is also taking his own step in this direction. His concern is particularly with the relationship between the church and the Roman Empire, but he also uses the earlier traditions of Hellenistic Jewish Mission Christianity.

As stated above the speeches attributed to Paul in Acts do not emphasize Paul's thoughts as known from Paul's letters. Taken as a whole the speeches in Acts are examples of the preaching of Hellenistic Jewish Mission Christianity. Paul's Sermon in Acts 13 is not a report of a speech delivered on a specific occasion, but a sample of what Paul must have said many times to Jews and "God-fearers." Likewise, the speech in Athens (Acts 17:16–31) is not so much a record of one attempt to convert the intellectual center of the Hellenistic world as a sample of what Paul and others must have tried a hundred times as they preached to the Gentile world whenever and wherever they found oppor-tunity. In the same way, Peter's speech in Acts 2 or Stephen's in Acts 7 are samples of how Hellenistic Jewish Christianity came to understand itself in tension with traditional Judaism. In the ancient world it was customary for authors of historical works to put speeches on the lips of the main characters in which they, the authors, represented their understanding of the narrative's events and of the speaker's role. The speeches in Acts certainly represent the author's understanding of what was going on in the narrative, but he also has access to some traditions from the past (the past of Hellenistic Jewish Mission Christianity rather than of Palestinian Christianity) as well as knowledge of the missionary preaching of his own day. So the speeches he writes are examples of the characteristic preaching of Hellenistic Jewish Mission Christianity, and they reflect its traditions.

You will recall from chapter 3 that Hellenistic Jewish Mission Christianity was influenced by a number of ideas, including Biblical traditions as they were transmitted in the Septuagint and the widespread Greco-Roman mythology about immortals. Though Luke's first volume does not stress formula quota-tions from Scripture as explicitly as does Matthew's "book," Luke is, nonethe-less, concerned to show that the events he portrays fulfill Scripture, and he indicates this clearly by his references to the Septuagint in the Acts speeches and especially at the beginning and end of his gospel.[5] Especially crucial is his view that God's foreordained plan is being carried out by the fulfillment of prophecies about the suffering servant of Isaiah. So imbued with the Septua-gint is his thinking that he can imitate its Hebraicized style of Greek ("Septu-agintisms"). While breathing the air of Old Testament prophecy and fulfillment through the Septuagint, Luke-Acts also reflects ideas characteristic of the Hellenistic Jewish portrayal of "Savior Gods" and wandering philos-ophers. In general, Jewish conceptions of prophets, priests, kings, miracle workers, teachers, and the like were viewed somewhat differently when in-fused with, or replaced by, conceptions of exceptional human beings wide-

---

[5] A. Hultgren, "Interpreting the Gospel of Luke," in J.L. Mays, *Interpreting the Gospels*, pp. 183–96.

spread in the Greco-Roman world at large.[6] Hellenistic Jewish Mission Christianity adapted its views of Jesus to widespread beliefs about popular miracle workers and philosophic conceptions, as well as to especially endowed healers and emperors who, because of their words and deeds, were believed to have ascended to the realm of the gods. Some heroes were said to have been begotten by a god and a human mother, and some were said to have appeared to followers after death. The Lukan Jesus is certainly portrayed as a figure of supernatural birth who is especially endowed with extraordinary powers, and as a wandering teacher whose way of life was exemplary for his followers. He is a great benefactor who offers salvation and peace to the whole world; he ascends to heaven from where he pours out his spirit to the church. Similar themes are transferred to Jesus' disciples. In presenting Peter as one whose rebuke can bring Ananias to death (Acts 5:3–5) and Simon to penitence (8:14–24), or Paul as one whose garments have the power to heal and whose name has power over demons (19:11–15), the author is reflecting the tendency of his movement to think of its heroes as especially endowed human beings. In short, Hellenistic Jewish Mission Christianity claimed Peter as a supporter, Paul as its hero, and Jesus as its savior; all three have the aura of divinity, are human and yet more than human, and they are presented according to the conventions of the Hellenistic world.

THE AUTHOR AND THE PROBLEMS OF THE CHRISTIANITY OF HIS DAY

Though the author of Luke-Acts is a product of and utilizes the traditions of the Hellenistic Jewish Christian mission, the problems of the churches he represents were different from those of Paul and his colleagues. Consider the account of the Jerusalem Conference in Acts 15. The probable historical occasion for this "summit conference" was the success of the mission to the Jews, "God-fearers," and Gentiles in Antioch and other predominantly Gentile communities, which contrasted dramatically with the comparative failure of the mission to the Jews in Palestine and other predominantly Jewish communities. The decision of this Conference, historically speaking, was to commission Paul and his companions to go to the Gentiles, to the predominantly Gentile communities, and to send Peter to the Jews, to the predominantly Jewish communities. If Paul is correct, circumcision was not required of Gentiles, but he and his companions were requested to remember "the poor" (cf. Gal 2:1–10). The result was the mission of Paul and Barnabas to the island of Cyprus and to the southern part of Asia Minor. The sequence of events and the decision of the Conference in Acts 15, however, is quite different. Acts 13–14 places the mission to Cyprus and Asia Minor prior to the Conference, not after, and in Acts 15, the decision of the Conference is to find a procedure to regulate social relationships between Jews and Gentiles in a Christian community. As Gala-

---

[6] See chapter 1, pp. 13–15.

tians 2:11–21 testifies, they became a problem in the Hellenistic Jewish Christian mission *after* the Jerusalem Council. Historically, the Jerusalem Council authorized Paul's missionary activity; it did not deal with a later compromise about social relationships that grew out of the mission. Acts 15:23–29, however, describes this compromise as having been achieved during the Conference because it had become a problem at the time Luke-Acts was written.

But though the social relationship of Jew and Gentile in the Christian church is a problem for the author of Luke-Acts, it is not major, nor is it the occasion for his writing his two-volume work. His major concerns are the fall of Jerusalem and the destruction of its Temple, the delay of the parousia, and the need to help the church normalize its relations with the Roman Empire and its members settle down to Christian witness in a continuing world.

The Destruction of Jerusalem and the Temple

The treatment of Jerusalem in Luke-Acts is a very special feature of the two-volume work. Though the gospel follows Mark in using the spelling *'Ierosolyma* at 13:22 (= Mark 10:32) and 19:28 (= Mark 11:1), the author infinitely prefers *'Ierousalēm,* which Luke-Acts uses some sixty-three times out of an approximate total of seventy-four uses in the whole New Testament. Our author has both a special concern and a special word for Jerusalem. He uses almost exclusively a form of the city's name not used frequently elsewhere in the New Testament, and he refers to the city many times.

We can approach the question of what Luke-Acts has to say about Jerusalem by observing a very important element in the composition of the gospel. If we compare the structure of the gospel with the structure of Mark, its source, we see that one major change is the insertion of a long, rambling travel narrative (Luke 9:51–18:14). It begins with a statement of Jesus' intent, "When the days drew near for his ascension he set his face to go to Jerusalem" (9:51),[7] and the rest of the gospel's narrative is about the fulfillment of that intent (cf. also 13:33b: ". . . for it cannot be that a prophet should perish away from Jerusalem"). Jesus goes up to Jerusalem and there endures the passion, which in Luke-Acts climaxes in the ascension, the act of Jesus being taken up into heaven: "While he blessed them, he parted from them and was carried up into heaven.[8] And they returned to Jerusalem with great joy and were continually in the temple blessing God" (24:51–53). Thus, the gospel anticipates the passion and ascension of its hero at Jerusalem, and from there the mission will be launched. The Acts of the Apostles exhibits the same compositional feature as

[7] This is our own translation. RSV says, "When the days drew near for him to be received up"; NEB, "when he was to be taken up into heaven"; TEV, "would be taken up into heaven." The Greek text uses *analēmpsis,* the technical term for "ascension" in Greek, hence our translation.

[8] Most modern translations relegate the second half of this verse to the margin. However, the reference forward to the ascension in 9:51 indicates that the gospel was intended to end on this note by its author; so we include the second half of the verse despite the ambiguous textual evidence.

Luke; it too has a long, rambling travel narrative beginning with a statement of intent. Acts 19:21 reads, "Paul resolved in the Spirit to pass through Macedonia and Achaia and go to Jerusalem, saying, 'After I have been there, I must also see Rome,' " and from that point the narrative is about Paul's journey to Jerusalem and Rome, ending with Paul preaching in Rome "quite openly and unhindered" (28:31).

So the narrative of Luke-Acts leads quite deliberately from Jerusalem, the place of Jesus' passion-ascension, to Rome, the place of Paul's preaching. That it is deliberate can be seen not only in Luke 9:51 and Acts 19:21 but also in many other references—Luke 9:31 (compare Mark 9:4); 9:53; 23:27–31—all emphasizing Jerusalem as the place of the passion. In Luke-Acts all the resurrection appearances take place in or near Jerusalem. But after the ascension the thrust is consistently from Jerusalem to Rome (Acts 1:4–6, 8). Each of the three accounts of Paul's conversion (9:1–30; 22:3–21; 26:9–23) has him begin his witnessing in Jerusalem immediately after his conversion. It is important that Paul, the exemplary witness, carry the gospel from Jerusalem to Rome; hence the references to Jerusalem in the conversion accounts, and hence 19:21 and the ending in 28:31. In fact, Paul did not go to Jerusalem immediately after his conversion, and his journey to Rome ended with his death. But to the author of Acts, the gospel events must climax in Jerusalem, the gospel must be brought from Jerusalem to Rome, and the gospel must take root in Rome. To portray all this in his narrative he has to take liberties with the historical events—limit the resurrection appearances to Jerusalem, have Paul go to Jerusalem immediately after his conversion, give the impression that Rome posed no problems for Paul's preaching—good examples of myth overcoming history. The myth is needed because Jerusalem is fallen, and the needs of the myth overrule the facts of history. According to Matthew and John, there were resurrection appearances in Galilee; Paul himself denies going to Jerusalem after his conversion (Gal 1:17); and Rome martyred him. But none of this matters compared to the needs of the myth.

The author of Luke-Acts interprets Jerusalem as the place of the passion of Jesus and regards its destruction as a consequence of that; Rome is the new center of gravity for Christians. Jerusalem and its Temple are gone, but the preaching of the gospel in the world of which Rome is the center remains.

The Delay of the Parousia

Like all the authors of the middle period of New Testament history, the author of Luke-Acts wrestles with the delay of the parousia, Jesus' return on the clouds of heaven, which should have happened and did not. At first glance certain passages appear to stress the near expectation of the parousia (cf. Luke 3:9, 17; 10:9; 21:32) and the author even seems to add to them (Luke 10:11; 18:7–8). Yet, these passages should be interpreted in relation to what is clearly Luke's more dominant and formative view: the parousia will take place in some indefinite future. One can make sense of the extended interim by regarding it as the time of the church, the time of the church's work and witness in the world.[9]

The author defers the time of the parousia by his treatment of certain key passages in the gospel of Mark, one of his sources. Mark 1:14–15 has Jesus coming into Galilee and proclaiming, "The time is fulfilled, and the Kingdom of God is at hand," a proclamation intended to arouse a fervent expectation that the End is imminent. Luke 4:14 simply says, "Jesus returned in the power of the Spirit into Galilee," and makes a comment about his growing fame. Luke 4:15 says, "And he taught in their synagogues, being glorified by all." The key passage for Luke, as we shall see, is found in the *next* verses (Luke 4:16–30) where Jesus is teaching in the synagogue at Nazareth. The theme is the fulfillment of Isaianic prophecies about preaching good news to the poor and healing by an anointed, spirit-filled prophet, with an anticipation of rejection and a movement toward the Gentiles. Mark's significant apocalyptic theme has been replaced by Luke's equally significant nonapocalyptic theme in which the element of imminent expectation has neatly been replaced by a focus on the past ministry of Jesus as the savior of all. But perhaps even more important for the specific question of the parousia is Luke's reworking of the synoptic apocalypse (Mark 13 = Luke 21). For the gospel of Mark, the warning is made not to identify the End specifically with the coming of false prophets announcing the immediate parousia (which, for the gospel writer, occurs in connection with the destruction of Jerusalem, Mark 13:5b, 14, 21–23), but it will, *nonetheless*, be soon thereafter (13:24: "But in those days, after that tribulation . . ."). For Luke, the close proximity of the destruction of Jerusalem and the parousia has been severed. The reference to the destruction of Jerusalem is made more specific (21:20, 24a), but he omits the reference to the false prophets at this point (cf. 17:20–23) and adds a reference to an interim period, ". . . until the times of the Gentiles are fulfilled" (21:24b). Luke has thereby lengthened the time between the earthly signs in relation to the destruction (21:7–24) and the cosmic signs of the parousia of the Son of Man (21:25–28).[10] There are other indications of this delay of the parousia in Luke's version of the apocalypse. He adds "The time is at hand!" as part of the false expectation of the prophets and warns, "Do not go after them" (21:8); he changes Mark's "the end is not yet" to "the end will not be at once," noting what must take place "first" (21:9). In this context the apparent references to the near expectation in Luke 21:32 ("Truly, I say to you, this generation will not pass away till all has taken place") would refer not to Jesus'—or even Mark's!—generation, but to a generation that stretches into the incalculable future. Thus, Luke stresses that the parousia is indefinitely postponed, an emphasis that can be illustrated throughout Luke-Acts.

The author of Luke-Acts also makes theological sense of the extended

[9] The extent to which Luke eliminated the parousia (following H. Conzelmann, see below, pp. 301–09) has been highly debated; cf. C. Talbert, "The Recent Study of the Gospel of Luke," in J.L. Mays, *Interpreting the Gospels*, pp. 203–04; W.C. Robinson, "Luke, Gospel of," *IDB Suppl.*, pp. 558–60.

[10] W. C. Robinson, p. 559.

interim period; it is the period of the "witness" of the church. This is very clear in the words of the resurrected Jesus to the disciples: "You shall be my witnesses in Jerusalem and all Judea and Samaria and to the end of the earth" (Acts 1:8). Now that is both a geographical and an ethnic progression. Judea surrounds Jerusalem and is still Jewish. The movement outward from Jerusalem toward Rome brings one to Samaria, regarded as only half-Jewish, and still moving toward Rome one comes to Gentile Syria and eventually to "the end of the earth," Rome itself. The Acts of the Apostles does indeed follow this geographical and ethnic progression, and very significantly, it ends on the note of Paul witnessing "openly and unhindered" in Rome (Acts 28:31). The extended time before the parousia is for the author of Luke-Acts the period of the church and her witness in the wide world.

A good example of the consequences of this viewpoint is Luke's treatment of the teaching on discipleship found in Mark 8:34–9:1. In Mark this teaching deals with the urgent demands of the brief period before the parousia; it is an interim ethic. But Luke 9:23–27 introduces a series of subtle changes. The disciple must now take up his cross *daily;* the Son of Man will come, but not "in this adulterous and sinful generation"; the martyr witnesses will be sustained by a vision of the Kingdom of God, but they will not see it come "in power." The effect is to change the tone of the whole passage so that it becomes concerned with an ongoing witness in a world that has a long history before it.

The Relations Between Christians and the Roman Empire

In our earlier discussion of apocalyptic Christianity we saw that persecution was an ever-present possibility for New Testament Christians, as true in the middle period of New Testament Christianity as in the earlier or later periods. But in Luke-Acts persecution is only a part of the whole problem of relations between the Christians and the Empire. As the author thinks of the long period of history before the parousia, he has also to consider Christians living within that history, and that means living within historical circumstances dominated by Rome and the Roman Empire. As long as Christians expected the world to pass away shortly, they could revile Rome and its Empire in anticipation of its imminent destruction, as John of Patmos does in Revelation 18. But to live in the Empire for a considerable period of time, they must come to terms with it, as the author of Luke-Acts, and no doubt the churches he represents, try to do.

To help his readers do so, the author of Luke-Acts consistently presents Roman authorities as sympathetic to the Christian movement: Pilate finds no fault in Jesus (Luke 23:4); in Cyprus the proconsul "believes" (Acts 13:12); Gallio, proconsul of Achaia, takes Paul's side against the Jews (Acts 18:14–15); and so on. The Christians' difficulties are not the hostility of Roman authorities but the machinations of the Jews (Acts 13:28; 14:2, 19; 18:12, etc.). At the same time the Christian movement is consistently represented as descended directly from, and indeed the proper fulfillment of, Judaism, especially in the speeches in Acts (e.g., 13:16–41). Not only was this the theme of Christian preaching to Jews, it also implied a claim that Christians share the Jews' privilege of having their faith declared a "legal religion" by the Romans, with its implications of toleration and freedom to practice their rites. Thus the author attempts to present Roman authority to Christians, and the Christians to Roman authorities, in the best possible light, in the hope of fostering good relations between them.

SALVATION HISTORY IN LUKE-ACTS

We have frequently observed the penchant of apocalyptic writers to portray historical epochs by means of symbols, and we have noted that several Biblical writers think in terms of the theme of salvation history. Among the evangelists, however, the one most dominated by the idea of salvation history is the author of Luke-Acts, who has sometimes been called "Luke the historian."[11] To place Luke-Acts' particular view of salvation history in proper perspective, it will be important to recall something of the nature of historical writing in antiquity.[12] Ancient Greek historians tended to pick key events and personalities, especially from their own time, because they illustrated the human drama of political life, they were important for moral instruction or exhortation, they illustrated national aspirations, or because they were simply interesting or entertaining. Characteristically, these historians created speeches for their heroes in order to give an impression of some of the great ideas of the age.

Roman historians, writing in Greek and Latin not long after Luke-Acts, generally followed these precedents. Lucian of Samosata, in his *How to Write History*, stressed that the task of the historian is not, as with many of his contemporary historians, entertainment, but description of things as they actually happened; yet, at the same time, he says, the historian would be well-advised to indicate in the foreword that what he will say is "important, essential, personal, or useful";[13] and like his forebears, Lucian chose to describe only the very important matters, such as political events and wars, and the very important people, such as generals, politicians, or poets; and he freely placed programmatic speeches in their mouths on subjects that he considered appropriate for the occasion. Livy's *Annals of the Roman People*, however, tends to

---

[11] In connection with Luke-Acts, H. Conzelmann's *The Theology of St. Luke* has been the center of all contemporary discussion, even among those who disagree with him, cf. *n. 9* above. Conzelmann himself writes in German and uses the term *Heilsgeschichte*, which the English translation of his book renders as "redemptive history." We prefer to use "salvation history" to avoid suggestion that history itself is redemptive. In the thought of the author of Luke-Acts it is not that history is redemptive but that redemption has a history.

[12] See especially M. L. Finley, *The Portable Greek Historians: The Essence of Herodotus, Thucydides, Xenophon, Polybius.*

[13] Lucian, *How to Write History* (Loeb), chapter 53.

combine history and legend in the interest of writing "inspiring history." Indeed, Livy clearly states his rationale: to perpetuate the memory of "the first people in the world" and to hold before the reader models of moral behavior. Even Tacitus, one of the most accurate Roman historians of the period, chose his material with a political prejudice and freely wrote the speeches of the Roman emperors.[14]

If we turn to Israelite and Jewish history writing, we see something of the same orientation. The Court History of David (2 Samuel 9:1–20:26; 1 Kings 1–2) appears to be almost eyewitness in character, but underlying it is the salvation history concept of the Deuteronomist which attempts to show how God is operating in the affairs of men to fulfill his promises to David (2 Samuel 7). History yields to salvation history. Closer to New Testament times 1 Maccabees develops fairly accurate Jewish history but, in a manner similar to Greco-Roman history, inserts pious addresses and prayers into the mouths of its heroes. Finally, Josephus, a Jewish historian who was a contemporary of Luke-Acts, not only writes to glorify his national heritage (and indeed, to defend his participation in the Jewish wars with Rome); he follows the general practice of composing speeches appropriate to the occasion, reflecting the ideas he himself believed were important. One need only read the masterfully written speech of the Zealot revolutionary Eleazar atop Masada to grasp the point.

If such were the general methods of writing history in that period, one further point should be mentioned: "Luke" was not only a historian; he was a religious writer and as well as a gospel writer. Here it should be recalled that ancient Greco-Roman biography was not like modern biography, but ranged from rather loose collections of sayings and anecdotes, such as Diogenes Laertius' *Lives and Opinions of Famous Philosophers*, to the Hellenistic romance calculated to evoke praise of the hero's virtues, such as Plutarch's *Lives* or Philostratus' sketch of the divinely begotten, miracle working Apollonius of Tyana. With this observation, one is back to the controversial question as to what extent the gospels in general, and the third gospel in particular, can be seen in relation to ancient romantic biographies of especially endowed human beings.[15] Even if the gospel as created by Mark is distinctive, Luke's version of it comes closest to the popular biographies of the period.

Thus, when thinking of Luke-Acts as historical writing, four points must be kept in mind: (1) the character of Hellenistic and Roman historical writing, especially in relation to the Acts of the Apostles; (2) the character and diversity of the Greco-Roman popular romance as a biographical form, especially in connection with the gospel of Luke; (3) the tradition of salvation historical writing in the Old Testament with prophecy and fulfillment as major themes; and (4) the actual modification by Luke of his source Mark, examples of which have been noted in connection with Luke's reorientation of Mark's understanding of the synoptic apocalypse. We shall comment on the latter point in conclusion.

As history, then, Luke-Acts is not modern history, but a special example

---

[14] C. K. Barrett, *Luke the Historian in Recent Study.*
[15] See above, pp. 13–15; cf. pp. 40, 234.

of Hellenistic-Roman historical writing ruled by a Biblical concept of salvation history, that is, it is not a mere chronicle of events but a history that portrays God's activity in saving all people. As a salvation history, it is an account of a remote past, an immediate past, a present, an immediate future, and a remote future. It looks back to a remote past, the time of the creation of the first man (taking the genealogy of Jesus back to Adam, Luke 3:38), and toward the distant future, the time of the parousia, now delayed. The salvation history of God's activity on behalf of all people began before the creation of man and before the beginning of world history, and it will continue after the parousia has brought world history to an end. Within these outer limits lies world history. It is a history of everyday events, of emperors, governors, kings, and high priests, of taxation and censuses (Luke 2:1; 3:1–2). As in no other New Testament writing, Luke-Acts is concerned with locating its story in a particular time and with reference to particular locations. But this history is also a history in which the promises of God are made, the word of God is proclaimed, and the salvific message is made known to the world. In this history the Spirit of God is operating in Jesus and in the church. But salvation history is also beyond world history, for it is the history from which the Spirit comes and to which Jesus ascends after his resurrection.

Viewing history in the context of salvation history, the author of Luke-Acts thinks of it as divided into a series of three epochs. At least two of the three epochs are indicated by Luke 16:16. The first is the era of "the law and the prophets" down to the mission of John the Baptist, a transitional figure. Then comes an interim period represented by the birth and infancy stories of John and Jesus and the activity of John as forerunner. The second era is the era of "the proclamation of the Kingdom of God," the time of Jesus and of the church (Luke 16:16; Acts 28:31). This second era is further subdivided, for it begins with the descent of the Spirit on Jesus at his baptism and is divided at the Cross where Jesus returns the Spirit to the Father (Luke 23:46). Then there follows an interim period in which Jesus is raised from the dead and reveals to the disciples the secret of the second part of the era of the Kingdom of God, an interim culminating in the ascension (Luke 24:51; Acts 1:1–11). This is followed by the third era, the period of the church, inaugurated by the descent of the Spirit at Pentecost (which is a baptism, Acts 1:5) and epitomized by Paul preaching the Kingdom of God "openly and unhindered" in Rome (Acts 28:31). This era will end with the parousia (Luke 21:25–28), which will be at some indefinite point in the future (Luke 9:27; 17:20–21; 19:11; 21:8–9; cf. Acts 1:7). The whole conception may be represented as follows:

First era: The time of "the law and the prophets," from Adam to John the Baptist.

Interim period: The time of the birth and infancy of John and Jesus and of the ministry of the forerunner John.

Second era: The time of the proclamation of the Kingdom of God by Jesus, from the descent of the Spirit on Jesus to the return of the Spirit to the Father at the Cross.

Interim period: The time of the resurrection, revelatory teaching to the disciples by the risen Jesus, and the ascension.

Third era: The time of the proclamation of the Kingdom of God by the church, from the descent of the Spirit at Pentecost to the parousia.

We will now say something about each of these divisions.

The Time of "the Law and the Prophets"

The key to understanding this epoch is Luke 16:16. "The law and the prophets were until John; since then the good news of the Kingdom of God is preached" is certainly crucial to understanding the thought of the author of Luke-Acts. He has made the text very much his own with its distinction between the time of the law and the prophets and that of the preaching of the Kingdom of God; consider his use of "kingdom of God" in Acts 1:3; 19:8; 28:23. This epoch is most characterized by prophecy, which the author of Luke-Acts sees as fulfilled, as well as renewed, in the succeeding periods of Jesus and the church.

The Interim Period of the Birth and Infancy of John and and Jesus and of the Ministry of the Forerunner John

The second epoch marked by Luke 16:16 may be stated: "since then the good news of the Kingdom of God is preached." The place of John the Baptist in Luke's schema ("since then") is difficult to determine, and it may be that he is seen as a transitional figure somewhat structurally analogous to the interim period between Jesus and the church. On the one hand, John does not preach "the good news of the Kingdom of God" (contrast Matt 3:2) and the author of Luke-Acts brings forward the imprisonment of John to a time before Jesus' public ministry is inaugurated (3:20; cf. Mark 6:17–18), thus seeming to stress further the tradition of John's subordination (3:15–16; Acts 13:25). Yet an analysis of Luke 1–2, which should be included in the overall plan of Luke-Acts,[16] shows a clear parallelism between the birth of John and the birth of Jesus with a symbolic six-month overlap in the pregnancies of their mothers, Elizabeth and Mary (1:24, 26, 36, 41–45). Also, John's birth is announced in Old Testament prophetic fashion by the old age of his parents (1:7), and he is called "prophet of the Most High" who will "prepare his ways" and "give knowledge of salvation to his people in the forgiveness of their sins" (1:76–77). Indeed, in Luke 3:18 John's exhortations are viewed as preaching the good news! Thus, it would appear that Luke's ambiguous "since then" (16:16) would

---

[16] P. Minear, "Luke's Use of the Birth Stories," *Studies in Luke-Acts*, pp. 111–30.

see John as at least a transition figure who, while clearly subordinate, prepares the way for the time of proclamation of the Kingdom of God by Jesus.

The Time of the Proclamation of the Kingdom of God by Jesus

The descent of the Holy Spirit on Jesus at his baptism (3:21–22) more clearly marks a time when "the good news of the Kingdom of God is preached," a time which will be continued in the third major epoch, the time of the church, which is also given the Spirit (at Pentecost, Acts 2). Thus, the coming of the Spirit, in addition to Book 1 and Book 2 of the two-volume work, shows the subdivision of the period of preaching the Kingdom into two epochs. Luke stresses that Jesus is identified as God's son at the descent of the Holy Spirit. Further, "full of the Holy Spirit" and "led by the Spirit" (4:1), the Son of God is tested by Satan in the wilderness (4:3,9). In the "power of the Spirit" Jesus returns to Galilee. It is at this point that Luke places the programmatic scene in the synagogue at Nazareth (4:16–30).[17] He moves it forward from its location in Mark 6, and places it directly before the healing scene in the synagogue at Capernaum; he adds the crucial prophecy about the Spirit from Isaiah, indicating that Jesus has fulfilled the prophecy "today." With Elijah/Elisha healing miracles he shows that Jesus is rejected because he implies that it is God's will that his offer of salvation go to the Gentiles. The Nazareth scene deliberately presents the reader with an announcement ahead of time of events to follow—a typical literary technique of Luke—and thereby an understanding of the time of Jesus as a time when prophecy is fulfilled, specifically Isa 61:1–2 (cf. also Isa 58:6). That prophecy concerns the coming of the Spirit of God, proclaiming the good news to the poor, their release to the captives, recovery of sight by the blind, setting the oppressed at liberty, and "the acceptable year of the Lord." These themes dominate the presentation of the time of Jesus in the gospel of Luke. Here we find the parables of the Lost Sheep, the Lost Coin, and the Lost Son (Luke 15). In this gospel is told the story of the tax collector who beats his breast; cries out to God, "God, be merciful to me a sinner!"; and goes down to his house, justified (Luke 18:9–14). Here too the poor widow successfully importunes an unjust judge (Luke 18:1–8), and paradise is promised to the penitent thief on his cross (Luke 23:43). The gospel of Luke is the gospel of the poor and the outcast, of Jesus' concern with them, and of God's gracious dealing with them through Jesus. There is a strong christological theme in this passage. Jesus is not only the Son of God associated with all mankind ("Adam," 3:38), he is also the Servant-Messiah whom God anointed "with the Holy Spirit and power" (Acts 10:38), and whose time offers salvation, especially healing, to all.

The author of Luke-Acts also emphasizes that during the time of Jesus, Jesus is not again directly hindered by Satan until the passion in Jerusalem,

---

[17] R. Tannehill, "The Mission of Jesus According to Luke IV 16–30," in E. Grässer, A. Strobel, and R. Tannehill, *Jesus in Nazareth*.

which also fulfills prophecy. To be sure, the activity of Satan lies behind the sick and possessed whom Jesus heals (cf. 10:18; 11:16–18; 13:16); yet, Jesus himself is free from Satan's malevolent activity. After the temptation of Jesus the devil "departed from him until an opportune time" (Luke 4:13; compare Matt 4:11), and that opportune time does not come until Jesus is in Jerusalem, the place of his passion and death, where "Satan entered into Judas called Iscariot, who was of the number of the twelve" (Luke 22:3).

The time of Jesus presented by the author of Luke-Acts has been appropriately called "the center of time."[18] It is the central time, the hinge of history, in which both the meaning of the past and the course of the future are revealed. The author recognizes that he and the people he is writing for are involved in the ongoing flow of history in the world, but in effect he is claiming that one epoch in that history, the time of Jesus, is also the decisive epoch in salvation history, the time when the good news of God's activity on behalf of man and man's salvation was proclaimed in the world. Now the world lives out of its relationship to that time of proclamation; now men and women know salvation as they relate to the center of time and history.

The Interim Period of Jesus' Resurrection, Revelatory Teaching to the Disciples, and Ascension

Between Jesus' act of committing his spirit to God at the Cross and the return of the Spirit to the church at Pentecost, there is an interim period of resurrection, teaching, and ascension. Luke stresses the resurrection of Jesus more than either Mark or Matthew. Mark has no resurrection appearances at all, while Matthew has one and then the commissioning scene. But Luke has the appearance on the Emmaus road (24:13–35), the appearance in Jerusalem itself (24:36–43), and also mentions an appearance to Peter (24:34). Further, Luke-Acts has a period in which the risen Jesus is with his disciples, teaching them (Luke 24:44–49; Acts 1:6–8), and then the ascension is an event separate from the resurrection (Luke 24:51, RSV margin; Acts 1:9). As far as we know, the author of Luke-Acts is the first man to conceive of the ascension as separate from the resurrection. Normally in the New Testament the resurrection-ascension is conceived of as one act. But Luke needs a separate ascension to have a place in his narrative for the revelatory teachings of the risen Jesus to his disciples. This teaching is very important. It is in Luke 24:44–49 and Acts 1:4–8 that the heart of the Lukan understanding of things is revealed. Here we find the necessity for repentance and forgiveness of sins to be preached by the disciples, who are "witnesses." Here we find, further, the "beginning from Jerusalem" and the moving "to the end of the earth," and finally the baptism with the Spirit that will make it all possible. These themes are crucial to the author of Luke-Acts, and they are all given in this interim period of revelatory teaching.

---

[18] This is Conzelmann's phrase. The German is *Die Mitte der Zeit*, which in the translation of Conzelmann's book is rendered as "the center of history."

The Time of the Proclamation of the Kingdom
of God by the Church, from Jerusalem to Rome

The *time of Jesus*, the center of time, is the time of the work of the Spirit through *Jesus*, the time of preaching the good news of the Kingdom of God. The *time of the church* is the time of the work of the Spirit through the *church*, the time of the proclamation of the Kingdom of God in the form of the church preaching repentance and the forgiveness of sins, the time of witnessing from Jerusalem to Rome. This time of the church will continue until the parousia, and it is the time of the author of Luke-Acts and of his readers. Just as the gospel of Mark ends symbolically with the reader's situation in mind, so also does Acts. Paul preaching and teaching in Rome "quite openly and unhindered" symbolizes the situation of the church in the world and also the situation of the reader in the world.

The presentation of the time of the church in Acts is extraordinarily realistic. For all the legendary elements, for all that Peter and Paul are "divine men" in accordance with the practice of religious propaganda in the Hellenistic world, the narratives of Acts are full of elements taken directly from the life and experience of the church in that world. Baptism, the laying on of hands and the experience of the Spirit, revelation by dreams and visions, the receptiveness of "God-fearers" to the gospel and the hostility of Jews—all this and more is taken by the author directly from the experience of the church in which and for which he was writing. Furthermore, the author carefully draws parallels between the time of Jesus and the time of the church. In particular he makes Jesus himself a model, or paradigm, of Christian piety. Jesus is empowered by the Spirit, as is the believer, and he prays and attends worship regularly as the believer should also. Moreover, the death of Jesus is not "a ransom for many," but Jesus is "one who serves" (Luke 22:27; compare Mark 10:45). The author of Luke-Acts consistently plays down the differences between Jesus as the Christ and other men. A good example is the reply to the question of the High Priest. In Mark 14:62, Jesus accepts the titles of "Christ" and "Son of the living God" by using the formula "I am." But in Luke 22:70, when Jesus is asked if he is the Son of God, he replies, "You say that I am." A very striking parallel between Jesus and the believer is that drawn between the passion of Jesus and the fate of Stephen, the first martyr. In his account of the trial of Jesus, Luke has no reference to the false witnesses found in Mark (Luke 22:66–71; compare Mark 14:56–64). But in Acts 6:13–14, false witnesses appear at Stephen's trial with the testimony that Mark has them give at the trial of Jesus. At his stoning Stephen cries with a loud voice, "Lord, do not hold this sin against them" (Acts 7:60), just as Jesus had cried from his Cross, "Father, forgive them; for they know not what they do" (Luke 23:34).

The effect of these parallels between the time of Jesus and that of the church, and between Jesus and the Christian believer, is to make it possible for the believer to relate directly to the time of Jesus and to Jesus himself as the model of Christian piety. The author of Luke-Acts is carefully providing his readers with an understanding of their place in salvation history and of their role in the world. The believer lives by the power of the spirit as he "preaches repentance and the forgiveness of sins" and joins in the worldwide witness of the church. It was observed in the chapter on Matthew that there is a correlation between Matthew's move toward salvation history and a foundation myth. This is so also for Luke. If Jesus is the Messiah who offers peace and salvation to the world, he functions as a mythical redeemer similar to those supernaturally endowed figures of the Greco-Roman world; and insofar as he offers a model for Christian piety, the era of Jesus is foundational. In fact, Luke's idealization of the early church might function in precisely the same way. Yet, salvation history in Luke *does* intersect with world history, and there is also a definite sense of "secular" time and movement to his story. Thus, salvation history in Luke-Acts provides one illustration for the intersection of history and myth so characteristic of the New Testament. We shall have further reflections on this phenomenon in our observations on the interpretation of Mark by the author of Luke-Acts.

The Lukan Community

The author of Luke-Acts, as a writer of salvation history in epochs, is clearly conscious that he writes in the middle period of the history of early Christianity, that he is a second, perhaps even a third, generation Christian. To that extent he distinguishes himself and his period from earlier periods. Yet, it should be recalled that he is a Hellenistic historian and writer and that his idealizations are intended to convey problems and solutions to his readers in his own time. Though the whole of Luke-Acts could illustrate this statement, two examples will highlight it: the growing institutionalization of the church and the issue of poor and rich in the Lukan community.

The Acts of the Apostles reflects the growing institutionalization of the church when it portrays the smooth and almost noncontroversial movement (internally) from Jesus to Peter and the apostles, and then to Paul and his mission to the Gentiles. Twelve apostles bear witness to the life of Jesus from the point of his baptism (1:21–26); Peter emerges as the leader of the Jerusalem church (2–5; 8–10; 15); people are now commanded and missionaries are sent; the Spirit is received by the "laying on of hands" (e.g., 8:17; 9:17; 19:6); and the seven (6:1–6) and elders are appointed (e.g., 14:23). "Apostles and elders" seem to be in charge, and Paul seems to entrust the elders of Ephesus with pastoral authority (20:28–35). Such passages should probably not be understood to mean that there exists here a well-developed idea of "apostolic succession," though it could be in its infancy. Certainly there is no concept of an institution so developed that it has a sacramental system and is itself the guarantor of the Spirit and of salvation. Yet, there can be no doubt that there are those who wield authority, and in portraying the church in this manner, Luke-

Acts reflects its own period. We have noted this also in connection with the Jerusalem Conference.[19]

As is clear from the concern for the poor and outcast, women and children, Samaritans and Gentiles, the author of Luke-Acts thinks of salvation in universal terms. Luke-Acts is concerned with those of low status and outsiders. To take only the poor as an example, Jesus proclaims good news to the poor (4:16–20; 7:22), blesses the poor (6:20), tells parables in behalf of the poor (e.g., 12:13–21; 16:19–31), condemns the Pharisees as lovers of money (16:14), and says it is impossible to serve God and mammon (16:13). Peter is poor (Acts 3:6) and his miraculous powers are not for sale (Acts 8:18–24). Cornelius the Gentile is praised for his almsgiving (Acts 10:2) and Paul observes the same practice (24:17). Certainly, the author of Luke-Acts stresses, "A man's life does not consist in the abundance of possessions" (Luke 13:15) and ". . . where your treasure is, there will your heart be also" (12:34). If any judgment can be made about what this implies about the Lukan community, it would appear that there are a number of rich within it and Luke is suggesting that if it is not in every case necessary to sell everything (19:8), the message of the Kingdom brings with it social concern in the community for the poor.[20]

THE STRUCTURE OF LUKE-ACTS

Of all the New Testament writings, Luke-Acts contains a set of episodes which are parallel in structure. It might even be said that Luke-Acts is a work of art organized according to the "law of duality."[21] The most obvious structural element is the addition of the Acts of the Apostles to the gospel. Parallels between the gospel and Acts are especially apparent, namely, the introductions to each volume (Luke 1:1–4; Acts 1:1–5), the careful parallelism of the baptism and descent of the Spirit in each volume, the parallelism of the journey motif of Jesus to Jerusalem and Paul to Rome, and the great significance of the teaching of the risen Jesus (Luke 24:46–49; Acts 1:8). In the gospel itself five major changes in relation to Mark's structure stand out: (a) the addition of an infancy narrative (1–2) as part of the introduction to the ministry of Jesus; (b) the Sermon on the Plain (6:20–49), which is much shorter than Matthew's Sermon on the Mount; (c) at 9:17 the "Great Omission" of a portion of Mark (6:45–8:26, consisting primarily of miracles, parts of which are duplicated by

---

[19] For the view that the author of Luke-Acts subdivides the era of the church into an Apostolic Age and a Post-Apostolic Age, and that there are possibly four epochs, each passing on authority in the manner of a teacher to his pupil in the philosophic schools, see C. Talbert, *Literary Patterns, Theological Themes, and the Genre of Luke-Acts*, chapter 6.

[20] R. Karras, "Poor and Rich: The Lukan *Sitz im Leben*," *Perspectives on Luke-Acts*, pp. 112–24; *What Are They Saying About Luke and Acts?* chapter 7.

[21] C. Talbert, *Literary Patterns*, develops this point of view extensively.

Luke-Acts elsewhere); (d) the long journey to Jerusalem (9:51–19:27); and (e) the resurrection and ascension accounts at the end (24:13–53). In addition, it should be observed in relation to the two-source theory that over one-third of the gospel is from special L, and that this is very often creatively combined with Q material in blocks (6:20–8:3; 9:51–18:14) which alternate with Markan blocks (3:1–6:19; 8:4–9:50; 18:15–24:11), though on occasion special L is also found in the Markan sequence.[22] This observation is most significant with respect to the creation of the journey to Jerusalem (9:51–19:27). Finally, the gospel is noted for its lack of accurate knowledge of the precise geography of Palestine, suggesting that the author uses it and topography in the service of his overall theology. This has been pointed out especially in reference to the Jerusalem theme.

There are also structural considerations in the plan of Acts. At critical moments in the geographical progression of the narrative there are formula-like summaries of the action: 2:43–47; 5:42; 9:31; 12:24; 15:35; 19:20. Coming where they do in the plot of the narrative, they provide us with the clues to its structure.[23] The following structure then emerges for the two-volume work:

Gospel of Luke
> Introduction to the two volumes, 1:1–4
> **Book One: The Ministry of the Spirit Through Jesus**
> Introduction of the Ministry of the Spirit through Jesus, 1:5–4:13
> The Ministry in Galilee, 4:14–9:50
> The Journey of Jesus to Jerusalem, 9:51–19:27
> Jesus in Jerusalem 19:28–21:38
> The Passion Narrative, 22:1–23:49
> Burial, Resurrection, Ascension, 23:50–24:53

Acts of the Apostles
> Introduction to the second volume, 1:1–5
> **Book Two: The Ministry of the Spirit Through the Church**
> Introduction to the Ministry of the Spirit through the Church, 1:6–26
> The descent of the Spirit on the Church, 2:1–42
>> SUMMARY, 2:43–47
> The Church in Jerusalem, 3:1–5:41
>> SUMMARY, 5:42
> The Movement into Judea and Samaria, 6:1–9:30
>> SUMMARY, 9:31

---

[22] This phenomenon, plus others (especially variations in the Lukan passion story) have given rise to the view that the author first composed a gospel combining Q and special L ("Proto-Luke"), into which he inserted parts of Mark, finally prefixing the infancy story (1–2). This theory is especially associated with B.H. Streeter, *The Four Gospels* (1924). Some scholars still support this view; it lays weight on sources rather than redaction.

[23] We shall note that similar formula-like expressions are used elsewhere in the narrative of Acts to mark divisions within it. Our contention is that the combination of a formula summary and a geographical shift mark the major divisions in the narrative.

The Movement into the Gentile World, 9:32–12:23
  SUMMARY, 12:24
To the End of the Earth (1): Paul's First Missionary Journey and Its
  Consequence, the Conference at Jerusalem, 12:25–15:33
  SUMMARY, 15:35
To the End of the Earth (2): Paul's Second Missionary Journey, the
  Movement into Europe and the Decision to Go to Rome, 15:36–19:19
  SUMMARY, 19:20
The Journey of Paul to Rome, 19:21–28:16
Paul in Rome, 28:17–31

EXEGETICAL SURVEY OF LUKE-ACTS

Because of the limitations of space it will not be possible in this exegesis to do more than indicate the outline and flow of the narrative and call attention to particular emphases and concerns of the author. We give the parallels to Mark or Matthew where the parallelism is close.

Introduction to the Two-Volume Work, Luke 1:1–4

The introduction is couched in the conventional language of Hellenistic literature and indicates that the author is deliberately attempting to compose a literary work. Note that he calls his work a "narrative" and wants to put matters into "an orderly account." But note also that his orderly account is a careful blending of secular history and salvation history.

Book One: The Ministry of the Spirit Through Jesus

Introduction to the Ministry of the Spirit Through Jesus, 1:5–4:13

1:5–80 *The birth of John the Baptist and the announcement of the birth of Jesus.* This introduction is written in a Greek characteristic of the Septuagint, the Greek translation of the Hebrew Scriptures. John's birth is parallel in structure to Jesus' birth, but John is a prophet who is clearly subordinate (1:39–45); he will announce salvation and forgiveness of sins (1:77); he is of priestly descent, while Jesus will be called "Son of the Most High" (1:32), a clear reference to the King of David's royal line (2 Sam 7:13–16; Ps 89:26–29). Mary's role is highlighted in the anticipation of Jesus' supernatural birth (1:25–56).

2:1–52 *The birth and infancy of Jesus.* Now salvation history and world history approach the point of intersection. Whereas Matthew concentrated in his infancy stories on the fulfillment of scriptural prophecy, Luke is concerned particularly with the promise that Jesus holds for the future, and

311

his infancy stories are designed particularly to interpret the "center of time" of salvation history in advance (e.g., 2:30–32, 34). Again the spirit inspires prophecy (2:25–38).

3:1–18   *Activity of John the Baptist* (= Mark 1:1–8 = Matt 3:1–12). This is close to Mark and Matthew and hence in general from Mark and Q. Luke extends the Isaiah quotation with its comment, "all flesh shall see the salvation of God," but omits its conclusion (3:6). He tones down the note of apocalyptic urgency in John's proclamation and adds the general ethical teaching of verses 10–14.

3:19–20   *The imprisonment of the Baptist.* This is a remarkable passage. In the service of his understanding of the periodization of salvation history, Luke has John shut up in prison *before* the baptism of Jesus.

3:21–22   *The descent of the Spirit on Jesus* (= Mark 1:9–11; Matt 3:13–17). What in the other gospels is the baptism of Jesus becomes in Luke the descent of the Spirit on him. Note the characteristic introduction of "and was praying" in verse 21. Luke places Jesus at prayer at critical turning points in his salvation history (3:21; 6:12; 9:18; 9:28; 11:1; 22:41); he is the master at prayer, teaching the church to pray (6:28; 10:2; 11:1–3; 18:1–8; 21:36).

3:23–28   *The genealogy of Jesus* (= Matt 1:1–16). Here the descent of Jesus is traced back to Adam, the first man, and not, as in Matthew, only to Abraham. Jesus is the Son of God; his salvation is for all.

4:1–13   *The temptation of Jesus* (= Mark 1:12–13; Matt 4:1–11). Jesus, full of the Holy Spirit, is led by the spirit and tempted as the Son of God. The devil, unsuccessful, departs "until an opportune time" (22:3).

The Ministry in Galilee, 4:14–9:50

4:14–15   *The first preaching in Galilee* (= Mark 1:14–15). Luke carefully omits the eschatological content of Jesus' preaching.

4:16–30   *The synagogue scene* (= Mark 6:1–6). What in Mark is an account of the rejection of Jesus by "his own" in Galilee is in Luke a carefully staged introduction to the whole ministry of Jesus. Here is a key statement of themes sounded constantly throughout the gospel; this scene is designed to introduce the reader to the whole ministry of Jesus and to help him understand it.

4:31–41   *The Sabbath day at Capernaum* (= Mark 1:21–34). Luke here omits the call of the first disciples, thereby showing how Jesus' success at Capernaum follows his rejection at Nazareth, but fulfills the programmatic intent of the Nazareth scene. He follows Mark with only minor modifications.

4:42–44 *A preaching journey* (= Mark 1:35–39). Verse 43 represents Luke's view of the ministry.

5:1–6:11 *Incidents of the ministry in Galilee* (= Mark 1:40–3:6). With the exception of the miraculous catch of fish, which is a hint forward to the world-wide mission of the church (5:1–11), Luke is with minor variations following Mark.

6:12–16 *The call of the twelve* (= Mark 3:13–19). This follows Mark in general, but note the characteristic Lukan emphasis on Jesus spending the night in prayer before choosing the twelve.

6:17–19 *Jesus heals the multitudes* (= Mark 3:7–12).

6:20–49 *The Sermon on the Plain.* Luke 6:20–8:3 combines Q and special L, deviating from the Markan order. The Sermon on the Plain is Luke's equivalent of Matthew's Sermon on the Mount, though it lacks Matthew's characteristic understanding of it as the first book of the new revelation. That both Matthew and Luke have such a sermon indicates that the tradition of bringing together teaching material and giving it a brief narrative setting was already a feature of the sayings source Q. Like Matthew, Luke also gives the sermon an eschatological setting, the Beatitudes (6:20–23), as Q must therefore have done. Luke, the gospel of the poor and outcast, characteristically adds a series of woes on the rich and happy (6:24–26). The remainder of the sermon parallels various places in Matthew; it is Q material, and probably in the same order as Q.

7:1–8:3 *Further incidents of the ministry in Galilee.* Now we have a series of incidents reflecting Luke's interests and concerns. The Centurion's Slave emphasizes the faith of a Gentile (7:1–10); the Widow's Son portrays Jesus' concern for a widow (7:11–17); the Baptist's Question (7:18–23) echoes the key note of the Nazareth synagogue scene; Jesus' testimony to John the Baptist stresses John's preparatory role in the history of salvation (7:24–35; cf. 1:76–77; the quotation of Mal 3:1 [Mark 1:2] was omitted in 3:4); the Woman with the Ointment highlights Jesus' concern for a sinner (7:36–50), and the Ministering Woman his preparedness to help and be helped by women (8:1–3). Some parts have parallels in Matthew (Luke 7:18–35 = Matt 11:2–19), but the configuration and concerns are those of Luke and his gospel.

8:4–18 *The parable of the Sower and the purpose of parables* (= Mark 4:1–29). Here Luke picks up the Markan order again. He follows Mark's parable chapter except that he omits Mark's parable of the Seed Growing Secretly and transposes the Mustard Seed to a different setting (Luke 13:18–19). Also, the three sayings in 8:16–18 are from Mark 4:21–25, but Luke has doublets of them at 11:33; 12:2; and 19:26, each time with a Matthean parallel. Clearly, different versions of these sayings were known to Mark and to the Q community.

Luke 8:16 is particularly interesting. Mark 4:21 has a saying about a lamp being put on a stand. Matt 5:15 has a version in which the lamp "gives light to all in the house"; "he is thinking of a reform within Judaism; Luke's lamp is placed, as in a Roman house, in the vestibule, that those who enter [i.e., the Gentiles] may see the light!"[24] The reinterpretation of traditional sayings in accordance with the interests and concerns of the evangelists is a complex and fascinating process.

8:19–21 *Jesus' true relatives* (= Mark 3:31–35).

8:22–25 *The stilling of the storm* (= Mark 4:35–41).

8:26–39 *The Gerasene demoniac* (= Mark 5:1–20).

8:40–56 *Jairus' daughter and the woman with the hemorrhage* (= Mark 5:21–43).

9:1–6 *The mission of the twelve* (= Mark 6:6b–13).

9:7–9 *Herod thinks Jesus is John, risen* (= Mark 6:14–16).

9:10–17 *The return of the twelve and the feeding of the five thousand* (= Mark 6:30–44). Luke is here following Mark, with some transpositions of order, but he omits Mark's account of the fate of the Baptist (Mark 6:17–29), because he has John in prison before the baptism of Jesus.

9:18–27 *Caesarea Philippi* (= Mark 8:27–9:1). Like Matthew, Luke omits the healing of the blind man at Bethsaida (Mark 8:22–26). But in Luke's case it is left out along with other material, the whole block being called the "Great Omission" (Mark 6:45–8:26). Luke's version of Mark's first prediction unit introduces a characteristic emphasis on Jesus at prayer (9:18), and he omits the misunderstanding and rebuke of Peter, most probably in the interest of honoring a hero of the church. Also, the eschatological note of Mark 9:1 is minimized in Luke 9:27 and the delay of the parousia is indicated in 9:23 ("daily").

9:28–36 *The transfiguration* (= Mark 9:2–8). Luke follows Mark but omits the eschatological note of the reference to the coming of Elijah in Mark 9:9–13 and places Jesus at prayer for this major event in salvation history.

9:37–43a *The healing of the epileptic boy* (= Mark 9:14–29). Luke omits Mark's identification of John the Baptist with Elijah (Mark 9:9–13; cf. 7:24–35; 8:19–21) who was expected to return at the End, i.e., he is consistent with his view that the parousia is delayed and that Elijah themes are related to Jesus himself. His special use of prayer will explain its omission in an exorcism (cf. Mark 9:29).

9:43b–48 *The second prediction unit* (= Mark 9:30–37). Luke greatly abbreviates Mark at this point, almost obliterating the passion prediction. This is a consequence of his particular understanding of the passion, which we discuss later in connection with his passion narrative.

[24] G.B. Caird, *The Gospel of St. Luke* (Pelican Gospel Commentaries), p. 119.

9:49–50 *The strange exorcist* (= Mark 9:38–41). Again, an abbreviation of Mark.

The Journey to Jerusalem, 9:51–19:27

Luke begins this section with a key verse: "When the days drew near for him to be received up, he set his face to go to Jerusalem" (9:51). The reference is actually to the ascension—"received up" (RSV) is a translation of the technical term for the ascension in Greek—and from this point forward the gospel moves toward Jerusalem and the ascension. Luke 9:51–18:14 is a long, rambling section loosely organized around the journey to Jerusalem, until in 18:15 Luke rejoins Mark's narrative at Mark 10:13. The material in this section of Luke is his longest non-Markan block, being derived partly from Q and partly from Luke's own special traditions. We will content ourselves with calling attention only to some features that particularly represent the characteristic concerns of this gospel.

10:1–20 *The mission of the seventy.* Only Luke has this mission, probably a symbolic anticipation of the church's mission to the Gentiles, since in Jewish thinking seventy was the traditional number of Gentile nations.

10:29–37 *The parable of the Good Samaritan.* The parable reflects Luke's concern for the outcast since the Jews regarded the Samaritans with real hostility (compare 9:51–56). Luke has created an introduction from Mark 12:28–31 and Q (Matt 22:34–40).

10:38–42 *Mary and Martha.* The characteristic approach to women in Luke's gospel: the woman disciple is praised; the woman domestic is chided.

11:1–13 *Prayer.* Again Luke portrays Jesus at prayer (11:1) as a prelude to Jesus' teaching about prayer to the disciples (and to the church). The Lord's Prayer (11:1–4) is followed by a parable (11:5–7) and a series of sayings about persistence and God's willingness to give the Holy Spirit, all dealing with prayer.

12:1–53 *Teaching to the disciples.* Jesus stresses the risks of discipleship and the importance of devotion to his way. Note especially the parable of the Rich Fool (12:13–21), the theme of the Holy Spirit (12:10, 12), and the notation about the delay of the parousia (12:45).

13:22, 31–35 *Jerusalem themes.* Luke reminds his readers of the journey to Jerusalem (13:22); in sayings of Jesus he stresses that a prophet should perish in Jerusalem (13:33) and gives the lament over Jerusalem (13:34–35).

14:7–14 *Teaching on humility.* The characteristic attitude toward wealth and concern for the poor.

15:1–32 *The Lost Sheep, the Lost Coin, and the Lost Son.* This is one of the great chapters in the New Testament. The banquet theme, which was associated with the Kingdom in the previous chapter (14:15–30) and stressed inviting the uninvited (14:21–24), is picked up with Jesus' banquet with the outcast tax collectors and sinners (15:1). In three parables Luke presents what he believes to be Jesus' intense concern for the lost. The sheep is lost from the flock, the coin from the woman's meager store, the boy from the land and standards of his father. But all are found again and in this Luke sees a symbol of God's love and concern for the lost and the outcast as epitomized by Jesus and to be echoed by the believer.

16:1–31 *Riches and the Kingdom.* The parable of the Unjust Judge, told to the disciples, becomes the occasion for sayings culminating in the theme, "You cannot serve God and mammon" (16:13). The Pharisees, who observed Jesus' banquet with sinners (15:2), are now accused as lovers of money (16:14–15). Luke 16:16 gives a clue to salvation history by contrasting the era of the law and prophets with the era of the proclamation of the good news of the Kingdom of God. The parable of the Rich Man and Lazarus (16:19–31) continues the theme of riches and concern for the poor.

17:11–19 *The faith of the Samaritan leper.* Ten lepers are cleansed "on the way to Jerusalem . . . between Samaria and Galilee." Only the Samaritan gives thanks. Jesus notes that the faith of "this foreigner" has healed him.

17:20–21 *The Kingdom of God and the day of the Son of Man.* The question "when" the Kingdom will come is answered with a denial of signs and denial of place; it is "in the midst of you." Luke 17:22–23 reflects the delay of the parousia.

18:1–14 *The parables of the Unjust Judge and the Publican.* Characteristic piety in the form of prayer, encouraged by the stories of a poor widow who successfully importunes an unjust judge and a tax collector who successfully prays for mercy.

18:15–19:27 *Jesus draws near to Jerusalem.* Luke now rejoins Mark's narrative. The blessing of the children (18:15–17 = Mark 10:13–16) would obviously appeal to Luke, as would the story of the rich young man (18:18–30 = Mark 10:17–31). Mark's third prediction unit (Mark 10:32–45) is itself composite, since the teaching on discipleship was probably originally in a Eucharistic setting, where Luke has it (Luke 22:24–27). Luke 18:31–34 has the third prediction of the passion, and 18:35–43 the healing of the blind man with only minor variations from Mark. Luke 19:1–10 has the story of Zacchaeus, in this instance a tax collector, only in Luke and characteristic of his concern for the ministry of Jesus to the outcast. The parable of the pounds (19:11–27) is told "because he was near to Jerusalem, and because they [wrongly] supposed that the Kingdom of God was to appear immediately" (19:11).

Jesus in Jerusalem, 19:28–21:38

This basically follows Mark 11:1–13:37. Luke 19:39–44 adds a prediction of the destruction of Jerusalem, which interprets that catastrophe as a judgment on the city, "because you did not know the time of your visitation." Luke maintains the apocalyptic discourse of Mark 13 because he accepts the parousia (Luke 21:25–38). He even adds a note of his own (Luke 21:34–36) that stresses the universal nature of the event. We have already noted how he redacts the chapter to separate the destruction of Jerusalem (21:20–24) from the more remote parousia (21:25–36), the "times of the Gentiles" falling between (21:24; cf. 21:8–9).

The Passion Narrative, 22:1–23:49

This is rather different from the account in Mark 14:1–16:8, and it has been suggested that Luke is following another source.[25] But the general framework of his narrative is from Mark, and the divergencies can be explained partly by his use of special material at some points and partly by a particular interpretation of the passion that causes him to undertake a rather extensive redaction of the Markan narrative in some places.

Luke understands the passion of Jesus as the legal murder of Jesus by the Jews, achieved despite a favorable attitude to Jesus by the Roman and Herodian authorities. The Jews and the Jews alone bear the guilt for the death of Jesus. A second major deviation from Mark is that Luke does not regard the Cross as an atonement for sin: the death of Jesus is not the basis for man's salvation. In Luke's version of the Last Supper the Cross of Jesus is interpreted as an act of service, not as in Mark 10:45 as a "ransom for many." There is even doubt as to whether the words of interpretation of the bread and wine at the Supper—a body "given for you" and blood "poured out for you"—belong in the original text of the gospel (Luke 22:19b–20).[26] The Lukan passion narrative has to be reviewed with some care.

22:1–2 *The conspiracy against Jesus* (= Mark 14:1–2).

22:3–6 *Satan returns to the scene* (= Mark 14:10–11). This is Luke's account of Judas Iscariot's agreement to betray Jesus, with the special note on the return of Satan, who was absent from Luke's narrative since the Temptation (4:13).

---

[25] V. Taylor, *The Passion Narrative of St. Luke*.

[26] The textual evidence indicates that Luke 22:19b–20 was added to the original text in the course of its transmission in the church. NEB and TEV relegate these verses to the margin.

22:7–13 *Preparation for the Supper* (= Mark 14:12–16).

22:14–38 *The Last Supper* (= Mark 14:17–25, but with significant variations). Luke begins his account of the Supper with the institution of the Eucharist and follows it with the announcement of the traitor, an inversion of the order in Mark. In itself this is of no great moment. More important is that Luke 22:15–16 has the reference forward to eating in the Kingdom of God before the words of interpretation, 22:17–19a (?19b–20), whereas Mark has the reverse order. It is entirely possible that Luke is minimizing the impact of the words of interpretation by deliberately preceding them with the reference to the future of the Kingdom of God.

Luke 22:24–27 is his version of Mark 10:42–45, and it is certainly independent of what Mark represented. The two versions of the teaching developed separately in the tradition of the church, and Luke chooses this one rather than what is in Mark because it avoids the ransom saying of Mark 10:45. Verses 28–30 seem to be from Q; Matt 19:28 has the saying in a different context. Verses 31–34 and 35–38 are special Lukan tradition.

22:39–53 *Jesus in Gethsemane* (= Mark 14:26–52). A somewhat abbreviated version of Mark's narrative.

22:54–71 *The trial before the Sanhedrin and Peter's denial* (= Mark 14:53–72). Luke finishes the account of the denial before beginning the trial, whereas Mark intercalates the trial into the denial story.

23:1–5 *Jesus before Pilate* (= Mark 15:1–5). Luke develops Mark's account in accordance with his wish to stress the positive attitude of Pilate to Jesus and the guilt of the Jews.

23:6–12 *Jesus before Herod.* A further demonstration of Luke's emphasis: the innocence of Jesus, the guilt of the Jews, the favor of the authorities toward Jesus.

23:13–25 *The sentencing of Jesus* (= Mark 15:6–15). Luke adds verses 13–16 to Mark's narrative, reiterating his emphases.

23:26–32 *The road to Golgatha.* Luke adds verses 27–31, the lamenting of the women of Jerusalem, to Mark 15:21.

23:33–43 *The crucifixion* (= Mark 15:22–32). Particular Lukan emphases are the prayer for forgiveness (verse 34), and the Penitent Thief (verses 39–43).

23:44–49 *The return of the Spirit to the Father* (= Mark 15:33–41). Luke rewrites the account of the death of Jesus in accordance with his concept of the role of the spirit in salvation history. The centurion's confession becomes a declaration of the innocence of Jesus, not a confession of his status as Son of God, as it is in Mark 15:39.

Burial, Resurrection, Ascension, 23:50–24:53

23:50–24:11 *The burial of Jesus and the empty tomb.* Basically follows Mark 15:42–47; 16:1–8.

24:13–35 *The road to Emmaus.* This is the first of the Lukan resurrection appearances, and verses 19–21 represent Luke's view of Jesus. It is located near Jerusalem (24:13). The story stresses that the preceding events fulfill Scripture.

24:36–49 *The risen Christ in Jerusalem.* This is the gospel version of the risen Jesus' teaching to his disciples. A further version is given in Acts 1:6–9, and Luke uses the opportunity of the repetition to develop slightly different emphases each time. These two sets of teaching are the key to the Lukan enterprise, and our overall exegesis of Luke-Acts builds heavily on them. Again, the prophecy-fulfillment theme is predominant.

24:50–53 *The ascension.* In accordance with 9:51 the reference to the ascension should be read in verse 51b and not relegated to the margin as in the Revised Standard Version.

Introduction to the Second Volume (Acts of the Apostles), Acts 1:1–5

Book Two: The Ministry of the Spirit Through the Church

Introduction to the Ministry of the Spirit Through the Church: the Risen Lord and His Disciples, 1:6–26.

1:6–11 *The risen Lord with his disciples.* This is Luke's second version of the interim period of special revelation. Note the emphasis on the empowering by the Spirit, the work of witnessing, and the geographical progression from Jerusalem to the end of the earth (Rome). This is a statement of the theme of Acts. Note further that the expectation of the parousia is still maintained (verse 11).

1:12–26 *The replacement of Judas.* The author of Luke-Acts is moving toward the church as an institution, and the fact that it is headed by a formal group of twelve apostles is important to him. Note the emphasis on prayer in verse 24, no doubt deliberately reminiscent of Jesus at prayer before the appointment of the twelve in the gospel.

The Descent of the Spirit on the Church, 2:1–42

This descent of the Spirit had already been interpreted as a baptism in 1:5 and so carefully parallels the beginning of the ministry of Jesus. The gift of tongues symbolizes the worldwide mission of the church. We have already pointed out that Peter's speech in verses 14–36 and 38–39 is built on an example of the *pesher* method of the interpretation of Scripture in the early church. As it stands in its present context, the speech represents Luke's understanding of things. Note especially the emphasis on the humanity of Jesus (verse 22), the guilt of the Jews (verse 23), the resurrection of Jesus and the witness of the church (verse 32), the subordination of Jesus to God (verse 36), and repentance and the forgiveness of sins (verse 38).

The section closes with a summary, 2:43–47.

The Church in Jerusalem, 3:1–5:41

The witness of the church begins in Jerusalem, in accordance with the programmatic statement in 1:8. Luke may be drawing on early traditions about the church in Jerusalem, but he clearly stamps them with his own emphases and concerns, especially in the speeches: 3:12–26 (Peter at Solomon's Porch), 4:8–12 and 5:29–32 (Peter before the Sanhedrin). Here, for example, Jesus is understood as a prophet (3:22); there is also an emphasis on the resurrection (3:26; 5:30) and on the guilt of the Jews (4:11; 5:30). For the most part, however, the legends are about the early days of the church, developed in the church for the edification of the believers. Such legends are common to all religious movements.

The section closes with a summary, 5:42.

The Movement into Judea and Samaria, 6:1–9:30

Following on the programmatic statement in 1:8, the witness now moves outward to Judea, the territory immediately surrounding Jerusalem, and Samaria. Here we begin to have some contact with the history of the early church as distinct from myths and legends about it. Behind the narrative of the dispute between Hellenists and Hebrews in Jerusalem (6:1–6) and the persecution of the church in Jerusalem (8:1), there lies the reminiscence of a real division in the church and the persecution of one part of it and not another. For all its legendary overlay and its reworking by the author of Luke-Acts in his understanding of things, this section of Acts does echo the historical origins of the Hellenistic Jewish Christian mission.

Stephen's speech (7:2–53) must be regarded as an example of the exegesis of Scripture and the interpretation of events by which Hellenistic Jewish Mission Christianity justified its break with Judaism. We noted earlier the parallels the author of Luke-Acts carefully draws between the passion of Stephen, the proto-martyr, and that of Jesus. In 8:1 Paul appears for the first time, and there can be no doubt that he did in fact persecute the church in some such manner as is here depicted. Luke 8:4–24 is a collection of legends about the origin of the Hellenistic Jewish Christian mission, remarkable in that it associates Peter firmly with that movement and presents both Philip and Peter as Hellenistic "divine men." Luke 8:25 is a summary reflecting a division in the narrative, not major since it is not associated with a geographical shift, but a division nonetheless. It is followed by the incident of Philip and the Ethiopian Eunuch (8:26–39). Then comes a summary of Philip's further activity (8:40), making it probable that the author of Luke-Acts has deliberately inserted this narrative here. It certainly represents two of the author's characteristic concerns. The eunuch was an outcast since the Jews would not have accepted a mutilated man as a proselyte, and the quotation from Isaiah 53 carefully avoids any interpretation of the death of Jesus as an atonement for sin.

Luke 9:1–30 is the first of the three accounts of the conversion of Paul in Acts (see also 22:3–21; 26:9–23). That this event is narrated three times indicates its importance to the author of Luke-Acts and the Hellenistic Jewish Mission Christianity he represents. We have already discussed the conversion of Paul, and here we need only note that the account is deliberately redacted in line with the programmatic statement of 1:8. Paul's witness did not begin in Jerusalem as all three accounts of his conversion insist it did, but the program announced in 1:8 is here dominant for our author. The myth is overtaking the history.

The section closes with a summary, 9:31.

The Movement into the Gentile World, 9:32–12:23

Still following the programmatic statement of 1:8, the narrative now moves to an account of the first Christian witness in the purely Gentile world. The author of Luke-Acts emphasizes the role of Peter in this movement, as he had previously emphasized the role of Peter in the beginning of Hellenistic Jewish Mission Christianity. In part the author wants to bring Peter and Paul, the two great heroes of early Christianity, into essential agreement with each other. But that Peter did in fact take part in the Hellenistic Jewish Christian mission is attested by his appearance in Antioch and Paul's passionate altercation with him there (Gal 2:11–21).

Characteristically Lukan themes recur in Peter's speech (10:34–43) and the founding of the church at Antioch (11:19–21). The latter marks the true beginning of the Christian mission to the purely Gentile world, and the fact—and it probably is a fact—that "in Antioch the disciples were for the first time called Christians" (11:26) is symbolic testimony to the importance of this moment in the history of New Testament Christianity.

The section closes with a summary, 12:24.

The Movement to the "End of the Earth" (1): Paul's First Missionary Journey and Its Consequence, the Conference at Jerusalem, 12:25–15:33

A feature of Acts is the presentation of Paul's missionary work in the form of three missionary journeys: 13:13–14:28; 15:36–18:21; 18:23–19:19. Clearly Paul must have undertaken missionary journeys; however, in view of the fondness of the author of Luke-Acts for the literary theme of "journeys" (Luke 9:51 and Jesus' journey to Jerusalem; Acts 19:21 and Paul's journey to Rome) these missionary journeys in Acts are probably a literary device around which the author organizes his presentation of Paul's work.

The first "missionary journey" features the first major speech by Paul in Acts, at Pisidian Antioch, 13:16–41. It rehearses themes characteristic of Luke-Acts: the guilt of the Jews, an emphasis on the resurrection, the witness of Christians, the proclamation of the forgiveness of sins as the heart of the Christian message, and so on. It represents the mind of the author of Luke-Acts far more than it does anything appropriate to the Paul of the New Testament letters. We have already indicated our reasons for believing that the Conference was the start of Paul's missionary journeys into the world beyond Antioch and that the "decree" of 15:29 represents a solution to a problem that arose as a consequence of Paul's work rather than during the course of it. At the same time, the activity and experiences depicted here in connection with Paul and Barnabas must have been typical of Hellenistic Jewish Christian missionaries in general as known to the author of Luke-Acts.

This section ends with a summary, 15:35.

The Movement to the "End of the Earth" (2): Paul's Second Missionary Journey, the Movement into Europe and the Decision to Go to Rome, 15:36–19:19

This section of Acts is dominated by Paul's decision to carry the Christian witness from Asia into Europe, presented as a direct consequence of the activity of the Spirit, and it leads to Paul's decision to go to Rome (19:21), which in Acts structurally parallels Jesus' decision to go to Jerusalem in Luke 9:51. Paul's experiences as presented here must have been very like those of most Hellenistic Jewish Christian missionaries, as Paul's speech at Athens (17:22–31) no doubt represents typical Christian preaching to the Hellenistic world. Note also the characteristic themes of the favor of the Roman authorities toward the Christians and the guilt of the Jews (18:14–17).

The section ends with a summary, 19:20.

The Journey of Paul to Rome, 19:21–28:16

We now find in Acts the same long, rambling travel narrative beginning with the chief protagonist's resolve that is in the gospel of Luke beginning with 9:51. It is a literary device obviously dear to the author of Luke-Acts. The narrative has been composed of a mixture of traditions and legends about the work of the apostle Paul on which the author of Luke-Acts has imposed his own understanding of things—as, for example, in the second and third accounts of the conversion of Paul (22:3–21; 26:9–23), where Paul's Christian witness always begins in Jerusalem and moves toward Rome.

A feature of this section of Acts is long passages written in the first-person plural, the so-called "we passages." These had first appeared in the previous section of the work (16:10–17), but now they are extensive (20:5–15; 21:1–18; 27:1–28:16).

Paul in Rome, 28:17–31

Luke-Acts ends with the establishment of Paul and his mission in Rome and the programmatic note of Paul preaching the gospel "openly and unhindered" there. It is the climax of the narrative as depicted in 1:8 and represents the situation of the readers of Luke-Acts as the author understands that situation.

THE INTERPRETATION OF THE GOSPEL OF MARK BY THE AUTHOR OF LUKE-ACTS

The author of Luke-Acts uses the gospel of Mark as a major source, that use revealing clearly his own emphases and concerns. We have indicated something of his literary use of Mark for his overall structure and in certain passages of the exegetical survey, most notably in his view of salvation history and the "law of duality." It will now be important to observe how he transforms Mark's Christology, that is, his understanding of Jesus, and the way that understanding relates to his total view.

The evangelist Mark wants to present Jesus as Christ and Son of God and to interpret those designations by a careful and systematic use of Son of Man, leading up to the climactic interpretation of Jesus as Son of Man in 14:62 and the climactic confession of him as Son of God by the centurion in 15:39. In the gospel of Luke all this changes. The confession of the centurion becomes in Luke 23:47 simply a declaration, "Certainly this man was innocent," and the formal acceptance and reinterpretation of the titles "Christ" and "Son of God" by Jesus in Mark 14:61–62 is in Luke 22:67–70 an indiscriminate use without any sensitivity to the nuances of meaning attaching to these titles. The author of Luke-Acts does not have either the same Christology or the same christological concerns as the evangelist Mark. In Luke-Acts, Jesus is the "center of time." He is portrayed, on the one hand, as the fulfillment of Old Testament prophecies, especially as the Spirit-filled, anointed Davidic Servant-Messiah and prophet who brings salvation to all, especially by preaching to the poor and outcast, and by healing (Luke 4:16–43; 24:19, 27). He also fulfills the prophecies when he is condemned by the Jews, suffers and dies, and is vindicated as Christ, Lord, and Son of God in his resurrection and ascension to God's side (Luke 24:25–26, 44–53; Acts 2:33, 36; 13:26–41). On the other hand, Jesus is portrayed as a Son of God by a human mother and supernatural agency, as full of the Spirit, as a wandering teacher and healer whose ways of life, teaching, and healing were bequeathed to his disciple-followers, as a figure who appeared after death and was taken up to heaven, and as a Savior who offered peace and salvation to the whole world. Such an account read by any high-ranking Gentile or Gentile group would indicate that the Jewish Messiah who fulfilled the Scriptures shared much in common with all manner of Savior figures throughout the Eastern Mediterranean, from the miracle workers and wandering philosophers, whose disciples learned and passed on their teacher's teaching and total way of life,[27] to the emperors whose inscriptions proclaimed peace and salvation to the world.[28] These overall views in Luke-Acts contrast sharply with dominant Son of God as Son of Man Christology in the gospel of Mark.

It is interesting to consider the interpretation of Mark's predictions of the passion and resurrection (Mark 8:31; 9:31; 10:33-34) in Luke (Luke 9:22; 9:44; 18:31-33). In all the predictions Mark stresses the authority of Jesus in that Jesus is said to "rise again" or "rise." But in Luke 9:22 the verb goes into the passive voice, and it is said that Jesus will "be raised." Luke-Acts emphasizes the resurrection throughout but as the act of God on behalf of the man Jesus. The impact of the gospel of Mark is strong enough for Jesus simply to "rise" in Luke 18:33, but the concern of the author of Luke-Acts in general is to subordinate Jesus to God and to stress the resurrection as an act of God's power, for example, as in Acts 2:33,36; 4:10; 5:30, and elsewhere.

Examining Luke's interpretation of Mark's predictions of the passion and resurrection leads to Luke's understanding of the passion of Jesus altogether. For Mark, the passion and death of Jesus is the means of man's salvation. Jesus comes "to give his life as a ransom for many" (Mark 10:45), and his Cross is a sacrifice in which his blood is "poured out for many" (Mark 14:24). None of this survives in the gospel of Luke. In Luke's equivalent to Mark 10:45 (Luke 22:27), the Cross of Jesus is simply an act of service and not the means of man's salvation, and Luke's account of the Last Supper omits the word of interpretation of the wine, Luke 22:19b-20 having little claim to being part of the original text of the gospel of Luke. Moreover, this understanding of the Cross of Jesus as determinative for man's salvation was reached in early Christianity by interpreting that Cross in terms of the great suffering servant passage of Isaiah 53, to which Mark 10:45 and 14:24 certainly allude. But when this passage comes up in Acts 8:32-33, it is most emphatically not used to interpret the death of Jesus as an atonement for sin.

The author of Luke-Acts simply does not understand the passion and death of Jesus in the same way as does the evangelist Mark. For Mark the death of Jesus is the means of man's salvation, the gospel of Jesus Christ is the proclamation that the Cross of Christ has made possible the salvation of man, and Christian discipleship is following Jesus in the way of his Cross. For the author of Luke-Acts the death of Jesus is an act of legal murder by the Jews, and the gospel as preached by Jesus and the church is a proclamation that if men will repent and turn to God they will receive the forgiveness of their sins.

---

[27] C. Talbert, *Literary Patterns*, chapters 6-8, stresses the popular philosopher.

[28] F. Danker, *Luke* (Proclamation Commentaries), chapters 1-4, stresses the Isaianic Servant-Hellenistic Benefactor.

The death of Jesus does not have the role in Luke-Acts it has in the gospel of Mark, and in Luke-Acts Christian discipleship is a witnessing to the resurrection of Jesus rather than a following of Jesus in the way of his Cross.

But the major difference between Mark and Luke-Acts is, of course, the sheer existence of the Acts of the Apostles itself. It is not likely that Mark would have written any such volume since he was anticipating an imminent parousia and envisaging his readers as preparing themselves for that event. The author of Luke-Acts, however, sees the parousia as deferred to the indefinite future and his readers as necessarily settling down to a long period of witnessing in the world. Under these circumstances an Acts of Apostles becomes necessary to help its readers understand how they came to be in their present position and gives them a paradigm they can follow. This is the twofold purpose of Acts: it helps the readers understand their place and function in the world and its history by explaining to them the origin and development of the movement of which they are a part, and it helps them fulfill their functions by giving them a model. In the Acts of the Apostles the almost legendary heroes of the early days of the church are deliberately presented as models of Christian witness in the world. Historically speaking, there were all kinds of differences between Peter and Paul, but in Acts they speak with one voice, share the same concerns, preach the same gospel; and the voice, concerns, and gospel are those of the church of Luke's own time. Or perhaps it would be more accurate to say they are the voice, concerns, and gospel as Luke hopes they will become in his own time. It is certainly in this light also that Luke's Jesus is portrayed in highly "ethical" terms, as the Savior of all, including the poor, the outcast, women, the lost, the sick, Samaritans, and Gentiles. In this, Luke goes far beyond Mark.

The authors of Mark and the Acts of the Apostles write didactic history, a history of the past told to instruct the reader in the present. But they go about their task differently. The evangelist Mark puts his message on the lips of the authoritative figure of Jesus, who is Christ, Son of God and Son of Man. The author of Luke-Acts presents his message through the heroes of the church, Peter and Paul, who become models to be imitated, paradigmatic figures whose example should be followed. But the use of model figures does not end with the presentation of Peter and Paul in the Acts; it is extended to the figure of Jesus in the gospel of Luke. A remarkable feature of the gospel of Luke is the way Jesus is presented as a model of Christian piety, and the way parallels are carefully drawn between the practice of Jesus in the gospel and that of the apostles in the Acts. These parallels are then extended by implication to the readers of Luke-Acts, and the readers find themselves at one with Peter, Paul, Stephen, *and Jesus* in the world. For this reason the author of Luke-Acts plays down the christological emphases of his source, the gospel of Mark, and also avoids any soteriological emphasis in connection with the Cross. The Jesus of the gospel of Luke is the first Christian, living out of the power of the Spirit of God in the world. He is not the Jewish Messiah whose death ransoms men from the power of sin over them.

It is interesting to compare the different and yet sometimes similar reinterpretations of the gospel of Mark by the evangelist Matthew and by the author of Luke-Acts. The similarity is that both carefully separate the time of Jesus from all preceding or succeeding times. Matthew does so by birth stories at the beginning and the commissioning scene at the end; Luke by the descent of the Spirit at the beginning and the ascension at the end. Moreover, the similarity continues in that both emphasize the special nature of the time of Jesus; for both the time of Jesus is the time of fulfillment. Matthew does this with his constant use of formula quotations; Luke with his insistence on the absence of Satan between the temptation of Jesus and the plot to betray him, and also with the various portrayals of the time of Jesus as the center of time, distinct both from the time of "the law and the prophets" before it and the time of the preaching of "repentance and the forgiveness of sins to all nations" after it. There is a sense, therefore, in which both Matthew and Luke transform what is essentially the apocalypse of Mark into a foundation myth of Christian origins, and this becomes most evident in the Lukan form of salvation history.

But if Matthew and Luke both transform the apocalypse of Mark into a foundation myth, they go very different ways in portraying how their readers may relate to this foundation myth. For Matthew, the means is an authoritative interpretation of the verbal revelation that occurred in the Sacred Time of Jesus. For Luke, the means is an imitation of the Jesus of the Sacred Time, because for him Jesus is quite simply the first Christian. Luke sees Jesus as the primary example to be imitated, as he sees the heroes of the Christian church as secondary examples to be imitated. For him, Christian faith means essentially the imitation of Jesus and following the example of those heroes of the early church who did successfully imitate him.

THE INTERPRETATION OF LUKE-ACTS

The author of Luke-Acts is the father of all presentations of the life of Jesus in which Jesus is an example to be imitated and the early church is a challenge to and exemplar of what is expected of Christians in the world—and of what Christians may expect of their life in the world. The author of Luke-Acts deliberately presents Jesus and the heroes of the early church as models of the challenge and possibilities of Christian existence in the world. Whereas the evangelist Matthew encouraged the interpretation of the gospel as a verbal revelation to be authoritatively interpreted, the author of Luke-Acts encourages the interpretation of that gospel as an example to be followed in the world. What Jesus, Peter, Stephen, and Paul did, so may and must we also do: that is the message and challenge of the author of Luke-Acts.

Further Reading

All our resource books discuss Luke-Acts:

W.G. Kümmel, *Intro*, pp. 122–88 (17th ed.).
W. Marxsen, *Intro*, pp. 155–62; 167–73.

R. Fuller, *Intro*, pp. 118–32.

PCB, pp. 820–43; 882–926 (G. W. H. Lampe).

JBC, pp. 115–64 (C. Stuhlmueller); 165–214 (R. J. Dillon and J. A. Fitzmyer).

IDB, vol. 3, pp. 180–88 (V. Taylor); vol. 1, pp. 28–42 (H. J. Cadbury, and particularly important).

IDB Suppl., pp. 558–60 (W. C. Robinson).

The interpretation of Luke-Acts presented by the present writers stands generally in the tradition represented by Dibelius, Haenchen, and Conzelmann.

M. Dibelius, *Studies in the Acts of the Apostles.*
E. Haenchen, *The Acts of the Apostles.*
H. Conzelmann, *The Theology of St. Luke.*

Certain modifications in Conzelmann's view of salvation history have been made, especially with respect to his interpretation of Luke 16:16 in regard to Luke 1–2 and the role of John the Baptist. On this, one may consult P. Minear, "Luke's Use of the Birth Stories," in *Studies in Luke-Acts*, edited by L. Keck and J.L. Martin. This volume contains other important essays. A more recent collection is *Perspectives on Luke-Acts*, edited by C. Talbert.

A valuable set of articles on the gospel of Luke is found in the journal *Interpretation* 19 (1975), pp. 3–74. These are reprinted in J.L. Mays, *Interpreting the Gospels*, pp. 183–246. Especially helpful is C. Talbert, "Shifting Sands: The Recent Study of the Gospel of Luke," pp. 197–213.

Two important articles are:

R. Tannehill, "The Mission of Jesus According to Luke IV 16–30," in E. Grässer, A. Strobel, and R. Tannehill, *Jesus in Nazareth.*
W. G. Kümmel, "Current Theological Accusations Against Luke," *Andover Newton Quarterly* 16 (1975), pp. 131–45, raises some questions about Conzelmann's important study.

Among the many recent books breaking new ground on Luke and Acts are these:

F. Danker, *Luke* (Proclamation Commentaries).
M. Hengel, *Acts and the History of Earliest Christianity.*
C. Talbert, *Literary Patterns, Theological Themes, and the Genre of Luke-Acts.*
D. Tiede, *Prophecy and History in Luke-Acts.*

A readable introduction is:

R. Karras, *What Are They Saying About Luke and Acts?*

Recent commentaries are:

F. Danker, *Jesus and the New Age.*
J. Fitzmyer, *The Gospel According to Luke* (I-IX, 1982) (Anchor Bible).

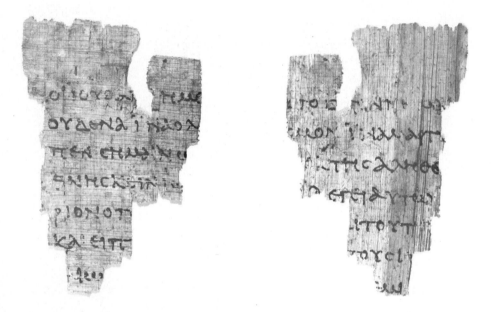

Rylands Greek Papyrus 457, a fragment of John 18. Known also as P 52, it is the oldest surviving New Testament text (middle of the second century).

CHAPTER ELEVEN

THE GOSPEL AND LETTERS OF JOHN:
The Literature of the Johannine School

Traditionally, five of the texts in the New Testament are regarded as having been written by the apostle John: the fourth gospel, the three letters of John, and the book of Revelation. The last, however, has at best only a tenuous relationship to the others and is so representative of apocalyptic Christianity that we do not discuss it further here. Neither in style nor in content does it have a claim to a place in the "Johannine corpus," the collection of literature attributed to the apostle John. But the other four texts exhibit a unity of style and content that shows that they certainly belong together, whatever the details of their origins may turn out to have been. They use the same language in the same way. They present stark contrasts between light and darkness, truth and falsehood, life and death, faith and unbelief. Striking indeed is the fact that the long discourses attributed to Jesus in the gospel and the contents of the first letter exhibit a habit of thinking in what has been called a "spiral structure": "The author states a thought, contemplates it from every angle, and apparently finishes up where he started. Yet, there is a slight but perceptible movement to another thought, and the process is repeated."[1] Above all, even the most casual reader can sense that here he is in the presence of someone who has meditated long and earnestly on the verities of the Christian faith: on God, who is light and in whom is no darkness at all; on Jesus Christ his Son whom he sent into the world to save it; on the Christian life as essentially the recognition of being loved and the act of loving. Every line of the gospel and letters of John breathes the spirit of this meditation, and this quality has made these writings the fundamental literature of Christian mystics through the long centuries of Christian history.

[1] R. Fuller, *Intro.*, p. 178.

In reading the literature about the gospel and letters of John, we are struck by the frequent images of artistic and especially musical composition. Amos Wilder, a scholar extremely sensitive to literary forms, says that in John's gospel "we have a kind of sacred drama or oratorio,"[2] and the *Oxford Annotated Bible* says of the first letter that its various themes "are frequently reintroduced, and often blend into one another, like the leading refrains of a great musical composition."[3] This imagery extends even to individual parts of the gospel. Bultmann speaks for many commentators when he describes the prologue to the gospel (John 1:1–18) as an "overture . . . singling out particular motifs from the action to be unfolded."[4] The gospel and letters of John give the impression of carefully composed wholes, of being a response to the internal dynamics of the genius and vision of the author. As a consequence, it is difficult to answer historical questions about these works. Nonetheless, there has been a good deal of progress recently in attempting to identify the traditions behind the gospel and the communities that transmitted them, as well as the contexts of the gospel and letters themselves. This progress will be reflected in what follows. But our comments in this instance are more tentative than they were in our discussions of the synoptic gospels.

HISTORICAL QUESTIONS CONCERNING THE GOSPEL AND LETTERS

Authorship

John 21:20–24 identifies its author, or at least the one who "caused these things to be written," as "the disciple whom Jesus loved, who had lain close to his breast at the supper and had said, 'Lord, who is it that is going to betray you?'" This passage clearly refers to "the beloved disciple" mentioned at the Last Supper (13:23–25) and entrusted by Jesus on the Cross with his mother (19:26–27). The gospel elsewhere identifies him as "the other disciple" (20:2), as one known to the high priest and present at Jesus' trial before him (18:15–16), and as linked with Peter (18:15; 21:7), in fact as one who outran Peter to the tomb (20:2–8). Moreover, 21:20–23 most probably implies that he is dead and attempts to correct the false impression that Jesus said he would still be alive at Jesus' parousia. It is stated that "his testimony is true" (21:24) and if 19:35 refers to him, he is said to be also an eyewitness to the death of Jesus. Though the "disciple whom Jesus loved" is never named, church tradition in the second century A.D. identified him as John, the son of Zebedee, one of the inner group of twelve disciples singled out for special mention in the gospel of Mark. He was supposed to have lived to a ripe old age in Ephesus

[2] A. Wilder, *Early Christian Rhetoric*, p. 30.
[3] *Oxford Annotated Bible*, p. 1482.
[4] R. Bultmann, *The Gospel of John*, p. 13.

and to have written the gospel there (Irenaeus, *Against Heresies* 3.1.2, ca. A.D. 180; cf. Bishop Polycrates of Ephesus in Eusebius, *Ecclesiastical History* 5.24.2ff., ca. A.D. 190). However, this tradition is not unanimous in the ancient world and its main source, Irenaeus, was not always correct about John (Eusebius, *Ecclesiastical History* 3.39.1–7). In addition, the author of the second and third letters identifies himself simply as the "presbyter" ("elder," cf. 2 John 1:1; 3 John 1:1) and there is a presbyter John who is a shadowy figure in early Christian tradition (Eusebius, *Ecclesiastical History* 3.39.1–7). Therefore, the identity of the author(s) of the gospel and letters poses a knotty problem. Before considering it further, however, several other issues need to be discussed.

The Integrity of the Text of the Gospel: Chapter 21

No text of the gospel ever circulated that did not include chapter 21. Yet that chapter is all but universally recognized to have been a supplement to the original text of the gospel.[5] In the first place, 20:30–31 reads like the original ending to the gospel. Then in 21:2 the sons of Zebedee, who are missing in chapters 1–20, suddenly appear. Further, like the commissioning scene in Matthew 28, the resurrection appearance of Jesus in Chapter 21 takes place in Galilee, whereas in chapter 20 the appearances are located in Jerusalem, as in Luke-Acts. The traditions are here in conflict. John 21:24 seems designed to identify the "disciple whom Jesus loved" as the author of the gospel. This remark could refer to everything up to that point, including 21:1–23. But the differentiation should come earlier, at the beginning of chapter 21, because in addition to the factors we have already mentioned there are some important differences between the Greek of chapter 21 and that of chapters 1–20.[6] It seems probable, therefore, that chapter 21, the chapter that relates to the origins of the gospel, was added to the original chapters 1–20 of the gospel, but before the text of the gospel had actually circulated beyond those who were certifying it (21:24: "we").[7]

---

[5] W. G. Kümmel, *Intro.*, pp. 207–08.

[6] Given in W. G. Kümmel, *Intro.*, p. 208.

[7] Another passage related to the integrity of the text of the woman taken into adultery, John 7:53–8:11. Most responsible modern translations relegate the story to the margin, because the best Greek manuscripts do not include it at all; when it does appear, it is either marked with asterisks or other signs to indicate that it is dubious, or it is included at different places. Some manuscripts have it after John 7:36, others after John 21:24, others after Luke 21:38. It is a traditional story about Jesus that circulated in the church and that various scribes inserted at various places throughout the New Testament as they transcribed it. It so happened that the texts from which the King James Version was translated had it at John 7:53–8:11, but it is not written in the Johannine style and has no claim to a place in John. Indeed, it has no claim to a place in the text of the New Testament at all, which is in some ways tragic, since it is one of the most challenging of all the stories told about Jesus.

Who added chapter 21 to the gospel of John? A natural answer would be some member(s) of a Johannine "school." We shall consider this possibility later; at this point it will be helpful to go in the opposite direction and ask what kinds of sources and traditions lie behind the gospel.

The Gospel of John and the Synoptic Gospels

Was the gospel of John written with a knowledge of any or all of the synoptic gospels? That question has never been resolved by a consensus of scholarly opinion. There are obvious and immediate differences between John and the synoptics in style and presentation of material. The long discourses on symbolic themes such as "light" and "life," which are not pieced together out of separate sayings as are the discourses in the synoptics but evolve as complex monologues or dramatic dialogues, are a good example. Then the chronological and topographical framework of the gospel is different. John envisages a ministry of Jesus beginning with the joint activity with the Baptist and featuring several extended ministries in Jerusalem. The synoptics have Jesus begin his ministry only after John was imprisoned, and it lasts one year and includes only one visit to Jerusalem. Further, only a limited number of incidents in John have parallels in the synoptics: a call of disciples (1:35–51); the healing of the official's son (4:46–53); a feeding followed by a sea miracle (6:1–21); Peter's confession (6:66–70); the triumphal entry into Jerusalem (12:12–15); the cleansing of the Temple (2:13–22); the anointing at Bethany (12:1–8); the Last Supper with a prophecy of betrayal (13:1–11); and the general story of the passion itself. By the same token, John has incidents unknown to the synoptics: the wedding at Cana (2:1–11); the narratives concerning Nicodemus (3:1–21) and the Samaritan woman (4:7–42); the healing at the pool of Bethzatha (5:1–9);[8] the healing of the man born blind (9:1–12); and the raising of Lazarus (11:1–44), which is the direct cause of the plot to put Jesus to death (11:45–53). John also has a lengthy farewell discourse and prayer of Jesus (13–17). Furthermore, there is no Kingdom of God teaching and there are no exorcisms and no developed parables, all of which are integral to the synoptic gospels. This combination of agreement and disagreement between the gospel of John and the synoptic gospels makes the question of John's knowledge of the synoptic gospels very difficult to resolve.

Differences in Style and Presentation

The differences in style and presentation can be illustrated by the parallels and contrasts between John 12:25–26 and Mark 8:34–35.

---

[8] Note, however, the striking parallels between the command to the paralytic here and that to the paralytic at Capernaum in Mark 2:9. They are identical.

John 12:25–26	Mark 8:34–35
He who loves his life	If any man would come
loses it, and he who hates	after me, let him deny
his life in this world will	himself and take up
keep it for eternal life.	his cross and follow me.
If anyone serves me he	For whoever would
must follow me; and where	save his life will lose
I am, there shall my servant	it; and whoever loses
be also; if any one serves me	his life for my sake and
the Father will honor him.	the gospel's will save it.

The parallels of the theme of following Jesus and losing and saving one's life indicate a relationship between the two. The differences are so great, however, that we might conclude that the texts were not related to one another directly but to a common tradition that had undergone independent development in different directions before each evangelist used it. But then we note that the differences between John and Mark represent the redactional interests of each author. In Mark's version, there are characteristic emphases on the passion and "the gospel." In John, these are absent, and what one finds are important Johannine themes: "hating life in this world"; "eternal life"; "where I am, there shall my servant be also"; "the Father will honor him." When we recognize that the Johannine material has gone through a considerable period and process of reflection and meditation it is by no means evident that John 12:25–26 does not exhibit knowledge of Mark 8:34–35.

Differences in the Order of Events

The differences in the order of the events between John and the synoptic gospels (really between John and Mark since Matthew and Luke in general follow the order of Mark) are also not grounds for denying John's knowledge of the synoptic gospels. John is simply not following the order of Mark; down to 12:37–38 he is probably building around his "signs source," which we shall discuss presently; 13–17 are thematic discourses and a prayer; from 18:1 onward we have the passion narrative. Whether he *knows* the order of Mark is a different matter, dependent on the sequence of agreements with Mark and whether John knows a passion narrative independent of that in Mark.

Sequence of Agreements with the Markan Order

Despite the great differences between John and Mark, the following events occur in the same sequence: the work of the Baptist, Jesus' departure to Galilee, the feeding of a multitude, walking on the water, Peter's confession, the departure to Jerusalem, the entry into Jerusalem and the anointing (order of

333

these two transposed by John), the supper with predictions of betrayal and denial, the arrest and the passion narrative. Apart from the fact that the gospel story necessarily climaxes in a passion narrative, this is an impressive list and can be weakened only by supposing an independent cycle of tradition linking the feeding and the walking on the water,[9] which would depend on a prior decision on other grounds that John does not know Mark. We have taken the list from C. K. Barrett's *The Gospel According to St. John*, pages 43–46, where Barrett considerably strengthens the case by pointing to a whole series of verbal similarities between John and Mark in precisely these passages that occur in the same order.

The Passion Narrative in John and Mark

The similarities and differences we have mentioned neither demonstrate that John knew the gospel of Mark nor necessarily deny it. In the passion narrative, however, the correspondence between the two gospels becomes much closer. For a long time the general opinion of New Testament scholars was that the passion narrative existed as a connected unit before the gospel of Mark was written, and it was easy and natural to think that John had known and used a version of that pre-Markan narrative rather than the gospel of Mark. But today the tendency is to ascribe more and more of the composition of the passion narrative to the evangelist Mark himself[10] and to doubt the very existence of a pre-Markan and non-Markan passion narrative extensive enough to have been the basis for the gospel of John. A particular consideration is the fact that the trial before the High Priest (John 18:19–24) is set in the context of the denial by Peter (18:15–18, 25–27), as it is also in the gospel of Mark. But there is a strong case that Mark himself originally composed this account of the trial at night before the Jewish authorities and then set it in the context of the story of Peter's denial. If this is so, the evangelist John must necessarily have known the gospel of Mark.[11]

Verbal Similarities Between John and the Other Gospels

For all the differences between the gospel of John and the other gospels, there are some verbal parallels at various points. In John and Mark there is the command to (different) paralytics in John 5:8 = Mark 2:11, "Rise, take up your pallet and go home." Equally striking are John 6:7 = Mark 6:37, "bread

---

[9] As for example in R. Fuller, *Intro.*, p. 82, n. 2.

[10] See especially W. Kelber, ed., *The Passion in Mark.*

[11] J. Donahue, *Are You the Christ? The Trial Narrative in the Gospel of Mark*, makes a convincing argument for the supposition that Mark composed the trial scene and intercalated it into the denial story in his gospel. If this is the case then John must have known Mark since he also has the trial scene and he has it in the same place.

(worth) two hundred denarii," and John 12:3 = Mark 14:3, "a pound (jar) of costly ointment of pure nard." In all three, only John and Mark among the gospels share this wording.[12] In John and Luke the argument really turns on the account of the anointing (John 12:3–8 = Luke 7:36–50). All the names in John occur in Luke at various places, and John's version of the anointing (Mary anoints Jesus' feet and wipes them with her hair, itself a not very reasonable process) is explicable if John knew the gospel of Luke, where the woman wipes Jesus' feet with her hair and then anoints them. In Mark 14:3–9, by contrast, the woman anoints Jesus' head, and there is no mention of her hair. The references to the woman anointing the feet and drying them with her hair that Luke and John have in common may indicate that John knew the Lukan account.

These are the considerations on which a decision as to whether the evangelist John knew the other gospels must be based. Obviously, they do not point overwhelmingly in one direction or the other, but they have convinced us that the gospel of John shows knowledge of the gospel of Mark, and perhaps also of the gospel of Luke. Thus, it would appear that among the sources behind the gospel lies at least one, perhaps two, of the synoptic gospels—even if the author of John did not always follow them closely.[13]

THE GOSPEL OF JOHN AND ITS SPECIAL SOURCES

Rudolf Bultmann in his important commentary of 1941 proposed that three special sources lie behind the gospel of John: a discourse source derived from Gnostic revelation discourses; a miracle collection called a "signs source"; and a passion story.[14] Long extended discourses are in fact a striking feature of the gospel; but the language and style of these discourses are so thoroughly Johannine and their thought so integral to the gospel and letters as a whole that the hypothesis of a discourse source has not found general acceptance.[15] Thus, the discourses will be considered along with John's major ideas.

The theory of a "signs source," on the other hand, has had a much more positive reception, especially in recent years.[16] In 2:11 Jesus' miracle at Cana is

---

[12] W. G. Kümmel, *Intro.*, pp. 202–03 with references.

[13] *Knowing* a gospel and following it closely as though it lay before him are not to be equated. For recent study, cf. R. Kysar, *The Fourth Evangelist and His Gospel*, pp. 54–66, and D. M. Smith, "John and the Synoptics: Some Dimensions of the Problem," *New Testament Studies* 26 (1979/80), pp. 425–44 (who evaluates the above analysis positively and still takes into account other sources behind the gospel).

[14] R. Bultmann, *The Gospel of John, passim.* Bultmann came to believe that John was independent of the synoptics.

[15] W. Marxsen is a member of the "Bultmann school" and hence sympathetic to Bultmann's views. So his judgment that Bultmann's suggestion of a discourse source is "by no means so certain as is the use of the 'signs source' " is particularly important (*Intro.*, p. 253). For a recent theory, see W. Temple, *The Core of the Fourth Gospel*.

[16] R. Kysar, *Fourth Evangelist*, pp. 13–37, discusses five theories. All agree that (*a*) the source contained seven signs, and (*b*) it ended at 20:30, perhaps including 20:31. J. Becker, a German scholar, includes 12:37–38.

described as "the first of his signs." Further signs are mentioned in general terms in 2:23, and in 4:54 the healing of the official's son at Capernaum is described as "the second sign that Jesus did when he had come from Judea to Galilee." Then 12:37 says, "Though he had done so many signs before them, yet they did not believe in him," and this note is sounded again in the closing summary of the gospel proper, 20:30–31: "Now Jesus did many other signs in the presence of the disciples, which are not written in this book; but these are written that you may believe. . . ." The possibility that in his narrative up to 12:37 the evangelist has used a source other than the synoptic gospels or the tradition represented by those gospels is strengthened since all the other miracles in John that are not paralleled in the synoptic gospels occur before 12:37: the healing at the pool of Bethzatha (5:1–9); the healing of the blind man (9:1–12); the raising of Lazarus (11:1–44). These miracles are generally on a grander and more elaborate scale than those in the synoptic gospels and seem to go further in presenting Jesus as a Hellenistic "divine man." Throughout the gospel until 12:37–38, and again in 20:30–31, the miracles are presented as intending to call forth faith: 2:11; 4:53; 6:14; 7:31; 11:45, 47b–48; 12:37–38; 20:31. Whereas in the synoptic gospels the emphasis is on faith as the prerequisite for miracles (e.g., Mark 6:5–6), here in the gospel of John miracles induce faith. These references not only contrast with the synoptic gospels, they also contrast with the remainder of the gospel of John itself. In 2:23–25 as in 4:48, Jesus repudiates the kind of faith induced by signs. The conversation with Nicodemus contrasts such faith unfavorably with rebirth "from above" and "of the spirit" (3:2, 3, 5–6). These factors make it very probable that the author of the gospel of John is using as a source and *reinterpreting* a book of signs that presents Jesus as a Hellenistic "divine man" whose miracles induce faith.[17]

The third major source, a passion story, has met with mixed responses. Some have argued that John is not dependent on the synoptics, but that the source for his passion story was also known and used by Mark and Luke, a view sometimes held by defenders of the signs source. Robert Fortna, whose views have stimulated a great deal of discussion, has taken the logical step and proposed that John used a source that contained both miracle stories *and* a passion story, that is, a "signs gospel."[18] If Fortna is correct, it would be possible to explain many of the similarities between John and the synoptics, including similarities in their passion stories, without recourse to John's dependence on one or another of the synoptics. This is precisely Fortna's position. Nonetheless, the inclusion of the passion story is not without its critics, and many still opt for a "signs source" without a passion story. If it did not contain a passion story, passion story contacts could also be explained by a knowledge of one or more of the synoptics, as argued above. If it did, it would still be

---

[17] R. Fortna, *The Gospels of Signs*, p. 231, cautiously made this connection; but he has recently raised questions about it; cf. "Christology in the Fourth Gospel; Redaction Critical Perspectives," *New Testament Studies* 21 (1974/75), pp. 489–94. A number of scholars have defended it, recently the Germans J. Becker and L. Schottroff. "Hellenistic" here should not be meant to exclude Hellenistic Judaism.

[18] R. Fortna, pp. 113–58. Cf. also H. Teeple, *The Literary Origin of the Gospel of John.*

possible to admit John knew one or more of the synoptics, though such a view would make for a far more complex relationship between the signs gospel and the synoptics.[19] Whereas a "signs source" has won a measure of acceptance and a "discourse source" has not, the verdict on the passion source is still out. If John's knowledge of Mark and perhaps Luke is maintained, as stated above, an independent passion source, whether linked with the "signs" or not, can be accepted only with extreme caution.

THE GOSPEL AND THE LETTERS

Having considered some sources behind the gospel, we now take up the question of the literary relationship between the gospel and the letters. Are they by the same author? They have a unity of general style, tone, and thought that seems to indicate they are, especially in the case of the letters and the discourses in the gospel. But a closer examination reveals a poverty of style in the first letter compared to the gospel—"the author works to death a few favorite constructions, and his vocabulary is more limited than that of the gospel"[20]—and some real differences in thought. The latter aspect of the matter is particularly important since these differences concern eschatology and the sacraments. The author of the letter has a strong hope for the future, a version of the traditional Christian hope for the parousia (2:17, 18, 28; 3:2, 3; 4:17), and he has a great interest in the sacraments of the church (2:12, 20, 27; 3:9; 5:1, 6). In the gospel of John the main thrust is toward a denial of the hope of the parousia, on the grounds that the first coming of Jesus was the decisive event and no further coming, no further judgment, is to be expected (3:16–21, 36, and elsewhere). But throughout the gospel are individual sayings that express the more traditional Christian hope (5:27–29; 6:39–40, 44b, 54; 12:48). Similarly with the sacraments: the gospel as a whole puts its major emphasis on the idea that men are brought to faith by their response to the church's proclamation (3:31–36 and elsewhere), and has no particular concern for the sacraments. Yet the words "water and" in 3:5 make that verse an unmistakable reference to baptism, where no such reference exists apart from those two words; 6:51b–58 makes the discourse on the bread of life sacramental, whereas without those verses it is not; and 19:34b–35 introduces an allusion to baptism as it interrupts the continuity of the narrative.

These indications suggest that the gospel has been redacted from an original text with no future parousia hope or concern for the sacraments, and that such hope and concern were introduced into the gospel by the author of the first letter.[21] If this is the case (and it is all very tentative), the main text of the

---

[19] D. M. Smith, who has in the past tended to favor independence to the extent of suggesting a plausible context for a Fortna-like "signs gospel," appears now to lean more toward John's *knowledge* of the synoptics as based on the above arguments, cf. *n*. 13 above.

[20] R. Fuller, *Intro.*, p. 178.

[21] Suggested by W. Marxsen, *Intro.*, p. 262, who sees the author of 1 John as a member of a group who redacted the original text of the gospel in the interests of the church's views on eschatology and the sacraments.

gospel is by one author and the first letter by another. Are either of these authors the "presbyter" who wrote the second and third letters? There are similarities of language and thought, yet there are small subtle differences.[22] We simply do not know; the most we can say is that probably at least two authors are involved in the gospels and letters of John, and perhaps three.

A natural question is whether the same person, who may possibly have been the author of the first letter, added chapter 21 and the redaction in the interest of the parousia and the sacraments. This is another question whose answer we simply do not have, but it is interesting that in 21:22 the traditional Christian parousia hope is implied.

Though it is possible that the original gospel of John had been redacted by someone with more interest in the parousia hope and sacraments of the church, there is no textual evidence for this redaction of the gospel. We do not know of any text of the gospel ever circulated that did not include the references to the future hope and sacraments of the church. If the redaction took place—and we think it did—it occurred before any text of the gospel actually circulated outside the persons who redacted it.

THE EVANGELIST AND THE PROBLEMS OF THE CHRISTIANITY OF HIS DAY

In speaking of "the evangelist," we have in mind the author of John apart from 7:53–8:11, the story of the adulteress, and chapter 21.[23] John 21:20–24, as we noted above, probably names him as "the disciple whom Jesus loved," which later church tradition took to be the disciple of Jesus, John son of Zebedee.[24] Literary, source, form, and redaction studies, by positing sources and traditions behind the gospel and additions to it, make the second-century traditional belief that he was one of the Twelve highly unlikely.[25] Some have sought a mediating position by suggesting the Johannine traditions *go back* to one of the Twelve, i.e., the son of Zebedee is "author" indirectly. Most modern critics, however, believe that the evangelist is anonymous; one view is that he is "the disciple whom Jesus loved," an anonymous disciple from the time of Jesus but outside the Twelve, and therefore not the son of Zebedee. More common is the view that maintains that the anonymous evangelist's traditions *went back* to an equally anonymous eyewitness disciple outside the Twelve, who again is not the author.[26] Others suggest that the anonymous evangelist draws on traditions from the Beloved Disciple who was not an eyewitness, but a revered member of the Johannine community, or that he is a symbolic figure with no actual historical reality. What is clear among modern critics is that he

---

[22] The differences are listed in W. G. Kümmel, *Intro.*, p. 315, but Kümmel himself dismisses them as "too trivial to be taken seriously."

[23] See above, n. 7.

[24] See the discussion in R. Kysar, *Fourth Gospel*, pp. 86–101 for the views that follow.

[25] See pp. 330–31, above.

[26] This is now the revised view of R. Brown, *The Community of the Beloved Disciple*, pp. 31–34.

is anonymous, but that he relies heavily on his special traditions, which he then modifies to meet the needs of his community.

Even if the identity of the author is unknown, more can be said about problems of his own day. To those we now turn.

The Destruction of Jerusalem

In attempting to date all of the gospels, we have noted possible oblique references to the destruction of Jerusalem in A.D. 70. John's gospel seems to make such a reference in the mouths of the chief priests and Pharisees: "If we let him go on thus (performing signs), every one will believe in him, and the Romans will come and destroy both our holy place and our nation" (11:48). Such a reference points to a date after the destruction of Jerusalem.

The Question of the Delay of the Parousia

If Q and Mark still maintained the nearness of the parousia, if Matthew held on to the parousia hope but reflected more consciously on the nature of the church, and if the author of Luke-Acts pushed the parousia off into the indefinite future in line with his view of salvation history, there is a sense in which the gospel of John has dispensed with it altogether—or better, he has so reinterpreted eschatology that its realities are already present in Christ. We noted this feature above and we shall note this again in connection with his major ideas, but it should be said at this point that John does not maintain views characteristic of traditional Jewish Christian apocalyptic.

The Conflict with the Jewish Synagogue

J. Louis Martyn is a recent proponent of a view that has won much acceptance, namely, that the gospel of John represents a "two-level drama": on one level there is his account of Jesus, on the other there is his concern for his community's present conflict with the synagogue.[27] We might say that if Matthew's account reflects a Christianity still in dialogue with the "synagogue across the street," John's story reflects an outright antagonism to those he labels "the Jews." Thus, the fourth evangelist seems to suggest a break with the synagogue. In three instances he refers to those who are "put out of the synagogue" (9:22; 12:42; 16:2). "The picture is that of a defensive Jewish community attempting to preserve its identity over against the onslaught of Christian evangelism, experiencing a growing number of apostates in its midst, and even harboring 'secret Christians' who held a private Christian faith in the effort to maintain their identification with the Jewish community."[28] An illuminating

---

[27] J. L. Martyn, *History and Theology in the Fourth Gospel; The Gospel of John in Christian History.*
[28] R. Kysar, *Fourth Evangelist,* p. 150.

example is found in the story of the healing of the man born blind in chapter 9 where we read, "the Jews had already agreed that if anyone should confess him to be Christ, he was to be put out of the synagogue" (9:22). This is to be considered a reference to a benediction introduced into Jewish synagogue worship by the rabbis meeting at Jamnia after the fall of Jerusalem.[29] It ran as follows:

> For the apostates let there be no hope
> And let the arrogant government be
> speedily uprooted in our days.
> Let the Nazarenes [Christians] and
> the Minim [heretics] be destroyed
> in a moment.
> And let them be blotted out of the
> Book of life and not be inscribed
> together with the righteous.
> Blessed art thou, O Lord, who humblest
> the proud!

The reorganization of Judaism that became necessary after the catastrophe of the Jewish War needed to establish the unity of the Jewish community and guard it against the threat of heresy. The worldwide Jewish community no longer had the geographical center of Jerusalem and its Temple; it became urgent to establish a center of theological belief and religious practice and to protect that center against the corrosion of heterodoxy and heresy. The benediction was one way of achieving this end, because its presence in the synagogue liturgy would force out of the synagogue community those who knew themselves to be designated Nazarenes or Minim. The most plausible date for the composition of this benediction and its introduction into the synagogue liturgy is A.D. 80–90.

The Date of the Gospel of John

The reference to the destruction of Jerusalem, the paucity of traditional Jewish Christian apocalyptic thought, and the conflict of the Johannine community with the Jewish synagogue all point to a context in the late first century A.D. This is reinforced by John's knowledge of Mark and possibly Luke. Moreover, textual evidence at the other end is supportive. The earliest text we have of any part of the New Testament is a fragment of the gospel of John. It is a papyrus fragment containing parts of John 18:31–33, 37–38, discovered in Egypt, and scholars consider it to have been written in the first half of the second century.[30] The gospel must have been written early enough for it to have circulated in Egypt early in the second century. A date later than A.D. 100

---

[29] R. Brown, *The Gospel According to John*, vol. 1, p. LXXXV.
[30] R. Brown, p. LXXXIII with references.

is, therefore, hardly likely. It seems probable that the gospel of John is to be dated about A.D. 90–100.

THE THOUGHT WORLD AND MAJOR IDEAS OF THE GOSPEL OF JOHN

It is one of the interesting facts of Christian history that the gospel of John became the favorite gospel of many Gnostic churches which were viewed as heretical by the Great Church,[31] while at the same time it became determinative for the Catholic Church's formulation of its official view of Jesus Christ in the fourth and fifth century creeds. It will be useful at this point to examine briefly the intellectual ambiance from which the gospel emerged.

The Intellectual Environment of the Evangelist

As the section above indicates, the fourth gospel was written sometime near the end of the first Christian century in a place where some members of John's community had been excluded from the synagogue. This points to a Jewish environment. There are many other aspects of the gospel which suggest a Jewish atmosphere: the detection of Aramaic language background; clear knowledge of the Old Testament; parallels with Aramaic paraphrases of the Old Testament (the Targums); interpretation of the Old Testament typical of rabbinic midrash (e.g., John 6); a Christology deeply indebted to myth of a descending and ascending figure of Wisdom; and connections of John's dualism with the light and darkness dualism of the Dead Sea Scrolls. Yet the gospel was written in Greek and, as noted, apocalyptic is not a characteristic feature of the gospel. Moreover, there are other features that indicate contact with the far-flung Hellenistic mystery religions and a quasi-Gnostic dualism. These features point to a highly diversified and complex religious background. Can one be more precise about late first-century Judaism? C. K. Barrett has studied this problem and concludes the following:[32] (a) that this period—with few exceptions—saw the end of Jewish apocalyptic, for this expression of Jewish faith had fulfilled its purpose; (b) that Gnostic concepts had already before A.D. 70 penetrated Judaism, as Qumran shows, but the gnosticizing of Judaism continued, particularly in those circles in which Judaism came into contact with Christianity (Ignatius); that (c) at the same time a new institutional development began, for after the destruction of the Temple increased emphasis was laid upon those observances whose execution was not bound to the Temple, and it was these which furthered the cohesiveness of the nation and strengthened it against the threat of heresy and disintegration. Some scholars,

---

[31] T. Pollard, *Johannine Christology and the Early Church*; D. Duling, *Jesus Christ Through History*, chapter III.

[32] C. K. Barrett, *The Gospel of John and Judaism*, p. 58.

partly in reaction against Bultmann, would reject the Gnostic background in point (b).[33] Others, however, still defend some connection with an early form of Gnosticism citing among other things the parallels in the newly discovered Coptic Gnostic texts from Nag Hammadi.[34] Certainly no one would deny the diversified nature of John's Jewish environment, a milieu which may also include the influence of rabbinic-type interpretation of the Old Testament and Samaritan thinking about Moses! It seems all observers acknowledge a highly complex environment which might, for want of precise language, be called syncretistic Hellenistic Judaism.

Johannine Theological Ideas

The major Johannine theological ideas can be outlined as follows.[35]

1. Christology. For John, Jesus fulfills all the Old Testament messianic expectations—Lamb of God, Chosen One of God, Messiah, King of Israel, the new Elijah—and in all of these, he is vastly superior to John the Baptist (1:19–51). But the center of John's Christology is that Jesus is the mysterious "man from heaven,"[36] the Son of Man, or simply Son (of the Father). He is not the *apocalyptic* Son of Man derived from Daniel and characteristic of certain passages in the synoptic gospels; rather, he originates from his Father in heaven, *descends* to earth as one "sent" from his Father (8:42) or as one who "came" from God, stays for a period (7:33), and *ascends* to his Father again (3:13–15; 6:62; 8:14; 16:28). He is as close to the Father as one can imagine (10:30) and yet he is subordinate to the Father (14:28) and is the Father's representative dispensing judgment (5:22, 27) and "eternal life" (3:13–15; 6:27; 6:53). He reveals God's "glory" (13:31). His ascent is also his being "lifted up," which is given a double meaning in terms of his being "lifted up" on the Cross (3:13–15; 8:28; 13:34–36). He is God's *only* son (3:16,18), and responding to Jesus is equivalent to responding to the Father. "The Jews" and a disciple do not understand his origins (6:41–42; 3:11–13). Ultimately, he is a stranger from another world (8:23).

It was noted in the discussion of sources that the revelation discourses represent John's own theology. One of the central themes of the discourses is the statement "I Am," sometimes without a predicate, sometimes with an implied predicate, sometimes with an explicit predicate (6:35: "I am the bread of life"; 8:12: "I am the light of the world"; 10:11,14: "I am the good shepherd,"

---

[33] R. Kysar, *Fourth Evangelist*, p. 145, argues that the pre-Christian syncretistic Gnostic hypothesis is on the decline in recent research.

[34] G. MacRae, "The Ego-Proclamation in Gnostic Sources," *The Trial of Jesus*, ed. E. Bammel, pp. 123–39; cf. also D. M. Smith, "Johannine Christianity: Some Reflections on Its Character and Delineation," *New Testament Studies* 21 (1974/75), pp. 238–44; *John* (Proclamation Commentaries), chapter 1.

[35] R. Kysar, *John, the Maverick Gospel; Fourth Evangelist*, Part III.

[36] W. Meeks, "The Man from Heaven in Johannine Sectarianism," *Journal of Biblical Literature* 91 (1972), pp. 44–72.

etc.). The sayings with no predicate seem to have a background in the Old Testament (Exod 3:14); those with a predicate are like those known in various Hellenistic religions (the Coptic Gnostic texts; the Hermetic literature; the Mandaean literature; the Isis mystery cult). One example comes from the Hermatic literature in connection with the revealer Poimandres:

> [The revealer appears to the speaker in a vision] "Who are you?" I said. "I am Poimandres," said he, "the Mind of the Sovereignty. I know what you wish, and I am with you everywhere. . . . Keep in mind the things you wish to learn and I will teach you."[37]

Clearly, the "I Am" sayings are intended to signal the revelation of a god.

We may also note the concept of the *Logos*, or "Word," the preexistent mythical wisdom figure who participates in the act of creation, a figure from the realm of Light. This idea, well known in Hellenistic Judaism, will be discussed in connection with the Johannine prologue (1:1–18).

The Christology of John's gospel is one of the best illustrations of myth in the New Testament; it should be noted this Johannine myth would naturally be an irritant to Judaism as understood at the Council of Jamnia.

2. Dualism. The fourth gospel is characterized by a set of symbolic opposites: light/darkness; life/death; God/Satan; above/below; heaven/earth; spirit/flesh; truth/falsehood; (true) Israel/"the Jews"; belief/unbelief. This dualism is not simply the *temporal*, or horizontal, dualism which contrasts "this world" and "the world to come" as known in Jewish apocalyptic eschatology; it may have roots in this type of thinking, but it is much more "cosmic" (*kosmos* = "world"), or *vertical*, a contrast between the heavenly world above and the earthly world below. But this dualism also has a human, personal dimension, that is, the way of "the world" is a sinful, inauthentic existence contrary to God's plan. In short, "the world" has become so corrupted by Satan (12:31) that it falls on the negative, earthly side of "darkness" (8:12), and is in need of redemption by a loving God who sends the man from another world (3:16), the world of light. Clearly, a document that is so negative to "the world" implies that it—like apocalyptic literature—proceeds out of a community that has experienced alienation from the dominant political and religious structures, an observation which corresponds with the theory of expulsion from the synagogue.

3. Signs and Faith. Above, it was suggested that the evangelist reinterpreted a "signs source" which presented Jesus as a "divine man" whose miracles induce faith. If so, how did John reinterpret them? The clearest point is that the evangelist used them as the basis for the first part of his work (2:1–12:50), viewing them as actions which become the occasion for lengthy monologues and dialogues. With regard to specific miracles, it seems at first that the evangelist used them in the same manner as the source, that is, they lead disciples and others to faith (cf. 2:11, 25; 20:30–31), and they prove his Messiahship

[37] C. H. Dodd, *The Interpretation of the Fourth Gospel*, pp. 10–53; C. K. Barrett, *New Testament Background*, pp. 80–90. Our quote is from Barrett, p. 82.

(2:18). Yet, "seeing" a sign can mean *more* than understanding Jesus as a wonder-worker miraculously capable of providing basic needs, such as food (6:26); and others do *not* respond to signs with faith (12:37). These subtleties about the impact of signs seem to be reinforced by 4:48 where Jesus responds to the request of the Capernaum official's son for healing by what appears on the surface to be a negative statement: "Unless you see signs and wonders you will not believe." Thus, the evangelist understands "signs" in a more complex manner: (*a*) not all who see signs *truly* "see" and believe; (*b*) some do "see" and believe, or perhaps "see" *because* they are open to faith; (*c*) some who "see" see more than the mere performance of a sign, that is, they "see" spiritually, beyond material needs;[38] (*d*) and some may not need signs at all: "Blessed are those who have not seen and yet believe" (20:29). There seem, then, to be different levels of perception of "signs," and some qualitative difference among them, suggesting to at least one scholar stages in the maturation of faith.[39] Whether this is the case or not, it seems clear that John sees a multileveled, dynamic interaction between signs and faith, or to put it another way, between religious experience and religious knowledge. This view can be correlated with his subtle view of faith and knowledge throughout the gospel.[40]

4. Eschatology. The eschatology of the fourth evangelist is rooted in his Christology, that is, acts that are normally associated with the *future*—the coming of the Messiah, resurrection, judgment, eternal life—are already *present* for the believer in the encounter with Jesus. If for Mark past, present, and future flow together in an apocalyptic drama that nonetheless throws the momentum toward the near future, in John past, present, and future are collapsed into a focus on the present. In contemporary scholarship, such a view has been called "realized eschatology" (C. H. Dodd). It is one way of responding to the delay of the parousia. To be sure, futurist eschatology in John is not totally lacking (cf. e.g., 5:28–29; 6:39–40, 44, 54; 12:48). There may also be a *type* of parousia that suggests Jesus will return and take the Christian to his heavenly home, perhaps at death (14:2–3). This, of course, is not the traditional apocalyptic view, but neither is it realized eschatology. In general, the futurist eschatology might have been preserved from the tradition or, as suggested above, it might have come from a member of a Johannine "school" who subsequently redacted the gospel to bring it more into line with traditional views. The evangelist's own view is characterized more by 5:24: "Truly, truly, I say to you, he who hears my word and believes him who sent me, has eternal life; he does not come into judgment, but has passed from death to life."

5. Spirit, Church, and Sacraments. The stress on the present in John's eschatology is matched by his view of the presence of the Spirit among believers. The special term for the Spirit in John 14–16 is Paraclete (Greek *paraklētos*; cf. 14:15–17, 25–26; 15:26–27; 16:5–11, 12–15). Literally, it means "the one called beside," but it can mean (*a*) "Advocate" or "Intercessor," that is, a defense

---

[38] R. Fortna, *The Gospel of Signs*, makes this his major focus.
[39] R. Kysar, *John, The Maverick Gospel*, pp. 70–73.
[40] R. Kysar, *John, The Maverick Gospel*, pp. 73–82.

attorney before God in behalf of the Christian; (*b*) "Comforter" or "Counselor" to the Christian; and (*c*) "Exhorter" or "Proclaimer." Like the Stranger from heaven, the Paraclete comes from the Father at the request of Jesus, or in Jesus' name after Jesus departs, or alternatively he is sent by the departed Jesus himself. He represents, then, the continued and recognized presence of Christ. He is a prophet teaching his believers and bearing witness and glorifying Christ, recalling all that Jesus said. In fact, Jesus is viewed as the first Paraclete in relation to "another Paraclete" (14:16). Like Jesus, the Paraclete is rejected by "the world"; it does not recognize him. But the Paraclete convicts "the world" of sin because it did not believe in Jesus.

The fourth evangelist, unlike Matthew and Luke, seems to have no interest in the organized institutional church. He mentions no church officials and he normally refers simply to "the disciples." In fact, Peter's role (and the apostolic church related to him) is devalued in contrast to the role of the Beloved Disciple. John seems more concerned with believers in general. As Christ is one with the Father and manifests his glory, so believers are one in Christ and manifest his glory (17:22–23); as God loved "the world" and gave his Son (3:16), so the Son loves his followers and they are to love one another (15:17). It would appear that John shares an important characteristic with apocalyptic Christianity: its "expulsion" from the synagogue seems to have led to a somewhat sectarian, "free" association with regard to the "church." We shall return to this issue in our conclusion.

Finally, the fourth evangelist did not lay emphasis on the sacraments; true, we catch glimpses of *possible* sacramental language (3:5: "water and"; 6:51–58), but these are highly debated, and in any case they may be the product of a member of the Johannine school wishing to be more explicit about sacramental matters.

In summary, the major Johannine ideas may be stated: "the world" below has become dominated by sin so that God the Father in his love sends his preexistent Son who descends, works signs, reveals himself in revelatory discourses, undergoes a passion and ascends, his Spirit-Paraclete being an Advocate and Comforter of believers who, without necessity of ecclesiastical structures and sacraments, already experience resurrection and eternal life now, in the present.

DISPLACEMENTS WITHIN THE TEXT OF THE GOSPEL

The redaction critical approach to determining the main emphases of a gospel writer relies in part on the ability to determine how an evangelist modifies and interprets his sources. It also attempts to learn about the writer's intentions by the way he structures his material as a whole and, as we noted in the case of Mark, this becomes especially important when the sources used are more tentative. The problems with regard to structure are especially complicated in this particular instance. The careful reader of the gospel of John is struck by a number of inconsistencies in the narrative. For example, 3:31–36 simply does not fit the theme of the testimony of the Baptist but reads more like a follow-up of 3:16–21. Is it possible that 3:22–30 is out of place and should be read as following 2:12? Again, in 6:1 it is presupposed that Jesus is in Galilee, though in 5:1 he is already in Jerusalem. Should chapters 5, 6, and 7 be read in the order 6, 5, 7? John 7:15–24 is concerned with the plot against Jesus' life reported in 5:18 and reads like the natural continuation of 5:47, whereas 14:1, 25–31 is also a very natural sequence. Did 7:15–24 originally follow 5:47? In 14:31 Jesus says "Rise, let us go hence," yet the discourses continue for three more chapters. Does 14:31 belong after 17:26 as the conclusion of the discourses?

There is no doubt that the flow of the narrative would be improved by answering these questions in the affirmative and making the necessary transpositions. However, once we begin to do this the question becomes, where do we stop? Bultmann, for example, in *The Gospel of John* comments on the text in an order that is extraordinarily complex, and one has the feeling that equally good arguments could be made for a different arrangement. In a text as reflective and meditative in character as the gospel of John, narrative consistency is not to be expected, and if there are displacements within the text they do not affect our general understanding of it. In our exegetical survey below we shall accept only the first of the possibilities mentioned here.

THE STRUCTURE OF THE GOSPEL[41]

The gospel of John falls naturally into five main parts:

1. **Introduction: Prologue and Testimony, 1:1–51.** In the prologue (1:1–18) a christological hymn is presented with comments, and then a series of incidents bring John the Baptist on the scene to give his testimony to Jesus, testimony confirmed by some of his disciples.

2. **The Book of Signs, 2:1–12:50.** Even before the general recognition of the use of a "signs source" in this part of the gospel, C. H. Dodd recognized the essential nature of these narratives by giving it this title.

3. **Farewell Discourses and Prayer for the Church, 13:1–17:26.** These discourses and the prayer are found in the context of the Lord's Supper (13:2; compare 1 Cor 11:20), and they meditate on the nature, meaning, and significance of the passion of Jesus.

4. **Passion Narrative, 18:1–20:30.**

5. **Epilogue: The Appearance in Galilee, 21:1–25.**

Dodd points out that there is a characteristic Johannine pattern of narration.[42] It consists of the following elements, as seen in John, chapter 5:

---

[41] In what follows we are deeply indebted to C. H. Dodd, *The Interpretation of the Fourth Gospel*.
[42] C. H. Dodd, p. 400.

Action: 5:1-9 (healing at Bethzatha)
Dialogue: 5:10-18 (Sabbath healing)
Monologue: 5:19-40
Appendix: 5:41-47

Or it can be, as in chapter 6:

Action and Dramatic Dialogue: 6:1-23 (feeding of the multitude)
Dialogue Tending to Monologue: 6:24-59 (bread of life)
Two Brief Concluding Dialogues: 6:60-65, 66-71

Or it can be, as in chapters 9 and 10:

Action: 9:1-7 (healing at Siloam)
Dialogues: 9:8-41 (trial scene and two brief colloquies)
Monologue: 10:1-18
Brief Concluding Dialogue: 10:19-21
Appendix: 10:22-39

The farewell discourses and prayer follow this pattern, except that in this instance we have the action, the passion narrative, coming last and not first.

Opening Dramatic Scene: 13:1-30
Dialogue: 13:31-14:31 (on Christ's departure and return)
Monologue: 15:1-16:15 (on Christ and his Church)
Concluding Dialogue: 16:16-33
Appendix: 17:1-26 (the prayer for the Church)
Action: 18:1-20:31 (the passion narrative; anticipated in 13:1-3)

This is a very important structural observation, and we take it seriously as we attempt the following exegetical survey of the gospel, though at some points our analysis differs slightly from Dodd's; for example, our experience with the other gospels has led us to pay particular attention to transitional passages.

EXEGETICAL SURVEY OF THE GOSPEL OF JOHN

Introduction: Prologue and Testimony, 1:1-51

Prologue, 1:1-18

The prologue consists of a hymn with comments. As reconstructed and translated by R. E. Brown, the hymn reads as follows:[43]

---

[43] Excerpts from *The Gospel According to John* by Raymond E. Brown, copyright © 1970 by Doubleday & Company, Inc. Brown's translation and discussion of the hymn are in vol. 1, pp. 3-23. See also D. M. Smith, *John* (Proclamation Commentaries), chapter 3.

1 In the beginning was the Word;
   the Word was in God's presence,
   and the Word was God.

2 He was present with God in the beginning.

3 Through him all things came into being,
   and apart from him not a thing came to be.

4 That which had come to be in him was life,
   and this life was the light of men.

5 The light shines in darkness,
   for the darkness did not overcome it.

10 He was in the world,
   and the world was made by him;
   Yet the world did not recognize him.

11 To his own he came;
   Yet his own people did not accept him.

12 But all those who did accept him
   he empowered to become God's children.

14 And the Word became flesh
   and made his dwelling among us.
   And we have seen his glory,
   the glory of an only Son coming from the Father,
   filled with enduring love.

16 And of his fullness
   we have all had a share—
   love in place of love.

The comments on this hymn are in effect the testimony of the Baptist (verses 6–8), the reference to being born "of God" (verse 13), further testimony of the Baptist (verse 15), and the evangelist's climactic summary (verses 17–18). These comments all represent important themes to the evangelist, which are further developed in the gospel: the testimony of the Baptist (1:19–42); being born of God is the theme of the dialogue with Nicodemus (3:1–15); while verses 17–18 are a summary of the whole gospel, not only of the prologue. The hymn itself presents features foreign to the gospel—in the gospel after the prologue Jesus is never called the Logos nor is the phrase *grace and truth* found—but its presentation of Jesus as the preexistent redeemer who manifested his glory in the world matches exactly the major aspects of the gospel's presentation of Jesus. In its presentation of Jesus as the redeemer who descends to the world the hymn shares the emphasis of the other christological hymns we discussed in chapter 3.

Testimony, 1:19–51; 3:22–30

The theme of testimony, prominent in the comments on the hymn in the prologue is now developed with regard to John the Baptist, and with regard to some of his disciples who become disciples of Jesus. Originally, 3:22–30 followed 1:51. It has been accidentally displaced.

The Book of Signs, 2:1–12:50

The first major section of the gospel, the Book of Signs, is built on the skeleton framework of seven miracle stories or "signs." These are as follows:

- Changing water into wine at Cana (2:1–11)
- Curing the official's son at Cana (4:46–54)
- Curing the paralytic at Bethzatha (5:1–15)
- Miraculous feeding in Galilee (6:1–15)
- Walking on the water (6:16–21)
- Curing the blind man in Jerusalem (9)
- Raising of Lazarus in Bethany (11)

In addition, there is a series of three consecutive thematic concerns:[44]

- (a) From Cana to Cana—Jesus manifests his glory in various ways and elicits various responses (2:1–4:42)
- (b) Jesus and the principal feasts of the Jews (5:1–10:39)
- (c) Jesus moves toward the hour of his glorification (11:1–12:50)

With these observations as our starting point and with Dodd's compositional insight as our guide, we offer the following exegetical survey of the Book of Signs.

Manifestation and Response, 2:1–4:42

Action
The first sign: the miracle at Cana, 2:1–11. It is explicitly stated that this is the first of the signs through which Jesus manifested his glory, and that it elicited the response of faith (verse 11).

    Transition, 2:12.

The anticipation of the final sign: the cleansing of the Temple in Jerusalem, 2:13–22. The cleansing of the Temple is not itself a sign, but it anticipates the climactic sign, the resurrection. In turn, the resurrection elicits the response of faith (verse 22).

    Transitional summary, 2:23–25.

Dialogue
Jesus and Nicodemus, 3:1–15. This dialogue is built on the theme of the new birth (compare the theme of being born "of God" in the prologue). It climaxes in a Son of Man saying (verses 14–15), which is itself a major statement of the Johannine theology of "the man from heaven."

---

[44] On this we are indebted to R. E. Brown, *John,* vol. 1, CXL–CXLI.

Monologue

The power of the Son to give eternal life to the believer, 3:16–21. The evangelist now
moves into a monologue developing the theme of the Son's power to give
eternal life to the believer, stated in the preceding verse. The traditional
Christian future eschatology has been replaced by an eschatology realized
in the present (a realized eschatology): "This is the judgment . . ." (verse
19). The farewell discourses parallel the same theme (12:46–48), where,
however, the traditional eschatology has been restored ("the word that I
have spoken will be his judge on the last day," 12:48). An editor has
apparently made the reference to baptism more explicit in 3:5.

A displaced section of monologue, 3:31–36. John 3:22–30 originally belonged after
1:51. But what about 3:31–36, obviously part of a monologue by the Johannine Jesus on the theme of witness, testimony, and belief? It does not
fit well after 3:21; perhaps it originally belonged after 3:15, where it would
certainly fit better, but we cannot be sure.

Action

Jesus moves to Samaria, 4:1–6.

Dialogue

Jesus with the woman, 4:7–21. The dialogue turns on two themes, "living water"
and worship "in spirit and truth." Water is a universal symbol for life, and
worship is a universal religious practice. John develops them in his characteristic dualism by contrasting "this" and "living" water, false worship
and true.

Monologue

The coming of the true worship, 4:22–26. The second theme of the dialogue now
develops in a short but characteristic monologue culminating in an interchange between Jesus and the woman and in a messianic claim by Jesus.
The theme of living water is not further developed here; the evangelist
will return to that later.

Appendix

Further dialogue and testimony in Samaria, 4:27–42.

Transition to Galilee, 4:43–45.

The second sign: the official's son in Capernaum, 4:46–54. While in Cana, Jesus heals
an official's son from a distance. This second sign in Cana marks the end
of the first section of the Book of Signs. It ends as it had begun—in Cana
and with a sign.

Jesus and the Jewish Festivals, 5:1–10:39

The second section of the Book of Signs explores the significance of Jesus
as understood in the symbolism and meaning of the great Jewish religious
festivals and observances.

Jesus and the Sabbath, 5:1–47. The Sabbath is a weekly observance, built on
Gen 2:3: "so God blessed the seventh day and hallowed it, because on it God

rested from all his work which he had done in creation." The Jews kept, and still keep, this day of the week free from work for religious observance, to link themselves ever more closely with God. This observance led to the question of what was to be considered "work" on the Sabbath, which is the background for such synoptic gospel controversy stories as Mark 2:23–27, the Plucking of the Grain. In the fourth gospel, however, the aspect of controversy between Jesus and the Jews as to what "work" was lawful on the Sabbath has been transformed into a meditation on the fact that Jesus "works" as God "works," to give life to the dead and to judge.

Transitional verse, 5:1. This verse speaks of a "feast," i.e., a religious festival, but the term is used broadly, since the concern is not with an annual religious observance but with the Sabbath.

Action

Jesus heals a lame man on the Sabbath, 5:2–9. The exact parallelism between the command to this paralytic (5:8) and that to a paralytic in Capernaum in Mark 2:9 is striking; it is cause for arguing that John knew the gospel of Mark. But the meditative character of the Johannine narrative is such that it leaves in the dark how far and in what ways this story is related to Mark 2:1–12. All the narratives in the Book of Signs have been so transformed into vehicles for meditation on the significance of Jesus for the believer that historical questions about them are all but impossible to answer.

Dialogue

A series of dialogues between the Jews, the man, and Jesus, 5:10–18. By means of these dialogues, the evangelist introduces the theme of the relationship between Jesus and God. Jesus is the Son of the Father, and equal with God.

Monologue

Jesus' relation to God, 5:19–47. This monologue explores the relationship of Jesus and God. Jesus is the Son of God, and as such his actions are identical with those of God: he judges, and he gives life to the dead.

Jesus and the Passover, 6:1–71. The passover celebrates the deliverance of the Jewish people from Egypt. It is observed annually by a meal in which the food eaten and the wine drunk symbolize this deliverance and anticipate the final eschatological deliverance. The Christian Eucharist was based on the Passover and uses much of the same symbolism. The evangelist John now explores the significance of Jesus in terms of Passover and Eucharistic symbols.

Action

The feeding of the multitude, 6:1–14. Transitional verse, 6:15.

The walking on the water, 6:16–21. The two incidents of a miraculous feeding and a sea miracle undoubtedly come to John through the tradition of the church, and probably through the gospel of Mark, which has them in exactly the same sequence: Mark 6:30–44 (feeding); 45–51 (walking on the water). John's gospel maintains them because they both have parallels in the narrative of the deliverance from Egypt: the Jews miraculously crossed the sea (Exod 14:21–25) and were equally miraculously fed in the wilderness (Exod 16:13–16, "It is the bread which the Lord has given you to eat." In Exod 16:31 this bread is called *manna*).

Dialogue

A dialogue between Jesus and the Jews on the bread that God gives to man, 6:22–34. John follows his usual pattern of introducing the theme of the ensuing monologue by means of a dialogue. The theme is the "bread of life," and it evokes both the manna of the wilderness and the bread of the Eucharist.

Monologue

Jesus as the bread of life, 6:35–40.

Dialogue

The bread of life is the flesh of Jesus, the bread of the Eucharist, 6:41–59. The theme of Jesus as the "bread of life" is developed in a monologue, which in turn is followed by a dramatic dialogue. The manna the Jews ate in the wilderness has become a symbol of the life-giving power of God to his people, which is now fulfilled forever in Jesus. The life-giving power of Jesus is in turn symbolized in the bread of the Christian Eucharist.

Appendix

Jesus and his disciples, 6:60–70. In its theme, this passage is strikingly reminiscent of the misunderstanding and confession in Mark 8:14–21.

Transition to the feast of Tabernacles, 7:1–13. Jesus is now to be considered in light of the symbolism of a further major Jewish festival, the feast of Tabernacles.

Jesus and the feast of Tabernacles, 7:14–10:21. The feast of Tabernacles was held in the autumn. It was originally an agricultural festival celebrating the harvest, but in the course of time it came also to celebrate the constant renewal of the covenant between God and his people. This latter fact makes it natural to take up here the theme of Jesus as the one who fulfills the old covenant as the Jewish Messiah. So in this section the evangelist explores the messianic claims of Jesus and also makes extensive use of the literary device of dramatic dialogues between Jesus and his Jewish opponents about those claims.

Action

Jesus in the Temple at Tabernacles, 7:14.

Dialogue

The claim of Jesus to be the Christ, 7:15–36. This is a series of three dramatic dialogues. The first (verses 15–24) concerns the authority of Jesus to heal on the Sabbath; the second (verses 25–31) deals with the claim of Jesus to be the Christ by the signs he has done; the third (verses 32–36) introduces the theme of the death of Jesus. This last will loom larger and larger from this point on in the gospel, until it dominates everything else as the theme of the farewell discourses.

Action

Jesus makes a personal claim to be the Living Water, 7:37–39. At the feast of Tabernacles, water was ceremoniously carried from the Pool of Siloam to the Temple as a reminder of the water miraculously supplied in the wilderness (Num 20:2–13) and as a symbol of the coming of the Messiah as the "water of life" (Isa 12:3). The evangelist has the opportunity to return to the theme of Jesus as the water of life, which he had first stated in the dialogue between Jesus and the woman of Samaria in chapter 4.

Dialogue

The Jews dispute among themselves concerning the claim of Jesus to be the Christ, 7:40–52. Unlike the previous dialogues, these do not feature Jesus at all but present the Jews in dispute among themselves concerning the validity of his claims.

[The adulteress story, 7:53–8:11, is not part of the original text of the gospel.]

Action

Jesus makes a personal claim to be the Light of the World, 8:12. A further feature of the symbolism of the feast of Tabernacles was the ceremonious lighting of lamps in the Temple court. The evangelist can return to the theme of Jesus as the Light of the World, a theme first stated in the prologue (1:4–5, 9).

Dialogue

The validity of Jesus' claims, 8:13–20. The Jews are presented as disputing with Jesus the validity of the claims he is making. This dialogue concludes on a further note of anticipation of the passion (verse 20).

Action

Jesus condemns the Jews, 8:21. The theme of the death of Jesus understood as his going where he cannot be followed (i.e., back to the heavenly region he came from) is developed at length in the farewell discourses (13:31–14:7). Here is its first statement in the context of a condemnation of the Jews, who cannot follow him. In the farewell discourses, the disciples are promised that they will be able to follow them.

Dialogue

Jesus and the Jews who do not believe in him, 8:22–30. Jesus is here presented as debating vigorously with, and condemning, the Jews who did not believe in him.

Action

Jesus and the Jews who did believe in him, 8:31–32. Jesus is now presented as making promises to the Jews who did believe in him.

Dialogue

Jesus and the natural claims of the Jews on God, 8:33–59. This dialogue begins with the Jews who did believe in Jesus and ends with those same Jews taking up stones to throw at him: here is the evangelist wrestling with the problem of the Jewish rejection of Jesus. Jesus himself had had some success in his mission to the Jewish people—he had attracted disciples—yet the Jews had finally engineered his crucifixion. Similarly, the Christians had had some success in their mission to the Jews, especially among the Greek-speaking Jews of the Dispersion, yet the Jews at Jamnia had finally produced the benediction that drove the Christian Jews out of the Jewish community. The evangelist anguishes over this tragic pattern in the literary form of a dialogue between Jesus and his Jewish contemporaries.

Action

Jesus gives sight to a man born blind, 9:1-7. Continuing the theme of Jesus as the Light of the World, the evangelist now presents an account of Jesus giving light to a man born blind.

Dialogue

The fate of Jesus and his followers in the Jewish community, 9:8-41. In many ways this is the most interesting and complex of the dialogues in the fourth gospel. But the complexities can be unraveled once we realize that what is at issue here in this series of dialogues is the fate of Jesus and his followers in the Jewish community.[45]

The first dialogue is between the man and his neighbors (verses 8-12). It reflects the original impact of Jesus on his Jewish contemporaries and the questions it gave rise to.

The second dialogue is between the man and the Pharisees (verses 13-17). Here the Pharisees represent not only the Jewish authorities who finally condemned Jesus, but also those at Jamnia who produced the benediction banning the Christian Jews from the synagogue.

The third dialogue is between the Jews and the man's parents (verses 18-23). It reflects the problems and divisions within the Jewish community produced by Jesus and his followers and their claims. As we indicated above, verse 22 refers to the benediction against the Nazarenes and the Minim, which came into use in Jewish communities toward the end of the first century A.D.

The fourth dialogue concerns the man himself and his fate at the hands of the Jewish authorities (verses 24-34). It reflects the fate of the Jewish convert to Christianity as the evangelist knows it; perhaps even the fate of the evangelist himself.

The fifth dialogue mirrors the further fate of the man who, now rejected by the Jewish community, finds his new home in the community of those who come to faith in Jesus (verses 35-41). The members of this community in turn reject the community that had rejected them.

These dialogues reveal the actual situation of the evangelist and his readers, just as Mark 13 revealed the situation of the evangelist Mark and his readers. John and his readers are Hellenistic Jewish Christians who have been rejected from the synagogue community in their city as a consequence of the introduction of the benediction against Nazarenes and Minim.

---

[45] In what follows we are heavily indebted to J. L. Martyn, *History and Theology in the Fourth Gospel;* cf. *The Gospel of John in Christian History;* D. M. Smith, *John,* chapter 4.

Concluding Monologue

Jesus as the shepherd and the sheepgate, 10:1–18. The evangelist closes this section with a monologue and a dialogue on the messianic claims of Jesus and the response of the Jews. The monologue concerns Jesus as the shepherd and the sheepgate. The discourse is an involved allegory in which various images on the care of sheep appear in connection with Jesus. In verses 1–6 Jesus is the shepherd responsible for the sheep and to whom the sheep are responsive. In verses 7–10 he is the gate through which sheep enter and leave their fold. Verses 11–15 introduce the theme of Jesus as the good shepherd prepared to die for his sheep, and Jesus is contrasted in this respect with other "shepherds." Finally, in verses 16–18 Jesus is the shepherd who lays down his life not only for his flock, the Jewish people, but also for the Gentiles.

Concluding Dialogue

The Jews disagree as to the claims of Jesus, 10:19–21. The section concludes with a dialogue on the varied responses of the Jews to Jesus. This dialogue no doubt reflects the experience of the evangelist as he became a Christian in his own Jewish community.

Jesus and the feast of Dedication, 10:22–39. The feast of Dedication celebrates the rededication of the Temple in 164 B.C. after its desecration by Antiochus Epiphanes, who erected an altar to the Greek god Zeus in the Jerusalem Temple. This is the "abomination of desolation" to which such frequent reference is made in Jewish and Christian apocalyptic (e.g., Mark 13:14). Since the festival celebrated a major victory of the people of God against their enemies and was seen as a renewal of the covenant between God and his people, it becomes a suitable occasion for the evangelist to return to his theme of the messianic claims of Jesus.

Action

Jesus at the feast of Dedication, 10:22–23.

Dialogue

The climactic claims of Jesus and the response of the Jews to them, 10:24–39. In this dialogue the evangelist presents Jesus as summarizing the claims he has already made for himself. He is the shepherd and the giver of life; he and the Father are one. At the same time a new note is introduced in accordance with the symbolism of the rededication of the Temple which lies behind the feast of Dedication: Jesus is the one consecrated by God and sent into the world (verse 36). Similarly, the negative response of the Jews is also summarized, and it is presented as reaching a climax. The Jews attempt to stone Jesus (verse 31) as they had before in 8:59; they also attempt to arrest him (verse 39) as they had before in 7:30, 32, 44; 8:20.

Transition: The End of the Public Ministry of Jesus, 10:40–42.

The thought of the evangelist is now turning more strongly to the Cross, and the last section of his Book of Signs deals with the meaning of the death of

Jesus. So this transitional passage marks the end of the public ministry of Jesus; from this point forward we are concerned only with the death of Jesus and its meaning. But the evangelist John thinks in a circular manner. We pointed out that the first part of the Book of Signs began and ended in Cana. Similarly, Jesus appeared on the scene for the first time in this gospel at the place where John was baptizing (1:29–34), and his public ministry must end at that same place, as it does in these transitional verses.

Jesus Moves Toward the Hour of His Glorification, 11:1–12:50

This is the last section of the Book of Signs. Jesus is still presented as working and teaching in public, but in the mind of the evangelist the public ministry is over, and now everything is dominated by the Cross. In this section, therefore, the evangelist begins the meditation on the death of Jesus and its meaning.

Action
The raising of Lazarus, 11:1–44. For the reader who comes to the gospel of John after a reading of the synoptic gospels this is a most startling narrative. Not only is it a major miracle of Jesus about which the synoptic gospels appear to know nothing, but also it is presented as the actual occasion for the crucifixion (verses 45–53). Moreover, the Martha and Mary of this story appear also in the gospel of Luke (Luke 10:38–42), where, however, there is absolutely no mention of Lazarus. The historical problems in connection with the story are all but insurmountable, and the best that scholars can do is suggest that the evangelist John is meditating upon an element of early Christian tradition otherwise lost to us.[46] But when all is done and said, the existence of this story alone is evidence that the gospel of John is simply not written at the level of history as "what actually happened." The evangelist is concerned rather with history as the believer's historical existence in the world and the difference that belief in Christ can make to that existence. At this level the story comes alive as a dramatic presentation of Jesus as the resurrection and the life to those who believe in him.

Reaction
The Jewish authorities condemn Jesus to death, 11:45–53. The normal pattern of the Johannine literary construction is shattered by the nearness of the Cross. So here we have the reaction of the Jewish authorities to the raising of Lazarus rather than the dialogue and monologue that would normally follow the action.

[46] R. Brown, *John,* vol. 1, pp. 427–30.

Transition: Will Jesus come to Jerusalem for the Passover? 11:54–57. The evangelist dramatically heightens the tension of his narrative in this transitional section.

Action

The anointing at Bethany, 12:1–8. This scene relates both to Mark 14:3–9, the anointing at Bethany, and to Luke 7:36–38, an anointing of Jesus in Galilee. In the gospel of John, as in Mark, the anointing anticipates the burial of Jesus.

Transition: The tension in Jerusalem heightens, 12:9–11.

Action

Jesus enters Jerusalem in triumph, 12:12–19. This parallels the synoptic gospel accounts of the same incident (Mark 11:1–10; Matt 21:1–9; Luke 19:28–38). In John, however, the incident is interpreted as an anticipation of the glorification of Jesus (verse 16).

Action

The Greeks come to Jesus, 12:20–22. The evangelist has been concerned thus far in his narrative with Jesus and the Jews, which no doubt reflects his personal position as a member of a Jewish community who became a Christian. But now he turns to Jesus and the Greeks in an incident referring to his being a Christian in a Greek city and preaching the gospel to the Greek world.

Dialogue

The meaning of the Cross, 12:23–36. The evangelist now returns to his favorite literary device and explores the meaning of the Cross in dialogue between Jesus and the voice from heaven and between Jesus and the crowd.

The ending of the Book of Signs, 12:37–50. The evangelist brings his Book of Signs to an end with a summary of the meaning of the signs of Jesus, meditating on their meeting with the reactions of both nonbelief and belief.

Farewell Discourses and Prayer for the Church, 13:1–17:26

In this third major section of the gospel the evangelist explores the meaning of Christ for the believer and the church in a series of discourses and a prayer by Jesus as the Last Supper. They probably originated as a series of meditations at the celebration of the Christian Eucharist.

Opening Dramatic Scene

The Last Supper, 13:1–30. This is the Johannine version of the Last Supper between Jesus and his disciples, narratives of which we also find in 1 Cor 11:23–26; Mark 14:17–25; Matt 26:20–29; Luke 22:14–38. Unlike those, John does not mention the "Eucharistic words," words of interpretation spoken by Jesus over the bread or the wine, and he has an incident of foot washing the other narratives do not. We have no idea why the Eucharistic words are missing. Earlier we suggested that the evangelist has no concern for the sacraments and puts his emphasis elsewhere, and the omission of the Eucharistic words may be part of this general trend. On the other hand, these "words" were especially sacred to Christians and the evangelist may have regarded this aspect of the narrative as too sacred to be written down. The matter of the washing of the feet lends itself more readily to an explanation. The evangelist thinks in plastic terms; it is natural for him to cast his thought in the imagery of incident and dramatic dialogue. So here he dramatizes the sacrifice of Jesus and its significance by means of an acted parable of humility and service. The humility of the action is the more striking in light of the evangelist's concentration on the passion of Jesus as his "glorification." This section contains the first reference to the disciple "whom Jesus loved" who "was lying close to the breast of Jesus" (13:23, 25).

Dialogue

Christ's departure and return, 13:31–14:31. In this dialogue between Jesus and his disciples, the evangelist explores the glory of the relationship between the believer and the glorified Christ.

Monologue

Christ and the believer, 15:1–16:15. The evangelist now turns to the pattern of the Christian believer's life in the world. The believer *abides* in Jesus (15:1–11); he enters into a relationship of *love* with the fellow believer (15:12–17); and he *separates* himself from the world (15:18–27). In this last connection we are introduced to a particular Johannine conception, the *paraklētos*, the Paraclete (15:26: RSV, "Counselor"; NEB, "Advocate"; TEV, "Helper"). In John's thinking it represents the thought that the risen Lord is spiritually present to the believer as that believer wrestles with the problems of Christian existence in the world.

Dialogue

Jesus and his disciples, 16:16–33. Turning now from monologue to dialogue, the evangelist explores the relationship of the risen Lord with those who believe in him. As is uniformly the case in these discourses, the Lord who speaks is the Jesus who died and rose again from the dead, who came from the Father and returned to him, and whose spiritual presence can now be known by the believer in the world.

Monologue

Christ's prayer for his church, 17:1–26. This is the evangelist's climactic statement of the significance of Jesus for the believer. It falls naturally into three parts. In part one (verses 1–5), the prayer is concerned with Jesus himself, with his death as his glorification, and with his power to give eternal life to those who believe in him. In part two (verses 6–19), the thought turns to the believer who is still in the world. Jesus is now glorified, but the believer still has to live out his life in the world and to represent Christ in the world. Finally, part three (verses 20–26) considers the corporate body of believers, the church, and the prayer is that the church may know the indwelling love of God as it fulfills its mission in the world of leading that world to belief in God.

The Passion Narrative, 18:1–20:31

The fourth major section of the gospel of John is the passion narrative. John covers the same ground as do the synoptic gospels, and we note the parallels between John and Mark. But the narrative in John has its own particular emphases. In the first place it has a distinctively apologetic tendency. The Jews are presented as "the sole villains of the plot," while Pilate becomes "a sympathetic figure, earnestly interested in Jesus' welfare."[47] Second, the Jesus of the Johannine passion narrative is a sovereign figure. In this narrative, "Jesus goes through the passion not as a victim, but as a sovereign and superhuman Being who at any moment could bring the process to a halt."[48]

The betrayal in the garden, 18:1–11 (compare Mark 14:32–48). John omits any reference to the prayer of Jesus, but then he has just completed the great prayer for the church. The saying of Jesus "Rise, let us be going" (Mark 14:42) is found earlier in John (John 14:31).

Jesus before the high priest and Peter's denial, 18:12–27 (compare Mark 14:53–72). The narrative follows the structure in Mark, even to the extent of intercalating the trial scene into the account of the denial by Peter. But compared with the Markan narrative there are some new elements. There is the informal appearance before Annas (18:12–14), which has the effect of bringing Jesus before *two* high priests: "the high priest then questioned Jesus . . ." (verse 19) and "Annas then sent him bound to Caiaphas the high priest" (verse 24). The historical fact was that Annas was deposed from the high priesthood by the Romans in A.D. 15, but he remained enormously influential, and it may well have been that the Jews continued to grant him the courtesy of the title, if only as a protest against the Roman power to appoint and depose the chief representative of the Jewish people before God. In itself then, there is nothing intrinsically improbable about the Johannine narrative of the two hearings, and it may be that John here does have access to a tradition about the appearance of Jesus before Jewish authorities that is otherwise lost to us. At the same time, however, it is obvious from the comment in verse 14 that John's interest is in the symbolic significance of the high priest as the chief representative of the people before God. With dramatic irony he puts on the lips of Caiaphas the key to understanding the meaning of the death of Jesus.

Another new element in the Johannine narrative is the appearance of "another disciple" who was "known to the high priest" and who brings Peter into the courtyard (verses 15–16). This disciple appears again in 20:2–10, where Mary Magdalene runs to Peter "and the other disciple" to tell them that Jesus' body is not in the tomb. In that context the "other disciple" is identified as "the one whom Jesus loved" (20:2), and this brings us to other references to the

[47] R. Brown, vol. 2, p. 787.
[48] R. Brown, vol. 2, p. 787.

"beloved disciple," of which there are five in the gospel. In 13:23–26 the disciple "whom Jesus loved" is intimately close to Jesus at the Last Supper. In 19:25–27 Jesus from the Cross commits his mother to the care of "the disciple whom he loved." In 21:7 "that disciple whom Jesus loved" recognizes the resurrected Jesus, and in 21:20–23 there is a dialogue between the risen Jesus and Peter about "the disciple whom Jesus loved, who had lain close to his breast at the supper." Finally, in 21:24 this disciple is identified as the ultimate source for the tradition in the gospel of John: "This is the disciple who is bearing witness to these things, and who has written these things; and we know that his testimony is true." We have indicated several views on the fascinating problem of his identity and importance for the Johannine community above.

Jesus before Pilate, 18:28–19:16 (compare Mark 15:1–15). This narrative is particularly interesting for its presentation of Pilate as a sympathetic figure earnestly interested in Jesus' welfare and of "the Jews" as the real villains of the plot. One gets a very strong impression that the author is himself a Jew reacting bitterly to the treatment of Jesus by his own people. The bitter note of rejection in John 19:15 is an echo of that in Matthew's gospel (Matt 27:25). There is no evidence that John knows the gospel of Matthew; it is rather the case that both John and Matthew are reacting equally strongly to a situation in which they feel themselves, as Jews, personally involved.

The crucifixion, 19:17–37 (compare Mark 15:22–41 and Luke 23:33–49). This narrative is close to Mark's with the exception of the mention of "the disciple whom he loved," and the reference to the giving up of the spirit (verse 30), which is reminiscent of Luke 23:46.

The burial, 19:38–42 (compare Mark 15:42–47). All the gospels stress the role of Joseph of Arimathea in the burial of Jesus (Mark 15:43; Matt 27:57; Luke 23:50), but John is alone in introducing the figure of Nicodemus, whom he carefully identifies as the one who had come to Jesus by night (verse 39; compare 3:1–15; 7:50–52).

The discovery of the empty tomb, 20:1–10 (compare Mark 16:1–8). All the gospel narratives diverge dramatically after the point at which Mark ends: the discovery of the empty tomb and the astonishment of the women. In Matthew the women run to tell the disciples and are met by the risen Jesus on the way, (Matt 28:9–10); then the risen Lord appears to the disciples in Galilee. In Luke the women tell of their discovery of the empty tomb, but they are not believed until a series of resurrection appearances in and around Jerusalem convinces the disciples that "The Lord has risen indeed!" (Luke 24:36). In John's gospel Mary Magdalene tells Peter and the "other disciple" of the empty tomb, and Jesus appears to her and to the disciples both in Jerusalem (20:19–23, 26–29) and in Galilee (21:1–14).

The appearance to Mary Magdalene, 20:11–18. The gospel of John puts a major emphasis on the spiritual presence of Jesus with the believer. Both in

6:62–63 and 16:7 the evangelist emphasizes the eventual return of Jesus to the heavenly realm from which he came and the consequent possibility of his spiritual presence with the believer. Now he returns to this note in the story of the appearance to Mary Magdalene as Jesus tells her that he is about to ascend to the Father. That will make possible his spiritual presence with the believer and the promise of that presence is the point of the next story.

The appearance to the disciples as a group, 20:19–23. The evangelist now dramatizes the possibility of the spiritual presence of Christ with the believer through this story of the risen Lord appearing to his disciples and breathing on them. Both in Hebrew and Greek the word for "spirit" is the same as the word for "breath."

The appearance to Thomas, 20:24–29. In this story the evangelist brings his gospel to a climax by dramatizing doubt so as to highlight the possibility of belief. "Thomas has become here the personification of an attitude,"[49] and by means of this story of his coming to faith the evangelist presents a paradigm of the possibility for all men everywhere to reach the point of saying to the risen Jesus, "My Lord and my God."

The purpose of the gospel, 20:30–31. The evangelist climaxes his work with a statement of its purpose: to bring the reader to belief in Jesus and to the life that belief makes possible.

Epilogue: The Appearance in Galilee, 21:1–23

Surely the evangelist intended his gospel to end at 20:31, and chapter 21 has been added as an epilogue by another writer. The language is not quite that of the evangelist; yet the epilogue certainly echoes his concerns. It emphasizes the role of Peter, it uses the imagery of shepherd and sheep, and it features "the disciple whom Jesus loved." In many respects it is like the prologue to the gospel (1:1–18), which also shares the concerns of the gospel and yet at the same time differs in language from the text of the gospel itself. R. E. Brown makes the interesting suggestion that both the prologue and the epilogue may have been added to the main text of the gospel by the same redactor.[50]

The purpose of the epilogue seems to be ecclesiastical. The author is now concerned with the ongoing life and work of the church in the world and appears to feel that from this viewpoint something needs to be added to the gospel narrative. In particular, four matters concern him. He knows a tradition of a resurrection appearance to the disciples in Galilee as they were fishing, and he preserves it as a supplement to the accounts of the appearances in Jerusalem (verses 1–8). Second, he is concerned with the Christian sacred meal,

---

[49] R. Brown, *John*, vol. 2, p. 1031.
[50] R. Brown, vol. 1, XXXVIII.

the Eucharist, and he presents here an account of a meal between the risen Lord and his disciples (verses 9–14), which is deliberately evocative of the Eucharist (Jesus "takes the bread" and "gives" it to the disciples in a solemn manner, verse 13). The Eucharist celebrated in the church is interpreted as a solemn meal between the risen Lord and those who believe in him. Third, there is the restoration of Peter after his denial of Jesus (verse 15–19). The gospel of Mark already hinted at the restoration of Peter and of a resurrection appearance to him: "tell his disciples *and Peter* that he is going before you into Galilee; there you will see him" (Mark 16:7). The epilogue to the gospel of John develops this theme further. Finally, the author of the epilogue identifies the "disciple whom Jesus loved" as the ultimate author of the gospel. As we have said, we do not know whether this disciple is a historical or an ideal figure.

THE FIRST LETTER OF JOHN

Much of what we wish to say about 1 John has already been said at various places in this chapter and now only needs to be brought together. It is probably not from the same author as the main text of the gospel. We noted the poverty of the style of this letter compared to that of the gospel and the real differences in thought between them on eschatology and the sacraments. At the same time we joined Bultmann, Marxsen, and others in holding that it was possible that the author of 1 John had redacted the main text of the gospel.

A few other points need to be noted. The author is not mentioned by name or title. The date of 1 John will not have been long after the gospel, the major reason being that the attention has shifted from *external* opponents ("the world"; "the Jews") to false teachers *within* the community. What do they teach? In a word, a Christology that denied that Jesus is the Christ, the Son of God (2:22–23), and especially that he came in the flesh (4:2–3). How might this false teaching have arisen?

The Christology of the Johannine writings stresses Jesus as the Son of God who came into the world to empower and glorify those who accept him. Nevertheless, the gospel and letters of John show a strong dualism, a strong sense of the contrast between above and below, light and dark, good and evil, the spirit and the flesh. Under these conditions it was natural that Christians particularly influenced by these writings and their authors should be susceptible to the view that the world and the flesh were essentially evil and that the heavenly redeemer could not truly have come in the flesh, but must have maintained his heavenly nature while only appearing to be in the flesh. This way of thinking was natural in the Hellenistic world, and when it was applied to Jesus it became the christological heresy "docetism," that is, he only "seemed" to be human (Greek *dokeō* = "I seem"). It was especially characteristic of later Gnosticism. In any case, a schism over true and false Christology arose within the Johannine church. For the author of 1 John, the opponents' docetic Christology led to disobeying the commandments, to hating one's brother, to lies and falsehood.

The *Oxford Annotated Bible* says that 1 John is not really a letter at all, but "in form and content it resembles a theological treatise or sermon, written with obvious affection and concern for the spiritual welfare of those to whom it is addressed."[51] Indeed, some have supposed that behind 1 John lies a source.[52] For our purpose, it will suffice to note that the text of 1 John exhibits a balance of proclamation and parenesis, and it may be analyzed as follows:

1:1–4 *Proclamation.* The eternal life has been made manifest.

1:5–2:17 *Parenesis.* Right behavior depends on true knowledge of God.

2:18–27 *Proclamation.* True knowledge of God depends on recognizing that Jesus is the true and only Son of God. He rewards with eternal life those who abide in him now.

2:28–3:24 *Parenesis.* Those who abide in him now and exhibit the love that naturally flows from that relationship have no need to fear his parousia.

4:1–6 *Proclamation.* Jesus Christ actually came in the flesh as the Son of God.

4:7–5:5 *Parenesis.* To abide in God is to be "of God," and to be "of God" is to exhibit love in the world. "We love because he first loved us."

5:6–12 *Proclamation.* Jesus Christ is the Son of God, and acceptance of him is the means to eternal life.

THE SECOND AND THIRD LETTERS OF JOHN

These are true letters written by a member of the Johannine school who calls himself the "presbyter" (elder). This word came to designate a given official in the church, e.g., 1 Tim 5:17 "Let the elders who rule well . . ." and probably the author is simply referring to himself by the title of his office in the church. The letters have no formal structure.

One interesting question is the kind of authority the author exercises over the churches he writes to. It seems to have been moral or even spiritual rather than formal, for the writer could not do much about Diotrephes, "who likes to put himself first," except appeal to his readers on moral grounds (3 John 9–12). This fact, together with the very nature of the gospel and letters of John themselves, indicates that the writer's authority stems primarily from his function as a preacher prominent in the conduct of Christian worship. It is perhaps not too much to say that in the second and third letters of John we have a much-loved leader of Christian worship and celebrator of the Eucharist attempting to extend his influence into matters of doctrine and polity.

[51] *Oxford Annotated Bible*, p. 1482.
[52] R. Bultmann, *The Johannine Epistles*; J. C. O'Neill, *The Puzzle of 1 John 2–7.*

The second letter of John is notable for its reference to churches as "the elect lady" and the "elect sister" and to the members of the churches as "her children" (2 John 1, 13). This indicates that the Christian church is now a definite and separate entity in the Hellenistic world and that individual churches are coming to be recognized as integral units in that entity. We are now in the middle period of New Testament Christianity. The second letter of John also continues the argument of the first letter against docetism (2 John 7–11).

The third letter of John reflects the authority of the writer as moral or spiritual rather than formal and, like 2 John, it emphasizes the importance of the physical presence of the writer in exercising such authority as he may possess (3 John 13; compare 2 John 12). For the rest, the letter testifies that the Christian Churches are recognizing that they are separate entities in the world and as such, have a definite responsibility for Christians who come to them from another place (3 John 5–8). This hospitality to other Christians was to become an important sociological factor in the development of the church.

THE JOHANNINE SCHOOL

After our exegetical surveys of the gospel and letters of John we are now able to make further tentative statements about these texts and their authors. As far as the gospel is concerned, it is evident that the author is or was a member of the Jewish community in a predominantly Greek city. His concern for Christian Jews and their exclusion from the Jewish community (John 9:22; 12:42; 16:2) indicate his Jewish background, as does his intense desire to explore the meaning of Jesus in terms of the symbolism of the Jewish festivals (John 5:1–10:39). At the same time, there is an equally unmistakable wish to interpret the meaning of Jesus to the believer in terms that would be realistic to the Greek world, symbolized by the story of the Greeks coming to Jesus in John 12:20–22, but evident throughout the gospel. So the evangelist is a Christian Jew living somewhere in a major population center in the Hellenistic world. Ephesus is that center according to ancient Christian tradition, but almost any city in Syria or Asia Minor would meet the requirements, and recently Alexandria in Egypt has been suggested as a possibility.[53] We do not know where the gospel of John originated, except that it was somewhere in the Hellenistic world where Greek culture was dominant but where there was a strong Jewish community.

We are on somewhat firmer ground when we claim that the gospel and letters of John emerged out of a Johannine "school". We have suggested that behind John's gospel lies one (or more) of the synoptics, but that the evangelist preferred his own individual sources, especially his "signs source." He undoubtedly had other traditions at his disposal as well. Furthermore, not only has chapter 21 been added to the gospel relating it to the witness of the Be-

---

[53] J. L. Martyn, *History and Theology*, p. 8.

loved Disciple; the text of the gospel was redacted in various ways, and certainly a second author was involved in the letters, perhaps even a third. As we consider the gospel and letters, the homogeneity of style, thought, and emphasis, with sometimes marked and sometimes subtle differences, indicate the activity of a close-knit group rather than a single person. The differences in literary form seem to make the same point. One person could indeed have written the gospel, the first letter (which is not really a letter at all, but a theological homily), and the second and third letters (which are indeed letters). But when these differences in literary form are linked with differences in style and thought, it becomes probable that we are dealing with related members of a closely knit group.

As we noted in chapter 1, "schools" were a common feature of the environment of the New Testament, from the rabbinical schools and schools of scribes such as those at Qumran to the many schools of the Greco-Roman world.[54]

Within Christianity itself there was the tradition of Jesus and his disciples, and in chapter 7 we discussed the school of Paul and his followers. The existence of a Johannine school is, therefore, in itself most likely, and the literary features of the gospel and letters of John make it virtually certain. The gospel and letters are the literary product of a tight-knit group that shared a common vision of the nature and meaning of Christian faith.

Can we be more specific about "the Johannine school"? Recent studies have attempted to describe the history of the unique Johannine community or communities, and the eventual formation of a Johannine school as the center of activity there.[55] Though much is debated, we shall attempt something of a scenario, drawing on several recent viewpoints. It seems likely that the community had its origins in connection with an anonymous, authoritative teacher in the community who had died, the Beloved Disciple. The later community believed he was a historical witness to the ministry of Jesus; though this may be a subsequent theological interpretation, he is certainly used in later times to authenticate the community's unique traditions, perhaps in contrast to Peter who represents alternative Jewish Christian traditions (Brown); in many respects his functions are described as analogous to those of the Spirit-Paraclete. Whether these later beliefs have any historical validity has been debated; some scholars believe the Beloved Disciple is purely symbolic. But there is greater agreement that the earliest Johannine community had a more traditional view of Jesus, either as a Davidic Messiah (Brown), and perhaps also as an Elijah

---

[54] Cf. above, p. 10, based on R. A. Culpepper, *The Johannine School.*

[55] R. A. Culpepper; see drawing on studies by Lindars, Freed, and Borgen; J. L. Martyn, *History and Theology; The Gospel of John in Christian History;* R. Brown, *The Community of the Beloved Disciple,* who in Appendix I gives 5 scholars' theories about the history of the Johannine community (Martyn, Richter, Cullmann, Boismard, Longbrandtner); cf. also D. M. Smith, "Johannine Christianity"; R. Kysar, "Community and Gospel: Vectors in Fourth Gospel Criticism," *Interpretation* 31 (1977), reprinted in J. L. Mays, ed., *Interpreting the Gospels,* pp. 265–77. In the sketch that follows we are most indebted to Brown, but it is slanted more toward the notion of sectarian Christianity and allows more room for source theories.

figure in terms of his miracle working and translation to heaven (Martyn). This group may have been located in Palestine. Adherents of the Baptist entered the community. At some point—or perhaps already from the beginning (Cullmann, Richter)—the group began to stress a Christology of Jesus as a Mosaic Prophet perhaps related to Samaritan views of one who brought a message from God to the people. It may have also polemicized against the Temple (Cullmann). Possibly the miracle tradition was now developed into a "signs source," or "gospel of signs" with a passion story. The tendency grew to see Jesus more and more as a preexistent, divine figure who descended and reascended to God, indicating a syncretistic Jewish environment.

Such a mythical conception brought about increasing conflicts with more traditional, monotheistic Jews. This may have been exacerbated by the inclusion of Gentiles. Did the Johannine Christians at this point move to a major Gentile city, such as Ephesus? In any case, by the late first century, in the wake of the Council of Jamnia, some of these Jewish Christians were expelled from a synagogue, thus experiencing persecution and becoming increasingly alienated from the religious traditions out of which they came. Now the evangelist writes. He is a creative author, drawing on special traditions in the community. He knows of Mark and perhaps Luke, but is more concerned to develop his theology of "signs," acknowledging the rightful place of the passion, and to affirm the Christology of the "man from heaven" in an alien "world," especially marked by disbelief on the part of "the Jews." He notes the Beloved Disciple, allowing him to overshadow Peter. In general, however, he avoids any emphasis on church officials, sacraments, and futurist eschatology, developing his view of the Spirit-Paraclete and a more generalized conception of discipleship.

With the separation from traditional Judaism complete, alternative interpretations of the dualistic emphasis of the evangelist now lead to schism within the community. One group stresses the divinity of the "man from heaven" for salvation, presumably to the detriment of his humanity, and develops John's realized eschatology in terms of salvation in the present. It also stresses prophecy and gifts of the Spirit. In the second century this leads in the direction of Gnostic and Montanist Christianity.[56] The other group follows the writers of the letters, holding onto the humanity of Jesus and believing that their opponents are false prophets who hold a "docetic" Christology, disrupt the community, and abandon the love commandment. One of this group (the writer of 1 John?) edits the gospel to bring out a slightly stronger emphasis on traditional eschatology and sacraments, perhaps also adding chapter 21 to trace the tradition to the Beloved Disciple. The writer of 1 John defends the Johannine Christ against docetism.

Another letter (2 John) has similar views and a third wrestles with the problem of church government.

If this sketch has any validity, there developed within the Johannine ("sec-

---

[56] Montanus drew on John's Paraclete idea for grounding his prophetic career. The Great Church considered him heretical.

tarian") community a "school" that made its objective the preservation of the "true" Johannine tradition;[57] at the point of schism, the group out of which the edited gospel and letters came thus made its own moves toward a more institutionalized Christianity, perhaps saving the Johannine literature for the Great Church in the late second century when Irenaeus claimed that it had been written by John, Son of Zebedee. In any case, the gospel and letters were ultimately accepted into the canon and gave support to the church's "high Christology" in the fourth and fifth centuries.

Further Reading

W. G. Kümmel, *Intro.* Gospel, pp. 188–247; Letters, pp. 434–52.

W. Marxsen, *Intro.*, pp. 251–69.

X R. Fuller, *Intro.*, pp. 168–83.

PCB, Gospel, pp. 844–69 (C. K. Barrett); Letters, pp. 1035–40 (G. Johnston).

JBC, Gospel, pp. 414–66 (B. Vawter); Letters, pp. 404–13 (B. Vawter).

IDB, vol. 2, Gospel, pp. 932–46 (J. N. Sanders); Letters, pp. 946–52 (G. B. Caird).

X 'IDB Suppl., Gospel, pp. 482–86 (D. M. Smith); Letters, pp. 486–87 (D. M. Smith).

There is voluminous literature about the gospel and letters of John. Good surveys of the literature are:

I. H. Howard and C. K. Barrett, *The Fourth Gospel in Recent Criticism and Interpretation.* (Barrett revised Howard's volume to bring the survey down to the work of Bultmann.)

J. M. Robinson, "The Johannine Trajectory" in J. M. Robinson and H. Koester, *Trajectories Through Early Christianity*, pp. 232–68. Surveys the situation from Bultmann down to about 1970.

E. Malatesta, *St. John's Gospel 1920–1965.*

R. Kysar, *The Fourth Evangelist and His Gospel. An Examination of Contemporary Scholarship.* An excellent survey of recent Johannine research down to 1975.

——, "Community and Gospel: Vectors in Fourth Gospel Criticism," *Interpretation* (1977), reprinted in J. L. Mays, ed., *Interpreting the Gospels*, pp. 265–77. The issue contains other important articles on John's gospel.

---

[57] R. A. Culpepper, *The Johannine School*, p. 259: "A sect is characterized by its devotion to the person or teachings of a founder or its adherence to a set of principles. Sects, therefore, share many of the characteristics of schools. . . . Schools, however, have the additional characteristic of preoccupation with teaching, learning, studying, writing." Compare and contrast the remarks of W. Meeks, "Man from Heaven," and R. Brown, *Community of the Beloved Disciple.* From a sociological perspective, the "sect" stands against "the world," cf. chapter 3 above.

There are a number of useful introductory studies on John and the Johannine literature:

R. Brown, *The Community of the Beloved Disciple.*
R. Kysar, *John the Maverick Gospel.*
G. MacRae, *Faith in the Word: The Fourth Gospel.*
J. Painter, *John: Witness and Theologian.*
D. M. Smith, *John* (Proclamation Commentaries).
D. G. Vanderlip, *Christianity According to John.*
———, *John, the Gospel of Life.*

On the background of John, see:

C. K. Barrett, *The Gospel of John and Judaism.*
J. H. Charlesworth, ed., *John and Qumran.*

Important recent studies include the following:

P. Borgen, *Bread from Heaven.*
O. Cullmann, *The Johannine Circle.*
R. A. Culpepper, *The Johannine School.*
C. H. Dodd, *The Interpretation of the Fourth Gospel.*
R. Fortna, *The Gospel of Signs; A Reconstruction of the Narrative Source Underlying the Fourth Gospel.*
E. Käsemann, *The Testament of Jesus.*
B. Lindars, *Behind the Fourth Gospel.*
J. L. Martyn, *History and Theology in the Fourth Gospel.*
———, *The Gospel of John in Christian History.*
W. Meeks, *The Prophet-King.*
D. M. Smith, *The Composition and Order of the Fourth Gospel.*

Among the many recent articles in this area, we note:

G. MacRae, "The Fourth Gospel and *Religionsgeschichte,*" *Catholic Biblical Quarterly* 32 (1970), pp. 13–24.
W. Meeks, "The Man from Heaven in Johannine Sectarianism," *Journal of Biblical Literature* 91 (1972), pp. 44–72.
D. M. Smith, "Johannine Christianity: Some Reflections on Its Character and Delineation," *New Testament Studies* 21 (1974/75), pp. 222–48.
———, "John and the Synoptics: Some Dimensions of the Problem," *New Testament Studies* 26 (1979/80), pp. 425–44.
C. Talbert, "The Myth of a Descending-Ascending Redeemer in Mediterranean Antiquity," *New Testament Studies* 22 (1975/76), pp. 418–40.

Among the many commentaries available the following are particularly important:

C. K. Barrett, *The Gospel According to St. John.*
R. Brown, *The Gospel According to John.* 2 vols (The Anchor Bible). Massive and encyclopedic.

R. Bultmann, *The Gospel of John.*

———, *The Johannine Epistles* (Hermeneia Series).

C. H. Dodd, *The Johannine Epistles.* Moffatt New Testament Commentary.

E. Hoskyns and N. Davey, *The Fourth Gospel.*

J. L. Houlden, *The Johannine Epistles.*

R. H. Lightfoot, *St. John's Gospel.*

R. Schnackenburg, *The Gospel According to St. John.* Two volumes are translated from German.

An introductory theological commentary is:

P. Perkins, *The Gospel According to St. John.*

It will be evident from our own presentation that we are particularly indebted to Dodd's *Interpretation of the Fourth Gospel,* to Martyn's *History and Theology in the Fourth Gospel* and *The Gospel of John in Christian History,* to the studies of Barrett, Brown, Culpepper, Fortna, Kysar, Meeks, and Smith, and to the commentaries of Bultmann and Brown, respectively.

Wall painting of a Eucharistic banquet from the catacomb of Priscilla, in Rome (early third century).

CHAPTER TWELVE

THE CHURCH ON THE WAY TO BECOMING AN INSTITUTION

Traditionally, the letters in the New Testament are divided into two groups: "the Pauline epistles" (including Colossians, Ephesians, the Pastorals, and Hebrews) and "the Catholic epistles" (James; 1, 2 Peter; Jude; and 1, 2, 3 John). The latter group is called "Catholic" because the letters are addressed to the church in general rather than to a particular congregation or individual. We have preferred to group the letters according to literary and historical considerations. In chapter 6 we discussed the letters actually written by Paul and then in chapter 7 those written in his name by pupils and immediate followers, that is, the Pauline school. In chapter 11, we grouped 1, 2, and 3 John with the gospel of John because the four texts have literary and theological connections as products of the Johannine school. We now consider the Pastorals, James, 1 and 2 Peter, and Jude together because they are the common products of the final period of New Testament history. We follow the order of the New Testament except that we put Jude before 2 Peter because 2 Peter reproduces Jude almost in its entirety. Furthermore, the connection between Jude and 2 Peter has led us to discuss 2 Peter before the Pastorals, although we recognize that, of the texts accepted into the New Testament canon, 2 Peter was probably the last to be written. The Pastorals and 2 Peter stand together as the most complete representatives of the emerging institutional church, and so the order of their treatment is comparatively unimportant.

The final period of New Testament history is marked by the growing institutionalization of the church. In the period roughly A.D. 100–140 the Christian movement is approaching the end of the first century of its existence. Though old problems—for example the delay of the parousia—continue to exist, new difficulties and needs are developing.

The major characteristic of this period is that the Christian movement has settled down to the task of being the church in the world. The parousia is no longer immediately expected, the Christians have learned to adjust to the destruction of Jerusalem and the Temple, and relations with Judaism and the Roman Empire are assuming an established norm. The church, therefore, now has to develop its own institutions in order to be the church in the world. After almost a hundred years the Christian movement exists in its own right. But the sheer fact of existing in its own right creates a new set of demands. A religious movement needs a creedal or confessional basis that makes clear what it stands for. Further, a movement stemming ultimately from Judaism, with its consciousness of revelation enshrined in written texts, needs its own texts defined carefully from other texts. To survive and function in the world the movement also requires an organizational structure, a decision-making apparatus, and a definition of the function of its officers and servants. To meet these needs the Christian church at the end of the New Testament period was rapidly establishing a creed, a canon, and an organized ordained ministry.

Some Christian literature of this period did not find a place in the final canon of the New Testament: a letter written by Clement, bishop of Rome, to the church at Corinth; letters written by Ignatius, bishop of Antioch, to various churches as he was on his way to martyrdom in Rome; and the Didache ("Teaching of the Lord to the Gentiles by the Twelve Apostles"), a church order from Syria. In addition, some Christians of this period were being influenced by a growing Gnostic movement still in contact with Judaism. We do not discuss any of these pieces of Christian literature, or the possibility of Christian Gnosticism in any detail, but we refer to the "Apostolic Fathers" in our concluding summary about the growth of institutional Christianity, and we note the opposition to apparent Gnostic threats (esp. 2 Peter and 1 Timothy) in the canonical literature.[1]

Our procedure in this chapter is to discuss the texts in this order: James, 1 Peter, Jude, 2 Peter, the Pastorals. Then we offer a summary of the characteristics of emerging institutional Christianity and some remarks on the interpretation of its literature.

THE LETTER OF JAMES

Despite the fact that it begins with greetings, James is not a letter.[2] Nor may we call it a sermon, because there is absolutely no proclamation within it. Unlike 1 John and Hebrews, it does not alternate and weave together procla-

---

[1] Information about the "Apostolic Fathers" is readily available in *IDB* under "Clement, Epistles of," vol. 1, pp. 648–49; "Didache," vol. 1, pp. 841–43; "Ignatius, Epistles of," vol. 2, pp. 678–80. See also R. Kraft, "Apostolic Fathers," *IDB Suppl.*, pp. 36–38.

[2] M. Dibelius and H. Greeven, *James*, p. 3: "we may designate the 'Letter' of James as paraenesis." See also G. Sloyan, "The Letter of James," in G. Krodel, ed., *Hebrews-James-1 and 2 Peter-Jude-Revelation*, p. 28. R. B. Ward, "James, Letter of," *IDB Suppl.*, p. 469, suggests that it conforms to a first-century form, the "parenetic letter." W. G. Kümmel, *Intro.*, p. 408, suggests a parenetic "essay."

mation and parenesis, but consists of nothing but parenesis. In its 108 verses it has 54 verbs in the imperative![3]

Parenesis, or moral exhortation, is a feature of the literature of the ancient world—Hellenistic, Jewish, and Christian. "Household codes" existed in Hellenistic moral philosophy and were borrowed by Christians. In the Jewish world the teaching of the rabbis and such books as Proverbs and Sirach, both virtually without proclamation, were popular. Before the writing of James, there were in the New Testament collections of ethical teachings ascribed to Jesus in the gospels (especially Matthew's Sermon on the Mount) and the parenetical sections of the Pauline and deutero-Pauline letters. We have every reason to believe that there was a strong tradition of moral exhortation in the Christian movement and that it borrowed freely from Hellenistic and Jewish parenetical material, as well as vigorously developing its own. The existence of a vigorous Christian parenetical tradition is important because a consequence is that verbal similarities between James and other New Testament texts do not mean that James necessarily knows those texts; all may have depended on a common tradition.

James shows knowledge of a tradition that uses sayings ascribed to Jesus in the gospels: 5:12 (compare Matt 5:36-37); 1:5, 17 (compare Matt 7:7-12); 1:22 (compare Matt 7:24-27); 4:12 (compare Matt 7:1); 1:6 (compare Mark 11:23-24). There is, further, parenetical material also used in 1 Peter: Jas 1:2-3 (compare 1 Pet 1:6-7); Jas 4:1-2 (compare 1 Pet 2:11). It is not that James necessarily knows the gospels or 1 Peter, but rather that there is a Christian parenetical tradition into which sayings ascribed to Jesus in the gospels have been taken up, although not in the form of sayings of Jesus, and of which both James and 1 Peter make use.

A further feature of James, as incidentally also of 1 Peter, is that the author uses Hellenistic Greek literary rhetorical devices. There are plays on words: 4:14, "That appears for a little time and then vanishes" (Greek: *phainomenē/aphanizomenē*); 1:1-2, "greeting/joy" (*chairein/charan*); 2:4, "made distinctions/become judges" (*diekrithēte/kritai*); and others. There is alliteration: 1:2, "you meet various trials" (*peirasmois/peripesēte/poikilois*); 3:5, "little member/great things" (*mikron/melos/megala*). James also uses the Hellenistic literary device of the diatribe, presenting an argument in the form of a dialogue between the writer and an imaginary interlocutor: 2:18-26; 5:13-15.[4]

Moral exhortation is very much the same throughout the various elements in a given culture. By the same token parenesis itself has little doctrinal concern, and James, a wholly parenetical work, has almost nothing distinctively Christian about it. Jesus Christ is mentioned only twice (1:1; 2:1), and both verses could be omitted without any harm to the flow of thought in the text. When the "coming of the Lord" is mentioned (5:7) there is nothing to denote the specifically Christian hope of the parousia; it could equally be a reference

---

[3] W. Marxsen, *Intro.*, p. 226.
[4] W. G. Kümmel, *Intro.*, p. 411.

to the coming of the Lord God. "Faith" in this text is not specifically Christian faith but rather the acceptance of monotheism (2:19). These facts have led some scholars to suggest that the text is a Jewish homily lightly Christianized. But a number of features seem to speak of Christian origin, especially the evidence of contacts with Christian parenetical tradition already noted and the discussion of "faith and works" in 2:14–26. The latter seems to presuppose an awareness of Paul's teaching in Galatians 3 and Romans 4. The discussion of faith and works in Jas 2:14–26 caused Martin Luther to contrast James unfavorably with the main texts in the New Testament as "a right strawy epistle in comparison with them, for it has no evangelical matter about it";[5] and this passage remains a problem.

Who is the James who identifies himself as the author of this parenetic collection? The tradition has been to identify him with James, the brother of Jesus. But the comparatively late date of James, the author's use of Hellenistic Greek rhetorical devices, his lack of specific references to Jesus, and his failure to exhibit any of the conservatism with regard to the Jewish Law we know to have been characteristic of Jesus' brother all make this quite impossible.

Structure

James defies the categories of our approach to the New Testament in more ways than one. Not only is it purely parenetical, it also has no discernible structure. It simply moves from theme to theme as the mind of the author takes him, on the principle of association of ideas or sometimes merely on catchwords. In our exegesis we follow the analysis given in Kümmel, *Introduction to the New Testament,* pages 404–405, which recognizes the nature of the text. The insights we used in our structural analysis of other texts in the New Testament simply do not apply to the homily of James.

Exegetical Survey

1:1 *Address.*

1:2–18 *Trials.* Rejoice over trials because trials are a way of being tested before God, and endurance in them leads to the rewards that only God can give.

1:19–27 Both hear and do the word of God.

2:1–12 Show no partiality, but fulfill the royal law of love.

2:13 *The necessity of mercy,* a verse attached by a catchword to the preceding.

[5] W. G. Kümmel, *Intro.,* p. 406.

2:14–26 *Faith and works.* This passage is obviously concerned either to controvert the Pauline doctrine of "justification by faith" or, more probably, to argue against an irresponsible development of that view that denied the necessity for "works" at all. Paul and James see "faith" in very different terms. For Paul faith is a dynamic relationship to the risen Lord allowing man to appropriate for himself that which God has wrought for man through Jesus. For James it is subscription to a sound monotheism. The two views could scarcely be further apart within the same tradition, and the difference characterizes those between emerging institutional Christianity and the earlier periods of the New Testament history. Paul himself would never have denied what James is saying, because it would have been self-evident to him that faith must have consequences in one's behavior in the world. James is arguing against the libertarians of his own day, whose view of faith was no doubt closer to the homilist's than to Paul's. There can be no direct comparison between James and Paul because they come from very different periods in New Testament history.

3:1–12 Watch your tongue.

3:13–18 Abandon earthly wisdom and seek heavenly wisdom.

4:1–10 Seek the peace that comes only from God.

4:11–12 Do not speak evil against one another.

4:13–16 The plans of merchants are subject to God.

4:17 Appended by catchword: the necessity of doing right.

5:1–6 Woes upon the rich.

5:7–11 The judgment of God is imminent.

5:12 Swear not.

5:13–18 The power of prayer.

5:19–20 Be concerned for the erring brother.

James has no formal conclusion.

THE FIRST LETTER OF PETER

In the First Letter of Peter the proclamation is not so much a challenge to accept some aspect of the Christian faith as it is a recognition that those being addressed have already accepted that faith. Thus, for example: "without having seen him you love him" and "as the outcome of your faith you obtain the salvation of your souls" (1:8–9); or "having purified your souls by your obedience to the truth" (1:22) and "To you therefore who believe" (2:7); or "You are a chosen race . . . now you are God's people . . . now you have received mercy" (2:9–10). Another feature of this proclamation is the constant baptismal theme: being born again or being like sheep who had been straying "but have now returned to the Shepherd and Guardian" of their souls (2:25); or the salvation of Noah by water as a type of the salvation of the readers by baptism (3:20–21). Hence the very plausible suggestion that the fundamental thrust of 1 Peter is that of a baptismal homily.

Another feature of this letter is that there seems to be a real difference in the references to suffering and persecution after 4:11. In 1:6; 3:14; and 4:1; "trials," suffering "for righteousness' sake," and "abuse" are real possibilities the readers must contend with. But in 4:12 the readers are actually enduring a "fiery ordeal," and in 5:8 they are warned that their "adversary the devil prowls around like a roaring lion, seeking some one to devour." This has led to the equally plausible suggestion that up until 4:11 we are dealing with the general possibility of suffering, but that after 4:11 we are in a concrete situation of persecution. Moreover, the reference to the one adversary seems to require that the persecution be general and not simply local, and 4:14–16 seems to indicate that Christians were being persecuted simply because they were known to be Christians. The first certain reference we have to systematic and widespread persecution of Christians *as Christians* is from the reign of Trajan (A.D. 98–117). 1 Pet 4:12–5:11 seems to require conditions that as far as we know first obtained under Trajan, whereas 1:3–4:11 seems to anticipate only the general possibility of suffering for one's faith.

These considerations lead to the conclusion that 1:3–4:11 is based on a baptismal homily the author was in the habit of using, and which at a time of real persecution, probably under Trajan, serves as a reminder to his readers of the spirit in which they first became Christians. He then adds 4:12–5:11 as a reflection on their current situation and circulates the whole to comfort his readers in the face of persecution.

A third feature of 1 Peter is the incorporation of a variety of traditional materials, especially christological hymns or confessions. Though precise reconstructions are probably not possible, we recall one possibility in 1 Pet 3:18–19, 22:[6]

> Having been put to death in the flesh,
> Having been made alive in the spirit,
> Having gone to the spirits in prison,
> He preached.

> Who is at the right hand of God,
> Having gone into heaven,
> Angels and authorities and powers having been
>   made subject to him.

[6] See above, chapter 3, p. 84.

If this hymn were prefaced with 1 Pet 1:20, the preexistence, earthly existence, and post-earthly existence pattern would be evident.[7] Verse 1:20 reads:

> He was foreknown before the foundation of the world,
> He was made manifest at the end of the times.

A final feature of 1 Peter, as of the homily of James, is the use of Hellenistic Greek rhetorical devices: the play on word, e.g., "perishable/imperishable" (*phthartēs/aphthartou*) (1:23); carefully paralleled clauses, e.g., "whoever . . . as/whoever . . . as" (4:11); the series of similar compound words, e.g., "imperishable, undefiled and unfading" (all words constructed in Greek in the same way, with the alpha-privative) (1:4); and others. Furthermore, 1 Peter is written in excellent Greek, and all quotations from and allusions to the Jewish Scriptures come without exception from the Greek translation of those Scriptures, the Septuagint. This evidence, together with the fact that the most probable date for the circumstances envisaged in 4:12–5:11 is the reign of the emperor Trajan, 98–117, makes it impossible that the letter should have been written by the apostle Peter. It is best understood as a letter written at the end of the first century by someone who used the pseudonym of the apostle.

Structure

It is difficult to recognize a structure in 1 Peter because so much of it is parenesis, and even where there is some small proclamation celebrating what God has done or some aspect of the significance of Jesus, there is always parenesis interwoven with it. We can recognize the opening greeting (1:1–2), the baptismal homily (1:3–4:11), the exhortation to stand fast in the face of persecution (4:12–5:11), and the closing greetings (5:12–14). Beyond that, however, the most we can do is try to follow the writer's train of thought.

Exegetical Survey

1:1–2   *Opening greetings.*

1:3–4:11   *The baptismal homily.*
>   **1:3–9**   *An opening blessing.* It was (and is) customary in Jewish worship to bless God for what he had done on man's behalf. Here we have a Christian development of that liturgical practice. Note how the author moves from "him" to "us" to "you" as his thought moves from God to Christians in general and then to the group he is addressing.
>   **1:10–12**   *Christian salvation as the fulfillment of prophecy.*

[7] Based on an analysis by the German scholar R. Bultmann; see further, G. Krodel, "The First Letter of Peter," in G. Krodel, ed., *Hebrews-James-1 and 2 Peter-Jude-Revelation*, pp. 66–72.

1:13–2:10 *An exhortation to holiness.* Parenesis based upon "[You shall] be holy, for I am holy" (Lev 11:44–45). Interwoven with the parenesis is reflection upon the significance of Christ: he is the lamb of God; he is the precious stone. Both these concepts are developed from Old Testament passages much used in the New Testament, the lamb from Isaiah 53 and the stone from Psa 118:22. Here the latter has led to other scriptural passages mentioning stones.

2:11–3:12 *An exhortation on the obligation of Christians.* A long parenetical section dealing with the relation of Christians to the world. It begins with an emphasis on maintaining good conduct among the outsiders (2:11–12) and moves to the necessity for accepting the authority of earthly rulers (2:13–17). In this latter passage we see the practical necessity for Christians to adjust to the realities of life in the world. Just as the author of Luke-Acts addresses the subject of the Christian's relationship to the Empire, so the author of 1 Peter finds it necessary to speak to the Christian's relationship to those institutions of authority to which he is personally subject. Next the writer turns to a household code, a summary of duties and responsibilities. Here the code itself becomes the basis for homiletical development.

A remarkable feature of this development is the use of Isaiah 53. Let us compare 1 Pet 2:21–25 with Isaiah 53.[8]

1 Pet 2:21–25	Isaiah 53
21. (Christ) also suffered for you leaving you an example that ye should follow his steps.	4. he . . . is pained for us
22. Who did no sin neither was guile found in his mouth.	9. he did no sin nor guile was in his mouth
23. Who when he was reviled, reviled not again; when he suffered, threatened not; but committed himself to him that judgeth righteously;	(7. As a lamb before his shearers is dumb, so opens he not his mouth) (11. the Lord also is pleased to justify the just one)
24. Who his own self bare our sins in his body upon the tree, that we, having died unto sin, might live	11. and he shall bear their sins (compare 4–6)
unto righteousness; by whose bruise ye were healed.	5. by his bruise we were healed
25. For ye were going astray like sheep	6. all we like sheep have gone astray

The parallels are too close to be accidental. 1 Pet 2:21–25 is to all intents and purposes a meditation upon Isaiah 53 as fulfilled in the crucifixion of Jesus.

[8] We are now following E.C. Hoskyns and N. Davey, *The Riddle of the New Testament,* pp. 57–59, and quoting the ERV as the most literal modern translation.

3:13–4:6 *Further exhortation.* This passage deals in general with Christians preparing to suffer for their faith, and in their prospective suffering to follow the example of Christ. The passion of Jesus as an example for individual Christians to follow in their suffering is a major theme of the literature of the early church concerning martydom, and it is prominent in this passage.[9] We have noted the strong possibility that there are christological hymns and confessions in this section.

4:7–11 *The End is at hand.* The baptismal homily climaxes on the note of anticipation of the parousia, but even this is interwoven with parenesis.

4:12–5:11 *The persecution parenesis.* The suffering that was thought of as prospective in the baptismal homily has now become actual persecution. The writer exhorts his readers to stand fast and reiterates many of the themes of his homily.

5:12–14 *Closing greetings.*

THE LETTER OF JUDE

The letter of Jude is a polemic, a polemic against a group of heretics within the church who are creating dissidence. They are accused of all manner of evil and vice, but they claim to be Christians and participate in the cultic meals of the community (5:12). They are ecstatic visionaries, whom Jude calls false prophets, and consider themselves to be superior to the angelic powers. Who are they?

These heretics appear to have been Gnostics, because the word used of them and translated as "worldly" in verse 19 is *psychikoi,* a technical term used by Gnostics. They were certainly libertarians; despising the world of the flesh they saw no fault in abandoning themselves to fleshly practices (verses 8 and 12). The writer simply denounces these heretics; he does not discuss their views or argue against them, but calls them names and threatens them with dire examples of punishment taken from Jewish Scriptures. "Jude's method of dealing with the false teaching is the least creative in the New Testament."[10]

The author call himself Jude, the brother of James, which would make him also the brother of Jesus, and tradition has affirmed this (Mark 6:3). But the letter looks back on the time of the apostles as in the past (verse 17), and this, together with features of emerging institutional Christianity in the letter, make such an authorship impossible. The letter is pseudonymous, as is all the literature of the emergent church in the New Testament.

The most interesting features of this letter are the characteristics of emerging institutional Christianity it exhibits. The letter speaks of "the faith once for all delivered to the saints"; faith is the acceptance of authoritative tradition,

---

[9] On the problem of the "descent into hell" in 3:19, see especially J. Fitzmyer, *JBC,* p. 366.
[10] R. Fuller, *Intro.,* p. 161.

and the writer denounces the heretics and admonishes the faithful on the authority of that tradition. There is also evidence of a developing Christian liturgy. In verses 20–21, "pray in the Holy Spirit; keep yourselves in the love of God; wait for the mercy of our Lord Jesus Christ" testifies to the liturgical development of a trinitarian formula. The closing benediction is a magnificent piece of liturgical language, so different in style and tone from the remainder of the letter that the writer has probably taken it from the liturgy of his church.

Structure

This polemical letter defies structural analysis beyond the obvious fact that it opens with a greeting and closes with a doxology. The writer simply denounces the heretics and warns his readers against them.

Exegetical Survey

1–2 *Address and salutation.*

3–4 *The emergence of false teachers* makes it an urgent necessity to contend for the faith once and for all delivered to the saints.

5–7 *Scriptural instances of sin and punishment.* The writer warns his readers that God punishes sin, using as examples the tradition of God punishing the unfaithful Israelites in the wilderness (compare 1 Cor 10:1–11; Heb 3:7–4:11) and the fate of the rebellious angels (Gen 6) and of Sodom and Gomorrah (Gen 19). The reference to the fallen angels seems to exhibit an awareness of how this myth was developed in the apocalyptic works Enoch, Jubilees, and 2 Baruch.

8–16 *Denunciation of the false teachers.* The reference to the archangel Michael in verse 9 is a reference to a legend in an apocalyptic work, the Assumption of Moses, where Michael digs a grave to bury Moses, and Satan appears and unsuccessfully claims the body. Cain (Gen 4) and Balaam (Num 22–24) figure prominently in both Jewish and Christian tradition. Korah led a rebellion against Moses (Num 16:1–11). "Love feasts" are a form of the Christian sacred meal in which the cultic aspect was blended into a regular communal meal. In Corinth, and no doubt elsewhere, this blending led to excesses and loss of the cultic aspect (1 Cor 11:20–22), and the communal meals were eventually separated from the cultic Eucharist. The reference to the wandering stars is from the apocalpytic book of Enoch. The quote in verses 14–15 is from Enoch 1:9.

17–23 *Attitude required of the faithful.* If verse 19 is a quotation, we do not know its source. It may represent the author's understanding of apostolic teaching and is notably apocalyptic in tone.

24–25 *Closing doxology.*

Jude's Use of Apocalyptic Texts

A remarkable aspect of Jude is its use of apocalyptic texts. Apocalyptic flourished in both Judaism and Christianity throughout the New Testament period, and its Jewish and Christian forms were closely related. Jude is eloquent testimony to this relation because he is aware of the myth of the fallen angels in Jewish apocalpytic in general, and he knows the myth of the burial of Moses from a Jewish-Christian apocalypse, the Assumption of Moses. He also alludes to a major apocalyptic work, the book of Enoch, in the matter of the wandering stars, and he explicitly quotes Enoch 1:9. His own understanding of apostolic faith is notably apocalyptic. The letter shows that apocalyptic is still a living force in the period of emerging institutionalism. Nevertheless, when Jude is reused in 2 Pet 2, the author of 2 Peter is careful to remove all references and allusions to apocalyptic works that were excluded from the Jewish canon of Scripture.

THE SECOND LETTER OF PETER

The Second Letter of Peter is, together with the Pastorals, the most thoroughgoing representation in the New Testament of the views of emerging institutional Christianity. Furthermore, 2 Pet 2 is based on Jude 4–16. This evidence makes it impossible for the apostle Peter to have written it, and it is universally recognized as pseudonymous. The writer knows the synoptic gospel account of the transfiguration (1:17–18); he knows 1 Peter (3:1) and the letters of Paul as a collection and as Scripture (3:15–16). He is probably the latest of all the New Testament writers, and a date about A.D. 140 would be appropriate.

This "letter" has a double purpose: to reiterate the hope for the parousia against a growing skepticism and to combat false teachers in the church. The two have a single root in that the false teachers were most probably Christian Gnostics who emphasized knowledge of salvation now and eventual translation to the heavenly sphere, despised the world and the body, and therefore had no concern for a future parousia. The sheer passage of time and the continuing delay of the parousia had undoubtedly sharpened their polemic against the traditional Christian hope.

Although 2 Peter has an opening greeting, it has no further literary characteristics of a letter. Its main text is a manifesto, a strong statement of what the author regards as correct and authoritative teaching against false and disruptive teaching in the church. It opens with a greeting we would find in a Christian letter, but the greeting, like the pseudonymity, is characteristic of emerging institutional Christianity itself.

Structure[11]

The structure of 2 Peter is simple.

Salutation, 1:1–2
Exhortation to holiness, 1:3–21
    1:3–11 Exhortation.
    1:12–18 The certainty of the promise is grounded in the revelation the
        apostle encountered.
    1:19–21 An appeal to scriptural prophecy.
Attack upon the false teachers, 2:1–22
True teaching concerning the day of the Lord, 3:1–10
Parenesis and concluding doxology, 3:11–18

Exegetical Survey

1:1–2 *Salutation.* The salutation is important for an understanding of the author's viewpoint and the emerging institutional Christianity he represents.
It sees faith as something originally obtained by the apostles and now
available to those who stand in succession to them.

1:3–21 *Exhortation to holiness.*
    1:3–11 *Exhortation.* Note the characteristic Hellenistic emphasis on the
    corruption of the world and on escaping it to partake of the divine
    nature (verse 4). It is only a short step from this to the Gnosticism of
    the false teachers. The list of virtues in verses 5 and 6 is a Christian-
    ization of the kind of lists of virtues popular in the Hellenistic world.
    Verse 11 represents a Hellenizing of much earlier Christian language
    about "entering the Kingdom of God."
    1:12–18 *The certainty of the promise is grounded in the revelation encountered by
    the apostle.* This is a difficult passage, but its general meaning seems
    clear. The apostles were eyewitnesses to the transfiguration of Jesus
    and so eyewitnesses of his majesty—i.e., they saw him partake of the
    divine nature on one occasion in anticipation of the moment after his
    resurrection when he would partake of it fully. Having been granted
    this vision, the apostles can testify to the reality of the promise that
    Christians also will one day partake of that divine nature.
    1:19–21 *An appeal to scriptural prophecy.* The promise is also guaranteed
    by the Scriptures. All Scripture is understood as prophecy, not only

---

[11] In the remainder of our discussion of 2 Peter we are deeply indebted to E. Käsemann, "An
Apologia for Primitive Christian Eschatology," now in his collected essays, *Essays on New Testament Themes,* pp. 169–95.

particular books or passages, and a very high, albeit somewhat mechanical, view of the inspiration of Scripture is presented. In such a view the question of canonicity is crucial, and we shall see that 2 Peter is in fact our earliest witness to the development of a definite, distinct, and limited view of the canon of Christian Scripture.

2:1–22 *Attack on the false teachers.* This is based on Jude 4–16. It portrays the false teachers in Jude's language and uses many of his examples. It is interesting that 2 Peter carefully purges Jude of all references to works outside the canonical Scriptures, as the Jewish canon was by this time coming to be defined. Jude has a reference to the myth of the burial of Moses from the Assumption of Moses, an allusion to the book of Enoch in the reference to the wandering stars, and a quotation from Enoch 1:9. The myth of the burial of Moses, the wandering stars, and the quotation are all missing in 2 Peter. It is not that the author of 2 Peter has an objection to apocalyptic; far from it. His objection is to the use of books now regarded as suspect insofar as a canon was developing among the Jews and as it should be accepted by Christians.

3:1–10 *True teaching concerning the day of the Lord.* This section begins with a renewal of the pseudonymous claim to Petrine authorship, which is at the same time a recognition that, for the writer, 1 Peter was already achieving the status of Scripture (verse 1). It continues with a clear recognition of the sacredness of the apostolic age, which is now past (verse 2). The present of the writer is separated from that age as "the last days" (verse 3; compare Jude 17–18 where we have exactly the same distinction between the apostolic age and "the last time"). The scoffing of the false teachers is met by claiming that God's time is different from man's and that the parousia is imminent in God's time and certain in man's. It is an ingenious argument, but it loses the dynamic of the imminence of the parousia in Mark or of the attempt to make theological sense of the delay of the parousia in Matthew or Luke. Verse 10 represents a theme known to us from the synoptic gospels (Matt 24:43 = Luke 12:39) and from 1 Thess 5:2, except that it is considerably embellished.

3:11–18 *Parenesis and concluding doxology.* The most interesting element in this concluding passage is the reference to Paul's letters. In verses 15–17 they are clearly known as a collection and regarded as "Scripture." We are approaching a Christian canon that excludes Jewish apocalyptic works that the Jews themselves were excluding from their canon and that includes Christian writings. The Christian writings embrace at least the synoptic gospels (see 2 Pet 1:17 and its reference to the Transfiguration—this is scriptural because 2 Peter does not use nonscriptural material in this way), 1 Peter (see 2 Pet 3:1), and a collection of the letters of Paul. Another important aspect of these references is the characterization of the letters of Paul as "hard to understand, which the ignorant and unstable twist to their own destruction . . ." (verse 16). This seems to imply that the false teachers the author is directing his polemic against are using the letters of Paul, or some aspects of them, as a basis for their position. The remainder of this passage is parenesis based on reiterating the expectation of the "day of the Lord" in 3:1–10.

THE PASTORAL LETTERS: 1 TIMOTHY, 2 TIMOTHY, TITUS

These letters are known as the "Pastoral Letters" because of their obvious pastoral concern for churches and their ministry. They purport to be written by the apostle Paul, but this is impossible on the following grounds:

Vocabulary. While statistics are not always as meaningful as they may seem, of 848 words (excluding proper names) found in the Pastorals, 306 are not in the remainder of the Pauline corpus, even including the deutero-Pauline 2 Thessalonians, Colossians, and Ephesians. Of these 306 words, 175 do not occur elsewhere in the New Testament, while 211 are part of the general vocabulary of Christian writers of the second century. Indeed, the vocabulary of the Pastorals is closer to that of popular Hellenistic philosophy than it is to the vocabulary of Paul or the deutero-Pauline letters. Furthermore, the Pastorals use Pauline words in a non-Pauline sense: *dikaios* in Paul means "righteous" and here means "upright"; *pistis*, "faith," has become "the body of Christian faith"; and so on.

Literary style. Paul writes a characteristically dynamic Greek, with dramatic arguments, emotional outbursts, and the introduction of real or imaginary opponents and partners in dialogue. The Pastorals are in a quiet meditative style, far more characteristic of Hebrews or 1 Peter, or even of literary Hellenistic Greek in general, than of the Corinthian correspondence or of Romans, to say nothing of Galatians.

The situation of the apostle implied in the letters. Paul's situation as envisaged in the Pastorals can in no way be fitted into any reconstruction of Paul's life and work as we know it from the other letters or can deduce it from the Acts of the Apostles. If Paul wrote these letters, then he must have been released from his first Roman imprisonment and have traveled in the West. But such meager tradition as we have seems to be more a deduction of what must have happened from his plans as detailed in Romans than a reflection of known historical reality.

The letters as reflecting the characteristics of emerging institutional Christianity. The arguments presented above are forceful, but a last consideration is overwhelming, namely, that together with 2 Peter, the Pastorals are of all the texts in the New Testament the most distinctive representatives of the emphases of emerging institutional Christianity. The apostle Paul could no more have written the Pastorals than the apostle Peter could have written 2 Peter.

The Pastorals are, therefore, pseudonymous and the question is why the author, whom we will call the Pastor, following R. H. Fuller, chose to write in the name of the apostle Paul. Vocabulary, style, viewpoint, and concerns in the three letters are sufficiently homogeneous to make it virtually certain that they were written by the same person. The answer probably is that the author believed himself to be in the tradition of Paul; he may have been a second- or third-generation member of the Pauline school. Perhaps also the false teachers against whom he writes were using Pauline material in their teaching, and he wished to present a true understanding of Paul against this.

The affinity of perspective between the Pastorals and 2 Peter, and of language between the Pastorals and second-century Christian literature in general, indicates a date for these letters somewhere in the first half of the second century, perhaps around A.D. 125.

The form of the Pastorals as letters must have been a stratagem by the Pastor. They were directed to the church at large or to churches in a particular area, and the address to individuals known to be companions of Paul is a literary device to lend plausibility. Despite their literary form, like 2 Peter, they are essentially manifestos, written in response to the threat of a spreading Gnosticism within the church. Furthermore, they are also an answer to the growing need for organizational structure in the church.

The structure of the Pastorals is simple; the Pastor argues against the false teachers and urges organizational structure on the church. He urges on "Timothy" or "Titus" correct behavior and practice as ordained ministers of the church. He characteristically holds up the false teachers as bad examples to avoid and the apostle Paul (according to his literary device, himself) as a good one to follow. The structures are too simple to warrant separate discussion, so we proceed immediately to the exegetical survey, in the course of which the structure will become evident.

Exegetical Survey of 1 Timothy

1:1-2 *Salutation.*

1:3-20 *Attack on the doctrine of the false teachers.* The false teaching is apparently a form of Gnosticism with a strong Jewish element. The reference to "myths and endless genealogies" (verse 4) would fit the Gnostic tendency to speculate about the hierarchy of heavenly beings, and the reference to the Law in verses 8-9 indicates the Jewish element. Faith in this passage has become a synonym for "the Christian religion." In verse 5, "sincere faith" can be read as "sincere profession of the Christian religion" (see also 5:8; 6:10, 21). Moreover, that faith has become a matter of accepting doctrinal propositions (verse 15).

2:1-3:16 *A church order: part one.* Reflecting institutional Christianity's concern with the organizational structure of the church, 1 Timothy includes what is to all intents and purposes a church order, divided into two parts, 2:1–3:16 and 4:11–6:19. The first part covers worship in the church (2:1–15) and the ordained ministry (3:1–16).

2:1–15 *Worship in the church.* The regulation to pray "for kings and all who are in high positions" and the grounds given for it (2:1–2) reflect the concern of emerging institutional Christianity for the world outside the church and for the good reputation of Christians in that world.

3:1–16 *The ordained ministry.* In emerging institutional Christianity the bishop is becoming the chief officer of the church, which we also find in the letters of Ignatius. The office of deacon is mentioned here; the term "deacon" is also found in Phil 1:1, and as well in Rom 16:1 where Phoebe is a "deaconess." This section climaxes in one of the great New Testament christological hymns (3:16), no doubt taken by the Pastor from the liturgy of his church.

4:1–10 *An attack on the ethics of the false teachers.* The writer contrasts the ethics of the false teachers with the behavior expected of the true teacher.

4:11–6:19 *A church order: part two.* In the form of instructions to "Timothy" the Pastor develops the ideal of a Christian minister (4:11–5:2). He details regulations concerning widows, who are also a recognized group in the church in the letters of Ignatius (5:3–16), and elders. Earlier in the New Testament *elder* is synonymous with *bishop* (Acts 20:17, 28), but now the bishop is separated as the chief officer (5:17–22). There follow some further instructions to the ideal minister (5:23–25; 6:3–19), and to slaves (6:1–2).

6:20–21 *Conclusion.* Even in his concluding greeting the Pastor continues his polemic against the false teachers. The reference to "what is falsely called knowledge" strengthens the case that the false teaching was a form of Gnosticism.

Exegetical Survey of 2 Timothy

This was the perhaps the first Pastoral written; certainly it is most concerned with creating an impression of personal relationship between Paul and "Timothy," showing a desire to authenticate the manifesto comparable to the "This is now the second letter I have written to you" of 2 Peter 3:1. The Pastor seems to have drawn his material for this from Acts.[12]

---

[12] On the general relationship of the Pastorals to Acts, apart from the question of the personal references being taken from Acts, see C. F. D. Moule, *The Birth of the New Testament,* pp. 220–21. On the question of the Pastor's use of Acts in his personal references to Paul, see R. Fuller, *Intro.,* pp. 139–40. Helpful also is J. L. Houlden, *The Pastoral Epistles,* pp. 23–25, who draws on the studies of the German scholar, A. Strobel.

1:1–2 *Salutation.*

1:3–2:13 *Exhortation to witness on the basis of the example of Paul.* Verses 13 and 14 of chapter 1 exhibit the view of Christian faith characteristic of the emerging institutional church. In essence it is the "pattern of sound words" which was heard from the apostles, and which is to be guarded and followed. Note also 2:2, which has a similar understanding, and 2:8, alluding to Rom 1:3; the Pastor knows a collection of the Pauline letters.

2:14–4:8 *Exhortation to good behavior in all respects.* The Pastor now turns to the behavior expected of the true minister of God. Characteristically, the false teachers are examples to avoid and the apostle Paul an example to follow. In this section we learn more about the false teaching: it is "godless chatter" (2:16); it holds that "the resurrection is past already" (2:18); it features "myths" (4:4). We also learn more about the characteristics of the emerging institutional church: it regards its time as the last time, separate from the time of the apostles (3:1; compare Jude 18; 2 Pet 3:3); it is coming to regard Scripture in a very formal way as "inspired by God" and "profitable" (3:16).

4:9–18 *Paul's personal situation.* This has been constructed to add verisimilitude to the pseudonymity.

4:19–22 *Closing greetings.*

Exegetical Survey of Titus

1:1–4 *Salutation.*

1:5–9 *The ordained ministry.* This section is not a church order such as we find in 1 Timothy but rather some directions with regard to bishops and elders. It seems to equate the two offices, whereas 1 Timothy separated them. Either Titus is considerably earlier than 1 Timothy or, more likely, the situation with regard to the relationship between the two offices was still fluid, and separation of the two was only beginning to take place at the time of the writing of the Pastorals.

1:10–16 *An attack on the false teaching.* The false teaching apparently had some connection with Crete (1:12) and certainly with Judaism (1:14).

2:1–3:7 *Exhortation to a proper Christian behavior.* Here is the kind of moral teaching standard in the literature of emerging institutional Christianity (compare 1 Pet 2:11–3:7). Note also the renewed parousia hope and the description of Jesus as "our great God and Savior" (2:13; compare 2 Pet 1:1).

3:8–11 *Renewed attack on the false teaching.*

3:12–14   *Personal notes.*

3:15   *Closing greetings.*

THE CHARACTERISTICS OF THE EMERGING INSTITUTIONAL CHURCH

In the era of the emerging institutional church, the church needed organization and structure. At the same time, it was faced with a threat from within, the growing influence of Gnosticism, and with the need to relate to those outside, especially those in positions of influence or power. In meeting these various needs the church developed the characteristics of the emerging institutional church.

The Apostolic Tradition

Perhaps the most obvious characteristic of the emerging institutional church is its concern for the apostolic age and its reliance on the idea of apostolic tradition. The church is now separated from the age of the apostles by a considerable period, and the tendency is to look back on that time as one of perfection, as the golden age of the church, as the time of revelation by God through Jesus to the church in the persons of the apostles. This process begins in the legends of the early church in the Acts of the Apostles, but the author of Luke-Acts himself deliberately stresses the parallels between that heroic age and his readers'. The writers in this period, however, characteristically see themselves and their readers as separated from the age of the apostles. That time was the time of revelation and perfection; theirs is the time of apostasy, of falling away. These are the "last days," and they are days of trial and corruption (Jude 17–18; 2 Pet 3:3; 2 Tim 3:1–5).

In many respects this understanding is strikingly parallel to the apocalyptic writers' understanding their days as the last days of a history hastening to its close. The representatives of the emerging institutional church shared the Christian apocalyptic hope of the parousia. Yet there is an important difference. The apocalyptic writers looked to the future *and lived out of that future;* the representatives of the emerging institutional church looked to the future but *lived out of the past,* the past of the apostolic age. An apocalyptic writer's expectation of the future dominates his whole understanding of things; a representative of emerging institutional Christianity, such as the author of 2 Peter, has an expectation of the future but is dominated by the past of the apostolic age, and the tradition that he believes comes to him out of that past.

The concept of an apostolic tradition is, therefore, essential to emerging institutional Christianity and this tradition must be guaranteed both in its origin and transmission. If it is to carry the authority of the apostles, then the apostles must themselves be the guarantors of the origin of the tradition. But if it is to carry the authority of the apostles into the "last days," there must be a separate agent guaranteeing its purity in transmission. That agent is the Holy Spirit; as the apostles are guarantors of the origin of the tradition, so the Spirit is the guarantor of its transmission (Jude 3; 2 Pet 1:12–18; 2 Tim 1:14).

In these circumstances these writers have a particular way of meeting the false teaching. They do not argue the issues or debate with the false teachers. Instead they confront the teaching and the teachers and, standing squarely on the authority of the apostolic tradition, denounce both as not being in accord with the apostolic truth.

The Concept of Faith

Emerging institutional Christianity conceived of revelation as given in the past, in the apostolic age, and handed on in the church as an object, sacred to be sure but nonetheless an object. It follows from this that its concept of faith is very different from that of earlier periods of the church's history. It is no longer a dynamic belief in the imminent coming of Jesus as Son of Man, nor is it a similarly dynamic relationship to the risen Lord; it has become the acceptance of a revealed truth that can be expressed in propositional sentences. It is even a synonym for the Christian religion. The gospel of Matthew prepares for this with its concept of obedience to a verbal revelation authoritatively interpreted; and Hebrews, where faith is "the assurance of things hoped for, the conviction of things not seen" (Heb 11:1), represents a transitional stage. But in the literature of emerging institutional Christianity, faith becomes the acceptance of monotheism (Jas 2:19), the acceptance of authoritative tradition (Jude 20), something originally obtained by the apostles and available to those who stand in true succession to them (2 Pet 1:1–2), and a synonym for the Christian religion (1 Tim 1:5). The key passages are, however, 2 Tim 1:13–14 with its "pattern of sound words" to be guarded and passed on; 2 Tim 2:2 with a similar emphasis; and the propositional statements scattered through the Pastorals that are "sure"—i.e., part of the structure of faith, the adjective coming from the same root as the noun "faith" (1 Tim 1:15; 3:1; 4:9; 2 Tim 2:11; Tit 3:8).

The View of Scripture

The emphasis on authoritative apostolic tradition and on the Spirit as its guardian leads naturally to a high view of the written deposit of that tradition and of its Jewish counterpart, Scripture. In 2 Pet 1:20–21, Scripture does not come "by the impulse of man, but men moved by the Holy Spirit spoke from God," and in 2 Tim 3:16, "All scripture is inspired by God. . . ." This view of Scripture naturally brought with it a concern for defining what constituted

Scripture and what did not. The concern for a canon was intensified by the successful Jewish definition of Scriptures in this period (about A.D. 90, at Jamnia) and also by the fact that the Gnostic false teachers depended on their own "Scriptures," which were often "secret" books or writings (for example, the Gnostic gospel of Thomas, whose opening reads: "These are the secret words which the living Jesus spake"). Motivated by their own high view of Scripture, challenged by the successful Jewish promulgation of a canon, and confronted by the necessity for authoritative writings with which to confront the Gnostic false teachers and their secret books, the representatives of the emerging institutional church took the first step toward defining a Christian canon of Scripture.

The most dramatic example is the contrast between Jude and 2 Peter 2. Jude makes indiscriminate use of the texts the Jews were accepting into their canon—what Christians were to call the Old Testament—and the texts the Jews were rejecting; in this instance apocalyptic texts. Jude is here typical of earlier phases of the Christian movement. But when Jude is used as the basis for 2 Peter 2, all reference to anything outside the Jewish canon of Scripture is carefully removed. The author of 2 Peter is paying eloquent testimony to the force of the Jewish example. In his own work he takes significant steps toward a Christian equivalent. By his treatment of Jude he has already revealed himself to be the first Christian writer to accept the Jewish canon of the Old Testament. Similarly, he is the first Christian writer to refer to Paul's letters as "Scripture" (2 Pet 3:15–16), and in his treatment of the transfiguration of Jesus (2 Pet 1:16–19) and in his reference to "the second letter I have written to you" (2 Pet 3:1), he is also prepared to accept the gospels and 1 Peter as "Scripture," and incidentally is not too reluctant to put his own letter in that category.

An Ordained Ministry

A natural outgrowth of the emerging institutional church's concern for its organizational structure was its emphasis on a regular ordained ministry. There is in its literature, especially in the Pastorals, the beginning of the separation of the offices of bishop and elder (1 Tim 3:1–7), explicit instructions for the offices of deacon (1 Tim 3:8–13) and elder and bishop, apparently here synonymous (Tit 1:5–9), and reference to the actual act of ordination to the ministry of the church, the laying on of hands (2 Tim 1:6).

The Concern for "Those Outside" the Church

The church settling down to the task of witnessing in the world must necessarily deal with its relations with the world at large, as the author of Luke-Acts dealt with the Roman Empire and its authorities. In the literature of the emerging institutional church, there is a parallel concern for authorities—

governors, kings, etc.—and also for the good reputation of Christians and the church among "those outside" (1 Pet 2:11–17; Tit 2:7–8; 3:1–2).

The Epistolary Form

Outstanding in the literature of the emerging institutional church is the deliberate use of the form of the letter. Only one of the texts is actually a letter (1 Peter), and the bulk of that is a baptismal homily. Of the others, James is parenesis and the remainder—Jude, 2 Peter, and the Pastorals—are manifestos. Why then are they all given, artificially, the form of letters? The answer is probably twofold. In the first place, at this time the letters of Paul were known and were being circulated as Scripture. To imitate the literary form was to present the churches with something familiar and hence more likely to be accepted. In the second place, and actually much more important, imitating the form of a letter provided an opportunity for pseudonymity—an opportunity to write in the name of a man from the apostolic age—and pseudonymity is crucial to this literature.

Pseudonymity

We have already discussed pseudonymity in the New Testament at several points,[13] but since pseudonymity is a major characteristic of the literature of the emerging institutional church, we must now give the subject closer attention. We discuss, first, pseudonymity in the New Testament apart from the literature of the emerging institutional church, and then we turn to the phenomenon in that literature itself.

Pseudonymity in the New Testament Apart from the Literature of the Emerging Institutional Church

The synoptic gospels and the Acts of the Apostles are not pseudonymous; they are anonymous. They were originally circulated without any author's name, and the names they now bear were ascribed to them in the early church. Similarly, the literature of the Johannine school first circulated anonymously, except that the writer of the second and third letters identifies himself as "the elder," and the author of the appendix to the gospel, chapter 21, identifies the evangelist as "the disciple whom Jesus loved." The apocalyptic author of the book of Revelation identifies himself as "John" with no further qualification,

---

[13] A brief general discussion of the authorship of the books of the N.T. is given in chapter 2, pp. 41-43. The pseudonymity of the deutero-Pauline literature is discussed in chapter 7: pp. 207-08 (general), pp. 208-09 (2 Thess), pp. 209-12 (Col), pp. 218-22 (Eph).

and we have no reason to doubt that a John "of Patmos" was in fact the author of the book, though we have every reason to doubt that we may identify him with any other "John" known to us from the early days of the church.

Outside the literature of the emerging institutional church, pseudonymity confronts us in the New Testament only in the case of the deutero-Pauline letters: 2 Thessalonians, Colossians, and Ephesians. These are in a sense a special case, for they are an instance of pupils deliberately writing in the name of the master. This was a wholly acceptable practice in the ancient world—Plato wrote in the name of Socrates—and need occasion no further comment. Analogous to the pseudonymity of the deutero-Pauline letters is the quite remarkable gospel practice of putting everything in the form of sayings of Jesus and stories about him, even when the contents come from the church.

Pseudonymity in the Literature of the Emerging Institutional Church

It is in the literature of the emerging institutional church that pseudonymity becomes a major factor in the New Testament. Every single text in this literature is pseudonymous! Neither James nor Jude, the brothers of Jesus, nor Peter nor Paul are the authors of the texts claiming their names in this literature. There is no single text in this literature that bears the name of its author; all without exception are written in the name of a figure from the apostolic age.

In claiming authorship, the other Christian literature of this period is also interesting. Clement of Rome does not write to the church at Corinth in his own name, but in the name of the church at Rome. The letter begins, "The church of God which sojourns in Rome to the church of God which sojourns in Corinth," and the actual author is nowhere mentioned in the letter. Ignatius of Antioch writes in his own name, but he is writing personal letters to churches and to an individual (Polycarp). The Didache is technically "The Teaching of the Lord to the Gentiles by the Twelve Apostles." In other words, in this period there was a reluctance to write in one's own name; the important thing is not oneself, but the church one represents, or still more, the apostolic tradition in which one stands. Ignatius is the exception, but then his letters are distinctly personal letters; they are not parenesis, manifestos, or incipient church orders.

We say "Ignatius is the exception," but what we should perhaps say is that Paul, Ignatius, and John of Patmos are all the exceptions. Of all the literature we are discussing—the New Testament literature plus 1 Clement, the letters of Ignatius, and the Didache—only these few intensely personal texts are written in the names of their authors. Paul writes personal letters to churches he has founded, to an individual he knows, and to a church from which he hopes to get support. John of Patmos writes an account of a personal revelation granted to him. Ignatius writes personal letters to churches and to an individual, Polycarp, known to him. The gospels and Acts are anonymous, as are 1 John, Hebrews, and the Didache. The second and third letters of John are written by someone who identifies himself with his office in the church, and 1

Clement is written in the name of the church in Rome. The deutero-Pauline letters are written in the name of Paul, and the literature of the emerging institutional church is written in the names of men from the apostolic age, including Paul.

We can see that the pseudonymity of the literature of the emerging institutional church is not something exceptional that must be accounted for; rather, it is part of a pattern. What we need to do in the early Christian literature is distinguish the highly personal from the remainder. Paul and Ignatius are writing very personal letters, and John of Patmos is giving an account of a personal revelation granted to him. But the others do not think of their work in this way. They are writing by the authority of the risen Lord, or of the church, or of an office within the church, or of their teacher, or of the apostolic age. So anonymity or pseudonymity is the rule; it is personal authorship that is the exception.

Once we recognize this, the pseudonymity of the literature of the emerging institutional church becomes readily understandable. The writers viewed themselves as defenders of a faith once and for all delivered to the apostles and transmitted in the church by means of an apostolic tradition. So they wrote in the name of apostles and even went to considerable lengths to establish "authenticity," as when the Pastor carefully constructs situations in the life of Paul out of which to write. The apostolic age and the apostolic tradition are the source of their inspiration and their authority. To write in the name of a man from the apostolic age is for them the next step.

THE INTERPRETATION OF THE LITERATURE OF THE EMERGING INSTITUTIONAL CHURCH

The interpretation of this literature depends very much on the personal standpoint of the interpreter (as does the interpretation of any literature). One who shares the concern of the writers for the apostolic age and tradition will find that these texts speak directly to him, as will one who shares the concern of the authors for proper order and sound doctrine. Others will perhaps see these texts as representing the church hammering out a new vision of its faith and purpose in drastically changing historical circumstances, which is what in fact they do represent, and will find that they speak to a similar situation of drastically changing historical circumstances.

Further Reading

We are immensely indebted to the work and insights of Ernst Käsemann, especially his epoch-making essay on 2 Peter, "An Apologia for Primitive Christian Eschatology," now found in his collected *Essays on New Testament*

Themes, pp. 169–95. Further, J. C. Beker's contributions to *IDB* on Jude, 2 Peter, and especially the Pastorals were of considerable help.

One may also consult N. A. Dahl, "Letter," *IDB Suppl.*, pp. 538–41; H. Koester, "Literature, Early Christian," *IDB Suppl.*, pp. 551–56; D. Schroeder, "Parenesis," *IDB Suppl.*, p. 643 and "Exhortation," pp. 303–04.

Helpful summaries with recent bibliography can be found in G. Krodel, ed., *Ephesians, Colossians, 2 Thessalonians, The Pastoral Epistles* (R. H. Fuller) and *Hebrews-James* (G. S. Sloyan)-*1 and 2 Peter* (G. Krodel; F. W. Danker)-*Jude* (G. Krodel)-*Revelation.*

Important commentaries on this literature are:

M. Dibelius and H. Greeven, *James* (Hermeneia).
J. N. D. Kelley, *A Commentary on the Epistles of Peter and Jude.*
M. Dibelius and H. Conzelmann, *The Pastoral Epistles* (Hermeneia).
J. L. Houlden, *The Pastoral Epistles* (Pelican New Testament Commentaries).

For the Letter of James, see:

PCB, pp. 1022–25 (L. E. Elliott-Binns).
JBC, pp. 369–77 (T. W. Leahy).
IDB, vol. 2, pp. 794–99 (A. E. Barnett).
X IDB Suppl., pp. 469–70 (R. B. Ward).
W. G. Kümmel, *Intro.*, pp. 403–16.
W. Marxsen, *Intro.*, pp. 226–32.
R. Fuller, *Intro.*, pp. 151–55.

For the First Letter of Peter, see:

PCB, pp. 1026–30 (C. E. B. Cranfield).
JBC, pp. 362–68 (J. A. Fitzmyer).
Δ X IDB, vol. 3, pp. 758–66 (J. C. van Unnik).
W. G. Kümmel, *Intro.*, pp. 416–24.
W. Marxsen, *Intro.*, pp. 233–38.
R. Fuller, *Intro.*, pp. 155–60.

For the Letter of Jude, see:

PCB, pp. 1041–42 (G. H. Boobyer).
X JBC, pp. 378–80 (T. W. Leahy).
IDB, vol. 2, pp. 1009–11 (J. C. Beker).
W. G. Kümmel, *Intro.*, pp. 425–29.
W. Marxsen, *Intro.*, pp. 239–40.
R. Fuller, *Intro.*, pp. 160–62.

For the Second Letter of Peter, see:

PCB, pp. 1031–34 (G. H. Boobyer).
JBC, pp. 494–98 (T. W. Leahy).

IDB, vol. 3, pp. 767–71 (J. C. Beker).
W. G. Kümmel, *Intro.*, pp. 429–34.
W. Marxsen, *Intro.*, pp. 241–45.
R. Fuller, *Intro.*, pp. 162–67.

The great work on this letter is, however, E. Käsemann's essay.

For the Pastoral Letters, see:

PCB, pp. 1001–07 (A. J. B. Higgins).
JBC, pp. 350–61 (G. A. Denzer).
IDB, vol. 3, pp. 668–75 (J. C. Beker).
W. G. Kümmel, *Intro.*, pp. 366–87.
W. Marxsen, *Intro.*, pp. 199–216.
R. Fuller, *Intro.*, pp. 133–44. (Especially valuable for a discussion of the Pastor's creation of circumstances in the life of Paul as background to his letters.)

Rembrandt's The Return of the Prodigal Son *(ca. 1665) is based on the parable of Jesus recorded in Luke 15:11–32.*

CHAPTER THIRTEEN

THE PRESUPPOSITION
OF THE NEW TESTAMENT:
JESUS

The ministry and message of Jesus is the presupposition for everything else in the New Testament. Had Jesus bar ("son of") Joseph from Nazareth not proclaimed his message concerning the Kingdom of God to the men and women of Galilee and Judea, had the Romans not executed him as a politically dangerous revolutionary, had some of those who heard him in his lifetime not come to believe that God had raised him from the dead, there would have been no Christian church and no New Testament. It is equally true that the books of the New Testament were produced for the service of the church by Christians who were far more interested in the living Lord they believed present in their midst and whom they expected to come soon on the clouds of heaven "to judge the quick and the dead" than they were in the historical Jesus bar Joseph from Nazareth. On this the modern view differs radically from that of the ancient church, and we must say something further about it.

THE FIGURE "JESUS" IN THE NEW TESTAMENT

In earliest Christianity the figure of Jesus was central to the belief and expectation of the group. But by our standards this figure was extremely complex. In part he was the Jesus who had lived and proclaimed his message in Galilee and Judea—whom we would mean by the "historical Jesus." But in still larger part he was the risen Lord present in the Christian communities, still conducting his ministry to them and through them. The early Christians took the extraordinary step of recording his teaching-through-prophets in the form of Jesus' speaking to his disciples in Galilee and Judea, recording their arguments with their fellow Jews in the form of Jesus disputing with scribes and Pharisees, and recording the success and failure of the Christian mission in

397

terms of people coming to Jesus from various places in and around Palestine. Then, finally, the Jesus they spoke and wrote of was the one whom they expected suddenly to appear "on the clouds of heaven" to judge and redeem, to destroy and remake, and they created a whole tradition portraying him already in his earthly ministry as exercising the authority that would be his when he came as Son of Man. In other words, earliest Christianity created a Jesus tradition—a tradition of sayings of Jesus and stories about him—based partly on actual reminiscence of his ministry and teaching, partly on experience of him in their present, and partly on an expectation of him in the future. But in all this the *form* was the form of sayings and stories of Jesus in what we would call his earthly ministry.

When in due course the authors of the various books of the New Testament came to write about Jesus, they were heirs to this complex way of thinking about him, and they added new dimensions and emphases. Paul concentrates his attention almost exclusively on the crucifixion and resurrection of Jesus and is virtually uninterested in his life; the unknown author of Hebrews sees Jesus as the fulfillment of whatever is truly valid about Jewish Temple worship; the evangelist Matthew sees him as the embodiment of the new and final revelation of God to his people; and so on. Only the author of Luke-Acts comes close to a modern historical interest when he depicts Jesus in his ministry as a paradigm of Christian piety. But he was in turn reinterpreting traditional materials so that though he has something approaching a modern historical concern, his gospel is just as far from being a life of Jesus in any modern sense as are the others.

Furthermore, earliest Christianity also treated Jesus as the Hellenistic world in general treated its heroic figures: it developed legends increasingly depicting him as a man of miraculous knowledge and power. There are legendary stories in the gospels, such as the Stilling of the Storm (Mark 4:35–41) and the Walking on the Water (Mark 6:45–52) and many more in the later apocryphal gospels.

This varied treatment of the figure of Jesus in the New Testament makes the task of arriving at historical information about him very difficult, but some progress is possible. We will now say something about how that progress has been made, and for the sake of convenience we will treat the life and the message of Jesus separately.

The Life of Jesus from a Historical Standpoint

The Outline of the Story of Jesus in the Gospels

Serious historical presentations of the life of Jesus emerged in the nineteenth century,[1] and the writers took the obvious step of building on the

---

[1] The classic account of this movement is, of course, A. Schweitzer, *The Quest of the Historical Jesus.* D. Duling, *Jesus Christ Through History,* gives a broader view and contains sections on the Social Gospel in the United States, Bousset and the History of Religions School, Loisy and Roman Catholic Modernism, Machen and American Evangelical Christianity, Fundamentalism, the Bultmannians, and recent movements in this century.

framework of the narrative outline in the gospels. With the development of the "Markan hypothesis," that the gospel of Mark was the earliest gospel and fundamentally a historical presentation of the ministry of Jesus, the outline of that gospel came more and more to be used in this way.[2] The outline seemed reasonable when it was treated as historical: a beginning in Galilee; the gathering of disciples on the one hand and the rise of opposition on the other; the movement toward Jerusalem and the intensive private instruction of the disciples; the final ministry in Jerusalem and the narrative of the passion. But then in 1901 William Wrede published his book *Das Messiasgeheimnis in den Evangelien* (*The Messianic Secret in the Gospels*) and showed that those who saw history in the gospel of Mark were reading that history into the gospel; the evangelist himself was motivated by theological concerns and his outline was dogmatic rather than historical.[3] In 1919 Karl Ludwig Schmidt's *Der Rahmen der Geschichte Jesu* (*The Framework of the Story of Jesus*) showed that the evangelist had in fact constructed his own outline, and this began the movement toward the kind of understanding of the gospel and its outline we presented in chapter 8. Clearly, if this understanding of the gospel and its outline is correct, and it does represent a consensus of contemporary scholarly opinion, the outline of the gospel of Mark has no historical value.

But if that is true of the Markan outline, it is certainly true of the outlines of the gospels of Matthew and Luke. We saw in chapters 9 and 10 that these gospels follow the outline of Mark in general, and where they differ they do so for theological reasons. Their outlines, therefore, also have no historical value. The gospel of John is even more intensely theologically motivated than Mark, and its outline also has no historical value. Though in some respects where the gospel of John differs from the synoptic gospels it could be historically correct (e.g., in implying more than one visit to Jerusalem), this does not make the outline any less theological or more historical in purpose. The several visits to Jerusalem by Jesus are theologically motivated; they provide the evangelist with the opportunity to introduce the symbolism of some of the major discourses.

The most that can be argued for the gospel outlines is that some aspects of the story they tell have an element of inherent historical probability. For example, it is inherently probable that Jesus was baptized by John the Baptist and that his ministry had some connection with that of the Baptist. Whether the connection was that of Jesus beginning his ministry while John was still at work (according to the gospel of John) or only after John was "delivered up" (according to the synoptic gospels) we do not know, but that there was some continuity between the two ministries is inherently probable.

Other aspects of the story of the life of Jesus can be accepted on the basis of extrapolation from known historical data. A calling and training of disciples is certain in view of the role of Peter and others in the early church, and some

---

[2] For a discussion of this hypothesis and its rise and fall, see N. Perrin, *What Is Redaction Criticism?*, pp. 3–13.

[3] W. Wrede's work is presented and discussed in N. Perrin, *What Is Redaction Criticism?* pp. 7–13; D. Duling, *Jesus Christ Through History*, pp. 233–36.

kind of table fellowship between Jesus and the disciples as a group is extremely probable considering the role of sacred meals in earliest Christianity. Other elements of the story can be accepted on the basis of extrapolation from aspects of the teaching of Jesus that are established as authentic: that Jesus proclaimed the Kingdom of God, that he had a special concern for the group known as "tax collectors and sinners," that he did not attempt to lead a revolt against Rome, and so on.

The Old Testament and Events in the Life of Jesus

A further problem for historical research into the life of Jesus is that so many of the events portrayed in the gospels are narrated as the fulfillment of Old Testament texts, or their details are allusions to the Old Testament. This is especially the case in the "formula quotations" in the gospel of Matthew, but it is a phenomenon in all the gospels. Good examples from the pre-Matthean stage of gospel writing are the Triumphal Entry and the Crucifixion in Mark. The former (Mark 11:1–10) fulfills Zech 9:9, and almost all the narrative details in the latter (Mark 15:22–37) are from the Psalms.

This phenomenon inevitably raises the question as to whether the details of the events, or even the events themselves, have been built up out of the Old Testament and whether, therefore, they "actually happened." To add narrative details from the Old Testament to interpret an event or even to create an event from an Old Testament text to interpret a person or movement would be quite in keeping with ancient Jewish practice, and certainly Christians did both of these things. We can see Matthew adding the detail of the second animal from Zech 9:9 to his account of the triumphal entry (Matt 21:7; compare his source, Mark 11:7), and it would be all but universally agreed that the birth and infancy stories in Matthew's gospel were created from the Old Testament texts they are held to fulfill. On the other hand, Jesus did enter Jerusalem as a pilgrim and he *was* crucified. Each event or narrative detail in which there is a quotation from or an allusion to the Old Testament—very many indeed—has to be investigated on its own merit.

The Historical Reconstruction of the Message of Jesus from the New Testament

Though it is virtually impossible to say very much about the life of Jesus on the basis of the New Testament, the same is not true of his message. Here our resources are greater, and historical scholarship has arrived at satisfactory criteria for determining the authenticity of material attributed to the Jesus of the New Testament.

For the sake of convenience we summarize here what we have said in earlier chapters and, indeed, in some part earlier in this chapter. The New Testament writers present us with material put on the lips of the Jesus of the gospels by the church. But this Jesus is not the historical Jesus and the material attributed to him in fact had a long and complex history of transmission in the tradition of the church before it reached the form in which we find it. It came in part from Jesus himself, but also from anonymous prophets and scribes in the community, and even from the evangelists themselves. It had constantly been edited and interpreted in response to the changing needs and insights of the communities of Christians through which it passed. Our problem is, therefore, twofold: we have to find a way of working back through the tradition to the earliest form of the material we can reach, and then we have to devise criteria for determining whether in that form it can be attributed to the historical Jesus.

Working back through the tradition to Jesus requires, in the first place, an acknowledgment of the nature of the gospels as we understand them through the perspective of *Redaktionsgeschichte*, or redaction criticism, as presented in chapters 8–11. As pointed out, the Johannine discourses do not seem to come from sources but represent the theology, or better, the "high Christology," of the evangelist himself. Thus, Jesus' teaching in John is John's redaction. In the synoptic gospels, we remember that Matthew and Luke share with other New Testament documents (2 Thessalonians, Ephesians, 2 Peter) the incorporation of previously written documents, or parts of them. In this case, the documents are Mark and Q, as well as other sources. In addition, there were undoubtedly other editions of Mark. All of this is what we called the reinterpretation of tradition in chapter 2, and this process continues among the copyists, as the four endings of Mark and a number of interpolations indicate. Moreover, all of the evangelists share in the interpretative process when they place Jesus' teachings at various locations in their writings, and give them time and place. It was Mark who created the Messianic confessions at Caesarea Philippi and before the high priest in Jerusalem; it was Matthew who created the long discourses out of isolated pieces of tradition; and it was Luke who created the programmatic scene of Jesus teaching in the Nazareth synagogue. These contexts, then, must be set aside and the isolated teachings themselves studied.

The study of the isolated units of tradition apart from their present context in order to describe their forms and theorize about their histories as they functioned in the various religious contexts of early Christian communities is called *Formgeschichte*, or form criticism (literally, the history of forms). It was developed in Germany, especially in the period after World War I, when scholars became aware that the New Testament writers had made extensive use of traditional material. Form criticism has not been limited to an analysis of the gospels; in fact, we have already used its results in suggesting that Paul and other writers in the New Testament constantly quote hymns, confessions, benedictions, and other elements from the liturgies of the New Testament churches. Similarly, they use lists of virtues and vices and lists of the duties of the various members of a household, which were consulted for the purpose of ethical instruction not only in the Christian churches, but also in the Jewish synagogues and in the schools of Greek moral philosophy. But perhaps more startling, it became apparent from form criticism that much of the material presented by the evangelists in the gospels was also in a more or less fixed form and that it functioned in the life and work of the Christian churches before its use by the evangelists in their gospels. Moreover, these forms were by no means unique to the Christian movement but were found in the literary traditions of other religious and philosophical movements in the Hellenistic world.

Bultmann, whose classic form critical work has become the foundation for further refinements,[4] divided the synoptic material into two general categories, narratives about Jesus and discourses of Jesus. The narratives about Jesus, like the biographical framework of the total story of Jesus itself, were judged to have little actual historical value, though historical events might lie hidden in them. Miracle stories, for example, were so retold that they often sounded like the miracle stories so common in the Greco-Roman world. Jesus was undoubtedly an exorcist, but the specifics of his healing activity have become clouded by tradition. Likewise, legendary accounts such as the birth and baptism have some historical material in them—for example, Mary, the mother of Jesus, or Jesus' baptism by John—but the stories as they came to be written became religious stories with a point of view. In the discourses, we are on more solid ground. Bultmann divided them into a number of forms, the broadest categories being apothegms, "words of Jesus," "I-Sayings," and parables. We shall have more to say about such forms and their subgroups below; here, we shall only illustrate the general problem of form and how an analysis of form can contribute to historical understanding.

One of Bultmann's forms was the *biographical apothegm*,[5] a story from the life of a wise man that culminates in a pregnant saying, or sayings, or in a brief dialogue. It is the characteristic of these biographical apothegms that when they occur in several versions, the biographical setting is the variant but the saying, sayings, or dialogue remain constant. Such stories were extraordinarily popular in the ancient world, and we find them in every possible cultural context, including the New Testament with its stories about Jesus. Examples of each of the possibilities we have mentioned from the New Testament stories about Jesus would be: Mark 3:19b–22 = Matt 12:22–24 = Luke 11:14–16 (story culminating in a single saying, in this instance to the effect that Jesus casts out demons by the power of the prince of demons); Matt 8:18–22 = Luke 9:57–60 (story culminating in two sayings, one about the homelessness of the

---

[4] R. Bultmann, *The History of the Synoptic Tradition* (originally 1921); N. Perrin, *Rediscovering the Teaching of Jesus*, chapter 1; E.V. McKnight, *What Is Form Criticism?* For Bultmann's perspective on Jesus, see D. Duling, *Jesus Christ Through History*, pp. 262–81. It would be generally acknowledged today that Bultmann's form criticism has to be expanded or revised by views of oral tradition studied in anthropology, the relation of form and function in literary criticism, and the "setting in life" suggested by social historiographical analysis; cf. C. Carlston, "Form Criticism, NT," *IDB Suppl.*, pp. 345–48 (bibliography). Some literary critical orientations think in terms of a need for criticism of the historical presuppositions of classical form criticism, e.g., N. Petersen, *Literary Criticism for New Testament Critics*.

[5] For a recent analysis of the apothegm oriented to literary criticism, see R. Tannehill et al., *Semeia*, vol. 20.

Son of Man, and one about the dead burying their dead); Mark 3:31–35 = Matt 12:46–50 = Luke 8:19–21 (story about Jesus' true relatives, culminating in a dialogue). In each of these instances, and in the many others that might be quoted, the relative freedom of the story compared to the relatively fixed nature of the saying, sayings, or dialogue indicates the evangelists' understanding of the essential nature of this category. Even knowing the version in Mark, Matthew and Luke do not consider themselves bound by its biographical element, and either vary it themselves or follow another version known to them. What this means for the historical study of the life of Jesus is clear: if the saying, sayings, or dialogue remains constant and the biographical setting varies from case to case, one will look for the preservation of Jesus' teaching in the saying, sayings, or dialogue, not the biographical setting.

The first concern of form criticism is with distinctive literary forms; the second is with the religious situation or context in which the form had a definite function. This can be illustrated by the parable of the Great Supper in Luke 14:16–24 and Matthew 22:1–10, with a third version found in the Coptic Gnostic Gospel of Thomas discovered at Nag Hammadi, designated Gos. Thos. 92:10–35.[6] In the Matthean version, the story is about a king who gives a wedding feast for his son; he sends his servants to fetch those who have been invited, but they do not come; he sends "other servants" who explain all the preparations for the wedding feast. Now the invited guests make excuses and some abuse the servants and kill them (verse 6). The king is angry. He sends his troops and destroys the murderers and burns their city (verse 7). Then he sends servants to the thoroughfares and they invite everyone they find, "both good and bad," and the wedding hall is filled.

The reader of Matthew's gospel will have just read the previous story about the wicked tenants who have killed the son of the owner of the vineyard (cf. Isa 5:2) and he responds by putting "those wretches to a miserable death" (21:41), after which comes a quotation from Scripture, "The very stone which the builders rejected has become the cornerstone . . ." (cf. 21:42). Prior to that is another parable about two sons, one of whom is obedient, the other is not, with the point being that tax collectors and harlots will go into the Kingdom of God before the chief priests and the elders of the people (cf. 21:23, 45). *After* the story of the wedding feast, the reader will learn—somewhat surprisingly and abruptly—that even though the wedding hall is filled with people from the thoroughfares, a man without a wedding garment is bound and cast into the outer darkness where men weep and gnash their teeth. All of this shows that Matthew is thinking in terms of at least a two-phase salvation history in which the church is the true successor to Israel, even though those *in* the church can also be excluded at the final judgment (the wedding garment).

This whole section indicates that Matthew is interpreting the story of the wedding feast as an allegory about Israel and the church: when Israel does not

---

[6] J. Jeremias, *The Parables of Jesus*, chapter 2; N. Perrin, *Rediscovering*, pp. 110–14; J. D. Crossan, *In Parables*, pp. 70–73.

respond to the wedding feast for God's son, and indeed, kills his servants (by persecution), God destroys them, burns their holy city, Jerusalem, and invites the outsiders, "both good and bad." In effect, the allegory states that in the light of the Jewish wars with Rome, the church has succeeded Israel as the people of God.

The Lukan version is different, different enough that some wonder whether it comes from the Q source. In Luke 14:16–24, there is no king, but a man; no wedding feast, but a great banquet; and no son. Hints of allegorization are present in the two sets of servants (14:21, 23), but there is no suggestion of the developed allegory in Matthew's story. Rather, the story contains a point typical of Luke: those who are subsequently invited are "the poor and maimed and blind and lame" (14:21). What we observe here is that Luke, who has a highly developed salvation history in his writings as a whole, does not have a version of the story with nearly as much salvation history allegory. The story is simpler, more to the point, with a general moral teaching. A natural conclusion would be that Luke's version of the story is earlier and reflects less of the special Lukan point of view.

Is this the version that Jesus told? Was Luke's concern about the "poor, maimed, blind, and lame" also typical of Jesus? Before drawing any conclusion, we must note a third version of the story, that found in Gos. Thos. 92:10–35. In this version the man who prepares a dinner sends out no advance invitations and there are four refusals instead of three. More importantly, the conclusion of the Thomas version is "tradesmen and merchants [shall] not [enter] the places of my Father." There is no invitation to special groups, but only to those whom the servant finds on the roads (92:31–34). In this version what is new, apart from the unusual fourfold refusal, is the suddenness of the invitation and the moral condemnation of the rich.

In all these versions, we can observe different interpretations of an original story: God's rejection of Israel and acceptance of the Christians; the good news for the "poor, maimed, blind, and lame"; and the condemnation of materialism (in Thomas materialism is a hindrance to achieving true *gnosis*, or "knowledge"). These interpretations represent the interests of the early churches; certainly concern for the poor was prior to Luke and even part of Jesus' teaching. However, in terms of *form*, the original parable of Jesus was a simple story that had none of these applications. He spoke simply of a man who held a sudden dinner, and without advance warning, invited guests who could not come. So a servant was sent to invite anyone who could come. The story beckons the hearer into a world where the unusual occurs: the invited do not come, the uninvited do. This reversal of the customary is quite like many of Jesus' parables, and the original version probably was something like it. In the process we can see the various ways in which Christians of later times interpreted it. For them, it functioned differently. From time to time, then, we can observe differing interpretations of the same material, and occasionally we can hypothesize about what the original form of the story was. In some cases, it is possible to plot a trajectory of its development.

We have attempted to illustrate something about form and function in the various communities of early Christianity, and noted the possibility of tracing the history of certain forms in early Christianity. When we work back through the material to the earliest possible form, how can we decide whether it came from Jesus? This requires some criteria for authenticity: a subject of some discussion.[7]

Criteria for Authenticity

A remarkable feature of work on this subject is that R. H. Fuller and N. Perrin, working independently of each other, arrived at virtually identical conclusions.[8] Fuller has four criteria, Perrin three. They may be tabulated as follows.

(a) Fuller: Distinctiveness
Perrin: Dissimilarity

(b) Fuller: The cross-section method
Perrin: Multiple attestation

(c) Fuller: Consistency
Perrin: Coherence

(d) Fuller: Linguistic and environmental tests
Perrin: Assumed this, but did not define it.

The criterion of dissimilarity. Dissimilarity is the fundamental criterion. Sayings and parables may be accepted as authentic if they can be shown to be dissimilar to characteristic emphases of both ancient Judaism and early Christianity. A good example of this is the use of "Father" (Aramaic: *Abba*) in addressing God. It is found in the Lord's Prayer (Luke 11:2) and on Jesus' lips in the Gethsemane story (Mark 14:36). It is a familiar mode of address that the Jews at the time of Jesus did not use for God, preferring "Our Heavenly Father," or something similar. Matthew (6:9) and the church following him revert to the Jewish mode of address.[9]

The obvious problems with the criterion of dissimilarity are that it misses material in which Jesus is at one with his Jewish heritage and the later church at one with him, and that by concentrating on what is different it may present a distorted picture of the message of Jesus. On the other hand, it is a relatively certain criterion, and its judicious use has led us to the distinctive elements in such fundamental things as Jesus' proclamation of the Kingdom, his use of

---

[7] D. Lührmann, "Sayings of Jesus," *IDB Suppl.*, p. 789; J. Gager, "The Gospels and Jesus: Some Doubts About Method," *Journal of Religion* 54 (1974), pp. 244–72, give recent critiques of the method; cf. C. Carlston, "Form Criticism," *IDB Suppl.*, pp. 347–48.

[8] R. H. Fuller, *Intro.*, pp. 94–98; N. Perrin, *Rediscovering the Teaching of Jesus*, pp. 39–47.

[9] For a further discussion of this example and for other examples, see N. Perrin, *Rediscovering*, pp. 40–43.

parables and proverbial sayings, and the prayer he taught his disciples. More-over, it is only a starting point; its use must always be supplemented by the use of other criteria.

The criterion of multiple attestation. This criterion tends to determine the authenticity of themes or concerns rather than of particular sayings, and it is immensely important because it tends to focus attention on themes or concerns that occur most frequently in the message of Jesus. Briefly, themes or concerns may be accepted as authentic if they occur in different literary forms within the tradition. So, for example, the concern for "tax collectors and sinners" is au-thentic because it is attested to in sayings, parables, and controversy stories, and that Jesus had a distinctive eschatology is evident from the fact that a particular view of the End Time is stamped on Kingdom sayings, proverbial sayings, and parables.

The criterion of coherence. This criterion grew out of a desire to go beyond the rather narrow limits of what can be established through dissimilarity and multiple attestation. Material may be accepted as authentic if it coheres with, or is consistent with, material established as authentic by other criteria. The validity of this criterion is self-evident.

The criterion of linguistic and environmental tests. This criterion tends to be negative rather than positive. Material is rejected if it is incompatible with the languages or environment of the ministry of Jesus. The interpretation of the parable of the Sower in Mark 4:13–20, for example, cannot be authentic because it uses language from the technical vocabulary of the early church,[10] and the teaching on divorce in Mark 10 cannot go back to Jesus in its present form because it presupposes Roman and not Jewish divorce law. The criterion does not work in the opposite direction. Material cannot be accepted as au-thentic only because it reflects the linguistic or environmental circumstances of the ministry of Jesus for the obvious reason that the earliest Palestinian church shared those circumstances.

JESUS IN SOURCES OTHER THAN THE NEW TESTAMENT

Thus far we have been discussing the use of New Testament material in our attempt to reach the historical Jesus. To begin here is justifiable because the New Testament is the major source for any possible historical knowledge of Jesus. But there are other sources and we must examine them to see whether they offer us any help in our quest for the historical Jesus.

---

[10] On this see J. Jeremias, *The Parables of Jesus*, pp. 77–79. It is important to note that the argument is not based simply on the fact that the language is Greek; the decisive point is that the particular Greek terms used in this passage reflect the technical vocabulary of the early church. Greek may well have been in use in Palestine at the time of Jesus and hence spoken by him. See J. Fitzmyer, "The Languages of Palestine in the First Century A.D.," *Catholic Biblical Quarterly*, vol. 32 (1970), pp. 501–31.

Non-Christian Sources

There are references to Jesus in both ancient Roman and ancient Jewish literature. The first of the Roman sources[11] is a work of the historian Tacitus written in A.D. 112–113. He describes a great fire in Rome in the summer of A.D. 64 while Nero was emperor, and he says that the emperor used the Christians as scapegoats to account for the fire. He then gives a brief account of the sect.

> The founder of this sect, Christus, was given the death penalty in the reign of Tiberius [A.D. 14–37] by the procurator Pontius Pilate; suppressed for the moment, the detestable superstition broke out again, not only in Judea where the evil originated, but also in the city [i.e., Rome] to which everything horrible and shameful flows and where it grows.
>
> Tacitus, *Annals* xv. 44

This represents the information available to the Roman historian at the beginning of the second century. It is probably based on the police interrogation of Christians and so is not actually independent of the New Testament or Christian tradition.

The second reference is also from a Roman historian, Suetonius, who published his *Lives of the Caesars* around A.D. 121. He says that Claudius, who was emperor A.D. 41–54, "expelled from Rome the Jews who were constantly rioting at the instigation of a certain Chrestus" (Suetonius, *Claudius,* 25). This is the expulsion referred to in Acts 18:2, and the reference is to disturbances in the Jewish community resulting from the preaching of Christian missionaries. Suetonius understood Chrestus to be the individual responsible for the riots.

The Roman sources do not offer us any information beyond that which could be deduced from the New Testament itself. They show that Christian missionaries reached Rome quite early, but that is evident from Paul's letter to the Romans. Only Tacitus says anything about Jesus, and his information probably comes indirectly from Christians. He tells us in effect that Roman historians accepted as factual the Christian tradition that the founder of the Christian movement had been crucified by Pontius Pilate.

There are several possible references to Jesus in the Jewish sources, of which the two most important occur together in the Babylonian Talmud.[12] There we find, first, a *Baraitha* (a tradition ascribed to the first or second centuries A.D.) which reads as follows:

> On the eve of Passover they hanged Yeshu [of Nazareth] and the herald went before him forty days saying, "[Yeshu of Nazareth] is going forth to

---

[11] A particularly valuable discussion of these is R. M. Grant, *A Historical Introduction to the New Testament,* pp. 290–94, to whom we are indebted at a number of points.

[12] The standard discussion of all the possible references to Jesus in the ancient Jewish literature is J. Klausner, *Jesus of Nazareth,* pp. 18–54. We are indebted to that discussion at a number of points in what follows.

be stoned in that he hath practiced sorcery and beguiled and led astray Israel. Let everyone knowing ought in his defense come and plead for him." But they found nought in his defense and hanged him on the eve of Passover.

b Sanhedrin 43a

This is a reference of quite extraordinary interest. Independent of any Christian sources, it offers us three items of information. It tells us that the Jews remembered Jesus as one who "practiced sorcery and beguiled and led astray Israel"; it links the death of Jesus with Passover, as do the Christian gospels; and the reference to pleading in his defense implies that Jesus was executed after a formal trial before Jewish authorities.

The second reference to Jesus in the ancient Jewish literature directly follows the first in the Babylonian Talmud.

Jesus had five disciples, Mattai, Maqai, Metser, Buni and Todah.

b Sanhedrin 43a

The names given here are different from any we find in the New Testament, although Mattai could be a corruption of Matthew and Todah a corruption of Thaddeus. However the important thing is not the names but the testimony to the fact that Jesus "had disciples."

There are several other possible references to Jesus in ancient Jewish literature[13] but they are either indirect or cryptic or both, and they do not add anything to what we have already learned. In summary, the Jewish sources tell us four things about Jesus. First, he "practiced sorcery and beguiled and led astray Israel." This must mean that Jesus had a reputation as a miracle worker, perhaps particularly as a successful exorcist, and that he had made a strong impression on the Jewish people. This latter point is reinforced by the second thing we are told by these references, namely that Jesus "had disciples." His ministry to the people was successful in that he attracted disciples who carried on his work after him. Then, there is the implication that Jesus was formally tried by the Jewish authorities, and finally, that he was executed on the eve before a Passover.

Jesus in Christian Sources Other Than the New Testament

Isolated Sayings Attributed to Jesus

There are several isolated sayings attributed to Jesus in Christian sources outside the New Testament, and indeed also in non-Christian sources.[14] The two most interesting are the following.

---

[13] M. Goguel, *Jesus and the Origins of Christianity*, vol. 1, pp. 70–91; D. Duling, *Jesus Christ Through History*, pp. 5–7; F. F. Bruce, *Jesus and Christian Origins Outside the New Testament* contains a study of the materials.

[14] On this, see especially J. Jeremias, *Unknown Sayings of Jesus*, and also E. Hennecke and W. Schneemelcher, *New Testament Apocrypha*, vol. 1, pp. 85–90, "Isolated Sayings of the Lord."

> When on the same day he saw a man doing work on the Sabbath, he said to him: Man! if you know what you are doing then you are blessed. But if you do not know what you are doing then you are cursed and a transgressor of the law.

This is found in one manuscript of the New Testament (Codex D) after Luke 6:4. Otherwise unattested, it coheres perfectly with something that has multiple attestation in the canonical tradition: the challenge of Jesus to make one's own decisions. It is to be accepted as authentic.

> Jesus, on whom be peace, has said: The world is a bridge, go over it, but do not install yourselves on it.

This is found inscribed on the south portal of a mosque in India and is also attested elsewhere in Islamic literature. It is a very beautiful saying, but it does not have the same claim to authenticity as the first one.

Apocryphal Gospels

There are a number of *apocryphal gospels,* gospels which did not achieve recognition in the final formation of the canon of the New Testament. They are known as "apocryphal" ("secret" or "hidden") because they were to be kept from the faithful in the church. Some of them simply develop the tendency of the tradition to create legends about Jesus; others are the vehicles for teaching that came to be regarded as heretical in the church. By and large they offer nothing that can help the historian in his quest for the historical Jesus. There is, however, one exception to this judgment: the gospel of Thomas.

The gospel of Thomas is a document known to us from the discovery in 1945–46 of a whole library of Gnostic Christian documents at a place called Nag Hammadi in Egypt.[15] It is written in Coptic and begins, "These are the secret words which the living Jesus spoke and Didymus Judas Thomas wrote." At the end it is identified as the "Gospel According to Thomas." It has no narrative, but is in the form of a series of sayings and parables attributed to Jesus, usually introduced by "Jesus said" or the like. Its form, therefore, is exactly parallel to that attributed by scholars to the hypothetical synoptic gospel source Q. What is particularly important about it in the context of the historical Jesus, however, is that it has versions of sayings and parables of Jesus that in some ways appear to be independent of the versions we find in the New Testament, and which therefore offer us an additional source to use in our attempt to reconstruct the original form of the saying or parable. Further, it offers us new sayings and parables, some of which have claims to authenticity on the basis of the criterion of coherence. A particularly interesting example of this latter type is the parable of the Assassin.

> Jesus said: "The Kingdom of the Father is like a man who wishes to kill a powerful man. He drew the sword in his house, he stuck it into the

---

[15] A convenient English translation is by R. McL. Wilson in E. Hennecke and W. Schneemelcher, *New Testament Apocrypha,* vol. 1, pp. 511–22. Cf. Appendix 4 for the discovery of the Nag Hammadi texts.

wall, in order to know whether his hand would carry it through; then he slew the powerful [man]."

Thomas 98

On the basis of the fact that this passage coheres with the Tower Builder and the King Going to War in Luke 14:28–32, it has claims to authenticity. The gospel of Thomas does therefore offer us some new material to use in our attempt to reconstruct the teaching of Jesus.[16]

THE LIFE AND MESSAGE OF JESUS

Our discussion thus far has established that the New Testament itself is our major source for knowledge of the historical Jesus, though it can be supplemented by limited information derived from Jewish sources and some teaching material preserved in various places, especially in the gospel of Thomas. But within the New Testament itself there is a distinction to be made: here, when we refer to the New Testament, we really mean the synoptic gospels.

Outside of the synoptic gospels the New Testament offers little resource for arriving at historical knowledge of Jesus. The gospel of John is so much the end product of intensive meditation and reflection, and so absorbed with the interpretation of Christ as the descending-ascending redeemer, that no way has yet been found of deriving historical information about Jesus from it. The Acts of the Apostles offers us an isolated saying (20:35, "It is more blessed to give than to receive"); Paul betrays no interest in anything about Jesus beyond his death and resurrection; the remainder of the New Testament by its very nature cannot be expected to reveal the historical Jesus. We are limited, therefore, to the synoptic gospels, with some small supplementary help from the Jewish sources, the gospel of Thomas, and some isolated sayings preserved in various places. It is on this basis that we proceed.

The Situation of the Jews in Palestine at the Time of Jesus

It is impossible to understand the life or the message of Jesus without recalling the situation of the Jews in Palestine at the time.[17] They were living in a territory under the control of the Romans, whom they regarded as godless Gentiles. Moreover, this territory was sacred to them as the people of God, and it was sacred also to God himself since its center was Jerusalem with its Temple and Holy of Holies, the very special place of God. They were convinced that Roman control of the Holy Land and the Sacred Place of the Temple and the Holy of Holies was an abomination in the sight of God and they were further convinced that God himself was about to remedy the matter. The only questions were how soon would God act and in what ways.

The answers given to these questions were varied and complex. Most Jews

[16] Both J. Jeremias, *Parables*, and N. Perrin, *Rediscovering the Teaching of Jesus*, make use of the Thomas material in this way.
[17] For a survey of the history of the Jews in the New Testament period, see chapter 1, pp. 15–22.

held some form of the apocalyptic hope and believed that God was about to irrupt into history to deliver his people. Inspired by this hope some were anxious to start a war against Rome that they believed God would terminate in their favor. The most extreme among this group were the Zealots, who spearheaded the war against Rome when it actually began in A.D. 66. But almost all Jews, except the Sadducees, shared this hope in one form or another and were prepared to take up arms against Rome when the time came. It was also widely accepted that the speed with which God would act to deliver his people depended in some respects on their state of purity in his eyes. The very presence of the godless Gentiles in the Holy City, it was felt, must be due to the sins of the people of God; they must therefore cleanse themselves in God's eyes so that he might find them more worthy, and also so that they might prepare themselves for his coming act of deliverance.

This demand for purity among the people of God had one tragic consequence: it bred a spirit of division within the Jewish community. Those who sought to keep the standards despised those who did not because the latter were thought to make the community as a whole unworthy of God's act of deliverance. This spiritual division was to reach a drastic climax during the revolt against Rome, the Jewish War of A.D. 66–70. During that time Jew murdered Jew in the name of God and his Law, and there was a vicious internecine strife in Jerusalem itself which must have aided the Romans in their siege of the city.

During the time of Jesus a group of people especially despised by their fellow Jews were known as "tax collectors and sinners." Tax collectors were hated not only because they were extortioners, which most of them were, but also because, directly or indirectly, they worked for the godless Gentile authorities occupying the land, collecting taxes imposed by the Romans. "Sinners" in this phrase are people whose activities or occupations are an offense to God and his Law. Prostitutes would be an obvious example, especially if their clientele included Roman soldiers. Swineherds would be another, for the care of animals made it impossible to observe the Sabbath, and swine were themselves ritually unclean. It is a crucial point in the parable of the Prodigal Son that the boy becomes a swineherd. That made him an outcast as far as the Jewish community was concerned, and his father should thereafter have rejected him. "Tax collectors and sinners" is, therefore, a general term for Jews who were outcasts in their own community because their activities or occupations were an offense to God, and hence perhaps their very existence was delaying God's act of deliverance of his people.

The Life of Jesus

We are now in a position to make a general statement about the life of Jesus. Jesus was born about 4 B.C. to Joseph, a carpenter from Nazareth of Galilee, and his wife Mary. He had brothers, one of whom (James) became prominent in the Palestinian church, and sisters (Mark 6:3). He grew up and was educated in the environment of the rural village life of Galilee, and his native tongue was the language of Palestine, Aramaic. He was baptized by John the Baptist, and the beginning of his ministry was in some way linked with that of the Baptist. In his own ministry Jesus was above all the one who proclaimed the Kingdom of God and who challenged his hearers to respond to the reality he was proclaiming. The authority and effectiveness of Jesus as proclaimer of the Kingdom of God was reinforced by an apparently deserved reputation as an exorcist. In a world that believed in gods, in powers of good and evil, and in demons, he was able, in the name of God and his Kingdom, to help those who believed themselves to be possessed by demons. Thus, he moved from village to village, from town to town, preaching the Kingdom, exorcizing demons, healing the sick, and offering hope to the poor. The general portrait of Jesus here is that of a spirit-filled ("charismatic") prophet, preacher, exorcist, and healer, often unconcerned about, or willing to break with, the legal-ritual traditions of purity which so concerned most of his fellow Jews.

A fundamental concern of Jesus was to bring together into a unified group those who responded to his proclamation of the Kingdom of God irrespective of their sex, previous background, or history. A central feature of the life of this group was eating together, sharing a common meal that celebrated their unity in the new relationship with God, which they enjoyed on the basis of their response to Jesus' proclamation of the Kingdom. In this concern for the unity of the group of those who responded to the proclamation, Jesus challenged the tendency of the Jewish community of his day to fragment itself and in the name of God to reject certain of its own members. This aroused a deep-rooted opposition to him, which reached a climax during a Passover celebration in Jerusalem when he was arrested, tried by the Jewish authorities on a charge of blasphemy and by the Romans on a charge of sedition, and crucified. During his lifetime he had chosen from among his followers a small group of disciples who had exhibited in their work in his name something of his power and authority. Thus arose a "Jesus movement," spearheaded by a band of itinerant radicals who, like Jesus, moved about the villages and towns of Palestine, preaching and healing in his name.

That, or something very like it, is all that we can know; it is enough.

The Message of Jesus[18]

Intensive work on the material in the synoptic gospels shows that there are four aspects of that material where we can come close to the words of the historical Jesus. These are the proclamation of the Kingdom of God, the proverbial sayings, the parables, and the Lord's Prayer.

The Proclamation of the Kingdom of God

Contemporary scholars generally agree that *at least* three sayings about the Kingdom of God have very strong claims to authenticity.

[18] N. Perrin, *Jesus and the Language of the Kingdom*, chapter 2; cf. D. Duling, *Jesus Christ Through History*, pp. 19–23. For further study, see B. Chilton, *God in Strength. Jesus' Announcement of the Kingdom*. An alternative view is offered by R. Hiers, *Jesus and the Future*.

The kingdom of God is not coming with signs to be observed; nor will they say, "Lo, here it is!" or "There!" for behold, the kingdom of God is in the midst of you.

LUKE 17:20–21

From the days of John the Baptist until now the kingdom of Heaven has suffered violence, and men of violence plunder it.[19]

MATT 11:12

But if it is by the finger of God that I cast out demons, then the kingdom of God has come upon you.

LUKE 11:20

There is no doubt that the proclamation of the Kingdom of God is the central aspect of the message of Jesus. But having said that, one has to ask what it means to say that Jesus proclaimed the Kingdom of God. To clarify this meaning, it is necessary to remember that in ancient Israel, prior to the time of the Babylonian Exile, there arose a myth about God and his Kingdom. This is not surprising since the political form of government in the ancient Near East was a monarchy. God was imagined as a great king who was so powerful that he created the world, brought his enslaved people out of Egypt, guided them through the wilderness, defeated their enemies like a conquering warrior, and gave them the promised land. He was a universal king, judging the nations, and his "reign" was thought to encompass his whole creation. This universal "reign" was the "Kingdom of God" (*malkuth Yahweh*, 1 Chron 28:5). The myth of the God who created the world and constantly acted to preserve, protect, and judge his people became the very foundation of the nation Israel. As the stories of the origins and destiny of Israel were told again and again, they gave meaning to the world and life.

But when "Israel" was finally destroyed and taken into exile by Babylon, the myth that had been the basis for national solidarity began to be more of a future hope than a present reality. It became an "eschatological myth," a myth to which the people held in times of trouble and persecution. When the myth was taken up by apocalyptic seers in the years before the birth of Jesus, the tendency was to think in terms of "this (evil) age" and "the (good) age to come," "this age" being marked by a succession of four evil kingdoms which God, in one great cataclysmic and cosmic event, will overthrow and judge, preparing the way for an everlasting and victorious paradisical kingdom like his kingdom of old. For the apocalypticist, the more difficult and tragic things became in this world, the closer the end of time was—and all of this was observable by signs, the political and cosmic signs of the times. Many apocalypticists undoubtedly took signs quite literally.

Examples of this kind of thinking are frequent in Jewish and early Christian apocalyptic writing, as we have seen. However, not all of Jewish thought stressed literal apocalyptic "signs to be observed" in connection with the coming of God's Kingdom (for example, the daily synagogue prayer called the

---

[19] This is Perrin's translation. For its exegetical justification, see N. Perrin, *The Kingdom of God in the Teaching of Jesus*, pp. 171–74, and *Rediscovering*, pp. 74–77.

Kaddish prayer: ". . . May he establish his kingdom in your lifetime and in your days and in the lifetime of all the house of Israel even speedily and at a near time"). But whether literal apocalyptic signs were stressed or not, it is clear that the use of the phrase "Kingdom of God" would call up in the consciousness of any Jewish person the totality of the experience of Israel, that is, it was a *symbolic phrase recalling the kingdom myth*, the myth in which God created the world and his people, protected and sustained all that he had created, judging and defeating enemies, even judging the people when they did not conform to the convenant. This language would also give an accent to the future: the hope in Jesus' time was for the reestablishment of God's Kingdom.

Luke 17:20–21 uses the symbol of the Kingdom, but it denies the literal apocalyptic interpretation of the eschatological myth: the Kingdom is not coming "with signs to be observed"; no one will be able to say "Lo, here it is!" or "There!" Jesus denies that the coming of the Kingdom of God is a historical event in the way that a king's actions, or a war, or the persecution of a people are historical events. In a number of passages, Jesus refuses to give a sign (Matt 12:39; 16:4; Luke 11:29–32; Mark 8:11–12). Most characteristic, and probably going back to the historical Jesus, is a tradition like this:

> The Pharisees came and began to argue with him, seeking from him a sign from heaven, to test him. And he sighed deeply in his spirit, and said, "Why does this generation seek a sign? Truly, I say to you, no sign shall be given to this generation."
>
> MARK 8:11–12

If this passage refers to apocalyptic signs, as seems likely, it helps to interpret the Kingdom saying in Luke 17:20–21: Jesus was not an apocalypticist of the literal sort because he refused to give apocalyptic signs about the coming of the Kingdom. Nonetheless, the phrase "Kingdom of God" is symbolic and will have called up the myth of God's Kingdom. Here Jesus says that the Kingdom of God "is among you." This means that the eschatological mythical reality symbolized by Kingdom language is confronting the hearers of Jesus already in the present, that it has already begun to be part of human experience, that one is not simply to expect it, but to respond to it now. The Kingdom is not coming with "signs to be observed"; it is *already* "in the midst of you," "among you."

What more might be said about the Kingdom symbol calling forth the myth of God's relation to his people? It is in the nature of such language that it cannot be limited to literal, descriptive statements.[20] A symbol calls forth a whole set of interrelated ideas and emotions. But another aspect of the Kingdom can be seen in the second saying above, Matthew 11:12, "From the days of John the Baptist until now, the Kingdom of Heaven has suffered violence, and men of violence plunder it." Part of the eschatological myth in Judaism involved a cosmic battle between God and Satan, between the forces of good and the forces of evil, in which God and the forces of good would ultimately triumph. In this light, the saying expresses the view that the death of John the

[20] See above, chapter 2, pp. 51–53, for this view of symbol.

Baptist and the prospective suffering of Jesus and his followers is part of the eschatological war. The future battle is already taking place, now, in the present.

We come, then, to the third saying, Luke 11:20: "But if it is by the finger of God that I cast out demons, then the kingdom of God has come upon you." This saying refers to the activity of Jesus as exorcist in the battle against the forces of evil, the demons. As exorcist, Jesus acts in behalf of God, or manifests his power to defeat evil. Again, the Kingdom "has come" in this activity; it is a present reality, certainly for those who are exorcised, and more, for those who can accept the saying itself. One aspect of "Kingdom reality" is exorcism, and exorcism challenges the hearers of Jesus' message to recall the Kingdom myth and to take it seriously as an aspect of their own present experience.

To summarize from these three sayings, then, "Kingdom of God" is a symbol that evokes the whole range of meanings associated with the myth of God's activity as King, of his visiting and redeeming his people, not in the sense that it is simply a future reality proved by the demonstration of literal signs, but as a present reality available already through the preaching and activity of Jesus. This Kingdom reality is the central theme of the message of Jesus. It will now be helpful to clarify it through a discussion of other aspects of his message.

The Parables

Modern research on the parables of Jesus has established a number of points about them which may be stated in summary fashion.

(a) Jesus taught in parables, but the early church readily translated them into allegories. The difference is that a parable makes its point as a totality. Moreover, the point is never exhausted by any one apprehension of it, but can be apprehended afresh as the parable is retold in different situations. For that reason the message of the parable can never adequately be expressed except in the metaphorical language of the parable itself; it cannot be translated into a propositional statement.[21] In an allegory on the other hand, the parts count and each individual part bears a one-to-one relationship with what it represents. Once that relationship has been discerned, the message of the allegory becomes clear, and the allegory itself can be abandoned, for its cryptic message

---

[21] This point has only recently come to be appreciated. It means, for example, that we cannot say that the message of the Sower (Mark 4:3–9) is "Have confidence in God's future!" as Perrin came near to claiming in *Rediscovering*, p. 156. That may be its message to one person in one time and one place, but such a direct statement by no means exhausts the parable's potential meaning. It should be noted that a parable shares this metaphorical quality with a myth. But there are contrasts: a parable is an imaginary story from normal, everyday human life which can be localized in time and place, a story which challenges established and conventional perceptions of reality; a myth is usually about the gods, or if it is drawn from events of the past, takes on a world constructing and maintaining function, and is usually celebrated ritually. Cf. J. D. Crossan, *In Parables*, p. 15.

can now be—and should be—expressed in noncryptic language.[22] A good example of allegory in the New Testament is the interpretation of the Sower in Mark 4:13-20.

(b) Both the allegorizing of the parables and their present context and application in the gospels are the work of the church and the evangelists. To interpret a parable as a parable of Jesus, therefore, one must first reconstruct the original nonallegorical form of the parable[23] and then interpret it as a parable in the context of the message of Jesus without reference to its context or function in the gospel narratives.[24]

(c) The fundamental element in a parable is the element of metaphor. A is compared to B so that meaning may be carried over from B to A. Normally, A is the lesser known and B the better known. For example, when the Kingdom of God is the lesser known, aspects of its meaning are illuminated by something better known or more readily envisaged: the story of a man finding a treasure in a field, or of a merchant finding a pearl (Matt 13:44-46).

(d) There is, therefore, in the parable a literal point, the meaning of the story or image, and also a metaphorical point, the meaning, the story, or image as it is transferred to what it is intended to refer to.

(e) The purpose of a parable is normally pedagogical; Jewish rabbis used it extensively to illuminate, illustrate, and instruct. In the case of Jesus, however, this normal use of the literary form "parable" seems to have been subordinated to another and different one. In the hands of Jesus the parable is not only a means of instruction but also a form of proclamation.[25]

Let us take as a concrete example the parable of the Good Samaritan (Luke 10:30-36).

> Jesus replied, "A man was going down from Jerusalem to Jericho, and he fell among robbers, who stripped him and beat him, and departed, leaving him half dead. Now by chance a priest was going down that road; and when he saw him he passed by on the other side. So likewise a Levite, when he came to the place and saw him, passed by on the other side. But a Samaritan, as he journeyed, came to where he was; and he saw him, he had compassion, and went to him and bound up his wounds, pouring on

---

[22] On this, see especially J. D. Crossan, "Parable and Example in the Teaching of Jesus," *New Testament Studies*, vol. 18 (1971/72), pp. 285-307 (reprinted in *Semeia* 1, ed. R. Funk, pp. 63-104), especially pp. 304-05. Crossan summarizes the distinction as follows: "Allegory is always logically and functionally secondary with regard to abstract proposition and statement . . . parable is that which is never so subordinate but which essentially says what cannot be said in any other better or clearer fashion. When allegory is seen as fundamentally reducible to abstract proposition, and parable as essentially irreducible to such a statement, the gulf between them is absolute . . . ." Crossan's whole article is immensely important and we are indebted to it at a number of points in what follows.

[23] This insight is the basic contribution of J. Jeremias, *The Parables of Jesus*, and all subsequent work builds on his in this connection.

[24] Crossan points out, correctly, that despite their recognition of the validity of this point, most modern exegetes (including Perrin) have failed to carry it out in practice. "Parable and Example," pp. 286-87.

[25] This is Crossan's fundamental point, and on this we are following him closely.

oil and wine; then he set him on his own beast and brought him to an inn, and took care of him. And the next day he took out two denarii and gave them to the innkeeper, saying, 'Take care of him; and whatever more you spend, I will repay you when I come back.' Which of these three, do you think, proved neighbor to the man who fell among the robbers?"

This is the form of the parable as Jesus taught it. The present context of the discussion with the lawyer (10:25–29, 37) has been supplied by the early church and must be ignored in an attempt to understand the parable as a parable *of Jesus*. In its present context the parable is an exemplary story, illustrating by example the principle of neighborliness. This is absolutely in keeping with the use of parables by Jewish rabbis. However, if we ignore the setting given to the story by the early church, as we must, then it is not an exemplary story. Crossan points out that if it were an exemplary story it would be better to have the Samaritan as the victim and the Israelite as the good "neighbor." No, the story *in itself* focuses attention on the deed of the Samaritan rather than on the need of the injured man. "The focal point must remain, not on the good deed itself, but on the *goodness* of the *Samaritan*. When the story is read as one told to a Jewish audience by the Jewish Jesus, it is impossible to avoid facing the good man not just as good, but as Samaritan."[26] But the Jews of Jesus' day despised the Samaritans on both racial and religious grounds, and relations between the two groups were such that no one could expect hospitality in a Samaritan village if he were on his way to Jerusalem (Luke 9:52–56). So when the parable confronts the hearer of Jesus at the literal level with the combination *good* and *Samaritan*, it is asking that the hearer conceive the inconceivable. "The whole thrust of the story demands that he say what cannot be said: Good + Samaritan."[27]

What happens when one is confronted by the demand to conceive the inconceivable, to say what cannot be said? Either the demand is rejected, or the person concerned begins to question all that he has taken for granted up to that moment. He is confronted by the necessity suddenly to reexamine the very grounds of his being, by a challenge that is effective at the deepest level of existential reality. The parable has become proclamation.

Crossan speaks of moving from the literal point of the parable to its metaphorical point, and his conclusion is worth quoting in full.

The literal point confronted the hearers with the necessity of saying the impossible and having their world turned upside down and radically questioned in its presuppositions. The metaphorical point is that *just so* does the Kingdom of God break abruptly into a person's consciousness and demand the overturn of prior values, closed options, set judgments, and established conclusions. . . . The hearer struggling with the dualism Good Samaritan is actually experiencing in and through this the inbreak-

[26] J. D. Crossan, "Parable and Example," p. 294.
[27] J. D. Crossan, p. 295.

ing of the Kingdom upon him. *Not only does it happen like this, it happens in this.*[28]

This conclusion from the Good Samaritan can be supported by a consideration of other parables. An almost exact parallel is the parable of the Unjust Steward (Luke 16:1–7).

> He also said to the disciples, "There was a rich man who had a steward, and charges were brought to him that this man was wasting his goods. And he called him and said to him, 'What is this that I hear about you? Turn in the account of your stewardship, for you can no longer be steward.' And the steward said to himself, 'What shall I do, since my master is taking the stewardship away from me? I am not strong enough to dig, and I am ashamed to beg. I have decided what to do, so that people may receive me into their houses when I am put out of the stewardship.' So, summoning his master's debtors one by one, he said to the first, 'How much do you owe my master?' He said, 'A hundred measure of oil.' And he said to him, 'Take your bill, and sit down quickly and write fifty.' Then he said to another, 'And how much do you owe?' He said, 'A hundred measures of wheat.' He said to him, 'Take your bill, and write eighty.'

Beginning in verse 8 ("The master commended the dishonest steward for his shrewdness; for the sons of this world are more shrewd in dealing with their own generation than the sons of light") there are moral applications to the story. These must be ignored as later attempts to understand how it is that Jesus told a story about a character who was dishonest and compounded his dishonesty in the solution to his problem.

Instead of asking how this character can be seen as admirable, as did the author of verse 8, we should rather recognize the dramatic affront to all moral standards that the unjust steward in himself represents. In the case of the Good Samaritan, one needs to be aware of the situation between Jews and Samaritans at the time of Jesus in order to appreciate the impossibility of putting together "Good" and "Samaritan," but with the Unjust Steward, the character's decision and actions are an affront to the common moral standards that make possible any business relationship, any delegation of responsibility in the world. The story itself focuses attention on the steward's dialogue with himself and his decision, and it implies that he was successful in his endeavor to avoid the evil consequences of his first dishonesty by compounding it. In a sense, then, the exegesis that concentrates on his "shrewdness" or the element of decision is correct in that this is the focal point of the story itself. But we should not remain content with recognizing that the story teases the mind of the hearer into applauding an act of decision in critical circumstances.[29] We must go on to understand that the content of that decision is an affront to the

---

[28] J. D. Crossan, p. 295. Italics ours.
[29] This is in effect what Perrin did in his previous treatment of the parable. See *Rediscovering*, p. 115.

accepted canons of moral behavior that make possible an ongoing world of business relationships. This story is as effective a challenge to the hearer to do what cannot be done, i.e., to applaud a decision of this nature, as the Good Samaritan is a challenge to say what cannot be said. The point of the parable as parable, then, is to admit the presence of an order of reality that at the very moment of the telling of the story is challenging all accepted canons of behavior and forms of human relationships. In a sense, the Unjust Steward is a more radical form of proclamation than is the Good Samaritan, for there is a sense of intrinsic rightness in allowing an act of mercy to challenge religious and racial prejudice. But it is very different to applaud a decision that involves such blatant dishonesty; yet that is what Jesus challenged his hearers to do as this parable became a form of his proclamation.

Having argued the matter in some detail with regard to these two parables, we may now proceed in a more summary fashion with others. A major theme of the proclamation of Jesus was reversal, and Crossan points to this theme in a number of the parables. In Luke 16:19-31, the Rich Man and Lazarus: "Jesus was . . . interested in . . . the reversal of human situation in which the Kingdom's disruptive advent could be metaphorically portrayed and linguistically made known." In the case of the Pharisee and the Publican (Luke 18:10-14), "the metaphorical point is . . . the complete and radical reversal of accepted human judgment, even of religious judgment, whereby the Kingdom forces its way into human awareness." The Wedding Guest (Luke 14:7-11) as an example of situational reversal on the literal level "points towards . . . [the way in which] the Kingdom arrives and breaks in on a man so that he experiences God's rule at the moment when his own world is turned upside down and radically reversed."[30]

In the hands of Jesus the parable becomes a form of the proclamation of the Kingdom. As the hearers are challenged to say what cannot be said, to applaud what should not be applauded, to recognize in the reversal of human judgments and human situations the sign of the breaking in of God's Kingdom, so the Kingdom "comes." The power of Jesus to transform the parable into a form of proclamation was at the same time a power to mediate to his hearers the experience of the Kingdom as existential reality.

But Jesus did not always use the parable form in this way. Many of his parables instruct or teach or, to use the word we have been using throughout this book, function as *parenesis.* This must have been so, because the message of Jesus could never have been as effective as its historical consequences demonstrate had it not included instruction in the mode of response to the proclamation. In turning to this aspect of Jesus' use of parables, we are dealing with what is uniformly acknowledged and thoroughly discussed in all the literature on the subject; so we may again proceed in summary fashion.

The Jew of Jesus' day who heard the Hid Treasure and the Pearl (Matt 13:44-46) would certainly have understood the metaphorical point to be the recognition that "a man can suddenly be confronted by the experience of [the

---

[30] J. D. Crossan, "Parable and Example," pp. 296-303.

Kingdom of] God and find the subsequent joy overwhelming and all-determinative." To the Tower Builder and the King going to War (Luke 14:28–32) we may now add the Assassin from the gospel of Thomas. "Here we have three vivid pictures of men from very different walks of life who have one thing in common: a willingness to prepare themselves realistically for the responsibility they assume . . . The . . . [builder] . . . calculates his resources, the King estimates his strength against his enemy's, the assassin assures himself that his hand has not lost its skill."[31] The metaphorical point of these parables is recognizing that, as Perrin heard T.W. Manson put it, "Salvation may be free, but it is not cheap." The Importuned Friend (the Friend at Midnight, Luke 11:5–8) and the Importuned Judge (the Unjust Judge, Luke 18:1–8) are rabbinical arguments from the lesser to the greater. The metaphorical position in both is the same. The friend is no real friend at all—otherwise he would be out of bed immediately—and the judge is certainly no true judge; yet both could be importuned into doing what they should. If they can be so importuned, how much more can we not trust God who needs no importuning?

We lack the space here to discuss all the parables of Jesus, but we have said enough to make the point that some of the parables of Jesus functioned as proclamation and others as parenesis. Some mediated the experience of the Kingdom of God as an existential reality to those who heard them, while others instructed the hearer to respond in various concrete ways to the experience mediated by the proclamation. An aspect of the use of the parables by Jesus we have not discussed is that which has apparent reference to the future; we return to this under the rubric "Jesus and the future" below.

The Proverbial Sayings[32]

The essence of a proverbial saying is that it is based on observation of how things are in the world. It is a flash of insight into the repeatable situations of life in the world, and its aphoristic form not only represents insight but also compels it. "A prophet is not without honor, except in his own country" (Mark 6:4a). The proverb readily becomes imperative, basing instruction on common-sense observation. "Do not throw your pearls before swine, lest they trample them underfoot" (Matt 7:6). The proverb can also be expressed in interrogative form, again compelling insight. "Which of you by being anxious can add one cubit to his span of life?" (Matt 6:27). Naturally, in the context of a firm belief in God, the proverb comes to express insight into the way things are, or should be, in the world ordered by God and a challenge to behavior that God will reward.

---

[31] We are repeating here Perrin's previous exegesis of these parables. See Perrin, *Rediscovering*, pp. 89, 127–28, 128–30.

[32] In the following discussion we are consciously indebted to R. Bultmann, *History of the Synoptic Tradition*, pp. 69–108, especially pp. 104–05, and to W. Beardslee, *Literary Criticism and the New Testament*, pp. 30–41, "The Proverb," and "Uses of the Proverb in the Synoptic Gospels," *Interpretation*, vol. 24 (1970), pp. 61–73.

> For the Lord honored the father above the children,
>> and he confirmed the right of the mother over her sons.
>
> Whoever honors his father atones for sins,
>> and whoever glorifies his mother is like one who lays up treasure.
>> Sir 3:2–4

In this context the proverb is an affirmation of faith in God's just and orderly rule of the world, as are the Jewish proverbs in collections such as the book of Proverbs in the Old Testament, or the Wisdom of Solomon and the Wisdom of Jesus the Son of Sirach in the Apocrypha.

This, then, is the general background against which we must set Jesus' use of the proverb. We limit ourselves to the proverbial sayings that Bultmann established as authentic on the basis of what later came to be called the criterion of dissimilarity: Luke 9:60a; Matt 5:39b–41; Mark 8:35; 10:23b, 25; 10:31; Luke 14:11; Mark 3:27; 3:24–26; Luke 9:62; Matt 7:13–14; Mark 7:15; 10:15; Matt 5:44–48.[33] We examine these in groups according to our own analysis.

(a) The most radical sayings: Luke 9:60a; Matt 5:39b–41

Luke 9:60a Leave the dead to bury their own dead.

Matt 5:39b–41 If any one strikes you on the right cheek, turn to him the other also; and if any one would sue you and take your coat, let him have your cloak as well; and if any one forces you to go one mile, go with him two miles.

These are the most radical of the proverbial sayings of Jesus. Indeed, they are so radical they shatter the form of proverbial saying altogether and become something quite different. Where proverbial sayings normally reflect on life in the world and, as Beardslee puts it, "make a continuous whole out of one's existence,"[34] these sayings overturn the whole idea of orderly existence in the world. To "leave the dead to bury their own dead" is to act so irresponsibly as to deny the kind of personal and communal sense of responsibility that makes possible the act of living in community in the world. Giving the "cloak as well" and going the "second mile" are commandments that are impossible to take literally as moral imperatives. The Palestinian peasant at the time of Jesus wore only those two garments, and so the result would have been indecent exposure. The second command refers to the privilege of Roman soldiers to impress local citizens into service; the result of obeying it would be a lifetime of forced servitude.

The history of the interpretation of these sayings is a mellowing down to the point where they become barely possible of fulfillment and hence extraordinarily radical challenges. In connection with the first the evangelist Luke adds, "but as for you, go and proclaim the kingdom of God" (Luke 9:60b), and so makes the saying a dramatic and radical challenge to Christian discipleship. In connection with the second, T.W. Manson says of the second mile: "The

---

[33] R. Bultmann, *History of the Synoptic Tradition*, p. 105.
[34] W. Beardslee, "Uses of the Proverb," p. 71.

first mile renders to Caesar the things that are Caesar's; the second mile, by meeting opposition with kindness, renders to God the things that are God's"[35] but these ancient or modern interpretations are irrelevant to a historical understanding of the message of Jesus.

As the message of Jesus these are not radical demands but part of the proclamation of the Kingdom of God. They challenge the hearer, not to radical obedience, but to radical questioning. They jolt him out of the effort to make a continuous whole of his existence and into a judgment about that existence. They exactly match the function of the parable as proclamation in the message of Jesus.

(b) The eschatological reversal sayings: Mark 8:35; 10:23b, 25; 10:31; Luke 14:11

Mark 8:35	For whoever would save his life will lose it; and whoever loses his life for my sake and the gospel's will save it. (The original probably ran something like ". . . for the sake of the kingdom of God").
Mark 10:23b, 25	How hard it will be for those who have riches to enter the kingdom of God! . . . it is easier for a camel to go through the eye of a needle than for a rich man to enter the kingdom of God.
Mark 10:31	But many that are first will be last, and the last first.
Luke 14:11	Every one who exalts himself will be humbled, and he who humbles himself will be exalted.

These sayings need not delay us. The theme of eschatological reversal is one of the best-attested themes of the message of Jesus. It proclaims the Kingdom as eschatological reversal of the present and so invites, indeed demands, judgment on that present. Again, this use of the proverb exactly parallels a use of the parable in the message of Jesus.

(c) The conflict sayings: Mark 3:27; 3:24–26

Mark 3:27	No one can enter a strong man's house and plunder his goods, unless he first binds the strong man; then indeed he may plunder his house.
Mark 3:24–26	If a kingdom is divided against itself, that kingdom cannot stand. And if a house is divided against itself, that house will not be able to stand. And if Satan has risen up against himself and is divided, he cannot stand, but is coming to an end.

Here we have the same kind of thinking expressed in proverbial sayings as in the Kingdom sayings Luke 11:20 and Matt 11:12. In the latter the Kingdom is proclaimed in terms of the exorcisms of Jesus, the fate of the Baptist, and the potential fate of Jesus and his disciples. The proverbial sayings are an aphoristic expression of an understanding of existence as essentially an arena

[35] T. W. Manson, *Sayings of Jesus*, p. 160.

of conflict in terms of which the Kingdom of God becomes a matter of human experience.

(d) The parenetical sayings: Luke 9:62; Matt 7:13–14; Mark 7:15; 10:15; Matt 5:44–48

Luke 9:62   No one who puts his hand to the plough and looks back is fit for the kingdom of God.

Matt 7:13–14   Enter by the narrow gate; for the gate is wide and the way is easy, that leads to destruction, and those who enter by it are many. For the gate is narrow and the way is hard, that leads to life, and those who find it are few.

Mark 7:15   There is nothing outside a man which by going into him can defile him; but the things which come out of a man are what defile him.

Mark 10:15   Whoever does not receive the kingdom of God like a child shall not enter it.

Matt 5:44–48   Love your enemies and pray for those who persecute you, so that you may be sons of your Father . . . for he makes his sun rise on the evil and on the good, and sends rain on the just and on the unjust. For if you love those who love you, what reward have you? Do not even the tax collectors do the same? And if you salute only your brethren, what more are you doing than others? Do not even the Gentiles do the same? You, therefore, must be perfect, as your heavenly Father is perfect.

In these sayings the normal use of the proverbial saying as parenesis reasserts itself, and Jesus uses the form exactly as his contemporaries among the rabbis would have. There is, of course, one great difference: these sayings are set in the context of the proclamation of the Kingdom of God. Like all the pareneses of Jesus, they are concerned with response to the reality of the Kingdom. Thus, though Jesus did not have a system of ethics in the usual sense, there are here some implications for ethical reflection: the radical questioning of one's easy acceptance of his or her current state of existence, the reversal of conventional morality, the battle against the forces of evil, and the necessity of responding to the Kingdom proclamation with spontaneous, radical, self-giving love.

The Lord's Prayer

We will not discuss the prayer in any detail here[36] but wish to call attention to a comparison between the prayer Jesus taught his disciples and the prayers of his Jewish contemporaries. A made-up parallel to the Lord's Prayer taken from Jewish sources is as follows:

[36] Perrin offered an exegesis of the prayer in *Kingdom,* pp. 191–98.

Our Father, who art in Heaven. Hallowed by Thine exalted Name in the world which Thou didst create according to Thy will. May Thy Kingdom and Thy lordship come speedily, and be acknowledged by all the world, that Thy Name may be praised in all eternity. May Thy will be done in Heaven, and also on earth give tranquillity of spirit to those that fear thee, yet in all things do what seemeth good to Thee. Let us enjoy the bread daily apportioned to us. Forgive us, our Father, for we have sinned; forgive also all who have done us injury; even as we also forgive all. And lead us not into temptation, but keep us far from all evil. For thine is the greatness and the power and the dominion, the victory and the majesty, yea all in Heaven and on earth. Thine is the Kingdom, and Thou art Lord of all beings forever. Amen.[37]

The Lukan version of the Lord's Prayer (Luke 11:2–4), generally recognized as being close to the prayer Jesus taught his disciples, reads as follows.

Father,
Hallowed be thy name. Thy Kingdom come.
Give us each day our daily bread;
and forgive us our sins,
  for we ourselves forgive
  everyone who is indebted to [i.e.,
  who has sinned against] us;
and lead us not into temptation.

In sentiment and meaning the two prayers are exactly parallel, and clearly Jesus was echoing his Jewish heritage. Yet the language of the two can be contrasted. The simplicity and brevity of the second express a less formal and majestic, but more intimate, understanding of the relationship between the petitioner and his God than do the sonorous phrases of the first. For many persons who can pray the prayer of Jesus, in a very real sense the Kingdom has already come.

Jesus and the Future

We come now to an extraordinarily difficult point in the message of Jesus, his expectation and teaching concerning the future. We are convinced that all sayings or teaching ascribed to Jesus in the gospels that give a definite form to a future expectation—for example, a future coming of the Son of Man—fail the test of the criteria for authenticity.[38] But to say this is not to resolve the problem, for the question is not whether Jesus expected a future coming of the Son of Man, but whether he looked toward the future for something different from what was already present in the experience of those confronted by the reality of his ministry and his message.

[37] Taken from T. W. Manson, *The Sayings of Jesus*, pp. 167–68.
[38] Perrin gives a detailed discussion of this claim in chapter 4 of *Rediscovering the Teaching of Jesus*.

To bring this question into focus we must call attention to one result of our discussion of the message of Jesus, namely, that Jesus claimed to mediate the reality of the Kingdom of God to his hearers in a way that had not been done before. His proclamation of the Kingdom of God necessarily claims to mediate an experience of existential reality to those of his hearers who responded in the right way to the proclamation. He took the literary form of the parable and pushed it beyond its normal limits, so that it became a medium of proclamation, and the hearers found the Kingdom breaking abruptly into their consciousness as they were forced to say what could not be said and to applaud what should not be applauded. Similarly, on the lips of Jesus the proverbial saying also became a medium of proclamation in its power to jolt the hearer out of the effort to make a continual whole of existence in the world and into a judgment about that existence. In this "jolting" the Kingdom is also "breaking in." Finally, the Lord's Prayer envisages and gives expression to a relationship with God so different from that in the Jewish prayers that for many persons who can pray that prayer the Kingdom has, in a real sense, already "come."

But there is another aspect, for within the Lord's Prayer itself we find the petition "Thy Kingdom come." Since we have already recognized it to parallel the petitions of the Jewish prayers in sentiment and meaning, we are forced to recognize that this petition looks toward the future, as the petitions in the Jewish prayers certainly did. Furthermore, there is a group of parables, the Sower (Mark 4:3–9), the Mustard Seed (Mark 4:30–32), the Leaven (Matt 13:33), and the Seed Growing of Itself (Mark 4:26–29), all bearing the stamp of authenticity and all challenging the hearer to look toward the future. At the literal level they move from the present of the sowing, or of the leavening of the dough, to the future of the result of the sowing or the leavening. At the metaphorical level also, therefore, they must be held to challenge the hearer to move from his present to a future. Finally, the eschatological reversal sayings seem to have an accent on the future in so far as the present is unacceptable.

At this point it becomes important to remind ourselves of several things. First, it is not necessarily the case that a modern conception of time and history can be ascribed to Jesus, a man of the first century. This consideration is reinforced by recalling that at one time, when first-century Jewish apocalyptic came very close to a modern understanding of signs as relating in a one-to-one relationship to temporal, historical events and figures, Jesus dissociated himself from such thinking. We are therefore justified in claiming that Jesus looked toward a future, but not necessarily a future conceived in what we would recognize as literal apocalyptic or temporal and historical terms. His message promised his followers a future that would be a consummation of what they already knew in the present of their response to the challenge of his proclamation. In their turn, they came to interpret this message in terms of a temporal and historical event drawn from apocalyptic expectations, the coming of the Son of Man whom they now identified with Jesus. They were not necessarily correct in so doing.

FROM JESUS TO THE NEW TESTAMENT

The Jesus we can reconstruct historically from the New Testament is, therefore, the proclaimer of the Kingdom of God. More than that, he is one who had the power to mediate to his hearers the existential reality of that which he proclaimed, and who instructed them in ways of responding to that reality so that they might enter ever more deeply into their experience of it. On this basis he taught those who responded to the proclamation to look to the future with confidence.

There are two things conspicuously absent from this picture compared to that given in the gospels. The first is a specific claim by Jesus himself to be the Messiah. It is a striking feature of modern historical research that there is general agreement that the Messianic claims put on the lips of the Jesus of the gospels are exactly that: claims *put on* the lips of the Jesus of the gospels. So far as we can tell, Jesus proclaimed the Kingdom of God but made no explicit claims for himself. Of course, the very fact that he proclaimed the Kingdom of God and challenged his hearers as he did no doubt *implied* claims about himself, but no such claims were ever made explicit. The explicit claims in the gospels reflect the piety and understanding of the early church, not historical data about Jesus of Nazareth.

The second element conspicuously absent from this picture is an interpretation by Jesus of his own death. The fact is that we simply do not known how Jesus thought about his own death. In view of the fate of the Baptist and of the saying Matt 11:12, it is inherently probable that Jesus did recognize the dangers to himself of his last visit to Jerusalem, but the sayings in the gospels and in 1 Corinthians 11 that reflect on his death are also products of the piety and understanding of the early church, and they do not tell us anything about Jesus himself. "The greatest embarrassment to the attempt to reconstruct a portrait of Jesus is the fact that we cannot know how Jesus understood his end, his death."[39] That is Bultmann's statement of the case, and it is valid.

We do know, however, that within a short time after his death the followers of Jesus were claiming that God had raised him from the dead. Where he himself had proclaimed the Kingdom of God, they began to proclaim him. The proclaimer became the proclaimed.[40] We have traced the various forms of this proclamation throughout the New Testament; our concern now is simply to

---

[39] R. Bultmann, "The Primitive Christian Kerygma and the Historical Jesus," in *The Historical Jesus and the Kerygmatic Christ*, ed. C. Braaten and R. Harrisville, p. 23.

[40] This is Bultmann's famous formulation of the matter. In the essay quoted immediately above, for example, he says: "While the preaching of Jesus is the eschatological message of the coming—more, of the breaking-in of the Kingdom of God—in the kerygma [message of the church] Jesus Christ is proclaimed as the one who died vicariously on the cross for the sins of men and was miraculously raised by God for our salvation" (p. 16).

note that he who proclaimed the Kingdom of God began himself to be proclaimed as (*a*) the one who was about to return on the clouds of heaven as Son of Man and agent of God's final judgment and redemption of the world (so apocalyptic Christianity); (*b*) as the one who "died for our sins and was raised for our justification" (so Paul); and (*c*) as "the lamb of God, who takes away the sin of the world" (so the Johannine school). The historical details of the movement from the Jesus who proclaimed the Kingdom of God to the New Testament and its various proclamations of Jesus as the Christ, the Son of God, are probably forever lost to us. What we have is the New Testament itself, its proclamation and its parenesis, its myth and its history.

Further Reading

Three of our resource books have a discussion of Jesus.

R. Fuller, *Intro.*, pp. 69–103. This is a discussion of gospel criticism and its consequence for life of Jesus research, of criteria for authenticity, and of our fundamental knowledge of Jesus and his message. The reader will find that though Fuller and Perrin share the same general approach, Fuller is much more ready than Perrin to accept material as authentic. We have made reference to his work at appropriate points in the chapter above.

PCB, pp. 733–47 (J. S. Bowman).

IDB, vol. 2, pp. 869–96 (F. C. Grant). Both Bowman and Grant write from a viewpoint reached before the full force of the impact of the form-critical view of the gospels on life of Jesus research was appreciated.

IDB *Suppl.*, pp. 863–68, "Teaching of Jesus" (W. R. Farmer); pp. 345–48, "Form Criticism, NT" (C. E. Carlston); pp. 641–42, "Parable" (C. E. Carlston); pp. 917–19, "Trial of Jesus" (D. R. Catchpole).

The literature on Jesus is immense, though recently it has been diminishing. Perrin gave an annotated bibliography of general work on the [life and] teaching of Jesus in *Rediscovering*, pp. 249–51. We will now give again some of the works listed there, together with a selection from the works published since 1967.

R. Bultmann, *Jesus and the Word*. Originally published in German in 1926, this is the starting point for all responsible work on Jesus being carried on today. A careful reading of this book is absolutely indispensable to any study of the subject.

G. Bornkamm, *Jesus of Nazareth*. This was published in Germany as scholarship was becoming possible again after the dislocations of the Hitler period, and of the Second World War and its aftermath. It attempted to present a general picture of the life and teaching of Jesus in accordance with the methods and findings of contemporary

New Testament scholarship, and it succeeded magnificently. It is the classic of the "new quest" of the historical Jesus.

H. Braun, *Jesus of Nazareth*, an important study by a post-Bultmannian which, like Bornkamm's work, is intended for the general reader. Written in 1969, it appeared in English in 1978.

D. Duling, *Jesus Christ Through History*. Chapter 1 has a brief sketch of the life and teachings of Jesus; chapter 2, Jesus Christ in earliest Christianity; chapters 3–10 contain discussions of important views of Jesus Christ in Christendom, including many biographical sketches. It culminates in some recent, general trends.

H. Conzelmann, *Jesus*. An expanded and updated translation of Conzelmann's article "Jesus Christ" in the German encyclopedia *Religion in Geschichte und Gegenwart*. Contains excellent bibliography down to 1973.

N. Perrin, *Jesus and the Language of the Kingdom*. Building on previous studies, this work attempts to interpret the Kingdom in terms of "tensive symbol" (P. Wheelwright) and "opaque symbol" (P. Ricoeur). It also has an extensive discussion of the history of parable interpretation and makes several advances in interpretation on particular passages.

M. Smith, *Jesus the Magician*. Though most modern critics find Smith's views eccentric, this renowned historian offers some fresh insights and the book is a mine of information about Greco-Roman magic.

G. Theissen, *Sociology of Early Palestinian Christianity*. Not specifically a book on Jesus, Theissen attempts to break new ground by giving a social-historiographical account of the "Jesus movement."

G. Vermes, *Jesus the Jew*. An excellent book offering many new insights from the Jewish literature by an acknowledged expert in the field of the history and religion of Palestinian Judaism.

A. Vögtle, "Jesus Christ," in *Sacramentum Verbi* (ed. J. B. Bauer), vol. 3, pp. 419–37. A presentation by a leading European Roman Catholic scholar.

H. McArthur, *In Search of the Historical Jesus*. A selection of articles on various aspects of the subject by representative scholars.

H. Kee, *Jesus in History*. A valuable discussion of the problems and issues.

A question that has been deliberately omitted from the discussion in this chapter is the "question of the historical Jesus," that is, the question of the significance of historical knowledge of Jesus for Christian faith. This question has been the subject of intensive discussion by scholars since the end of the nineteenth century, when doubts first began to be felt about the position of liberal scholarship that the historical Jesus was the source of Christian faith and hence historical knowledge of him was the foundation of that faith. The debate shows no signs of abating, and any attempt to outline its progress or to indicate the issues currently at stake in it would burst the bounds of this or any introduction to the New Testament. Perrin devoted chapter 5 of *Rediscovering* (pp. 207–48) to it, and gave there an annotated bibliography (pp. 262–65). Two extremely important books on the subject published since the completion of the manuscript of that book in 1967 are the following:

V. Harvey, *The Historian and the Believer.*
L. Keck, *A Future for the Historical Jesus.*

For an extensive bibliographical review of studies on Jesus, see J. Reumann (forthcoming).

EPILOGUE
Ways of Being Religious in the New Testament

It is not possible to read the New Testament without being impressed by its immense variety, and especially by the variety of ways of being religious it exhibits. Although the New Testament is a unity in that all of its books accept the centrality of Jesus Christ, nonetheless it is diverse in that both the understanding of Jesus as the Christ and the understanding of what it means to accept him as the Christ are almost infinitely varied. Ascetic and mystic, warrior priest and worker priest, apocalyptic visionary and social revolutionary, ecclesiastical dignitary and street-corner pamphleteer—all these and many more have taken their inspiration from the New Testament or from some part of it. We have constantly been calling attention to this variety within the New Testament; now in this epilogue we briefly summarize some of its orientations.

APOCALYPTICISM

The Christian movement began as an apocalyptic sect and apocalypticism is a major element in the synoptic gospel source Q, in portions of Paul's letters, in the gospel of Mark and, of course, in the book of Revelation, itself an apocalypse. The apocalyptic visionary is one caught up in the drama of a history hurrying to its close, preparing himself for the imminent future in which all will be different. Christian apocalypticism developed the concept of Jesus as the Son of Man, the powerful redeemer who would descend to the earth on the clouds of heaven to judge and redeem, destroy and remake. But it did more than that, because not only was Jesus the Son of Man; the Son of Man was Jesus. That meant that characteristics of the redeemer figure were always subject to the control of the lineaments of Jesus. (So the evangelist Mark was able to blend together the elements of power and authority and the

431

necessity of suffering.) In many respects, Christian apocalyptic was indistinguishable from Jewish, and certainly Christian apocalyptic writers made extensive use of Jewish apocalyptic literature. But the central feature of their visions was always Jesus. Nonetheless, the movement was apocalyptic, with its sense of a world being caught up in the throes of catastrophic change and its belief in the imminence of the final intervention of God that would make all things new and different. Like all apocalypticists, the Christian apocalypticist was alienated from the dominant social and religious structures; so the apocalypticist despaired of the world and its history but had faith in God who was about to change it. As a Christian he believed that Jesus would be the means of that change, and he prepared himself for the imminent coming of Jesus as Son of Man by obeying the teaching that was given in the name of Jesus.

THE APOSTLE PAUL

"For I am not ashamed of the gospel: it is the power of God for salvation to everyone who has faith, to the Jew first and also to the Greek. For in it the righteousness of God is revealed through faith for faith, as it is written, 'He who through faith is righteous shall live.' . . . There is therefore now no condemnation for those who are in Christ Jesus. For the law of the Spirit of life in Christ Jesus has set me free from the law of sin and death" (Rom 1:16–17; 8:1–2). With this deeply rooted conviction Paul put forth his view of the good news about Christ and his Cross-resurrection. That which he could not do himself, that which he believed the Law could not help him to do, Christ has done for him. He can now stand in the presence of God, from which presence he would before have had to flee, for he now bears not his own righteousness but Christ's. He now lives in the world not the life of fear and condemnation but of freedom and power within the bounds of faith and love. This life is Christ's gift to him. Here we recognize a classical form of the Christian experience of religious reality. It is the revelation that one is justified in the sight of God, and the discovery that this can be received only as a gift. Central to this understanding is a concentration on the Cross of Christ, interpreting it as a means of reconciling man to God. This understanding of religion is loaded with the symbolism of evil and focuses attention on the means whereby that evil is overcome and a quality of life from it can be known.

THE EVANGELIST MATTHEW

With the evangelist Matthew we reach another of the classical options of New Testament religion. Here the central point is the concept of a verbal revelation authoritatively interpreted. The essence of religion is obedience to the revealed truth, and such obedience is possible because the world and life are ordered by the God who has revealed this truth to man. There is order and stability to be experienced, there is the firm basis of a revealed truth on which to build; there are appointed means both to make possible the necessary understanding and also to help attain the necessary level of obedience. These means are present in the church, in the structure and organization of the community of which the individual is a member and in which the risen and glorified Christ is present. In this understanding of what it means to be religious in the world the essential elements are those of revelation and of obedience to revelation, and the conviction that there is a correspondence between the revealed truth and the experienced reality of life in the world such that life in the world can be successfully organized on the basis of obedience to the revelation, and only on that basis.

THE AUTHOR OF LUKE-ACTS

The author of Luke-Acts is also concerned with revelation but with revelation in the form of a sacred person and a sacred time, and with a structured means of relating to that time. That person is Jesus, and his time is that between the descent of the Spirit upon him at his baptism and the return of the Spirit to the Father at the Cross. One relates to him and to his time by means of the Spirit, which returned to the church and the believer at the baptism of Pentecost. In his own life Jesus was a paradigm of the possibilities for human existence in the world and the model of what it means to be religious in the world. The presence of the spirit of Jesus in the world, linking the believer with the sacred life and sacred time of Jesus, empowers the believer to exhibit the same quality of life in the world that Jesus did. This is borne out by the heroes of the church whose lives paralleled Jesus' in many respects. To be religious in the world is to imitate Jesus, an imitation made possible by the presence and work of his spirit in the world. To imitate Jesus means to care for the outcast, to concern oneself for the neighbor, to live the life of love in the world and for the world.

THE EVANGELIST JOHN

In the case of the evangelist John we have a concentration on the Cross of Christ almost as strong as that in the case of the apostle Paul. In John, however, the context is not the symbolism of evil but rather the symbolism of glory. The Christ of John's gospel is the descending/ascending redeemer, and the Cross is the moment of his glorious return whence he came—having achieved that for which he was sent. While the Cross itself is the moment of supreme glorification, there is a series of earlier majestic "signs" by means of which the Christ also manifests his glory. Moreover, a series of solemn discourses explores the glory of this Christ by using primary symbols of life-giving power—water, light, bread—and by claiming explicitly that he gives life and "eternal life" to those who believe in him. Further, he does the Father's work; he is at one with God. Combined with this emphasis on glory and power and on the Christ's

433

oneness with God is an emphasis on the concern of the Christ for the believer—for example, by the use of shepherd and sheep symbolism—and on the believer's oneness with him.

This last point is the key to the Johannine understanding of what it means to be religious in the world. The believer contemplates the glorious majesty of the Christ and of the Christ's oneness with the Father, and then finds himself at one with the Christ in a mystical union by means of which he experiences the life of love in the world. But the emphasis now is on the rapture of love as experienced in the world through knowledge of Christ, whereas in Luke-Acts the emphasis is on the manifestation of love in human relationships. Of course, neither excludes the other (see 1 John 2:1-11), but the emphasis is different.

The gospel and letters of John are the charter of Christian mysticism.

THE OTHER WAYS

There are other understandings of what it means to be religious in the world in the New Testament, but they are all variations, sometimes very important variations, on the themes we have already established. So, for example, the gospel of Mark reshapes the apocalyptic way of being religious in the world by systematizing the apocalyptic drama, by developing the theme of the Son of Man who "must" suffer, and by showing what these things mean to faith and discipleship. Similarly, the writers of the period of the emerging institutional church develop, systematize—and further institutionalize—the "way" of the gospel of Matthew. But we have said enough, we believe, to indicate something of the classical options the New Testament presents.

APPENDIX 1
The Canon of the Bible

When we speak of the "canon" of the Bible we are referring to a *list* of books authoritatively accepted as comprising the Old and New Testaments. The word *canon* is derived from Greek (*kanōn*), meaning something "made of reeds" or "straight like reeds"—for example, a stave, a rod, or a ruler for drawing or measuring. Metaphorically it can mean a rule, a standard, a model, a paradigm, and so on. The Greek and Latin church fathers used this word, or forms of it, in connection with many things, including lists of church rules (hence "canon law") and lists of clergyman or saints (hence "canonized"). On the occasion of the Easter festival of 367, Athanasius, bishop of Alexandria, used it in a letter to his churches giving a list of books to be accepted as constituting the New Testament. This letter settles the New Testament canon in the West, and it is because of its wording that we use the term *canon* in connection with the Old Testament, the New Testament, or the Bible as a whole.

THE CANON OF THE OLD TESTAMENT

The Hebrew Canon

The movement toward a Jewish canon of Scripture began in 621 B.C., when a book was found in the collection box of the Temple of Jerusalem and accepted by King Josiah and the people as the authoritative revelation of God to the Jews (2 Kings 22–23; 2 Chronicles 34). This book was in effect the book of Deuteronomy, and King Josiah and the Jews accepted it as the verbal revelation of the will of God to them and as the basis of their relationship with God. It was accepted as "the law [Torah] of the Lord given through Moses" (2 Chron 34:14) to govern their life in the world, and with this the idea of religion as essentially obedience to a verbal revelation was born. But if religion is essentially obedience to a verbal revelation, then the question becomes, what constitutes the verbal revelation? In addition to the book of Deuteronomy, the Jews had historical and legal traditions associated with the figure of Moses, and they also had prophets and prophetic traditions. Further, they developed liturgical literature and literature concerned with moral instruction, and eventually also apocalyptic literature. It therefore became a matter of practical necessity to define the extent of the verbal revelation.

The process toward the definition of a Jewish canon was a gradual one. First to be defined was the Law, the Torah. Gradually, historical and legal traditions associated with the figure of Moses were gathered together around the nucleus of the book of Deuteronomy. This collection of texts eventually became the Torah as it is now known: the five "books of Moses," Genesis, Exodus, Leviticus, Numbers, and Deuteronomy. We do not know the exact date of the acceptance of these five books as God's Law, but it must have been after the return from the Babylonian exile and before the separation of the Samaritans from the Jews (since the Samaritans also accept these five books as Scripture). A date about 400 B.C. is therefore probable.

In 400 B.C., however, the Jews had other books that spoke to them of God. Specifically, there were books concerning prophets, either narratives in which they were heavily involved or accounts of their oracles. This class of literature came to be known simply as "the Prophets," and eventually it encompassed eight books: Joshua, Judges, (1 and 2) Samuel, (1 and 2) Kings—the so-called Former Prophets—and Isaiah, Jeremiah, Ezekiel, and the book of the twelve minor prophets—the so-called Latter Prophets. These achieved the form in which we know them and were accepted as authoritative by 180 B.C., at which date Jesus, son of Sirach, speaks of "the law and the prophets," reads the poems of Second Isaiah as part of the book of Isaiah, and knows the twelve minor prophets as one volume (Sir Prologue; 48:24; 49:10).

After "the Law and the Prophets" were accepted as Scripture other works were attracted into their orbit. This process was going on in Judaism through the New Testament period and eventually it produced a group of books known as "the Writings." This group consisted of poetry (Psalms, Proverbs, Job); texts read at annual festivals (Song of Solomon, Ruth, Lamentations, Ecclesiastes, Esther); prophecy (Daniel); and history (Ezra, Nehemiah, [1 and 2] Chronicles). This group was achieving authoritative status in the New Testament period. Matthew is conservative in this regard, accepting only "the law and the prophets" (Matt 5:17), whereas Luke accepts "the law . . . the prophets and the psalms" (Luke 24:44), "the psalms" meaning here the Writings. A similar division of opinion existed among Jewish writers of the period.

The final canon of Jewish Scripture was fixed by the Pharisees meeting at Jamnia after the destruction of Jerusalem, and a date about A.D. 90 would be appropriate for it. The first known references to the Jewish canon as thus defined are 2 Esdras 14:44–46, which speaks of twenty-four books, and Josephus, *Apion* I:viii, who speaks of twenty-two. The writer of 2 Esdras is counting five books of the Law (Genesis, Exodus, Leviticus, Numbers, Deuteronomy), eight of the Prophets (Joshua, Judges, [1 and 2] Samuel, [1 and 2] Kings, Isaiah, Jeremiah, Ezekiel, the twelve minor prophets) and eleven of the Writings (Psalms, Proverbs, Job, Song of Solomon, Ruth, Lamentations, Ecclesiastes, Esther, Daniel, Ezra-Nehemiah [counted as one book], and [1 and 2] Chronicles). Josephus probably unites Ruth with Judges and Lamentations with Jeremiah to get twenty-two books. This canon is called the "Hebrew canon," since the fact that a book was written in Hebrew was a criterion used by the Pharisees at Jamnia in their selection.

The Greek Canon

Although the Pharisees at Jamnia spoke for the Judaism of the future, in New Testament times the Hellenistic Judaism of the Diaspora was going its own way with regard to the canon as in other matters. Hellenistic Judaism tended to accept as authoritative books that the more conservative Palestinian Judaism represented at Jamnia was beginning to reject. Moreover, the Greek-speaking Judaism of the Diaspora tended to obliterate the Palestinian Jewish division Torah/Prophets/Writings in favor of a division according to literary types. So the "Bible" of the Greek-speaking Jews of the Diaspora was more extensive than that accepted at Jamnia. It is somewhat misleading, however, to speak of it as a "Greek canon," because so far as we know no formal list of books was ever established by Greek-speaking Jews, and the lists we have are those implied by *Christians* as they transmitted texts of the Old Testament in Greek. Here the earlier codices are not in agreement. But it would be fair to say that Hellenistic Judaism produced and used books rejected by the Jews at Jamnia but preserved by Christians. The Jamnia Jewish canon was not followed by Christians until the rise of Protestantism, when a threefold distinction began to be made: Old Testament (according to the Jamnia canon), New Testament, and Apocrypha. The latter were Jewish books (or parts thereof) used by Christians that the Jamnia canon did not include.

The Apocrypha represents, therefore, a Christian collection of the literature of Hellenistic Judaism, but it nonetheless shows characteristic interests and concerns of Hellenistic Judaism. It tends to fall into six classes.

1. Historical Books

1 Esdras (concerned with reforms of Jewish worship carried out by Josiah, Zerubbabel, and Ezra)

1 Maccabees (an account of Maccabean revolt and part of the Hasmonean period)

2 Maccabees (an account of the Maccabean period written in the Hellenistic sytle known as "pathetic history," i.e., history recounted in a way intended to stir the emotions)

437

2. Imaginative History
Tobit
Judith
Susanna (in Daniel)
Bel and the Dragon (in Daniel)
These are actually moralistic novels.

3. Wisdom Books
Wisdom of Solomon
Wisdom of Jesus, Son of Sirach

4. Devotional Literature
Prayer of Manasseh
Prayer of Azariah and the Song of the Three Young Men (in Daniel)
Baruch (two prayers and a Wisdom homily)

5. A Letter
The Letter of Jeremiah (a pseudonymous homily and in form, therefore, parallel to some of the "letters" in the New Testament; sometimes it is chapter 6 of Baruch)

6. Miscellaneous
The Additions to Esther ("historical" episodes, letters, prayers, a dream interpretation, a claim of validation)

The Christian Canon of the Old Testament

The Christians transmitted the Jewish Scriptures in Greek as part of their Bible, for the most part as they were found in the Hellenistic Judaism of the Diaspora. Although in some quarters there was a tendency to accept the decisions made at Jamnia, this tendency did not persist. The Christians in general accepted a canon of the Old Testament that was broader than the canon of Jewish Scripture defined at Jamnia, and when Jerome produced his Latin version of the Bible, the Vulgate, he included in the Old Testament the books listed above, plus a largely apocalyptic work, 2 Esdras.

But the knowledge persisted that the Hebrew canon of Scripture was different from the Christian Old Testament as defined by the Latin Vulgate. At the Reformation, Martin Luther and his followers were anxious to differentiate themselves from the Catholic church. They also found that some of the doctrines they came to despise had their only scriptural support in books the Hebrew canon had rejected; for example, the doctrine of purgatory had its only possible scriptural support in 2 Macc 12:43–45. At the same time it was absolutely essential for Luther to define the limits of Scripture, since he was rejecting the authority of the Papacy and substituting for it that of Scripture. In his epoch-making translation of the Bible (1534), Luther published only the books of the Hebrew canon in his Old Testament. He relegated the others to a separate section following the end of the Old Testament, under the heading "Apocrypha: these are books which are not held equal to the sacred Scriptures, and yet are useful and good for reading." The details of what followed do not concern us; it is sufficient to say that this gradually became the practice of Protestantism as a whole. Such authoritative modern English translations as the Revised Standard Version and the New English Bible do not include the books of the Apocrypha in the Old Testament.

In reaction to the practice of the Protestant reformers, the Roman Catholic church reaffirmed the canonicity of all the books of the Vulgate Old Testament but the Prayer of Manasseh and 1–2 Esdras. Catholic scholars are sensitive to the problem and tend to distinguish between "protocanonical" books (the Hebrew canon) and the "deutero-canonical" books (the Protestant "Apocrypha"), as do, for example, the writers in the *Jerome Biblical Commentary*.

THE CANON OF THE NEW TESTAMENT

The process that led to the formation of the New Testament canon and the recognition of the New Testament as one book was a gradual one, beginning with the first collection of the letters of Paul and reaching its climax in 367 with Athanasius's letter giving a list of the "books that are canonized and handed down to us and believed to be divine." His list gives the books of the Old Testament and then the twenty-seven books that comprise the New Testament. It became authoritative for the church in the West, although it was resisted in the East, as we shall see below.

The Collection and Circulation of Pauline Letters

The first collection of letters attributed to Paul probably consisted of nine letters (1, 2 Thessalonians; 1, 2 Corinthians; Romans; Galatians; Philippians; Colossians; and Philemon) with a tenth, Ephesians, added as a covering letter to the whole collection. It is this collection, which must have been in circulation by the end of the first century, that the author of 2 Peter regards as "scripture" (2 Pet 3:15–16).

In the course of time the Pastorals and Hebrews were added to the collection. The Pastorals were added sometime in the second half of the second century; they are in the Muratorian Canon, a list of the books of the New Testament with remarks, in Greek, perhaps written in Rome near the end of the second century and preserved for us in a Latin translation discovered and published in 1740. The Muratorian Canon does not include Hebrews, but early in the third century, Origen, who succeeded Clement as head of the Christian school in Alexandria in 203, reports that it was accepted everywhere. Although he himself had doubts about Pauline authorship, he justified the acceptance on the grounds that the thought was Pauline.

With the general acceptance of Hebrews as part of the Pauline corpus, this aspect of the New Testament was complete. Other letters circulated in the name of Paul, but these were not accepted. The Muratorian Canon refers to several "which cannot be received into the catholic church, for gold ought not to be mixed with honey."

The Acceptance of the Four Gospels

There were a comparatively large number of gospels written in the early church, some covering in a more legendary fashion much the same ground as the four that became canonical, others developing the themes of the infancy of Jesus or the post-resurrection instruction of the disciples by the risen Lord.[1] These competed with the gospels of Matthew, Mark, Luke, and John in the early church, but the latter rapidly gained an ascendancy they never lost.

The earliest testimony to the four gospels as "scripture" comes from the middle of the second century. At that time a homily was written that was ascribed (falsely) to Clement, bishop of Rome, author of the letter to the Corinthians known as 1 Clement. The homily is known as 2 Clement. 2 Clement 2 reads, "And again another scripture says, 'I came not to call the righteous, but sinners,' " and so treats Matt 9:13 as Scripture. At about the same time, Justin Martyr, a church father who died as a martyr in Rome somewhere between 163 and 167, in describing an act of Christian worship, speaks of "the memoirs of the Apostles or the writings of the Prophets [which] are read, as long as time permits" (Justin, *Apol.* 1. 67). Elsewhere he speaks of the "memoirs made by [the apostles], which are called gospels" (*Apol.* 2, 33, 66). From these references we can see that the gospels are gaining scriptural status and that although they originally circulated anonymously they are now being attributed to "apostles." This latter fact is a tribute to the developing dependence on apostolic tradition.

The Influence of the Heretic Marcion

The next step in the formation of the New Testament canon was taken by a heretic, Marcion, who flourished in the middle of the second century. An altogether remarkable man, he had been raised in the East as an orthodox Christian but was strongly influenced by Gnosticism, so that he came to believe that the creator God of the Old Testament was an inferior deity and that Jesus had revealed the supreme God, the God of love, previously unknown. He further came to believe that the revelation by Jesus had been hopelessly corrupted by the Twelve but preserved by the one true apostle, Paul. In support of his teaching Marcion constructed the first Christian canon, consisting of ten letters of Paul and an edited version of the gospel of Luke. The ten letters of Paul were the extent of the Pauline corpus in his day, and the gospel of Luke was accepted because it was attributed to a companion of Paul. Marcion apparently edited his text of the gospel of Luke, and perhaps also that of the Pauline

---

[1] The most convenient discussion of this whole literature is E. Hennecke and W. Schneemelcher, *New Testament Apocrypha*, vol. 1, *Gospels and Related Writings*.

letters, to bring it into accord with his understanding of the revelation of God by Jesus.

Marcion was extraordinarily successful. Although condemned by the orthodox as a heretic, he attracted a wide following. And in the very course of the struggle against him, his influence was crucial to the development of the New Testament canon.

The Formation of a Canon of the New Testament as Distinct from the Old Testament

Before Marcion, the tendency was to add new writings to the Jewish Scriptures to make up the Christian Scriptures. For example, 2 Pet 3:15–16 adds the letters of Paul to the "other scriptures," that is, to the Jewish Scriptures. Then Justin Martyr adds the "memoirs of the Apostles" to "the Prophets," the Prophets being a Jewish designation for a part of their Scriptures. But with Marcion all this changes, for Marcion flatly repudiated the Jewish Scriptures and substituted for them a new Christian Scripture, consisting of the "gospel" and the "apostle"—the gospel of Luke and the letters of the apostle Paul. The orthodox churches were ultimately successful in their struggle against Marcion, but in Christianity the Jewish Scriptures were henceforth separated from the Christian, a tendency that had not been evident before. The very conception of a New Testament as distinct from the Old may well go back to Marcion's repudiation of the Jewish Scriptures.

The New Testament as the "Gospel" and the "Apostle"

Marcion's division of Christian Scriptures into "gospel" and "apostle" also survived the success of the orthodox Christian struggle against him. The orthodox churches did not repudiate this division but added to it. They fought to add other gospels to that of Luke, and other letters to those of Paul, including the Pastorals, written in the name of Paul and representing the viewpoint of emergent Catholicism rather than that of Marcion. The Pastorals were undoubtedly the more readily accepted because they were effective weapons against Marcion. The division of the Christian canon into "gospel" and "apostle" became as traditional as that of the Jewish canon into "law," "prophets," and "writings."

The Influence of Gnosticism

Marcion was the first important heretic, and his appearance in the middle of the second century was a foretaste of things to come. As we have said, Marcion was influenced by Gnosticism, and beginning with him Gnosticism became more and more influential in the Christian churches. In fact, late in the second century and in the third Gnosticism developed as a specific Christian heresy. At this point there is a problem in terminology, because traditionally the term Gnosticism has designated that specific Christian heresy. However, we now know that Gnosticism was in fact a much broader movement and that the Christian heresy was but one form it took. At various places in this book we have discussed the broader movement, being especially concerned with its earlier phases and its influence on the New Testament. But now we are concerned with the specific Christian heresy.[2]

As a Christian heresy Gnosticism claimed to be an improved or perfected version of the Christian faith. Among other things, it said it possessed secret books of the teaching of Jesus and the apostles above and beyond those used in the orthodox churches. A good example is the Gnostic gospel of Thomas, which begins, "These are the secret words which the living Jesus spake, and Didymus Judas Thomas wrote them down." Marcion is not typical of Gnosticism in his view of Scripture, for he limited the Christian canon: Gnosticism normally expanded it. This Gnostic tendency forced the churches to struggle to limit the canon (as compared with the fight against Marcion, where they struggled to expand it) and to emphasize the apostolic authority of their sacred books. Both Gnostic Christian and orthodox Christian churches accepted the idea of apostolic authority as normative.

The combined impact of Marcion and the development of Gnostic Christianity led therefore to (a) the idea of a Christian canon separate from the Jewish, (b) the struggle to expand the Christian canon over against Marcion and limit it over against Gnostic Christianity, and (c) an emphasis on apostolic authority, and ultimately on apostolic authorship for the books of the orthodox Christian canon.

The Muratorian Canon

The Muratorian Canon, perhaps from Rome toward the end of the second century,[3] is definitely anti-Marcionite in tone. It speaks of a letter "to the Laodiceans, another to the Alexandrians, forged in Paul's name for the sect of Marcion."[4] This canon consists of the four gospels, Matthew, Mark, Luke, John; the Acts of the Apostles; thirteen letters of Paul (including the Pastorals but omitting Hebrews); Jude; 1 and 2 John; the Wisdom of Solomon; and two apocalypses (the book of Revelation and the apocalypse of Peter).

---

[2] A convenient and good account of the specific Christian heresy is given by R. M. Grant, "Gnosticism," *IDB*, vol. 2, pp. 404–06. Grant restricts the term to the Christian heresy, the traditional use.

[3] A. C. Sundberg, Jr., "Muratorian Fragment," *IDB Suppl.*, pp. 609–10, argues that the Muratorian Canon is not from Rome, but from the eastern churches, and from the fourth century. If he is correct, one of the major turning points in the development of the canon cannot be sustained as is usual.

[4] We quote the translation conveniently available in E. Hennecke and W. Schneemelcher, *New Testament Apocrypha*, vol. 1, pp. 43–45.

From this point forward the orthodox church maintained the four gospels as canonical, strenuously resisting the inclusion of any others. Acts also had a firm place in the canon, as did the thirteen letters attributed to Paul. But the others mentioned remained in dispute for some time. Some were dropped and others added. However, the tendency was to accept more and more of what we called the literature of emergent Catholicism, an understandable tendency in view of the characteristics of that literature.

THE CANON IN THE THIRD CENTURY

In the third century there are two representative figures: Tertullian (about 160–220) who wrote in Latin in the West, mainly in Carthage, and Origen (185–254) who wrote in Greek in the East, mainly in Alexandria.[5] Tertullian is the first writer to speak of the "New Testament" (*Novum Testamentum*) as distinct from the Old, and he accepts the following books as constituting that New Testament: the four gospels, the thirteen letters attributed to Paul, Acts, Revelation, 1 Peter, 1 John, and Jude. Comparing this list with the Muratorian Canon, we see that 2 John, the apocalypse of Peter, and the Wisdom of Solomon are missing, but that 1 Peter has been added. Origen had traveled widely and concerned himself with the acceptance of books by the Christian churches everywhere. He distinguishes between those "acknowledged" and those "disputed." Those generally acknowledged were the four gospels, the fourteen letters attributed to Paul (including Hebrews, as we noted earlier), Acts, 1 John, 1 Peter, and Revelation. Among those disputed in some places he includes James, Jude, 2 Peter, 2 and 3 John. This means that by the time of Origen all the books that finally constituted the canon of the New Testament were known and in circulation, but some were disputed. Origen is the first writer to mention the letter of James.

A feature of the later third century in the East was a dispute about the status of the book of Revelation. In the second half of the century it came to be generally rejected in Alexandria and Antioch, and although it was eventually restored to the canon it never achieved the same status as the other books in Greek-speaking Christianity, and it never achieved canonical status in the Syrian churches.

The Canon in the Fourth Century

About 325 Eusebius of Caesarea completed his famous *Ecclesiastical History.* In it he reports on the state of the New Testament canon in the Greek-

---

[5] In the second century Latin was established as the dominant language in the western Mediterranean, while Greek was maintained in the eastern Mediterranean. By the end of the second century Latin was in general use in the churches of North Africa, Gaul, and Spain, while Greek continued in use in the East. The church at Rome became predominantly Latin-speaking about the middle of the third century.

speaking churches of the eastern Mediterranean. He is the first writer to speak of a distinct group of the "seven so-called Catholic epistles" (1, 2, 3 John; 1, 2 Peter; James; Jude) but he notes that James, Jude, 2 Peter and 2, 3 John are all "disputed." He is ambiguous about Revelation. Unambiguously accepted are the four gospels, Acts, the fourteen letters attributed to Paul (with a note that some reject Hebrews because the church at Rome does not accept it as Pauline), 1 John, and 1 Peter.

The great event in the fourth century in the East is, however, the festal letter of Athanasius, bishop of Alexandria, circulated among the churches under his charge in 367. The crucial passage reads as follows.

> Continuing, I must without hesitation mention the Scriptures of the New Testament; they are the following: the four Gospels according to Matthew, Mark, Luke and John, after them the Acts of the Apostles and the seven so-called catholic epistles of the apostles—namely, one of James, two of Peter, then three of John and after these one of Jude. In addition to this there are fourteen epistles of the apostle Paul written in the following order; the first to the Romans, then two to the Corinthians and then after these the one to the Galatians, following it the one to the Ephesians, thereafter the one to the Philippians and the one to the Colossians and two to the Thessalonians and the epistle to the Hebrews and then immediately two to Timothy, one to Titus and lastly the one to Philemon. Yet further the Revelation of John.[6]

In the first part of the fourth century the Latin-speaking churches in the western Mediterranean generally accepted a canon consisting of the four gospels, the thirteen letters of the Pauline collection, 1 John, 1 Peter, and Revelation. That is Tertullian's canon minus Jude. In the latter half of the century, however, the influence of Alexandria made itself felt, and when Jerome made the Latin translation of the New Testament that became the standard translation in the West (the so-called Vulgate), he followed the canon as set forth by Athanasius. In a letter to Paulinus written about 385, he defends the canonicity of the seven Catholic epistles, Hebrews, and Revelation, while acknowledging the difficulties some have with them.

Further History of the New Testament Canon

The festal letter of Athanasius in the East and the work of Jerome in the West mark the formation of the New Testament canon as we know it. This canon gradually became accepted everywhere except in Syria. In Syria until the end of the fourth century the canon was the Diatessaron (a harmony of the four gospels rather than four separate gospels), Acts, and fifteen letters of Paul (including a third letter to Corinth). About 400, a list substitutes the four sepa-

---

[6] As quoted in E. Hennecke and W. Schneemelcher, *New Testament Apocrypha*, vol. 1, pp. 59–60.

rate gospels for the Diatessaron and omits 3 Corinthians. In the first quarter of the fifth century Syria moved nearer to the remainder of the church by accepting the four gospels, Acts, fourteen Pauline letters, James, 1 Peter, and 1 John. The accommodation would doubtless have gone further, but in the fifth century fierce christological controversies split the Syrian church and separated it from the rest of the church.

The only other factor that needs mention here is that for some time books were accepted in some places in addition to the twenty-seven-book canon of Athanasius and Jerome; for example, Codex Alexandrinus, a fifth-century Greek manuscript, includes 1 and 2 Clement in the New Testament. Gradually, however, the twenty-seven-book canon gained general acceptance. The acceptance was by common consent rather than by formal pronouncement of general church council.

The New Testament Apocrypha

We have seen that several works hovered on the edge of acceptance into the canon of the New Testament, for example, 1 and 2 Clement. Others in this category are the Shepherd of Hermas, the epistle of Barnabas, and the Didache (Teaching of the Twelve Apostles). Although these were not included in the final canon of the New Testament, they continued to exercise considerable influence and came to be known as the "Apostolic Fathers," a designation that also included the letters of Ignatius and some other works. Beyond these, however, a vast quantity of other early Christian literature, some but not all of it Gnostic in character, was definitely rejected by the orthodox churches. This included all gospels except the four, all letters attributed to Paul except the fourteen, acts of various apostles, and many apocalypses. These came to be called New Testament *Apocrypha*. *Apocrypha* means "hidden," "secret," and these books were to be hidden from the faithful. They are conveniently discussed and in part translated in Hennecke-Schneemelcher, *New Testament Apocrypha*, vols. 1 and 2. An older translation is M. R. James, *The Apocryphal New Testament*.

Further Reading

W. G. Kümmel, *Intro.*, pp. 475–510.
W. Marxsen, *Intro.*, pp. 279–84.
R. H. Fuller, *Intro.*, pp. 191–99.
PCB, pp. 73–75 (O. T. canon: B. J. Roberts); pp. 676–82 (N. T. canon: J. N. Sanders).
JBC, pp. 516–22 (O. T. canon: R. E. Brown and J. C. Turro); pp. 525–31 (N. T. canon: R. E. Brown); pp. 543–46 (Apocrypha: R. E. Brown).

IDB, vol. 1, pp. 498–520 (O. T. canon: R. H. Pfeiffer); pp. 520–32 (N. T. canon: F. W. Beare); pp. 161–69 (Apocrypha: M. S. Enslin).

IDB Suppl., pp. 130–36 (O. T. canon: D. N. Freedman); pp. 136–40 (N. T. canon: A. C. Sundberg, Jr.); pp. 34–36 (Apocrypha: R. McL. Wilson); pp. 609–10 (Muratorian Fragment: A. C. Sundburg, Jr.; cf. note 3 above).

APPENDIX 2
The Text
of the New Testament

GREEK MANUSCRIPTS

The various books of the New Testament were originally written in *koinē* ("common") Greek, a later form of classical Greek that was the common language of the Hellenistic world. The church at large continued to use Greek for several centuries, and when in 313 the Christian church became the church of the Empire under Constantine and had the resources to produce fine manuscripts, they were written in Greek. Greek continued to be the official language of a major branch of the Christian church in the East, and manuscripts of the New Testament continued to be produced in Greek until the invention of printing. These manuscripts may be classified as follows.

Papyrus Codices

These manuscripts are on sheets of papyrus bound together as a book (codex). The use of codices rather than continuous rolls (as in Jewish manuscripts such as the Dead Sea Scrolls) is a feature of earliest Christian literary activity. These codices are either of individual books, or of partial collections such as the gospels and Acts or the Pauline corpus. Some eighty-eight papyri are now known, all discovered in modern times in Egypt, where the climate preserves papyrus. They date from the second to the eighth centuries and vary in size from fragments of leaves to considerable remnants of a codex. The contents of these codices follow the developing categories of Christian Scripture. The collections of books found together are the "gospel" (the four gospels and Acts), the "apostle" (a collection of Pauline letters), and the "catholic epistles" (some of the catholic epistles, often together with books that were not included in the final canon). These papyrus codices are designated by the letter

447

P followed by a number. They include the earliest known texts of books of the New Testament, the earliest of them all being P 52, a small scrap of papyrus containing four verses of John 18. This is dated on paleographical grounds (the age of the form of the letters used) in the first half of the second century, possibly about A.D. 125.

The Great Uncial Codices

These are manuscripts of the complete New Testament, indeed, of the complete Bible, since they include the Greek Old Testament, known as the "Septuagint." They date from the fourth century onward and some of them include books excluded from the canon of Athanasius (discussed in Appendix 1). They are written on parchment in uncial characters (large or "capital" letters) and are designated by letters, or by numbers prefixed by a zero, since scholars have run out of alphabets! Some of the more important are the following.

S 01 Codex Sinaiticus (middle fourth century). This manuscript was discovered by Konstantin von Tischendorf in the monastery of Saint Catherine at the foot of Mount Sinai in the period 1844–1859.[1] Its subsequent preservation for the world of scholarship was a dramatic and fitting climax to Tischendorf's life-long devotion to the search for and evaluation of manuscripts of the Greek New Testament. This codex is the greatest of the uncials since it is the only one in which the New Testament is completely preserved. It also includes the epistle of Barnabas and the Shepherd of Hermas. Enamored of his discovery and recognizing its value, Tischendorf designated it Aleph, the first letter of the Hebrew alphabet, since Roman A was already used to designate Alexandrinus. Today, since Hebrew characters are often unavailable to printers and are not recognized by most readers, it is often designated S (for Sinaiticus).

A 02 Codex Alexandrinus (early fifth century). This manuscript originally contained the Old Testament, the New Testament, 1 and 2 Clement, and the Psalms of Solomon (a collection of noncanonical Jewish psalms composed shortly before the time of Jesus). Originally kept in Alexandria, it was presented to Charles I of England in 1627 and is now in the British Museum.

B 03 Codex Vaticanus (early fourth century). This codex, which originally contained the whole Greek Bible, is the earliest of the great uncials. It has been in the Vatican Library in Rome since before the publication of the first catalogue of that library in 1475; no one knows how it came to be there in the first place.

D 05 Codex Bezae (fifth or sixth century). Another manuscript with a dramatic history, this one, which contains the gospels and Acts, first appears in the hands of the bishop of Clermont at the Council of Trent, where it was used by

[1] Recently eight missing pages have also turned up! See below, p. 463, *n.* 1.

that worthy in an attempt to lay a biblical foundation for celibacy. (At John 21:22, D reads: "If I wish him to remain *thus* until I come." It is the only Greek manuscript that has "thus" in this passage, although this reading is found in the Latin Vulgate.) After a subsequent checkered history the manuscript finally came into the possession of Theodore Beza, the heir of John Calvin in Geneva, who presented it to Cambridge University in 1581. It is important to scholars in two respects. First, it is the earliest known New Testament manuscript written in both Greek and Latin, having a Greek text and a Latin translation on facing pages. Second, the text of the books it contains is very different from that of other Greek manuscripts. This text—called "Western" because it has much in common with some Latin versions that come from the West—has presented, and continues to present, a major problem to critics attempting to reconstruct the original text of the gospels and Acts.

The Minuscule Codices

Until the ninth century all biblical manuscripts were written in uncial characters, but then something of a revolution set in and small cursive (run together) characters began to be used. From then on we have minuscule manuscripts, that is, codices written in a cursive script. The use of cursive writing made manuscript production much less laborious, and from the ninth century until 1450 (the invention of printing), we have some 2800 minuscules, compared with some 274 uncials from the earlier period. The minuscule manuscripts are designated by Arabic numerals (1,2, etc.).

EARLY "VERSIONS" OF THE NEW TESTAMENT

At the time of the writing of the books of the New Testament and for several centuries thereafter, Greek was the common language of the world in which the New Testament circulated. Gradually, however, the universality of the Greek language diminished and local languages became dominant in various areas: Latin in the West, Syriac in the East, Coptic in Egypt, and so on. Consequently, Christian literature was produced in these languages and books of the New Testament were translated into them. These translations are now known as "versions." The process began well before the establishment of the canon of the New Testament and before the church had the resources to sponsor careful and official translations. A confusing plethora of texts and translations emerged, and in at least two of the linguistic areas of the church, the Latin and the Syriac, this fact, together with the need to either accept the Athanasian canon or establish a variant one, led in turn to the establishment of an "official" text and translation. In the West this task was entrusted to the great scholar Jerome at the end of the fourth century; the result is now known as the Latin Vulgate. Previously existing Latin versions are now designated Old Latin versions. Jerome accepted the canon as promulgated by Athanasius and from his time on there is no dispute about the New Testament canon in the West. Athanasius had spoken for the Greek-speaking church, and in the Latin church the influence of the Vulgate was all determinative.

In the Syriac-speaking church the books of the New Testament were also variously translated, but although the four gospels common in the West were translated as separate entities, this version was almost never used. In its place was a harmony of the four gospels, a weaving together of their texts to produce a continuous narrative, prepared in the second half of the second century by the Syrian Tatian, born about 110, who lived for years in Rome and was a disciple of Justin Martyr. It was known as Tatian's Diatessaron ("[one] through four") and was immensely popular. The same multiplicity of texts and translations, and a similar need for a canon, developed in the Syrian church as in the Latin. Early in the fifth century an "official" version was prepared, the Peshitta (from a Syriac word meaning "simple"). It had the four separated gospels. The Diatessaron was subsequently suppressed and no complete original language copy of it has survived to us. In addition to the gospels, the Peshitta contained Acts, the Pauline corpus (including Hebrews), James, 1 Peter, and 1 John. It did not have 2 Peter, 2 and 3 John, Jude, or Revelation. Syriac versions earlier than the Peshitta are now known as Old Syriac versions.

Other ancient versions of the New Testament in Coptic, Armenian, Ethiopic, and Georgian are less important than the Latin and the Syriac, although the Ethiopic Bible is remarkable in that it preserves complete versions of two Jewish apocalyptic works, the works of Enoch and Jubilees, which would otherwise be known to us only in fragments.

We have now reviewed briefly the manuscripts and versions through which the New Testament has been transmitted to us. The next matter to be considered is that of its text. When we read the New Testament, how near are we to what the original authors actually wrote?

THE SEARCH FOR THE ORIGINAL TEXT OF THE NEW TESTAMENT

From the very beginning the books that now make up the New Testament were copied and recopied. Possibly Paul himself had his letter to the Romans copied and sent to churches other than Rome. Certainly churches having letters from him circulated them to other churches, and it was not long before there was a Pauline corpus, a collection of his letters, in general circulation. Similarly, the other books now included in the New Testament were copied and circulated. Copies of the gospel of Mark, for example, were available to the authors of Matthew and Luke. Indeed, constant copying and circulation could almost be described as a prerequisite to final inclusion in the New Testament, for books not found generally useful, and hence not copied and circulated, would not have found their way into the canon. But all this was going on in circumstances that made any kind of control over the texts very difficult. For the first three centuries the church rarely had the resources to employ professional scribes, or sufficient peace and stability to be able to establish careful control of the texts being copied. Moreover, for a large part of this time the books did not have the status of sacred Scripture and its consequent reverential handling. It was not until the epoch of the great uncials that these conditions prevailed, and by this time the damage had been done. Scribal errors of all kinds had crept into the manuscripts, devotional and theological factors had affected them in numerous places, reminiscence of one passage had influenced the text of another, and so on.

The various major church centers undertook revisions of the text of the New Testament in an attempt to bring order out of the chaos, and today we can identify readings characteristic of such revisions, as in the great uncials BSA, which are in part products of a revision or revisions undertaken in Egypt. But by and large the production of manuscripts went on uncritically, and even though more scribal care was now exercised than had been in the past, older corruptions were passed on and newer ones entered the tradition.

The Greek New Testament was first printed, as distinct from being copied by hand, early in the sixteenth century. The initial editions were uncritical printings of late and therefore necessarily defective Greek manuscripts. The first to appear was prepared by the Dutch humanist Desiderius Erasmus (1516), and it was so uncritical that where his few manuscripts were defective Erasmus simply retranslated into Greek the Latin of the Vulgate! Nevertheless, the printing met a real need and the volume went through edition after edition. The second edition of 1519 formed the basis for Luther's German New Testament. In 1522 the Catholic Bishop Ximenes published a Greek New Testament as part of his Complutensian Polyglot (a version of the Bible with Hebrew, Aramaic, Greek, and Latin in parallel columns), and in 1546 the Protestant printer-editor Robert Estienne (Stephanus) began to publish a Greek New Testament that was essentially a reproduction of a later edition of Erasmus' text, but which gave an apparatus of variant readings found in different manuscripts. It too went through edition after edition. The third (1550) became very influential in England and was used in the preparation of the English King James Version translation. The fourth (1557) first introduced the verse divisions we use today.

The Stephanus text became the *Textus Receptus* ("received text") in the English-speaking world and the object of what can only be called veneration. The availability of a printed Greek text had made possible the translation of the New Testament from the original Greek into the vernacular languages, and this had become an essential part of the great religious vitality of the Reformation. The role of the Luther Bible in Germany and of the various English translations culminating in the King James Version in the England cannot possibly be exaggerated; and men who were part of this revitalization naturally felt themselves indebted to the printed Greek texts. But despite its religious importance the Erasmus-Stephanus text was in fact somewhat far removed from the earliest Greek manuscripts, and to accept it uncritically was to ignore the immense problems involved in the reconstruction of a reasonably accurate text of the New Testament. Since the Erasmus-Stephanus text achieved real religious significance, we can of course ask, why tamper with it in an attempt to reconstruct an earlier text nearer to that written by the authors of the various books? The answer is comparatively simple. Erasmus was a man of the Renaissance, in fact the greatest of the northern Renaissance, and his concern was, first, to bring the more learned of his contemporaries back from the Latin Vulgate, then dominant in the West, to the original Greek of the New Testament, and, second, to make a vernacular translation of that Greek available to every man and woman. In this connection he wrote a passage that became famous:

> I could wish that every woman might read the Gospel and the Epistles of St. Paul. Would that these were translated into each and every language. . . . Would that the farmer might sing snatches of Scripture at his plough, that the weaver might hum phrases of Scripture to the tune of his shuttle, that the traveler might lighten with stories from Scripture the weariness of his journey.

These lines are a memorable expression of the driving force behind the work of Erasmus, of Stephanus, and of the men who translated their texts into the vernacular languages. But this is the Renaissance and the Reformation; it is not yet the Enlightenment. These men were concerned with a text in the original Greek; they were not yet concerned with the text as it was actually written by the original authors. But the Enlightenment came, and with it an intense interest in history "as it actually happened," in things as they actually were. Men of the Enlightenment could not rest content with the Erasmus-Stephanus "received text"; they were driven by the spirit of the age in which they lived to go beyond it to the original text of the Greek New Testament, as far as it could be reconstructed. This has remained a major concern of Biblical scholarship.

After the establishment of the Erasmus-Stephanus "received text," at least three factors combined to undermine its authority. In the first place, the growth of the Enlightenment spirit made inevitable the search for a more historically authentic text. Second, the discovery, publication, and study of the great uncials and other ancient Greek manuscripts dramatically called attention to ancient manuscripts with readings very different from those of the "received text." In 1707 an Englishman, John Mill, climaxed thirty years of searching ancient manuscripts by publishing an edition of the Greek New Testament in which he reported having found some thirty thousand variant readings, that is, readings varying from the "received text." This was a serious blow to the authority of that text. Third, great strides were made in the textual criticism of ancient classical texts in Greek and Latin, and the techniques learned in this discipline were than applied to the study of the text of the New Testament. Richard Bentley, one of the great figures in the history of classical scholarship, published in 1720 a set of *Proposals* for the preparation of an edition of the Greek New Testament in which he explained that he would base his text on the oldest manuscripts and restore the text known to Origen, which was the standard of the church fathers at the Council of Nicea. He did not in fact produce his edition of the Greek New Testament, but after his day resources developed in the field of classical scholarship were freely used by scholars of the Greek New Testament.

Three hundred years of scholarship in all nations climaxed in the work of B. F. Westcott and F. J. A. Hort, whose *New Testament in the Original Greek* (1881–82) sounded the death knell for the "received text" and established the critical text that provides the basis for all modern work on the Greek New Testament. Westcott and Hort recognized that the ancient manuscripts could be sorted into various groups, each representing the text of a given area of the ancient church, and they went on to claim that one of these groups did in fact represent almost the original text of the New Testament transmitted in a comparatively uncorrupted form. This was for them the "Neutral Text," essentially that of the great uncials Vaticanus and Sinaiticus. Their Greek New Testament was built upon the foundation of these two witnesses.

The non-Greek-reading student can readily grasp what was involved in this overthrow of the "received text" by comparing the English Revised Version (or the American Standard Version) with the King James Version, for Westcott-Hort provided the basis for the former as Erasmus-Stephanus had for the latter.[2] A few examples at random follow.

Mark 1:2
KJV: As it is written in the prophets,
ERV: Even as it is written in Isaiah the prophet,

The later manuscripts had corrected an error; the quotation being introduced actually is a combination of Malachi and Isaiah.

Luke 11:2
KJV: When ye pray, say, Our Father which art in heaven, Hallowed be thy name.
ERV: When ye pray, say, Father, Hallowed be thy name.

The original reading of Luke, "Father," had been conformed to the Matthean "Our Father which art in heaven." The Lukan reading becomes important in the study of the teaching of Jesus.

Acts 8:37
KJV: And Philip said, If thou believest with all thine heart, thou mayest. And he answered and said, I believe that Jesus Christ is the Son of God.

ERV omits the above verse. Some ancient scribe had inserted into the account of the conversion of the Ethiopian eunuch this dialogue he thought fitting and that probably reflected the baptismal practice of the church of his own day.

---

[2] The ERV was published in 1881 at the same time as the publication of the Westcott-Hort text. Both Westcott and Hort were active members of the committee that prepared the text for the translators. That committee originally had two other members, but one of them, S. P. Tregelles, was prevented by ill health from taking any part in the work of the committee. The fourth member, F. H. A. Scrivener, was of a conservative persuasion, leaning toward the Byzantine text (virtually the same as the "received text"). It is said that the decisions of the committee were regularly reached on the basis of a vote of two to one.

1 John 5:7, 8

KJV: For there are three that bear record in heaven, the Father, the Word, and the Holy Ghost: and these three are one. And there are three that bear witness in earth, the Spirit, and the water, and the blood; and these three agree in one.

ERV: For there are three who bear witness, the Spirit, and the water, and the blood: and the three agree in one.

An ancient scribe, in the West, had added a reference to the Trinity.

1 John 4:19

KJV: We love him because he first loved us.

ERV: We love, because he first loved us.

The omission of the pronoun makes a considerable difference to the teaching in this passage.

Since the work of Westcott and Hort it has been shown that their Neutral Text, although ancient, had in fact been subjected to considerable editing. It could not be, therefore, as near to the original as Westcott and Hort claimed. Today, thanks to renewed study of the texts represented by the various groups of manuscripts, to extensive investigation of the texts represented by the ancient versions, and above all to the discovery of the papyrus codices, we know that there was a period of such significant disturbance of the text in the earliest times that it may well be that the original text of the New Testament will lie forever beyond our grasp. But we are constantly making new discoveries and textual critics are constantly refining their tools, and the various revisions of the Greek New Testament text published by the Bible societies do represent better and better texts.

Further Reading

W. G. Kümmel, *Intro.*, pp. 360–86.

PCB, pp. 663–70 (Text: K. W. Clark); pp. 671–75 (Versions: B. M. Metzger).

JBC, pp. 561–89 (P. W. Skehan, G. W. MacRae, R. E. Brown).

IDB, vol. 4, pp. 594–614 (M. M. Parvis).

IDB Suppl., pp. 884–86 (Text: C. M. Martini); pp. 891–95 (Textual criticism, NT: E. J. Epp).

The most comprehensive discussion of this material is B. M. Metzger, *The Text of the New Testament*, 2nd ed. (1968). See also W. Birdsall, "The NT Text," *The Cambridge History of the Bible*, vol. I (1970), pp. 308–77.

APPENDIX 3
English Translations
of the Greek New Testament

THE TRADITION OF THE KING JAMES VERSION

The Path to the King James Version

The translation of the New Testament from the original Greek into the vernacular languages of Europe was an aim of Renaissance humanism, and it gathered impetus in the Reformation, becoming indeed a main goal of the Reformers. Luther's translation of the New Testament into German, published in 1522, was an example followed in other lands. In England William Tyndale (1494?–1536) undertook the task, but he had great difficulties because of English hostility to Luther, led by King Henry VIII. He carried out his work in Reformed Europe, therefore, and finally got his translation printed in Worms in Germany in 1526.

Tyndale's translation aroused great controversy in England when it appeared. But the political climate was changing: King Henry quarreled with the Pope, and although Tyndale continued to be considered a dangerous heretic and was never able to return to England, the demand for copies of the New Testament in English was allowed to grow. Tyndale's translation was often printed in pirated editions and with unauthorized revisions. Motivated in part by a desire to counteract changes in his work of which he disapproved, Tyndale in 1534 published his own revised version of his translation. This 1534 translation is an altogether magnificent one so far as its language is concerned, and much of the force and power of the King James Version is Tyndale's. "Nine tenths of the Authorized New Testament is still Tyndale, and the best is still his."[1]

---

[1] H. W. Robinson, quoted in F. F. Bruce, *The English Bible* (rev. ed., 1970), p. 44.

The following is the opening paragraph of Hebrews in Tyndale's 1534 edition.

> God in tyme past diversly and many wayes, spake vnto the fathers by Prophetes: but in these last dayes he hath spoken unto vs by his sonne, whom he hath made heyre of all thinges: by whom also he made the worlde. Which sonne beynge the brightnes of his glory, and very ymage of his substance, bearinge vp all thinges with the worde of his power, hath in his awne person pourged oure synnes, and is sitten on the right honde of the maiestie an hye, and is more excellent then the angels, in as moche as he hath by inheritaunce obteyned an excellenter name then have they.

In the Greek text this is all one long sentence with its clauses carefully organized according to the principles of Hellenistic Greek rhetoric.

Tyndale died for his work. He spent his last years in the free city of Antwerp but was kidnapped in 1536 and taken into Catholic Europe, where he was tried and executed for heresy. He is said to have died with the prayer on his lips, "Lord, open the King of England's eyes."

The next major English translator is Myles Coverdale (1488–1569), who, like most of the translators of this period, did his work in the safety of Reformed Europe. In 1535 he published the first complete printed Bible in English. It was printed in continental Europe, probably in Cologne, but copies imported into England carried a dedication to Henry VIII. It was hoped that the king would authorize the translation to be read in English churches; he did not do so formally but neither did he forbid its circulation. A second edition in 1537 was authorized and appeared with the words, "Set forth with the kinge's most gracyous license" on the title page. In the same year another English Bible was authorized by the king—"Matthew's Bible," translated by one Thomas Matthew. But "Thomas Matthew" was a pseudonym. Matthew's Bible was in fact Tyndale's translation of the New Testament and, as far as it had been completed, the Old Testament also. Gaps in the Old Testament were filled by using Coverdale's translation. It is ironic but fitting that within a year of his death Tyndale's New Testament was circulating in England with the king's authorization.

Coverdale was not proficient in Hebrew and Greek, so he did not translate from the original text. What he did was to prepare a version using five existing translations: Tyndale's, the Latin Vulgate, a more recent Latin translation published in 1528, Luther's German translation, and a version of Luther's German translation adapted to the Swiss dialect of German. His New Testament was basically Tyndale's revised, not always very happily, in the light of the German translations.

There is no need for us to follow the vicissitudes of the English translations of the Bible through the closing years of Henry's reign (died 1547), the brief reigns of Edward VI (1547–53) and Mary (1553–58), or the long years of Elizabeth I (1558–1603). The English Bible came to achieve an influence over the English people that was not to be shaken, despite the various efforts to contain or nullify the effects of the Reformation. But the various versions of the New Testament published during these years were all basically revisions of Tyndale, not new translations.

The King James Version

At the death of Elizabeth in 1603 the crown passed to James I, who was already ruling in Scotland as James VI. To regulate the affairs of the English church he called a conference of churchmen and theologians at Hampton Court in 1604, which agreed on only one thing, that a new translation should be made of the whole Bible and that it should be authorized for use in the churches of England. King James liked the suggestion and took a leading part in organizing the work of translation. The result appeared in 1611: the Authorized Version (AV), as it is known in England, the King James Version (KJV), as it is known in America.

This translation of the Bible became a landmark in the religious history of English-speaking people, and indeed in their general cultural history. Its phrases and its images are deeply embedded in English-speaking piety and culture. For many it is still *the* Bible, and one who has grown up with it finds himself forever returning to it. Its translation of the opening paragraph of Hebrews is as follows.

> God, who at sundry times and in diverse manners spake in time past unto the fathers by the prophets, hath in these last times spoken unto us by his Son, whom he hath appointed heir of all things, by whom also he made the worlds; who being the brightness of his glory, and the express image of his person, and upholding all things by the word of his power, when he had by himself purged our sins, sat down on the right hand of the Majesty on high; being made so much better than the angels, as he hath by inheritance obtained a more excellent name than they.

The sonorous phrases of what is in effect Elizabethan English, the language of Shakespeare, match the rhetorical flourishes of the long Greek sentence.

The Revision of the King James Version

That the KJV established itself at the heart of English-language piety and culture does not change the fact that it was a translation from a late and comparatively poor Greek text, and with the passage of time better texts came to be established. English-language usage also changed, so that while some of the phrases of the KJV proved unforgettable, others became unintelligible. The result was that in England in 1870, after more than two and a half centuries, a revision of the KJV was undertaken.

The terms under which this revision was undertaken testify to the hold of the KJV, for the revisers were instructed to introduce as few changes as possible and, where possible, to take the language for those changes either from the language of the KJV or earlier English versions. Almost the only freedom the scholars were permitted was to work from a better Greek text. The result was the English Revised Version (RV or ERV) of the New Testament, published in 1881. The American scholars involved in the project had been rather unhappy about the very conservative conditions imposed upon the revisers, but they agreed to give the new version twenty years before publishing a further revision. In 1901, therefore, they published their own version of this revision, the American Standard Version (SV or ASV). The changes over against the RV were, however, only minor. Here is the RV translation of the opening paragraph of Hebrews.

> God, having of old time spoken unto the fathers in the prophets by divers portions and in divers manners, hath at the end of these days spoken unto us in his Son, whom he appointed heir of all things, through whom also he made the worlds; who being the effulgence of his glory, and the very image of his substance, and upholding all things by the word of his power, when he had made purification of sins, sat down on the right hand of the Majesty on high; having become by so much better than the angels, as he hath inherited a more excellent name than they.

In one respect the ERV was a success: it translated a good Greek text. But in other respects the terms laid down for the revision made an effective new translation impossible, and the ASV could make only minor changes. As translations, therefore, these versions were never a success. In 1937 in America a decision was made to undertake a further revision of the KJV or, more accurately, a revision of the ASV. The result was the Revised Standard Version. The New Testament appeared in 1946 and the whole Bible in 1952. In the 1952 edition there were further minor changes in the New Testament. In the RSV the opening paragraph of Hebrews reads as follows.

> In many and various ways God spoke of old to our fathers by the prophets; but in these last days he has spoken to us by a Son, whom he appointed the heir of all things, through whom also he created the world. He reflects the glory of God and bears the very stamp of his nature, upholding the universe by his word of power. When he had made purification for sins, he sat down at the right hand of the Majesty on high, having become as much superior to angels as the name he has obtained is more excellent than theirs.

For the first time in this tradition the long sentence has been broken up to correspond more readily to English diction, and the archaic English usages are gone ("hath" has become "has," etc.). The result is a good translation, which succeeds in blending the twin responsibilities of remaining as true as possible to the original Greek text and at the same time representing the meaning of that text effectively in English.

BREAKING WITH THE TRADITION
OF THE KING JAMES VERSION

The New English Bible

In 1946 the Church of Scotland suggested that a completely new translation of the Bible be made, translating the Greek text afresh and not simply
revising further the tradition of the KJV. The suggestion was eagerly adopted
by the Church of England and the major denominational churches, and the
translation of the New Testament was entrusted to a committee under the
convenership of C. H. Dodd (General Director of the whole project after 1949).
The result was the New English Bible (NEB), of which the New Testament was
published in 1961 and the whole Bible, with a slightly revised New Testament,
in 1970. This is the opening paragraph of Hebrews in the NEB.

> When in former times God spoke to our forefathers, he spoke in
> fragmentary and varied fashion through the prophets. But in this the final
> age he has spoken to us in the Son whom he has made heir to the whole
> universe, and through whom he created all orders of existence: the Son
> who is the effulgence of God's splendour and the stamp of God's very
> being, and sustains the universe by his word of power. When he had
> brought about the purgation of sins, he took his seat at the right hand of
> Majesty on high, raised as far above the angels, as the title he has inher-
> ited is superior to theirs.

The NEB is a very effective translation, and any choice between it and the
RSV would have to be made on personal grounds.

Today's English Version

The break with the tradition of the KJV in America came from the American Bible Society, which in 1966 published *Good News for Modern Man: The New
Testament in Today's English,* a translation of the New Testament by Robert G.
Bratcher. This is usually known as Today's English Version (TEV). It is a good
translation, published in paperback and considerably enhanced by some very
effective line drawings by Annie Vallotton. Here is the opening paragraph of
Hebrews in Today's English.

> In the past God spoke to our ancestors many times and in many
> ways through the prophets, but in these last days he has spoken to us
> through his Son. He is the one through whom God created the universe,
> the one whom God has chosen to possess all things at the end. He shines
> with the brightness of God's glory; he is the exact likeness of God's own
> being, and sustains the universe with his powerful word. After he had
> made men clean from their sins, he sat down in heaven at the right hand
> of God, the Supreme Power.

PRIVATE TRANSLATIONS

The translations reviewed above are all "official" in that they have been produced by committees or societies representing major churches or associations of churches. Moreover, they are the best-known and most widely circulated translations. But anyone is free at any time to publish a translation of the New Testament, and many such "private" translations have in fact been published. The three most important are probably those by James Moffatt, Edgar J. Goodspeed, and J. B. Phillips. Moffatt, a Scottish New Testament scholar, published a translation of the New Testament in 1913 as *The New Testament: A New Translation* and of the Old Testament in 1924. His translation of the whole Bible appeared in one volume in 1928 as *The Bible: A New Translation.* Moffatt's translation is fresh and vigorous and he does not hesitate to trust his own scholarly judgment in such matters as the rearrangement of the text of the gospel of John. Goodspeed, an American New Testament scholar, published a translation of the New Testament in 1923. A parallel version of the Old Testament appeared in 1927, translated by several scholars, and the two were published together by the University of Chicago Press in 1931 as *The Bible: An American Translation,* often called the Chicago Bible. Goodspeed's translation of the New Testament ranks with the best ever achieved. Phillips, a vicar of the Church of England, published between 1947 and 1957 a translation of the New Testament in four volumes. In 1958 they were brought together and published in one volume as *The New Testament in Modern English.* It is a lively and readable translation, but Phillips exercises great freedom in his handling of the original Greek text so that his translation frequently approaches paraphrase. He is sometimes very successful, as in his translation of the Pauline letters ("Letters to Young Churches"), which makes them sound "as if they had just come through the mail."[2]

ROMAN CATHOLIC TRANSLATIONS

Until recently, Roman Catholic translations of the New Testament have not been translations of the Greek New Testament but of a Latin version, usually the Vulgate. A change came, however, beginning in 1935 with the publication of the Westminster Version in England and continuing in America in 1954 with the publication of the Kleist-Lilly New Testament, "an attempt to do for Catholic circles what Goodspeed had done for non-Catholic circles."[3] Neither of these translations was particularly successful but they were important pioneering efforts. Then from 1948 to 1954 a translation of the whole Bible

---

[2] R. E. Brown in *JBC,* p. 587.
[3] R. E. Brown, *JBC,* p. 588.

with introductions and footnotes appeared in French under the editorship of the Jerusalem Dominicans. A one-volume abridgement of the French work has been translated as the Jerusalem Bible (1966). Though it is an important achievement of contemporary Roman Catholic Biblical scholarship, the translation is essentially a translation of a translation: the Greek reaches English via French.

The first major Roman Catholic translation of the Greek New Testament directly into English is the New American Bible, published in 1970. Both in title and in style it resembles the NEB, for the translators deliberately abandoned the tradition of revising former translations, in this case translations of a Latin text, in favor of a completely new translation from the Greek into modern English. Protestant scholars were invited to assist in the final stages of the project. The NAB renders the opening paragraph of Hebrews as follows.

> In times past, God spoke in fragmentary and varied ways to our fathers through the prophets; in this, the final age, he has spoken to us through his Son, whom he has made heir of all things and through whom he first created the universe. This Son is the reflection of the Father's glory, the exact representation of the Father's being, and he sustains all things by his powerful word. When he had cleansed us from our sins, he took his seat at the right hand of the Majesty in heaven, as far superior to the angels as the name he has inherited is superior to theirs.

It can be seen that responsible modern translations are drawing very close together, and that a choice between them will now almost always be made on grounds other than the validity of the translation itself. Each translation has its own virtues.

Further Reading

PCB, pp. 24–28 (A. Wikgren).
JBC, pp. 586–89 (R. E. Brown).
IDB Suppl., pp. 933–38 (Versions, English: K. R. Crim).

The most complete survey of the subject is F. F. Bruce, *The English Bible: A History of Translations*, rev. ed. (1970).

APPENDIX 4
Major Archeological, Textual Discoveries, and Publications

Archeological and textual discoveries and publications relating to the period of the New Testament are much too numerous to describe in a short appendix. They cover the whole arena of the Greco-Roman empires from Britain to Babylonia and include literally thousands of manuscripts and artifacts. In Palestine alone well over 200 sites have been excavated since World War II! We have already indicated some of the exciting finds in the area of New Testament manuscripts (Appendix 2), and recently another major discovery of papyrus and parchment turned up at the Monastery of Saint Catherine at the foot of Mount Sinai, including the eight missing pages from Codex Sinaiticus![1] Fascinating discoveries, then, are always possible and continue to the present. What follows is only a sample of the rich treasures recently discovered; for further information, consult the bibliography at the end of this section.

THE DEAD SEA SCROLLS AND KHIRBET QUMRAN

In the spring of 1947 two Arab shepherd boys of the Bedouin Ta'amireh tribe were grazing their flocks of sheep and goats at the foot of the cliffs about a mile west of the Dead Sea, twelve miles east of Jerusalem, in the vacinity of the ancient ruins of the Wadi Qumran (a *wadi* is a dry river bed in summer, but it fills with flash flood waters in the rainy season).[2] According to the boys, one of the animals strayed and in their search, Muhammed ed-Dib threw a

---

[1] S. Agourides and J. H. Charlesworth, "A New Discovery of Old Manuscripts on Mt. Sinai: A Preliminary Report," *Biblical Archeologist* 41 (1978), pp. 29–31; J. H. Charlesworth, "St. Catherine's Monastery: Myths and Mysteries," *Biblical Archeologist* 42 (1979), pp. 174–79; "The Manuscripts of St. Catherine's Monastery," *Biblical Archeologist* 43 (1980), pp. 26–34.

[2] This account is based on F. M. Cross, *The Ancient Library of Qumran*, chapter 1.

stone into one of the cave openings high up the face of the cliff. Instead of the thud of stone against stone, he heard a shattering sound and, perhaps because of fear of demons, he fled. Later, when his fear subsided, Muhammed and his companion, Ahmed Muhammed, returned to the cave, went exploring, and found elongated jars partly buried in the cave floor, one of them containing leather scrolls. Muhammed ed-Dib had discovered the first of what became known as the Dead Sea Scrolls, a discovery the eminent American archeologist, W. F. Albright, has called "the greatest manuscript discovery of modern times. . . ."[3]

The following period was characterized by clandestine and illegal excavations and by the intrigue of buying and selling the valuable manuscripts. Some of the scrolls were finally purchased in a Jerusalem antiquities shop by Prof. E. L. Sukenik for the Hebrew University in Jerusalem; another lot was acquired from the Bethlehem shoemaker and middleman Kando by the Syrian Orthodox Metropolitan of Jerusalem, identified by scholars at the American School of Oriental Research in Jerusalem, smuggled to the United States by the Metropolitan, and finally purchased for the Hebrew University at the highly inflated price of $250,000 in 1954. In the meantime, the Arab-Israeli fighting frustrated attempts to find the site of the discovery and carry out scientific excavations until the spring of 1949. The episode seemed closed. But further digging by the Ta'amireh tribesmen in 1951 uncovered more scrolls in caves at nearby Wadi Murabba'at, which again ended up in the hands of antiquities dealers. More bargaining took place, and a series of scientific excavations of the caves was begun in the general area.

The first digging at Khirbet ("ruin") Qumran in 1951 convinced scholars that the site was the ancient monastery of the Essenes who were described by Josephus, Philo of Alexandria, and Pliny the Elder.[4] More discoveries by the Ta'amireh tribesmen and further scientific excavations in a total of eleven caves unearthed the remains of about 600 manuscripts, including 10 complete scrolls. Most were written on parchment (leather), though a few were on papyrus, and two were on copper. The most valuable finds were discovered in Cave I (the first discovered), Cave IV, and Cave XI; because of the fragmentary nature of the material in Cave IV, almost 75 percent still await publication. The present location of the scrolls is in the Shrine of the Book in Jerusalem.

Archeological excavation of the ruins of Khirbet Qumran have shown that on top of an eighth-seventh century B.C. fortress the Essene community built a monastery which it occupied in two periods, the first from about 135 B.C. to 31 B.C., when it was destroyed by an earthquake, the second from about 1 B.C. to A.D. 68, when it was destroyed by the Romans. The site was quite elaborate and contained a water supply system with aqueduct, cisterns and baths, assembly and banquet hall, kitchen and pantry, laundry, scriptorium (a room for copying texts), pottery workshops, storerooms, stables, watchtower, and ceme-

---

[3] In a letter to Dr. John Trevor of the American School of Oriental Research when Trevor correctly identified their antiquity and value.

[4] Their accounts are discussed in A. Dupont-Sommer, *The Essene Writings from Qumran*, chapter 1.

tery nearby. Other excavations were undertaken two miles south at 'En Feskhah where there was an agricultural complex, nine miles inland at Khirbet Mird where there was a Hasmonean fortress, and twelve miles south at Wadi Murabba'at where there were four caves containing Greek, Aramaic, and Hebrew materials related to the bar Cochba Revolt of A.D. 132-35, including letters of Simon bar Kosibah himself! A few other valleys and caves to the south were explored.

About one-fourth of the Dead Sea Scrolls are books that were eventually included in the Hebrew Bible, all thirty-nine books being represented except the book of Esther. Other categories of literature in the scrolls are Apocrypha and Pseudepigrapha;[5] Biblical commentaries exemplifying the *pesher* method of interpretation;[6] apocalyptic, sectarian writings such as the War of the Sons of Light Against the Sons of Darkness; and Rules for the community (the Manual of Discipline). All three languages—Hebrew, Aramaic, and Greek—are found in the scrolls, Hebrew predominating. The presence of books from the Apocrypha and Pseudepigrapha is further testimony that the scholars of Jamnia in the late first century A.D. narrowed down the sacred texts from a much larger and more diversified body of literature in use prior to A.D. 70; furthermore, variations in some of the Biblical texts show that the Jamnia scholars chose particular *types* (recensions) of manuscripts.

The organization of the community was based on several texts, especially the Manual of Discipline. It included divisions into priests and laity; the domination of the priests including a priest-president who presided at the sacred meal; an overseer who had power over admissions, instruction, and various practical matters; a guardian of all the "camps"; a Council of the Community; a future lay leader (perhaps the royal Messiah); a Court of Inquiry to try offenders; an annual assembly at the Feast of the Renewal of the Covenant; nightly study and prayer; and a two-year initiation for new members. Several important beliefs and practices were that the community is the elect, purified remnant of Israel which will be vindicated in the final days (apocalyptic eschatology); that the Jerusalem Temple and its priesthood are polluted and are replaced by the community and its worship life; close adherence to ritual laws and seasonal festivals according to a solar calendar; the maintenance of purity by ritual baths; a sacred meal in which bread and wine are served and which anticipates the Messianic banquet (see Appendix 5); a dualistic eschatology which opposes light, good, and angelic powers against darkness, evil, and the demonic powers; the hope for a prophet, as well as a Messiah of Aaron (priestly) and a Messiah of Israel (royal); and the anticipation of a postmessianic age that includes a new Jerusalem.

The discovery of the Dead Sea Scrolls was an amazing event. Old Testament texts in Hebrew were uncovered that predated previously known texts by a thousand years; the history of the Old Testament textual traditions was illuminated; knowledge of a little-known Jewish sect was impressively re-

---

[5] On the Pseudepigrapha, see below, pp. 468–69.
[6] The *pesher* method is discussed in chapter 1.

vealed; the understanding of pre-A.D. 70 Judaism was transformed; and a parallel sectarian movement to early Christianity was uncovered, one that continues to provide invaluable information for the environment of Christian origins.[7]

MASADA

About thirty miles south of Khirbet Qumran along the Dead Sea is a magnificent mesa, the flat top of which covers about twenty acres, with steep rock cliffs rising about 600 feet on the west side and about 820 feet on the east.[8] This natural fortress was accessible only by two paths, one of which was a treacherous "snake path," and the other was a path which narrowed at one point. On the top Herod the Great built a fortress which he named Masada ("mountain stronghold"). The Jewish writer Josephus has immortalized the location with his exciting, but tragic, tale of the last stand of the Zealots and their mass suicide in order not to be taken alive by the Romans (*Wars* VII.viii-ix).

Initial surveys of the well-known site in 1953 and 1955-56 led to a full-scale archeological expedition in 1963–65 headed by the noted Israeli archeologist, Yigael Yadin. The discoveries revealed three main periods of occupation: (1) Herodian (37–4 B.C.); (2) the period of the Jewish-Roman wars and their aftermath (A.D. 66–73); and (3) the Byzantine period (fifth-sixth century A.D.). Since there was no water supply, Herod built dams on two small wadis below, and in the rainy season the water flowed by channels to two huge reservoirs cut in the cliff on the northwest side; from there the water was carried by slaves to cisterns on the top, all together the cisterns holding about 1,400,000 cubic feet of water. His casemate wall surrounding the top (except for the villa) had thirty towers and four gates. Also on the top Herod constructed a series of storerooms for provisions, an intimate and luxurious three-tiered palace-villa at the north end, a hugh western palace for administration and ceremony, several small palaces for family members and high-ranking officials, a luxurious bathhouse, and a swimming pool.

Prior to the beginning of the revolt in A.D. 66, a Roman garrison was bivouacked on Masada but, at the outbreak of the war, the Zealots took it by trickery and adapted it for themselves and their families. They also constructed ritual baths, a synagogue, and what may be a "religious study house." Excavators uncovered in the western palace many burnt arrows and coins and in the smaller palaces scrolls of the Scriptures, of ben Sirach, and of some Qumran literature, indicating that some point of contact existed between the Essenes and the Zealots. About 700 ostraca (pieces of pottery often used for ballots) show not only Hebrew and Aramaic writing, but also Greek and Latin. There is still visible a gigantic dirt ramp, on which a huge battering ram was brought

---

[7] The last of the complete scrolls, the Temple Scroll, has recently been published by Prof. Yigael Yadin; see J. Milgrom, "The Temple Scroll," *The Biblical Archeologist* 41 (1978), pp. 105–20.

[8] Y. Yadin, "Masada," *IDB Suppl.*, pp. 577–80; *Masada*.

forward by the Romans in their siege of the fortress. A Roman garrison remained after the siege. Subsequently, Masada was deserted until some Christian monks settled there and built a church, as well as a few rooms and cells.

THE NAG HAMMADI TEXTS

The precise details leading up to the discovery at Nag Hammadi are not clear. Late in 1945, an Egyptian peasant boy, Abu al-Majd, discovered twelve papyrus codices plus part of a thirteenth (tucked into Codex VI) bound in portfolio-like leather covers and stored in a ceramic jar under an overhanging rock at the base of the Gebel el-Tarif, located near the Nile River towns of Chenoboskia, a monastic center, and Nag Hammadi, both in southern ("Upper") Egypt.[9] The peasant boy was accompanied by six others, one of whom was his oldest brother, Muhammad 'Ali, who took charge. Muhammed broke open the jar and, upon finding the codices, decided to divide them up among the seven camel drivers present; when the fearful and unknowing drivers refused their shares, Muhammed put them in a pile, wrapped them in his white headdress, and slinging them over his shoulder, mounted his camel and headed for his home in Chenoboskia. The usual confusion and intrigue followed: the scrolls made their way to middlemen, then to antiquities dealers, and finally to the Coptic Museum in Old Cairo, Egypt. The Jung Codex was an exception; it made its way out of Egypt to the United States and then to Brussels, where it was purchased for the C. G. Jung Institute in Zurich and presented to the eminent psychiatrist as a birthday present; subsequently (after its publication) it was returned to Cairo.

The announcement of the discovery of the Nag Hammadi texts was made by the French scholar Jean Doresse, and work on the texts officially began in 1956. The texts consist of copies of Coptic translations of 51 Greek texts (Coptic is an Egyptian language written with mostly Greek letters).[10] In their present form as copies, they date from about the middle of the fourth century A.D., but some of the autographs are much older and the original Greek still earlier. The collection represents many different literary types (genres), some like those of the canonical New Testament. It contains gospels, apocalypses, acts, letters, dialogues, secret books, speculative treatises, wisdom literature, exegeses, revelation discourses, and prayers. The texts also represent various types of Gnosticism known from the early Church Fathers, as well as the Egyptian Hermetic literature and non-Gnostic writings, such as Plato's *Republic*. Moreover, the texts show strong influence of Jewish traditions and interpretations, for example, the Genesis myth of creation, the Wisdom myth, various techniques of scriptural interpretation, and the apocalyptic periodization of history.

The question of the possible origin of Gnosticism has been hotly debated;

---

[9] J. M. Robinson, "The Discovery of the Nag Hammadi Codices," *Biblical Archeologist* 42 (1979), pp. 206–24.

[10] G. MacRae, "Nag Hammadi," *IDB Suppl.*, pp. 613–19 describes the library and gives a chart of each of the books, the codex in which they are found, and their names. See also B. Layton, "Coptic Language," *IDB Suppl.*, pp. 174–79.

some of the texts seem to be non-Christian, but this does not answer the question whether they are pre-Christian. Nonetheless, it has been demonstrated that a non-Christian text in the collection (Eugostos the Blessed) has been reworked and made into a Christian version (the Sophia of Jesus Christ), that is, a Gnostic Christian has made use of a non-Christian text. This is all the more interesting when it is observed that the Nag Hammadi text called The Apocalypse of Adam appears to be non-Christian, maybe dating as early as the second century A.D., yet it contains the full-blown Gnostic Redeemer Myth. Such an instance would seem to support the *possibility* that early Christianity could have been influenced by such a myth in its interpretation of Jesus. Another important text for the interpretation of Christian literature is the Coptic Gnostic Gospel of Thomas, which contains a collection of Jesus' sayings, including some thirteen parables which are variants of synoptic gospel parables. The genre of a "sayings-collection" is important for the Q hypothesis; moreover, a comparison of the forms of the Thomas parables with those of the synoptic tradition shows that the Gospel of Thomas has preserved simpler, perhaps earlier, forms of Jesus' parables.

Until the discovery of the Nag Hammadi texts, what was known about Gnosticism came primarily through the anti-Gnostic polemics of early Christian writers. Now there is available a group of texts that show what some of the Gnostics themselves believed. They are extremely valuable for the light they shed not only on the Gnostic movement but also on the history of Judaism and early Christianity which came to terms with it.

THE PSEUDEPIGRAPHA

The term "Pseudepigrapha" means literally "false writings," not because they are not true, that is, spurious, but because they are non-canonical writings which for the most part are inspired by, in honor of, and attributed to Old Testament heroes who did not write them; that is, they are pseudonymous.[11] The term is not totally satisfactory because Old Testament writings, like those in the New Testament, are also pseudonymous; on the other hand, not every book in the collection called Pseudepigrapha is pseudonymous. No better term has been found for these books. Briefly, they are books that are either partially or totally Jewish or Jewish-Christian, from the approximate period 200 B.C. to A.D. 200, they are normally considered to be inspired or related to the Jewish Scriptures (Old Testament), and are usually attributed to some Old Testament figure. Usually excluded are most (but not all) of the books from the same period called the Apocrypha (though most of the Apocrypha is found at various places in the Old Testament canon for Roman Catholics; the Protestant churches returned to the Hebrew Bible); also excluded are the Dead Sea Scrolls as a special discovery, and the Coptic Gnostic Nag Hammadi Texts as another special discovery, though some would like to include the (apparently non-Christian) Apocalypse of Adam, and certainly *by definition* many of the Dead

[11] J. H. Charlesworth, *The Pseudepigrapha and Modern Research,* p. 21.

Sea Scrolls could be included. The rabbinic literature (especially the Mishnah and the Talmuds) which has been preserved among Jewish scholars for centuries since its earliest sections were codified about A.D. 200 is excluded as well; this body of literature has traditions that go back to the period covered by the Pseudepigrapha, though most of it is later.

The primary modern edition of the Pseudepigrapha in English is volume 2 of the two-volume collection by R. H. Charles called *Apocrypha and Pseudepigrapha of the Old Testament.* It contains seventeen writings, introduced and extensively annotated. Soon to be published, however, is a new edition edited by J. H. Charlesworth (autumn 1982). Because of new discoveries, publications of little known manuscripts, and further evaluation of previously known documents, the new pseudepigrapha will contain fifty-two documents with introductions and annotations. This is clearly a significant increase in the amount of material available to the Biblical student for historical and literary study. There are a wide variety of forms and genres, including apocalypses, testaments, prayers, psalms, hymns, odes, oracles, and legends, and the material contains not only apocalyptic eschatology, but much information about some of the more esoteric aspects of Judaism and Jewish Christianity; for example, astrology and magic. In short, though the new Pseudepigrapha is not a completely new discovery in the sense of the Dead Sea Scrolls or the Nag Hammadi texts, much of it is either new or scarcely known and it will be an exciting addition to the non-canonical materials of the period.

There are a number of major literary sources for understanding the period of the New Testament, collections of which are cited in the bibliography at the end of chapter 1. But beyond the texts, there are the excavations themselves. All of this material vastly expands the knowledge of the period of the New Testament and Christian origins, and is thus an invaluable aid to understanding the New Testament itself.

Further Reading

The literature in this area is vast; the following represents a minimal selection, and focuses primarily on Palestinian archeology.

The Dead Sea Scrolls and the Khirbet Qumran Area:

F. M. Cross, *The Ancient Library of Qumran and Modern Biblical Studies.*

J. T. Milik, *Discoveries in the Judean Desert* (standard edition, several volumes).

H. Ringgren, *The Faith of Qumran.*

K. Stendahl, *The Scrolls and the New Testament.*

G. Vermes, *The Dead Sea Scrolls in English.*

Among our reference works, see:

PBC, pp. 55–57, from "The Archeology of Palestine" (J. Grey).

JBC, pp. 546–57, "Dead Sea Scrolls" (R. Brown).

IDB, vol. 1, pp. 790–802, "Dead Sea Scrolls" (O. Betz).

IDB Suppl., pp. 210–19, "Dead Sea Scrolls" (G. Vermes).

Additional bibliography may be found in J. Fitzmyer, *The Dead Sea Scrolls. Major Publications and Tools for Study.*

Masada:

Y. Yadin, *Masada.*
IDB, vol. 3, pp. 293–94, "Masada" (R. Funk).
IDB Suppl., pp. 577–80, "Masada" (Y. Yadin).

Nag Hammadi Texts:

J. Doresse, *The Secret Books of the Egyptian Gnostics.*
J. M. Robinson, ed., *The Nag Hammadi Library.*
IDB Suppl., pp. 613–19, "Nag Hammadi" (G. MacRae).
Biblical Archeologist 42/4 (Fall, 1979) is devoted to the discoveries.

Pseudepigrapha:

R. H. Charles, *Apocrypha and Pseudepigrapha of the Old Testament*, vol. 2.
J. H. Charlesworth, *Pseudepigrapha* (projected for 1982).
J. H. Charlesworth, *The Pseudepigrapha and Modern Research* (2nd ed.).
IDB Suppl., pp. 710–12, "Pseudepigrapha" (M. E. Stone).

Miscellaneous:

W. F. Albright and W. G. Dever, *The Archeology of Palestine.*
Archeological Discoveries in the Holy Land (Archeological Institute of America), Part III: "Post-Biblical Palestine."
Biblical Archeologist.
I. Browning, *Petra.*
J. Finnegan, *The Archeology of the New Testament.*
E. R. Goodenough, *Jewish Symbols in the Greco-Roman Period.*
J. Finnegan, *The Archeology of the New Testament.*
K. Kenyon, *Jerusalem. Excavating 3,000 Years of History.*
A. Negev, *Archeological Encyclopedia of the Holy Land.*
D. W. O'Connor, *Peter in Rome. The Literary, Liturgical and Archeological Evidence* (cf. F. Snyder, "Survey and 'New' Thesis on the Bones of Peter," *Biblical Archeologist* 32 [1969], pp. 2–24).
Y. Yonah, *Oriental Art in Roman Palestine.*
JBC, pp. 653–74, "Biblical Archeology" (R. North).
IDB, vol. 1, pp. 195–207, "Archeology" (G. W. Van Beek).
IDB Suppl., pp. 44–52, "Archeology" (W. G. Dever); pp. 992–93 (map of archeological sites); pp. 994–95, "Archeological Sites" (listed); pp. 563–66, "Manuscripts from the Judean Desert" (G. Vermes).

There are numerous other archeological studies in the *IDB Suppl.* listed by location; the student will also find quite interesting pp. 199–201, "Crucifixion" (O. Wintermute).

For the discoveries in the Monastery of Saint Catherine's on Mount Sinai, see above, *n.* 1.

APPENDIX 5
Religious and Philosophical Texts from the Greco-Roman World

PHILOSOPHY

Plato's allegory of the cave[1]

In his allegory of the cave, Plato (d. 347 B.C.) presented the view that the transient material world we perceive through the senses is only a shadow of the true reality, the eternal world of abstract ideas known by reason.

> And now, I said, let me show in a figure how far our nature is enlightened or unenlightened:—Behold! human beings living in an underground den which has a mouth open towards the light and reaching all along the den; here they have been from their childhood, and have their legs and necks chained so that they cannot move, and can only see before them, being prevented by the chains from turning round their heads. Above and behind them a fire is blazing at a distance, and between the fire and the prisoners there is a raised way; and you will see, if you look, a low wall built along the way, like the screen which marionette players have in front of them, over which they show the puppets.
> I see.
> And do you see, I said, men passing all along the wall carrying all sorts of vessels, and statues and figures of animals made of wood and stone and various materials, which appear over the wall? Some of them are talking, others silent.
> You have shown me a strange image, and they are strange prisoners.
> Like ourselves, I replied; and they see only their own shadows, or the shadows of one another, which the fire throws on the opposite wall of the cave?

[1] From *The Republic*, Bk. VII, as quoted in C. K. Barrett, *The New Testament Background*, pp. 58–59.

True, he said; how could they see anything but the shadows if they were never allowed to move their heads?

And of the objects which are being carried in like manner they would only see the shadows?

Yes, he said.

And if they were able to converse with one another, would they not suppose that they were naming what was actually before them?

Very true.

And suppose further that the prison had an echo which came from the other side, would they not be sure to fancy when one of the passers-by spoke that the voice which they heard came from the passing shadows?

No question, he replied.

To them, I said, the truth would be literally nothing but the shadows of the images.

That is certain.

(The rest of the allegory pictures a human being who gets free from the chains, ascends from the cave, sees the true reality, experiences blindness from the light, but is unable to convince the others of what he has seen.)

Cleanthes: Hymn to Zeus

Cleanthes was a Greek Stoic philosopher of the third century B.C. (Stoicism takes its name from *stoa*, "a painted portico" in Athens where its founder, Zeno [ca. 336–263 B.C.], taught). The Stoics believed that the world was ordered by a divine reason, the Logos, associated with fire, and capable of being identified with God, or Zeus. The closeness of philosophy and religion can be seen in Cleanthes' *Hymn to Zeus*, where the law of God is right reason. It begins:[2]

> Thou, O Zeus, art praised above all gods:
> many are thy names and thine is all power for ever.
>   The beginning of the world was from thee:
> and with law thou rulest over all things.
>   Unto thee may all flesh speak: for we are
> thy offspring.
>   Therefore will I raise a hymn unto thee:
> and will ever sing of thy power.
>   The whole order of the heavens obeyeth thy
> word: as it moveth around the earth:
>   With little and great lights mixed together:
> how great art thou, King above all forever!

[2] As quoted in C. K. Barrett, *Background*, p. 63.

Epictetus: Discourses

The Cynics' stress on ethics and right living was gradually absorbed into the more moderate and philosophically reflective Stoicism of the lecture hall, but the Cynic way of life was revived as an ideal among first-century Stoics who wished to appeal to the masses. Thus, later Stoics like the ex-slave Epictetus (late first, early second century A.D.) and the emperor Marcus Aurelius (ruled 161–180 A.D.) highlighted the ethical life. The following passage from Epictetus, recorded by his follower Arrian, illustrates how the Cynic-Stoic view of ordering one's self correctly and proclaiming it to others is the way to cope with the unpredictability of life in the Hellenistic world.[3]

First then you must make your Governing Principle pure, and hold fast this rule of life, "henceforth my mind is the material I have to work on, as the carpenter has his timber and the shoemaker his leather: my business is to deal with my impressions aright. My wretched body is nothing to me, its parts are nothing to me. Death? Let it come when it will, whether to my whole body or to part of it. Exile? Can one be sent into exile beyond the Universe? One cannot. Wherever I go, there is the sun, there is the moon, there are the stars, dreams, auguries, conversation with the gods."

The true Cynic when he has ordered himself thus cannot be satisfied with this: he must know that he is sent as a messenger from God to men concerning things good and evil, to show them that they have gone astray and are seeking the true nature of good and evil where it is not to be found, and take no thought where it really is: he must realize, in the words of Diogenes when brought before Philip [II, king of Macedon, father of Alexander the Great] after the battle of Chaeronea, that he is sent "to reconnoitre." For indeed the Cynic has to discover what things are friendly to men and what are hostile: and when he has accurately made his observations he must return and report the truth, not driven by fear to point out enemies where there are none, nor in any other way disturbed or confounded by his impressions.

He must then be able, if chance so offer, to come forward on the tragic stage, and with a loud voice utter the word of Socrates: "Oh race of men, whither are ye hurrying? What are you doing, miserable creatures? You wander up and down like blind folk: you have left the true path and go away on a vain errand, you seek peace and happiness elsewhere, where it is not to be found, and believe not when another shows the way.

The following example of Epictetus' ethical thinking shows the stress on one's will, that is, to control things in one's power is to be in accord with God's will.[4]

---

[3] As quoted in C. K. Barrett, *Background*, pp. 75–76.

[4] *Discourses of Epictetus*, Book IV, chapter 1, as quoted from W. J. Oates, *The Stoic and Epicurean Philosophers*, p. 418.

Come now and let us review the conclusions we have agreed to. He is free whom none can hinder, the man who can deal with things as he wishes. But the man who can be hindered or compelled or fettered or driven into anything against his will, is a slave. And who is he whom none can hinder? The man who fixes his aim on nothing that is not his own. And what does "not his own" mean? All that it does not lies in our power to have or not to have, or to have of a particular quality or under particular conditions. The body then does not belong to us, its parts do not belong to us, our property does not belong to us. If then you set your heart on one of these as though it were your own, you will pay the penalty deserved by him who desires what does not belong to him. The road that leads to freedom, the only release from slavery is this, to be able to say with your whole soul:

Lead me, O Zeus, and lead me, Destiny,
Whether ordained is by your decree.

Epicurus: Epistle to Menoeceus

The name of Epicurus (ca. 342–270 B.C.) has become synonymous with "pleasure." The following extract gives an impression of Epicurus' view of pleasure.[5]

When, therefore, we maintain that pleasure is the end, we do not mean the pleasures of profligates and those that consist in sensuality, as is supposed by some who are either ignorant or disagree with us or do not understand, but freedom from pain in the body and from trouble in the mind. For it is not continuous drinkings and revellings, nor the satisfaction of lusts, nor the enjoyment of fish and other luxuries of the wealthy table, which produce a pleasant life, but sober reasoning, searching out the motives for all choice and avoidance, and banishing mere opinions, to which are due the greatest disturbance of the spirit.

ASTROLOGY

Astrology was extremely widespread in the Hellenistic world, affecting almost every religion or religious philosophy, and when wed with Greek mathematics, it became quite complex. The following comment was written by the second-century A.D. Roman author, Vettius Valens.[6]

Fate has decreed as a law for each person the unalterable consequences of his horoscope, controlled by many causes of good and evil; and their results are watched over by two self-begotten deities who are

[5] As quoted in C. K. Barrett, *Background*, p. 75.
[6] As quoted in F. C. Grant, *Hellenistic Religions*, pp. 60–61.

her ministers, Hope (Elpis) and Chance (Tyche); these rule over life, and by both deception and compulsion see to it that everyone obeys the law.

MAGIC

One of the areas where astrology was highly visible was magic. The following selection from Egyptian magical papyri shows the influence of Hebrew language names in magic, including that of Jesus.[7]

For those possessed by daemons, an approved charm by Pibechis.

Take oil made from unripe olives, together with the plant mastigia and lotus pith, and boil it with majoram (very colorless), saying: "Joel, Ossarthiomi, Emori, Theochipsoith, Sithemeoch, Sothe, Joe, Mimi-psothiooph, Phersothi, Aeeioyo, Joe, Eochariphtha: come out of such a one (and other usual formulae)."

But write this phylactery upon a little sheet of tin: "Jaeo, Abraothioch, Phtha, Mesentiniao, Pheoch, Jaeo, Charsoc," and hang it round the sufferer: it is of every demon a thing to be trembled at, which he fears. Standing opposite, adjure him. The adjuration is this: "I adjure thee by the god of the Hebrews Jesu, Jaba, Jae, Abraoth, Aia, Thoth, Ele, Elo, Aeo, Eu, Jiibaech, Abarmas, Jabarau, Abelbel, Lona, Abra, Maroia, arm, thou that appearest in fire, thou that art in the midst of earth and snow and vapour. . . .

INITIATION INTO THE MYSTERIES

Apuleius, in *The Golden Ass* (11.22–26), comes almost to the point of telling what his initiation into the most secret mysteries was like. According to a dream, Isis instructed him to find an old high priest, Mithras by name, who led him to the temple, performed sacrifices, and from secret holy books instructed him in his preparations. When Apuleius had purchased the necessary materials, the priest ritually washed and purified him, presented him to the goddess in the temple, and taught him "certain secret things unlawful to be uttered." Apuleius then fasted for 10 days. His account continues:[8]

Then behold the day approached when as the sacrifice of dedication should be done; and when the sun declined and evening came, there arrived on every coast a great multitude of priests who according to their ancient order offered me many presents and gifts. Then was all the laity and profane people commanded to depart, and when they had put on my back a new linen robe, the priest took my hand and brought me to the most secret and sacred place of the temple. Thou wouldest peradventure

---

[7] As quoted in C. K. Barrett, *Background*, pp. 31–32.
[8] As quoted from C. K. Barrett, *Background*, pp. 98–99.

demand, thou studious reader, what was said and done there: verily I would tell thee if it were lawful for me to tell, thou wouldest know if it were convenient for thee to hear; but both thy ears and my tongue should incur the like pain of rash curiosity. Howbeit I will not long torment thy mind, which peradventure is somewhat religious and given to some devotion; listen therefore, and believe it to be true. Thou shalt understand that I approached near unto hell, even to the gates of Proserpine [Persephone], and after that I was ravished throughout all the elements, I returned to my proper place: about midnight I saw the sun brightly shine, I saw likewise the gods celestial and the gods infernal, before whom I presented myself and worshipped them. Behold now have I told thee, which although thou has heard, yet it is necessary that thou conceal it; wherefore this only will I tell, which may be declared without offence for the understanding of the profane.

Apuleius continued by reporting that he was then sanctified with twelve stoles and dressed in a religious habit. Torch in hand, garland of flowers on his head, he was permitted to be seen by the people, an act which solemnized the feast. Apuleius then gave an oration to Isis and embraced his spiritual father.

GNOSTIC TEXTS

The Corpus Hermeticum, the Odes of Solomon, and the Gospel of Thomas

In the Hermetic literature, composed sometime in the second century A.D., the Egyptian God Thoth, who is given the Greek name Hermes Trismegistus ("Thrice-Greatest Hermes"), is usually the revealer of secret knowledge (*gnōsis*) to a disciple about God, creation, and salvation. The following extract tells of the fall of the Primal Man leading to the slavery of man to the lower powers and to his death. The passage, *Corpus Hermeticum* tractate Poimandres 14-15, illustrates Gnostic dualism.[9]

And he who had all authority over the world of mortal beings and of beasts without reason bent down through the harmony [of the spheres], broke through the encirclement, and disclosed God's godly form to the lower nature. When she [the lower nature] saw him who had in himself infinite beauty, all power over the governors, and the form of God, she smiled in love, because she beheld man's most beautiful form reflected in the water and in the shadow upon the earth. When he beheld in the water the figure like himself that was to be found in [the lower] nature, he loved it too and willed to dwell there. But the fulfillment followed at once with his intention, and thus he took his abode in the form devoid of

---

[9] As quoted in E. Lohse, *Environment*, pp. 264–65, taken from W. Foerster, *Gnosis: A Selection of Gnostic Texts*, vol. 2.

reason. And nature [thereby] received the beloved and wholly embraced him, and they were united and loved each other. (14) Therefore man, in contrast to all other living creatures on earth, is a dual being, mortal, to be sure, because of the body, but immortal because of the essential man. Although he is immortal and is given power over all things, he suffers the lot of a mortal and is subject to fate. Although he is placed above the harmony [of the spheres], he became a slave within this harmony. Although he is bisexual, because he is born of a bisexual father, and although he is sleepless, because he comes from one who is sleepless, he is under the dominion [of desire and the longing for sleep]. (15)

The Odes of Solomon were probably written in Greek about A.D. 100 either by a Jew whose work was subsequently Christianized or by a Jewish Christian. They show signs of some relationship to the Dead Sea Scrolls, yet most scholars see them as Gnostic. The following is a thanksgiving prayer for redemption, Ode 21.[10]

> My arms I lifted up on high
> To the grace of the Lord,
> because he cast off my fetters from me
> and my helper lifted me up to his grace and redemption.
> I put off darkness
> and put on the light.
> And my soul acquired members
> in which there was no sickness,
> nor misery, nor pain.
> And extremely helpful to me was the counsel of the Lord,
> and his imperishable fellowship.
> And I was lifted up into the light
> and I passed before his face
> and I came near to him
> praising and confessing him.
> He made my heart overflow, and it was found in my mouth
> and arose upon my lips.
> And upon my face the exultation over the Lord and his
>   praise increased.
> Hallelujah!

Although previously known by title, *The Gospel of Thomas* was first discovered among the Nag Hammadi texts.[11] It is called a gospel, but it has no narrative or miracle stories; rather, it is (like Q) a collection of sayings usually beginning with a formula like "And Jesus said. . . ." A number of parables in *Thomas* are close to the synoptic gospel parables and, in fact, some of them appear to be earlier in form that those preserved there, even though the writing

---

[10] As quoted in E. Lohse, *Environment*, p. 276.
[11] See Appendix 4.

was probably not done until about the middle of the second century. Its author was a Christian Gnostic who wrote in Coptic.[12]

> These are the secret words which the living Jesus spoke, and Didymos Judas Thomas wrote them down.
> 1. And he said, "He who finds the meaning of these words will not taste death."
> 2. Jesus said, "Let him who seeks not cease seeking until he finds, and when he finds, he shall be troubled, and when he is troubled, he will marvel, and he will rule over the All."

> 20. The disciples said to Jesus, "Tell us, what is the Kingdom of Heaven like?" He said to them, "It is like a mustard seed, smaller than all seeds. But when it falls on plowed ground, it puts forth a large shrub and becomes a shelter for the birds of heaven."

> 107. Jesus said, "The Kingdom is like a shepherd who had a hundred sheep. One of them, which was the largest, wandered off. He left the ninety-nine; he searched for the one until he found it. After he tired himself, he said to the sheep, 'I love you more than the ninety-nine.' "

THE HERO ("DIVINE MAN")

Apollonios of Tyana was said to have been sired by the Egyptian God Proteus, and to have gathered followers, taught, helped the poor, healed the sick, raised the dead, cast out demons, and appeared to his followers after death to discourse on immortality. He lived through most of the first Christian century and shortly after 217 a "Life" of him was written by Philostratus. The following account is an exorcism story about Apollonios reminiscent of the type found in the synoptic gospels.[13]

> And when he told them to have handles on the cup and to pour over the handles—this being a purer part of the cup since no one's mouth touches that part—a young boy began laughing raucously, scattering his discourse to the winds. Apollonios stopped and, looking up at him, said, "It is not you that does this arrogant thing but the demon who drives you unwittingly," for unknown to everyone the youth was actually possessed by a demon, for he used to laugh at things no one else did and would fall to weeping for no reason and would talk and sing to himself. Most people thought it was the jumpiness of youth which brought him to do such things and at this point he really seemed carried away by drunkenness. But it was actually a demon which spoke through him.
>   Now as Apollonios was staring at him the phantom in the boy let

---

[12] D. R. Cartlidge and D. L. Dungan, *Documents for the Study of the Gospel*, pp. 25, 27, 35.
[13] D. R. Cartlidge and D. L. Dungan, *Documents*, pp. 229–30.

out horrible cries of fear and rage, sounding just like someone being burned alive or stretched on the rack, and then he began to promise that he would leave the young boy and never possess anyone else among men. But Apollonios spoke to him angrily such as a master might to a cunning and shameless slave and he commanded him to come out of him, giving definite proof of it. "I will knock down that statue there," it said, pointing toward one of those around the Porch of the King. And when the statue tottered and then fell over, who can describe the shout of amazement that went up and how everyone clapped their hands from astonishment! But the young boy opened his eyes as if from sleep and looked at the rays of the sun. Now all those observing these events revered the boy for he no longer appeared to be as coarse as he had been, nor did he look disorderly, but he had come back to his own nature just as if he had drunk some medicine. He threw aside his fancy soft clothes and, stripping off the rest of his luxuriousness, came to love poverty and a threadbare cloak and the customs of Apollonios.

THE JEWISH HIGH PRIEST

Ben Sirach 50:5–11

The following text describes Simon, son of Onias, who was High Priest in the Jerusalem Temple about 219–196 B.C.[14]

> 5) How glorious he was when the people gathered round him
>   as he came out of the inner sanctuary!
> 6) Like the morning star among the clouds,
>   like the moon when it is full;
> 7) Like the sun shining upon the temple of the Most High,
>   and like the rainbow gleaming in glorious clouds;
> 8) like roses in the days of the first fruits,
>   like lilies by a spring of water,
>   like a green shoot on Lebanon on a summer day;
> 9) like fire and incense in the censer,
>   like a vessel of hammered gold adorned with all kinds
>   of precious stones;
> 10) like an olive tree putting forth its fruit,
>   and like a cypress towering in the clouds.
> 11) When he put on his glorious robe and clothed himself
>   with superb perfection
>   and went up to the holy altar, he made the court of
>   the sanctuary glorious.

[14] As quoted from *The Oxford Annotated Bible* (RSV).

JEWISH ESCHATOLOGY

Apocalyptic: The Assumption of Moses 10:1–10

The Assumption of Moses, a work contemporary with the New Testament, is particularly interesting because of its use of "Kingdom of God," a key concept in the teaching of Jesus.[15]

And then his [God's] kingdom shall appear throughout all his creation,
And then Satan shall be no more.
And sorrow shall depart with him.
Then the hands of the angel shall be filled
Who has been appointed chief,
And he shall forthwith avenge them of their enemies.
For the Heavenly One will arise from his royal throne,
And he will go forth from his holy habitation
With indignation and wrath on account of his sons.
And the earth shall tremble: to its confines shall it be shaken.
And the high mountains shall be made low
And the hills shall be shaken and fall.
And the horns of the sun shall be broken and he shall be turned into
    darkness;
And the moon shall not give her light, and be turned wholly into blood.
And the circle of the stars shall be disturbed.
And the sea shall retire into the abyss,
And the fountains of waters shall fail,
And the rivers shall dry up.
For the Most High will arise, the Eternal God alone,
And he will appear to punish the Gentiles,
And he will destroy all their idols.
Then thou, O Israel, shalt be happy,
And thou shalt mount upon the necks and wings of the eagle,
And they shall be ended.
And God will exalt thee,
And he will cause thee to approach to the heaven of the stars,
In the place of their habitation.
And thou shalt look from on high and shalt see thy enemies in Gehenna,
And thou shalt recognize them and rejoice,
And thou shalt give thanks and confess thy Creator.

[15] R. H. Charles, *The Apocrypha and Pseudepigrapha of the Old Testament in English*, vol. II: *Pseudepigrapha*, pp. 421–22.

Nationalistic: Psalms of Solomon 17:23–35

The Psalms of Solomon, probably dating from Pompey's coming into Palestine in 63 B.C. (cf. 2:1–2, 30; 17:14), expresses a hope for the coming of the "son of David."[16]

Behold, O Lord, and raise up unto them their king, the son of David,
At the time in which thou seest, O God, that he may reign over Israel thy
    servant.
And gird him with strength, that he may shatter unrighteous rulers,
And that he may purge Jerusalem from nations that trample her down
    to destruction.
Wisely, righteously he shall thrust out sinners from the inheritance,
He shall destroy the godless nations with the word of his mouth;
At his rebuke nations shall flee before him,
    And he shall reprove sinners for the thoughts of their heart.
And he shall gather together a holy people, whom he shall lead in
    righteousness,
    And he shall judge the tribes of the people that has been sanctified
    by the Lord his God.
And he shall not suffer unrighteousness to lodge anymore in their midst,
    Nor shall there dwell with them any man that knoweth wickedness,
    For he shall know them, that they are all sons of their God.
And he shall divide them according to their tribes upon the land,
    And neither sojourner nor alien shall sojourn, with them any more.
He shall judge peoples and nations in the wisdom of his righteousness.
And he shall have the heathen nations to serve him under his yoke;
    And he shall glorify the Lord in a place to be seen of all the earth;
And he shall purge Jerusalem, making it holy as of old:
So that nations shall come from the ends of the earth to see his glory,
    Bringing as gifts her sons who had fainted,
    And to see the glory of the Lord, wherewith God hath glorified her.

SYNAGOGUE PRAYERS

The Eighteen Benedictions

Though the precise wording of the Eighteen Benedictions has never been fixed, the following version of some of its petitions is from the earliest form. The first petition praises God, the ninth asks for a good year, the fourteenth mentions the Messiah, and the last was a prayer against Christians and heretics

---

[16] R. H. Charles, *Pseudepigrapha*, pp. 649–50.

added sometime after the destruction of Jerusalem and the Temple in A.D. 70. The major emphasis of the prayers is redemption.[17]

1. Blessed art Thou, O Lord, God of Abraham, God of Isaac and God of Jacob, God Most High, who art the Possessor (Creator) of heaven and earth, our Shield and the Shield of our fathers. Blessed art Thou, O Lord, who quickenest the dead!

9. Bless for us, O Lord our God, this year and satisfy the world from the treasuries of Thy goodness. Blessed art Thou, O Lord, who blessest the years!

14. Be merciful, O Lord our God, towards Jerusalem, Thy City, and towards Zion, the abiding place of Thy glory, and towards the kingdom of the house of David, Thy righteous anointed one. Blessed art Thou, O Lord, God of David, the Builder of Jerusalem!

The prayer against the heretics was inserted after the eleventh benediction:

Let the Nazarenes and the heretics perish as in a moment, let them be blotted out of the book of the living and let them not be written with the righteous.

The Kaddish Prayer

The Kaddish is also a synagogue prayer. Jesus' prayer, "Hallowed by thy name, Thy kingdom come" (Matt 6:9–10; Luke 11:12), has often been compared to it.[18]

Magnified and sanctified be his great name in the world
   that he has created according to his will.
May he establish his kingdom in your lifetime and in your days
   and in the lifetime of all the house of Israel,
   even speedily and at a near time.

SACRAMENTAL TEXT

The Messianic Banquet at Qumran

The Rule Annexe (1QSa 11-22) was discovered in Cave I along the Dead Sea. It represents a liturgical meal in anticipation of the great banquet which will take place when the Messiahs of Aaron and Israel come. It is an Essene

---

[17] W. Foerster, *From the Exile to Christ*, pp. 228, 229, 157, based largely on C. W. Dugmore, *The Influence of the Synagogue upon the Divine Office*, pp. 115–24.
[18] Quoted from N. Perrin, *Jesus and the Language of the Kingdom*, p. 26.

sacrament using bread and wine. The brackets represent probable readings of the damaged text (lacunae).[19]

(11) [Concerning the mee]ting of the men of renown [called] to assembly for the Council of the Community when [the Lord] will have begotten (12) the Messiah (cf. Ps 2:7) among them.

[The Priest] shall enter [at] the head of all the Congregation of Israel, then all (13) [the chiefs of the sons] of Aaron, the priests called to the assembly, men of renown; and they shall sit (14) [before him], each according to his rank.

And afterwards, [the Mess]iah of Israel [shall enter]; and the chiefs (15) of [the tribes of Israel] shall sit before him, each according to his rank, . . . then all (16) the heads of the fa[milies of the Congre]gation, together with the wise me[n of the holy Congregation], shall sit before them, each according to (17) his rank.

And [when] they gather for the Community tab[le], [or to drink w]ine, and arrange the (18) Community table [and mix] the wine to drink, let no man [stretch out] his hand over the first-fruits of bread (19) and [wine] before the Priest; for [it is he who] shall bless the first-fruits of bread (20) and w[ine, and shall] first [stretch out] his hand over the bread. And after[wards], the Messiah of Israel shall [str]etch out his hands (21) over the bread. [And afterwards], all the Congregation of the Community shall [bl]ess, each according to his rank.

And they shall proceed according to this rite (22) at every mea[l where] at least ten persons [are as]sembled.

[19] A. Dupont-Sommer, *The Essene Writings from Qumran*, English translation from the French by G. Vermes, pp. 108–09; cf. D. R. Cartledge and D. L. Dungan, *Documents*, p. 171.

BIBLIOGRAPHY

Adams, H. *The Interests of Criticism: An Introduction to Literary Theory.* New York: Harcourt Brace Jovanovich, 1969.

Agourides, S., and Charlesworth, J. H. "A New Discovery of Old Manuscripts on Mt. Sinai: A Preliminary Report." *Biblical Archeologist,* vol. 41 (1978), pp. 29–31.

Aharoni, Y. *The Land of the Bible. A Historical Geography.* Philadelphia: Westminster Press, 1980.

Albright, W. F. *The Archeology of Palestine.* Baltimore: Penguin Books, 1960.

Althaus, P. *The So-Called Kerygma and the Historical Jesus.* Edinburgh: Oliver and Boyd, 1959.

Amiot, F. *The Key Concepts of St. Paul.* Trans. J. Dingle. New York: Herder and Herder, 1962.

Archeological Discoveries in the Holy Land. Compiled by the Archeological Institute of America. New York: Bonanza Books, 1967.

Auerbach, E. *Mimesis.* Garden City, N.Y.: Doubleday, Anchor Books, 1957.

Bacon, B. W. *Studies in Matthew.* New York: Holt, Reinhart & Winston, 1930.

Baron, S., and Blau, S., eds. *Judaism, Postbiblical and Talmudic Period.* New York: The Liberal Arts Press, 1954.

Barrett, C. K. *From First Adam to Last: A Study in Pauline Theology.* New York: Scribners, 1962.

———. *The Gospel According to St. John.* London: S.P.C.K., 1955.

———. *The Gospel of John and Judaism.* Philadelphia: Fortress Press, 1975.

———. *Luke the Historian in Recent Study.* London: The Epworth Press, 1961.

———. *The New Testament Background: Selected Documents.* Harper Torchbook No. 86. New York: Harper & Row, 1961.

———. "Paul's Opponents in II Corinthians." *New Testament Studies,* vol. 17 (1970–71), pp. 233–54.

Bartchy, S. Scott. *First Century Slavery and 1 Corinthians 7:21.* SBL Dissertation Series 11. Missoula, Mont.: The Society of Biblical Literature, 1973.

Barth, M. *Justification. Pauline Texts Interpreted in the Light of the Old and New Testaments.* Trans. A. M. Woodruff III. Grand Rapids: William B. Eerdmans, 1971.

Bartsch, H. W., ed. *Kerygma and Myth.* Harper Torchbook No. 80. New York: Harper & Row, 1961.

Beardslee, W. A. *Literary Criticism of the New Testament.* In *Guides to Biblical Scholarship.* New Testament Series. Ed. Dan O. Via, Jr. Philadelphia: Fortress Press, 1970.

———. "The Uses of the Proverb in the Synoptic Tradition." *Interpretation,* vol. 24 (1970), pp. 61–76.

Berger, K. "Zu den sogennanten Sätzen Heiligen Rechts." *New Testament Studies,* vol. 17 (1970–71), pp. 10–40.

Bettenson, H. *Documents of the Christian Church.* New York: Oxford University Press, 1942.

Betz, H. D. *Galatians.* Hermeneia Series. Philadelphia: Fortress Press, 1979.

Bickerman, E. *From Ezra to the Last of the Maccabees. Foundations of Postbiblical Judaism.* New York: Schocken Books, 1947.

Boobyer, G. H. "Galilee and Galileans in St. Mark's Gospel." *Bulletin of the John Rylands Library,* vol. 35 (1952-53), pp. 334–48.

Borgen, P. *Bread From Heaven.* Leiden: E. J. Brill, 1965.

Bornkamm, G. *Early Christian Experience.* Trans. P. L. Hammer. New York: Harper & Row, 1969.

———. *Jesus of Nazareth.* New York: Harper & Row, 1960.

———. *Paul.* New York: Harper & Row, 1971.

———. "The Risen Lord and the Earthly Jesus: Mt. 28:16–20." In *The Future of Our Religious Past.* J. M. Robinson, ed., pp. 203–09. New York: Harper & Row, 1971.

Bornkamm, G., Barth, G., and Held, H. J. *Tradition and Interpretation in Matthew.* Philadelphia: Westminster Press, 1963.

Bousset, Wilhelm. *Kyrios Christos.* Nashville and New York: Abingdon Press, 1970. German original 1913.

Bowman, J. W. "The Revelation to John. Its Dramatic Structure and Message." *Interpretation,* vol. 9 (1955), pp. 436–53.

Brandon, S. G. F. *The Fall of Jerusalem and the Christian Church.* London: S.P.C.K., 1951.

Braun, H. *Jesus of Nazareth.* Trans. E. R. Kalin. Philadelphia: Fortress Press, 1979.

Bright, J. *A History of Israel.* Philadelphia: Westminster Press, 1976.

Brown, R. E. *The Birth of the Messiah.* Garden City, N.Y.: Doubleday, 1977.

———. *The Community of the Beloved Disciple.* New York: Paulist Press, 1979.

———. *The Gospel According to John.* 2 vols. Garden City, N.Y.: Doubleday, 1966 (I–XII), 1970 (XIII–XXI).

———. *New Testament Essays.* Milwaukee: The Bruce Publishing Company, 1965.

Brown, R., Donfried, K. P., and Reumann, J. *Peter in the New Testament.* Minneapolis: Angsburg Publishing House, 1973.

Browning, I. *Petra.* Park Ridge, N.J.: Noyes Press, 1973.

Bruce, F. F. *The English Bible: A History of Translations.* Rev. ed. New York: Oxford University Press, 1970.

———. *Jesus and Christian Origins Outside the New Testament.* Grand Rapids: Eerdmans, 1974.

———. *New Testament History.* Garden City, N.Y.: Doubleday, Anchor Books, 1972.

Buchanan, G. W. *To the Hebrews.* Anchor Bible. Garden City, N.Y.: Doubleday, 1972.

Bultmann, R. *The Gospel of John: A Commentary.* Oxford: B. Blackwell, 1971.

———. *The History of the Synoptic Tradition.* New York: Harper & Row, 1968.

———. *Jesus and the Word.* New York: Scribners, 1934, 1958. German original 1926.

———. *Jesus Christ and Mythology.* New York: Scribners, 1958, and London: SCM Press, 1960.

———. *The Johannine Epistles.* Trans. R. P. O'Hara et al. Philadelphia: Fortress Press, 1973.

———. *Primitive Christianity in Its Contemporary Setting.* New York: Meridian, 1956.

———. "The Primitive Christian Kerygma and the Historical Jesus." In *The Historical Jesus and the Kerygmatic Christ.* Carl A. Braaten and Roy A. Harrisville, eds. New York and Nashville: Abingdon Press, 1964.

————. *Theology of the New Testament.* 2 vols. New York: Scribners, 1951 and 1955.

Caird, G. B. *The Gospel of St. Luke.* Pelican Gospel Commentaries. Baltimore: Penguin Books, 1963.

Cairns, D. *A Gospel Without Myth? Bultmann's Challenge to the Preacher.* London: SCM Press, 1960.

Cambridge History of the Bible II. The West from the Reformation to the Present Day. New York: Cambridge University Press, 1963.

Campbell, Joseph. *Myths to Live By.* New York: Viking Press, 1972.

Cartlidge, D. R., and Dungan, D. L. *Documents for the Study of the Gospels.* Cleveland: Collins, 1980.

Cerfaux, L. *Christ in the Theology of St. Paul.* Trans. G. Webb and A. Walker. New York: Herder and Herder, 1959.

————. *The Church in the Theology of St. Paul.* Trans. G. Webb and A. Walker. New York: Herder and Herder, 1959.

Charles, R. H. *The Apocrypha and Pseudepigrapha of the Old Testament in English.* 2 vols. Oxford: Clarendon Press, 1913.

Charlesworth, J. H. "The Manuscripts of St. Catherine's Monastery." *Biblical Archeologist,* vol. 43 (1980), pp. 26–34.

————. "St. Catherine's Monastery: Myths and Mysteries." *Biblical Archeologist,* vol. 42 (1979), pp. 174–79.

————. *The Pseudepigrapha & Modern Research* (with Supplement). Missoula, Mont.: Scholars Press, 1981.

Charlesworth, J. H., ed. *John and Qumran.* London: Geoffrey Chapman, 1972.

Collins, A. Yarbro. *The Combat Myth in the Book of Revelation.* Missoula, Mont.: Scholars Press, 1976.

————. "The Political Perspective of the Revelation to John." *Journal of Biblical Literature,* vol. 96 (1977), pp. 241–56.

Collins, J. "Pseudonymity, Historical Reviews and the Grace of the Revelation of John." *Catholic Biblical Quarterly,* vol. 39 (1977), pp. 329–43.

Conzelmann, Hans. *1 Corinthians.* Hermeneia Series. Philadelphia: Fortress Press, 1975.

————. *History of Primitive Christianity.* New York: Abingdon Press, 1973.

————. *Jesus.* Philadelphia: Fortress Press, 1973.

————. *The Theology of St. Luke.* New York: Harper & Row, 1960.

Cope, L. *Matthew, A Scribe Trained for the Kingdom of Heaven.* CBQ Monograph 5. Washington, D.C.: The Catholic Biblical Association of America, 1976.

Crane, R. S., ed. *Critics and Criticism, Essays in Method.* Abridged ed. Chicago: University of Chicago Press, 1957.

————. *The Languages of Criticism and the Structure of Poetry.* Toronto: University of Toronto Press, 1953.

Cross, F. M. *The Ancient Library of Qumran and Modern Biblical Studies.* Rev. ed. Garden City, N.Y.: Doubleday, 1961.

Crossan, J. D. "Parable and Example in the Teaching of Jesus." *New Testament Studies,* vol. 18 (1971–72), pp. 285–307.

Cullmann, O. *The Johannine Circle.* Trans. J. Bowden. Philadelphia: Westminster Press, 1976.

Culpepper, A. *The Johannine School.* SBL Dissertation Series. Missoula, Mont.: Scholars Press, 1975.

Cumont, F. *Oriental Religions in Roman Paganism.* New York: Dover Publications, 1956 [1911].

Dahl, N. A. *Studies in Paul.* Minneapolis: Augsburg, 1977.

Danker, F. W. *Jesus and the New Age, According to St. Luke.* St. Louis: Clayton Publishing House, 1972.

————. *Luke.* Proclamation Commentaries. Philadelphia: Fortress Press, 1976.

Davies, W. D. *Paul and Rabbinic Judaism.* Harper Torchbook. New York: Harper & Row, 1967.

———. *The Sermon on the Mount.* Cambridge: Cambridge University Press, 1966.
———. *The Setting of the Sermon on the Mount.* Cambridge: Cambridge University Press, 1964.
Dibelius, Martin. *From Tradition to Gospel.* New York: Scribners, 1935.
Dibelius, M., and Conzelmann, H. *The Pastoral Epistles.* Hermeneia Series. Philadelphia: Fortress Press, 1972.
Dibelius, M., and Greeven, H. *James.* Hermeneia Series. Philadelphia: Fortress Press, 1976.
Dodd, C. H. *The Interpretation of the Fourth Gospel.* Cambridge: Cambridge University Press, 1953.
———. *The Johannine Epistle.* Moffatt New Testament Commentary. London: Hodder and Stoughton, 1946.
———. *The Meaning of Paul for Today.* New York: Meridian Books, 1957.
Dodds, E. R. *The Greeks and the Irrational.* New York: W. W. Norton, 1966.
Donahue, John R. *Are You the Christ? The Trial Narrative in the Gospel of Mark.* SBL Dissertation Series 10, 1973.
———. "Tax Collectors and Sinners." *Catholic Biblical Quarterly,* vol. 33 (1971), pp. 39–61.
Donfried, K. P. *The Romans Debate.* Minneapolis: Augsburg, 1977.
Doresse, J. *The Secret Books of the Egyptian Gnostics.* New York: Viking Press, 1960.
Doty, W. G. *Letters in Primitive Christianity.* Guides to Biblical Scholarship. Philadelphia: Fortress Press, 1973.
Dugmore, C. W. *The Influence of the Synagogue upon the Divine Office.* Oxford: Oxford University Press, 1944.
Duling, D. *Jesus Christ Through History.* New York: Harcourt Brace Jovanovich, 1979.
———. "The Therapeutic Son of David: An Element in Matthew's Christological Apologetic." *New Testament Studies,* vol. 24 (1978), pp. 392–410.
———. "Interpreting the Markan Hodology." *Nexus,* vol. 17, no. 2 (1974), pp. 2–11.
Dupont-Sommer, A. *The Essene Writings from Qumran.* Trans. G. Vermes. Cleveland: The World Publishing Company, 1961.
Edwards, R. A. "An Approach to the Theology of Q." *Journal of Religion,* vol. 51 (1971), pp. 247–69.
———. *The Sign of Jonah in the Theology of the Evangelists and Q.* Studies in Biblical Theology. London: SCM Press, and Naperville, Ill.: Allenson, 1971.
———. *A Theology of Q.* Philadelphia: Fortress Press, 1976.
Eliade, Mircea. *Cosmos and History: The Myth of the Eternal Return.* Harper Torchbook No. 2050. New York: Harper & Row, 1959.
———. "Myth." *Encyclopaedia Britannica,* vol. 15 (1968), pp. 1132–42.
———. *Myth and Reality.* Harper Torchbook No. 1369. New York: Harper & Row, 1963.
———. *The Quest: History and Meaning in Religion.* Chicago: University of Chicago Press, 1969.
Evans, C. F. "I will go before you into Galilee." *Journal of Theological Studies,* n.s. 5 (1954), pp. 3–18.
Farmer, W. R. *The Synoptic Problem. A Critical Analysis.* New York: Macmillan, 1964.
Feine, P., Behm, J., and Kümmel, W. G. *Introduction to the New Testament.* New York and Nashville: Abingdon Press, 1966.
Fenton, J. C. *The Gospel of St. Matthew.* Pelican Gospel Commentaries. Baltimore: Penguin Books, 1963.
Festugière, A. J. *Personal Religion Among the Greeks.* Berkeley: University of California Press, 1960.
Filson, F. V. *A New Testament History.* Philadelphia: Westminster Press, 1964.
Finley, M. I., ed. *The Portable Greek Historians: The Essence of Herodotus, Thucydides, Xenophon, Polybius.* New York: The Viking Press, 1959.
———. *The Ancient Economy.* Berkeley: University of California Press, 1973.

Finnegan, J. *The Archeology of the New Testament.* Princeton: Princeton University Press, 1969.

Fiorenza, E. Schluessler. "Composition and Structure of the Book of Revelation." *Catholic Biblical Quarterly,* vol. 39 (1977), pp. 344–66.

Fitzmyer, J. A. *The Gospel According to Luke I–IX.* Anchor Bible. Garden City, N.Y.: Doubleday, 1981.

———. "The Languages of Palestine in the First Century A.D." *Catholic Biblical Quarterly,* vol. 32 (1970), pp. 501–31.

Foerster, W. *From the Exile to Christ.* Philadelphia: Fortress Press, 1964.

———. *Gnosis. A Selection of Gnostic Texts.* 2 vols. Trans. R. McL. Wilson. Oxford: Clarendon Press, 1972.

Fortna, R. T. "Christology in the Fourth Gospel: Redaction-Critical Perspectives." *New Testament Studies,* vol. 21 (1975–76), pp. 489–504.

———. *The Gospel of Signs: A Reconstruction of the Narrative Source Underlying the Fourth Gospel.* London: Cambridge University Press, 1970.

Francis, F. O. "Humility and Angelic Worship in Col 2:18." *Studia Theologica* 16 (1962), pp. 109–34.

Francis, F. O., and Meeks, W. *Conflicts at Colossae.* Missoula, Mont.: University of Montana, 1973.

Fuller, R. H. *A Critical Introduction to the New Testament.* London: Duckworth, 1966.

———. *The Foundations of New Testament Christology.* New York: Scribners, 1965.

———. "The 'Thou Art Peter' Pericope and the Easter Appearances." *McCormick Quarterly,* vol. 20 (1966–67), pp. 309–15.

Funk, R. W. *Language, Hermeneutic and Word of God.* New York: Harper & Row, 1966.

Funk, R. W., ed. *Journal for Theology and the Church. VI: Apocalypticism.* New York: Herder and Herder, 1969.

Furnish, V. P. *The Moral Teaching of Paul.* Nashville: Abingdon, 1979.

Furnish, V. P. *Theology and Ethics in Paul.* Nashville: Abingdon, 1968.

Gager, J. "The Gospels and Jesus: Some Doubts About Method." *Journal of Religion,* vol. 54 (1974), pp. 244–72.

———. *Kingdom and Community. The Social World of Early Christianity.* Englewood Cliffs, N.J.: Prentice-Hall, 1975.

Gaston, L. *No Stone on Another. Studies in the Significance of the Fall of Jerusalem in the Synoptic Gospels.* Leiden, The Netherlands: Brill, 1970.

Gennep, A. Van. *Rites of Passage.* Chicago: University of Chicago Press, 1960.

Georgi, D. "Forms of Religious Propaganda." In *Jesus in His Time.* H. J. Schultz, ed. Philadelphia: Fortress Press, 1971.

———. *Die Gegner des Paulus im 2. Korintherbrief: Studien zur religiosen Propaganda in der Spätantike.* WMANT II. Neurkirchen-Vluyn: Neukirchener Verlag, 1964.

Gogarten, F. *Demythologizing and History.* London: SCM Press, 1953.

Goguel, M. *Jesus and the Origins of Christianity.* Harper Torchbooks. 2 vols. New York: Harper & Row, 1960.

Goodenough, E. R. *An Introduction to Philo Judaeus.* Oxford: Basil Blackwell, 1962.

Goodspeed, E. J. *A History of Early Christian Literature.* Rev. and enlarged by R. M. Grant. Chicago: University of Chicago Press, 1966.

Goulder, M. *Midrash and Lection in Matthew.* London: S.P.C.K., 1974.

Gowan, D. E. *Bridge Between the Testaments.* Pittsburgh Theological Monograph Series. Pittsburgh: The Pickwick Press, 1980.

Grant, F. C. *Hellenistic Religions.* Indianapolis and New York: Bobbs-Merrill, 1953.

———. *Hellenistic Religions.* New York: Liberal Arts Press, 1953.

Grant, M. *The World of Rome.* Cleveland: World, 1960.

Grant, R. M. *The Bible in the Church: A Short History of Interpretation.* New York: Macmillan, 1948.

———. *A Historical Introduction to the New Testament.* London: Collins, 1963.

———. "The Origin of the Fourth Gospel." *Journal of Biblical Literature*, vol. 69 (1950), pp. 305–22.

Grant, R. M., ed. *Gnosticism: An Anthology.* London: Collins, 1961.

Green, H. *The Gospel According to Matthew.* London: Oxford University Press, 1975.

Gundry, R. *The Use of the Old Testament in St. Matthew's Gospel.* Leiden: E. J. Brill, 1967.

Hadas, M. *Hellenistic Culture.* New York: W. W. Norton, 1959.

———. *Imperial Rome.* New York: Time Inc., 1965.

Hadas, M., and Smith, M. *Heroes and Gods.* New York: Harper & Row, 1965.

Haenchen, E. *The Acts of the Apostles.* Philadelphia: Westminster Press, 1971.

Hanson, P. *The Dawn of Apocalyptic.* Philadelphia: Fortress Press, 1975.

Hare, D. *The Theme of Jewish Persecution of Christians in the Gospel According to St. Matthew.* Cambridge: Cambridge University Press, 1967.

Harnack, Adolf. *What Is Christianity?* New York: Harper & Row, 1957.

Harrington, D. "Matthean Studies Since Joachim Rhode." *Heythrop Journal*, 16/14 (1975), pp. 375–88.

Harris, R., and Mingana, A. *The Odes and Psalms of Solomon. II. The Translation.* New York: Longmans, Green, 1916–20.

Hartman, Lars. *Prophecy Interpreted.* Coniectanea Biblica New Testament Series No. 1. Lund, Sweden: G. W. K. Gleerup, 1966.

Harvey, Van A. *The Historian and the Believer.* New York: Macmillan, 1966.

Heitmüller, W. "Hellenistic Christianity Before Paul," in W. Meeks, *The Writings of St. Paul.* New York: W. W. Norton, 1972, pp. 308–19.

Hengel, M. *Acts and the History of Earliest Christianity.* Trans. J. Bowden. Philadelphia: Fortress Press, 1980.

———. *Judaism and Hellenism.* 2 vols. Philadelphia: Fortress Press, 1974.

Henderson, I. *Myth in the New Testament.* Chicago: H. Regner, 1952.

Hennecke, E., and Schneemelcher, W. *New Testament Apocrypha.* 2 vols. Philadelphia: Fortress Press, 1965.

Hock, R. F. *The Social Context of Paul's Ministry. Tentmaking and Apostleship.* Philadelphia: Fortress Press, 1980.

Holladay, C. H. *Theios Anēr (Divine Man) in Hellenistic Judaism: A Critique of This Category in New Testament Christology.* SBL Dissertation Series 40. Missoula, Mont.: Scholars Press, 1977.

Holmberg, B. *Paul and Power. The Structure of Authority in the Primitive Church as Reflected in the Pauline Epistles.* Philadelphia: Fortress Press, 1980.

Hoskyns, E. *The Fourth Gospel.* F. N. Davey, ed. London: Faber and Faber, 1940.

Hoskyns, Edwyn, and Davey, Noel. *The Riddle of the New Testament.* London: Faber and Faber, 1948.

Houlden, J. L. *Ethics in the New Testament.* New York: Oxford University Press, 1977.

———. *The Pastoral Epistles.* Pelican New Testament Commentary. New York: Penguin Books, 1976.

Howard, G. *Crisis in Galatia.* Cambridge: Cambridge University Press, 1979.

Howard, W. F. *The Fourth Gospel in Recent Criticism and Interpretation.* K. Barrett, ed. London: Epworth Press, 1955.

Hull, J. M. *Hellenistic Magic and the Synoptic Tradition.* SPT Second Series 28. Naperville, Ill.: SCM Press, 1974.

Hunter, A. M. *Paul and His Predecessors.* Philadelphia: Westminster Press, 1961.

The Interpreter's Dictionary of the Bible. 4 volumes. New York and Nashville: Abingdon Press, 1962 (Supplementary volume, 1976).

Jaspers, K., and Bultmann, R. *Myth and Christianity: An Inquiry into the Possibility of Religion Without Myth.* Trans. N. Guterman. New York: Noonday Press, 1958.

Jeremias, Joachim. *Jesus' Promise to the Nations.* Naperville, Ill.: Allenson, 1958.

———. *The Parables of Jesus.* Rev. ed. New York: Scribners, 1963.

———. *The Problem of the Historical Jesus.* Philadelphia: Fortress Press, 1964.

———. *Rediscovering the Parables.* London: SCM Press, 1966.

The Jerome Biblical Commentary. 2 volumes bound together. Englewood Cliffs, N.J.: Prentice-Hall, 1968.

Johnson, M. *The Purpose of the Biblical Genealogies.* London: Cambridge University Press, 1969.

Jonas, H. *The Gnostic Religion.* Boston: Beacon Paperback, 1963.

Jones, G. V. *Christology and Myth in the New Testament.* London: Allen and Unwin, 1956.

Judge, E. A. "St. Paul and Classical Society." *Jahrbuch für Antike und Christentum,* vol. 15 (1972), pp. 28–32.

Kähler, Martin. *The So-Called Historical Jesus and the Historic Biblical Christ.* Philadelphia: Fortress Press, 1964.

Karris, R. "Poor and Rich: The Lukan *Sitz im Leben.*" In C. Talbert, ed., *Perspectives on Luke-Acts.* Danville, Va.: Association of Baptist Professors of Religion, 1978, pp. 112–25.

———. *What Are They Saying About Luke and Acts?* New York: Paulist Press, 1979.

Käsemann, Ernst. "Epheserbrief." In *Die Religion in Geschichte und Gegenwart.* 3rd ed. Vol. II, pp. 518–19. Tübingen: J. C. B. Mohr, 1958.

———. *Essays on New Testament Themes.* Studies in Biblical Theology, 41. London: SCM Press, 1964.

———. *New Testament Questions of Today,* Philadelphia: Fortress Press, 1969.

———. *The Testament of Jesus: A Study of the Gospel of John in the Light of Chapter 17.* London: SCM Press, 1968.

Keck, L. E. *A Future for the Historical Jesus.* New York and Nashville: Abingdon Press, 1971.

Keck, L. E., and Martyn, J. L., eds. *Studies in Luke-Acts.* Nashville: Abingdon Press, 1966.

Kee, Howard C. *Christian Origins in Sociological Perspective.* Philadelphia: The Westminster Press, 1980.

———. *Community of the New Age: Studies in Mark's Gospel.* Philadelphia: Westminster Press, 1977.

———. *Jesus in History.* New York: Harcourt Brace Jovanovich, 1970.

———. *The Origins of Christianity.* Sources and Documents. Englewood Cliffs, N.J.: Prentice-Hall, 1973.

Kelber, W. *The Kingdom in Mark.* Philadelphia: Fortress Press, 1974.

———. *Mark's Story of Jesus.* Philadelphia: Fortress Press, 1979.

———. *The Passion in Mark.* Philadelphia: Fortress Press, 1976.

Kelber, W., Kalenkow, A., and Scroggs, R. "Reflections of the Question: Was There a Pre-Markan Passion Narrative?" In *The Society of Biblical Literature One Hundred Seventh Annual Meeting Seminar Papers* (1971), pp. 503–85.

Kelly, J. N. D. *A Commentary on the Epistles of Peter and Jude.* New York: Harper & Row, 1969.

Kenyon, K. *Jerusalem. Excavating 3,000 Years of History.* New York: McGraw-Hill, 1967.

Kingsbury, J. D. "The Jesus of History and Christ of Faith in Relation to Matthew's View of Time—Reactions to a New Approach." *Concordia Theological Monthly,* vol. 37 (1966), pp. 500–10.

———. *Matthew.* Proclamation Commentaries. Philadelphia: Fortress Press, 1977.

———. *Matthew: Structure, Christology, Kingdom.* Philadelphia: Fortress Press, 1975.

———. *The Parables of Jesus in Matthew 13.* London: S.P.C.K., 1969.

Klausner, J. *Jesus of Nazareth.* New York: Macmillan, 1925, and Boston: Beacon Press, 1964.

Knigge, H. D. "The Meaning of Mark." *Interpretation,* vol. 22 (1968), pp. 53–76.

Kock, K. *The Rediscovery of Apocalyptic.* SBT Second Series 22. London: SCM Press, 1972.

Krodel, G., ed. *Hebrews-James-1 and 2 Peter-Jude-Revelation.* Proclamation Commentaries. Philadelphia: Fortress Press, 1977.

———. *Ephesians, Colossians, 2 Thessalonians, the Pastoral Epistles.* Proclamation Commentaries. Philadelphia: Fortress Press, 1978.

Kümmel, W. G. "Current Theological Accusations Against Luke." *Andover Newton Quarterly*, vol. 16 (1975), pp. 131–45.

———. *The New Testament: The History of the Investigation of Its Problems*. New York and Nashville: Abingdon Press, 1972.

———. *The Theology of the New Testament*. New York: Abingdon Press, 1973.

Kümmel, W. G., ed. See Feine, P.

Kysar, R. "Community and Gospel: Vectors in Fourth Gospel Criticism." In J. L. Mays, ed., *Interpreting the Gospels*. Philadelphia: Fortress Press, 1981, pp. 265–77.

———. *John the Maverick Gospel*. Atlanta: John Knox Press, 1976.

———. *The Fourth Evangelist and His Gospel. An Examination of Contemporary Scholarship*. Atlanta: John Knox Press, 1976.

Liebermann, S. *Hellenism in Jewish Palestine*. New York: The Jewish Theological Seminary of America, 1950.

Lietzmann, H. *A History of the Early Church*. 4 vols. Trans. B. L. Woolf. Cleveland: World, 1961.

Lightfoot, R. H. *The Gospel Message of St. Mark*. Oxford Paperbacks 41. New York: Oxford University Press, 1962.

———. *History and Interpretation in the Gospels*. The Bampton Lectures. New York: Harper & Row, 1934.

———. *Locality and Doctrine in the Gospels*. New York: Harper & Row, 1936.

———. *St. John's Gospel*. Oxford: Clarendon Press, 1956.

Lindars, B. *Behind the Fourth Gospel*. London: S.P.C.K., 1971.

———. *New Testament Apologetic*. London: SCM Press, 1961.

Lohse, E. *Colossians and Philemon*. Hermeneia Series. Philadelphia: Fortress Press, 1971.

———. *The New Testament Environment*. Trans. J. E. Steely. Nashville: Abingdon, 1976.

MacMullen, R. *Roman Social Relations. 50 B.C. to A.D. 284*. New Haven: Yale University Press, 1974.

Macquarrie, J. *The Scope of Demythologizing; Bultmann and His Critics*. London: SCM Press, 1960.

MacRae, G. "The Ego-Proclamation in Gnostic Sources." In E. Bammel, ed. *The Trial of Jesus*. London: SCM Press, 1970, pp. 122–34.

———. *Faith in the Word: The Fourth Gospel*. Chicago: Franciscan Herald Press, 1973.

———. "The Fourth Gospel and *Religionsgeschichte*." *Catholic Biblical Quarterly*, vol. 32 (1970), pp. 13–24.

Malherbe, A. *Social Aspects of Early Christianity*. Baton Rouge, La.: State University Press, 1977.

Manson, T. W. *The Sayings of Jesus*. London: SCM Press, 1949.

———. *The Teaching of Jesus*. Cambridge: Cambridge University Press, 1931.

Martyn, J. L. *The Gospel of John in Christian History*. New York: Paulist Press, 1979.

———. *History and Theology in the Fourth Gospel*. New York: Harper & Row, 1968.

Marxsen, Willi. *Introduction to the New Testament*. Trans. G. Buswell. Philadelphia: Fortress Press, 1968.

———. *Mark the Evangelist*. Trans. R. Harrisville. New York and Nashville: Abingdon Press, 1969.

Mays, J. L., ed. *Interpreting the Gospels*. Philadelphia: Fortress Press, 1981.

McArthur, Harvey A. *In Search of the Historical Jesus*. New York: Scribners, 1969.

McKnight, E. V. *What Is Form Criticism?* In *Guides to Biblical Scholarship*, New Testament Series. Dan O. Via, Jr., ed. Philadelphia: Fortress Press, 1969.

McNamara, M. *Targum and Testament*. Grand Rapids: Eerdmans, 1972.

McNeill, W. *The Rise of the West*. Chicago: University of Chicago Press, 1963.

Meeks, W. A. "The Man from Heaven in Johannine Sectarianism." *Journal of Biblical Literature*, vol. 91 (1972), pp. 44–72.

———. "Since Then You Would Need to Go Out of the World; Group Boundaries in Pauline Christianity." In T. J. Ryan, ed. *Critical History and Biblical Faith. New Testament Perspectives*. Villanova, Pa.: Villanova University, 1979, pp. 4–29.

——. "The Social World of Pauline Christianity." *Aufstieg und Niedergang der römischen Welt.* (Forthcoming.)

——. *The Writings of St. Paul.* Norton Critical Editions. New York: W. W. Norton, 1972.

Meier, J. *Law and History in Matthew's Gospel.* Analecta Biblica 71. Rome: Biblical Institute Press, 1976.

——. *The Vision of Matthew.* New York: Paulist Press, 1979.

Metzger, B. M. *The Text of the New Testament.* 2nd ed. New York: Oxford University Press, 1968.

Milgrom, J. "The Temple Scroll." *The Biblical Archeologist,* vol. 41 (1978), pp. 105–20.

Milik, J. T. *Ten Years of Discovery in the Judean Desert.* SBT 26. Naperville, Ill.: Allenson, 1959.

Minear, P. "Luke's Use of the Birth Stories." In L. Keck and J. L. Martyn, eds. *Studies in Luke-Acts.* New York: Abingdon, 1966, pp. 111–30.

Moule, C. F. D. *The Birth of the New Testament.* London: A. & C. Black, 1962.

Munck, J. *Paul and the Salvation of Mankind.* Trans. F. Clarke. Richmond: John Knox Press, 1959.

Negev, A. *Archeological Encyclopedia of the Holy Land.* New York: G. P. Putnam's Sons, 1972.

Neihardt, G. *Black Elk Speaks.* Lincoln: University of Nebraska, 1960.

Neill, S. *The Interpretation of the New Testament, 1861–1961.* London: Oxford University Press, 1964.

Neusner, J. *The Rabbinic Traditions About the Pharisees Before 70.* 3 vols. Leiden: E. J. Brill, 1971.

——. "The Formation of Rabbinic Judaism: Yavneh (Jamnia) from A.D. 70 to 100." *Aufstieg und Niedergang der römischen Welt* II.10.2.

Nickle, K. *The Collection. A Study in Paul's Strategy.* SBT 48. Naperville, Ill.: Allenson, 1966.

Nineham, D. E. *The Gospel of St. Mark.* Middlesex: Penguin Books, 1963.

Nock, A. D. *Early Gentile Christianity and Its Gentile Background.* Harper Torchbook No. 111. New York: Harper & Row, 1964.

Noth, M. *The History of Israel.* Rev. ed. New York: Harper & Row, 1960.

Oates, W. J. *The Stoic and Epicurean Philosophers.* New York: Random House, 1940.

Ogden, S. M. *Christ Without Myth.* New York: Harper & Row, 1961.

O'Neill, J. C. *The Puzzle of 1 John 2–7.* London: S.P.C.K., 1966.

Painter, J. *John: Witness and Theologian.* London: S.P.C.K., 1976.

Peake's Commentary on the Bible. Rev. ed. London and New York: Thomas Nelson and Sons, 1962.

Perkins, P. *The Gospel According to St. John. A Theological Commentary.* Chicago: Franciscan Herald Press, 1978.

Perrin, Norman. "The Christology of Mark: A Study in Methodology." *Journal of Religion,* vol. 51 (1971), pp. 173–87.

——. "The Composition of Mark IX.1." *Novum Testamentum,* vol. 11 (1969), pp. 67–70.

——. *Jesus and the Language of the Kingdom.* Philadelphia: Fortress Press, 1976.

——. *The Kingdom of God in the Teaching of Jesus.* London: SCM Press, and Philadelphia: Westminster Press, 1963.

——. "The Literary Gattung 'Gospel'—Some Observations." *Expository Times,* vol. 82 (1970), pp. 4–7.

——. "The Modern Interpretation of the Parables of Jesus and the Problem of Hermeneutics." *Interpretation,* vol. 25 (1971), pp. 131–48.

——. "The Parables of Jesus as Parables, as Metaphors and as Aesthetic Objects." *Journal of Religion,* vol. 50 (1970), pp. 340–46.

——. *The Promise of Bultmann.* In the series *The Promise of Theology.* M. Marty, ed. Philadelphia and New York: J. B. Lippincott, 1969.

————. *Rediscovering the Teaching of Jesus*. London: SCM Press, and New York: Harper & Row, 1967.

————. "The Son of Man in the Synoptic Tradition." *Biblical Research*, vol. 13 (1968), pp. 1–23.

————. "Towards the Interpretation of the Gospel of Mark." In *Christology and a Modern Pilgrimage: A Discussion with Norman Perrin*. H. D. Betz, ed., pp. 1–78. Claremont, Calif.: New Testament Colloquium, 1971.

————. "The Use of *(para)didonai* in Connection with the Passion of Jesus in the New Testament." In *Der Ruf Jesu und die Anwort Der Gemeinde: Festscrift für Joachim Jeremias*. E. Lohse, ed. Göttingen: Vandenhoeck & Ruprecht, 1970.

————. *What Is Redaction Criticism?* Rev. ed. In *Guides to Biblical Scholarship*. New Testament Series. Dan O. Via, Jr., ed. Philadelphia: Fortress Press, 1971.

————. "Wisdom and Apocalyptic in the Message of Jesus." *Society of Biblical Literature One Hundred Eighth Annual Meeting (1972) Proceedings*. vol. 2, pp. 543–70.

Peters, F. E. *The Harvest of Hellenism*. New York: Simon and Schuster, 1970.

Petersen, N. R. *Literary Criticism for New Testament Critics*. Guides to Biblical Scholarship. Philadelphia: Fortress Press, 1978.

Pfeiffer, R. H. *History of New Testament Times with an Introduction to the Apocrypha*. New York: Harper & Row, 1949.

Pilch, J. *What Are They Saying About the Book of Revelation?* New York: Paulist Press, 1978.

Pollard, T. W. *Johannine Christology and the Early Church*. Cambridge: Cambridge University Press, 1970.

Reumann, J. *Jesus in the Church's Gospels*. Philadelphia: Fortress Press, 1968.

Richardson, P. *Paul's Ethic of Freedom*. Philadelphia: Westminster Press, 1979.

Ricoeur, Paul. *Le Conflit des interpretations: Essais d'hermeneutique*. Paris: Editions du Seuil, 1969.

————. *Freud and Philosophy: An Essay in Interpretation*. New Haven: Yale University Press, 1970.

————. *The Symbolism of Evil*. Boston: Beacon Press, 1969.

Ringgren, H. *The Faith of Qumran*. Philadelphia: Fortress Press, 1963.

Robbins, V. *The Christology of Mark*. Unpublished Ph.D. dissertation, University of Chicago Divinity School, 1969.

Robinson, J. M. "The Discovery of the Nag Hammadi Codices." *Biblical Archeologist*, vol. 42 (1979), pp. 206–24.

————. "The Johannine Trajectory." In J. M. Robinson and H. Koester, *Trajectories Through Early Christianity*. Philadelphia: Fortress Press, 1971.

————. "Hermeneutics Since Barth." In *The New Hermeneutic*. J. M. Robinson and J. B. Cobb, eds. New York: Harper & Row, 1964.

————. *The Nag Hammadi Library in English*. San Francisco: Harper & Row, 1977.

Robinson, J. M., and Cobb, J. B., eds. *The New Hermeneutic*. New York: Harper & Row, 1964.

Robinson, J. M., and Korester, H. *Trajectories Through Early Christianity*. Philadelphia: Fortress Press, 1971.

Roetzel, C. *The Letters of Paul. Conversations in Context*. Atlanta: John Knox Press, 1975.

Rohde, Joachim. *Rediscovering the Teaching of the Evangelists*. Philadelphia: Westminster Press, 1968.

Rowley, H. H. *The Relevance of Apocalyptic*. Rev. ed. New York: Association Press, 1964.

Rubenstein, R. *My Brother Paul*. New York: Harper & Row, 1972.

Russell, D. S. *Between the Testaments*. Philadelphia: Fortress Press, 1965.

————. *The Method and Message of Jewish Apocalyptic*. Philadelphia: Fortress Press, 1964.

Safrai, S., and Stern, M., eds. *The Jewish People in the First Century*. 2 vols. Philadelphia: Fortress Press, 1974.

Sanders, E. P. *Paul and Palestinian Judaism. A Comparison of Patterns of Religion*. Philadelphia: Fortress Press, 1977.

Sanders, J. T. *Ethics in the New Testament*. Philadelphia: Fortress Press, 1975.

——. *The New Testament Christological Hymns: Their Historical Religious Background.* SNTS Monograph Series. New York: Cambridge University Press, 1971.

Sandmel, S. *The Genius of Paul.* Philadelphia: Fortress Press, 1979.

Schauss, H. *The Jewish Festivals, History and Observances.* New York: Schocken Books, 1974.

Schelke, K. H. "The Letters of Paul." In K. Rahner, ed. *Sacramentum Mundi.* 6 vols. New York: Herder and Herder, 1968–70, vol. 4, pp. 198–203.

Schmidt, Karl L. *Die Rahmen der Geschichte Jesu.* Berlin: Trowitzsch & Sohn, 1919.

Schmithals, W. *Paul and the Gnostics.* Trans. J. E. Steely. Nashville: Abingdon Press, 1972.

Schnackenburg, R. *The Gospel According to St. John.* 2 vols. vol. 1, trans. K. Smyth. New York: Herder and Herder, 1968; vol. 2, trans. C. Hastings et al. New York: Seabury Press, 1980. Now published by Crossroads.

Scholes, R., and Kellog, R. *The Nature of Narrative.* New York: Oxford University Press, 1966.

Schürer, E., Vermes, G., and Miller, F. *The History of the Jewish People in the Age of Jesus Christ.* Vol. 1. Edinburgh: T. & T. Clark, 1973.

Schütz, J. *Paul and the Anatomy of Apostolic Authority.* Cambridge: Cambridge University Press, 1975.

Schweitzer, Albert. *The Quest of the Historical Jesus.* New York: Macmillan, 1964.

Schweizer, E. *The Good News According to Matthew.* Trans. D. E. Green. Atlanta: John Knox Press, 1975.

Scroggs, R. "The Earliest Christian Communities as Sectarian Movement." In J. Neusner, ed. *Christianity, Judaism and Other Greco-Roman Cults. Studies for Morton Smith at Sixty.* Part II. Leiden: E. J. Brill, 1975, pp. 1–23.

——. "Paul and the Eschatological Woman." *Journal of the American Academy of Religion,* vol. 40 (1972), pp. 283–303.

——. "The Sociological Interpretation of the New Testament: The Present State of Research." *New Testament Studies,* vol. 26 (1980), 164–79.

Senior, D. *The Passion Narrative According to Matthew.* Louvain: Leuven University Press, 1975.

Simon, M. *Jewish Sects at the Time of Jesus.* Philadelphia: Fortress Press, 1967.

Smith, D. M. "Johannine Christianity: Some Reflections on Its Character and Delineation." *New Testament Studies,* vol. 21 (1974–75), pp. 222–48.

——. *John.* Proclamation Commentaries. Philadelphia: Fortress Press, 1976.

——. "John and the Synoptics: Some Dimensions of the Problem." *New Testament Studies,* vol. 26 (1979–80), pp. 425–44.

Smith, J. Z. "Social Description of Early Christianity." *Religious Studies Review,* vol. 1 (1975), pp. 19–25.

Smith, M. *Jesus the Magician.* New York: Harper & Row, 1978.

Stendahl, K. *Paul Among Jews and Gentiles.* Philadelphia: Fortress Press, 1976.

——. *The School of St. Matthew.* Philadelphia: Fortress Press, 1968.

Stone, M. *Scriptures, Sects, and Visions. A Profile of Judaism from Ezra to the Jewish Revolts.* Philadelphia: Fortress Press, 1980.

Strauss, David Friedrich. *The Life of Jesus Critically Examined.* Philadelphia: Fortress Press, 1972.

Strecker, G. "The Concept of History in Matthew." *Journal of the American Academy of Religion,* vol. 35 (1967), pp. 219–30.

Streeter, B. J. *The Four Gospels.* London: Macmillan, 1924.

Suggs, M. Jack. *Wisdom, Christology and Law in Matthew's Gospel.* Cambridge: Harvard University Press, 1970.

Talbert, C. *Literary Patterns, Theological Themes, and the Genre of Luke-Acts.* SBL Monograph 20. Missoula, Mont.: Scholars Press, 1974.

——. "The Myth of a Descending-Ascending Redeemer in Mediterranean Antiquity." *New Testament Studies* 22 (1975/76), pp. 418–40.

———. "The Concept of Immortals in Mediterranean Antiquity." *Journal of Biblical Literature*, vol. 94 (1975), pp. 410–36.

———. *What Is a Gospel?* Philadelphia: Fortress Press, 1977.

Talbert, C., ed. *Perspectives on Luke-Acts*. Danville, Va.: Association of Baptist Professors of Religion, 1978.

Tannehill R. C. "The 'Focal Instance' as a Form of New Testament Speech: A Study of Matthew 5:39b–42." *Journal of Religion*, vol. 50 (1970), pp. 372–85.

———. "The Mission of Jesus According to Luke IV 16–30," in E. Grässer, A. Strobel, R. Tannehill, and W. Eltester. *Jesus in Nazareth*. New York: de Gruyter, 1972, pp. 51–75.

Tannehill, R. C., ed. *Semeia 20. Pronouncement Stories*. Chico, Ca.: Scholars Press, 1981.

Tarn, W., and Griffith, C. T. *Hellenistic Civilization*. 3rd ed. London: Arnold, 1952.

Taylor, V. *The Gospel According to St. Mark*. London: Macmillan, 1952.

———. *The Passion Narrative of St. Luke*. Cambridge: Cambridge University Press, 1972.

Tcherikover, V. A. *Hellenistic Civilization and the Jews*. New York: Atheneum, 1970.

Teeple, H. *The Literary Origin of the Gospel of John*. Evanston, Ill.: Religion and Ethics Institute, 1974.

Theissen, G. *The Social Setting of Pauline Christianity*. Trans. J. H. Schütz. Philadelphia: Fortress Press, 1982.

———. *Sociology of Early Palestinian Christianity*. Trans. J. Bowden. Philadelphia: Fortress Press, 1978.

Thompson, W. G. *Matthew's Advice to a Divided Community*. Analecta Biblica 44. Rome: Pontifical Biblical Institute, 1970.

Tiede, D. *The Charismatic Figure as Miracle Worker*. Missoula, Mont.: Society of Biblical Literature, 1972.

———. *Prophecy and History in Luke-Acts*. Philadelphia: Fortress Press, 1980.

Tilborg, S. van. *The Jewish Leaders in Matthew*. Leiden: E. J. Brill, 1972.

Tödt, H. E. *The Son of Man in the Synoptic Tradition*. Philadelphia: Westminster Press, 1965.

Toynbee, A., ed. *The Crucible of Christianity*. New York: World Publishing Co., 1969.

Vanderlip, D. G. *Christianity According to John*. Philadelphia: Westminster Press, 1975.

———. *John, The Gospel of Life*. Valley Forge, Pa.: Judson Press, 1979.

Vermes, G. *The Dead Sea Scrolls in English*. Baltimore: Penguin Books, 1962.

———. *Jesus the Jew*. New York: Macmillan, 1973.

Via, Dan O., Jr. *The Parables: Their Literary and Existential Dimension*. Philadelphia: Fortress Press, 1967.

Vögtle, A. "Jesus Christ." *Sacramentum Verbi II*. J. B. Bauer, ed. New York: Herder and Herder, 1970, pp. 419–37.

Weeden, T. J. *Mark—Traditions in Conflict*. Philadelphia: Fortress Press, 1971.

Weiss, J. *The Preaching of Jesus Concerning the Kingdom of God*. Philadelphia: Fortress Press, 1971.

Wheelwright, Philip. *The Burning Fountain*. Rev. ed. Bloomington: Indiana University Press, 1968.

———. *Metaphor and Reality*. Bloomington: Indiana University Press, 1962. Paperback 1968.

Whiteley, D. H. *The Theology of St. Paul*. Philadelphia: Fortress Press, 1964.

Wilder, A. N. *Early Christian Rhetoric: The Language of the Gospel*. New York: Harper & Row, 1964. Rev. ed., Cambridge: Harvard University Press, 1971.

———. "Eschatological Imagery and Earthly Circumstance." *New Testament Studies*, vol. 5 (1958–59), pp. 229–45.

———. "The Rhetoric of Ancient and Modern Apocalyptic." *Interpretation*, vol. 25 (1971), pp. 436–53.

Wilson, B. R. *Sects and Society*. Berkeley: University of California Press, 1961.

Wood, J. D. *The Interpretation of the Bible*. Studies in Theology. London: Duckworth, 1958.

Yadin, Y. *Masada*. New York: Random House, 1966.

BIBLIOGRAPHY
FOR RESEARCH PAPERS

This bibliography is not meant to be comprehensive, but is designed to be an English language aid in writing research papers in New Testament and related areas. Further bibliography can be found at the end of the relevant chapters and in many of the tools cited below.

I. Dictionaries and Encyclopedias

Bauer, J. B., ed. *Sacramentum Verbi: An Encyclopedia of Biblical Theology.* 3 vols. New York: Herder and Herder, 1970. Excellent Catholic European scholarship.

Encyclopaedia Britannica. Excellent scholarly work on some selected topics. Bibliographies.

Encyclopedia Judaica, ed. C. Roth. Jerusalem: Keter Press, 1972. 16 vols. plus supplement. The best, recent encyclopedia in English on topics pertaining to Judaism.

Encyclopedia of Archeological Excavations in the Holy Land, ed. M. Avi-Yonah. Jerusalem: Massada Press, 1975. English edition, Englewood Cliffs, N.J.: Prentice-Hall, 1978. 4 vols.

Harper's Bible Dictionary, M. S. and J. L. Miller. 8th ed. New York: Harper, 1973. Many illustrations and maps. No bibliographies.

Harper's Encyclopedia of Bible Life, M. S. and M. L. Miller. Rev. ed. B. M. Bennett and D. H. Scott. New York: Harper, 1978. Subject listings with illustrations, maps, and concluding bibliography.

Hastings, J. *Dictionary of the Bible.* Rev. ed. F. C. Grant and H. H. Rowley. New York: Scribners, 1963. Short articles. No bibliographies.

International Standard Bible Encyclopedia, ed. G. W. Bromiley. Grand Rapids: Eerdmans, 1979—. Conservative, A-D has appeared.

Interpreter's Dictionary of the Bible (IDB), ed. G. A. Buttrick et al. 4 vols. New York: Abingdon, 1962. Supplementary volume (1975). Brief to medium length, excellent articles. Bibliographies. The supplementary volume should always be checked for recent scholarship and bibliographies.

Jewish Encyclopedia, ed. I. Singer (1901–06). Reprinted 1966. 12 vols. New York: KTAV, 1901–1906. Dated, but still excellent on many subjects.

Leon-Dufour, X. *Dictionary of Biblical Theology.* Rev. ed. New York: Seabury Press, 1973. Brief articles with references to Biblical passages.

Leon-Dufour, X. *Dictionary of the New Testament.* New York: Harper & Row, 1980. Brief, cross-referenced word studies. Introductory survey article on the New Testament world.

McKenzie, John L. *Dictionary of the Bible.* Milwaukee: Bruce, 1965. One volume, paperback. Brief articles by Prof. McKenzie himself. No bibliographies with articles.

New Catholic Encyclopedia. New York: McGraw-Hill, 1967–74. 15 vols. plus 2 supplementary vols. Generally high quality. Short bibliographies.

The New International Dictionary of New Testament Theology, ed. C. Brown. 3 vols. Grand Rapids: Eerdmans, 1975–78. 3 vols. Bibliographies.

New Westminster Dictionary of the Bible, ed. H. S. Gehman. Philadelphia: Westminster Press, 1970. Short, useful entries. No bibliographies.

Pictorial Biblical Encyclopedia, ed. G. Cornfeld. New York: Macmillan, 1964.

Richardson, A., ed. *A Theological Word Book of the Bible.* New York: Macmillan, 1951. Still useful for short studies of important Biblical words.

Theological Dictionary of the New Testament, eds. G. Kittel and G. Friedrich. 10 vols. Grand Rapids: Eerdmans, 1964–76. Scholarly word-study reference tool listed alphabetically by Greek words. Occasionally helpful to non-Greek reading students. Some articles dated.

Turner, N. *Christian Words.* Edinburgh: T. & T. Clark, 1980. Arranged alphabetically by English translation of Greek words.

The Oxford Classical Dictionary, eds. N. G. L. Hammond and H. H. Scullard. Oxford: University Press, 1970. Bibliographies.

II. Periodicals, Indices, and Abstracts

Biblical Theology Bulletin (1971—). Summary articles.

Elenchus Bibliographicus Biblicus. Rome: Biblical Institute Press, 1920—. An excellent, very thorough index arranged by topics numbered for cross-references. Published as part of the journal *Biblica* until 1967. Annual. Now covers over 1100 journals.

Index on Articles on Jewish Studies. Jerusalem: Magnes Press, 1969.

Index to Religious Periodical Literature (see *Religion Index One*)

Internationale Zeitschriftenschau für Bibelwissenschaft und Grenzgebiete (1951—). Multilingual, topical, cross-referenced, including abstracts. Though more difficult to use, it will supplement *New Testament Abstracts.*

New Testament Abstracts. Cambridge, Mass.: Weston College School of Theology, 1956—. Most useful English language abstracts of articles, numbered for cross-reference; appears three times a year.

Religion Index One (formerly *Index to Religious Periodical Literature*) (1949—). Available in most college and university libraries, it is probably the most useful because it indexes the best journals in the field. Check "Bible, New Testament," and its subdivisions by New Testament book. Includes author index.

Religion Index Two (1976—). Supplements *Religion Index One* with volumes of collected essays. There are also two supplemental volumes back to 1960.

Wagner, Gunter. "NT Bibliographical Aids." This card-catalogue style bibliography, arranged by Biblical book and verse, will be published by Mercer Press in bound volumes.

III. Introductory Bibliographical Tools

Danker, F. W. *Multipurpose Tools for Bible Study.* 3rd ed. St. Louis: Concordia Publishing House, 1970. Narrative-style description of standard tools for Biblical research.

France, R. T., ed. *A Bibliographical Guide to New Testament Research.* Sheffield, England: JSOT Press, 1979. Excellent pamphlet describing 29 areas of New Testament study with standard works annotated.

Hurd, J. C. *A Bibliography of New Testament Bibliographies.* New York: Seabury Press, 1966. Dated, but still useful, this listing tells you where bibliographies are.

Kepple, R. J. *Reference Works for Theological Research.* Washington, D.C.: University Press of America, 1981. Recent, comprehensive, annotated. Chapters 19–25 list materials for Biblical studies.

Marrow, S. B. *Basic Tools of Biblical Exegesis: A Student's Manual.* Subsidia Biblica 2. Rome: Biblical Institute Press, 1976. Annotated Bibliography on tools for Biblical interpretation. Also covers materials outside the Bible.

Scholer, D. M. *A Basic Bibliographic Guide for New Testament Exegesis.* 2nd ed. Grand Rapids: Eerdmans, 1973. Little or no annotation, lists standard tools in areas of New Testament research.

Thiselton, A. C. *New Testament Commentary Survey.* Revised by D. Carson. Madison, Wis.: Theological Students Fellowship, 1977. Essay format listing and evaluating commentaries from an evangelical perspective.

IV. Specialized Bibliographical Books

Aune, D. E. *Jesus and the Synoptic Gospels: A Bibliographic Study Guide.* Madison, Wis.: Theological Students Fellowship, 1980. Selective, partially annotated.

Berlin, C. *Index to Festschriften (Memorial Volumes) in Jewish Studies.* New York: KTAV, 1971.

The Bible: Texts and Translations of the Bible and the Apocrypha and Their Books from the National Union Catalog, Pre-1956 Imprints. 5 vols. London: Mansell, 1980. The first four volumes list over 63,000 books; the last indexes the first four.

Brock, S. P., Fritsch, C. T., and Jellicoe, S. *A Classified Bibliography of the Septuagint.* Leiden: E. J. Brill, 1973.

Charlesworth, J. H. *The Pseudepigrapha and Modern Research* with Supplement. Missoula, Mont.: Scholars Press, 1981. Descriptions of documents plus bibliographies.

Fitzmyer, J. A. *The Dead Sea Scrolls: Major Publications and Tools for Study;* with an Addendum. Missoula, Mont.: Scholars Press, 1977. Texts, studies, authors, Biblical passages.

Gottcent, J. H. *The Bible as Literature: A Selective Bibliography.* Boston: G. K. Hall & Co., 1979. Annotated resources on various literary approaches to the Bible.

Grossfeld, B. *A Bibliography of Targum Literature.* Cincinnati: Hebrew Union College Press, 1972. Describes literature from 1500s to 1971.

———. *A Bibliography of Targum Literature,* vol. II. Cincinnati: Hebrew Union College Press, 1977. Supplements vol. I.

Hilgert, E. *A Bibliography of Philo Studies 1963–1970* and *Abstracts of Selected Articles on Philo 1966–1970* in *Studia Philonica* 1 (1972), pp. 57–91.

Kissinger, W. S. *The Parables of Jesus: A History of Interpretation and Bibliography.* ATLA Bibliography Series, No. 4. Metuchen, N.J.: Scarecrow Press, 1979. A history of parable interpretation and a bibliography.

Kissinger, W. S. *The Sermon on the Mount: A History of Interpretation and Bibliography.* ATLA Biblical Series, No. 3. Metuchen, N.J.: Scarecrow Press, 1975. History and bibliography.

Kümmel, W. G. *Introduction to the New Testament.* London: SCM Press, 1975. Contains bibliographies at beginning of each section.

Langevin, P.-E. *Bibliographie biblique, Biblical Bibliography, Biblische Bibliographie, Bibliografia Biblica, Bibliografía Bíblica,* vol. 1: 1930–1970; vol. 2: 1930–1975. Quebec: Les Presses de L'Université Laval, 1972, 1978.

Malatesta, E. *St John's Gospel, 1920–1965: A Cumulative and Classified Bibliography of Books and Periodical Literature on the Fourth Gospel.* Rome: Pontifical Biblical Institute, 1967. Derived from *Elenchus Bibliographicus* and its supplement, *Verbum Domini.*

Mattill, A. J., and Mattill, M. B. *A Classified Bibliography of Literature on the Acts of the Apostles.* Leiden: E. J. Brill, 1966.

Metzger, B. M. *Index to Periodical Literature on Christ and the Gospels.* Leiden: E. J. Brill, 1965. Topical arrangement plus author index.

———. *Index to Periodical Literature on the Apostle Paul.* Rev. ed. Leiden: E. J. Brill, 1970.

——. *Index of Articles on the New Testament and the Early Church Published in Festschriften (Memorial Volumes)*. SBL Monograph No. 5. Philadelphia: Society of Biblical Literature, 1951: supplement 1955. Dated.

Neusner, J., ed. *The Study of Judaism: Bibliographical Essays*. New York: KTAV, 1972.

Nickels, P. *Targum and New Testament: A Bibliography, Together with a New Testament Index*. Rome: Pontifical Biblical Institute, 1967. Part I by author, Part II by New Testament passage.

Rounds, D. *Articles on Antiquity in Festschriften (Memorial Volumes): the Ancient East, the Old Testament, Greece, Rome, Roman Law, Byzantium*. An Index.

St. John's University Library Index to Biblical Journals. Collegeville, Minn.: St. John's University Press, 1971.

Scholer, D. M. *Nag Hammadi Bibliography 1948–1969*. Leiden: E. J. Brill, 1971. Supplemented annually in the periodical *Novum Testamentum*.

Schreckenburg, H. *Bibliographie zu Flavius Josephus*. Leiden: E. J. Brill, 1968.

——. *Bibliographie zu Flavius Josephus: Supplementband mit Gesamtregister*. Leiden: E. J. Brill, 1979.

Vermes, G. *The Dead Sea Scrolls: Qumran in Perspective*. London: Collins, 1977. Select bibliographies.

Vogel, E. K. *Bibliography of Holy Land Sites: Compiled in Dr. Nelson Glueck*. Cincinnati: Hebrew Union College/Jewish Institute of Religion, 1974. Reprint of Hebrew Union College Annual, vol. 42. Arranged alphabetically by place. Over 200 sites.

V. Concordances

There are many concordances (alphabetized word lists with their contextual references by chapter and verse) to the original languages and the various translations. The Revised Standard Version is used in this book. A recent important concordance is:

Morrison, C. *An Analytical Concordance to the Revised Standard Version of the New Testament*. Philadelphia: Westminster Press, 1979. It contains the English terms, Greek original with a transliteration, book, chapter, verse, and usually a phrase in which the term occurs.

VI. Commentaries

One-volume commentaries on the whole Bible are cited on p. xii, "A Note About the Resource Books." Commentary series project commentaries on all the books of the New Testament or Bible. Each volume contains one or more books depending on length. Likewise, one scholar will often do only one volume in the series. Important series include:

The Anchor Bible, 1964—. Scholarly, mostly excellent. (Doubleday)

Barclay, W. *The Daily Study Bible Series*. 17 vols. Rev. ed. Philadelphia: Westminster Press, 1975. Simple and helpful British conservative scholarship.

Harper's New Testament Commentaries. 1960 (Harper & Row).

Hermeneia—A Critical and Historical Commentary on the Bible. 1971— (Fortress Press). Mostly translated from German. Excellent.

International Critical Commentary. 1930–60 (T. & T. Clark). Old Standard reprinted.

Interpreter's Bible. 12 vols. 1952–57 (Abingdon). Clear and still useful.

New Century Bible. 1967— (Nelson).

New Testament Message: A Biblical-Theological Commentary. 22 vols. 1979–81 (M. Glazier). Varies in quality, but generally good.

VII. Atlases

Aharoni, Y., and Avi-Yonah, M. *The Macmillan Bible Atlas*. New York: Macmillan, 1977. Main events of the Bible are stressed by maps.

Grollenberg, L. H. *Atlas of the Bible*. Trans. J. M. H. Reid and H. H. Rowley. New York: Nelson, 1956. Maps, narrative, and photography.

May, H. G. et al. *Oxford Bible Atlas*. 2nd ed. London: Oxford University Press, 1974.

Topographical maps, archeology, narrative, occasional photographs, and plan of Jerusalem.

Negenman, J. H. *New Atlas of the Bible*, ed. H. H. Rowley et al. Trans. H. Hoskins and R. Beckley. Garden City, N.Y.: Doubleday, 1969. Photographs, narrative, occasional maps, and helpful charts.

Wright, G. E., and Filson, F. *The Westminster Historical Atlas to the Bible*. Philadelphia: Westminster Press, 1956. Narrative, photographs, and excellent maps stressing geography.

GLOSSARY

Apocalypse   An apocalyptic writing.

Apocalyptic   From the Greek *apokalypsis*, "an uncovering." The word is used to describe a movement in Judaism and Christianity in which the writers characteristically claimed that God had "uncovered" for them (revealed to them) the secrets of the imminent end of the world. The movement is described in detail in chapter 4. Apocalyptic is a feature of religions in the Hellenistic world other than Judaism and Christianity, but we are concerned only with its Jewish and Christian forms.

Apocrypha   From the Greek *apocryphos*, "hidden." The word is used of books that were not accepted into the final canon of Jewish or Christian Scripture. Such books were to be "hidden" from the faithful in the church. When used alone, *Apocrypha* refers to the Apocrypha of the Old Testament, that is, to the books rejected from the final Jewish canon of Scripture but transmitted by Christians as part of the Old Testament. After the Reformation, the Protestant churches accepted the Jewish canon of Scripture as defining the Old Testament. The Roman Catholic church continued to accept the broader canon of the ancient church.

Canon   From the Greek *kanōn*, which means something made of reeds or something straight like reeds. It came to be used of an authoritative list. In the Christian church it was used of a list of regulations, hence "canon law"; of a list of clergy or saints, hence "canonize"; and of a list of books to be read in the churches, hence "canon of the New Testament," and "canon of the Old Testament."

Catholic   From the Latin *catholicus*, "universal" or "general." It is used in connection with the later letters in the New Testament, the "Catholic Epistles," because they are addressed to the church at large rather than to individuals or separate churches. It is then used of the church as a whole as distinct from one

501

particular part of the church, e.g., the "catholic church" as distinct from the "Syrian church." In discussing the period after the Reformation it distinguishes the Roman Catholic church from the Protestant churches. In that last context it is always capitalized, "Catholic."

Christology From the Greek *Christos* (=Hebrew *Messiah*) and *logos*, "word" or "teaching." Hence, teaching concerning the person of Christ.

Church order A text setting out the polity and discipline of a church with regard to its officers and members.

Corpus The Latin word for "body." It is used of a complete or comprehensive body of writings. The "Pauline corpus" is the body of writings attributed to the apostle Paul.

Demythologizing program A proposal by Rudolf Bultmann to understand the myths in the New Testament as essentially expressions of ideas about the existential reality of human existence in the world and to interpret them in that way.

Diaspora (or **Dispersion**) From the Greek *diaspora*, "a dispersion." The community of Jews living outside their ancestral homeland, Palestine (Israel).

Doxology From the Greek *doxologia*, "a praising." The act of praising God. In New Testament studies specifically used in connection with formal praises of God to be found in prayers, letters, and the liturgy of the church.

Eschatology From the Greek *eschatos*, "furthest," and *logos*, "word" or "teaching," teaching concerning the last things, the end of the world or the end of history. It is related to apocalyptic in that apocalyptic features a particular kind of eschatology.

Evangelist From the Greek *euangelion*, "good news." A preacher of the gospel, or, more especially in New Testament studies, the author of one of the gospels.

Form criticism A translation of the German *Formgeschichte*, literally "form history." A description of this movement in New Testament scholarship is given in chapters 3, 13.

Gospel From the Middle English *godspell*, "good spell," i.e., "good news." It translated Greek *euangelion* "good news." Originally, it referred to the good news of what God had done in Christ, then to the literary form created to narrate and proclaim the event.

Hellenism (adjective: **Hellenistic**) From the Greek *Hellenismos*, "imitation of the Greeks." The culture that developed in the world conquered by Alexander the Great as that world adopted the Greek language and imitated Greek ways.

Hermeneutics From the Greek *hermēneutēs*, "an interpreter." The science of interpretation, especially the interpretation of written texts. It is becoming usual to use *hermeneutic* of a particular method of interpretation and *hermeneutics* of the science as a whole.

History of religion A translation of the German *Religionsgeschichte*. It denotes the comparative study and analysis of religions, e.g., the study and analysis of early Christianity in comparison with the religions and philosophies of the Hellenistic world.

Kerygma   The Greek word for proclamation. It is used to denote the preaching, proclamation, or central message of the New Testament as a whole or of any part of it, and similarly of the church as a whole or of any part of it.

Koine   The Greek word for "common." It describes the form of Greek which became the lingua franca, the common language, of the Hellenistic world.

Life of Jesus research   A comprehensive term designating every possible kind of historical research in connection with the life and teaching of Jesus.

Life of Jesus theology   The theology based on the conviction that the results of Life of Jesus research are normative for Christian faith.

Mimesis (adjective: **Mimetic**)   The Greek word for "imitation." It is used as a technical term for literature that is deliberately realistic, i.e., imitative of life.

Parenesis   From the Greek *parainesis*, "exhortation," "advice." A technical term used to denote exhortation, advice, instruction, encouragement, etc.

Parousia   The Greek word for "presence." In Hellenistic Greek it became a technical term for the visit of a high official, especially a king or emperor, to a province or place. In the New Testament it came to be used of the expected coming of Christ in glory to judge the world and redeem his people, and in this sense it has become a technical term of theological and Biblical scholarship.

Passion   When used alone ("Passion" or "the passion") this term always refers to the suffering and death of Jesus. The "passion narrative" is the narrative account of that suffering and death.

Pastorals (Pastoral Epistles or **Letters)**   The letters written in the name of Paul and addressed to Timothy or Titus. They give advice to a "pastor" of a church with regard to his responsibilities to his "flock," hence their designation.

Pericope   From the Greek *peri*, "about," and *koptein*, "to cut": An extract from a larger work, a unit of narrative or discourse.

Pseudonymity   From the Greek *pseudos*, "false," and *onyma*, "name." The practice of writing under a false name.

Redaction criticism   The usual translation of the German *Redaktionsgeschichte* (literally "redaction history"). The study of the redaction or editing of traditional material as it is transmitted or used. A description of this aspect of New Testament scholarship is given in chapters 3, 8.

Septuagint   From the Latin *septuaginta* ("seventy"). The Greek translation of the Jewish Scriptures, transmitted to the Old Testament by Christians. It received its name from the legend that it was translated in seventy days by seventy-two translators, six from each of the twelve Jewish tribes.

Sitz im Leben   A German term meaning "setting in life." It is used as a technical term for the context in which a given oral or literary form functions (e.g., sermon, ethical instruction, etc.) and for the purposes for which it was developed. It is discussed in the section on form criticism in chapter 8.

Social history   The study of historical documents from the perspective of sociological theory, attempting thereby to understand what such documents (usually unintentionally) reveal about the "social world" of early Christian communities. It is concerned with such issues as the distribution of power, social organization, status, rural and urban environments, relation to the "world," and the like; it attempts to understand individuals and communities by analogy with comparable models known from sociology in general.

Soteriology   From the Greek *sōtēr*, "savior," and *logos*, "word" or "teaching." Teaching about the death of Jesus as the means of man's salvation.

Synoptic gospels   From the Greek *synoptikos*, "seeing the whole together." The gospels of Matthew, Mark, and Luke are called the "synoptic gospels" because they tell the same general story in the same kind of way. A contrast is intended to the gospel of John.

Synoptic tradition   The traditional material that has been used in the synoptic gospels.

Witness   One who bears testmony to his or her faith, or the act of bearing testimony. The Greek work is *martyr*, and later it came to be used specifically of those who "witnessed" to their faith to the point of dying for it.

PICTURE CREDITS

p. xx   From Vincent and Steve, *Jerusalem de l'Ancien Testament* (Paris: J. Gabalda & Cie)

p. 2   From *The Mainstream of Civilization,* 3rd ed, by Joseph R. Strayer and Hans W. Gatzke. Copyright © 1979 by Harcourt Brace Jovanovich, Inc., p. 50

p. 38   The British Library

p. 64   Photo by Elliot Faye from *In the Footsteps of St. Paul* by Wolfgang E. Pax. Copyright © 1977 by Nateev, Printing and Publishing Enterprises Ltd., Israel, p. 111

p. 94   M.644, f.174v. The Pierpont Morgan Library

p. 126   Éditions d'Art Albert Skira S.A.

p. 206   Institute for Antiquity and Christianity, Claremont, California. Photo by Jean Doresse

p. 232   The Bettmann Archive Inc.

p. 262   Archie Lieberman

p. 292   Alinari/Editorial Photocolor Archives

p. 328   The John Rylands University Library of Manchester

p. 370   André Held

p. 396   The Hermitage Museum, Leningrad

INDEX

Q

T

V

W

Y

Z

3
C 4
D 5
E 6
F 7
G 8
H 9
I 0
J 1